The Structure of Emotion

Peter J. Lang

The Structure of Emotion

Psychophysiological, Cognitive and Clinical Aspects

Edited by

Niels Birbaumer

University of Tübingen
Tübingen, Germany

Arne Öhman

University of Uppsala
Uppsala, Sweden

Hogrefe & Huber Publishers
Seattle · Toronto · Bern · Göttingen

Canadian Cataloguing in Publication Data

Main entry under title:

The structure of emotion : psychophysiological, cognitive and clinical aspects
Includes bibliographical references and index.
ISBN 0-88937-055-9
1. Emotions. I. Birbaumer, Niels, 1945– . II. Öhman, Arne.
BF531.S87   1993   152.4   C91-094832-1

Library of Congress Cataloging-in-Publication Data

The Structure of emotion : psychophysiological, cognitive, and clinical aspects / edited by
Niels Birbaumer, Arne Öhman.
p. cm.
Includes indexes.
ISBN 0-88937-055-9 : $65.00
1. Emotions. 2. Emotions—Physiological aspects. 3. Conditioned response.
I. Birbaumer, Niels. II. Öhman, Arne.
[DNLM: 1. Emotions—physiology. WL 103 S927]
BF531.S84   1993   152.4—dc20
DNLM/DLC for Library of Congress   91-20856 CIP

P. O. Box 2487, Kirkland, WA 98083-2487
12–14 Bruce Park Ave., Toronto, Ontario M4P 2S3

ISBN 0-88937-055-9
Hogrefe & Huber Publishers · Seattle · Toronto · Bern · Göttingen
ISBN 3-456-82010-0
Hogrefe & Huber Publishers · Bern · Göttingen · Seattle · Toronto

Printed in Germany

Cover design by Carla Dal Brun (Padova)

Table of Contents

A. Basic Conceptual Issues

B. Organization of Emotion in Memory: Applications to Imagery, Clinical Problems and Experimental Esthetics

C. Acquisition of Fear

D. Emotion and Reflex Modification: Clinical Implications

Preface

*M'illumino
d'Immenso*

Giuseppe
Ungaretti

This book is dedicated to Peter J. Lang, in recognition of his profound contribution to the "illumination of the immense" universe of emotion. It is written by friends, colleagues and former students in deep appreciation of the inspiring guidance he has provided in our joint enterprise, the psychological and psychophysiological analysis of emotion. Its authors represent diverse backgrounds and cultural heritages but they have more in common than the friendship to a particular person; they are joined by a set of beliefs about how research on emotion should proceed. It is this set of beliefs that unite the various contributions to this volume into a coherent exposition of its subject matter. It is better described as a "set of beliefs" than as a "program", because it is an open system, and not a defined number of minimally agreed statements. It is inspired by Peter's writing and teaching, and developed over years of interactions, discussions, and mutual influences, typically during joyful circumstances. There is definitely room for arguments and disagreements, and expulsion because of failure to adhere to a program is alien to the friendly spirit of the group. Some of the basic beliefs are described in the first chapter of the book.

The purpose of the book is not to provide a polished explication of Peter's contribution to the study of emotion. As always, Peter's research and ideas are in a dynamic and continuous flux, and he consistently refuses to let himself be captured in anything even vaguely reminiscent of a shining monument. Thus, each author pursues his or her line of interest, inspired by ideas that we all share, and many of which can be traced back to Peter. This is emphasized in the organization of the book, which has sections introduced by some of Peter's texts, which then provide starting points for the authors of the chapters in the section. The scope of the book is not historical, but contemporary and future-oriented, as research should be.

Emotion, indeed, is an immense area of human experience and scientific inquiry. It ranges from the joy induced by shared food and Barolo wines, to the distress and anguish we meet in our patients, and from detailed assessments of miniscule physiological responses to conceptual tackling of some of the intellectual riddles that always have puzzled mankind. Its scientific elucidation provides an inspiring and exciting challenge, which, in the case of the authors of this book, is enhanced by our friendships and joint commitments. If something of this excitement is transmitted to the reader of the book, and contributes to recruiting new students to the field, it has served its purpose well, and, we are sure, to the great satisfaction of Peter Lang.

Tübingen and Uppsala, July, 1992
Niels Birbaumer
Arne Öhman

Section A.
Basic Conceptual Issues

Psychophysiological and Cognitive-Clinical Perspectives on Emotion: Introduction and Overview

Arne Öhman* and Niels Birbaumer**

Abstract

The purpose of this chapter is to provide an introductory discussion of some of the basic issues in the psychology of emotion. Thinking about emotional phenomena typically occurs within the constraints provided by the common language, which gives rise to serious problems in defining emotion. It is argued that emotional phenomena involve behavioral responses, physiological activity, and verbal reports of affective evaluation of the eliciting stimulus context. However, none of these data domains present unequivocal information for inferring emotion. In a second part, the chapter reviews the question of fundamental emotions and the three-system approach to emotion. It is suggested that the task for a scientific study of emotion is not to elucidate presumed fundamental emotional states derived from the common language, but to develop conceptual networks that tie situational aspects to personal characteristics and to emotional phenomena as revealed in behavioral, physiological and verbal responses. A third part of the chapter presents the perspective on emotion that is shared by the contributors, and which focuses on clinical and psychophysiological approaches and cognitive mechanisms. Finally, it presents an overview of the remaining chapters in the book.

Emotion pervades human psychology. There is an emotional aspect to virtually everything a person does. Even when we are engaged in the essence of cold, rational thought, logical deduction and mathematics, emotion intervenes with joy in success or frustration in failure, and these emotional reactions may influence the subsequent performance. Emotion links the person to his body and to his outside world. Thus, it provides a bridge to inner needs and wishes, and practically all psychological activity occurs in the context of avoiding some things or events or approaching others. Thus, anything we do takes place in a psychological space where emotion helps define the cardinal points.

This is recognized in cultural developments and in the different fields of aesthetic achievements. An important part of culture is to control and discipline emotion by developing conventions about how, for instance, bereavement, anger or joy can be handled and expressed. The essence of artistic creativity is to convey emotional experience to a reader or an audience, be it in the form of a poem, a painting, or a piece of music.

There is no question, therefore, that emotional phenomena are central to psychology. Yet the psychology of emotion often may seem hopelessly undeveloped. Indeed, we are not even close to providing a reasonable account of the emotional effects conveyed by Ungaretti's hermetic lines "M'illumino d'Immenso." If this

*   Uppsala University, Uppsala, Sweden
**   University of Tübingen, Tübingen, Germany & University of Padova, Padova, Italy
Acknowledgement: Arne Öhman was supported by the Swedish Council for Research in Humanities and Social Sciences and Niels Birbaumer by the German Research Society (Deutsche Forschungsgemeinschaft).

were what we aspired for in a science of emotion, we would have good reason to despair the slow progress. But even though our scientific tools may appear blunt, there are other areas for their use, which appear both more pressing and more tractable. For example, many persons are suffering from debilitating aversive emotions such as anxiety, where the subtlety of juxtaposed alliterative words appears superfluous to the scientific analysis. Thus, this book will definitely deal more with anxiety than with poetry, even though we include chapters on the emotional effects of music (Ch. 12) and movie clips (Ch. 3).

In this introductory chapter we shall first discuss delineations and definitions of emotion to help provide a frame for the rest of the book. Secondly, a couple of basic theoretical points will be briefly discussed. Thirdly, we shall describe the perspective on the scientific study of emotion that is shared by the authors, and which is very much influenced by the work of Peter Lang. Finally, we shall provide an overview of the contributions to the various sections of the book, thus helping the reader to prepare and orient to what is coming.

Delineating Emotional Phenomena

Problems in Defining Emotion

Part of the problems for a science of emotion is that emotions themselves, as phenomena, remains elusive. Primarily, they are manifested as subjective experience, and as such they are embedded within a network of mental events and mechanisms that pose serious philosophical and methodological problems to a natural science inclined investigator. As experience, emotion in a very real sense remains private and inaccessible to the scientific community. Thus, subjective experience does not fulfil the basic requirement of scientific data, that they can be objectively (i.e., intersubjectively) verified (e.g., Lang, 1978, see Ch. 2, this volume). They can be made public only through the use of language, and indeed, common language has a rich vocabulary for describing emotional states. Yet, because the very phenomenon that it denotes, the emotional experience, remains hidden inside the person, the verbal community is at a loss in shaping a precise use of the vocabulary (e.g., Skinner, 1974). Thus, a primary aim for a scientific theory of emotion becomes to dissociate itself from the views and limitations of the perspective on emotion which is implicit in the common language (Mandler, 1975). This language is a convenient vehicle to communicate and comment on emotion, but to achieve this

purpose it has to be vague, overinclusive, ambiguous and redundant. These are exactly the characteristics that would undermine the usefulness of a scientific language, because its purpose is unequivocal description and explanation. Thus, the two languages remains antithetical approaches to emotion (or to any psychological phenomenon).

Concentrating on the more tangible aspects of emotion, the behavioral and physiological concomitants, on the other hand, leaves investigators open to the criticism that they risk missing the very phenomenon that they intended to study. Emotion bear no necessary relation to behavior. Although we laugh with joy and may assault an opponent in anger, the behavioral concomitants can be more or less completely inhibited because of, for example, cultural display rules. Some emotions do not seem to be manifested in behavior at all. Sadness, for example, has been defined as "nonbehavior" (Frijda, 1986). And even behavior which is conventionally taken as related to emotion, such as avoidance, can occur without the intensity and heat we associate with emotion. For example, finding ones way through a known city late at night, one may avoid some streets and alleys without much thought and much emotion. However, if in an unknown area of the city one looks down an alley and sees a threatening figure disappear in the shadow, fear may be aroused, and as a consequence, one avoids walking down this particular alley. Thus, emotions are not amenable to simple operational definitions in behavior terms. Nor are they easy to define conceptually, if we want to come up with an explicit definition that unequivocally delineates what is emotional and what is not. Given the contemporary state of incomplete knowledge, an explicit definition of emotion may be premature, and it may merely risk to elaborate on the connotation of the term "emotion" in the common language (Mandler, 1975). For example, some emotions may be taken as given or basic, and efforts may be directed towards enumerating their blends and consequences rather than in analysing their antecedents, and how the consequences varies with the antecedents. A viable explicit definition should come as a result of research rather than being regarded as a prerequisite for it (Frijda, 1986; Mandler, 1975; Öhman, 1987). Given this state of affairs, a reasonable approach is to try to delineate the phenomena of interest, *the emotional phenomena* (Frijda, 1986) rather than to provide an explicit definition of the term emotion. Figure 1 pro-

vides the context for such a delineation. Thus, emotional phenomena occur in a stimulus context, and they are manifested in three types of observations: verbal reports, physiological responses and behavior.

The Stimulus Context

Although behavioral and physiological responses suggesting emotional phenomena unfold in continuous transactions between persons and environments, they are usually regarded as *elicited* by stimuli in the environment (e.g., Frijda, 1986; Skinner, 1974). For example, fear behavior may be seen as a response to threat, and expressions of anger as a response to an agent that thwarts goal-directed activity. Except perhaps for intensity, the physical dimensions of a stimulus is of only limited value in predicting whether it will elicit emotional responses. Rather it is the stimulus as perceived or processed by the person that is emotionally effective. What for one person is an innocuous and interesting spider, prompting approach, is for another a deadly threat most likely to elicit panic and head-on flight. Thus, a heavy emphasis has been put on cognitive appraisal processes evaluating the situation in accounts of emotion (e.g., Lazarus, Kanner & Folkman, 1980). However, such processes should not be identified with intentional, conscious thought. For example, to be identified as threatening, a stimulus must make contact with organized memory information where it is related to previous experience with aversive circumstances generating fear arousal (e.g., Lang, Ch. 6). Accessing such information is a largely automatic process, and does not require conscious thought. For example, phobic responses to snake or spider stimuli in phobics may be elicited by pictures that are presented under masking conditions preventing their conscious perception (Öhman & Soares, 1992; see Ch. 16). Some theorists have argued that such automatic arousal of affect, which precedes later cognitive inferences, provides a decisive ingredient in emotion (Zajonc, 1980).

From these considerations it is clear that it is not the stimulus as such, but its *meaning* or *sig-*

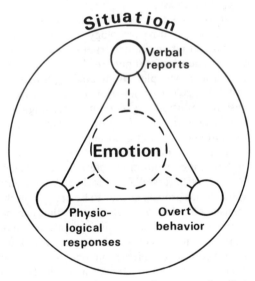

Figure 1. The structure of emotion, suggesting that emotional phenomena are evoked by situations and are manifested in verbal reports, physiological responses and behavior. (Reprinted from Öhman, 1987, by permission by the JAI Press)

nificance to the person that is decisive for its power to elicit emotion. From a cognitive perspective, therefore, emotion is closely tied with a cognitive interpretive system determining the meaning of stimuli (Mandler, 1975). The concept of significance provides a useful link between emotion and the psychophysiological literature on the orienting response (OR) (Öhman, 1987, pp. 104–107). The OR is a phasic response to novel or significant stimuli that is discernible in autonomic, cortical and skeletal measures (see Siddle, 1983). Like emotion, it sensitizes perceptual and primes efferent systems, interrupts and distracts ongoing performance, and mobilizes autonomic activation. Thus, it may play an important part in the initiation of emotional phenomena (Öhman, 1987). The OR, therefore, may provide a psychophysiological avenue to the identification of emotionally effective stimuli.

Verbal Reports

Phenomenologically, emotion *is* experience. Yet to equalize emotion with experience is to pay a heavy prize in terms of unused analytical power. It means that one dissociates oneself from emotional phenomena seen in other species than our own, and thus from a biological perspective on the topic. Furthermore, because experience cannot be objectively verified, it means also dissociating oneself from natural science. One solution to this dilemma is to exchange emotional experience *per se* with verbal reports about such experience, because such reports can be examined for interobserver agreements. The underlying assumption, of course, is that there is an orderly, but perhaps not isomorphic, relation between experience and report. But the verbal report puts emotion squarely within the domain of the common language, which, as we have already noted, introduces a host of problems (see also Ch. 7, for a discussion of related problems). For one thing, it introduces a dualistic conception, where the phenomenal emotion is taken as the given, "the real thing," in contrast to its capricious reflections in the observable world, in verbal reports, behavior and physiology. The task for the scientist, it is then held,

is to account for the given, the phenomenal emotion, rather than to embed the ensemble of emotional phenomena of which it is a part in a broad explanatory framework. Thus, as emphasized by several authors (Lang, 1978; Ch. 2; Mandler, 1975; Cuthbert & Melamed, Ch. 7)), a primary objective of a scientific analysis is to get beyond the notions of emotion that are inherent in the common language.

Lang (1978; Ch. 2) noted that the language system can have quite different roles and functions with regard to emotion. Most often, when we think about verbal reports of emotion, we think about reports of perceptual experience: "I feel ... " However, emotion can also be manifested in verbal reports on an expressive level, as a tone of voice or choice of particular wording, e. g., using a harsh language. Finally, verbal reports can have a control function, prompting changes in other response channels.

At the experiential level, emotion is intimately connected to *valence*, to liking and disliking. Indeed, a good case can be made for the contention that it is a necessary feature of emotion that the underlying appraisal be valenced either positively or negatively (Ortony, Clore, & Collins, 1988).

On the basis of experiential evidence, the founder of modern psychology, Wilhelm Wundt, suggested that emotional experience comprises three dimension (Wundt, 1874). One of these dimensions was pleasure-aversion ("Lust-Unlust," that is, *valence*), the second one was activation-inhibition ("Erregung-Beruhigung," that is, *arousal*), and the third one was tension-relaxation ("Spannung-Lösung").

A similar dimensional structure results from verbal ratings of emotional stimuli (Lang, Ch. 4; Russell, 1980; Russell & Bullock, 1985). At least valence and arousal appear to be prominent dimensions in the space of emotion that can be derived from verbal descriptions of emotional stimuli. A third factor labelled potency or dominance comes out as less prominent in the factor analytic work, but may nevertheless be helpful in accounting for emotional phenomena. For example, anger and fear are both negatively valenced, high arousal emotions, but they differ in dominance, where anger is dominant and fear submissive (see Ch. 4 and 5).

Behavior

Instrumental and noninstrumental behavior. Emotional concepts, Frijda (1986) noted, are invited as hypotheses "to explain behavior that has neither sufficient nor adequate external purpose or reason; the explanation, then, is sought 'within' the subject" (p. 2). Examples may be that behavior interacting effectively with the environment comes to a sudden stop, or becomes peculiarly ineffective, or shows unusual intensity or emphasis. To Frijda (1986), therefore, emotional phenomena are primarily reflected in *noninstrumental* aspects of behavior. A reasonable interpretation of this statement is that it refers to behavior which is not primarily maintained by instrumental contingencies, that is, it is not shaped by its consequences (see Skinner, 1974). While the notion of emotion as primarily reflected in noninstrumental behavior undoubtedly captures an important aspect of emotional phenomena, it is not unproblematic. One problem is that it appears to fly in the face of the commonly held notion that a dimension of approach-avoidance is basic to emotional behavior (e.g. Schneirla, 1959). This dimension corresponds to the valence dimension of verbal ratings of emotion, and it may be viewed as major strategic disposition of the organism vis-a-vis its environment (Lang, Bradley & Cuthbert, 1990; Ch. 17). It is certainly reasonable to claim that we approach what we like and avoid what we dislike, but then we are definitely talking about instrumental behavior. One way out of this dilemma is suggested by the previously discussed examples of different reasons for avoiding particular alleys when out walking at night. Thus, one can routinely and unemotionally avoid situations because of established habits, and it is only when fear is aroused, e.g. before an effective avoidance response has been learned (e.g., Overmier & Lawry, 1979), that efforts to avoid can be taken as related to emotion. Another case in point is provided by the often extensive avoidance behavior of phobics. Although this behavior clearly is instrumentally maintained, it goes way above what is "objectively" reasonable in terms of the instrumental contingency. Thus, it would be covered within Frijda's (1986) formulation of

having "neither sufficient nor adequate external purpose or reason." Thus, from this perspective, approach and avoidance would not be regarded as sufficient to incorporate particular behaviors among emotional phenomena. To do so, one would require that the behavior showed some "surplus," "inefficiency" or "irrationality" to suggest the involvement of emotion.

Expressive behavior. One instance of noninstrumental behaviors concerns what is typically called expressive behavior. For the moment, we may by-pass *what* it is that the behavior in question expresses. That is to say, one should not take for granted that it necessarily expresses a specific emotion. Rather it may be components of emotional phenomena that are relatively independently elicited by a particular stimulus situation (Mandler, 1975; Ortony & Turner, 1990). Expressive behavior is typically elicited by stimuli rather than shaped by consequences. This is not to deny that it may serve communicative purposes and thus come under instrumental control. In fact, parental reinforcements are likely to shape emotional expressions of the developing child to make them conform with cultural conventions. In the adult these instrumentally learned modifications of emotional responses largely have become automatized, which may hide their instrumental character to the observer. Yet careful comparisons of genuine and posed facial expressions related to joy, reveals that the elicited expression differs from the posed one (Ekman & Friesen, 1982). Although facial expressions have been taken as defining features of a set of basic emotions (e.g., Ekman, Friesen, & Ellsworth, 1982), one could plausibly argue that the facial muscle movements that constitute a particular emotional expression do not necessarily reflect an integrated pattern but rather quite independent components (Ortony & Turner, 1990). For example, the frowned eyebrows, which often are specifically associated with anger, also occurs during concentrated attention (Frijda, 1986), anticipated effort (Smith, 1989) or frustration or puzzlement (Cacioppo, Petty & Morris, 1985). Thus, expressive behaviors often provide helpful indices of emotional phenomena, but one cannot take for granted that they provide unequivocal pointers to emotional states.

Physiological Responses

Theoretical issues. William James (1884) popularized the notion, independently proposed by Lange (1885), that what we feel in emotion is our body reacting to the emotional stimulus. Thus, we do not attack an opponent out of anger but feel anger because we attack. For James and Lange, then, bodily reactions were necessary for emotions. Although the Jamesian view of emotion has been debated and criticised, the implied notion that bodily activation is necessary for emotion still has its adherents (see e. g., Harris & Katkin, 1975). For example, although disavowing James' focus on explaining the experience of emotion, Mandler (1975; 1984) holds reactions in the autonomic nervous system as necessary input to the cognitive meaning analysis which results in emotion. Indeed, it is hard to deny that physiological responses are important components of emotional phenomena. To take a perhaps extreme example, patients suffering from panic disorder often start their medical care career by seeking treatment for a failing heart, because the cardiovascular concomitants of a panic attack are so strong that they may overshadow its essential emotional connotation. Thus, there is no question that physiological responses are at the heart of emotional phenomena. At the theoretical level, this means that bodily reactions figure prominently in theories of emotion (e. g., James, 1884; Schachter & Singer, 1962; Mandler, 1975). Empirically, it has meant that psychophysiological recordings have been of heavy use in attempts to operationalize emotional phenomena (e. g., Lang, 1971; Lang, Rice & Sternbach, 1972; Öhman, 1987).

Physiological correlates of emotional phenomena. But psychophysiological responses provide no less complicated an avenue to emotional phenomena than does verbal reports and behavior. Thus, it is as hard to claim that physiological responses provide specific pointers to particular emotions as it is for behavioral measures. There are some reports of a limited specificity in the sense that the cardiovascular pattern of reactions appears different in fear and anger (Ax, 1953; Schwartz, Weinberger, & Singer, 1981; Roberts & Weerts, 1982), but in general, physiological responses are more responsive to factors like metabolic demands than to emotional content. Cannon (1936) argued that autonomic, and particularly sympathetic, responses peak in intense emotion, associated with emergency, because it is in such situations that bodily resources have to be maximally recruited to meet threat and challenges. In agreement with such notions, Smith (1989) reported a strong relation between heart rate and anticipated effort using imagery as stimuli. Similarly, Obrist (1981) and coworkers have shown that situations involving active coping with a hardly controllable stressor induce cardiovascular responses even above what is metabolically justified from the muscular work involved.

But physiological reactivity is not restricted to situations manipulating metabolic demands. There is also reason to consider cognitive determinants related to the transaction between the individual and the environment. In a classical chapter, Lacey (1967) argued that the cardiovascular system helps modulate the sensitivity of the brain to take in or reject sensory information. Even disregarding this innovative theory, the data suggest that heart rate deceleration is associated with intake of sensory information in nonthreatening situations (e. g., Jennings, van der Molen, Somsen, & Brock, 1991), whereas demanding cognitive activity such as mental arithmetic accelerates heart rate and elevates blood pressure (e. g., Linden, 1991).

From these considerations, it is clear that what may appear as patterned psychophysiological effects during specific emotions in effect may reflect independent effects referable to specific elements of the particular stimulus configuration that is present. Just as the frowned eyebrow and the wide opened eyes seen in anger may be due to concentrated visual attention on an opponent, the heart rate deceleration sometimes seen in anger (e. g. Ax, 1953) may reflect the externally directed attention rather than the emotion itself. In contrast, fear with its readiness to escape rather than fixate and approach the eliciting stimulus, may engage much less focused attention, and, as a consequence, heart rate acceleration remains unconstrained and becomes part of the metabolic mobilization for taxing flight responses.

Even though there are good reason to question intrinsic relations between physiological responses and specific emotions, some recent data suggest striking relationships between some physiological responses and the emotional dimension of valence and arousal. Thus, Greenwald, Cook and Lang (1989) reported a strong relation between electromyographically recorded activity in facial muscles (the *corrugator*, mediating frowned eyebrows, and the *zygomatic*, mediating smiles) and independently rated valence of pictorial emotional stimuli. Skin conductance changes, on the other hand, were closely related to the independently rated arousal value of the stimuli. Subsequent research from Lang's laboratory has launched inhibition of the probe-elicited eye-blink startle reflex component as closely related to stimulus valence (Bradley, Cuthbert, & Lang, 1990; see Ch. 5 and Ch. 19).

Physiological substrates of emotion. So far, our discussion of the physiological response level in emotion has been restricted to physiological *correlates* of emotion, which in principle have no different status as emotional output than behavioral and verbal correlates of emotion. However, recording of physiological activity points more unequivocally towards potential physiological mechanisms for the phenomena under scrutiny than does behavioral and verbal measures. Thus, documenting physiological correlates invariably seems to raise, but should be carefully distinguished from, the question of the underlying physiological *substrates* of emotion. Such substrates, of course, are located in the brain, which ultimately organizes external and internal emotional stimuli into a more or less coherent emotional response.

In recent years, new technology has made the human brain much more accessible to direct study than it was before. In particular, positron-emission tomography (PET) allows visualization of neural activity in quite precisely located cortical and subcortical areas of the awake human brain, as it reacts to stimuli, controls behavior or imagines emotional scenes. For example, PET-studies show that in the negative

response to pain, the sensory (including the memory) function of the pain response is organized primarily in the cortical postcentral gyrus, whereas the emotional, valence-part of the response depends on limbic-forebrain activity, particularly in the cingulate region (Talbot, Marrett, Evans et al., 1991). By help of the more precise cortical localization which is possible on the basis of the brain's electrical and magnetic activity (electroencephalogram and magnetoencephalogram), it can be demonstrated that the cortical organization of emotional responses appears separable from non-emotional, "cold" cognitive operations (Nauman & Bartussek, 1991).

In general, these examples of the fruitfulness of the new technology provide results which are consistent with the animal literature and observations on humans patients during brain surgery. These data overwhelmingly suggest that the crucial ingredients of emotion, valence and arousal, primarily depend on subcortical and limbic-hypothalamic structures (e. g. Panksepp, 1982; Panksepp, Sacks, Crepeau, & Abbott, 1991). However, memory and the culturally shaped expressions of emotion rely on cortical networks, diffusely distributed over the neocortical surface (see Ch. 9 for references and further discussion of these issues).

In closing this section, let us point out that neurophysiological and neurochemical studies, although promising to delineate the neural substrates of emotional phenomena, cannot substitute for, but rather is dependent on, studies at other levels. Even with perfect knowledge about neurophysiological mechanisms, the definition of emotional phenomena requires the contextual-situational, the subjective-verbal, the peripheral physiological, and the behavioral components (see Figure 1) to be complete.

A Tentative Definition of "Emotional Phenomena"

Emotional phenomena are evoked by stimuli (external or internal) that are processed as significant to the person. They involve behavioral responses (particularly noninstrumental aspects of such responses), physiological activity, and subjective experiences which are reflected in verbal reports focused on affective

(i.e., positive-negative) evaluations of the stimuli (cf. Frijda, 1986).

Theoretical Issues

The Question of Fundamental Emotions

Some emotional states, such as fear, anger, joy, and sadness appear to be more consensual and prototypic emotions than others (Fehr & Russell, 1984; Shaver, Schwartz, Kirson, & O'Connor, 1987). These prototypic emotions have quite unambiguous counterparts in other mammals, which suggests that they have an origin in biological evolution. Furthermore, they have distinct facial expression, which shows a reasonable degree of invariance across cultures (Ekman, 1972). It appears an attractive notion, therefore, to give this basic set of emotion a special status of basic or fundamental emotions. As such, they would be expected to have a hard-wired neurophysiological basis and specific physiological correlates. Further, they would provide the building block for other less basic and more mixed emotions, and they would be transferable to new eliciting conditions through Pavlovian conditioning, perhaps constrained by biological preparedness (e.g., Öhman, 1987).

However, in an incisive analysis, Ortony and Turner (1990) showed that this view, in spite of its attractions, encounters problems that are hard to deal with. One problem concerns which emotions to include in the basic set. Although a reasonable consensus exists with regard to some emotions (like the ones listed above), there is a marked disagreement regarding others, even to the extent that what some theorists regard as basic emotions are not even recognized as emotions by others. A strong reason in favor of basic emotions would be if they could be demonstrated to have distinct neural substrates. However, neurophysiological data suggest that there are a limited number of response systems in the mammalian brain that are relevant for families of emotions (like flight,

caution, anxiety, fear, horror) rather than for individual emotions (Panksepp, 1982). Indeed, rather than to delineate the emotion of interest from other related emotional states in the common language, investigators of the neural mechanisms behind a specific emotion prefer to reverse the problem and use the neural circuitry to define the emotion. Thus, Panksepp et al. (1990), proposed that "*fear* is the central state that arises from the activity of a specific transdiencephalic emotional circuit which is recruited when body safety is threatened" (p. 9). Clearly, such an approach begs the question of whether fear as understood in the common language should be regarded as a basic emotion.

The facial expression data provide some of the best support for the notion of basic emotion, but the support can be challenged. At the basic conceptual level one can question what it is that the facial expressions "express." With Mandler (1975) one can argue that the notion of fundamental emotions accepts the common language view that there are palpable and invariant "emotions" which underlie and "cause" expressive behavior: "the fact that the common language has established broad and rather vague categories of emotions easily leads to the belief that these categories represent real and underlying dimensions of thought and experience" (Mandler, 1975, p. 86). But emotions are not things bearing an invariable relation to expressive behavior. Rather, in humans, these expressions are flexibly tied to a multitude of situational and motivational circumstances, some of which would not be included among emotional phenomena. Not the least are they used for communicative purposes, which led Mandler (1975, p. 147) to conclude that "the fine muscular patterns with which we are dealing (in facial expression) are probably remnants of communicative acts, not expressions of some underlying palpable emotion." Ortony and Turner (1990) pushed this analysis further by examining the pattern of facial muscle activation taken to be specific for anger. They argued that each of the components (frown, compressed lips, raised upper eye-lids, and tensed posture) can be tied to particular situational circumstances or psychological processes rather than being specifically indicative of anger. As we have already noted, open eyes under a frown may be related to concentrated visual attention, tense posture may indicate an impending attack and be absent if this course of action is impossible, and the compressed lips may be related to determination to remove the obstacle directly causing the anger. From this view, a seemingly specific pattern of facial actions tend to co-occur with the experience of anger because anger-inducing situations often include the stimuli for each of the specific components in the "pattern." The implication, then, is that the "patterning effect" may originate in patterns of external stimuli and their cognitive processing rather than in the internal patterning of responses. Thus, according to Ortony and Turner (1990, p. 322) such patterns of responses do not indicate "so much the presence of specific emotions as the presence of certain dissociable components of emotion, namely specific appraisals and their corresponding responses."

Refuting the basic emotion view in this way suggests an alternative that goes beyond common language categories of emotion to analyse specific relations between situational antecedents, psychological processes, and physiological and behavioral responses at a more detailed level. Also, it opens the vistas for a dimensional view of emotion. Such a view may deal with specific emotions as points in a dimensional space, but its emphasis is on the dimensions and their correlates (Ch. 4 and 5) and theoretical meaning (Ch. 17)

Independent Indicators versus a Three-System View of Emotion

The three response channels shown in Figure 1 and discussed above can be viewed as overt manifestations of emotion. Consequently, they may be useful in *inferring* emotion. From the perspective of the common language, behavior, peripheral physiology and verbal reports can be used to indicate the underlying, supposedly palpable emotion. Alternatively, they could be taken as the operational anchoring of hypothetical constructs of emotion embedded in a network of theoretical terms (Kozak & Miller, 1982). In either case, one would expect the various response channels to provide alternative and overlapping routes to the emotion. In other words, the different measures would be expected to be highly correlated with each other because they would be indicators of the same construct. However, as shown by Öhman (1987), it is quite complicated to decide what is meant with a "high correlation" in this instance. Because behavior, physiology and verbal reports represent very diverse data domains, most of the variance in each of the measure would be attributable to factors that would not contribute to the variance in the others. For example, a peripheral physiological measure such as heart rate is primarily constrained by the design and demands of the cardiovascular system, and the variance left for psychological factors to play with is necessarily small. Similarly, verbal reports would be shaped by cultural conventions including linguistic limitations, that would not affect heart rate at all. Because a high correlation between two measures requires that their variance is determined by the same sources of variance in approximately the same proportions, high correlations between, say, heart rate and verbal reports, would be unlikely. In fact, using the theorems of factor analysis for a theoretical treatment of this problem, Öhman (1987) was able to show that the maximal between-response channel correlation one could realistically opt for in the present case would rather be .30 than .70. Indeed, even within one of the response domain, autonomic responses, covariations between measures to various emotional stimuli often barely reach statistical significance, typically ranging between .2 and .3 (Fahrenberg, Walschburger, & Foerster, 1979). Given this limitation on the expected covariation, one would be likely to encounter frequent cases where, say, behavior and physiology, would provide discordant bases for inferring an emotion.

The inference of emotion is not a simple empirical operation, even if different measures should prove consistent. As argued by Miller and Kozak (Ch. 3) the emotion construct has to be put in some theoretical framework to guide the decision of when emotional processes are in operation. This consideration is easy to oversee if one's view of emotion is rooted in the common language wisdom that emotions are palpable underlying states that manifest themselves in behavior, peripheral physiology, and verbal reports.

A critical aspect of Lang's (1968) dismissal of the unitary fear construct in favor of the now famous three-system view (Ch. 2 and 3) was that he provided a radical break with the way that fear is treated in the common language. From his behavioral therapist vantage point, he had discovered that the effects of behavioral interventions to alleviate fear was partly dependent on which outcome measures were used. Being a behaviorist and behaviorally focused therapist he realized that

what he was treating was fear behavior rather than a construct of "fear" as we regard it in the common language. From this insight he went on to argue that fear is not a unitary construct but a loosely woven fabric of responses that only partially correlate with each other. This formulation has had a profound impact both on the clinical assessment of fear (e. g., Cone, 1979) and ideas of how it should be treated. For example, it has inspired attempts to match treatment modality to the most affected response system in phobics (e. g., Öst, 1987). The development of Lang's work from this starting point is traced in Chapters 2, 3 and 7. For the purpose of the present discussion, we may note that the three-system view is more compatible with a dimensional than with a categorical view of emotion (Ch. 4 & 5), as we have argued above. Furthermore, this research may serve as an example that it is an essential ingredient of scientific psychology to break away from, and go beyond, the "folk psychology" inherent in the common language.

Perspective on Emotion

The contributors to this book share a set of beliefs which together provide a perspective on the study of emotion. Part of the shared perspective can be traced to similar but independent backgrounds and experience, and part of it reflects mutual influences in more or less structured situations. The perspective has two conceptual and spatial points of departure, the psychological clinic and the psychophysiological laboratory.

The Role of Clinical Psychology

Psychopathology is an area where considerations about emotion are inevitable. Emotional phenomena seen in the clinic are focused on aversive emotion, including the agony of anxiety and the despondency of depression, as well as the inappropriate affect sometimes seen in schizophrenia. Seeing clinical patients, therefore, provides many invitations to reflect on the role of emotion in psychology and pathology. Indeed, following Freud, it has been a popular

conception that the phenomena of psychopathology throw light on normal psychology. Most of the contributors to this volume would probably emphasize the reverse direction of influence, the need to use models and theories from general psychology to enlighten the work of the clinician. Nevertheless, the clinical experience brings with it an interest in emotions and some preconceptions about their nature. Given the reason that bring people to seek professional help from clinical psychologists, a bias in favor of interest in aversive emotion is unavoidable. Thus, it is clear that the emotional content of this book goes much more in the direction of fear, anxiety and panic than in the direction or joy or positive excitement.

Many of the contributors have a background in clinical psychology with a behavioral orientation, and many still combine research and teaching with clinical work. This is important in several ways. Experience with patients provides an inescapable link to the real world and the problems that plague people there. Thus, one realizes that the emotional phenomena of interest occur in a real persons in their total life-contexts, and not only under limited experimental conditions. This experience provides an inoculation to the commonly felt pull of the ivory tower, to concentrate on esoteric phenomena that at best can be repeatedly produced in the laboratory, but that has unclear relations to what goes on in the outside world. Thus, encounters with patients give opportunity for informal and intuitive test of the usefulness of theoretical ideas, and the relevance of data.

The behavioral orientation involves a commitment to observe, measure, and influence, rather than to merely talk about, behavior. It allows the practitioner to go beyond mere intuition and collect data in the clinical situation through the use of formal behavioral assessment techniques and potentially stringent single-case experimental designs. In this way systematic bodies of clinical data can be developed, which puts the clinically interested researcher into an advantageous position compared to his colleagues in purely basic research areas of psychology. Thus, the clinician has a good notion of the type of phenomena in real life that the theories are supposed to explain, which contrast to the merely anecdotal, informal and limited real-life observations that are available in other areas of psychology. Thus, if one's interest is fears and phobias, not only should the theoretical notions one advances accounts for laboratory findings of fear, but they should also address the spectrum of more or less peculiar behavior displayed by phobics in real life as it is documented in clinical descriptions (see e. g., Öhman, Dimberg, & Öst, 1985).

The Psychophysiological Laboratory

The other point of departure is the psychophysiological laboratory, which sometimes may happen to be located in a clinical setting, but sometimes merely is an academic research laboratory. In either case, however, it would be a conceptual branch of the Science Building. Thus, the contributors to this volume share a natural science outlook on psychological research and a preference to ground psychological research in biomedical science. Training as a psychophysiologist necessarily involves acquiring a broad biological background with particular emphasis on general physiology. Furthermore, it provides generalizable experience of measurement techniques and a taste for measurement precision, sound statistics and experimental control. In short, the methodological approach of psychophysiology falls squarely within the mainstream of science. At the theoretical level, the psychophysiologist is likely to take seriously the notion of peripheral physiology as of primary importance for emotion. However, rather than to rest content talking about the importance of physiological responses for emotional processes, he or she is likely to ask him- or herself about the physiological mechanisms involved and whether they are amenable to measurement. Once the questions are asked, the next step is to find ways of examining the issues empirically. Thus, the contributors to this book has a decided bias in favor of empirical research. For an area like the psychology of emotion, which has been dominated by grand theoretical attempts often going far beyond the available empirical knowledge, efforts to develop the data base are clearly called for. However, for the present contributors, the predilection for empirical approaches does not bring with it an antitheoretical stance. Quite to the contrary, several of the chapters have a clear theoretical scope. However, an important point with the theoretical endeavours is that they opt to interact with data, to be tested and reformulated, if found wanting.

Cognitive Mechanisms

Both the clinical and the psychophysiological perspectives converge in stimulating theoretical developments in terms of cognitive mechanisms. Thus, both these areas, as the rest of psychology, have taken a cognitive tack when it comes to theory. Behavior therapy has evolved into and intermingled with cognitive approaches to provide a compelling theoretical frame for clinical phenomena (see e. g., Brewin, 1988). Rather than to rest content with the

analysis and change in reinforcement contingencies, therapists have become interested in
the way in which their patients construe the
world, the way that they interpret and act on the
available information from the environment
and in their memory. For example, a cognitive
analysis of panic (e. g., Clark, 1988) has paved
the way for powerful intervention techniques
(e. g., Öst, 1988).

Psychophysiology has seen a similar development in interest in cognitive mechanisms,
where articulated information processing constructs have been used to analyse common psychophysiological phenomena like the orienting
response (e. g., Öhman, 1979). Lang's (e. g.,
1979) work on the cognitive analysis of imagery
and the organization of emotional information
in memory can be taken as paradigmatic examples (Ch. 6).

In keeping with their basic science orientation, rather than accepting notions of cognitions derived from the common language, the
authors prefer formal treatments of cognitive
processes derived from an information processing perspective (e. g. Ch. 6, 8, 10, 15, 16). In
particular, many of the contributions more or
less explicitly deals with the organization of

emotional information in memory from a
memory network perspective launched by
Lang (Ch. 6). According to this model, emotion
is represented in memory as interconnected
nodes comprising stimulus, response, and
meaning information.

To sum up, the behavior therapy and the
psychophysiology background of the contributors combine to foster a tough-minded data-
oriented approach to the tender-minded phenomena of human emotion. We think that the
this volume shows that the time has come for
the ripening of such an approach. Coupled with
the cognitive theoretical orientation, the behavioral and psychophysiological origins naturally promote a three-system view on emotion.
Thus, virtually all of the contributors would regard this view as a conceptual cornerstone for
their approach to emotion. Other common
threads that run through the chapters are the
focus on clinically relevant aversive emotions
such as fear and anxiety, the concern for psychophysiological measurements, and the theoretical focus on the cognitive structure of emotions in memory as determinants of meaning,
behavior, physiological responses and verbal
reports of affective experience.

Organization and Overview of the Book

The book is organized in four sections, each
including between 4 and 7 chapters. The first
section, of which the present chapter is a part,
deals with *Basic Conceptual Issues*. The chapters in this section are focused on the three-system approach and a dimensional view on emotion. The three-system approach can be viewed
as a way of organizing the out-put side of
emotional phenomena, whereas the dimensional view serves the complementary function
of organizing the input side, by providing dimensions for evaluating emotional stimuli.
Both these notions are introduced in the present chapter. Chapter 2 then contains some of
Lang's most important writing on the three-system theory, which is followed up and analysed
in Chapter 3 by Miller and Kozak. Chapter 4
provides a fuller introduction of the dimen-

sional model, which is then developed empirically by Bradley, Greenwald and Hamm in
Chapter 5. This section, then, provide an important conceptual foundation for the following
chapters.

The second section of the book is devoted to
*Organization of Emotion in Memory: Applica-
tions to Imagery, Clinical Problems, and Experimental Aesthetics*. This is the central theoretical
part of the exposition. The theory is presented
by Lang in Chapter 5, and in Chapter 7 Cuthbert
and Melamed trace its development over three
decades of studies of anxiety disorder in the
Madison and Gainesville laboratories. Foa and
Kozak have developed a related theoretical
position, and in Chapter 8 they provide a review
of their view with special emphasis on the meaning component of the emotional memory net-

work. So far, the data discussed have almost exclusively concerned more or less peripheral physiological correlates of emotion. In Chapter 9, Birbaumer, Lutzenberger, Flor, Rockstroh and Elbert discuss the use of measures of central nervous system activity to get at the neurophysiological substrate of emotional imagery. Sexual activity provides opportunities to examine positively valenced emotions. In contrast to the emphasis on aversive emotion in most of the other chapters, Geer, Lapour, and Humphrey in Chapter 10 examine cognitive approaches to sexual behavior with a special emphasis on the usefulness of Lang's model in this new context. The remaining two chapters in this section, Chapter 11 by Palomba and Stegagno and Chapter 12 by Vaitl, Vehrs and Sternagel, examine implications of Lang's theorizing for the emotional effects of movies and music. Using a laboratory approach, Palomba and Stegagno examine psychophysiological effects of movie clips with an emotional content. Vaitl et at., on the other hand, provides a theoretical analysis of the emotional impact of music (and particularly Richard Wagner's operas) in terms of memory network theory, and then proceed to illustrate the analyses by data from a field study at a real opera performance.

The third section deals with the *Acquisition of Fear*, primarily from a memory network perspective. After a brief introduction by Lang in Chapter 13, Sartory provides an overview of fear acquisition in terms of modification of associative networks in Chapter 14. Hamm and Vaitl in Chapter 15 combine network notions with conditioning theory and report a series of studies demonstrating the fruitfulness of their approach. Finally, in Chapter 16, Öhman reviews studies on the effect of genetically prepotent stimuli on fear acquisition with particular emphasis on his own work, before proceed-

ing to discuss theoretical implications, again with special emphasis on the memory network notion.

The concluding section of the book brings us to the center of Lang's most recent work, which concerns modification of simple reflexes such as startle depending on the emotional context *(Emotion and Reflex Modification)*. In Chapter 17, Lang, Bradley and Cuthbert present a theoretical perspective incorporating a dimensional view on emotion into a construct of strategical emotional dispositions, where the organism may be overall inclined to approach or avoid with various degrees of intensity or activation. The central idea is that strategical approach disposition facilitates appetitive reflexes and inhibits defensive ones, whereas the reverse is true for an avoidance disposition. Chapter 17 by Requin and Bonnet presents a neurophysiologically oriented exposition of the startle reflex and its modifications. In Chapter 19 Bradley and Vrana examine the implications of startle modification data for research on emotion and emotional disorders. In Chapter 20 Simons, Fitzgibbons, and Fiorito uses the startle probe technique to analyse an emotionally interesting population of anhedonic subjects presumed to be at elevated risk for psychopathology and particularly for schizophrenia.

To sum up, this books presents a coherent view on emotion starting from basic perspective stressing multiple system measurements and a dimensional view of emotion; at the theoretical core lies a conception of emotion as organized in memory network comprising information about stimuli, responses and meaning. These theoretical notions are then applied to several different areas, including the study of fear and anxiety, human sexuality, fear acquisition, and experimental aesthetics.

References

Ax, A. (1953). The physiological differentiation between anger and fear in humans. *Psychosomatic Medicine, 15*, 433–442.

Brewin, C. R. (1988). *Cognitive foundations of clinical psychology*. Hillsdale, NJ: Erlbaum.

Cacioppo, J. T., Petty, R. E., & Morris, K. J. (1985). Semantic, evaluative, and self-referent processing: Memory, cognitive effort, and somatovisceral activity. *Psychophysiology, 22*, 371–384.

Cannon, W. B. (1936). *Bodily changes in pain, hunger,*

fear, and rage. New York: Appleton-Century-Crofts.

Clark, D. M. (1988). A cognitive model of panic attacks. In S. Rachman & J. D. Maser (Eds.) *Panic: Psychological perspectives* (pp. 71–90). Hillsdale, NJ: Erlbaum.

Cone, J. D. (1979). Confounded comparisons in triple response mode assessment research. *Behavioral Assessment, 1,* 85–95.

Ekman, P. (1972). Universals and cultural differences in facial expressions of emotion. In J. K. Cole (Ed.) *Nebraska symposium on motivation* (Vol. 19). Lincoln: University of Nebraska Press.

Ekman, P., & Friesen, W. V. (1982). Felt, false, and miserable smiles. *Journal of Nonverbal Behavior, 6,* 238–252.

Ekman, P., Friesen, W. V. & Ellsworth, P. (1982). What emotion categories or dimensions can observers judge from facial behavior? In P. Ekman (Ed.) *Emotion in the human face* (pp. 39–55). New York: Cambridge University Press.

Fahrenberg, J., Walschburger, P., & Foerster, F. (1979). *Psychophysiologische Aktivierungsforschung.* München: Minerva.

Fehr, B., & Russell, J. A. (1984). Concept of emotion viewed from a prototype perspective. *Journal of Experimental Psychology: General, 113,* 464–486.

Frijda, N. H. (1986). *The emotions.* Cambridge: Cambridge University Press.

Greenwald, M. K., Cook, E. W., III, & Lang, P. J. (1989). Affective judgement and psychophysiological response: Dimensional covariation in the evaluation of pictorial stimuli. *Journal of Psychophysiology, 3,* 51–64.

Harris, V. A., & Katkin, E. S. (1975). Primary and secondary emotional behavior: An analysis of the role of autonomic feedback in affect, arousal, and attribution. *Psychological Bulletin, 82,* 904–916.

James. W. (1884). What is an emotion? *Mind, 9,* 188–205.

Jennings, J. R., van der Molen, M. W., Somsen, R. J. M., & Brock, K. (1991). Weak sensory stimuli induce a phase sensitive bradycardia. *Psychophysiology, 28,* 1–10.

Kozak, M. J., & Miller, G. A. (1982). Hypothetical constructs vs. intervening variables: A re-appraisal of the three-system model of anxiety assessment. *Behavioral Assessment, 4,* 347–358.

Lacey, J. I. (1967). Somatic response patterning and stress: Some revisions of activation theory. In M. H. Appley & R. Trumbull (Eds.) *Psychological stress: Issues in research* (pp. 14–38). New York: Appleton-Century-Crofts

Lang, P. J. (1968). Fear reduction and fear behavior: Problems in treating a construct. In J. M. Shlien

(Ed.) *Research in psychotherapy* (Vol. 3) (pp. 90–102). Washington, D. C.: American Psychological Association.

Lang, P. J. (1971). The application of psychophysiological methods to the study of psychotherapy and behavior modification. In A. E. Bergin & S. L. Garfield (Eds.) *Handbook of psychotherapy and behavioral change: An empirical analysis* (pp. 75–125). New York: Wiley.

Lang, P. J. (1978). Anxiety: Toward a psychophysiological definition. In H. S. Akiskal & W. L. Webb (Eds.) *Psychiatric diagnosis: Explorations of biological predictors* (pp. 365–389). New York: Spectrum.

Lang, P. J. (1979). A bio-informational theory of emotional imagery. *Psychophysiology, 16,* 495–512.

Lang, P. J., Bradley, M. M., & Cuthbert, B. N. (1990). Emotion, attention, and the startle reflex. *Psychological Review, 97,* 377–395.

Lang, P. J., Rice, D. G., & Sternbach, R. A. (1972). The psychophysiology of emotion. In N. S. Greenfield & R. A. Sternbach (Eds.) *Handbook of psychophysiology* (pp. 623–643). New York: Holt, Rinehart, & Winston.

Lange, C. G. (1885). *Om sindsbevegelser: Et psykofysiologisk studie.* Köbenhavn.

Lazarus, R. S., Kanner, A. D., & Folkman, S. (1980). Emotions: A cognitive phenomenological analysis. In R. Plutchik & H. Kellerman (Eds.) *Emotion: Theory, research and experience* (Vol. 1) (pp. 189–217). New York: Academic Press.

Linden, W. (1991). What do arithmetic stress tests measure? Protocol variations and cardiovascular responses. *Psychophysiology, 28,* 91–102.

Mandler, G. (1975). *Mind and emotion.* New York: Wiley.

Mandler, G. (1984). *Mind and body.* New York: Norton.

Naumann, E., & Bartussek, D. (in press). Emotionality and event-related potential. In H.J. Heinze (Ed.) *New developments in event-related potentials.* Boston: Birkhäuser.

Obrist, P. A. (1981). *Cardiovascular psychophysiology: A perspective.* New York: Plenum.

Öhman, A. (1979). The orienting response, attention, and learning: An information-processing perspective. In H. D. Kimmel, E. H. van Olst, & J. F. Orlebeke (Eds.) *The orienting reflex in humans* (pp. 443–471). Hillsdale, NJ: Erlbaum.

Öhman, A. (1987). The psychophysiology of emotion: An evolutionary-cognitive perspective. In P. K. Ackles, J. R. Jennings, & M. G. H. Coles (Eds.) *Advances in psychophysiology* (Vol. 2) (pp. 79–127). Greenwich: J. A. I. Press.

Öhman, A., Dimberg, U., & Öst, L.-G. (1985). Animal and social phobias: Biological constraints on learned fear responses. In S. Reiss & R. R. Bootzin (Eds.) *Theoretical issues in behavior therapy* (pp. 123–175). New York: Academic Press.

Öhman, A., & Soares, J. J. F. (1992). *Unconscious anxiety: Phobic responses to masked stimuli.* Paper submitted for publication.

Ortony, A., Clore, G. L., & Collins, A. (1988). *The cognitive structure of emotions.* New York: Cambridge University Press.

Ortony, A., & Turner, T. J. (1990). What's basic about basic emotions? *Psychological Review, 97,* 315–331.

Öst, L.-G. (1987). Individual response patterns and the effect of different behavioral methods in the treatment of phobias. In D. Magnusson & A. Öhman (Eds.) *Psychopathology: An interactional perspective* (pp. 177–196). Orlando, FL: Academic Press.

Öst, L.-G. (1988). Applied relaxation vs. progressive relaxation in the treatment of panic. *Behaviour Research and Therapy, 26,* 13–22.

Overmier, J. B., & Lawry, J. A. (1979).Pavlovian conditioning and the mediation of behavior. In G. H. Bower (Ed.) *The psychology of learning and motivation* (Vol. 13) (pp. 1–55). New York: Academic Press.

Panksepp, J. (1982). Toward a general psychobiological theory of emotions. *Behavioral and Brain Sciences, 5,* 407–468.

Panksepp, J., Sacks, D. S., Crepeau, L. J., & Abbott, B. B. (1991). The psycho- and neurobiology of fear systems in the brain. In M. R. Denny (Ed.) *Fear, avoidance and phobias: A fundamental analysis* (pp. 7–59). Hillsdale, NJ: Erlbaum.

Roberts, R. J., & Weerts, T. C. (1982). Cardiovascular responding during anger and fear imagery. *Psychological Reports, 50,* 219–230.

Russell, J. A. (1980). A circumplex model of affect. *Journal of Personality and Social Psychology, 39,* 1161–1178.

Russell, J. A., & Bullock, M. (1985). Multidimensional scaling of emotional facial expressions: Similarity from preschoolers to adults. *Journal of Personality and Social Psychology, 48,* 1290–1298.

Schachter, S., & Singer, J. (1962). Cognitive, social and physiological determinants of emotional state. *Psychological Review, 69,* 379–399.

Schneirla, T. C. (1959). An evolutionary and developmental theory of biphasic processes underlying approach and withdrawal. *Nebraska Symposium of Motivation: 1959* (pp. 1–42). Lincoln: University of Nebraska Press.

Schwartz, G. E., Weinberger, D. A., & Singer, J. A. (1981). Cardiovascular differentiation of happiness, sadness, anger and fear following imagery and exercise. *Psychosomatic Medicine, 43,* 343–364.

Shaver, P., Schwartz, J., Kirson, D., & O'Connor, C. (1987). Emotion knowledge: Further exploration of a prototype approach. *Journal of Personality and Social Psychology, 52,* 1061–1086.

Siddle, D. (Ed.) *Orienting and habituation: Perspectives in human research.* Chichester: Wiley.

Skinner, B. F. (1974). *About behaviorism.* New York: Knopf.

Smith, C. A. (1989). Dimensions of appraisal and physiological reponse in emotion. *Journal of Personality and Social Psychology, 56,* 339–353.

Talbot, J. D., Marrett, S., Evans, A. C., Meyer, E., Bushnell, M. C., & Duncan, G. H. (1991). Multiple representation of pain in the human cerebral cortex. *Science, 251,* 1355–1358.

Wundt, W. (1874). *Grundzüge der Physiologischen Psychologie.* Leipzig: Engelmann.

Zajonc, R. B. (1984). Feeling and thinking. Preferences need no inferences. *American Psychologist, 35,* 151–175.

The Three-System Approach to Emotion

Peter J. Lang*

Philosophical and Theoretical Problems

In this chapter I would like to propose an alternative to the view that anxiety can best be understood as a phenomenon of human experience. I undertake the task with some "anxiety". Given the long history of this approach, its firm place in the conceptions of intellectuals of every persuasion, both clinicians and laymen, there must be very compelling reasons for its rejection. I believe such reasons exist.

The primary problem with the phenomenological model of anxiety lies in the fact that behavioral and physiological measurements in emotion often bear little relationship to each other, and are in turn poorly correlated with a verbal report of the subjective state. Furthermore, when responses are in dispute, the hypothesized true world of subjective experience remains private. Thus, there are no objective criteria which tell us which system to believe.

The failure of covariation is not a new phenomenon, and dynamic theories of psychopathology are primarily efforts at coping with this truth. Skinner, in a classic confrontation with Else Frenkel-Brunswick, illuminated this problem in the context of early psychoanalytic theory. Like most of his contemporaries, Freud held that behavior was a consequence of subjective intention or feeling. Thus, we would expect a close covariation between verbal report of feeling and behavioral consequences. However, it is exactly in the context of pathology that this covariation is most diminished. Thus, the patient with a hysterical disorder reports that he does not *intend* to immobilize his legs or discontinue vision. These things occur, he says, in the absence of an appropriate subjective state. It is of course possible to simply assume that the patient refuses to give an accurate report – he's either malingering or he doesn't understand the question. This is the view of some physicians today as well as in Charcot's time. However, other evidence seemed to Freud inconsistent with this simple explanation. Nevertheless, if he accepted the failure of covariation as fact, it flew in the face of a more fundamental theory which held that subjective states control behavior. Freud's solution was ingenious. He invented another state of subjectivity which had all the properties of intention, thought, and feeling associated with consciousness, which could also determine behavior, but which was unknown to the usual subjectivity about which people can report verbally. In effect, the invention of the unconscious mind was a device designed to save a more important theory, the view that behavior was determined by subjective feeling and intention. Out of this line of reasoning came such con-

* University of Florida

Reprinted from: Lang, P. J. (1978). Anxiety: Toward a psychophysiological definition. In H. S. Akiskal & W. L. Webb (Eds.) *Psychiatric Diagnosis: Explorations of Biological Predictors*. New York: Spectrum Publications, Inc., pp. 365–389. Excerpts: pp. 368–370 and 376–382.

Lang, P. J. (1971). The application of psychophysiological methods to the study of psychotherapy and behavior modification. In A. E. Bergin & S. L. Garfield (Eds.) *Handbook of Psychotherapy and Behavior Change: An Empirical Analysis*. New York: John Wiley and Sons, pp. 75–125. Excerpts: pp. 105–109.

cepts as "unconscious anxiety", e.g., the appearance of visceral arousal or behavioral avoidance in the absence of an appropriate verbal report.

It is easy to see a parallel between the unconscious of Freud and many other "theory saving" constructs in science. The epicycles of Ptolemy were designed to explain how the observed movements of the planets could be understood without violating the then accepted geocentric view of the universe. Much later physicists thought that space must be filled with "ether" because physical theory seemed to demand a medium for the propagation of light. In both these instances, new, more potent of more inclusive theories accommodated the data, and the necessity of the saving construct was undermined.

Skinner's solution to Freud's dilemma is a vigorous application of Occam's razor. Accordingly, behavior is a consequent of environmental contingencies, and subjective experience may be dispensed with as a theoretical construct without objective utility. However, we may question whether Skinner's concepts really have the power to exorcize the "ghost in the machine".

Science and Subjectivity

It may be inferred from the arguments presented above that there are two ways in which a theory of anxiety can consider subjective states. On the one hand, the content of subjective experience may be considered part of the raw phenomenon of science, i.e., as data. We are encouraged to dispense with anxious feelings as data by the scientific dictum that all events considered by science must be measurable, operationally defined, and through this definition available to shared observation. Traditional notions of subjective experience do not meet this criteria.

On the other hand, the theoretical constructs of subjective idealism might be used, as Freud used them, as models for organizing measurable events. It is perhaps less clear that such a theory does not lead to any useful explanation. Skinner's abrupt rejection of both conscious and unconscious determinism may seem premature to the clinician who sees unconscious processes at work when a rapid heart rate is accompanied by reports of emotional calm. Skinner counters by invoking the law of parsimony, and others have noted that such explanations are almost always *post hoc*, generating little predictive power. To this argument let us add the suggestion that subjective constructs have become somewhat shopworn. Psychology and psychiatry have for many years borrowed heavily from the philosophies of experience, with only a modest advance in scientific understanding and technological development to show for it. We constantly demand that theories which interrelate measurable responses remain isomorphic with theories of subjective experience. It may be necessary to escape from this pattern of conceptual thinking. Physics could not begin a new advance until it accepted counterintuitive theories (e.g., that apparently solid, stable objects are made up of small, widely spaced points of moving energy). Progress in psychopathology may require a similar flexibility of thought from the next generation of theorists.

Anxiety as a Response

From an empirical perspective, behavior culturally defined as anxious includes events in three broadly defined response systems. These are language responses, organized motor acts, and changes in the tonic activity levels of the somatic muscles and the viscera. All these responses may be prompted by external events through the mediation of the central nervous system (CNS) or may be occasioned directly by spontaneously occurring nervous or neuro-hormonal activity.

A variety of data tell us that all responses may act back on the central nervous system either through feedback at the effector or through distance receptors. Thus, it is reasonable to hypothesize that there is potential interaction and covariation between systems in emotion, which both precedes and follows the occurrence of any responses. The central task for researchers is to define the conditions under which these systems function in concert and under what conditions the systems operate independently, and to relate these phenomena to measurable antecedent events, both within the nervous system, and as far as possible, in the reactional biography of individuals. The central task for theorists is to provide us with guiding, explanatory constructs, models or analogies which organize these data, and ultimately provide a basis for practical prediction and control. It is not important to either the scientific or clinical enterprise that our explanations parallel phenomenological psychology, indeed, as I have already suggested, we should be ready to accept models which mathematically interrelate these events that may be quite alien to a psychology of experience.

System Interaction

The experiments of S. Schachter and his associates illustrate some important aspects of inter-system influence. Instructional set (information that permits the subjects to interpret exteroceptively perceived autonomic change) will block an emotional response that would have resulted from the coincidence of an appropriate external stimulus and sympathetic arousal. Lazarus and his colleagues (Lazarus and Opton, 1966; Lazarus, Speisman, Mordkoff, and Davison, 1962) have shown similar effects when external emotional stimuli are presented without the catechol supplement. In their studies, autonomic responses were recorded while subjects watched a stressful film (such as a film dealing with the subincision rites of Australian aborigines). They found that tonic autonomic activity was reduced if subjects are encouraged to intellectualize or deny the painful circumstances of the operation.

On the other hand, if the organism is cognitively set to be angry or afraid, autonomic activity or appropriate external stimuli will prompt a more intense response. Under the right conditions, instructions alone can lead to both the physiological and behavioral output of emotion. Thus, Graham and his colleagues (Graham, Kabler, and Graham, 1962) gave normal subjects waking or hypnotic suggestions to assume emotional attitudes previously found to be associated with specific psychosomatic syndromes. They found physiological change appearing in their subjects, in the same organ systems that were afflicted in the parallel patient group. Sternbach (1964) found that gastric motility (as measured by the movement of an ingested magnet) varied with instructions concerning a pill he administered to a small group of subjects. Those told that it would relax the stomach showed a reduction in activity relative to an uninformed group, while subjects told it was a gastric stimulant showed a significant increase in motility. In our own laboratory, Melamed (1969) found that instructional set grossly altered the physiological tonus and habituation rate of subjects to filmed fear stimuli, and that these changes were correlated with subsequent verbal reports of fear reduction. Thus, subjects instructed to intensify their emotional experience showed greatest autonomic arousal and least post-experiment change in fear; subjects instructed in muscular relaxation showed lower levels of arousal and more fear reduction.

It is also clear from clinical data that a mutually augmenting feedback loop may be generated between systems. Thus, the patient who is "set" to be distressed may become aware of autonomic feedback (such as heart rate increase) that confirms the cognition. A rapid pulse may then achieve the status of a discriminative stimulus for further anxious cognitions. In this manner, tachycardia begets tachycardia. A recent study by Lang, Sroufe, and Hastings (1967) suggests that such feedback effects are not dependent on awareness. In this experiment subjects tracked a meter, pressing a button when the pointer passed specific numbers on the meter face. They were unaware that the movements of the pointer were determined by their own heart rate. These subjects showed a significant increase in heart-rate variability during the task, relative to simultaneously run, yoked control subjects. This latter control group worked with the same meter display, but the meter was driven by their yokemates' heart rate rather than their own. The experiment clearly shows changes in an autonomic response which are a direct result of the subject's participation (albeit unaware) in an exteroceptively mediated feedback loop. It is reasonable to assume that such interactions may develop spontaneously, with important consequences for the development and maintenance of emotional behavior.

We have already alluded to neurophysiological evidence that suggests that autonomic activity may feed back *interoceptively* to influence striate-muscle reflexes and cortical activity. Such feedback is potentially disruptive, and in emotion, could contribute to the unskillful execution or blocking of motor acts. Furthermore, such failure of psychomotor functioning is *exteroceptively* perceived, and its negative valence can add to an ascending spiral of verbal, behavioral, and autonomic activation and disorganization.

Stimuli that prompt affects are less likely to instigate a general, disorganizing emotion when psychomotor responses are not disrupted. If an act is well-practiced, the individual may maintain good motor control, despite the presence of excessive autonomic arousal or anxious cognitions. Furthermore, repeated successes in generating effective behavior in the face of provocative stimuli break the link between augmenting systems. Under these conditions, it becomes possible to adapt out or unlearn the unsuitable emotional self-instruction and the associated physiological activity. Athletes, actors, musicians, and students have long used overlearning to reduce or prevent the debilitating effects of stress. Recently, this method has become a more explicit part of psychotherapeutic treatment (Wolpe and Lazarus, 1966). Social behaviors are practiced and overprac-

ticed with the therapist. After these roleplaying sessions, the patient begins supervised trials in the natural environment, proceeding on a regular schedule from low-stress to high-stress situations.

Jacobson (1938), Gellhorn (1964), Wolpe (1958), and Schultze and Luthe (1959) have all advocated the retraining of the peripheral physiological system as the best method to break the emotional-response loop. It is assumed that feedback of autonomic events is an integral part of emotion, and that efforts to attenuate this source of stimulation will favorably modify motor and cognitive response components.

Jacobson and Wolpe emphasize muscle relaxation as the vehicle for change. Instructional control of striate muscles is first achieved, and then employed to reduce tonus throughout the body. It is assumed that somatic-autonomic connections will function to reduce levels of sympathetic activity in the viscera. Schultze and Luthe's method is more similar to hypnosis, in that direct suggestions are made to reduce activity in specific body parts.

Recently, techniques have developed for the direct training of autonomic systems through the use of exteroceptive feedback and operant shaping techniques. Shearn (1962) first showed the operant conditioning of heart rate accelerations, and subsequent studies have also demonstrated shaping of tonic deceleration (Brenner, 1966; Engel and Hanson, 1966). Other experiments suggest that blood pressure (Hnatiow, 1968; Shapiro et al., 1969), sweatgland activity (Crider, Shapiro, and Tursky, 1966), and blood volume (Lisina, 1958) may be similarly influenced.

In our own laboratory, exteroceptive feedback has been used in training human subjects to reduce sinus arrythmia and stabilize their heart rates within narrowly defined limits (Hnatiow and Lang, 1965; Lang, Sroufe, and Hastings, 1967). In these experiments subjects observed a meterlike display that was in parallel circuit with a cardiotachometer (thus, pointer movements indicated beat-by-beat changes in rate). When provided with this display and given instructions to enter the pointer on the scale within a six B/M area, subjects significantly increased the total time their heart rate fell in the target area. Furthermore, they showed significantly greater reduction in heart rate standard deviation than uninstructed or nonfeedback controls.

More recent experiments from our laboratory suggest that these effects may be achieved with respiration experimentally controlled (Sroufe, 1969). Furthermore, systematic changes in the *P-R* interval of the EKG waveform appear to be associated with learned stabilization (Hnatiow, 1968). This would suggest that such heart-rate control is effected neurally (that is, through variation in vagal inhibitory impulses to the heart) and is perhaps independent of striate mediators. Animal experiments accomplished by Miller and his associates (Miller and DiCarra, 1967; Miller, 1969) support this latter hypothesis. In their research, rats were curarized and artificially respirated. Positive brain stimulation was then employed to reinforce either increases or decreases in heart rate. The appropriate directional changes shown by the shaped subjects greatly exceeded those of control animals. These investigators also reported *P*-wave changes in the EKG to be associated with experimental modification of heart rate.

Although autonomic feedback effects may not depend on muscle or respiratory mediation, Lisina (1958) suggests that the use of "voluntary" striate mediators early in training facilitates autonomic learning, and that these somatic responses then drop out when control is well learned. In a recent experiment we found some support for Lisina's first hypothesis; subjects given explicit instruction in relevant respiration patterns achieved rapid control of heart rate, which readily transferred to non-feedback conditions (Sroufe, Hnatiow, and Lang, 1967).

Stoyva (1968) has reported success in producing states of general psychophysiological relaxation using electromyograph feedback from striate muscles. The interaction of somatic and autonomic systems in the context of learned physiological control merits continued study.

Recently, the investigation of operant-feedback control of EEG frequency has been undertaken. In this research, a band-pass filter is used to separate out the frequency to be incremented from the total cortical signal. A predetermined amplitude of this frequency triggers an auditory stimulus. Subjects are instructed that task success is determined by the total time they can keep on the auditory stimulus. Kamiya (1962, 1968) reports that the proportion of the EEG falling within the alpha range may be significantly increased by this method. Furthermore, the psychophysiological state accompanying alpha increase involves a reduction in tonic autonomic levels, a verbal report of lessened anxiety, and an increased sense of well-being.

Much research remains to be done before the mechanism of change or the clinical value of operant-feedback methods of physiological control is clearly established. However, these techniques show promise of providing an avenue for modifying the physiological substrate of emotion. While drugs have long been used for this purpose, their effectiveness is often lessened by lack of specificity, unwanted side effects, and an absence of positive transfer to the non-drug state. If the persistence of emotional states is dependent even in part on physiological feedback, the retraining of the critical organ systems in the direction of reduced sympathetic activity could become a powerful new therapeutic intervention.

System Independence

It is proposed that emotional behaviors are multiple system responses – verbal-cognitive, motor, and physiological events that interact through interoceptive (neural and hormonal) and exteroceptive channels of communication. All systems are controlled or influenced by brain mechanisms, but the level of the important centers of influence (cortical or subcorti-

cal, limbic or brainstem) are varied, and like the resulting behaviors, partially independent. Because of this imperfect coupling, it is possible and even usual to generate emotional cognitions without autonomic arousal, aggressive behavior without a hostile motive, or the autonomic and avoidant behavior of fear without insight (proper labeling).

A coincidence of activity in more than one system is what we most confidently refer to as an emotion, and a highly general response characterizes states of intense affect. Perhaps the most obvious examples of system independence are apparent when emotion is attenuated. With a reduction in intensity, systems are often diminished in an unbalanced way, and evidence of arousal may actually disappear from one system and not another. So-called mild feeling states may involve no more than the verbal report, and we might find little specific activity in the autonomic or behavioral sphere. This points up the additional fact that systems differ in their sensitivity and the subtlety of their response. For example, the verbal behavior of a human being is capable or reflecting gradations of affect, to which the cruder autonomic system may be completely insensitive (Lang, Geer, and Hnatiow, 1963).

A variety of empirical data (Eriksen, 1958; Lang, 1968; Mischel, 1968) support the hypothesis that the behavior systems that we have described as active in the emotional response are partially independent. In our own work on the desensitization of phobias (Lang and Lazovik, 1963), we have found repeatedly that some subjects will show rapid change in overt behavior (for example, show less avoidance of the phobic object), but no initial lessening of fear in questionnaires or interview report. Later this verbal system often "catches up." On the other hand, some subjects report diminution of fear, but continue to show performance deficit. Similarly, the low correlations found between physiological and behavioral data are legion (see Lacey, 1959; Martin, 1961; Martin and Sroufe, in press). While it is possible to assume that the poor relationships obtained are attributable to inadequate measurement, they have appeared so often as to merit serious consideration as real phenomena. From this perspective, these findings argue that behavioral systems are to some extent capable of independent change – they can be shaped separately by environmental influence.

With reference to the development of normal and pathological emotion, this theoretical position implies that most affects do not arise all of a piece – with a viewing of the primal scene

(Freud, 1938) or the hearing of loud noises near small animals (Watson and Rayner, 1920). It suggests that emotional responses may be constructed element by element as the organism develops. We have already described the operant-feedback training of the autonomic nervous system. Similar effects may occur in nature, as they have been shown to do in the laboratory. Thus, states of general or organ-specific sympathetic activity could develop through a fortuitous occurrence of negative or positive reinforcers in the environment, in concert with specifically vulnerable developmental stages. The systematic delay of food or attention until heart-rate and blood-pressure variability increase, could produce a chronically hyperactive cardiovascular system. As Miller (1969) has suggested, such unintended but specific operant schedules may determine the development of psychosomatic disease. Furthermore, Russian studies of interoceptive conditioning suggest that conditioned stimuli can impinge on autonomically innervated organs (for example, the intestinal wall), and through contiguity with an aversive event, come to mediate widespread autonomic change (Razran, 1961). In these cases, no explicit language behavior or motor acts may be attached to the stimulus-response sequence. Nevertheless, stimulation of the gut produces an aversive psychophysiological state. Of course, language components could be added to the sequence later through further conditioning, or as a function of behavioral or semantic generalization from emotional learning in other situations.

On the other hand, individuals may develop emotional responses out of primarily verbal learning experiences. Thus, parents may reinforce the statement "I am afraid" in specific stimulus contexts. The child may learn to emit the language response reliably. However, whether the verbal statement becomes associated with behavioral acts or autonomic activity, depends on other learning. Similarly, it is possible that emotions might be started from overt aggressive acts or avoidance behavior, and the language and autonomic activity added later.

That the language system comes to catalogue, and to some extent control and direct, other behaviors is clear (although the method by which this is accomplished is not). However, it is also true that considerable independence is maintained. Emotions, almost by definition, are events that are outside the control of language (that is, conscious motives or intent). Furthermore, the breadth and tonicity of a subject's verbal emotional gradient may be considerably at variance with the same dimension's characteristics in another response system. Thus, some individuals have learned to signal anxiety as intense, when only minimal sympathetic arousal or behavioral deficit can be measured. In these cases, treatment might be directed primarily at the alteration of verbal-adaptation levels, and the acceptance of some upset as a normal part of living. On the other hand, some patients fail to note the debilitating effects of stress despite gross changes in performance or physiological deterioration. They may need an opposite, sensitization therapy, so they can begin to cope earlier in the sequence of emotion-generating events.

This analysis suggests that we are unlikely to find in the autonomic system an isomorphic representation of verbal report of feelings, or reliable precursors of emotional acts. It further suggests that human behavior may not be so smoothly integrated as introspective analysis sometimes prompts us to think. If we insist on locating a controlling homunculus in the cortex of man, we must also recognize the limitations of the beast. He is not going to have awareness of many important behaviors – much learning and unlearning is going to take place without and despite him. Furthermore, it does not seem reasonable to solve the problem by inventing another homunculus (that is, the unconscious), contenting ourselves that a sensitive bedside

manner can alone encourage an internal dialogue. We will need to confine ourselves to measurable behaviors in all systems, and discover the laws that determine their interaction. The data suggest that we must deal with each behavior system in its own terms. Treatment programs will have to be tailored to each behavior in the light of what we know about its educability. Thus, a patient who reports anxiety, fails to cope or perform effectively under stress, and evidences autonomic activity that varies widely from the practical energy demands of the situation, needs to receive treatment for all these disorders. He should be administered a treatment directed simultaneously at shaping verbal sets (so as to reduce reported stress over the variety of situations in which it appears), assisted in building effective coping behaviors and practicing them in appropriate contexts, and finally, administered a program for attenuating autonomic arousal and excessive muscle tonus, with the goal of reducing the distraction and interference of peripheral physiological feedback. In short, psychotherapy should be a vigorous multisystem training program, tailored to the unique behavioral topography presented by the patient. Fortunately, it is not infrequent that successes in the control of one system seem to precipitate broad change throughout the individual's behavioral repertoire. It may come about through a new insightful conceptualization, or relief from aversive autonomic feedback, or the generation of a new, active coping behaviour. However, all these things may be required to achieve a lasting cure. At this stage of development we know too little about the interaction between response systems to depend on the broad generalization of narrow therapeutic programs.

The Language of Anxiety

In this discussion we have so far treated the patient's language behavior in emotion as verbal report data, without distinguishing the context in which the verbal response was obtained or considering its functional significance. However, it is clear that anxious verbalizations do not *mean* the same things in all situations.

Furthermore, language is a system of signs and symbols specialized for communication and information processing. Thus, language can serve a special function in integrating response systems. One of the reasons that we might anticipate poorer response concordance in young children than adults is because the child's linguistic skills have not developed to a point where they could serve him adequately in the role of observer of his own behavior. Furthermore, it is language responses which suggest the greatest differentiation in emotion. The large vocabulary of emotion implies that verbal discriminations among stress stimuli are many times more subtle than might be found if we were to depend on such measures as skin conductance changes or gross motor acts to define emotional states. Indeed, one of the important factors which prompted Cannon to criticize James' theory was the failure of psychophysiologists to readily translate the myriad of reported feeling states into an equally differentiated physiological language. A similar assessment prompted Schachter and Mandler to presume that physiological activation is the same in all emotions, and plays no role in defining specific emotional states. However, it may still be too early to close this issue, and the relationship between subjective judgment and arousal may very well not be the terrain on which the battle should be fought.

In studying the relationship between verbal report and other measures of emotion, the results obtained often seem to depend on the function of language behavior that is being measured. Several different verbal response modes can be distinguished which have been examined in studies of affective behavior. Thus, researchers have analyzed the expressive or instrumental use of language in the context of arousing stimuli. I include here the vocalization of an angry patient who yells "I hate you" at the therapist, screams and cries of distress when a phobic patient is exposed to the fear object, systematic avoidance of certain topics of discussion at interview and other so-called defensive behavior. Some of these behaviors have obvious face validity as emotional expression; others are very difficult to code. In general, the less primitive the expressive dimension, the more complex and arbitrary becomes our measurement system. Another mode, closely related to the above category, is linguistic performance deficit. This category includes stuttering, stammering, memory loss, disorganized speech, blocking – all disturbances of verbal behavior which *may* be contingent on emotional stress. The third mode

is probably the most popular among investigators. This is the verbal response obtained by inquiring about the patient's subjective state, e. g., "How do you feel?" "How would you label your feeling state and what is the strength or clarity of this feeling?" In yet another mode, we employ the subject as an observer of his other responses that we hold to be associated with emotion. Most frequently we ask subjects to report on their physiology – "Were your palms sweaty? Did your heart skip a beat?" This line of inquiry has been called autonomic perception. Finally, it is also possible to conceptualize language specifically in terms of its control function. To what extent are subjects able to modulate physiological or gross motor responses in emotion on instruction? If subjects read a passage of text describing an emotionally arousing concept, to what extent is sympathetic activation occasioned by the material and does the pattern of somatic and visceral responses relate to the specific emotional situation (fearful, aggressive, or sexual)? Does visceral arousal accompany instructed emotional imagery? In experiments designed to answer these questions, language becomes the stimulus for a physiological response, rather than simply an output covariate. Of course, the verbal report of anxiety evoked by such instructions may also be obtained. Information on the subjects' response to this kind of instigated concordance may provide important clues to the cognitive structure of anxiety which are not obtained from responses to nonlinguistic stimuli.

The list of response modes presented here may not be exhaustive. Clinical inquiry and laboratory research may yet uncover other properties of verbal behavior in emotion that merit measurement. However, all measures probably can be related to three broad uses of affective language; these are *expressive, perceptual*, and *control* functions. Furthermore, we might anticipate different patterns of covariation between these separate language functions and concurrent physiological or gross behavioral responses in emotion. In fact, it could be argued that much of our confusion about emotional states stems from a failure to note explicitly which language function is being related to the other behaviors.

Autonomic Perception and Emotional Expression

Interest in autonomic perception stems directly from James' theory of emotion. If feeling states are to be understood as somato-visceral percepts, then it is reasonable for investigators to expect covariation between subjects' reports of physiological arousal and their actual reactivity. George Mandler has given the most systematic attention to this concept. In a series of studies published between 1958 and 1961, he and his colleagues carefully examined the covariation between subjects' report of physiological arousal and the evidence of bioelectric responses, recorded under stress. Mandler, Mander, and Uviller assessed verbal report of arousal through an Autonomic Perception Questionnaire. It consisted of three sections: (1) "Free response descriptions" of feelings and bodily reactions to anxiety and pleasurable situations; (2) 30 graphic scale items, dealing with the perception of specific bodily activity, e.g., "When you feel anxious, how often are you aware of any change in your heart action?"; and, (3) Items selected from the MMPI particularly from the Manifest Anxiety subscale, because they deal "with reports of internal bodily stimulation." Subjects scoring high in autonomic perception and a second group who scored low were placed in an "intellectual stress situation," and skin resistance, heart rate, respiration, skin temperature, and peripheral blood volume changes were assessed.

Mandler and associates found that, in general, subjects who reported that they experienced high levels of reactivity showed significantly higher autonomic arousal in a stress situation, on 3 of the 5 physiological channels measured, than did low perceivers. However, the two distributions did overlap. Furthermore, Mandler and colleagues noted a significant tendency for high perceivers to overestimate their own reactivity, and for low perceivers to underestimate their reactivity. That is to say, there was a clear reporting bias, such that given a constant level of autonomic response, some subjects systematically reported themselves to be highly aroused, while other individuals reported less or no arousal. In brief, self-descrip-

tions of autonomic symptoms are to some extent independent of ANS reactivity, and controlled by other factors in the environment. In further support of this view, Mandler and Kremen observed that the Autonomic Perception Questionnaire correlated only .22 with ANS activity. When it was combined with a psychological interview the prediction of ANS activity increased to only .30 (sharing only 9% of the total variance in the situation).

In a later study Mandler, Mandler, Kremen and Sholiton pursued a different approach. Instead of asking subjects to estimate their general responsivity, subjects were instructed to respond verbally to a series of statements tapping sexual, aggressive, and other emotional contents. The statements were highly provocative, and related to areas of potential emotional conflicts, e.g., "Boy beats mother into unconsciousness.", "He enjoys sleeping with men." The subjects' verbal behavior was analyzed in terms of such dimensions as avoidance (a long reaction time, or the subject did not discuss the content presented), interference in the subjects' usual speech patterns, or personal affective expressions (e.g., "That's horrible."). While the covariation between systems was still far from perfect, under these conditions concordance was improved. Mandler et al. reported one correlation of .72 between a total emotionality score, resulting from an analysis of the subject's speech productions, and an overall measure of physiological arousal. The investigators concluded that "there is a strong association between the amount of verbal disturbance a stimulus elicits and the degree of physiological response to it."

The categories of verbal behavior and the coding system developed by Mandler are certainly not ideal, and a full replication is needed before one may feel wholly confident in the data. However, the above results do suggest that the concordance of physiological arousal with *expressive* (instrumental or functionally disturbed) verbal behavior may be much greater than with a *perceptual* response, i.e., judgments of affective states or self-observations of physiological change. These results also encourage the view that language is better conceptualized as an output system, rather than as a murky window opening on a subjective world of feeling and desire.

Instructional Control and Physiological Arousal

From the perspective of phenomenology, emotional behavior differs from other responses of the organism in that it seems unintended by the person, and outside one's self control. We noted earlier that Kierkegaard referred to anxiety as an "alien power" that seizes control of the mind and body. For Fenichel too anxiety is "ego-alien", as are all neurotic symptoms. The alien nature of emotion is implied by the term *affect*. Anxiety is not conceived as a response *effected* by the organism, but as an experience which happens to the person. Thus, anxiety seems analogous to a percept, as if the individual were processing some information from an outside source. We have already questioned the indictment of the visceral physiology as the "alien" stimulus for feelings and emotional judgments. We would now like to consider a radical alternative to the perceptual view. We propose to examine physiological arousal not as a stimulus for feelings, but as an output system which is understood to be loosely coupled with (i.e., controlled by) verbal instructions.

John Lacey is fond of pointing out that the autonomic nervous system is rich in afferents; however, textbooks in physiology traditionally emphasize the efferent role of the ANS. It is viewed as a control system over organs which modulate the body's energy requirement. Furthermore, although we call the system autonomic, the autonomy is at best only partial, as the CNS exerts an impressive degree of control over all levels of visceral functioning. So-called voluntary, somatic muscle and ANS mediated visceral reactivity are closely coupled in all behaviors. As Obrist et al. notes, cardiovascular changes covary in a precise and refined way with changes in the tonus of the neuromusculature, and such coordination is instigated primarily at the level of the brain. Thus, there are no anatomical or functional neurophysiological barriers to a discussion of central control over arousal states. Furthermore, considering the rich neural connection downward from the cortex, it is hardly farfetched to consider the function of language in modulating the activity level of muscle and viscera. Indeed, it would be much more difficult to argue that such control is absent.

The role of the verbal system in anxiety is illuminated by considering the degree of physiological arousal prompted by an objective fear stimulus, relative to that occasioned by appropriate verbal instructions. Thus, a phobic patient may react physiologically to an alive spider with, for example, high heart rate when close to the animal. However, the objective fear stimulus is not inherently capable of evoking a strong autonomic response, as would a loud burst of white noise, or a puff of air on the cornea. Reactivity to the spider may depend importantly on the instructional context in which it is presented. Thus, if we tell the patient that the spider is a rare representative of a poisonous species, or that it is in reality a wind-up toy, differential physiological responsivity may reasonably be anticipated. Furthermore, instructions do not only influence responding by adding to or subtracting from information *about* the stimulus. We may also change responsivity by telling the subject how to react *to* the stimulus. Thus, Melamed found that phobic subjects' physiological responses to films of snakes were enhanced when they were told to react with an intense emotional experience, *as if* they were actually in the presence of an alive snake. Indeed, for some subjects the presence of an objective fear stimulus is wholly unnecessary to the evocation of a sympathetic response. We may obtain physiological change if we simply describe a fear context, and this may be further enhanced if we also instruct the subject to imagine the stimulus vividly and to respond emotionally.

The ability to react to language physiologically, to self-generate "off line" part or all of the physiological response to an external stimulus, is not found in all individuals. Marks and Huson reviewed a series of experiments in which physiological responses to fear imagery were obtained from a total of 77 psychiatric patients. "Significant differentiation of neutral from phobic imagery was found on skin conductance in two of the six studies, on heart rate in four of the studies, and on subjective anxiety in all six studies." Furthermore, when between system correlations were examined, "hardly any relationship was found between subjective anxiety and physiological measures." These data suggest that verbal report of anxiety is the most reliable consequent of instructions to imagine a frightening event. Such instructions will also increment sympathetic activation, but they seemingly accomplish it independently of emotional judgments, and apparently not in all subjects.

The relationship between physiological reactivity to fear imagery and therapeutic change was studied by Lang, Melamed and Hart. Heart rate activity was recorded during desensitization along with verbal report of anxiety to each scene presentation. When scenes reported to be maximally frightening were examined, no general covariation with heart rate was apparent. Thus, some subjects who described themselves as too fearful to continue scene imagery showed a consonant cardiac arousal; however, others offering the same verbal report of distress responded with no measurable increase in heart rate. Furthermore, a significant correlation was observed between heart rate during these high fear scenes and overall posttreatment reduction in phobic response. In brief, subjects who reported high scene fear but did not show cardiac reactivity (i. e., discordant subjects) showed little improvement. However, concordant subjects whose heart rates were high during scenes reported to be maximally fearful, showed the greatest fear reduction after treatment as measured by behavioral change and verbal report.

Schroeder and Rich recently reported a similar relationship between heart rate and therapeutic success. However, they measured heart rate after each desensitization session and prior to a series of postsession behavioral avoidance tests. They found that subjects who responded favorably to treatment had higher heart rates in anticipation of the avoidance test. Thus, both subjects who react autonomically to phobic imagery, and who react autonomically to instructions that a phobic stimulus will be presented, have good prognosis for therapeutic intervention. These results suggest that successful therapy may depend on the subjects' capacity to react cardiovascularly to instructions, and perhaps also on the generation within the therapy hour of physiological components of the fear response. I do not mean by this to suggest that behavior change is only mediated by intense emotional experience. It is now clear from studies of therapeutic flooding under tranquilizing medication that reduction of fear may be obtained under low levels of arousal. Furthermore, many of the significant differences in cardiac rate between subjects, to which we refer here, represent deviations of only a few beats per minute. However, the findings suggest that processing parts of the visceral anxiety response may be a key factor in prompting broader therapeutic change.

It is interesting to note that relationships between reactivity and performance, analogous to those noted above, have been observed for many simple laboratory tasks. Roessler studied the reaction time performance, reactivity to stressful films, and vigilance behavior of subjects divided into experimental groups on the basis of personality testing. He found consistent evidence of greater autonomic reactivity, coupled with better task performance, in subjects who scored high on Barron's Ego Strength scale. It will be recalled that this scale appears sensitive to such traits as self-confidence and competency, and has been shown to predict success in psychotherapy. It is tempting to consider language control over visceral reactivity as a factor in competency measurement, and as a basic mechanism in mobilizing the organism for behavior change. In any event, it seems clear that concordance between response systems, while characteristic of intense fear, may in some cases prompt a more hopeful prognosis than a discordant topography. Furthermore, the ability to self-generate arousal may also be a key to the central processing of emotion which is a goal of psychotherapy.

References

Brenner, J. Heart rate as an avoidance response. *Psychological Record*, 1966, 16, 329–336.

Crider, A., Shapiro, D., and Tursky, B. Reinforcement of spontaneous electrodermal activity. *Journal of Comparative and Physiological Psychology*, 1966, 61, 20–27.

Engel, B. T., and Hanson, S. P. Operant conditioning of heart rate slowing. *Psychophysiology*, 1966, 3, 176–187.

Eriksen, C. W. Unconcious processes. In M. R. Jones (Ed.), *Nebraska Symposium on Motivation*. Lincoln: University of Nebraska Press, 1958.

Freud, S. *The basic writing of Sigmund Freud*. A. A. Brill (Ed.), New York: Modern Library, 1938.

Gellhorn, E. Motion and emotion: The role of proprioception in the physiology and pathology of the emotions. *Psychological Review*, 1964, 71, 457–472.

Graham, D. T., Kabler, J. D., and Graham, F. K. Physiological response to the suggestion of attitudes specific for hives and hypertension. *Psychosomatic Medicine*, 1962, 24,159–169.

Hnatiow, M. Learned control of heart rate and blood pressure. Unpublished doctoral dissertation, University of Pittburgh, 1968.

Hnatiow, M., and Lang, P. J. Learned stabilization of cardiac rate. *Psychophysiology*, 1965,1, 330–336.

Jacobson, E. *Progressive Relaxation*. Chicago: University of Chicago Press, 1938.

Kamiya, J. Conditioned discrimination of the EEG alpha rhythm in humans. Paper presented at the Western Psychological Association Meeting, San Francisco, April 1962.

Kamiya, J. Conscious control of brain waves. *Psychology Today*, 1968,1, 57–60.

Lacey, J. I. Psychophysiological approaches to the evaluation of psychotherapeutic process and outcome. In E. A. Rubinstein and M. B. Parloff (Eds.), *Research in psychotherapy*, Vol. 1. Washington, D.C.: American Psychological Assiociation, 1959.

Lang, P. J., Fear reduction and fear behavior: Problems in treating a construct. In J. M. Shilieu (Ed.), *Research in Psychotherapy*, Vol. III. Washington: American Psychological Assiociation, 1968.

Lang, P. J., Geer, J., and Hnatiow, M. H. Semantic generalization of conditioned autonomic responses. *Journal of Expermental Psychology*, 1963, 65, 552–558.

Lang, P. J., and Lazovik, A. D. Experimental desensitization of a phobia. *Journal of Abnormal and Social Psychology*, 1963, 66, 519–525.

Lang, P. J., Sroufe, L. A., and Hastings, J. E. Effects of feetback and instructional set on the control of cardiac rate varability. *Journal of Experimental Psychology*, 1967, 75, 425–431.

Lazarus, R. S., and Opton, E. M. The study of psychological stress: A summary of theoretical formulations and experimental findings. In C. D. Spielberger (Ed.), *Anxiety and behavior*. New York: Academic Press, 1966.

Lazarus, R. S., Speisman, J. C., Mordkoff, A. M., and Davison, L. A. A laboratory study of psychological stress produced by motion picture film. *Psychological Monographs*, 1962, 76 (Whole No.553).

Lisina, M. I. The role of orienting in the conversion of involuntary into voluntary reations. In L. G. Voronin et al. (Eds.), *The orienting reflex and exploratory behavior*. Moscow: Acad. Pedag. Sci., 1958.

Martin, B. The assessment of anxiety by physiological-behavioral measures. *Psychological Bulletin*, 1961, 234–255.

Melamed, B. G. The habituation of psychophysiological responses to tones, and to filmed fear stimuli und varying conditions of instructional set. Unpublished doctoral dissertation, Universtiy of Wisconsin, 1969.

Miller, N. E. Learning of visceral and glandular responses. *Science*, 1969,163, 434–445.

Miller, N. E., and DiCara, L. V. Instrumental learning of heart rate changes in curarized rats: Shaping and specificity to descriminative stimulus. *Journal of Comparative and Physiological Psychology*, 1967, 63, 12–19.

Mischel, W. *Personality and assessment*. New York: Wiley, 1968.

Razran, G. The oberservable unconscious and inferable conscious in current Soviet psychophysiology: Interoceptive conditioning, semantic conditioning, and the orienting reflex. *Psychological Review*, 1961, 68, 81–147.

Schultze, J. H., and Luthe, W. *Autogenic training: A psycho-physiologic approach in psychotherapy*. New York: Grune and Stratton, 1959.

Shapiro, D., Tursky, B., Gershon, E., and Stern, M. Effects of feetback and reinforcement on the control of human systolic blood pressure. *Science,* 1962,163, 588–590.

Shearn, D. W. Operant conditioning of heart rate. *Science,* 1962,137, 530–531.

Sroufe, L. A. Learned stabilization of cardiac rate with respiration experimentally controlled. *Journal of Experimental Psychology,* 1969, 81, 391–393.

Sternbach, R. A. The effects of instructional sets on automatic responsivity. *Psychophysiology,* 1964, 1, 67–72.

Stoyva, J. Skinnerian Zen: Or control of psychological responses through information feetback. Paper read at Denver University Symposium on Behavior Modification, 1968.

Watson, J. B., and Rayner, R. Conditioned emotional reactions. *Journal of Experimental Psychology,* 1920, 3, 1–14.

Wolpe, J. *Psychotherapy by reciprocal inhibition.* California: Stanford University Press, 1958.

Wolpe, J., and Lazarus, A. A. *Behavior therapy techniques.* New York: Pergamon Press,1966.

Three-Systems Assessment and the Construct of Emotion

Gregory A. Miller* and Michael J. Kozak**

Abstract

The three-systems approach to assessing fear is historically important for having put physiology on a par with self-report and overt actions as indices of emotion and for having recognized the frequent poor covariation among the systems. This view has been widely embraced, but typically in ways that entail conceptual and practical problems. These problems are related to the distinction between data and the fear construct itself, and to the criteria for inferring fear from three-systems data. Issues of data, construct, and inferential rules are highly pertinent to newly developing psychophysiological methods of assessing fear, such as the facial action coding system, topographic EEG mapping, and startle-probe/dual-task paradigms. Functionally defined constructs of emotion can circumvent some problems in the application of multi-system assessment, provided that the implications of the "intentionality" that characterizes some functional constructs are appreciated.

Key words: three systems, psychophysiology, fear, assessment, intentionality, functional construct

From the modern vantage point it is easy to take the "three-systems" approach for granted, and it is often discussed without citation (e. g., Linehan & Wagner, 1990). Such historical oversight is a measure of the pervasive impact of Lang's articulation (1964), development (1968), and fundamental revision (1978) of the now-familiar notion that publicly observable fearful behavior may be classified as self-report, physiology, and overt behavior. Subsequent writers on the topic (e. g., Cone, 1979; Kozak & Miller, 1982; Rachman & Hodgson, 1974), though explicitly acknowledging their debt to Lang, are now sometimes mistakenly cited as the source of this notion. Again, such is the likely result of successful penetration into the basic assumptions of an entire field.

Including Physiology in Behavioral Assessment

Why does the three-systems notion matter? Lang (1968) made two radical points with which we are all still struggling. First, he portrayed physiology as on a par with self-report and overt behavior. The behaviorists of 25 years ago were devoted to the last of these and generally comfortable with self-report as well. Lang proposed that physiology belonged in the clinical assessment battery, and with an equal role. For behaviorists content with Skinner's sys-

*   University of Illinois at Urbana-Champaign
**   Medical College of Pennsylvania
     Order of authorship is arbitrary. This chapter was written with the support of NIMH grants MH39628, MH42178, and MH45404. The helpful suggestions of Arne Öhman and Niels Birbaumer on an earlier draft are gratefully acknowledged.

tematic neglect of the innards of the organism (and even for cognitive psychologists content with reliance on self-report and reaction time), Lang's proposal was radical.

Not everyone agrees to this day that physiology is an equal partner in measuring human functioning. Some still see it as technological overkill; some remain overly impressed with it. Lang claimed simply that it was an available source of data and that we as scientists should attend to it, as something neither more nor less important than other types of data. In general, it appears that most of the field has come to agree with him. However, we continue to struggle with when and how to obtain such data and especially with how to integrate the three domains and relate the data to a construct of emotion.

Covariation of Measures: A Conceptual Progression

Lang's other radical point was that the various sources of data often do not covary. A few other writers had noted the poor covariation of physiological measures (e. g., Maher, 1966; Martin, 1961), but it was Lang (1968) who made the case forcefully and persuaded clinical researchers to acknowledge the problem. The title of the paper, "Fear and Fear Behavior: Problems in Treating a Construct," states the dilemma simply. Lang was calling attention to a still-unsolved problem in the behavior therapy literature: if we are to treat fear, we must have clear operational measures of fear behavior. Lang argued further that fear behavior is multi-dimensional; i. e., there are three different domains of measures. A traditional unidimensional construal of fear (fear being the example Lang chose of a general problem) could not deal with the poor covariation commonly observed for the available measures of fear.

This problem bears some elaboration. Clinically, if we are to construe fear behavior as a unitary phenomenon, then the various behavioral exemplars of fear must be largely consistent in order to be of much use for inferring fear. That is, the early behaviorist approach assumed a simple relationship between fear behavior as a category and specific, relevant behaviors as measurable examples of that category. Lang's observation that the different behaviors frequently do not covary rendered this unidimensional concept of phobia and its treatment untenable. Thus, a more complex construct would be needed to make sense of these apparent inconsistencies. We have argued that a mere intervening variable must be inade-quate and that a hypothetical construct is required (Kozak & Miller, 1982; see Ohman, 1987, for a similar view). That is, one would need to propose a theory of (inferred) fear states and (observed) fear behavior. Part of that theory would have to spell out how to infer a fear state (an unobserved, hypothetical construct) from publicly observable behaviors. To recognize a fear behavior needing treatment, one needs a rule for deciding which behaviors are part of the phobia.

The importance of Lang's point about the poor covariation of measures does not depend on his effort to have us treat physiology like self-report and overt behavior. If one works only within one domain of measurement, one must still face the poor covariation among measures within each domain. As developed by Rachman and Hodgson (1974) and Rachman (1980), for example, observable clinical change often occurs at a very different pace in different response systems, and physiological data are particularly illustrative of the covariation problem.

In recent years, as Lang's efforts have increasingly emphasized the development of an elaborated theory of emotion and its expression, his position on the poor covariation of measures sometimes appears to have changed. Lang, Bradley, and Cuthbert (1990) state:

> *Biobehavioral and language dimensions* of arousal and valence *are presumed to be roughly coupled.* That is, language and behavior (and even to some extent its physiology) can be shaped independently (Lang, 1964, 1985), but *central associa-*

tive connections are assumed to exist between semantic and behavioral representations of emotion. Thus, barring an active dissociative process, subjective affective judgments about stimuli are expected to be *positively correlated* with related emotional behaviors. (p. 381; emphasis added)

This passage can be read to suggest a reversal of opinion about poor covariation among putative measures of fear. However, the emphasized text clarifies that this is not a change in view about the covariation of *measures*. Rather, the assertion is that there is a coherent whole (the associative network) represented in the brain. Accordingly, the dynamic nature of the connections in that network is such that its elements covary. Nevertheless, even if overt manifestations of the whole also covary, those manifestations merge with ongoing activity in each peripheral response system, thus potentially controlling only some portion of the observable variance in each system. Thus, the 1990 position still allows low covariation among observable measures. Atop those measures, Lang now explicitly posits a hypothetical construct adequate to co-exist with them: the associative network. Thus, Lang et al. (1990) have reconsidered the problem identified in the 1968 paper – "treating a construct" is indeed the goal. Effective therapy must alter the associative network, not just isolated, overt manifestations of it.

It should be kept in mind that Lang (1968) did not argue that measures are altogether uncorrelated. Indeed, the treatment study of Lang, Melamed, and Hart (1970) demonstrated that it is when multiple expressions of fear are well connected during therapeutic intervention that therapy is most effective. Specifically, when self-report of fear covaried with heart rate elevation, subjects benefitted most from treatment. Even so, correlations do not reach 1.0, and it was this imperfect correlation among measures that has been emphasized throughout Lang's writing. Lang (1968) called on researchers to face this fact. Lang et al. (1990) articulated a theoretical approach that accommodates imperfect correlations with an elaborated construct of emotion. This explicit embrace of hypothetical constructs represents a reorientation toward resolving the issue of

poor covariation which had been recognized earlier.

Lang et al. (1990) took the original point about poor covariation a step further with an important distinction, between strategic and tactical aspects of emotion. They suggested that a dimension such as valence or arousal is a broad, controlling factor which "differentially primes or inhibits subsequent behavior" (p. 380). In contrast, tactical factors are determined largely by the instrumental demands of a specific circumstance in pursuit of strategic goals. The optimal physiology to support performance in a given situation depends greatly on that situation. Different fearful situations might best be handled with different overt behavior, prompting inconsistent physiologies across situations which we consider to be consistent in the emotion elicited. Thus: "It is this tactical variability in emotional behavior that has frustrated efforts to [identify] specific and reliable psychophysiological response patterns" (p. 380–381). In other words, the problem of poor covariation among measures has now been localized to tactical factors, whereas hypothesized "covariation" of elements of the network is posited at a more abstract level.

For present purposes, what is important about Lang's position in recent years (beginning with a 1977 paper on imagery and including the passage quoted above, 1990, p. 381) is that the explicit reliance on a psychological construct (a cognitive one, not a behavioral one) moves Lang further away from the relatively fundamentalist behavioral position of the 1968 paper which touched so many other researchers. It is quite clear that overt manifestations of emotion are logically distinct from the inferred, hypothetical phenomena which drive them. An ambiguity in the 1968 paper concerning the distinction between data and construct, discussed below, has been removed: they are properly distinct.

A final historical note is that Lang (1964, 1968) was abandoning a unitary view of emotion and clinical change in behavior therapy at about the same time that Lacey (1967) was attacking a unitary concept of arousal in psychophysiology with a parallel argument: the poor covariation of measures. In both literatures, we have been struggling ever since to develop an adequate account of things. Other chapters in this volume consider Lang and colleagues' own attempt, a now heavily cognitive theory of emotional imagery (where image = activated network) based on yet another radical notion, that efferent activity (in all three systems) is not a *response to* the image but a *part of* the image. More generally, Lang has proposed that emotions are action dispositions; again, the efference is an inherent *part of* emotional processing

(Lang et al., 1990). In the present chapter we examine the three-systems proposal, its development in Lang's writings, and its impact on the field, including its relevance to some promising technologies. We then discuss how the proposal may be assimilated into theories of fear and offer a meta-theoretical approach to the issue of the poor covariation among observable measures, including a discussion of some philosophical problems with that approach.

The Three-Systems Perspective in Use by Others

Lang's most-cited discussion of the three-systems notion was not his most developed, and considerable confusion has been associated with it. Lang (1968) summarized the three-systems approach as follows. "Fear is a response, and further that it is expressed in three main behavioral systems: verbal (cognitive), overt-motor, and somatic" (p. 90). The statement appears to equate "verbal" and "cognitive" events. This perspective proved convenient as behavioral researchers began to allow cognitive phenomena and concepts into their thinking. However, this equation creates a problem. Cognitive events are not directly observable and therefore are not "behaviors" in the standard behaviorist meaning of that term. Thus, in this equation there is a confusion between observable data (verbal acts) and inferred constructs (cognition). Kozak and Miller (1982) discussed the conceptual problem this creates.

> ... the three-systems view deprives the term "fear" of the logical status of a hypothetical construct by failing to distinguish data and construct. This identification of data with the construct inferred from those data creates a serious practical difficulty for the assessor: one cannot specify principles of inference to bridge the gap between the data and the fear construct. Given a particular set

of data, we cannot know how or when to conclude that a person is afraid. (p. 348)

The 1982 paper also documented the pervasiveness of this confusion in the clinical research literature. For example,

> Nelson (1979), in an editorial statement for *Behavioral Assessment*, blurs the distinction between verbal report and cognition, as well as between physiological responses (data) and emotion (construct), by classifying behavior samples into "motor, verbal-cognitive, and physiological-emotional" response categories. It appears that cognition and emotion have somehow become observable behavior. (p. 354)

This conceptual confusion has continued in the literature in the past decade, even though Lang's (1978) revision of his position avoided this problem by explicitly distinguishing language behavior from cognitive activity. We have also noted (Miller, 1988; Miller & Ebert, 1988) a similar error in traditional, implicit presumptions that self-report data or brain-wave responses particularly reflect cognition and that peripheral physiological data particularly reflect emotion.* There is no logical necessity preventing cognition from having an equally direct

---

*   The literature on the social psychology of attitude exemplifies this traditional association. The influential "tripartite model" of Rosenberg and Hovland (1960; see historical review by Breckler, 1984) associated sympathetic nervous system responses with affect. Interestingly, their tripartite model – affect, behavior, and cognition – treated all three of its component parts as "hypothetical, unobservable classes of

impact on the autonomic nervous system, with measures of the latter thus good candidates for study of the former. Indeed, Ohman (1979, 1987), Dawson (1990), Packer and Siddle (1989), and others have utilized skin conductance (traditionally an "emotional" measure) in their studies of information processing, without invoking any concept of emotion. Conversely, brain-wave measures have been used in studies of emotion (e.g., Davidson, Ekman, Saron, Senulis, & Friesen, 1990; Johnston, Burleson, & D. Miller, 1987; Klorman & Ryan, 1980; Simons, Ohman, & Lang, 1979; Yee & Miller, 1988). Gray (1990) has recently argued the case against a clear separation of cognition and emotion on neurophysiological grounds.

To assume that certain measures are particularly related to certain hypothesized psychological functions is (at least implicitly) to make a theoretical proposal. If explicit, it can be tested and challenged. Unfortunately, a great deal of theorizing about the relationship between data and construct in emotion research has remained implicit and unexamined.

An interesting semantic implication of our critique of confusing data and construct involves the common usage of the term, "subjective." One often reads of "subjective report," usually meaning self-report of the subjects's conscious experience. However, "subjective physiology" and "subjective overt behavior" could be equally valid terms. "Subjective" would have to do with things – anything – about the subject, perhaps with the connotation of "from the subject's standpoint." For example, physiological data, in principle, could be just as valid and useful an indicator of someone's subjective experience as self-report is. Indeed, in daily life we routinely infer another person's subjective experience from his or her manifest physiology and overt behavior; in fact sometimes we infer our own subjective experience from these data channels. To take a position on the relevance of an individual's verbal assertions about their subjective experience – to call self-report "subjective report" – is implicitly to take a theoretical position on the relationship of data (self-report) to construct (subjective experience). As before, we believe that this may be defensible, if made explicit, but not necessarily more defensible than other positions that emphasize physiology or overt behavior as a basis for inferences about subjective experience. To refer to "subjective report" as *data* is to commit a logical error, which is quite common in the emotion literature. The *data* are not "subjective." What the experimenter makes inferences *about* is "subjective."

New Technologies for the Physiology of Emotion

In the years since the main statements of the three-systems perspective (Lang, 1968, 1978), measurement technologies have developed which appear to hold some promise for avoiding the problems discussed above. Three will be considered here, as examples of what such advances may or may not provide in light of Lang's analysis of the importance of measuring physiology and the poor covariation of measures.

Facial Expression

The Facial Action Coding System (Ekman & Friesen, 1976, 1978) is an increasingly influential contribution to the measurement of emotion. It is a highly developed observational coding scheme for classifying specific movements of specific muscle groups in the face.

---

response" to a stimulus (Breckler, 1984, p. 1191). This non-behaviorist view of "behavior" at least kept its components at a consistent logical level.

Considerable evidence is available for its reliability (Ekman, Davidson, & Friesen, 1990) and its cross-cultural utility (Ekman, 1971, 1989).

It might be tempting to see FACS codes of facial behavior as *the* criterion in the study of emotion. Indeed, FACS was developed, in part, as a basis for inferring emotion. However, the FACS *methodology* does not address the question of how one should relate facial coding data to emotion constructs. That is, one still needs to know how and when to infer *emotion* as a psychological *state* given a particular set of facial *data*. Ekman and colleagues wisely distinguish the rules for scoring facial expression from inferences about the presence of a specific emotion.

> The scorer identifies the action units, such as the one that pulls the lip corners up or that lowers the brow, *rather than making inferences about underlying emotional states* such as happiness or anger, or using descriptions that mix inference and description such as smile, scowl, or frown. (Ekman et al., 1990, p. 346; emphasis added)

Associated with, but distinct from, the facial scoring system are a set of inference rules on which Ekman and colleagues rely for characterizing a given facial expression as indicative of an acute state of emotion. For example, a certain type of smile is defined very precisely:

> The Duchenne smile (D-smile) was composed of all instances in which the smile was produced by the zygomatic major muscle and the lifting of the cheeks and gathering of the skin around the eye were produced by the orbicularis oculi muscle. (Ekman et al., 1990, p. 346)

This type of proposal is what is necessary for understanding emotion and its modification (Kozak & Miller, 1982). Other potential dependent measures are needed, and their relationship to facial behavior spelled out, in order to validate the inferential rules. The rules may warrant revision at some point, without entailing any flaw in the facial coding scheme. It remains to be seen how well FACS-categorized facial expressions will covary with other physiological data and with self-report and overt behavior (e. g., Chesney, Ekman, Friesen, Black, & Hecker, 1990; Davidson et al., 1990). To the extent that the covariation among these measures is low, this must also be understood (Ohman, 1987). Given the history of research on emotion, the null hypothesis must be that facial data will covary poorly with other putative measures of emotion under many circumstances.

One *could* posit that facial expression is the only, or at least a sufficient, criterion for inferring emotion. This, of course, would constitute a theoretical proposal, which could be endorsed, challenged, and tested. Although one might initially find the proposal appealing, upon reflection we are still left struggling with the role of other data channels of enduring interest in emotion such as a flushed face, avoidance or withdrawal behavior, vocal expressions of fear, or compulsive rituals.

Topographic Mapping

Another example of recently developing technology which may appear to promise some escape from the low covariation problem in the measurement of emotion is topographic brain mapping. Typically based on multi-channel EEG recording, such "topo maps" represent scalp voltage like isobars on a weather map, with lines or color bands indicating regions of similar voltage. The voltage pattern may be the momentary distribution of an event-related potential component or the amount of activity in the alpha band of the ongoing EEG at one point in time. The spatial relationship of activity in different EEG channels can be represented in a graph of the data, with a series of graphs representing sequential points in time. With such displays now being implemented on desktop computers, this technique has created much interest. Algorithms are also under development which infer brain sources of scalp-recorded voltages, essentially creating maps at arbitrary depths to complement the scalp maps. Though less readily obtainable than EEG, other types of physiological measures have been used to generate similar representations of brain activity, such as magnetoencephalography, positron emission tomography, and nuclear magnetic resonance. Will such an esthetically appealing representation of multi-channel data facilitate the study of emotion and the inference of emotional states?

Like FACS, topo mapping constitutes an important technical innovation that warrants extensive exploration. Significantly, however, it must be kept in mind that such mapping is a way of representing *data*, not a set of rules of inference about psychological *states* on the basis of those data. In this sense, then, a theory of emotion is not advanced. What spatial voltage pattern in the EEG evidences fear? joy? These are potentially answerable questions, in the sense that a scientist may propose rules of inference and conditions of data collection under which to apply those rules. As we have argued, such a proposal would constitute a theory, or the beginning of a theory (e. g., Davidson & Tomarken, 1989). It is not a property of the method of data collection, representation, or scoring. Indeed, such new configural methods of data representation are not so different from those which Lacey, Remond, and others proposed over 30 years ago for multi-channel data. A valuable feature of FACS and topo maps is that their configural data are based on the spatial relationships among the data channels. Nevertheless, there remains the logical problem of how to infer constructs of emotion from disparate data channels.

There is a further wrinkle to this issue which is especially apparent for topo mapping. Beyond using it for data representation, as noted above there are efforts to use such spatial data to infer brain electrical sources – to locate where in the brain the scalp-recorded voltage is generated. To the extent this proves feasible, might this contribute to theories of emotion? Will it allow us to localize emotion to a particular brain region? Will it allow us to get rid of a (psychological) concept of emotion entirely? The reader is referred to Fodor (1968) for a compelling argument against such reductionism.

Although topo maps may prove to be oversold visually and underspecified theoretically, recent studies in which gross regional EEG is analyzed more simply compel an interesting and potentially important expansion of the three-systems approach to fear assessment. Typically, the physiological measures assumed to be of interest in human studies have been peripheral – "patterns of visceral and somatic activation" (Lang, 1985, p. 134) – rather than involving more direct measures of central nervous system activity. This peripheral focus is a legacy of James (1884). However, a growing literature on regional EEG alpha during emotion provides a basis for inclusion of such measures in physiological assessment of emotion. The EEG alpha literature has been inconsistent in its interest in dimensional vs. categorical views of emotion. Thus, it is not yet clear exactly what sort of emotional state or processing is associated with specific EEG patterns. There is talk of frontal lateralization of emotional valence (e.g., Ekman et al., 1990), a similar lateralization of an approach/avoidance dimension (Davidson et al., 1990), and a more complex pattern of left frontal + right parietal vs. right frontal + left parietal linkage (Heller, 1990). However, the EEG alpha literature enriches the traditional three-systems approach by suggesting a new domain of assessment.

Startle-Probe and Dual-Task Paradigms

Indeed, implications extend beyond EEG assessment. For example, Bradley, Cuthbert, and Lang (1988) provided evidence for hemispheric specialization of affective processing in a study of the acoustic startle reflex. That study used a well established but only recently popularized paradigm in which the startle reflex is modulated by variations in startle stimulus qualities (intensity, modality, timing) in the context of other stimuli. A large body of work on startle with infants and adults by Graham and colleagues (reviewed by Anthony, 1985) has inspired a number of recent studies by Lang and his colleagues and former students. Based on a review of these studies, which involve startle probes during emotional imagery or exposure to affective stimuli such as slides, Lang et al. (1990) proposed a comprehensive theory of aspects of emotion.

Looked at more broadly, the startle-probe paradigm can be seen as a special case of a more general approach called the dual-task paradigm. Subjects are presented with two (or more) essentially simultaneous tasks, with a primary interest in the performance effects of processing load and resource-sharing between tasks. The archetypal applications are for design of displays for military pilots and air-traffic controllers at major airports, where both infor-

mation rate and performance demands are high. Psychophysiologists have been well represented in that literature, with an emphasis on brain-wave responses (reviewed by Donchin, Kramer, & Wickens, 1986).

However, the dual-task paradigm has also been used for autonomic studies of information processing and resource allocation (reviewed by Dawson, 1990). The Dawson procedure allows study of cognitive processes in the 100 ms range, unusual for skin conductance studies. Yee and Miller (1990) combined brain-wave and autonomic recordings in a study of resource allocation in clinical samples and have proposed an adaptation suitable for studies of emotion (Miller & Yee, in press). While not as esthetically appealing as topo maps, the startle-probe and dual-task paradigms are presently receiving wide attention and will surely contribute further to emotion research.

What New Technologies Will Not Do

To some extent, these potential technological advances, involving multiple measurement channels, are driven by a general engineering problem: how to represent lots of data in a way which allows fruitful perception by a human observer. This is an important question in many fields, and much interesting work is being done on it. However, in the absence of a theory of physiology in emotion, we cannot say what data should be in the display or what configuration in the display should be telling.

It is worth noting that the Ekman FACS approach, which does include Ekman's proposals for which facial event patterns constitute evidence for specific emotional states, is ripe for topographic presentation. It may seem uninteresting to take videotapes of facial expressions, FACS-code them, and generate a schematic face display, with the pixels a function of the FACS codes for various muscle groups. However, a (topographic) facial EMG version

of this display might prove as useful for tracking emotion as a topographic scalp EEG display. Either way, cute technology begs the question of which patterns of which data are theoretically interesting.

Another general caveat about these new technologies is that they may prove to be somewhat paradigm-specific. The procedures for collecting or scoring the data tend to be exceptionally intensive and relatively fragile. Selection of specific slides as emotional stimuli, decisions about alpha metrics, and details of stimulus properties in dual-task studies typically require exhaustive piloting before a successful experiment is possible. Furthermore, most of the new technologies rely heavily on within-subject manipulations. Whether generalizations drawn from them will endure in between-subjects comparisons remains to be seen.

Emotion Terms as Functional Constructs

Some may despair of any means to infer emotion from multi-channel scientific data. If the present paper seems to belabor the construct issue, it is because it remains highly pertinent to current thinking about emotion. The three-systems perspective has earned pervasive lip service, but it remains tempting to seek an easy way out to the problem of the poor covariation of measures. It has been argued, however, that such easy outs not only fail to account for the data (Lang, 1968) but are indeed *bound* to fail (Kozak & Miller, 1982; Ohman, 1987).

We believe that the notion of a functionally defined construct will be helpful in understanding the relationship between data and construct in the study of emotion. This idea was discussed in an earlier paper (Kozak & Miller, 1982) but was left relatively undeveloped. We will pursue it in the remainder of this paper.

To allow specification of the rules relating observed data to fear and other psychological constructs, fear is viewed as a hypothetical construct referring to, and descriptive of, a particular kind of functional state .... The relationship between the terms "psychological event" (e. g., fear, cognition) and "central nervous system (CNS) activity" is that of a functionally defined state to a case of its instantiation (as discussed at length in Fodor, 1968). Thus, fear is a functional state, in that it is recognized, across variations in CNS activity and observed peripheral events in the three systems, by the common functions served or roles played by these events when fear is said to be present – i. e., by some supposed common meaning or interpretation of varied response patterns in varied situations. Emotions are complex, unobserved, psychological events, which can be evidenced by observed organismic events [which include] overt acts, electrical potentials, tissue changes, or what is spoken, written, secreted, excreted, or otherwise emitted by the organism.

Thus, verbal data are no exclusive inferential pathway to central activity, nor a unique window on emotion. (Kozak & Miller, 1982, p. 356)

Fear as a Functional Construct

How might one construe an emotion such as fear as a functional state? There would be some function which would characterize "fear" behavior in all domains (self-report, physiology, overt behavior), whatever the context and whatever the specific behavior in that context. Behavior which could not serve that function would simply not be "fear" behavior. If we suspected that certain behavior was part of fear, but in fact it did not serve that function, we would necessarily conclude that that behavior was not "fearful" after all.

A function of any mousetrap, no matter how implemented, must be to catch mice. Something that looked much like a mousetrap, or worked much like one, or frequently co-occurred with one, but could not catch mice, would simply not be a mousetrap – though we might have to study it carefully in order to conclude that with confidence. Indeed, such may be the fate of some of the behavior we now routinely assume to be "fearful." We recognize that there can be difficulties with such a simple definition. For example, a broken mousetrap might still colloquially be called a mousetrap. A logically consistent, fully developed functional concept might in some cases violate conventional usage. We point out an example of this with a functional view of fear, below.

What is the function of fear behavior? What is fear *for*? We propose that fear is to prepare the individual for avoidance behavior. This proposal is consistent with some contemporary emotion theorists (e. g., Davidson et al., 1990; Lang et al., 1990) and with a variety of authors over the last century. Fear is a type of preparatory state, consistent with views of emotion as an "action set" (Lang, 1984, p. 195) or an "action tendency" (Frijda, 1986, p. 71), embodied in the propositional network of Lang (1977,

1979) or the "facial affect program" of Ekman (1971, p. 212). One might consider the object of the avoidance to be a physical stimulus (a knife), a perceived danger (the possibility of being knifed), or a psychological consequence of the stimulus or danger (the pain of a wound). In any case, let us consider fear as that functional state which prepares the organism for avoidance or withdrawal.

An interesting implication of this view is that the subject's perception of things matters. Whether or not the knife is a rubber toy, it matters whether the subject believes it to be dangerous. (A mousetrap need only capture mice, not intimidate them; whereas a scarecrow has the opposite function with birds, functioning successfully only to the extent that the birds are frightened away.) Thus, the subject's perception of a situation is important in understanding the function of behavior in that situa-tion. In judging the function of some behavior, it does not matter whether the behavior is appropriate to avoid a real danger. One must know certain aspects of the meaning of a situation for the subject (Foa & Kozak, this volume) in order to infer the function of behavior in that situation. Immediately this points to the relevance of historical and current context to judgments of function. As noted (Kozak & Miller, 1982; Lang, 1968), there is no specific observable phenomenon that invariably indicates fear, nor any specific behavior (e. g., freezing or running) which is a necessary consequence of fear. What constitutes "fearful" behavior depends on the context as perceived by the subject. In particular, we suggest that it depends on what behavior (in all three systems) serves the function of avoidance of an apparently dangerous possibility.

Implications for Three-Systems Assessment

A question arises about the respective roles of self-report, physiology, and overt behavior as manifestations of fear. A striking implication of the present view of fear as a functional state serving avoidance of danger is that self-ratings, as a subset of self-report, are not exemplars of fear behavior. Self-ratings presumably reflect the fear state, but they do not serve an avoidance function.* Self-ratings request the subject to act as an observer of the subject's situation and experience, which immediately changes the situation and the experience. More directly expressive language behavior (Lang, 1978) would qualify, however, if it could be seen to serve the goal of avoidance of danger.

Given the proposal to treat fear as a functional state and given that the function of this state is to avoid, how does physiology contribute to the avoidance goal? In other words, what sorts of physiological activity would be considered "fearful" under our proposal? Two categories are apparent. First, physiology may subserve that goal by supporting verbal-expressive and overt behavioral actions which in turn facilitate avoidance. Increased heart rate is useful for running or for immediate preparation to run. Second, it is conceivable that some physiological changes could facilitate avoidance in more subtle ways, similar to the lowered sensation threshold and slowed heart rate associated with orienting (Graham, 1979). For example, it is possible that a certain topographic EEG pattern reflects a configuration of gross brain activity which facilitates subsequent processing, much like the priming of motor neurons (Rockstroh, Elbert, Birbaumer, & Lutzenberger, 1982).

---

*   As an example of this distinction, consider that shouting about some danger is fear behavior, in contrast with offering a rating on a subjective units of discomfort scale: "My SUDS rating is 67." The observational readout is not the functioning. The rating can be evidence of fear and thus can be used to infer fear. But so can the actual presence of a snake be used to infer fear. The presence of the snake is not fear behavior. Nor is the rating fear behavior.

Problems with a Functional Approach to Emotion

Our 1982 proposal that fear (or any emotion) be viewed in functional terms did not attempt to work out the specifics of a functionalist view; we merely argued the general merits of such a view relative to a traditional behaviorist approach, as a major implication of Lang's point about measure covariation. The present attempt to begin to develop a specific functionalist position on fear reveals two problems with treating emotions as functional states. First, it is not clear what criteria one should use in determining what function a given class of emotion serves. Thus, one has to propose, on some logical or empirical grounds, the function of fear as an operational state of the organism. How does one decide?

Theorists may potentially offer diverse functions for fear, and we will not attempt to describe where these should come from. However, this problem of criteria for judging a proposed function may be approached the way one evaluates any theoretical proposal once made. Does it fit the available data? Does the fit survive various means of convergent validation of the construct? We believe that an avoidance function for fear accounts quite well for most behavior typically considered fearful, though we will not make that case at length here. It suffices to note that quite varied verbal, physiological, and overt behavior may be called for in diverse situations, but all in the service of the same function.

For example, the position of Lang et al. (1990), developed to account for their startle-probe data, fits the present functionalist view very well. What they call the "strategic" level of emotion can be construed in functional terms. The organism activates an associative network which includes a general (strategic) avoidance goal or program. The momentary, specific (tactical) implementation of this function will vary with the circumstance and the particular organism's history, repertoire, and resources. A detailed account of the churning of the linkages in the network would constitute a process theory of fear at the strategic level. Observable activity in the three systems consti-

tutes the outcome of that churning as shaped and filtered by the tactical factors.

The second problem with a functionalist approach to emotion is more difficult. There is arguably something about functional constructs which is qualitatively different and less satisfying than the constructs used in the behavioral approach Lang was addressing. To say that a given state has a function appears to impute purpose to the organism. This sounds disturbingly like the homunculus Lang has often criticized as a failure of scientific theorizing. It is accepted by many that a goal of science is to develop a fully mechanistic account of human behavior, without reference to what have been called "intentional" constructs.

To expand on a standard example of this distinction (Chisholm, 1952): For William James to *hunt* tigers in India, (a) he has to *think* about tigers in India, but (b) there do not have to *be* tigers in India. That is, "hunting" has to do with the person who has a goal, not with the object of that goal (tigers). In fact, the goal does not have to be realistic; the key is that there is a subject with a goal. For this reason, one can meaningfully speak of hunting unicorns as well as tigers, even though one does not believe that there *are* unicorns. Again, an intentional construct such as "hunting" depends for its meaning on someone having "hunting" as a goal. There is nothing about tigers or unicorns alone that allows for a concept of "hunting," nor is there any specific self-report, physiology, or overt behavior that uniquely signifies "hunting." It is not enough for William James and tigers to be located in the same jungle, for him to be armed, and for him to be on a trail of a tiger to describe the situation as "hunting." He must have the goal of shooting a tiger in order for his behavior to be described as "hunting." In fact, we could meaningfully say that he is hunting tigers even if there were no tigers in that particular jungle that day. Similarly, it would be meaningful to say that he is hunting unicorns. This is an intentional account of William James in the jungle.

In contrast, for William James to *shoot* tigers

in India, (a) he does not have to *think* about tigers in India, but (b) there must *be* tigers in India. That is, there must be objects and possible actions involving those objects; there do not have to be intentions or any other mental operations (he could just happen to pull the trigger and happen to hit a tiger without ever thinking of tigers or bullets). If a complete account of the events of the day in the jungle could be offered in such terms, we would have succeeded in supplying a fully mechanistic, non-homuncular, non-intentional explanation.

Thus, as scientists we might like a complete account of William James shooting tigers not to depend on postulates about his intentions. There should be an explanation which simply lays out how things unfold, a world of objects and events rather than of subjects willfully acting on objects. However, conceiving emotional states in functional terms does not necessarily meet this criterion. That is, functional terms are sometimes used in ways that are intentional. We might characterize William James' running as fear behavior if we supposed that, unarmed, he chanced upon a tiger and *wanted* to avoid it. We would say that the function of the running was to avoid the danger he perceived. In such a non-mechanistic account, William James is not merely running, nor running because a tiger is nearby; he is running because of his appraisal and goals – an intentional account. This problem is quite distinct from the issue of how one decides what the function of a given emotion is. Instead, the problem is that emotions may be said to have functions at all. If we are not careful, the function becomes the intention becomes the homunculus.

Can We Use Intentional Constructs in a Theory of Emotion?

Dennett (1978) offered a persuasive discussion of the role of intentional constructs in scientific psychology. Accordingly, one could view an organism as an intentional system (and make intentional predictions) by ascribing to the organism "the possession of certain information and supposing it to be directed by certain goals" (p. 6). Dennett asserted that it is a small step to call the information possessed "beliefs" and the goals "desires." That is to say, the idea of possession of information is as "intentional" as is that of belief. He argued that an intentional theory of behavior, which assumes a rational organism, must be ultimately unsatisfactory, because it presupposes rather than explains rationality or intelligence.

Nevertheless, Dennett noted that intentional predictions are useful in that they work surprisingly well for predicting behavior. Furthermore, they often work better than anything else available. It would be impractical simply to discard a useful intentional theory. The difficulty arises because, despite the usefulness of intentional predictions, they do not work perfectly, and then the organism's departure from rationality must be explained. Dennett argues that a non-intentional account is therefore eventually required. An intentional construct can thus be viewed as a kind of theoretical "loan," which allows one to make some predictions which could otherwise not be made at the time, but which must be paid back later in the form of non-intentional accounts. In sum, intentional theories of behavior are viewed as temporarily quite useful and important, but ultimately quite limited, and for that reason unsatisfactory.

Can We Have "Functional" without "Intentional"?

Given this case for tolerating intentional constructs in a science of emotion, as least for awhile, we now consider an alternative version of a functional view of emotion which does not involve intentionality at all. Consider the mousetrap discussed earlier. If we say that a mousetrap is functionally defined, then the necessary and sufficient condition for being a mousetrap is mouse-catching. That is, we define a mousetrap by what it *does*. Importantly, we need not impute any intention to it. We need not assume that the mousetrap *wants* to catch mice, or that a scarecrow *wants* to drive away birds. We observe that they just happen to perform certain functions.

Now, after watching a mousetrap in action one *could* propose that it was motivated to catch mice, as an (intentional) explanation of its behavior. But typically we come up with non-motivational (thus non-intentional) accounts of mousetrap behavior. So it might be with our hypotheses about William James and the tiger. Behavior which we *could* characterize as aggressively or fearfully motivated might instead be explicable in purely non-intentional terms.

The proposal here is that "functional" can be construed in two senses, only one of them intentional, and that we could attempt to build theories of emotion that treat emotional moments as functional states in the non-intentional sense of functional. Rather than trying to infer William James' motivations from available self-report, physiological, and overt behavior, we could use the same data to infer functions. He happens to go to India, well armed, ventures into areas inhabited by tigers, and shoots them when he sees them. If he runs out of bullets before he runs out of tigers, he runs, because he functions to avoid perceived danger. When we observe behavior which appears to be the sort that could avoid danger, we categorize that behavior as "fearful." We need not go the further step and infer that he *wanted* to avoid danger – that would be an intentional account

of his behavior. The intentional account relies on inferences of subjective purpose; the non-intentional account does not. In an intentional account, the explanation rests on purpose as intended by the subject. In a non-intentional account, it rests on possible outcomes as construed by the scientist-observer.

In developing theories of emotion, it will be tempting to generate functional accounts of emotional behavior which are intentional: William James *wants* to avoid the tiger, with that inference about his motivations aimed at accounting for diverse behavior which we may observe across response systems. We prefer, when possible, a non-intentional inference, such as: William James' diverse behaviors serve to avoid danger. Similarly, one could propose that the function of certain facial behavior is to communicate danger without further assuming that the individual *wants* to communicate danger or anything else.

Given that Lang has explicitly embraced a functionalist view of emotion (Lang et al., 1990), is it an intentional or non-intentional version? Is "having an associative network" necessarily intentional, as "having a motivation" is? We think not. It appears that one can describe a goal-serving network and its churning without requiring the subject to *intend* to achieve the goal. Recall the crucial notion in Lang's work that the efference is *part of*, not a *response to*, the network. The network does not "cause" the output. Rather, part of what it means to be in a state of fear is to execute an avoidance program. Thus, it appears that the network is not a(n intentional) homunculus.

Evaluating 'Avoidance' as the Function Fear Serves

As simple as it is to propose that "the function of fear behavior is to avoid" and thus to judge candidate fear behaviors by their apparent function, it may not be immediately apparent how one could validate or challenge that proposal. As Lang has often noted, it may not be that the most promising theories will map closely onto colloquial notions of fear. Some

criterion other than consistency with common assumptions about emotion is needed. We suggested above that this problem of criteria for judging a proposed function may be approached the way one evaluates any theoretical proposal. Does it fit the available data? Does the fit survive various means of convergent validation of the construct?

As noted earlier, an important subtlety in a proposal of fear as a functional construct is that the issue is not whether the behavior actually succeeds in accomplishing avoidance. William James need not outrun the tiger for us to consider the running to be avoidant.

Besides Lang et al. (1990), another recent theory of fear which seems to take a functionalist approach is Foa and Kozak's (1985, 1986) work on emotional processing. These authors construed both the subject's perception of danger and responses preparatory to escape or avoid it as central to understanding fear. Although the subject's perception is important to their concept of fear, such perception can but need not be intentional. Accordingly, self-reports of perceived danger and intent to escape would indeed "count" as evidence to infer fear, but non-introspective evidence of perceived danger could also "count." For example, a number of experimental paradigms in cognitive psychology can yield evidence that a semantically coded concept of "danger" is associated with a particular situation for a given individual (Foa & Kozak, this volume). Notably, these paradigms do not rely on self-reports of an introspective nature. Semantic meaning (danger) is inferred from non-introspective data, and its status in hypotheses about fear appears to be non-intentional.

For Foa and Kozak, William James differs from a mousetrap in that understanding his behavior requires understanding the "programs" which drive that behavior. Furthermore, stated intentions are only one possible way to make inferences about programs for behavior. Although they are not taken as isomorphic with those programs, they do "count" as evidence. It remains to be discovered empirically whether introspective or non-introspective evidence of semantic aspects of meaning will prove the more useful for understanding fear. This discovery would be expected to cast light on the question of whether intentional constructs can be eliminated from a scientific psychology.

The Function of Fear: An Alternative

What if, instead of "avoidance/withdrawal" of danger, the hypothesized function of fear behavior is: to *communicate* danger? Such a proposal fits very well with a social psychological view of emotion and with a focus on facial expression in emotional states (e. g., Smith, 1985). Some overt "fear" behavior could also be understood as communicating danger, though it may seem contrived to characterize the *function* of running away from the tiger as communication to someone else. The latter could serve as a *consequence* of running away but not as its function.

How does physiological activity fit with the hypothesis that the function of fear behavior is to communicate danger? Some physiological changes are apparent to an observer, but many are not, including heart rate and EEG patterns. Perhaps these covert changes exist to support the overt ones. More radically, one could propose that, if the avoidance function is not definitive of fear, then the covert changes are not part of the physiology of fear but of the physiology of running or of a certain type of information processing that is often useful when facing danger but not essential to communicating anything about danger, and this is not fear functioning.

To develop this further: one could choose to confine "emotion" to a relatively narrow domain of psychological functioning and overt expression and not include other phenomena which are often, but not invariably, associated with emotion. Thus, the poor covariation among putative "fear" behaviors would be due to at least many of those behaviors not being driven specifically by fear at all. On this view, the difficulty in construing some types of "fear" behavior as serving the function of communicating danger is not a problem with the proposed function but in construing too many types of behavior as part of "fear." This recalls the "tactical" concept of Lang et al. (1990) but goes beyond it, suggesting that what Lang considers to be tactical expressions of fear actually are not part of emotion at all. Emotion would exist only at his "strategic" level.

From this cursory consideration of an alternative functional definition of fear – communicating danger – , it does appear to be viable. However, it would do greater violence to colloquial notions of fear than the avoidance definition. Which view will prove a better fit for data remains to be seen.

Conclusion

Contained in the three-systems view of emotion behavior is an implicit hypothesis: that physiology is relevant to fear. This is a claim about the relationship between data and construct – therefore already a theoretical proposal. Lang's arguments that physiology should be considered as an equal partner in the assessment of emotional behavior and that diverse measurement systems covary poorly have stood the test of time. The three-systems view is holding up very well as a method for the study of emotion. It was, however, never intended as a full-blown theory of emotion. It does not define the sort of hypothetical construct fear is, nor specify how it relates to observable data. Its contribution continues to be to point to the domains of data for which a theory of fear must account. Our functional proposal is fully consistent with it and proposes a specific theoretical meaning for fear: a harm-avoidance function.

The idea that avoidance is the central fact about fear behavior is not innovative. We have suggested here a functional version of this idea, some criticisms of that version, and some responses to those criticisms. We believe that a functional approach offers promise for theorizing about emotion. However, we recognize the distinction between intentional and non-intentional functions and anticipate difficult challenges in developing functional theories of emotion of a strictly non-intentional sort.

References

Anthony, B.J. (1985). In the blink of an eye: Implications of reflex modification for information processing. In P.K. Ackles, J.R. Jennings, & M.G.H. Coles (Eds.), *Advances in psychophysiology, volume 1.* Greenwich, CT: JAI Press. (pp. 167–218)

Bradley, M.M., Cuthbert, B.N., & Lang, P.J. (1988). Lateral presentation of acoustic startle stimuli in a varying affective background. *Psychophysiology, 25,* 436.

Chesney, M.A., Ekman, P., Friesen, W.V., Black, G.W., & Hecker, M.H. (1990). Type A behavior pattern: Facial behavior and speech components. *Psychosomatic Medicine, 53,* 307–319.

Chisholm, R.M. (1952). Intentionality and the theory of signs. *Philosophical Studies, Volume 3.* Minneapolis: University of Minnesota Press.

Cone, J.D. (1979). Confounded comparisons in triple response mode assessment research. *Behavioral Assessment, 1,* 85–95.

Davidson, R.J., Ekman, P., Saron, C.D., Senulis, J.A., & Friesen, W.V. (1990). Approach-withdrawal and cerebral asymmetry: Emotional expression and brain physiology I. *Journal of Personality and Social Psychology, 58,* 330–441.

Davidson, R.J., & Tomarken, A.J. (1989). Laterality and emotion: An electrophysiological approach. In F. Boller & J. Grafman (Eds.), *Handbook of neuropsychology, Volume 3.* Amsterdam: Elsevier. (pp. 419–441)

Dawson, M.E. (1990). Psychophysiology at the interface of clinical science, cognitive science, and neuroscience. *Psychophysiology, 27,* 243–255.

Dennett, D. (1978). *Brainstorms: Philosophical essays on mind and psychology.* Cambridge, MA: MIT Press.

Donchin, E., Kramer, A.F., & Wickens, C. (1986). Applications of brain event-related potentials to problems in engineering psychology. In M.G.H. Coles, E. Donchin, & S.W. Porges (Eds.), *Psychophysiology: Systems, processes, and applications.* New York: Guilford. (pp. 702–718)

Ekman, P. (1971). Universals and cultural differences in facial expressions of emotion. In J. Cole (Ed.),

Nebraska symposium on motivation. Volume 19. (pp. 207–283). Lincoln: Univ. of Nebraska Press.

Ekman, P. (1989). The argument and evidence about universals in facial expressions of emotion. In H. Wagner & A. Manstead (Eds.), *Handbook of psychophysiology: The biological psychology of emotions and social processes* (pp. 143–164). London: John Wiley.

Ekman, P., Davidson, R.J., & Friesen, W.V. (1990). The Duchenne smile: Emotional expression and brain physiology II. *Journal of Personality and Social Psychology, 58,* 342–353.

Ekman, P., & Friesen, W.V. (1976). Measuring facial movement. *Journal of Environmental Psychology and Nonverbal Behavior, 1,* 56–75.

Ekman, P., & Friesen, W.V. (1978). *The facial action coding system.* Palo Alto, CA: Consulting Psychologists Press.

Foa, E.B., & Kozak, M.J. (1985). Treatment of anxiety disorders: Implications for psychopathology. In A.H. Tuma & J.D. Maser (Eds.), *Anxiety and the anxiety disorders.* Hillsdale, NJ: Erlbaum. (pp. 421–452)

Foa, E.B., & Kozak, M.J. (1986). Emotional processing of fear: Exposure to corrective information. *Psychological Bulletin, 99,* 20–35.

Foa, E.B., & Kozak, M.J. (this volume). Pathological anxiety: Meaning and the structure of fear. In N. Birbaumer & A. Ohman (Eds.), *The Organization of Emotions.* Toronto: Hogrefe International.

Fodor, J.A. (1968). *Psychological explanation.* New York: Random House.

Frijda, N.H. (1986). *The emotions.* New York: Cambridge University Press.

Graham, F.K. (1979). Distinguishing among orienting, defense, and startle reflexes. In H.D. Kimmel, E.H. van Olst, & J.F. Orlebeke (Eds.), *The orienting reflex in humans.* Hillsdale, NJ: Erlbaum. (pp. 137–167).

Gray, J.A. (1990). Brain systems that mediate both emotion and cognition. *Cognition & Emotion, 4,* 269–288.

Heller, W. (1990). The neuropsychology of emotion: Developmental patterns and implications for psychopathology. In N.L. Stein, B. Leventhal, & T. Trabasso (Eds.), *Psychological and biological approaches to emotion.* Hillsdale, NJ: Erlbaum. (pp. 167–211)

James, W. (1884). What is an emotion? *Mind, 9,* 188–205.

Johnston, V.S., Burleson, M.H., & Miller, D.R. (1987). Emotional value and late positive components of ERPs. In R. Johnson, Jr., J.W. Rohrbaugh, & R. Parasuraman (Eds.), *Current trends in event-related potential research, EEG Supplement 40,* 198–203.

Klorman, R., & Ryan, R.M. (1980). Heart rate, contingent negative variation, and evoked potentials during anticipation of affective stimulation. *Psychophysiology, 17,* 513–523.

Kozak, M.J., & Miller, G.A. (1982). Hypothetical constructs vs. intervening variables: A re-appraisal of the three-systems model of anxiety assessment. *Behavioral Assessment, 4,* 347–358.

Lacey, J.I. (1967). Somatic response patterning and stress: Some revisions of activation theory. In M.H. Appley & R. Trumbull (Eds.), *Psychological stress: Issues in research.* New York: Appleton-Century-Crofts. (pp. 14–38)

Lang, P.J. (1964). Experimental studies of desensitization psychotherapy. In J. Wolpe (Ed.), *The conditioning therapies.* New York: Holt, Rinehart, & Winston.

Lang, P.J. (1968). Fear reduction and fear behavior: Problems in treating a construct. In J.M. Shlien (Ed.), *Research in psychotherapy. Volume 3.* (pp. 90–102). Washington, D.C.: American Psychological Association.

Lang, P.J. (1977). Imagery in therapy: An information processing analysis of fear. *Behavior Therapy, 8,* 862–886.

Lang, P.J. (1978). Anxiety: Toward a psychophysiological definition. In H.S. Akiskal & W.L. Webb (Eds.), *Psychiatric diagnosis: Exploration of biological criteria.* (pp. 265–389). New York: Spectrum.

Lang, P.J. (1979). A bio-informational theory of emotional imagery. *Psychophysiology, 16,* 495–512.

Lang, P.J. (1984). Cognition in emotion: Concept and action. In C.E. Izard, J. Kagan, & R.B. Zajonc (Eds.), *Emotions, cognitions, and behavior.* New York: Cambridge University Press. (pp. 192–228)

Lang, P.J. (1985). The cognitive psychophysiology of emotion: Fear and anxiety. In A.H. Tuma & J.D. Maser (Eds.), *Anxiety and the anxiety disorders.* Hillsdale, NJ: Erlbaum. (pp. 131–170)

Lang, P.J., Bradley, M.M., & Cuthbert, B.N. (1990). Emotion, attention, and the startle reflex. *Psychological Review, 97,* 377–395.

Lang, P.J, Melamed, B.G., & Hart, J. (1970). A psychophysiological analysis of fear modification using an automated desensitization procedure. *Journal of Abnormal Psychology, 72,* 220–234.

Linehan, M.M., & Wagner, A.W. (1990). Dialectical behavior therapy: A feminist-behavioral treatment of borderline personality disorder. *The Behavior Therapist, 13,* 9–14.

Maher, B.A. (1966). *Principles of psychopathology:*

An experimental approach. New York: McGraw-Hill.

Martin, B. (1961). The assessment of anxiety by physiological behavioral measures. *Psychological Bulletin, 58,* 234–255.

Miller, G.A. (1988, March). *Measuring the brain's output: Boundaries between cognitive and emotional processing.* Invited address presented at the conference on Emotion: Image and Action, Gainesville, FL.

Miller, G.A., & Ebert, L. (1988). Conceptual boundaries in psychophysiology. *Journal of Psychophysiology, 2,* 13–16.

Miller, G.A., & Yee, C.M. (In press). Psychophysiological contributions to the behavioral highrisk paradigm. To appear in P.K. Ackles, J.R. Jennings, & M.G.H. Coles (Eds.), *Advances in psychophysiology, Volume 5.* Greenwich, CT: JAI Press.

Nelson, R.O. (1979). Editorial statement. *Behavioral Assessment, 1,* i.

Ohman, A. (1979). The orienting response, attention, and learning: An information-processing perspective. In H.D. Kimmel, E.H. van Olst, & J.F. Orlebeke (Eds.), *The orienting reflex in humans.* Hillsdale, NJ: Erlbaum. (pp. 443–471).

Ohman, A. (1987). The psychophysiology of emotion: An evolutionary-cognitive perspective. In P. Ackles, J.R. Jennings, & M.G.H. Coles (Eds.), *Advances in psychophysiology, v. 2.* Greenwich, CT: JAI Press. (pp. 79–127).

Packer, J.S., & Siddle, D.A.T. (1989). Stimulus miscuing, electrodermal activity, and the allocation of processing resources. *Psychophysiology, 26,* 192–199.

Rachman, S.J. (1980). Emotional processing. *Behaviour Research and Therapy, 18,* 51–60.

Rachman, S., & Hodgson, R. (1974). I. Synchrony and desynchrony in fear and avoidance. *Behaviour Research and Therapy, 12,* 311–318.

Rockstroh, B., Elbert, T., Birbaumer, N., & Lutzenberger, W. (1982). *Slow brain potentials and behavior.* Baltimore-Munich: Urban & Schwarzenberg.

Rosenberg, M.J., & Hovland, C.I. (1960). Cognitive, affective, and behavioral components of attitude. In M.J. Rosenberg, C.I. Hovland, W.J. McGuire, R.P. Abelson, & J.W. Brehm (Eds.), *Attitude organization and change: An analysis of consistency among attitude components.* New Haven: Yale University Press. (pp. 1–14)

Simons, R.F., Ohman, A., & Lang, P.J. (1979). Anticipation and response set: Cortical, cardiac, and electrodermal correlates. *Psychophysiology, 16,* 222–233.

Smith, W.J. (1985). Consistency and change in communication. In G. Zivin (Ed.), *The development of expressive behavior* (pp. 51–75). Orlando, FL: Academic Press.

Yee, C.M., & Miller, G.A. (1988). Emotional information processing: Modulation of fear in normal in and dysthymic subjects. *Journal of Abnormal Psychology, 97,* 54–63.

Yee, C.M., & Miller, G.A. (1990, November). *Resource allocation in dysthymia and anhedonia.* Annual meeting of the Society for Research in Psychopathology, Boulder.

Affective Picture Processing

Margaret M. Bradley*, Mark K. Greenwald* and Alfons O. Hamm**

Abstract

The development of a standardized set of emotionally evocative slide stimuli, called the International Affective Picture System (IAPS), is discussed here. These pictorial contents represent a broad range of semantic categories that vary in pleasantness and arousal, resulting in a wide distribution in the affective space defined by a dimensional view of emotion (e. g., Lang, chapter 4, this volume). Perceptual processing of such stimuli produces reliable changes in facial and visceral electrophysiology, interest level, and viewing behavior that covary with reports of affective experience. Recent studies investigating these relationships are reviewed, as well as those exploring the sensitivity of memory performance to these dimensions. While providing clear support for a dimensional model of emotion, these experiments also address the related role of discrete emotional states in determining physiological patterning. Coordination of methodological and empirical efforts among laboratories using the emotional stimuli in the IAPS offers an exciting opportunity to clarify mechanisms of emotional structure and expression.

Key words: emotion, affect, pictures, pleasure, arousal, memory, physiological response, facial expression, visceral response, heart rate, skin conductance, ratings, interest, attention, viewing time, emotional states, affective valence

Lang (1968; 1978) proposed that the data base of emotion can be defined by responses in three systems: verbal report, physiological response, and behavioral action. If sets of emotional stimuli with *known* effects on one or more of these response systems were available, an important tool for the study of emotion would exist. With this purpose in mind, the International Affective Picture System (IAPS; Lang, Öhman, & Vaitl; 1988) was developed to provide a set of normative emotional stimuli for experimental investigations. In this chapter, we discuss how the development and use of this (now extensive) picture system has allowed an orderly advance in understanding how emotion is organized, and we provide an overview of the empirical facts that render these stimuli attractive for use in a variety of explorations of emotional experience and expression.

Methodological Goal and Theoretical Orientation

The purpose of the IAPS is to provide a large set of standardized, emotionally-evocative, internationally-accessible, color photographs that samples contents across a wide range of semantic categories. The methodological goal of this (as it turns out, heroic and time-consum-

---

*   University of Florida
**   University of Giessen
       This research was supported by National Institute of Mental Health (NIMH) Grants MH37757, MH41950 and MH43975 to Peter J. Lang.

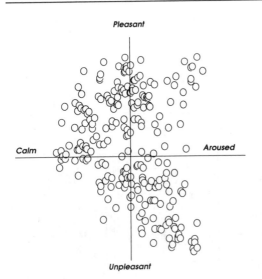

Figure 1. The placement of 240 pictures in the two-dimensional affective space defined by the mean rating of affective valence (pleasant-unpleasant) and arousal (calm-aroused) for each slide by subjects in the USA.

ing) task is to allow comparisons to be made across different investigations of emotion, and to encourage replication within and across research labs assessing basic or applied aspects in the study of emotion. Clearly, in an undertaking of this nature, the theoretical orientation underlying the work will not only define which dependent variables are measured, but will also govern the interpretation of the resulting data. The orientation taken by Lang and his colleagues (Greenwald, Cook, & Lang, 1989; Lang, Bradley, & Cuthbert, 1990; Lang, Greenwald, Bradley, & Hamm, in press) is founded on a dimensional view, which assumes emotion can be defined as a coincidence of values on a limited number of strategic dimensions. Empirical data supporting this conception is

found in Osgood's (Osgood, Suci, & Tannenbaum, 1957) seminal work with the semantic differential, in which factor analyses conducted on a slew of verbal judgments indicated that the variance in emotional assessments was accounted for by three major dimensions. The two primary dimensions were one of affective valence (ranging from pleasant to unpleasant) and one of arousal (ranging from calm to excited). A third, less strongly-related dimension was variously called 'dominance' or 'control'. In the research involving visual slides reported here, the control dimension has shown a high, positive correlation with valence, adding little discrimination beyond the two primary dimensions.* Views of emotion which similarly attribute a central role to the dimensions of valence and arousal have been more recently advocated by Tellegen (1985) and Russell (1980).

Assuming that emotion can be defined by independent dimensions of affective valence and arousal, a 2-dimensional space of the type illustrated in Figure 1 results. To explore the nature of this space, four separate slide studies, each consisting of 60 different slides, were conducted at the University of Florida**; these 240 slides comprise the current IAPS. In each experiment, the subject rated the valence, arousal, and dominance of each slide immediately after a 6-s slide viewing period, using the Self-Assessment Manikin (SAM) affective rating system devised by Lang (1980). In this system, a graphic figure depicting each dimension on a continuously varying scale is used to indicate emotional reactions. Figure 2 illustrates the paper-and-pencil version of SAM used in these rating experiments. As can be seen, SAM ranges from a smiling, happy figure to a frowning, unhappy figure when representing

---

*   Since dominance showed a high positive correlation with affective valence in the ratings of these visual slide materials, the dominance dimension will receive little attention in our discussion of the IAPS. It is likely that the dominance dimension is ill-suited for this type of static visual stimulus; this dimension may account for independent variance in stimuli describing or depicting dynamic, interactional emotional situations.

**   These four studies were conducted over the course of five years (1987–1992) by Peter Lang and members of his research group, including Andy Bertron, Margaret Bradley, Ed Cook, Bruce Cuthbert, Mark Greenwald, Chris Patrick, & Margaret Petry.

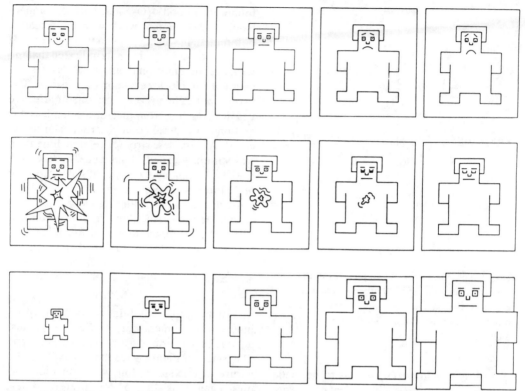

Figure 2. The Self-Assessment Manikin (SAM) used to rate the affective dimensions of valence (top panel), arousal (middle panel), and dominance (bottom panel).

the valence dimension; similarly, SAM ranges from an excited, wide-eyed figure to a relaxed, sleepy figure for the arousal dimension. In this version of SAM, the subject can place an 'X' over any of the 5 figures in each scale, or between any two figures, which results in a 9-point rating scale for each dimension. In addition to the paper-and-pencil version, SAM exists as a dynamic computer display on a variety of different systems, including DEC and IBM (Cook, Atkinson, & Lang, 1987) systems. The computer SAM instrument uses a 30-point scale, rendering more discrimination in each dimension than the paper-and-pencil version.

I. Verbal Reports

Using SAM, over 300 subjects have rated slides in the IAPS on the dimensions of valence, arousal, and dominance. The slides sample a wide range of semantic categories, and include pictures of babies, opposite-sex nudes, romantic couples, sports events, food, nature scenes, household objects, snakes, spiders, guns, cemeteries, mutilated bodies, and more. In Figure 1, each slide is located in the portion of the emotional space defined by its mean valence and arousal rating. There are several characteristic features of the resulting space. First, these stimulus materials evoke reactions across the entire range of each dimension: mean valence ratings for these slides range from extremely unpleasant (mean = 1.3) to extremely pleasant (mean = 8.5), and are distributed fairly evenly across the valence dimension. Similarly, a wide range of arousal levels are elicited by these materials. Secondly, it is clear that pleasant slides range continuously along the arousal dimension: the upper half of emotional space has exemplars at many positions along this dimension. These data suggest that the degree of arousal is uncorrelated with the pleasantness of the slide. Slides depicting unpleasant events, however, show a tendency to cluster in the quadrant of emotional space indicating high arousal: there are relatively fewer unpleasant items located in the calm quadrant of emotional space. Finally, for items rated as neutral in valence (i.e., those occurring at and near the midline of the valence dimension), arousal ratings do not attain the high levels associated with either pleasant or unpleasant materials.

These observations are supported by the statistics. Across the entire set of slides, the linear correlation between valence and arousal rating is low and not significant, indicating that these two dimensions are linearly independent. However, a significant quadratic relationship between valence and arousal captures their relationship: arousal ratings tend to be higher as the slides approach either end of the valence dimension (i.e., become increasingly more pleasant or unpleasant). As Figure 1 illustrates, this relationship between extreme valence categories and arousal ratings is more pronounced for unpleasant materials.

These empirical facts about affective space – at least as defined by these stimulus materials – identify the calm quadrant of negative emotional space as relatively less inhabited than other places in emotional space. The types of categories that currently reside here include slides depicting pollution, starving children, and cemeteries. If this portion of space remains difficult to fill, reasonable hypotheses concern limitations in the type of emotional stimuli used here (i.e., static visual images) and/or the underlying function of emotion (e.g., extremely aversive stimuli may require high mobilization). As Tellegen (1985) suggests, high negative affect may necessarily involve a high level of arousal.

Stability and Reliability of Ratings.

In addition to the four large rating experiments, several psychophysiological experiments have been conducted using subsets of these slide materials (Bradley et al., 1990; Greenwald et al., 1989; Lang et al., in press). Verbal report data (using SAM) gathered in all of these experiments suggest that the valence and arousal dimensions are highly salient in defining the emotional differences among the slides, and that these ratings are stable when assessing either within- or between-subject reliability. For example, mean ratings of slide valence and arousal are highly internally consistent. The split-half coefficients for the valence and arousal dimensions were highly reliable ($p < .001$), both for pencil-and-paper ($rs = .94$ and $.94$, respectively for 60 slides) and computer administration formats of SAM ($rs = .94$ and $.93$, respectively for 21 slides; Greenwald, 1987).

These affective judgments remain stable regardless of the local context in which a slide is processed – ratings of a particular slide by subjects in different experiments using different slide sets remain robust. For example, using the pencil-and-paper version of SAM, a small set of slides used in the first large-group normative rating study were re-presented in the second large-group normative study, in the context of a completely different set of to-be-rated slides. Independent sample t-tests of these replicate slides (which were distributed widely in the affective space) revealed no significant difference in either the mean valence or the mean arousal ratings. Using computer SAM, Lang et al. (in press) also found that the ratings of a subset of slides (n = 11) used in their study were highly similar to the same slides presented in an earlier experiment (Greenwald et al., 1989) in both mean valence ratings ($r = .99$) and mean arousal ratings ($r = .97$). Again, t-tests revealed no significant differences in slide valence or arousal means across studies.

The stability in affective ratings is independent of SAM administration format. The mean valence ratings for 21 slides across the two (i.e., paper & pencil SAM and computerized SAM) rating instruments produced a very high correlation (r = .99); arousal ratings were also significantly reliable, but somewhat lower in magnitude (r = .64). Closer inspection of the arousal data indicated that five specific slides (including three pictures of facial expressions) accounted for the lower correlation. While several factors may affect this difference, most obvious are differences in the viewing conditions (group classroom vs. individual isolation in the laboratory), including viewing distance, which was considerably closer in the lab. Subsequent data suggest that this arousal reliability estimate probably represents a lower boundary. Recent estimates from work in Lang's lab (Lang et al., in press) suggest a higher correlation (rs up to .94), although still lower than those obtained for valence ratings. Normalization of the slide ratings, which minimizes idiosyncratic subject variance, also tends to yield higher estimates.

Since it might be expected that emotional judgments would remain robust across extreme emotional categories (e. g., mutilated bodies, opposite sex nudes), data regarding the stability in measurement may seem somewhat trivial. However, the semantic categories included in the IAPS incorporate exemplars of more vague emotional status (e. g., an agate, fire hydrant, a lecturer, etc.). The high reliability in affective ratings within and between subject samples and slide contents suggests that these visual materials, however complex, reliably elicit consistent affective reactions.

Cross-Cultural Differences

The relationships discussed above were assessed using rating data from subjects living in a specific geographical and cultural enclave: undergraduate students at the University of Florida in the United States. As is true of most psychological research, one would like to generalize beyond this sample. One of the earliest goals in constructing IAPS, in fact, was to provide visual images that were relatively culture-free in terms of evoking emotional responses. To this end, researchers from several different European countries have conducted comparable pencil-and-paper SAM ratings on

the first set of 60 IAPS slides. Countries contributing to this highly valuable research effort are West Germany (Hamm & Vaitl, University of Giessen, N = 78), Sweden (Öhman; Uppsala University, N = 97), and Italy (Palomba & Stegnano, University of Padua, N = 126).

Preliminary analyses have uncovered both similarities and differences in slide affective judgments across countries. In general, the reliabilities of mean valence and arousal ratings across these four samples are high for both the valence and arousal dimensions (rs > .80). In addition, the correlation between the valence and arousal ratings for each country on this set of materials is similar, indicating that the two dimensions covary in the same way. These data suggest that the emotional stimuli comprising the IAPS are robust across both cultural and geographical distance.

One difference among the countries in affective assessment is worth noting – the distribution of slide arousal ratings was significantly different across countries. Relative to the U.S. and West German samples (which did not differ in mean arousal rating across all 60 slides, 4.84 and 4.88, respectively on the 1 to 9 scale), Swedish subjects generally assigned lower arousal ratings (X = 4.17) to the slides, indicating calmer emotional reactions, whereas the Italians rated slides as significantly more arousing overall (X = 5.36). Surprisingly, these data tend to support the general cultural stereotypes that exist for these countries. More importantly, these data indicate that the IAPS might reliably index cultural differences in emotional disposition, which renders it a potent set of stimuli for investigating cross-cultural affective experience. Since SAM is also a culture-free, language-free measuring instrument, the entire methodology is suitable for use in many different countries and cultures.

Sex Differences

Gender differences in affective judgments began to reliably appear with even the earliest investigation using IAPS stimuli. Thus, gender is now regularly included in the design of these experiments, and contributes to the between-subject variance in the measurement of slide reliability. In general, females tend to use a wider range along the valence dimension, rating more materials at the extremes of both pleasantness and unpleasantness, relative to males (Greenwald et al., 1989). A gender difference in arousal ratings was also found in the cross-cultural data above. Females assigned ratings which were significantly more arousing (X = 5.00) than those of males (X = 4.78), which was independent of country of origin.

Age Differences

Differences in the distribution of slides in emotional space have also been implicated as a function of age. In one study (Cuthbert, Bradley, & Lang, 1988), women from the ages of 18–60 viewed a subset of the IAPS; these subjects were part of a larger study of emotional changes across the lifespan. Whereas the younger, college-aged women produced a typically low and non-significant linear correlation between valence and arousal ($r = -.06$), the mature women in this sample (i.e., 45 and older) produced a linear correlation of $-.73$. Clearly, these mature subjects were viewing the emotional world differently (at least as defined by these stimuli). For these women, pleasant events were those that were non-activating; on the other hand, events that were arousing tended to be rated as unpleasant. This provocative finding (which should be assessed in older males as well) suggests that age, as well as culture and gender, influences how affective pictures are evaluated.

SAM and the Semantic Differential

Although it appears that SAM is measuring the dimensions identified as central in factor analyses using the semantic differential, it would clearly be helpful to validate this relationship with these emotional materials. Typically, factor analyses have been conducted on emotional materials that are verbal in nature. For instance, Mehrabian and Russell (1974) presented their subjects with descriptions of 64 situations thought to "elicit a large variety of emotional states" and asked subjects to rate their reactions to these textual descriptions. Ratings were made using a semantic differential scale that consisted of 18 different bipolar adjective pairs. The resulting matrix of correlations was factor analyzed and the solution indicated the typical three factors, with pleasure accounting for 27%, arousal accounting for 23%, and dominance accounting for 14% of the total variance, respectively.

Recently, Hamm (in press) used the semantic differential rating scale in conjunction with a set of slides from the IAPS. In his study, 93 subjects made ratings on all 18 bipolar adjective pairs immediately after each slide was viewed. Factor analysis produced an identical three factor solution with pleasure (valence) accounting for 26%, arousal for 19%, and dominance for 10% of the total variance, respectively. This dimensional structure was replicated in a second study in which a different 60-item slide set was used, again drawn from the IAPS, with an independent sample of 96 subjects. In this experiment, the valence factor accounted for 32%, arousal for 18% and dominance again for 10% of the total variance. Importantly, the distribution of the slides in the affective space was identical irrespective of whether the semantic differential or SAM was used to rate these slide stimuli. These data are encouraging, in that they indicate that the SAM ratings obtained for IAPS stimuli are identical to those obtained with another, verbal measure of affective reactions. Since SAM is a fast, reliable, and nonverbal method for measuring these dimensions, it might be preferred over the more cumbersome, and time-consuming semantic differential methodology.

Interest Ratings of IAPS Slides

In addition to SAM ratings, materials in the IAPS set have been rated as a function of how interesting the slide is to the subject (Bradley et al., 1990, 1991; Lang et al., in press). These ratings tend to correlate very highly with the arousal dimension (rs from .76 to .87), indicating that both very pleasant and very unpleasant slides are found to be of high interest. A similar finding occurs with viewing time data: if the subject is allowed to view the slides in the IAPS as long as desired (terminating the slide presentation with a button press), viewing time is longer for arousing slides – both pleasant and unpleasant – than for calm slides (*rs* from .45 to .61). As expected from these relationships, interest ratings and viewing times are positively correlated as well. These data widen the purview of the affective judgment data available for these materials, and suggest that additional ratings of attention and emotion might well prove interesting.

Taken together, the emotional judgment data reviewed above are encouraging and suggest that the slide stimuli comprising the IAPS are potent elicitors of affective states. Additionally, they indicate that the normative rating data obtained for these materials may be sufficient for categorizing and selecting emotional stimuli for future experimental efforts. Finally, they provide a solid data base from which to assess replication data, as well as to compare data from studies that utilize these stimuli in new ways.

II. Physiological Response

It seems clear that subjects' evaluations are sensitive to the dimensional variations in the slide stimuli. However, these judgments are not exhaustive in tapping the subject's affective data base. Indeed, the inherent plasticity in language and its sensitivity to experimental cues raise the possibility that subjects may respond to these slides as they think others should (i. e., in a socially appropriate manner). If this were true, one might expect to find that many subjects would show a divergence between these measures and physiological indices of emotional response. As Lang (1968) originally noted, correlations between measures of emotion are typically very modest. Part of the problem may relate to the general lack of standardized stimuli for assessing concordance across response systems.

Using the IAPS stimuli, covariation among emotional responses can easily be assessed. One method is to relate verbal reports to physiological responses by ranking the slide materials on the basis of their affective judgments. Once the slide stimuli are arrayed along a dimension (e. g., valence or arousal), one is able to assess the covariation between, for example, the physiological index of heart rate change, and the subject's judgments of pleasantness. This strategy optimizes the opportunity to observe unit changes in physiology coincident with changes in affective judgments, and allows one to determine the nature of the relationship

between verbal judgments and physiological response. This type of formulation essentially provides an 'emotional psychophysics' that is analogous to Stevens' (1961) classic law which relates subjective reports of stimulus magnitude to physical intensity of the stimulus.

In two experiments ($N = 108$) that examined the dimensional relationships of judgments to physiology (Greenwald et al., 1989; Lang et al., in press), a pairwise correlation between verbal judgments and physiological responses (along each dimension of valence and arousal) was computed for each subject. Clear, reliable relationships emerged from this work, as Figure 3 illustrates. First, the pattern of facial muscle responses strongly paralleled reports of affective valence. Second, the degree of heart rate acceleration was also sensitive to valence judgments but, not surprisingly, weaker than for facial expression. Third, skin conductance activity closely tracked changes in rated arousal. Finally, these relationships – especially the valence/ facial expression and arousal/conductance correlations – were present in the majority of people who viewed the slide materials. These observations suggest that the IAPS materials prompt complete expression of emotional engagement and are not solely responded to in a verbally appropriate manner.

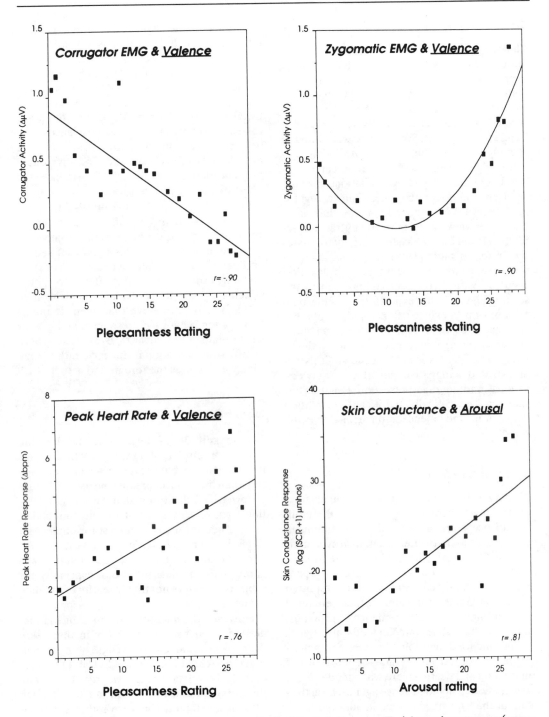

Figure 3. Relationship of affective ratings to psychophysiological responses. Facial muscle responses (corrugator and zygomatic EMG) and heart rate covaried closely with changes in pleasantness ratings whereas skin conductance activity was more closely associated with changes in rated arousal.

Corrugator EMG

The corrugator muscle is responsible for lowering the brow muscle, and is involved in facial expressions indicating distress (see Fridlund & Izard, 1983, for a review). In fact, significant contraction of this muscle appears when a slide is rated as unpleasant (Greenwald et al., 1989; Lang et al., in press). Specific materials reliably eliciting corrugator changes (from a 1 s base immediately preceding slide onset) greater than .5 µV were slides depicting mutilations, starving children, and pollution scenes. The corrugator response was lower (but still greater than baseline) when viewing slides rated neutral, and actually relaxed below baseline activity for materials rated as most pleasant. The most representative example of corrugator relaxation occurred with pictures of smiling babies. As seen in Figure 3 (upper left), the dimensional relationship between valence judgments and corrugator response (i. e., the correlation of the averaged corrugator response at each valence rank) was –.90. Over 80% of the subjects demonstrated a negative correlation between valence and corrugator response, with 50% showing a statistically significant correlation between judged valence and corrugator EMG activity.

Zygomatic EMG

Activity of the zygomatic muscle is involved in controlling the smile response, and therefore should occur primarily to pleasant stimuli. In fact, there is a sharp differentiation in zygomatic activity for stimuli which subjects rate as most pleasant. As can be seen in Figure 3 (upper right), zygomatic activity in the studies reported above was greatest for materials that were rated as very high in affective valence, and almost nonexistent for slides rated in moderate regions of the valence dimension. However, for materials rated as most unpleasant – often slides of mutilation and death – there was a tendency for zygomatic activity to increase again. The activation of the zygomatic muscle in addition to increases in corrugator response suggests that an expression of facial grimacing may accompany perception of these aversive materials.

Because of the slight increase in zygomatic EMG activity at the unpleasant end of the valence continuum (and the significant increase at the positive end) there is a reliable quadratic (more so than linear) correlation between reports of judged pleasantness and zygomatic EMG activity. The strength of this quadratic correlation ranged from .85 to .90 in each of the two studies conducted above. Overall, more than 70% of subjects showed a positive quadratic correlation, and about 50% demonstrated a statistically significant effect.

Interestingly, roughly two-thirds of female subjects showed this significant relationship, whereas only a quarter of male subjects responded appropriately. This significant gender difference indicates that the expression of emotion might primarily involve different response systems in females and males, with women more facially expressive than men. Identical findings for facial EMG responses and gender were obtained by Schwartz, Brown and Ahern (1980) when emotional imagery, rather than slide viewing, was the foreground activity.

Heart Rate

The magnitude of heart rate acceleration during mid-interval slide viewing was sensitive to slide valence, but showed a weaker relationship than the facial expressive measures. Figure 3 (lower left) illustrates that cardiac acceleration was typically greatest for pleasant slides, less for neutral slides, and least for unpleasant slides. Klorman, Wiesenfeld, and Austin (1975) also determined that cardiac deceleration was greatest for unpleasant slides, especially for subjects who were not highly fearful of the slide contents.

However, the data obtained in Lang's lab indicated considerable variability in these estimates, which reduces the strength of the dimensional correlation. Greenwald et al. (1989) reported a correlation of .50, whereas Lang et al. (in press) found a correlation of .76. Although 74% of the subjects in these samples demonstrated a positive correlation between valence judgments and cardiac acceleration, only 14% of subjects in the two studies produced a significant correlation. Cardiac response has several limitations as a measure of emotional state, in that heart rate acceleration can occur in judgment tasks that are affectively neutral (Bull & Lang, 1972; Gatchel & Lang, 1973). Furthermore, even in affective tasks, the direction of heart rate change varies with experimental context (Lang et al., in press; Hodes, Cook, & Lang, 1985). In addition, momentary fluctuations in cardiac activity (influenced by the housekeeping function of this organ) tend to minimize the correlation with affective judgments.

Although the heart rate response during slide viewing demonstrates a weaker relationship with slide valence than does the facial EMG, it remains a useful adjunct measure of slide processing. In several studies (e. g., Bradley et al., 1990, 1991), the direction of heart rate change during processing of aversive materials (i. e., deceleratory) allowed one to rule out simple attentional differences. In general, though, heart rate responses are best considered ancillary, rather than defining, measures of affective valence in emotional processing.

Skin Conductance

Electrodermal activity is advantageous as a measure of arousal since it is innervated entirely by the sympathetic nervous chain, whose output results in a broad state of activation. Indeed, in recent studies (Greenwald et al., 1989; Lang et al., in press), the amount of skin conductance activity increased linearly as ratings of arousal increased, regardless of emotional valence. This is illustrated in Figure 3 (lower right), in which the dimensional correlation between skin conductance activity and arousal reports was .81. This relationship is further validated by data indicating larger skin conductance responses to extremely pleasant or unpleasant materials. As noted above, valence ratings tend to show a quadratic relationship with reports of arousal. Thus, Winton, Putnam, & Krauss (1984) obtained data indicating larger skin conductance responses to slides that were rated as highly pleasant and highly unpleasant. Manning & Melchiori (1974) obtained similar skin conductance data when the stimulus items were words

that were rated as highly pleasant (e. g., sex) and highly unpleasant (e. g., violence).

In the studies conducted by Lang and his colleagues, over 80% of the subjects showed a positive correlation between arousal reports and conductance response; 31% showed a significant correlation. Interestingly, a larger proportion of males showed a significant correlation (46%), relative to females (16%). Thus, whereas females are more facially expressive, males are more reactive in the electrodermal system.

Startle Responses

The autonomic and somatic measures reviewed above were measured as spontaneous responses occurring during the slide viewing interval. A second method for measuring affective valence involves the presentation of a startle probe during emotional processing (see Bradley & Vrana, this volume; Lang et al., 1990; Vrana, Spence, & Lang, 1988). The startle stimulus consists of the sudden onset of an intense stimulus (e. g., a loud noise) and produces a reflexive response which includes an easily measurable eyeblink component. Lang and his colleagues (see Lang et al., 1990, for an overview) have determined that the magnitude of the blink reflex is systematically related to the pleasantness of the slide foreground material: eyeblink magnitude increases as the slide stimuli are rated more unpleasantly. The relationship between startle magnitude and slide valence is reliable, and has been replicated many times (Bradley et al., 1990, 1991; Hamm, Stark, & Vaitl, 1990; Cook, Hawk, & Stevenson (1990); Patrick, Bradley, & Lang, in press; Vrana et al., 1988).

While similar to the corrugator EMG data in showing a significant linear correlation with slide valence, the startle response has the additional desirable properties of being a discrete somatic event that occurs within milliseconds of probe onset, is reflexive (which eliminates interpretive problems based on demand characteristics), and is easily implemented in a laboratory setting. These characteristics make it an attractive index for measuring the affective valence of foreground processing.

III. Memory

The psychophysiological relationships reviewed above suggest that the valence and arousal dimensions are salient organizational parameters of emotion. The simple slide-viewing context thus appears sufficient to access affective response patterns stored in memory. Accordingly, it is reasonable to hypothesize that measures of memory performance would vary systematically with either the judged valence or arousal – or both – of the slide content.

Past research, as well as folklore, provides a basis for practically every prediction possible. Claims that unpleasant stimuli are well-remembered are supported by recent studies (e. g., Christianson & Loftus, 1987), while the opposite idea – that unpleasant events are 're-pressed' in memory – has an impressive history, spurred by Freud's psychodynamic viewpoint. On the other hand, Matlin & Stang (1978) produce data suggesting that pleasant events are at an advantage in memory (termed the 'Polly-anna' effect), which is bolstered by the commonsense notion that people tend to view the past through 'rosy-colored glasses'. A positive relationship between level of arousal and increased memory performance has been obtained numerous times (see Craik & Blank-stein, 1973, for a review), whereas, at least for short-term memory, high levels of stimulus arousal have been purported to reduce memory performance as well.

Free Recall Performance

Memory retrieval of stimuli from the IAPS was assessed in two different studies (Bradley, Greenwald, Petry, & Lang, 1992). In the first study, each subject viewed 60 slides, and rated each slide (immediately after offset) on the dimensions of valence, arousal, and dominance using paper-and-pencil SAM. No mention of a later memory test was given during the rating phase of the experiment. When all of the slides had been rated, a 5-minute, incidental free recall test was administered, in which the subject was instructed to write down a word or short phrase describing each slide that could be re-membered. Memory was assessed again a year later when a delayed incidental free recall test on the same materials was given. In this long-term memory portion of the experiment, the subject was contacted by telephone and again asked to recall as many of the slides as possible seen in the experiment the year before.

The results were provocative: at both immediate and delayed recall, the judged arousal level of a slide had a large influence on memory performance. Superior memory performance was consistently obtained for slides rated as highly arousing, relative to slides that received lower arousal ratings. A significant linear trend between recall and arousal rating was obtained both immediately and a year later, suggesting that the relationship between arousal and memory performance is a monotonically increasing function of the slides' arousal level. The parallel data obtained in immediate memory performance and a year later is impressive support for the role of the arousal dimension in memory processing.

The influence of judgments of affective valence on memory performance was less consistent. Significant quadratic trends relating judged valence to recall were obtained in both immediate and delayed recall. However, this effect could be explained as a function of the differences in the rated arousal of slides at the extreme positions of the valence dimension: as before, both highly pleasant and highly unpleasant slides received higher arousal ratings than neutral slides.

The independent contribution of valence and arousal was assessed by creating a factorial combination of these variables. For each subject, an estimate of recall was computed based on the proportion of slides remembered in each of four cells defined by covarying valence (unpleasant, pleasant) and arousal (low, high). Figure 4 (left-hand panel) illustrates the recall data obtained as a function of these two affective dimensions. As expected, arousal again showed a clear, significant main effect on memory performance. In addition, there was a modest, marginally significant advantage for pleasant materials at immediate recall. A year later, however, this mild effect for positive materials had disappeared, leaving a strong arousal effect intact. No interaction was obtained between valence and arousal at either recall test. These data suggest that the effect of valence on memory performance is minimal, showing only a slight bias for positive materials on an immediate memory test, whereas arousal shows a strong, consistent effect on memory retrieval.

Recognition Performance

A second study investigated the speed at which the subject could discriminate previously presented slides from slides never presented before in the experiment. During the encoding phase in this study, each subject viewed one of

two sets of 21 IAPS slides; each pair of slides in the two sets was matched as close as possible for rated valence, rated arousal, and semantic content. During encoding, each of the 21 slides was presented for 6 seconds. In a subsequent retrieval phase, all 42 slides (21 repeated slides and 21 new slides) were presented for a speeded recognition decision. The subject was instructed to press one of two buttons as quickly as possible, indicating whether the slide had been seen before or was new.

As the right-hand panel of Figure 4 indicates, the speed of recognition memory performance was significantly affected by the arousal level of the slides. However, the direction of the effect depended upon whether the slide was being *retrieved* from memory or whether it was being *encoded* for the first time. For slides that had pre-

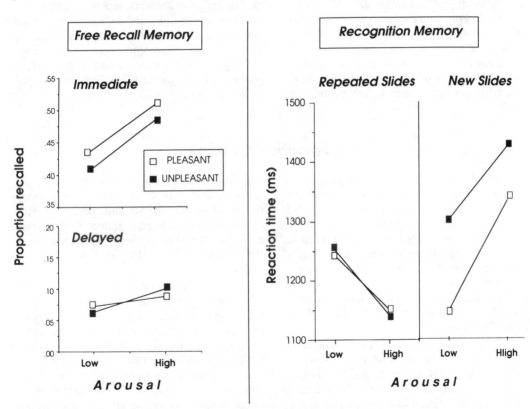

Figure 4. Memory performance for affective pictures. Left panel illustrates that rated arousal facilitates free recall on both an immediate and delayed (1 year later) test. The right panel illustrates data from a speeded recognition test, in which arousal facilitated performance for slides seen before and inhibited performance for new slides.

viously been encoded, high arousal *speeded* recognition decisions; for new slides, high arousal *slowed* recognition decisions. In addition, for new slides, slide valence had a significant impact on reaction time: unpleasant slides prompted longer decision times than pleasant slides.

These data suggest differences in the way the valence and arousal dimensions affect *encoding* and *retrieval* processes. As found for the free recall data, the major factor affecting retrieval performance is the arousal level of the slide stimulus: high arousal facilitates retrieval performance, whether measured by verbal recall, or speed of recognition. On the other hand, encoding processes appear to be sensitive to both dimensions: both high arousal and unpleasantness slowed recognition speed.

One way to interpret these effects is to note that pleasant events can be defined as those which primarily engage approach or appetitive behaviors, whereas unpleasant events are those prompting avoidance and defensive actions (see Lang et al., 1990, for further exposition of this theoretical viewpoint). In this analysis, the arousal dimension relates to the vigor of the designated behavioral set, and can range from high to low mobilization of resources. From this type of functional viewpoint, a memory system sensitive to the arousal level of the event makes sense: an organism will remember events that mobilize behavior, regardless of whether the purpose of action is to approach a desired object (e.g., a food source when hungry) or to avoid a feared one (e.g., a predator in one's environment). The mechanics underlying this effect – in terms of both its cognitive and neurophysiological aspects – remain to be explicated.

These data point to a strong role of arousal in memory, as assessed by recall and recognition of these affective pictures. In addition to being useful in determining the underlying organization of emotion in memory, it is likely that disorders of memory, especially emotional memory, can be indexed by measuring recall and/or recognition speed using stimuli in the IAPS. Finally, developmental questions concerning emotional memory and its maturation processes might similarly profit from this type of investigation.

IV. Specific Emotions

Thus far, the argument that the dimensions of valence and arousal are salient in organizing the affective materials comprising the IAPS is impressively supported. Judgments on both dimensions are internally reliable and replicable, and covary significantly with physiological measures of emotional response, as well as with memory performance. These data suggest that a dimensional view is – at the least – a useful one when considering how emotion might be centrally organized.

An alternative view argues that emotion is best conceptualized as a series of discrete, unique emotional states (e.g., fear, anger, happy, etc.) that are not necessarily linked by an underlying dimension of valence and/or arousal. This 'specific state' view of emotion has its virtues; one property it lacks, however, is parsimony. The linguistic emotional repertoire is quite large – a recent count of the number of emotional states that a sample of subjects could list (Fehr & Russell, 1984) produced an impressive total of 197! In fact, one goal in specific emotion work has been to reduce the list to account for the so-called "basic" or primary emotions (Izard, 1977; Oatley & Johnson-Laird, 1987).

It is likely that the dimensional and specific state views of emotion are *complementary* – rather than opposed – methods of studying emotion. For instance, it is possible to locate specific emotional states in the 2-dimensional affective space defined by valence and arousal. In a preliminary investigation of this sort, Lang et al. (in press) required their subjects to rate a series of slides along the affective dimensions of valence, arousal, and dominance (using SAM). In addition, a 7-alternative, forced choice emotion categorization task was conducted, in which each slide was labelled regarding the principal emotion evoked during the viewing period. Choices in the specific emotion categories were happy, surprised, angry, sad, fearful and disgusted (similar to Izard's [1977] list of primary emotions). In addition, a 'neutral' emotional category choice was included in the set. In this study, affective valence and arousal ratings could be computed as a function of the specific emotional state elicited by the slide context.

As expected, specific emotional states occupied different positions in space, with sad and fearful events, for example, both rated low in valence, but different in arousal level (sad events were lower in arousal). Interestingly, events that were classified as fearful were rated slightly higher in arousal than stimuli labelled disgusting, which may index the high mobilization for avoidance or escape for fear stimuli. Valence judgments of happy slides were clearly rated higher in valence and higher in arousal than neutral slides. Predictably, slides rated as neutral tended to be rated as low in arousal.

Because this investigation was only a preliminary assessment of specific emotions elicited by these slide materials, the rating procedure used was not optimal: it was difficult to balance the number of slides assigned to each emotion category and even more difficult to insure that all subjects responded in all emotion categories. Clearly, normative ratings of the slide materials using an established instrument for measuring specific states (such as the Differential Emotion Scale used by Izard, 1972) is necessary.

Nonetheless, several slide stimuli were reliably classified, across subjects, as producing a specific emotion state, including disgust, happiness, fear, and sadness. Slides reliably rated as producing these emotional states were used to investigate the relationship of specific state to physiological response. For the disgust category, pictures of mutilated faces reliably elicited reports of disgust (with about 75% reliability). Slides of smiling babies (90% agreement) clearly represented one type of happy category, associated perhaps with nurturance. A second category of slides reliably labelled happy, but with significantly higher arousal ratings were opposite-sex erotic stimuli (averaging 78% reliability for males, and 52% agreement

for females). The best fear-evoking slides (aimed pistol, 72%, and snake, 52%) and sadness-evoking slides (dead animal and starving child, each 59%) were used as exemplars of these categories. In addition to these emotion categories, household items were described as neutral with high agreement (about 95%). Since no specific slide was *reliably* judged as producing surprise or anger, these categories were excluded from analysis.

Assuming that emotional reactions for specific emotional states are defined by their underlying valence and arousal ratings, it is possible to assess whether specific emotional states show the predicted covariation with physiological response. Thus, the six emotional states defined here (i.e., fear, sadness, disgust, neutral, happy/ nurturant and happy/erotic) were arrayed by their mean affective valence (or arousal) ratings, and the magnitude of physiological responses assessed. Figure 5 illustrates the facial muscle (corrugator and zygomatic) responses for these emotion slide categories (upper two panels).

As in the concordance analysis between *dimensional* affective ratings and physiology, corrugator responses for this set of emotion categories showed a strong linear relationship with the mean valence rating ($r = .83$). Magnitude of the corrugator response for disgusting and sad materials (the two most negatively rated states) was large and significantly greater than for other emotions. As expected by the ordering in their valence ratings, happy/nurturant slides elicited significantly greater relaxation of the corrugator muscle than did happy/ erotic slides. Results were similar for zygomatic muscle activity: when plotted by their mean valence ratings, the predicted quadratic pattern was obtained across the six emotion categories. The most positive emotion (happy/nurturant) prompted significantly greater zygomatic response than all other emotion categories. The most negatively rated emotion – disgust – also prompted increased zygomatic activity, which is completely consistent with the quadratic relationship obtained in the dimensional analyses.

Autonomic responses as a function of specific emotion category are also presented in Figure 5 (two lower panels), with heart rate re-

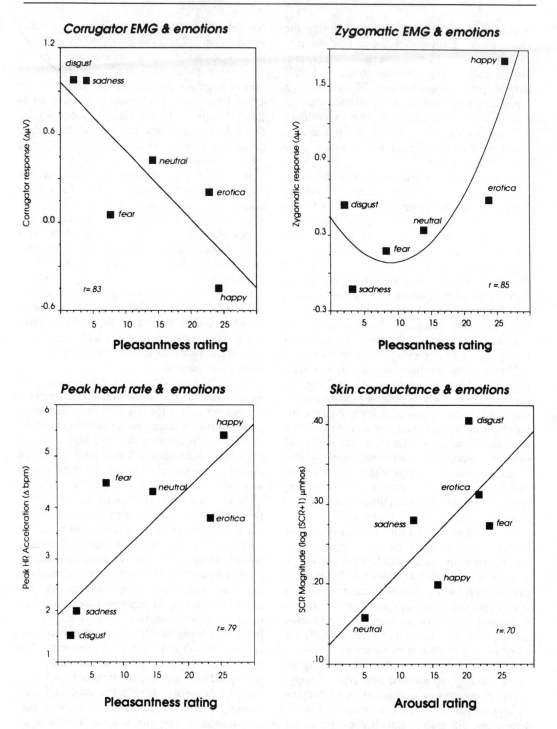

Figure 5. Relationship of psychophysiological responses to specific emotional states as defined by the affective ratings for slides reliably labelled as evoking fear, sadness, disgust, happy, or erotic pleasure.

sponse arrayed against valence ratings, and skin conductance response plotted against arousal ratings. Again, peak heart rate acceleration showed a significant linear relationship with valence ratings; as predicted, responses to unpleasant materials – disgust and sad slides – were equivalent and significantly smaller (by about 2–3 bpm) than responses prompted by slides rated higher on the valence dimension.

When arrayed by mean arousal ratings, the magnitude of skin conductance responses as a function of specific emotional state showed the expected linear relationship. Some aspects of this relationship seemed less than perfect, however. For example, the largest skin conductance responses occurred during the processing of slides rated as disgusting, even though fear materials were rated slightly higher in arousal. Furthermore, although sadness was rated as significantly lower in arousal than fear, these slides prompted equivalent conductance activity. On the other hand, skin conductance responses for the positive emotional states – nurturant and erotic – showed the predicted relationship, with larger responses for erotic materials than for the baby slides. In addition, consistent with arousal ratings, the 'neutral' emotional state prompted the least conductance activity.

While these data offer only a preliminary look at specific emotional states, the results encourage the view that the dimensional and specific emotion viewpoints are complementary. The differences in physiological response obtained for the specific emotional states investigated here seem to be well-accounted for by variations along the valence dimension; differences in arousal level were slightly less successful in predicting physiological responses. Clearly, these issues require more investigation before they are satisfactorily resolved. Interest-ingly, Shaver, Schwartz, Kirson & O'Connor (1987) recently concluded that arousal may be a relevant discriminator *within* specific emotions, rather than across emotions. Their conclusion was based on a hierarchical analysis of verbal emotional materials that had been used in a sorting task. Regardless of the ultimate resolution of these issues, it is clear that the slide stimuli are potentially useful for integrating dimensional and specific state viewpoints in the study of emotion.

Conclusion

The goal is well-met: the International Affective Picture System successfully offers a set of normative emotional materials for use in investigations of emotion. Indeed, the task continues, as new stimuli and new ratings are added to the collection. It is noteworthy that in developing these materials Lang and his colleagues have, in a sense, taken a step backward and attempted to define and organize emotion, in order to study it. The parsimonious viewpoint inherent in a dimensional theory of emotion provides an opportunity to simplify the phenomenon. In addition, an easy association can be made between the verbal dimensions of affective *valence* and *arousal* and the dimensions underlying behavior, earlier proposed by Hebb (1949) to be *direction* and *vigor*. This relationship provides a straightforward link between the sophisticated verbal behavior accompanying affective experience, and the physiological and behavioral aspects that have always been recognized as central to emotional engagement. This theoretical viewpoint, together with the large data base underlying the slide stimuli comprising the IAPS, promises to advance our understanding of the mechanisms underlying emotion.

References

Bradley, M. M., Cuthbert, B. N., & Lang, P. J. (1990). Startle reflex modification: Emotion or attention? *Psychophysiology, 27*, 513–523.

Bradley, M. M., Cuthbert, B. N., & Lang, P. J. (1991). Startle and emotion: Lateral acoustic probes and the bilateral blink. *Psychophysiology, 28*, 285–295.

Bradley, M. M., Greenwald, M. K., Petry, M., & Lang, P. J. (1992). Remembering pictures: Pleasure and arousal in memory. *Journal of Experimental Psychology: Learning, Memory and Cognition, 18,* 379–390.

Bull, K., & Lang. P. J. (1972). Intensity judgments and physiological amplitude. *Psychophysiology, 9,* 428–436.

Cacioppo, J. T., & Petty, R. E. (1981). Electromyograms as measures of extent of affectivity of information processing. *American Psychologist, 36,* 441–456.

Cacioppo, J. T., Petty, R. E., Losch, M. E., & Kim, H. S. (1986). Electromyographic activity over facial muscle regions can differentiate the valence and intensity of affective reactions. *Journal of Personality and Social Psychology, 50,* 260–268.

Christianson, S.-Å., & Loftus, E.F. (1987). Memory for traumatic events. *Applied Cognitive Psychology, 1,* 225–239.

Cook, E. W. III, Atkinson, L., & Lang, P. J. (1987). Stimulus control and data acquisition for IBM PC's and compatibles. *Psychophysiology, 24,* 726. [Abstract]

Craik, F. I. M., & Blankstein, K. R. (1975). Psychophysiology and human memory. In P. H. Venables & M. J. Christie (Eds.), *Research in psychophysiology* (pp. 388–417). Chichester, UK: Wiley.

Cuthbert, B.N., Bradley, M.M., & Lang, P.J. (1988). Psychophysiological responses to affective slides across the life span. *Psychophysiology, 25,* 441. [Abstract]

Fehr, B., & Russell, J. A. (1984). Concept of emotion viewed from a prototype perspective. *Journal of Experimental Psychology: General, 113,* 464–486.

Fridlund, A. J., & Izard, C. E. (1983). Electromyographic studies of facial expressions of emotions and patterns of emotions. In J. T. Cacioppo & R. E. Petty (Eds.), *Social psychophysiology.* NY: Guilford Press.

Gatchel, R. J., & Lang, P. J. (1973). Accuracy of psychophysical judgments and physiological response amplitude. *Journal of Experimental Psychology, 98,* 175–183.

Greenwald, M. K. (1987). *Affective judgments and their relation to physiological responses.* Unpublished masters thesis, University of Florida.

Greenwald, M. K., Cook, E. W., & Lang, P. J. (1989). Affective judgment and psychophysiological response: Dimensional covariation in the evaluation of pictorial stimuli. *Journal of Psychophysiology, 3,* 51–64.

Hamm, A. O. (in press). What can be perceived during the processing of emotions. In D. Vaitl and R. Schandry (Eds.), *Interoception and cardiovascular processes.* New York: Springer.

Hamm, A. O., Stark, R., & Vaitl, D. (1990). Startle reflex potentiation and electrodermal response differentiation: Two indicators of two different processes in Pavlovian conditioning. *Psychophysiology, 27,* S37. [Abstract]

Cook, E. W. III, Hawk, L. W., Jr., & Stevenson, V.E. (1990). Fearfulness and affective modulation of startle. *Psychophysiology, 27,* S7. [Abstract]

Hebb, D. O. (1949). *The organization of behavior: A neuropsychological theory.* NY: Wiley.

Hodes, R. L., Cook, E. W., & Lang, P. J. (1985). Individual differences in autonomic response: Conditioned association or conditioned fear? *Psychophysiology, 22,* 545–560.

Izard, C. E. (1972). *Patterns of emotions: A new analysis of anxiety and depression.* NY: Academic Press.

Izard, C.E. (1977). *Human emotions.* NY: Plenum Press.

Klorman, R., Wiesenfeld, A., & Austin, M. L. (1975). Autonomic responses to affective visual stimuli. *Psychophysiology, 12,* 553–560.

Lang, P.J. (1968). Fear reduction and fear behavior: Problems in treating a construct. In J. Schlien (Ed.), *Research in psychotherapy, III.* Washington, DC: APA.

Lang, P. J. (1978) . Anxiety: Toward a psychophysiological definition. In H. S. Akiskal & W. L. Webb (Eds.), *Psychiatric diagnosis: Exploration of biological predictors* (pp. 365–389). New York: Spectrum.

Lang, P. J. (1979). A bio-informational theory of emotional imagery. *Psychophysiology, 16,* 495–512.

Lang, P. J. (1980). Behavioral treatment and bio-behavioral assessment: Computer applications. In J. B. Sidowski, J. H. Johnson, & T. A. Williams (Eds.), *Technology in mental health care delivery systems* (pp. 119–137). Norwood, NJ: Ablex.

Lang, P. J., Bradley, M. M., & Cuthbert, B. N. (1990).

Emotion, attention, and the startle reflex. *Psychological Review, 97,* 377–398.

Lang, P. J., Greenwald, M. K., Bradley, M. M. & Hamm, A. O. (in press). Looking at pictures: Affective, facial, visceral and behavioral reactions. *Psychophysiology.*

Lang, P. J., Öhman, A., & Vaitl, D. (1988). *The international affective picture system* [photographic slides]. Gainesville, FL: The Center for Research in Psychophysiology, University of Florida.

Manning, S. K., & Melchiori, M. P. (1974). Words that upset urban college students: Measured with GSRs and rating scales. *Journal of Social Psychology, 94,* 305–306.

Matlin, M., & Stang, D. (1978). *The pollyanna principle: Selectivity in language, memory and thought.* Cambridge, MA: Schenkman.

Mehrabian, A., & Russell, J. A. (1974). *An approach to environmental psychology.* Cambridge, MA: MIT Press.

Oatley, K. & Johnson-Laird, P. (1987). Towards a cognitive theory of the emotions. *Cognition and Emotion, 1,* 29–50.

Osgood, C., Suci, G., & Tannenbaum, P. (1957). *The measurement of meaning.* Urbana, IL: University of Illinois.

Patrick, C. J., Bradley, M. M., & Lang, P. J. (in press). Emotion in the criminal psychopath: Startle reflex modulation. *Journal of Abnormal Psychology.*

Russell, J. (1980). A circumplex model of affect. *Journal of Personality and Social Psychology, 39,* 1161–1178.

Schlosberg, H.S. (1952). The description of facial expression in terms of two dimensions. *Journal of Experimental Psychology, 44,* 229–237.

Schwartz, G. E., Brown, S. L., & Shern, G. L. (1980). Facial muscle patterning and subjective experience during affective imagery: Sex differences. *Psychophysiology, 17,* 75–82.

Shaver, P., Schwartz, J., Kirson, D., & O'Connor, C. (1987). Emotion knowledge: Further exploration of a prototype approach. *Journal of Personality and Social Psychology, 52,* 1061–1086.

Stevens, S. S. (1961). To honor Fechner and repeal his law. *Science, 133,* 80–86.

Tellegen, A. (1985). Structures of mood and personality and their relevance to assessing anxiety, with an emphasis on self-report. In A. H. Tuma & J. D. Maser (Eds.), *Anxiety and the anxiety disorders* (pp. 681–706). Hillsdale, NJ: Erlbaum.

Vrana, S. R., Spence, E. L., & Lang, P. J. (1988). The startle probe response: A new measure of emotion? *Journal of Abnormal Psychology, 97,* 487–491.

Winton, W.M., Putnam, L.E., & Krauss, R.M. (1984). Facial and autonomic manifestations of the dimensional structure of emotion. *Journal of Experimental Social Psychology, 20,* 195–216.

Section B.
Organization of Emotion in Memory: Applications to Imagery, Clinical Problems and Experimental Esthetics

From Emotional Imagery to the Organization of Emotion in Memory

Peter J. Lang*

Imagery in Therapy

The role of imagery in therapy poses a perplexing question for a natural science of behaviour. Philosophers tell us that images are private events, available only to human introspection. As their observation cannot be shared or their dimensions measured by any instrument, they cannot be data in a scientific analysis. The founder of systematic desensitization therapy, Joseph Wolpe, recognized this limitation of the subjective construct. Thus, he proposed an alternative view, that images were "specific neural events" which formed part of the pattern or neural sequence previously evoked by specific external stimuli. As they shared a common neurophysiology, the image could "stand in" for an objective stimulus and the consequences of its manipulation were held to be similar to those that might be occasioned by the object itself. Speaking of desensitization, he states that "a basic assumption underlying this procedure is that the response to the imagined situation resembles that to the real situation" (Wolpe, 1958, p. 139). However, the initiating stimulus in therapy is not the "neural events"; it is a set of instructions, which include the admonition to adopt an imaginal set and a description of the things to be imagined. Furthermore, we are unable to manipulate directly the complex neurophysiology implied by Wolpe's

analysis. Thus, while the neural image may be an ultimate reality, the practical utility of the concept is limited. Nevertheless, we should not be wholly dismayed. As it not a knowledge of chemistry which guides the chef to a good bouillabaisse, but knowing which fish to use and how to cook them, so in trying to understand the practical effect of desensitization, the primary task may not be facilitated by reductionism, but by a direct analysis of the information content of the image and the manner of its functional processing.

A starting place for this enterprise is found in a study of systematic desensitization conducted by Lang, Melamed, and Hart (1970). They noted several consistent relationships between physiological reactivity to fear imagery and successful therapeutic outcomes. Subjects who profited from desensitization had faster heart rates during scenes said to evoke fear than during scenes they did not find frightening. Furthermore, successful subjects reported scenes to be unusually fearful during sessions when their tonic heart rates were relatively high. Finally, subjects who improved with treatment showed a systematic reduction in heart rate with repeated scene presentation, which was in turn associated with fewer fear signals. This covariation between verbal report and car-

* University of Florida.
Reprinted from: Lang, P.J. (1977). Imagery in therapy. *Behaviour Therapy,* 1977, 8, 862–886. Excerpts: pp. 862–870. Lang, P.J. (1984). Cognition and emotion: Concept and action. In C.E. Izard, J. Kagan, & R.B. Zajonc (Eds.) *Emotion, cognition, and behaviour.* New York: Cambridge University Press, pp. 192–226. Excerpts. pp. 196–214; 221–223.

diac activity was not found for those who failed to show improvement with treatment. These data suggest a relationship between the physiology of instructionally evoked imagery and emotional behaviour change. More specifically, they imply that the psychophysiological structure of imagined scenes may be a key to the emotional processing which the therapy is designed to accomplish.

In the following pages an information processing analysis of emotional imagery will be described. An effort will be made to show that the image can be a meaningful psychophysiological construct, that it can be defined in terms of measurable response events, and that these responses are controlled by identifiable external stimuli. Consideration is given to the recent thought of cognitive psychologists, as they have reexamined issues of imagery processing and storage. It will be argued that affective images are best conceptualized as propositional structures, rather than as reperceived raw, sensory representations. We will show that the former view logically permits experimental manipulation of the image through instructions and development of an imagery taxonomy of stimulus and response components. In the second part of the paper, the analysis will be further developed to encompass emotional phenomena more generally, and particularly the way that emotion may be organized in memory.

Imagery Processing and Storage

There are two basic ways in which the imaginal act has been conceptualized. From the first viewpoint, sensory images are presumed to be the primary products of external observation. They are stored in the brain as primitive, non-reducible units, having a fundamental geometric (if visual) or iconic representation in storage. The act of imagining involves the scanning, inward perceiving, or interpreting of this raw harvest of sensory observation. Advocates of the second viewpoint do not assume that the brain is such a silo of unprocessed *appearances*; the brain stores *knowledge* (to use the philosophic terms). We have information about objects or events, not pictures or representations of them. We are culturally conditioned to speak of "seeing" images in the "mind's eye", but this is no more than a compelling metaphor. The phenomenal image masks a more fundamental code. This alternative view begins with the assumption that the image in the brain is more like an elaborated description, an integration of specific affirmations about the world. The image is a functionally organized, finite set of propositions. Such propositions are assertions about relationships, descriptions, interpretations, labels, and tags, which prompt percept-like verbal reports, but which are more basically the units of a preparatory set to respond.

It will be argued in this paper that behaviour therapists and researchers in psychopathology should not adopt the picture metaphor, but should embrace the propositional conception of information storage, retrieval, and processing. We are guided in the following argument by an excellent theoretical paper by Pylyshyn (1973), whose explication of this problem is commended to serious students of cognitive imagery.

Pictures in the Head

For many psychologists, the verbal report of an image is viewed as a product of perceptual processing in the absence of an external stimulus. The mental image is a kind of picture in the head, which may be faint and fleeting, or in the case of idetics it may be so vivid as to ape an external observation. As Pylsyshyn (1973) points out, "The whole vocabulary of imagery uses a language appropriate to describing pictures and the process of perceiving pictures. We speak of clarity and vividness of images, of scanning images, of seeing new patterns in images, and of naming objects or properties depicted in images" (p. 8).

The implications of this language are that object representations are stored in the brain in analog form, that they may be removed from files and "subsequently scanned perceptually in order to obtain meaningful information regarding the presence of objects, attributes, relations, etc." While subjective experience clearly commends this view, there are practical and logical reasons for its rejection. To begin with, the assumption of analog representation places "an incredible burden on the storage capacity of the brain". If the "pictures" held in storage are really in raw form, containing in fine grain the same detail that could have been read off the retina or basilar membrane at the time of external observation, then no serious, current neural theory of memory could explain how the finite sum of cells in the human brain could accommodate this wealth of information. We would be inundated with neuronal snapshots well before the first month of life. Furthermore, the notion that perceptual scanning and interpretation are secondary to a retrieval process introduces at time delay, which is often inconsistent with the rapid efficiency of the brain in reviewing experience and generating behaviour. Phenomenological research also prompts a questioning of this view. Remembered scenes, only partially apprehended, are not recalled like jigsaw puzzles with pieces missing. Furthermore, images often seem to have attributional properties that are inextricably wedded to their objective content. Pylyshyn (1973) notes that a chess player may have an image of two pieces that could be described as "being attacked by"; a nonchess player would not have this element in his image, although he might report imagining the same spatial relations between pieces on a chessboard. Or similarly, one can have a vivid image of two lovers embracing without any specific sense of who was on the left or who was on the right.

Apartial solution to the storage problem might be to assume some kind of limited resolution representation. We could hypothesize a finite number of scan lines, as in a television picture, to be enhanced later by the brain for verbal report, as the computer enhances telemetered pictures of the near planets. A digital code might be even more efficient; however, we now stray even farther from the concept of a primary image. If a teleological statement may be risked, it seems unreasonable to suppose

that the purpose of the brain is to provide primary images for human beings to comment on. As Sperry noted many years ago (1952), the purpose of the brain is not to generate perceptual experience but to organize and facilitate responding. If this is true we might expect the image code not to be independent of behavioural function, as are scan lines or digital notation, but to be relational and to incorporate the responding organism. Descriptions of images, particularly emotional images, inevitably contain many of the editorial comments (e.g., "attacking", "embracing") alluded to above. They also include the observer, his point of view, and often his active participation.

The Image as a Propositional Construct

What subjects report about images does not sound like limited-resolution photographs. The reports include both more and less detail than such a system would suggest, as well as the interpretive elements that are not part of raw observations. Any representation having such properties "is much closer to being a description of the scene than a picture of it. A description is propositional, it contains a finite amount of information, it may contain abstract as well as concrete aspects and, especially relevant to the present discussion, it contains terms (symbols for objects, attributes, and relations) which are the results of-not inputs to-perceptual processes" (Pylyshyn, 1973, p. 11).

It is proposed that emotional images, of the sort evoked in the therapeutic context, are best understood as propositional constructions. A proposition is essentially what a string of words assert, e.g. "The book is on the desk". However, this does not mean that the propositions of an image are basically linguistic in form. Bower (1970) makes the distinction between an imagistic memory system and a contrasting verbal-propositional mode of thought and retention. The former is more active in processing concrete information whereas the latter is the common medium for abstract thought. These modes are identified with different hemispheres of the brain, and neurological evidence and studies of recognition memory offer support for the distinction (Sperry, 1968; Nebes, 1974). However, it is reasonable to assume that both of these storage modes have a common underlying code in the functional organization of the brain. We suggest that this deep structure of mentation must be propositional.

This is not meant to deny that so-called short-term memory could involve iconic forms in storage or that there may not be something like spatial schema which underlay such phenomena as face recognition. However, when emotion-laden images are evoked in patients, it is long-term storage which is being tapped. "The hypothesis favoured here is that the experience of an image itself arises out of 'constructive' processes (Neisser, 1967). The notion is that the units abstracted and interpreted during perception are stored in long-term memory in an abstract format and must be acted on by processes that serve to generate or to produce an experience of an image" (Kosslyn, 1975). Although some might question this view as an explanation of simple visual images, it seems highly consonant with the nature of affective imagery in therapy. These latter images have the property of serial narratives, that obviously include much more than sensory impressions. It is for this reason that they cannot be held to simply "stand in" for objective stimuli. They are

always processed with response elements as fundamental parts of the structure. In fact, the aim of therapy could be described as the reorganization of the image unit in a way that modifies the affective character of its response elements.

It is proposed that the image we seek to manipulate in using desensitization, catharsis, or flooding techniques is best comprehended as a finned network of specific propositional units which have designating and action functions. The logic of this structure and of its underlying neurophysiology is presently unknown. In practice, propositions are often added serially to a diachronic structure. That is to say, the emotional image is not always processed as a complete unit, nor does it necessarily impact on behaviour in the abrupt fashion of an external stimulus. Rather, the emotional image is recreated as it is evoked, and propositions may be added to or subtracted from this protean cognitive structure while it unfolds over time. We have noted that the emotional image involves behaviour, and it is to be anticipated that this behaviour will be measurable. In many practical contexts the emotional image is less usefully conceived of as an internal percept and more valuable when construed as a preparatory set to respond.

Emotional Imagery and Instructional Control

We have already been at some pain to emphasize the fundamental, nonlinguistic nature of the hypothesized propositional units. Furthermore, it is clear that emotional images may be evoked and elaborated by nonlinguistic external stimuli, such as models, pictures, or films. However, it is also true that propositional elements can be rendered as statements in a natural language. There is a long history of this enterprise in the written fiction, prose, and poetry of all civilized cultures, and an even more ancient oral tradition which the imagery therapist imitates.

It is therefore proposed as a methodological expedient that the emotional image be considered as a cognitive schema containing a

finite set of propositional units, each of which can be represented as a verbal statement or instruction. It is not at all clear at the outset what the basic units of such a structure might be. However, for the purposes of experimental investigation, it is suggested that the emotional image contains at least two fundamental classes of statements: stimulus propositions and response propositions. To the extent that we think of the image as a percept, it is logical to assume that its structure will include descriptors, or assertions about stimuli, e.g., a black snake writhing on the path, an auditorium of staring faces. However, emotional images also invariably contain assertions about behaviour, or response propositions; e. g., my palms are sweating, my heart is racing, I scream, I run away. The response components of the image are often more elaborate than the stimulus elements. They divide themselves naturally into the three response classes that we have come to associate with the empirical analysis of emotion [verbal responses, overt motor acts, and responses of the physiological organs, see Lang (1968, 1971, 1978)], as well as propositions which define characteristics of the subject's thinking processes, and sense organ adjustments or postural responses that determine point of view. Response propositions representing each of these classes can be observed in the script presented below, created by Watson and Marks (1971, p. 277). It is an example of imagery instructions used in their flooding research on the phobia-reducing effects of exposure to relevant and irrelevant fear stimuli.

Try and imagine yourself at home. You have to go out. You can't avoid it. You're uneasy at the thought. You have to go alone. Your boy is at school, you are on your own. You are already scared. You stumble as you leave your front door. You pull the door to with a bang. By the time you reach the pavement your heart is racing, your mouth is dry, you sweat. Just ten yards further on, past familiar landmarks, the panic starts. You dread losing control, and you shake like a leaf. You feel sick. You feel people are looking at you. You lose control of yourself. You lose control of your body. You vomit. You wet your underwear. You lose control of your mind. You cannot see things clearly. The world is unreal, seems unfriendly, a terrifying place. You cannot stop yourself from screaming. The noise attracts attention. You scream and scream and scream. Soon a crowd surrounds you. People are afraid to approach you, having hysterics as you are, and surrounded by your own vomit. You scream and shout and wave your arms and legs about like a child having a tantrum when it can't get its own way. Your thoughts are muddled, you are confused. You are lost, unable to control yourself, just a few yards away from your home. You continue screaming, crying, yelling, howling. The crowd grows. You go on making an exhibition of yourself. You feel ashamed. You no longer feel grown up and feel

you are a baby. No one in the crowd dares to approach you. You make a grotesque spectacle. In a way, some of the crowd enjoy your being out of control. No one comes to help. No one is on your side. All the hysterics fail to make you feel better. In fact, the panic gets worse. The crowd laughs at you, shouts, jeers, and points. You feel exposed. You realize they are seeing you as you really are. The panic just goes on. Finally everything goes black.

Image Taxonomy

A tentative propositional catalogue is presented in Table 6.1, which can be used in classifying imagery instructions for analysis or as a guide for creating balanced scripts for use in treatment and imagery experiments. It is interesting to note how few of the statements contained in the Watson and Marks (1971) script actually define stimulus propositions. Most of the flooding instructions assert the responses of the subject. It is clear that some of these statements are hard to classify. Feeling sick, for example, sounds like a stimulus proposition. However, the experience of sickness involves as much behaviour as sensation. Thus, our pulse may race, muscles tense, and stomach contract, we have difficulty maintaining a steady hand, and we feel sick. What are usually called feelings may fall into one or several different propositional classes, e. g., stimulus elements, self-referent statements, visceral events, and processor characteristics. Very few details of the internal stimulus configuration actually contribute to the propositional net. Consonant with the view of the emotional image as a response set, its potency is often instructionally augmented more by the elaboration of response propositions than by the refinement of stimulus elements.

It is suggested that the emotional image in the brain of a cooperative patient is more or less consonant with the propositional structure of the administered instructional set. Furthermore, if the image is indeed a preparatory set, we should observe partial responses in imagining subjects which are consistent with the response elements of the script. In point of fact,

Table 1. Propositional units of the emotional image.

I.   Stimulus propositions (auditory, visual, tactile, cutaneous, olfactory, vestibular, kinesthetic)
       A.   Physical details of the object or situation
       B.   Changes in object configuration
       C.   Object movement (approach or withdrawal)
       D.   Physical place or general location
       E.   Presence or absence of others as observers or participants
       F.   Comments made by others
       G.   Pain, location on the body: sharp, dull, etc.
II.   Response propositions
       A.   Verbal responses
              1.   Overt verbalizations, out loud comments or expressive cries
              2.   Covert verbalizations
                     a. Emotional labeling
                     b. Self-evaluative statements, e. g., feelings of inferiority
                     c. Attribution of attitudes to others
       B.   Somatomotor events
              1. Muscle tension
              2. Uncontrolled gross motor behaviour
              3. Organized motor acts, freezing, approach, avoidance
       C.   Visceral events
              1. Heart rate and pulse
              2. Body or palmar sweat
              3. Vascular changes, blanching or flushing
              4. Pilomotor response
              5. Salivary response, mouth dry
              6. Respirator change
              7. Intestinal upset
                     a. Vomiting
                     b. Incontinence
              8. Urinary dysfunction
       D.   Processor characteristics
              1. Perception unclear or unusually vivid or distorted
              2. Loss of control over thoughts, cannot think clearly
              3. Disoriented in time or space
       E.   Sense organ adjustments
              1. General postural changes
              2. Eye and head movements

in many experimental situations, no methodological distinction need be made between the imagery instructions and the hypothesized image in the brain. While this may not be expedient for individuals, who idiosyncratically add or subtract from the suggested propositional structure, the instructions will be very close to the image for groups of subjects, whose numbers improve the signal-to-noise ratio. Thus, if elaborate response propositions are part of the instructional set given to one group of subjects and not to another, then the premotor, verbal, and visceral responses during imaging will be relatively augmented for the group so instructed. To modify McLuhan's statement, "the media is the message", the proposed research strategy affirms that the message is the image.

Emotion as Information

In a further development of the bioformational analysis of emotional imagery (Lang, 1979), we now propose a more general framework for understanding affective behaviour. Emotion is conceived to be an action set, defined by a specific information structure in memory, which, when accessed, is processed as both a conceptual and a motor program. The data structure of an emotion includes three primary categories of information: (1) information about prompting external stimuli and the context in which they occur; (2) information about responding in this context, including expressive verbal behaviour, overt acts, and the visceral and somatic events that mediate arousal and action; (3) information that defines the meaning of the stimulus and response data.

In discussing emotional imagery we proposed that emotion information is coded in memory in the form of propositions and that these propositions are organized into an associative network of the general sort first described by Quillian (1966) for semantic knowledge and later adapted to accommodate other types of information (e.g., Anderson & Bower, 1975; Kieras, 1978). The emotion information network is a sort of prototype or schema, which is processed as a unit when a critical number of propositions are accessed. This processing is held to be the cognitive work of emotional expression. Efferent outflow and action are the output events occasioned by the processing of response information (i.e., efferent subroutines) in the network program.

Phobic reactions are characterized by unusually coherent and stable emotion prototypes, which can be accessed readily by a variety of internal and external instigating conditions. For this reason (in addition to the author's clinical interest in fear behaviour), phobia is used here as a model of an emotion prototype and as a laboratory illustration. However, other emotional states (e.g., individual conditions of sexual arousal) may be equally focused in content, involving similarly well-organized, readily

defined propositional elements of limited number, and might serve equally well as examples.

A Phobia Prototype

We have suggested elsewhere (Lang, 1979) that the conceptual network that organizes an emotional response includes two primary information categories, stimulus and response propositions. To this classification we now add a third, meaning propositions, which are construed as analytic and interpretive. To illustrate with a common focal phobia, the central data structure of the fear response might include the following propositions: (1) *Stimulus propositions* code information critical to the recognition of the frightening animal, including the relevant context of its appearance (e.g., the snake's skin has a diamond pattern; it's moving toward me; no one else is here); (2) *response propositions* describe all the overt and covert responses made in this context, including avoidance, self-referent verbal statements (e.g., God, I'm scared!), and the visceral and somatic responses of physiological arousal (e.g., tachycardia, sweating); (3) *meaning propositions* are interpretive, defining the significance of input and output events, probabilities of stimulus occurrence and consequences of action (e.g., snakes are dangerous and unpredictable; when your heart beats fast you're frightened). An abridged model of a network is presented in Figure 6.1.

The phobia prototype is a conceptual network of propositionally coded information, related by association, which has as functional output a visceral and somatomotor program. The prototype may be activated as a unit by instructional, media, or objective sensory input that contains information matching that in the network. The phobia prototype illustrated in Figure 6.1 could be rendered in descriptive, narrative English as follows: "I am in a wooded area when I see a large snake. It appears to be moving toward me. There's a diamond pattern on its back. This could be a dangerous snake.

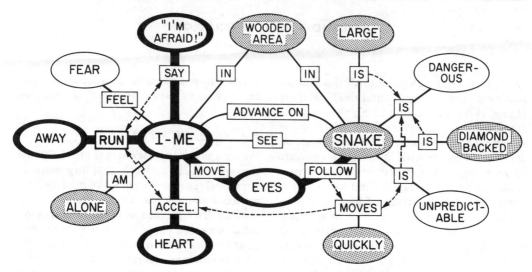

Figure 1. A phobia prototype: An associative network of propositionally coded information, presumed to be stored in long-term memory, which is accessed and processed in the expression of a fear response. The development of this propositional notation as a representation of emotional cognitions is described in Lang (1979).

My eyes jump in my head following a quick, sinuous movement. My heart starts racing. Snakes are unpredictable. 'I'm afraid!' I say it aloud, but nobody is there to hear me. I'm alone and very frightened. I start to run ... "

Propositions in the network are represented in Figure 6.1 by the oval nodes, containing the concept name, and the labelled, solid black lines that show the links between concepts. In the notation proposed by Kintsch (1974), the lines indicate predicators and the ovals are their arguments (e.g., MOVES, SNAKE, QUICK-LY). The dotted lines indicate some of the connections between propositions that could have particularly high probabilities of association. No attempt is made here to indicate all propositions or all possible connections. However, it is suggested that certain propositions are strongly bonded to others and may thus be keys to the broad recruitment of the network, with its action subprograms. For example, (MOVES, SNAKE, QUICKLY) may have a primitive high-probability connection to (ACCELERATE, I, HEART), which in turn unlocks the other fear response propositions, prompting rapid prototype activation.

The network includes three broad classes of information: stimulus, meaning, and response propositions. Stimulus concepts are indicated on the diagram by the shaded ovals, and meaning concepts by the clear ovals. Response propositions are represented by a heavy black connecting line. This is a reminder that such information is doubly coded, that response concepts are represented primitively as motor programs. The view taken here is that the deep structure of the prototype is an action set. Although the prototype can be described in a natural language and processed in part as an independent, exclusively semantic network, these programs are functionally organized to generate efferent output. Thus, the processing of conceptual emotional information always involves some degree of visceral and motor outflow.

An emotion prototype is accessed when a subject attends to information that matches propositions in the network. This matching process is very broadly analogous to the analyzer matching described by Sokolov (1963). However, instead of a mismatch, which prompts orienting, we propose a matching of input information with stored information in the prototype, which activates an associative network. Presently, we assume that a critical number of propositions must be matched for the entire conceptual network to be activated and the associated motor subprogram to be processed. However, certain propositions, or classes of propositions, may be more important than others in accessing an emotion program. Determining the properties of this intranetwork structure is seen as a priority task for future research.

At this point, however, it is sufficient to consider that an emotion prototype may be accessed from memory through a great variety of information input modes and that the instigating information can be from any of the three classes of propositions that determine such conceptual aggregates. Perhaps the most obvious means of evocation involves the exposure of the subject to the actual fear object or context. It is presumed that the fear network is more likely to be accessed by external input when this input includes a critical number of the stimulus propositions that are in the network and when there is no information inconsistent with the prototype. Thus, the sighting of a large snake, which has a diamond pattern on the dorsal surface, by a subject who is alone may be sufficient to initiate the fear prototype. However, the sighting of a 6-inch snake by a subject who is with a crowd of friends may not cause the fear program to be accessed. Alternatively, all stimulus propositions described in the first case might be present along with information that the snake is a battery-operated mechanical toy, which would again not cause the fear prototype to be accessed.

It is not necessary, however, for a fear object to be "real" to access the prototype and run the motor programs. The information in the prototype is conceptual and does not refer to any specific pattern of sensory input. Films, slides, or models may contain enough stimulus propositions to activate the network. Even a verbal description may be sufficient, particularly if the subject is told to process the input as an image. Finally, it is not only stimulus information that can access the prototype. If some of the visceral and somatic response propositions of an emotional prototype are active (perhaps prompted by very different circumstances, such as exercise or drugs; e. g., see Schachter, 1964), less stimulus information is required to prompt the total emotional response.

The phobic prototype is held to be relatively easy to activate. The stimulus and meaning information cohere more strongly to the response information and the stimuli are less readily processed independent of the prototype network. The coherence of the network may constitute a definition of severity of phobia. Coherence is defined, in turn, by the number of input propositions required for prototype processing (e. g., the degree to which stimulus information may be degraded and still occasion the efferent outflow of an action set).

Despite phobic prototype hypersensitivity and the high incidence of such fears in the normal population, the majority of phobias are never treated in the clinic. Phobics simply avoid all relevant input information and thus rarely process the fear network. Unless environmental circumstances force confrontation (a snake-phobic geologist is sent to a Central American jungle to evaluate an oil lease), treatment is seldom sought. Thus, the isolation of the network contributes to its stability. If the prototype never moves from the memory into the brain's work space, it is unlikely to undergo modification.

From the perspective presented here, treatment of phobia would involve a breakdown of network coherence and the attachment of the stimulus and meaning information to other response subroutines. Any processing of the prototype through exposure or imagery would facilitate this goal, as the processing context would necessarily add new, possible inhibitory or incompatible information to the prototype, reducing coherence through this broader association and encouraging a division into smaller subprograms that could be instigated independently by differing environmental circumstances.

Activating an Emotional Response

To restate our general view briefly, it is held that emotions are represented in memory as specific coherent data structures. The information is stored in propositional form, and these propositions are organized into an associative network called an emotion prototype. An entire network may be activated by a few prompting propositional units. However, probability of prototype access increase with quantity of matching input propositions. Although matching stimulus information provides a powerful prompt, independent instigation of response propositions and meaning propositions can be in many instances the key determinants of access.

The factors that determine emotional activation may be summarized as follows: (1) In general, the more complete and consistent the stimulus information matches the prototype, the more likely it is that the emotion response program will be accessed and run. To state this in terms of output, the probability of an emotional response is reduced with degradation of the input information. Thus, actual exposure to fear objects is more likely to occasion emotional processing than a film, slide show, or verbal description of the same stimulus. (2) Degraded stimulus input is more likely to access the prototype if other propositions in the prototype are independently instigated. For example, watching a film about poisonous snakes at a safari camp in an African jungle (meaning information: Dangerous snakes are nearby) is more likely to prompt fear than watching the same film in a Manhattan apartment. Similarly, watching the film in the New York apartment after unwritting epinepherine intake (response information: a pattern of physiological arousal generally consonant with fear) may increase the probability of an actual fear response (including verbal, behavioural components, and more focused physiology) to the African safari level. (3) The emotion response prototype can be accessed by instructions and/or description of provocative events in a natural language, as in emotional imagery. However, this is a degraded stimulus input situation relative to exposure and has a lower probability of access. It depends importantly on the subject's ability and inclination to convert semantic input into the deep structural code of the emotion prototype. (4) Because emotions are always about action, prototype activation involves the processing of efferent programs, which, in theory, can be monitored both centrally and at the end organs (muscles or glands).

Emotional Imagery: Text Processing and Efferent Patterning

It is clear that the evocation of emotional states in human organisms is not dependent on instigation by objective stimuli. Language cues, both as the spontaneous result of internal processing or through external communication, are often the medium of access to the emotional prototype. This occurs formally when descriptions of emotional events are administered to subjects who are under an implicit or explicit instructional set to experience them "as if" they were actually happening. The human response to the novelist's art, an imagery therapist's instructions, the stage hypnotist's commands, or an intimate letter from a close friend all depend on this common underlying process. In these cases the instigation of emotion is essentially a text-processing task. The emotion to be experienced is described by a script and the semantic and lexical structure of the script are critical both to the understanding or comprehension of the semantic content and to the accessing of the relevant emotional prototype from long-term memory storage.

Text-prompted emotional experience is similar to instructionally cued perceptual imagery, as both involve a reprocessing of stimulus information about objects or events that are not objectively present. They both also involve response information processing and the apparent regeneration of related motor programs. Thus, memory images formed during a variety of perceptual tasks have been shown to be accompanied at recall by patterns of efferent activity that are similar to those occurring during the original percept. As early as 1940, Shaw demonstrated that forearm muscle tension levels during imagery recall were proportional in amplitude to the heft of different weights previously employed in a weight-judging task. Several different investigators have found a similar result in visual memory, that is, when a perceptual task requires a stereotyped pattern of ocular scanning, recall trials are accompanied by parallel patterns of eye movement (Brady & Levitt, 1966; Brown, 1968; Deckert, 1964; Jacobson, 1930).

Text-instigated emotional experience has sometimes yielded analogous laboratory findings. In these instances, however, the emphasis is less on a regenerated perceptual physiology and more on a question of demonstrating the affective patterns of physiological arousal. Thus, both Lang, Melamed, and Hart (1970) and Van Egeren, Feather, and Hein (1971) found that passages of descriptive text, hierarchically arranged according to intensity of judged fear content, occasioned in fearful subjects a parallel gradient of visceral arousal, with the greatest heart-rate acceleration and skin conductance responses occurring in reaction to the most frightening text and the smallest responses to the neutral text. A variety of other studies have produced similar results (e. g., Grossberg, & Wilton, 1968; Schwartz, 1971). However, the experimental literature also includes negative findings, instances in which seemingly appropriate instructions and scripts failed to produce a physiologically affective image. For example, Marks and Huson (1973) reported that severely phobic patients showed the expected greater heart-rate acceleration to phobic than to neutral imagery instructions in only three of five experiments conducted at the Maudsley Hospital. Skin conductance fared even more poorly, differentiating these contents in only two of five experiments. Despite this absence of visceral arousal, the patients all reported subjective anxiety or fear during phobic imagery. In point of fact, anxiety reports to frightening or arousing imagery content are relatively easy to obtain; visceral response effects are more rare (e.g., see Weerts & Lang, 1978). This is particularly troubling in relation to research suggesting that therapeutic imagery may be ineffective unless it includes palpable autonomic activation (Lang et al., 1970; Levin, 1982; Schroeder & Rich, 1976).

Some Experimental Results

We have recently undertaken a series of experiments designed to explore the circumstances under which the processing of emotional descriptive text does or does not occasion a broad affective response. The previous inconsistent findings are expected by our view insofar as text, compared to fear-object exposure, represents a degraded input. To put this more explicitly: If accessing the fear prototype is facilitated by the number of matching propositional units in the stimulus material, then many previous studies may have failed to elicit responses because the experimental context did not contain enough appropriate information. One obvious difference between our approach and previous imagery theory concerns the role of response information. The classic view of imagery stresses only stimulus information, viewing any efferent activity that may occur as a response to the internal stimulus in the "mind's eye". However, the conception presented here presumes the image to be a network of both stimulus and response information. Thus, the probability of processing the image would be increased if both response and stimulus material were directly instigated, in this case by inclusion in the imagery script. To an extent, probability of prototype access should improve with an increase in the number of any relevant propositions in the input script. However, response propositions also have a special role. While they are coded in the script in a natural language and stored as semantic concepts in the brain, they are also linked to deep structure response propositions that constitute the information base for a motor command system. Thus, processing textual response codes facilitates the access of action programs from memory storage. Activation of the prototype includes innervation (usually at a subovert level) of the designated somatomotor or visceral organ systems. It seems clear that this efferent leakage comes from inhibited motor programs. In fact, such cognitive activity can, under the proper conditions, become dramatically manifest as overt behaviour. This occurs routinely in such laboratory tasks as the postural sway test, in which "thinking about" falling produces some sway in the average subject and may prompt actual loss of balance in a susceptible individual (examples abound, from Hull, 1933, to Hilgard, 1965).

It is also clear that the semantic information contained in a script can be processed as "knowledge about" an emotional situation quite independently of any underlying motor subroutines. We presume further that such content comprehension, or processing of the semantic network only, will prompt in many subjects a content-consonant verbal report of subjective distress. In this case, the subject is in effect providing an appraisal of the affective meaning of the script. The extent to which these two modes of processing are independent varies widely among individual: Some subjects cannot process in the imagery (or subovert action) mode; some subjects cannot process in the imagery mode; the vast majority of intelligent normals are able to do either, depending on context and instructions.

We have recently developed a brief training program designed to set subjects for imagery processing. Groups are administered imagery scripts and instructed to imagine vividly the events described. Subsequently, they are asked to recall their image and to report to a trainer all the details of the experience they can remember. The trainer then reinforces the subjects specifically for response details (i.e., actions the subject was performing, visceral and somatic responding), priming him or her with instructions to include more such material in subsequent images. In a series of studies, we have contrasted this training procedure with a type of training more oriented to the "mind's eye" view of imagery. In this latter procedure, subjects are reinforced postimagery for only stimulus detail (i.e., the characteristics of the external scene as presented to the receptors). Specifically, we tested the hypothesis that imaging subjects are more likely to generate a psychophysiology of emotion when the prompting text includes response propositions (as well as stimulus information), particularly when subjects have been trained to process response information from text.

The first two experiments were performed by Lang and his associates (1980). Imagery was manipulated by varying the content of the prompting instructions (either stimulus detail or active responding was emphasized in the image script) and by prior imagary training (in which subjects' postimage verbal reports were shaped to emphasize either stimulus or response material). Three thematic contents were examined: neutral, action, and fear scenes. Examples of each script content are presented in Table 6.2. In Experiment 1, a group that received response-oriented imagery training and response scripts was compared to a stimulus-oriented group. The results strongly supported our primary hypothesis. That is, response subjects showed greater physiological activity during imagery than did stimulus-trained subjects. Furthermore, the efferent patterns shown by response subjects generally followed the script content. In Experiment 2, one group again received response training and the other, stimulus training. However, half of each group was later tested on response-structured scripts and the other half on stimulus scripts. Thus, all cells in the interaction between training and script could be examined. Results again supported the primary hypothesis. As in Experiment 1, response-trained subjects tested on response scripts showed substantial, appropriate physiological activity. None of the other groups, which received stimulus training and/or stimulus scripts, showed significant physiological response during imagery. These effects are illustrated in Figure 6.2 for three of the dependent variables studied in Experiment 2.

The physiological patterns obtained in these experiments tended to differ according to type of content, without being wholly concordant with the propositional structure of the instigating text. Thus, although both fear and action scenes prompted more somatovisceral activity than did the neutral scripts, the pattern of physiological activity differed in these two scene types. Mean muscle potential levels were higher during action images than during fear imagery (the largest response was given to the isometric exercise scene, a context that would reasonably call for considerable muscular effort). On the other hand, heart rate and skin conductance tended to be higher for fear than for action scenes (maximal conductance oc-

Table 2: Experiment 1: Scene contents and sample texts for neutral, stimulus, and response scripts

Neutral scenes (Trials 1, 6)	Action scenes (Trials 2, 3, 9, 10)	Fear scenes (Trials 4, 5, 7, 8)
1. Sitting in the living room 2. On the sidewalk of a quiet street	1. Flying a kite 2. Playing ping pong 3. Isometric exercises 4. Studying a difficult text	1. Hornet in the car 2. Spider on the pillow 3. Trapped in a sauna 4. Snake in the water

Imagery scripts

Neutral scene

You are sitting in your living room reading on a Sunday afternoon. Sitting back, relaxed, you look out the window. It is a sunny autumn day. Red and brown leaves drift slowly down from the trees, and several cars and a truck go by in the street. Wind from the cars blows the leaves, which are lying in the street. They scatter onto the pavement and the thick green lawn.

Stimulus

1. You are flying a kite on the beach on a bright summer day. Your red kite shows clearly against the cloudless blue sky and whips quickly up and down in spirals with the wing. The sun glares at you from behind the kite and makes the white sandy beach sparkle with reflection. The long white tail dances from side to side beneath the soaring kite. A strong gust of wind catches the kite, sending it higher and higher into the sky. (Action).

2. You are alone in your car on an interstate highway and you notice an insect on the windshield. It is a large buzzing insect, a yellow jacket that has trapped itself inside your car. The bug has a yellow and black body, and moves back and forth, flying against the windshield trying to get out. It jumps onto the floor and crawls under the seat. It flies around in the back of the car where you can't see what it is doing, and there is no place on the roadside where you can stop so it can escape. (Fear)

Response

1. You breathe deeply as you run along the beach flying a kite. Your eyes trace its path as it whips up and down in spirals with the wind. The sun glares into your eyes from behind the kite, and you tense the muscles in your forehead and around your eyes, squinting to block out the bright sunlight. You follow with your eyes the long white tail, which dances from side to side beneath the soaring kite. (Action)

2. You are alone, driving your car on the interstate highway and you hear the buzzing of an insect on your windshield. Your heart begins to pound as you notice that it is a yellow jacket trapped in your car. You perspire heavily and your eyes dart from the insect to the roadside while you try to watch the bug and look for a place to stop. You tense the muscles of your face and neck as the yellow jacket buzzes to the back of the car where you can't see what it is doing. You breathe in short quick gasps, glancing to the rear to locate the bug. (Fear)

Note: The average number of response propositions per script for action topics was: heart 0.00; respiration .75; muscle 1.75; eye 2.00; sweat 0.00. For fear topics these values were: heart 1.00; respiration 1.00; muscle 1.25; eye 1.25; sweat 0.75. Thus, fear scripts were weighted in favor of heart, respiration, and sweat-gland responses, whereas eye-movement and muscle-tension responses were relatively more frequent in action scripts (Lang et al., 1980).

Source: Lang, P.J., Kozak, M.J., Miller, G.A., Levin, D.N., & McLean, A., Jr. (1080). Emotional imagery: Conceptual structure & pattern of somato-visceral response. *Psychophysiology, 17,* 179–192.

curred in response to a public-speaking script). Thus, the results obtained here cannot be attributed to some generalized instruction to be physiologically active, nor are they to be explained by a unidimensional concept of arousal. However, they are consistent with the hypothesis that the scripts instigated the processing of an affective prototype already stored in the brain.

In summary, response training and script do partially control the image. However, their influence is shaped by preexisting response dispositions. The image manipulations studied here appear to have interacted with conceptual

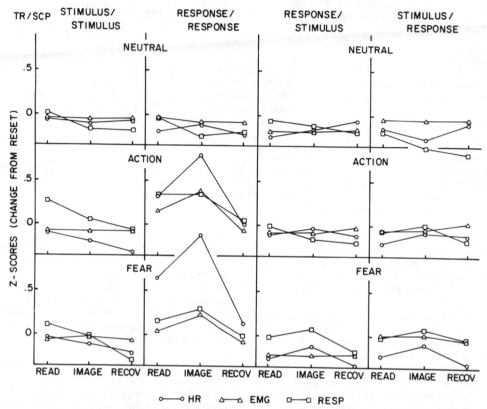

Figure 2. Mean change in median heart rate, muscle tension, and respiration cycle length during the presentation on imagery text (read), the imagery period, and an immediately following no-image recovery period. Each measurement period was 30 sec in duration. Experiment 2 results are shown for the four groups separately, during imagery of neutral, action, and fear scenes. The values shown are z-scores, based on the combined data of Experiments 1 and 2. Respiration cycle length change values were multiplied by -1 for plotting. Average heart-rate change for the response-trained/response-script group during the fear content image period was +7.31 bpm. Muscle tension change was +15.58 volts/min, and respiration cycle length change was -.64 sec (Lang et al., 1980).

structures already stored in long-term memory. The largest responses were obtained when both response and stimulus propositions in the scripts were consistent with a precoded perceptual and efferent arousal network, for example, muscle tension during isometric exercise or skin conductance during speech imagery. Training amplified response, increasing the strength of the subject's efferent signal to a level that could be readily measured (Lang et al., 1980).

These phenomena were placed in yet more vivid relief in a recent study conducted in our laboratory with two different populations of fearful subjects: snake phobic and socially anxious (Lang et al., 1983). Subjects in both groups were first exposed to both their own and the other group's actual fear situations (public speaking and a snake-avoidance test), and the different physiological patterns of response generated by these two tasks were noted. All subjects were also administered an imagery task, using scripts based on the two fear contents.

The pattern of means for the physiological responses observed during exposure readily differentiated the two fear groups. During the snake test, the snake-phobic subjects showed a pattern of high heart rate and verbal report of fear arousal significantly different from the low heart rates and low arousal reported by socially anxious subjects. As expected, socially anxious subjects reported greater arousal during the speech task. Curiously, however, the groups did not differ in heart rate during public speaking. Apparently, the task requirements of this performance, in terms of cardiovascular demand, are so great as to obscure any additional load prompted by a differential affective tone.

The group patterns of heart rate and arousal report means observed during imagery of speech and snake contexts paralleled those found at exposure. However, amplitude of physiological response during imagery was low and variance within the sample large, resulting in insignificant statistical tests. Therefore, two new populations of fearful subjects were selected according to the same criteria previously employed, and the experiment was performed again. This time half of each fear group was stimulus trained and half response trained before the administration of fear imagery test scenes. The heart-rate change during imagery found in both experiments is presented in Figure 6.3.

It is readily apparent that subjects respond more to fear material when response trained. As noted previously, the effects on heart rate of stimulus training are little different from those found without training. More pertinent to the present argument, it can be seen that snake phobics responded strongly to the snake scenes; however, even following response training, the reaction of socially anxious subjects to this material is negligible. On the other hand, both fear groups show cardiac acceleration to the speech scenes after response training. These are exactly the same effects found at exposure. The cardiovascular demands of the speech task itself are apparently so marked as to obscure a specifically affective response

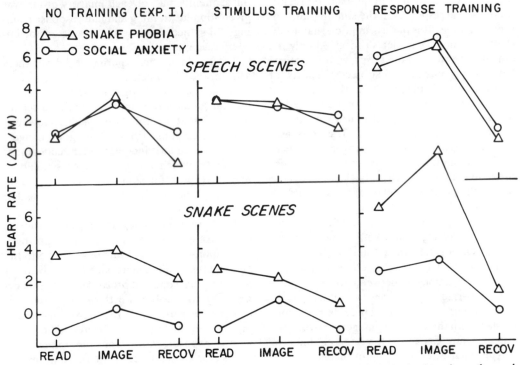

Figure 3. Average heart-rate change over read, imagery, and recovery periods for both snake and speech scenes. Data are presented for both no training (Experiment 1) and the comparison of training procedures (Experiment 2). See Lang et al. (1983).

in this system. However, the difference between groups is placed in vivid relief when subjects image themselves seated, passively observing a live snake.

It is important to note again that the effect of response training was not to impose a physiology on subjects. Despite having received the same training and response material as the snake phobics, socially anxious subjects did not show an affective physiology to the snake scene. Again, the effect of response information is only to facilitate the access of perceptual-motor programs that are already present in memory.

From a three-system perspective (Lang, 1978), it is also pertinent that response training occasioned greater concordance between ratings of arousal and visceral activation than was found for other subjects. That is, all groups reported arousal during fear and action scenes, and these verbal reports varied significantly with fear diagnosis. However, as already noted, this was accompanied by modest and nonsignificant visceral responses in the stimulus and untrained groups. It is our assumption that a substantial number of subjects processed only the semantic network of the script, with its natural language propositions. Subject's reports of arousal were appropriate to the emotional meaning of this information but did not reflect processing of the deep structure with its somatic and visceral programs. The response-training method, which encouraged subjects to attend to somatic and visceral information, probably had two effects: It both increased the probability that efferent programs would be accessed and increased the subject's discrimination of images that actually involved physiological processing. Thus, with response training, physiological arousal and verbal report varied in parallel over scene contents. Furthermore, the relationship between arousal reports and heart-rate response was basically the same as that found in exposure. These data are concordant with the view that imagery instructions and exposure can access the same phobia prototype. That is, different input media access a common data structure from memory.

It is our hypothesis that response training, by setting the subject to process response informa-tion, facilitates image mode retrieval and access of the deep structure emotional prototype. However, we further hypothesize that some subjects can perform in this manner spontaneously, with no more help than the instruction to process text in the image mode. Furthermore, if we are correct in assuming a structural similarity between perceptual imagery and emotional imagery, then subjects who profess to have particularly vivid imagery should show a more appropriate physiological response to simple imagery instruction and to the training manipulation (Miller et al., 1981).

In an experimental test of this view, two groups of subjects, good imagers and poor imagers, were selected on the basis of extreme response to the Questionnaire on Mental Imagery (QMI), originally created by Betts (1909) and more recently revised by Sheehan (1967). All subjects were first administered a psychophysiological imagery assessment procedure similar to that used in previous experiments. Subsequently, half of each imagery group was given stimulus training and half response training. All subjects were then reassessed for imagery response.

The results of this experiment did not show a difference between imagery groups before training. The physiological response of these normal subjects to standard emotional scenes was modest at the initial assessment. However, following response training, the good imagers showed a dramatic increase in text concordant reactivity, which the poor imagers failed to match. Results for standard scenes, for both heart rate and skin conductance are presented in Figure 6.4.

The reason good imagery subjects did not, in the above experiment, show a better pretraining response than poor imagers may lie in the fact that the scripted material employed did not match strong, coherent prototypes in these normal subjects. Support for this interpretation is provided by subsequent research with subjects preselected for high fear. Results indicating a greater exposure-concordant physiological response for good imagers than for poor imagers has been observed among both volunteer phobics (Levin, 1982) and phobic patients treated at a Fear Clinic (Levin, Cook, & Lang, 1982).

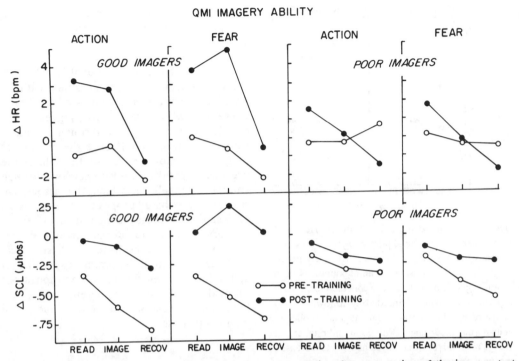

Figure 4. Average heart-rate and skin-conductance response during the presentation of the imagery text (read), the imagery period, and during the immediately following no-image recovery period. Each measurement period was 30 sec in duration. Average data for action and fear scenes are presented for both high and low imagery subjects (Bett's questionnaire), before and after response training. See Miller et al. (1981).

In both of these latter experiments the phobics had received no special imagery training before the administration of test imagery. Nevertheless, Levin and his associates (1982) found greater response by good imagers to personal anxiety scenes and a tendency for good imaging patients to begin their response to standard fear scenes earlier than poor imagers. Levin (1982) observed significantly greater initial heart-rate and skin-conductance responses in QMI-defined high-imagery phobic subjects responding to phobia-relevant text than for phobics classified as poor imagers on the QMI responding to the same material (Figure 6.5). Levin's good imaging, subjects also showed significant habituation of heart rate over fear imagery trials, whereas low QMI subjects were initially nonreactive and showed little change.

The experiments just described exploring text structure and the image mode of text pro-

cessing, have been a productive beginning. The findings are consistent with the hypothesis that emotional processing can be instigated through the response information included in an imagery script. We have developed a method (response training) that enhances the normal subject's ability to process text in the imagery mode. The use of this methodology leads subjects to generate, during text-prompted imagery, a subovert efferent pattern that is consistent with the specific arousal pattern shown at actual exposure to the referenced objects or contexts. We have traced a link between perceptual imagery and emotional imagery and shown that response-trained, questionnaire-selected "good" perceptual imagers are more likely to generate a physiology of affect from text than are similarly trained "poor" imagers. Furthermore, among subjects who are presumed to have a more coherent fear prototype

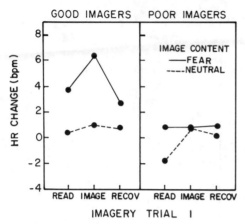

Figure 5. Untrained phobic volunteers: Heart-rate change scores of good and poor imagers (Bett's questionnaire) responding to both an affectively neutral script and a script describing an encounter with the phobic object. These data were collected for separate experimental groups immediately following actual exposure and thus represent an imaginal recollection of an actual experience. Both good and poor imager groups responded with marked heart-rate increase to the just preceding objective exposure. See Levin (1982).

(i.e., phobics), this difference between good and poor imagers appears even without supplementary training.

In future studies we plan a more systematic exploration of the propositional structure of emotion-generating text, as it interacts with the learning and retrieval activities of the brain. Bower's (1981) recent work suggests that emotional processing may, through spread of association, broadly influence the content of long-term memory. We intend to evaluate the organization of the prototype network through studies of recall, in which the associative strength of textbased propositions are assessed after subjects process the material in either the imagery or text-comprehension modes. We expect to relate these results to the physiological analyses reported in the present experimental series. It is our view that response propositions (as evidenced by relevant efferent activity) are the primary mediators of affective influence on memory process.

Accessing the Prototype: Media and Emotional Change

It is a current working hypotheses that the accessing of an emotion prototype from long-term storage, with its associated motor programs, is facilitated by the quantity of matching propositions at input. In the research just described, we have attempted to prompt such emotional processing by priming the response side of the network. However, a parallel line of research has also been under way in which the amount of stimulus information has been manipulated, as this predicts differences in both the imagery and the exposure physiology of emotion.

With such factors as imagery ability or familiarity of material being equal, it is held that the probability of emotional processing will increase with the quantity of matching stimulus information. Thus, for example, actual expo-

sure to a feared object is more likely to access the prototype than a filmed presentation, which in turn would be a better prompt than a written text. The hypothesis depends, of course, on the absence of serious mismatch, which might result in the access of different, competing material from memory. Furthermore, it will be obvious to the reader that we are entering here the realm of functional aesthetics and that the associative strength of specific stimulus propositions and the organization of the input, as well as the quantity of information, may be of importance. Thus, an artist might well create a poem that would be a surer path to an affective response than a Hollywood extravaganza on the same theme. Our effort here is to describe media differences in terms of their average quantity of information. We are for now skirting the formidable aesthetic problems, as well as the obvious fact that different media require the application of different transformation formulas before either raw stimulus material or semantic representations can be converted into the conceptual information of the prototype (e. g., text in a natural language must be comprehended in terms of the objects and events to which the semantic code refers).

McLean (1981) recently completed an experiment in our laboratory that examined the verbal report and physiological responses of untrained subjects to an imagery script, compared with their response to an elaborate dramatic presentation of the same affective content. The dramatic presentations or playlets took place in a realistic setting, employed trained actors, and engaged the subjects as participant observers. Two contents were studied: The first scenario (fear) involved a live snake that was being ineptly restrained by the actor-handler who described it as poisonous, while the subject watched from a position only a few feet away. The second playlet (anger) cast an actor as a teaching assistant who berated the subject for his lack of intelligence and poor performance on an examination. Both dramatic presentations had great verisimilitude. However, subjects were clearly informed that the events were not "real": for example, the snake was not poisonous, and the actor was only "saying" the subject was stupid for the purposes of the experiment. Thus, some of the meaning propositions in the situation were discordant with the presumed emotional prototypes. However, the stimulus information was rendered faithfully in all its physical parameters, and both the subjects watching the playlets and those hearing the text description were told to imagine the contexts vividly "as if" they were real.

The results of these interventions are presented in Figure 6.6. It is clear that the playlets generated heart-rate change in untrained subjects that was significantly greater than that shown by text-prompted imagery. The modest responses of these subjects to imagery scripts were similar to those observed in previous research by untrained normal subjects. The response to the playlets (with their enriched stimulus information) was comparable in

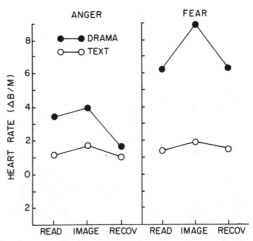

Figure 6. Average heart-rate changes observed during text and playlet (drama) prompted imagery. A script was read to the subject during the read period for the text condition; a playlet was presented during the read period in the drama condition. Descriptive fear-inducing (an encounter with a poisonous snake) and anger-inducing (receiving unjust verbal abuse) contents were examined. See McLean

amplitude of physiological response to that previously obtained from response-trained subjects reacting to text (e. g., see Figure 6.3). Furthermore, as with response training and scripted response material, the effect of the playlet on the physiological affective response was enhanced among questionnaire-selected "good" imagers. A comparison of differences between good and poor imagers in response to the playlets is presented in Figure 6.7. It will be noted that the response of females differs from that of males, according to content. Male good imagers responded more to both playlets than did their poor imaging peers. However, good imaging females, while showing a dramatically larger response to the fear scene, did not differ at all from poor imaging females when they visualized being criticized for poor performance. This reduced response to so-called anger stimuli is consistent with sex differences in affect noted by Frodi, Macaulay, and Thome (1977).

If quantity of matching propositions is the key to prototype access, it is expected that response training would have the same enhancing

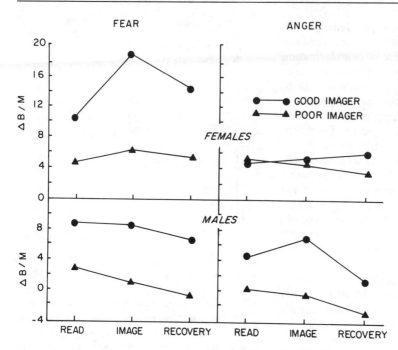

Figure 7. Average heart-rate responses of good imagery subjects (Betts's questionnaire) during imagery occasioned by fear- and anger-inducing dramatic presentations. Responses of the two sexes are separately indicated. See McLean (1981).

effect on efferent responding regardless of the input medium. Kozak (1982) recently explored this hypothesis, administering both stimulus and response training to subjects and examining the effects of these procedures on different stimulus materials. Subjects were both administered scripted text and exposed to some of the actual physical stimuli presumed to be part of the stimulus structure of a relevant fear proto-type (e.g., for speech anxiety, a view of an audience). For both the physically presented stimuli and the text, response training prompted the enhanced physiological fear pattern predicted; stimulus training occasioned a significantly smaller physiological response to the objective stimulus, as it did to the scripted rendering of the same material, and as it has in our previous comparisons of the effects of training method on emotion-instigating text (Lang et al., 1980).

Two other experiments merit mention in the present context. Both are concerned with emotional change and its relationship to imagery processing. In an earlier study (Lang et al., 1970) it was shown that phobic patients treated by systematic desensitization profited from the therapy to the extent that verbal re-

port of fear during therapy imagery was concordant with a physiology of fear arousal. Recently, Levin (1982) undertook an exploration of the mechanism of this effect. Snake-phobic subjects were exposed repeatedly to a live snake in a habituation paradigm. Between exposure trials, subjects imaged either the snake or a neutral scene (imagery was text prompted). On the basis of QMI scores, subjects were divided into good imager and poor imager groups. The results for good imagers indicated marked habituation of cardiac rate to repeated, objective exposure trials when phobic imagery intervened between these exposure trials; good imagers showed significantly less habituation when the intervening imagery was neutral in content. As noted earlier, the good imagers also showed a significantly greater initial heart-rate response to the intervening phobic imagery than to neutral imagery. Furthermore, the phobic imagery response of the good imagers (unlike their response to neutral content) habituated with repeated presentations of the scene. None of these same effects were obtained for poor imagers. That is, while poor imagers showed a marked heart-rate response with snake exposure, habituation was not hastened by intervening phobic imagery. Furthermore, again unlike good imagers, the poor imaging group showed no difference in physiological response between neutral and fear imagery.

These results suggest that text-generated imagery processing accesses the same emotion prototype for good imagers as does actual exposure. Furthermore, the prototype's modification over imagery trials transfers directly to the exposure situation. This prompts the hypothesis that for therapies other than those involving direct exposure, effectiveness may depend on the subject's previous ability to generate affect from linguistic representations (instructions to imagine, recall, or discuss emotional content) initiated in the therapeutic interaction. The results of a clinical series (Levin, Cook, & Lang, 1982), conducted in parallel with our laboratory work, provide some support for this view. Among a population of anxious and phobic patients, it was shown that clients who generated appropriate physiological patterning to imagery instructions at an initial diagnostic session were significantly more likely to successfully complete treatment than those who failed to show a palpable initial response. Furthermore, the successful subjects were significantly more likely to be high on the imagery questionnaire than were the subjects who failed to successfully complete the course of treatment.

Summary and Conclusions

This chapter is a speculation on the cognitive events that determine the central representation and expression of an emotional response. Cognition is defined here as conceptual information processing. We begin with a description of how the information base of an affective response disposition is organized and its form of representation in memory. An effort is then made to indicate some of the conditions under which such a disposition is accessed and processed as efferent output. Emotions are conceived to be action sets that can evolve three different response systems: verbal report, overt motor response, and expressive physiology. It is held that there is no clear demarcation between affective and nonaffective behaviour. However, popular consensus defines the terrain of emotion as including response that vary in valence, arousal, and control or dominance, and it is toward an explanation of these phenomena that the present chapter is oriented. Because of consistency of response and the realiability of stimulus-instigating conditions (as well as the importance of the clinical problem and the convenience of access to the subject population), focal phobia is used here as a primary case illustration of our approach.

This view of emotion is a development of the bio-informational theory of imagery previously described (Lang, 1979). Affective dispositions are held to be coded in memory in propositional form. Propositions are organized into networks related by association. The units of a network may be divided into three general information classes: stimulus, meaning, and response propositions. Response propositions are double coded, in that their deep structure is linked to the motor command system that generates efferent output. The information network determining a phobic response is closely bonded and richly interconnected. This coherence of information means that the network has a high probability of being activated as a unit, giving it the status of an action or emotion prototype.

A primary method of accessing the prototype is through input of matching stimulus information. The better the match to the prototype (perhaps optimal with presentation of an actual phobic object), the more likely that the emotion response program will be accessed and run. However, matching information other than stimulus propositions also facilitates access. Thus, under conditions of degraded input (e.g., imagery instructions), probability of access is increased by the simultaneous instigation of the response components in the network. Subjects vary in their basic ability to access affective response codes, independent of the relative coherence of an emotion prototype. This ability appears to be similar to that involved in perceptual imagery recall. Thus, good imagers are more likely to generate affect under conditions of degraded input than are poor imagers. Because of the link between response propositions and motor programs, processing of an affective prototype always involves efferent leakage (even if the implied overt action is inhibited). Therefore, the affective event, as it varies between subjects and/or contents, can be monitored in real time through bioelectric recording.

Two lines of research supporting this view are described. The first group of experiments represents an exploration of text-prompted emotional imagery. Subjects were instructed to imagine emotional situations described by propositionally coded scripts. It was determined that the inclusion of response propositions in the text, in conjunction with prior response training in processing this material, resulted in the largest and most concordant affective reactions (verbal report and physiological pattern). Emphasis on stimulus material, including a "mind's eye" oriented imagery training program, did not facilitate the affective imagery response. The same methodology was subsequently used in a study of two distinct types of fearful subjects. Following response training, reliable differences in the two fear groups were observed, consistent with exposure physiology and hypothesized differences in the two fear types. It was also established that questionnaire-defined good imagers, responding to scripted material, generated more appropriate affective responses than did poor imagers, and that these effects were particularly large and spontaneous when the good imagers were also phobics imaging phobic material.

The second research line involved a systematic varying of affective stimulus information. It was found that affective responses were larger when subjects reacted to a dramatic presentation than when they reacted to scripted text. Furthermore, good imagers showed the same superior performance with the dramatic scenes as they did in our previous studies of text based imagery. Good imagers also showed significant differentiation of response, according to the content of the dramatic scene and hypothesized individual differences in the target emotion prototypes (in this case the expected differences were based on sex rather than fear type). Again, comparable to studies of text, response training prior to objective stimulus presentation was significantly more effective than stimulus training in amplifying appropriate affective patterns or response. Finally, the results obtained for both phobic volunteers and clinical patients support the view that prototype access is crucial to therapeutic behaviour change.

In conclusion, it is noted that the present view is wholly consistent neither with the traditional conception of specific states of emotion (subsisting patterns of physiology and behaviour that are consistent with the phenomenology of fear, anger, joy, etc.), nor with the concept of emotion as a coincidence of unidimensional arousal and affect-appraising cognitions. The information processing view radically redefines theoretical categories in emotion studies. Emotion is held to be a differentiated action set, often context bound, based on a specific information structure in memory. The research problems this view poses for the future include: a further study of prototype structure and organization, and an assessment of the effects of prototype processing on other memory content; further exploration of individual differences in accessing of affective information; study of how quantity and quality of input information (including the significance of the specific transformational rules required by different media) influence ease of access of an emotional prototype; and finally, systematic examination of the processes of prototype consolidation and change, with a practical view to the improvement of methods for the therapeutic modification of aversive emotional states.

References

Anderson, J.R., & Bower, G.H. (1974). A propositional theory of recognition memory. *Memory and Cognition,* 2 (3), 406–412.

Betts, G.H. (1909). *The distributions and functions of mental imagery.* New York: Columbia University Teachers College. Contributions to Educational Series, No. 26.

Bower, G.H. (1970). Analysis of mnemonic device. *American Scientist, 58,* 496–510.

Bower, G.H. (1981). Mood and memory. *American Psychologist, 36,* 129–148.

Brady, K.P., & Levitt, E.E. (1966). Hypnotically induced visual hallucinations. *Psychosomatic Medicine, 28,* 351–353.

Brown, B.B. (1968). Visual recall ability and eye movements. *Psychophysiology, 4,* 300–306.

Deckert, G.H. (1964). Pursuit eye movements in the absence of a moving visual stimulus. *Science, 143,* 1192–1193.

Frodi, A., Macaulay, J., & Thome, P.R. (1977). Are women always less aggressive than men? A review of the experimental literature. *Psychological Bulletin, 84,* 634–660.

Grossberg, J.M., & Wilson, H.K. (1968). Physiological changes accompanying the visualization of fearful and neutral situations. *Journal of Personality and Social Psychology, 10,* 124–133.

Hilgard, E.R. (1965). *Hypnotic susceptibility.* New York: Harcourt, Brace, & World.

Hull, C.L. (1933). *Hypnosis and suggestibility: An experimental approach.* New York: Appleton-Century-Crofts.

Jacobson, E. (1930). Electrical measurements of neuromuscular state during mental activities: III. Visual imagination and recollections. *American Journal of Physiology, 95,* 694–702.

Kieras, D. (1978). Beyond pictures and words: Alternate information processing models for imagery effects in verbal memory. *Psychological Bulletin, 85,* 532–554.

Kintsch, W. (1974). *The representation of meaning in memory.* Hillsdale, N. J.: Erlbaum.

Kosslyn, S.M. (1975). Information representation in visual images. *Cognitive Psychology, 7,* 341–370.

Kozak, M.J. (1982). *The psychophysiological effects of training on variously elicited imaginings.* Unpublished doctoral dissertation, University of Wisconsin, Madison.

Lang, P.J. (1968). Fear reduction and fear behaviour: Problems in treating a construct. In J.M. Shlien (Ed.), *Research in psychotherapy* (Vol. 3), pp. 90–103. Washington, D.C.: American Psychological Association.

Lang, P.J. (1971). The application of psychophysiological methods to the study of psychotherapy and behaviour modification. In A.E. Bergin & S.L. Garfield (Eds.). *Handbook of psychotherapy and behaviour change.* New York: Wiley.

Lang, P.J. (1978). Anxiety: Toward a psychophysiological definition. In H.S. Akiskal & W.L. Webb (Eds.), *Psychiatric diagnosis: Exploration of biological predictors,* pp. 365–389. New York: Spectrum.

Lang, P.J. (1979). A bio-informational theory of emotional imagery. *Psychophysiology, 16,* 495–512.

Lang, P.J., Kozak, M.J., Miller, G.A., Levin, D.N., & McLean, A.Jr. (1980). Emotional imagery: Conceptual structure & pattern of somatovisceral response. *Psychophysiology, 17,* 179–192.

Lang, P.J., Levin, D.N., Miller, G.A., & Kozak, M.J. (1983). Fear behaviour, fear imagery and the psychophysiology of emotion: The problem of affective integration. *Journal of Abnormal Psychology, 92,* 276–306.

Lang, P.J., Melamed, B.G., & Hart, J.H. (1970). A psychophysiological analysis of fear modification using an automated desensitization procedure. *Journal of Abnormal Psychology, 76,* 220–234.

Levin, D.N. (1982). The psychophysiology of fear reduction: Role of response activation during emotioned imagery. Unpublished doctoral dissertation, University of Wisconsin – Madison.

Levin, D.N., Cook, E.W. III, & Lang, P.J. (1982). Fear imagery and fear behaviour: Psychophysiological analysis of clients receiving treatment for anxiety disorders. *Psychophysiology, 19,* 571–572 (abstract).

Marks, I.M., & Huson, J. (1973). Physiological aspects of neutral and phobic imagery. *British Journal of Psychiatry, 122,* 567–572.

McLean, A., Jr. (1981). *Emotional imagery: Stimulus information, imagery ability, and patterns of physiological response.* Unpublished doctoral dissertation. University of Wisconsin-Madison.

Miller, G.A., Levin, D.N., Kozak, M.J., Cook, E.W., Melanean, A., Carroll, J., & Lang, P.J. (1981). Emotional imagery: Individual differences in imagery ability and physiological responses. *Psychophysiology, 18,* 196 (Abstract).

Nebes, R.D. (1974). Hemispheric specialization in commissurolomized man. *Psychological Bulletin, 81,* 1–14.

Neisser, U. (1967). *Cognitive psychology*. New York: Appleton-Century-Crofts.

Pylyshyn, Z.W. (1973). What the minds eye tells the mind's brain: A critique of mental emagery. *Psychological Bulletin, 80*, 1–22.

Quillian, M.R. (1966). Semantic memory. In M.L. Minsky (Ed.). *Semantic information processing*. Cambridge, Mass.: MIT Press.

Schachter, S. (1964). The interaction of cognitive and physiological determinants of emotional state. In L. Berkowitz (Ed.), *Advances in experimental social psychology* (Vol. 1), pp. 48–80. New York: Academic Press.

Schroeder, H.E., & Rick, A.R. (1976). The process of fear reduction through systematic de-semitization. Journal of Consulting and Clinical Psychology, *44*, 191–199.

Schwartz, G.E. (1971). Cardiac responses to self-induced thoughts. *Psychophysiology, 8* (4), 462–467.

Shaw, W.A. (1940). The relation of muscular action potentials to imaginal weight lifting. *Archives of Psychology, 23*, 380–389.

Sheehan, P.Q. (1967). A shortened form of Bett'

questionnaire upon mental imagery. *Journal of Clinical Psychology, 23*, 386–389.

Sokolov, Y.N. (1963). *Perception and the conditioned reflex*. New York: MacMillan.

Sperry, R.W. (1952). Neurology and the mind-brain problem. *American Scientist, 40*, 291–312.

Sperry, R.W. (1968). Hemisphere deconnection and unity in conscious awareness. *American Psychologist, 23*, 723–733.

Van Egeren, L.F., Feather, B.W., & Hein, P.L. (1971). Desensitization of phobias: Some psychophysiological propositions. *Psychophysiology, 8*, 213–228.

Watson, J.P., & Marks, I.M. (1971). Relevant and irrelevant fear in flooding. *Behaviour Therapy, 2*, 275–293.

Weerts, T.C., & Lang, P.J. (1978). The psychophysiology of fear imagery. Differences between focal phobia and social-performance anxiety. *Consulting and Clinical Psychology, 46*, 1157–1159.

Wolpe, J. (1958). *Psychotherapy by reciprocal inhibition*. Stanford, CA: Stanford University Press.

Anxiety and Clinical Psychophysiology: Three Decades of Research on Three Response Systems in Three Anxiety Disorders

Bruce N. Cuthbert* and Barbara G. Melamed**

Abstract

Research on the psychophysiology of the anxiety disorders is selectively reviewed from the perspective of the emotion theories developed by Peter Lang and his associates. Lang's bioinformational theory of emotion developed from an effort to understand emotional imagery in fear research. In this theory, the memory organization underlying a phobia is considered to be an associative network of information. In addition to information about the situational context, the memory structure also stores the relevant responses to be made, and its activation results in measureable efferent activity. These responses can be observed in the "three systems" of overt behavior, verbal reports, and physiological responses. Responses to phobic imagery are smaller for patients with panic attacks compared to simple phobics, and less related to relevant variables such as imagery vividness. In addition, panic patients show less responding than social phobics in a speech test, and less effect of the introduction of new speech materials. These results are interpreted as indicating that the associative network in panic disorder shows the least cohesive organization, while simple phobics have the most tightly linked fear memory structure. The implications are briefly discussed in terms of the current status of the three-systems model and anxiety disorders research.

Key words: anxiety disorders, phobia, psychophysiology, bioinformational theory, emotion (three-systems model)

Peter Lang is generally credited with being one of the first investigators to point out that emotion is a construct which involves measurements in three response systems – overt behavior, verbal reports of affect, and physiological responding (e. g., Lang, 1968). This view of emotion has been most systematically considered in studying fear, both as a basic emotion and as a psychopathological condition, i. e., in phobias and other anxiety disorders. The purpose of this chapter is to review work on the anxiety disorders performed over the past three decades in Lang's laboratory. The three-systems model is considered in the context of an information processing theory of emotion and imagery, which has been applied to differences among the various anxiety disorders, particularly simple phobia, social phobia, and panic disorder. The relationship of each of the three systems to current anxiety disorders research is then considered briefly. It is concluded that psychophysiological measurement can be highly useful in exploring the psychopathology of the anxiety disorders.

*   University of Florida
**   Ferkauf Graduate School and Albert Einstein College of Medicine of Yeshiva University

Background

The development of systematic desensitization by Joseph Wolpe (1958) inaugurated the modern era of behavior therapy. Wolpe's techniques offered the first systematic, scientifically verifiable therapies applicable to clinical problems. Among others, two particular problems emerged in the research which ensued. First, as Wolpe's technique was especially suited for phobias, it became necessary to measure fear accurately and comprehensively; this, in turn, required some conceptualization of fear, and, by extension, of emotion in general. Lang's original statement of the three-systems model (1968) was not so much a fully elaborated theoretical model, as a recognition that fear was a construct used to refer to measurable variables which could be considered as occurring in three different response systems. Perhaps most evident in the clinical situation were verbal reports of fear – patients' statements about where and when they are afraid, and what the phenomenological experience of fear was like. Second was actual, overt behavior: Individuals or animals may be observed to run away, attack, or freeze in the presence of a feared object or situation. Finally, there is an expressive physiology associated with fear, such as increases in heart rate and blood pressure, excessive sweating, or changes in the frequency of elimination. The idea that fear is a unitary internal state would imply that measurements in these three systems should invariably agree with each other; however, the empirical literature indicates that responses in the three "systems" are frequently impressive by their lack of covariation. Thus, the challenge for research is to understand the circumstances under which three-system synchrony may or may not occur, and for the latter, to disentangle the variables controlling responding in the various systems.

The second problem was that not all clinical fear conditions responded equally well to the imagery-based systematic desensitization technique. A variety of investigators discovered, in particular, that social phobias and agoraphobia were less responsive to desensitization; the newer flooding techniques, in contrast, were frequently more successful (Marks, 1969). As these differences were not necessarily predicted by the reciprocal inhibition theory underlying desensitization, it was obviously important to understand more about the psychopathology of various fears.

In 1970, a pair of studies related to both of these concerns was published in a paper by Lang, Melamed, and Hart, which proved to adumbrate many of the issues addressed more fully in the subsequent literature. The initial study included some of the first physiological recording done during systematic desensitization therapy. Treatment controls were compared to snake-phobic subjects receiving eleven sessions of desensitization. Half of the latter subjects received a standard desensitization treatment, while the remainder were given therapy using a "Device for Automated Desensitization" (DAD). This was an electromechanical system in which the hierarchy scenes were prerecorded and presented on audio tape with a preprogrammed presentation protocol; subjects pressed a switch to signal fear, which caused the apparatus to terminate the item and immediately play a relaxation tape.

Fear reduction was comparable to previous studies (e. g., Lang, Lazovik, & Reynolds, 1965); interestingly, the automated DAD procedure actually resulted in slightly superior outcomes compared to live therapists. Even more intriguing, however, were the results for the psychophysiological recordings performed during DAD therapy. In particular, heart rates during therapy sessions were compared to treatment outcome (each subject's average rank on all the outcome measures). This analysis showed that subjects with greater fear reduction across treatment had higher heart rates during those trials where fear was signaled by a switch press; the correlation between fear reduction rank (1 = best) and heart rate was $-.75$ (p < .05). Successful subjects also showed more decrement in heart rate across successive presentations of the high-fear item ($r = -.91$, p < .01). Finally, subjects with more fear reduction tended to have higher heart rates during the initial, neutral scene of sessions with high fear trials ($r = -.75$, $p < .05$). Thus, as later studies would confirm, greater synchrony in verbal report and physiological activity was associated with more therapeutic gain.

The elevated physiological activity observed during high-fear trials implied that a gradient of autonomic response should exist, corresponding to the increasing fear items of the desensitization hierarchy. This possibility was tested in a second experiment. Volunteer phobics were selected as before to represent extremes of fear, with ten subjects each reporting fears of spiders and of public speaking; the initial questionnaire responses were confirmed by interview. Subjects constructed a 20-item fear hierarchy in collaboration with an experimenter. At a final session, physiological responses were recorded during visualization of five items, chosen to span the range of the hierarchy, in random order. The results generally confirmed the hypothesis: A strong linear trend was observed overall for both heart rate and skin conductance, with increased responding

for higher hierarchy items. However, consistent differences were observed between the two phobic categories. Within-group tests indicated a significant linear trend in skin conductance only for spider phobics; while the heart rate trend met conventional significance levels for both groups, the F value for spider phobics was six times larger (30.4 vs. 5.2), with a noticeable flattening of the trend line at high fear levels for socially anxious subjects. Finally, a linear trend in respiration variability was significant only for social phobics. In addition to these fear-related results, separate procedures also indicated more frequent spontaneous skin conductance responses and slower habituation rates for socially anxious subjects (cf. Lader, 1967). Overall, this study was one of the first to compare directly fear and non-fear material in focal and social phobics; combined with the results of the first study, these results illuminated the findings of other investigators regarding less successful outcomes for social phobics with desensitization (e. g., Lader, Gelder, & Marks, 1967).

Bio-informational Theory

These studies, in retrospect, spurred extensive theoretical development to account for the results. What was it about imagery that caused some people to have higher heart rates than others during high-fear scenes? And why should these people have better outcomes in therapy? Too, if all phobias are highly similar except for the type of phobic object or context, why should social phobics show a different gradient of response across a fear hierarchy as compared to simple phobics?

Basic Theory

The development of what has come to be known as bio-informational theory provided a framework in which to address these questions. The theory developed out of the need to organize findings indicating an organized nervous system – one which is designed to ensure the survival of the species, and one which differen-

tiates animal from man on the ability of the second signal system, i. e., language, to direct behavior at both the micro (internal physiological) and macro or overt level of movement and behavior. While the model was originally conceived as a theory of imagery (Lang, 1979), it has since been extended to a more general theory of emotion (Lang, 1984, 1985).

The bio-informational theory essentially adapts concepts from modern cognitive psychology regarding the representation and processing of information in memory, and applies these principles to the study of emotion. Thus, information about emotions is assumed to be stored in memory in associative networks consisting of logically linked elements, just as any other information. While the original depictions followed contemporary cognitive psychology in positing a linked series of logical propositions, more recently cognitive psychologists have debated a number of ways in which information may be stored (e.g., Johnson-Laird, Herrmann, & Chaffin, 1984). However, the statement of bio-informational theory is not critically dependent on the exact manner in which information is organized; rather, the emphasis is placed upon the types of information stored, and the results when the information is activated. The network can be activated by inputs (e.g., direct perceptual experience, imagery, textual descriptions, etc.) which match the information present; when a sufficient number of the nodes of the network are so accessed, the entire network is activated, resulting in the variety of behaviors and experience that are labeled as an emotion. Certain elements of the network may be particularly high in associative strength, so that activation of only a few key nodes may be sufficient to access the entire program; for example, a wriggling movement may be the only cue necessary to elicit a strong response in a snake phobic.

Three different kinds of information are hypothesized to be represented in emotional memory. The first concerns information about external stimuli, and corresponds to the usual descriptions of situations and/or objects which give rise to emotional behavior. Obviously, matching inputs here are important in defining emotional situations, and are the primary events usually thought of with respect to episodic memories. A more unusual departure was represented by the second class of information, which introduced the idea that the responses which occur in a situation are also encoded as an integral part of the emotional memory structure. Further, these are comprised of the three systems – behavioral, physiological, and verbal – discussed above. Finally, a third class consists of semantic concepts elaborating the meaning of the object or situation, to represent information not objectively present in the context. For instance, the statement "Someone died of a rattlesnake bite in these woods last month" adds information which may well augment the memory structure for a snake phobic, although it would not be present in any aspects of the objective situation.

One important innovation of this theory is the emphasis on response information coded directly as a constituent of the affective information structure. Thus, the responses which occur in emotion are a natural consequence of the activation of an appropriate information network. In imagery, of course, behavior is gated out before its full expression. However, by a process of "efferent leakage," some relevant physiological activity is hypothesized to occur during vivid imagery. This provides a rationale for why responses are observed in imagery (those denoted as emotional, and otherwise, e.g., Cuthbert & Lang, 1984), and suggests the functional nature of such responses. It also leads directly to the concept of vivid imagery as being more related to the response, rather than to the stimulus, aspect of imagery.

It may be noted that this network is described on a conceptual basis, i.e., it describes a functional software program or set of programs without necessarily implying specific anatomical locations. Thus, the model has the advantage of not being tied to particular brain sites in attempting to explain emotional responses (for an example of the difficulties involved in relating specific emotions to specific brain locations, see the target article and commentaries following Panksepp, 1982).

An Imagery Research Program

The bio-informational model fulfilled one of the important tests of a good theory, i.e., it has generated a substantial body of research, which has been supportive in most respects. In Lang's laboratory, a basic imagery protocol emerged which served to test several predictions derived from the model. The basic paradigm involved pre-recorded imagery scripts, with eleven different scenes tested in each session. Each trial involved a 30-second baseline period, 50 seconds for the playing of an imagery script, 30 seconds of imagery, and a 30-second recovery period (cued by a tone at the end of the imagery period). Subjects were instructed to begin imagining the scene when they heard the recording; when the script finished, they were to continue imagining the scene, starting at the beginning of the description, until they heard the tone. After the recovery period, they then rated their experience of the previous trial on affective dimensions of pleasant-unpleasant, aroused-calm, and dominant-controlled (Hodes, Cook, & Lang, 1985), as well as imagery vividness, using an interactive computer display. Physiological measurements were digitized on-line and recorded continuously throughout each trial. Median and inter-quartile range values were calculated separately for the four trial periods, i. e., the Base, script playback ("Read," only the last 30 seconds of which were analyzed), Imagery, and Recovery periods; scores for the latter three periods were then expressed as change scores relative to the Base period.

One of the first hypotheses was that scripts with stimulus descriptions only (the usual circumstance for emotional imagery studies) should show less physiological responding compared to scripts containing both stimulus and response propositions; not only would the latter contain more information to match the network, but the processing of script response information should lead to measureable efferent activity. Early studies by Cuthbert, Kozak, and Lang produced results consistent with this hypothesis, but with inconsistent or marginal statistical outcomes. Lang, Kozak, Miller, Levin, and McLean (1980) then explored the hypothesis that subjects might be processing response information in the scripts in a semantic manner only (as though simply listening to a story) without incorporating such propositions in their actual imagery production. Accordingly, Lang et al. developed two training procedures to explore this possibility. Each procedure involved working with small groups of subjects to shape verbally the reported content of their imagery over several practice trials involving a variety of images. One set of subjects was praised for elaborating stimulus aspects of an image, such as colors, sounds, textures, etc. The second set of subjects, in contrast, was reinforced for including mention of responses in the image – such as the feeling of one's heart pounding, sweat trickling off the brow, feeling muscles contract, etc. Thus, by the end of training, both groups reported that their imagery was now much more vivid than before, but with markedly different emphasis in content.

The usual imagery procedure followed the imagery training session. Scripts included three each neutral, fear, and action scenes, presented in randomized order. As a further manipulation of script effects, the scripts for half the subjects in each training condition included mention of both stimulus and response propositions, while for the remaining subjects the scripts contained stimulus items only. As predicted, subjects who had received the response training procedure, and whose scripts contained response information, showed significantly enhanced responding in heart rate and muscle tension compared to subjects in the other three training/script combinations. In addition, the effect was specific to scenes where activation could be expected, i. e., the fear and action scenes, but not the neutral scene; a significant three-way interaction between scene content, imagery training, and script content was observed. Thus, the response-oriented imagery training procedure appeared to function rather like an amplifier, augmenting response predispositions to a point where they could be measured reliably (Lang et al., 1980).

The next step in the experimental program involved testing the model with high-fear subjects, specifically, snake phobics and socially anxious subjects selected from undergraduate populations (Lang, Levin, Miller, & Kozak, 1983). In order to compare differences in task demands, both groups were exposed to their own and to the other group's fear situations, as well as other control (exercise and neutral) situations. In a first study, subjects imagined snake and public speaking situations both before and after actual exposure to these situations. While the results were complex, two main findings emerged. First, heart rate increases were greater for snake phobics than socially anxious subjects during snake exposure; while heart rates were higher overall for both groups during the speech test, no between-group differences were observed. Skin conductance patterns were similar, but less strong statistically. This effect was interpreted in terms of the metabolic requirements which are required to support speech performance, which were apparently obligatory irrespective of reports of fear. This inference was supported by the fact that reports of arousal during speech were higher for social than snake fear subjects. Second, while the differences in imagery were similar in pattern to those seen during exposure, the effects were smaller and non-significant. In fact, the imagery data were similar to the stimulus-trained subjects in the earlier Lang et al. (1980) study, in that the effects were in the predicted direction, but not sufficiently strong for statistical reliability.

Accordingly, in a second experiment, a new sample of snake- and social-fear subjects was selected. Half the subjects received the response-oriented imagery training procedure as before, while the others participated in stimulus training. All subjects then imagined scenes involving both snake exposure and public speaking, along with control exercise and neutral situations. Scripts were identical for all subjects, and contained both stimulus and response references. The data were now compellingly similar to the exposure situation: For response-trained subjects, heart rate increases differentiated the two groups in visualization of snake exposure, but not of public speaking. Stimulus training once again resulted in similar, but non-significant patterns. Further specificity was indicated by electromyograms recorded from the forehead and neck, which revealed higher tension during imagination of exercise than fear. Thus, the data overall supported the model: Patterns of physiological response during imagery were similar to that observed during exposure, supporting the hypothesis that the same memory information structure is accessed during imagery as in an actual situation. The results further confirmed that the response training procedure acted to amplify physiological response in imagery, but only for pre-existing response dispositions; neutral scenes failed to show appreciable reactivity, even for response-trained individuals. Finally, the results showed that the context must be considered in both exposure and imagery, in that tasks with intrinsic metabolic demands may show increases in physiological activity in the absence of any indication of fear.

Clinical Studies

Overall, this program of research has suggested many possibilities for the lack of consistency in earlier research with emotional imagery, given the variety of paradigms, scripts, etc. that have previously been employed (e. g., see Cuthbert, Vrana, & Bradley, 1991, for a more extensive review). The bio-informational theory has also stimulated further research in many other laboratories. Such studies have included similar investigations regarding fear in normal subjects (e. g., Hirota & Hirai, 1986; Robinson & Reading, 1985). In addition, the research has expanded into a variety of clinical areas, such as post-traumatic stress disorder (Pitman, Orr, Forgue, Altman, de Jong, & Herz, 1990), sexual dysfunction (Jones & Barlow, 1989), and agoraphobia (Zander & McNally, 1988). The focus of the work in Lang's laboratory has continued to be in the psychopathology of the anxiety disorders, with an emphasis on differentiating different subtypes. Thus, an Anxiety Disorders Clinic has been in operation for the past several years at the University of Florida as a clinical test bed to evaluate the theory with three primary phobic groups – simple, social, and panic disorders with agoraphobia.

The protocol that has been developed includes an interview, an imagery assessment session, behavior tests, and preliminary standardized therapy. The imagery session used the script playback and imagery periods described above, with some modifications for clinical use. In particular, five scenes were constructed uniquely for each patient on the basis of the clinical material and interview – two phobic scenes, one scene of personal danger or discomfort not involving the presenting problem, one pleasant scene, and one neutral scene. These scripts included responses that patients indicated as actually occurring in each situation, and were recorded for playback along with standard fear and action scenes. The latter included a dental examination and giving a speech, as well as control action and neutral situations.

The preliminary results of this work were reported previously (Cook, Melamed, Cuthbert, McNeil, & Lang, 1988), and revealed differences among the diagnostic groups. Simple phobics exhibited significantly greater heart rate and skin conductance change during imagery of their phobic material, as compared to social phobics and agoraphobics. In addition, better self-reported imagery ability (as assessed by the Questionnaire on Mental Imagery, Sheehan, 1967) was related to greater heart rate response for simple phobics, but not the other two groups. On the other hand, good imagers in all patient groups responded more to the standard aversive scene involving a dental examination. Interestingly, while social phobics were less responsive than simple phobics to their personal clinical scenes, they responded significantly more to the "standard" speech fear than the other two groups (both in heart rate and, for good imagers, in skin conductance).

These results led to the hypothesis that the memory associative networks mediating phobic behavior differ among the patient groups. Simple phobics have highly organized, coherent structures which are high in associative strength between elements; social phobics have networks marked more by vigilance and evaluative concerns; agoraphobics seem to be characterized by memory structures which are lower in associative strength, and much less reliable in their evocation. (See Öhman, 1986, for an extended discussion of possible evolutionary reasons for these differences.) Thus, it is primarily simple phobics who display a strong disposition for escape and avoidance as a part of the phobic prototype (Lang, 1985). One possibility to explain the lack of response by agoraphobics is that the situation-oriented scripts fail to capture their "real" fear, i.e., of having a panic attack. While this may be possible, all agoraphobic scripts contained several response propositions reflecting the DSM-IIIR criteria for panic attacks (e. g., dizziness, hyperventilation, palpitations); also, most of the scripts explicitly mentioned the fear of having an attack. Similarly, agoraphobic patients did not report the scenes to be subjectively less vivid or arousing than other patients. Thus, it is concluded that the lack of response is most likely to represent an inability of textual inputs to prompt an activation of anything like the cognitive pro-

duction involved in a panic attack. Also of interest is the stronger response of social phobics to the standard speech script than to personal phobic material; possibly personal scenes represent more those situations with which socially anxious individuals have learned to cope and cannot avoid (and indeed, may wish to approach), while the standard speech scene (a novel situation, involving an "impatient class") may invoke an avoidance program more like that of simple phobics.

This protocol has been continued, and samples of 20 to 25 patients are now available for each of the three phobic groups. Current analyses continue to indicate that simple phobics show the largest responses during imagery of personal phobic scripts, and agoraphobics the least. This result is still statistically significant for skin conductance, but not for heart rate. However, further multiple regression analyses of the latter measure have indicated some strong relationships with other variables for simple phobics: Together, over 80% of the variance in heart rate response to phobic scenes is accounted for by the QMI, post-trial imagery vividness ratings, Beck Depression Inventory scores (presumably reflecting the degree of phobic distress), and age (Cuthbert, Melamed, McNeil, Cook, Patrick & Lang, 1990). Each of these variables is individually significant within the model, and shows a Pearson r of over .40 with heart rate change. These same variables, however, account for small and non-significant amounts of variance in the responses of social phobics and agoraphobics. A similar finding for the latter group has recently been reported by Zander and McNally (1988).

Partial replication of these data, as well as previous results regarding distinctions between simple and social phobics, comes from a recent study by McNeil, Vrana, Melamed, Cuthbert, & Lang (in press). Groups of subjects were selected by questionnaire (and confirmed by interview) to be high on either social fear, dental fear, or both ("multiple" phobics); subjects in the first two groups were also required to be below the median on their non-fear category to enhance the distinctiveness of the groups. Subjects imagined situations pertaining to social confrontation or speaking, a dental injection or examination, and mixed dental/social situations. As in the earlier studies, heart rate change varied between the groups for imagery of a simple phobic situation (i. e., dental work), but failed to differentiate the groups when a public speaking or confrontation situation was visualized. In addition, questionnaire measures indicated significant relationships with physiological response only in the specific fear groups. Thus, QMI scores were significantly related to phobic fear heart rate response for simple and "multiple" subjects, but not for the socially anxious group.

This study was the first in the laboratory's research program in which a group was selected to be simultaneously high on two fears. This appeared to be a sort of "hyper-phobic" group, responding consistently more than the other groups to both dental and social situations, and to other scenes as well. Thus, while social phobia is often associated with diminished response to relevant fear imagery, generally exacerbated responding may be seen when social anxiety occurs in conjunction with a number of other specific fears. Other data were consistent with this hypothesis as well. The dental and multiple fear subjects were combined with the simple phobics from the preliminary anxiety disorders sample of the Cook et al. (1988) paper mentioned above, to provide more power for regression analyses and explore the continuity of response patterns. In this combined sample, the QMI and Fear Survey Schedule (FSS; Wolpe & Lang, 1964, a long inventory of various fears) together accounted for a significant amount of variance in the heart rate response to standard speech and dental scenes; thus, higher overall fear was associated with greater responsivity. Results for combined social fear subjects (questionnaire-selected students plus patients) did not approach significance. Similarly, Patrick, Cuthbert, and Lang

(1989) performed an imagery study with patients drawn from an outpatient psychology clinic. A variety of diagnoses were represented (about half in the anxiety disorders), and only standard scenes were used. Once again, however, subjects with higher FSS scores showed significantly higher heart rate reactions to fear scenes than low FSS patients.

It thus appears that the tendency to be highly fearful may be associated with a general temperamental characteristic of elevated psychophysiological reactivity. In support of this hypothesis, Melamed (1969; see also Lang, 1970) conducted a study in which groups of subjects high in snake fear listened to two series of 10 1000-Hz tones, one at a high intensity (100 dB) and the other at a low intensity (50 dB). At a subsequent session, subjects viewed two series of brief motion pictures of snakes, one with 10 repetitions of high-fear films and the other with 10 low-fear films. Between-group variables included the stimulus intensity order (low-high or high-low) and the instructed involvement of the subject in the film (Attend, Relaxation, or "Catharsis," i. e., maximized involvement). In the Attend group, subjects' habituation rates to the high-fear film and the high-intensity tone were highly related, with 75 percent of the variance in the former accounted for by the latter. Further, the order of the tone intensity levels significantly affected the overall low fear film series and the low-intensity tone series, a result predicted by adaptation level theory. Thus, both overall main effects and individual difference variables displayed similar patterns for fear stimuli and "non-affective" pure tones. More investigations with normative psychophysiological measures may accordingly contribute to a greater understanding of the psychopathology of anxiety disorders.

Agoraphobia vs. Social Phobia: Exposure

Evidence thus continues to mount that not only is the memorial structure in simple phobia linked together strongly and coherently, but that the reactions of simple phobics can be predicted systematically by such factors as phobic severity and the ability to access the deep structure of an information network from an image prompt. On the other hand, given the indications of the lack of a coherent avoidance program in social and agoraphobia, can psychophysiological measures be useful in distinguishing agoraphobics and social phobics in the clinic? While the standard speech fear imagery script (as discussed above) represents one possibility, a recent clinical study from our laboratory suggests a useful paradigm based on actual exposure. As a part of the larger clinical program described above, all patients were given a behavior test before treatment commenced. This test was generally related to the patient's own fears. Social phobics performed a 10-step speech avoidance test, while agoraphobics participated in a standardized "agoraphobia walk." However, these avoidance tests were given generally at the second or third session, often before a final diagnosis (always requiring the consensus of two or more doctoral-level raters) could be determined. Accordingly, several patients presenting with mixed social and agoraphobic symptoms were given both tests; of these, 12 were later diagnosed as agoraphobic. Thus, speech test data were available both for these agoraphobics, as well as the larger sample of 22 social phobic subjects.

The behavior test procedure was straight forward. The patient was seated in a comfortable chair with electrodes attached, and was instructed that s/he would perform a variety of public speaking tasks to a small audience. While patients were given the option to stop at any time, in the event this seldom occurred. The test consisted of ten steps, each consisting of a 30-second baseline and a 30-second speech or read period; the therapist gave instructions for each trial just before its onset. The first step was performed with the therapist and one opposite-sex stranger. The patient was asked to "describe

your trip to the clinic today," with a remote experimenter announcing, "Begin preparation" at the start of the baseline period; brief tones cued the start and end of the speech period. The next six steps involved the reading of brief scripts, with the patient instructed to begin reading at the first tone and stop reading at the second tone. A new script was introduced on trials 2, 4, and 6, and 8; once again, the remote experimenter announced "Begin preparation" as the baseline period started. On trials 3, 5, and 7 the scripts were the same as the preceding trial, but one new audience member entered the room just before the therapist's instruction; entry of audience members alternated by gender, with a resultant total of two male and two female strangers at the start of Trial 8. The patient was instructed on these three trials that there would be no preparation period (i.e., no remote announcement), although the 30-second baseline period was recorded as usual. The final two trials once again involved extemporaneous speeches: On trial 9 the patient described once again his or her trip to the clinic, and on trial 10 spoke about "a personal topic of your own choosing." While this situation may seem somewhat lacking in verisimilitude, its impact on patients was generally strong, with one patient describing it afterward as "the hardest thing I've ever done in my life."

The entire procedure was tape-recorded and subsequently scored for various measures of speech disturbance (Mahl, 1956). Physiological responses included heart rate and skin conductance recordings. The primary measures were change scores for each trial, calculated by subtracting baseline from speech/read period values for each trial. Not surprisingly, the physiological data showed a substantial degree of reactivity. In addition, the procedure was successful in differentiating the socially anxious and agoraphobic patients. As shown in Figure 1, skin conductance responses for the first six script-reading trials (2 through 7) were significantly higher for social phobics than agoraphobics ($F = 4.24$, $p < .05$). In addition, further specificity of the procedure was apparent. Sep-

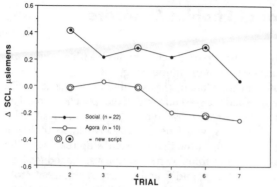

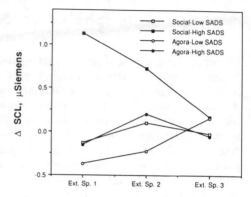

Figure 1. Skin conductance response during the 6 trials for scripts 1, 2, and 3. Overall, Socially Anxious patients responded more than Agoraphobics, $F = 4.24, p < .05$. In addition, for speech phobics, the first reading of a script (trials 2, 4, and 6) occasioned more skin conductance increase as compared to the second reading of each script (trials 3, 5, and 7): $F = 5.54, p < .03$. This effect was not found for agoraphobics ($F < 1$).

arate repeated-measures tests for each group indicated that for speech phobics, trials involving a new script (and the "Begin preparation" announcement) occasioned greater skin conductance change than trials with script repetition (new/old script F = 5.54, p < .03); this effect was not found for agoraphobics (F < 1). The same effect was observed for heart rate response: Although overall the group difference was not significant, only speech phobics exhibited greater acceleration during new as compared to repeated script reading (F = 6.95, p < .02).

Further differences emerged when scores on the Social Anxiety and Distress Scale (SADS; Watson & Friend, 1969) were taken into account. Overall, agoraphobics actually averaged substantially higher on the SADS than social phobics. However, only for social phobics were SADS scores related to speech test results. Figure 2 (top panel) shows that elevated SADS scores predicted greater skin conductance reaction during the extemporaneous speech trials for social, but not agoraphobics (Group F = 6.22; SADS F = 7.43, p < .02). In addition, a similar effect could be seen for the behavioral measure of disturbances in speaking: High-SADS social phobics exhibited markedly

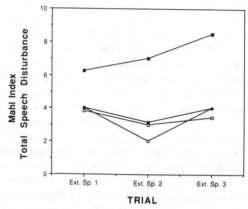

Figure 2 Top panel: Skin conductance responding during extemporaneous speeches (deviated from the preceding baseline). A positive relationship between SADS scores and skin conductance response was observed for Socially Anxious patients, but not for Agoraphobics. With SADS included in the analysis, the overall group effect was significant: Group $F = 6.22, p < .02$; SADS $F = 7.43, p < .02$; Trials $F = 3.22, p < .05$; Group X Trials interaction $F = 3.40$, $p < .05$. *Bottom panel:* Total speech disturbances (Mahl ratings) for Socially Anxious and Agoraphobic patients for the three extemporaneous speech trials. Greater speech disturbance was observed for those Socially Anxious patients with high SADS scores, while this relation was not observed for Agoraphobics. Group $F = 7.39, p < .02$; SADS $F = 10.05$, $p < .005$.

greater speech dysfluency than other patients (Group F = 7.39, p < .02; SADS F = 10.05, p < .005).

Finally, relationships between imagery and the speech test also demonstrated greater specificity for social phobics. For example, skin conductance increases during imagery of a stressful speech (in the preceding imagery session) were related to the level of skin conductance exhibited in immediate anticipation of the first speech test trial, but only for social phobic patients ($F = 7.7$, $p < .02$; agoraphobics, $F < 1$).

While most measures were thus consistent in showing greater reactivity and more specificity of response for social phobics, one index favoring the agoraphobics emerged. It was observed that agoraphobics appeared actually to increase skin conductance between trials, while social phobics tended to recover from responses during speech periods. To evaluate this effect, a second change score was calculated in which the Preparation period for trials 3 through 8 was deviated from the Speech period of the previous trial; the therapist read the next trial's instructions and new audience members were introduced on trials 3, 5, and 7 in the time between these two periods. In this analysis, agoraphobics now responded significantly more than socially anxious patients, $F = 6.28$, $p < 02$. There was also a trend for this effect to be larger for agoraphobics on trials when a new audience member was introduced; however, apparently due to the relatively small sample size of this group, the effect did not reach significance in separate within-group tests.

These results were to some extent serendipitous, and warrant replication: The availability of the agoraphobic group was not expected, and the effects were not predicted. Nevertheless, these results suggest that appropriate paradigms and recording procedures can reveal systematic differences among patient groups, related to relevant psychopathology, even in situations where considerable overlap of distress occurs. Social phobics reacted more to aspects of the situation related specifically to the social performance demands, i. e., giving an extemporaneous speech and delivering a reading of new verbal material. Furthermore, elevated physiological response was predicted by greater self-reports of social distress, and by response to speech fear material in imagery, only for social phobics. On the other hand, agoraphobics were more specifically responsive to those contextual aspects associated with greater social constraint, i. e., larger numbers of strangers and increasing time in the situation. Given the previous comments regarding avoidance programs and physiological systems, it is interesting that most of the effects observed here involved skin conductance, which seems associated to a greater degree with non-specific sympathetic arousal, as opposed to heart rate, which may reflect more a specific action disposition. Heart rate change did not differ overall between groups, and effects were observed only within the social phobic group for the new vs. repeated script effects. An expanded set of physiological measures would help to evaluate potential distinctions between avoidance/ escape reactions and non-specific distress or arousal responses, which would be relevant both to differential diagnosis between groups, and to distinctions among patients within current diagnostic groups, e. g., current suggestions that circumscribed speech fear may be a differentiated type of social anxiety.

The Three-Systems Model and Current Research

As mentioned above, outputs in the three response systems of verbal reports, overt behavior, and physiological activity are all seen as integral components of the information structure of fear and other emotions. While the experiments just reviewed provide strong support for the bio-informational theory, the data also continue to indicate the desynchrony of the three response systems. Thus, the verbal reports of all three groups of anxiety disorder patients following phobic imagery are similar in expressing increased arousal and distress, but with marked differences in physiological response (Cook et al., 1988). Such desynchrony is perhaps most remarkable in the current literature with respect to panic disorder patients, whose reports of massive physiological arousal are so extreme. In spite of this, ambulatory monitoring studies indicate that these patients frequently report panic attacks in the absence of palpable physiological activation, or, conversely, exhibit large-magnitude heart rate increases without experiencing panic (Barlow, 1988).

The importance of understanding such lack of covariation, accordingly, indicates that the three-systems model is still highly relevant to current concerns. Indeed, this model has come to occupy such a central place in modern emotion research that it is now virtually an obligatory starting point for any discussion of emotion. The concept, in fact, has even been honored by earning its own place in the jargon of psychological literature, e. g., the "triple response measurement" ("TRM") discussed by Himadi, Boice, and Barlow (1985). In spite of this theoretical cogency, different concerns have arisen in interpreting the outputs in each of these three systems, and some of these issues are considered briefly in the following sections.

Verbal Reports, Phenomenology and Cognition

In behavior therapy research, it is now a commonplace that behavior tends to lead verbal reports in therapeutic progress. Lang and his colleagues may have been one of the first to note this phenomenon, stating in their first paper that "Most frequently subjective report lags behind overt behavior. Thus, avoidance test scores differentiated between experimental and control subjects immediately following the experiment, but it was not until the follow-up interview that the subjective scales yielded the same finding." (Lang et al., 1963, p. 525) Recently, perhaps the best-known discussion of this point is Rachman and Hodgson's more thoroughly elaborated clinical account of desynchrony (1974).

While the basic three-systems concept is thus generally accepted, the nature of verbal reports remains more intensely debated. Although

Lang has written extensively about the problems of regarding verbal reports as a window into the internal world (e. g., Lang, 1979, 1984), a reliance on such an outlook still dominates much of the literature. Basically, "verbal reports" are generally interpreted by investigators in one of two ways. The first considers such reports to be a shorthand way of representing the phenomenological feelings that are assumed to be the core, indeed, the "real" emotion. Thus, "Differential emotions theory holds that anxiety can be analyzed phenomenologically in terms of patterns of emotions and emotion-cognition or affective-cognitive relationships ... a number of investigators with roots in the behavioristic tradition ... focus on response and cognitive characteristics of emotion and deliberately ignore or discount the importance of the feeling states or emotion components of anxiety." (Izard & Blumberg, 1985, pp. 123 & 109) Even writers with strong ties to neuroscience and animal research are swayed by the appeal of subjective states, as in Panksepp's creative article (1982) linking four hypothesized limbic circuits in rats to phenomenological experience in humans.

A second interpretation of verbal reports regards them as the output of "cognitions" that result in or contribute to emotions. For example, "Anxiety disorders are conceptualized as being comprised of three loosely interwoven dimensions, consisting of cognition, behavior and physiology." (Michelson, 1986) In these views, while emotions are also generally viewed as internal feeling states, the primary use of verbal reports in research is to gather information about the appraisal and evaluation operations leading to emotional distress. Thus, a distinction is drawn between cognitive (thinking) and affective (emotion/feeling state) processes. Leading exponents within this general purview include Ellis (1977), Lazarus (1974), and Beck (1985).

Many evaluations have been made of these positions, which do not need to be recapitulated here (e. g., Reisenzein, 1983; Hallam, 1985). Rather, a few comments can be made in the light of the three-systems model. First, an emphasis on the subjective can lead to the use of everyday language words as scientific terms, with resultant potential confusion for theory. For instance, in a recent theoretical account, Barlow (1988) equates panic with fear as an extreme of the "fight or flight" activation seen in moments of extreme distress or danger; anxiety, on the other hand, is regarded as more akin to worry, the chronic, nagging "feelings" of unhappiness and concern. Conversely, Beck considers that "Anxiety may be distinguished from fear in that the former is an emotional process while fear is a cognitive one. Fear involves the intellectual appraisal of a threatening stimulus; anxiety involves the emotional response to that appraisal." (Beck & Emery, 1985, p. 9) Thus, Beck's anxiety would seem more closely related to Barlow's fear. If these are common sense terms understood by everyone, how can two leading writers come up with such disparate definitions – are we to take these differences seriously, or ignore them on the basis that we really know what they are talking about anyway?

Another misleading term involves the basic word "cognition." As used by theorists in the cognitive behavior therapy tradition, cognitions refer to the largely conscious, deliberate thought processes of appraisal and evaluation that individuals go through to decide upon their responses to situations, which are considered separate from affect. On the other hand, theories based in experimental cognitive psychology, such as Lang's, regard all information processing as cognitions – no matter whether the content of such processing would be typically labeled emotional or otherwise. Running madly from a suddenly perceived snake, appraising an approaching stranger as threatening, and mentally computing the square root of 71 are all seen as equally "cognitive," in that they must be accomplished by the processing of appropriate brain programs for each task. As Lang recently pointed out, "Affective networks and their associated productions are not viewed as mechanistically different from other cognitive structures and their behavioural sequelae. Indeed, we can readily subscribe to the view that all contexts and behaviours have some degree of affective tone. Thus, the theory's business is not to define what is and what is not an emotion, but rather to try to explain the cogni-

tive bases of behaviours occurring in situations that the culture holds to be emotional." (1988, p. 423)

This point has been expanded upon ably by Richard Hallam (1985). Following Averill, Sarbin, and others, Hallam emphasizes the "social construction" of anxiety (like other emotions): "Anxiety is an acquired meaning which, I will assume, allows the individual to organise, label and therefore talk about certain kinds of perceptual experience." (p. 164) In brief, Hallam's thesis is that anxiety (like other emotions) is a "multireferential lay construct," i.e., a term in common use in every day language which has multiple internal and external referents for its use. As opposed to other advocates of the social construction position (e.g., see review by Kemper, 1987), Hallam's position seems more reminiscent of Skinner (1953), and explicitly allows for physiological and behavioral activity as part of the reference base for a report of anxiety: "I assume, then, that the appropriate use of the construct of anxiety does not entail the presence of a fixed and invariant set of referents. Whether there is a necessary set must be determined empirically, although it seems likely that there is a modal set, of which some are evaluated as aversive. In its everyday use, anxiety may therefore be regarded as a construct that has both public and private referents." (p. 164)

Thus, given the influence of Lang's theories to date, it will be of some interest from this perspective to observe what transpires with respect to the dominance of phenomenological approaches to emotion and anxiety. Are such discussions only the arcane province of the theoretician? Unfortunately not. The splintering of modern anxiety disorders research (e.g., as reflected in the diversity of approaches in Tuma & Maser, 1985) may well continue as long as the reports of feelings that patients bring to the clinic are regarded as the phenomena nonpareil which must be explained by a theory of emotion.

Behavior

Measures of behavior are in some sense the most objective of the three systems. Behavior is easier to measure and quantify, and lacks the interpretive difficulties of verbal reports and the intensive measurement problems of physiology. Differences in the nature of avoidance behavior may be important for an understanding of various disorders. For instance, Lang et al. (1983) observed that social phobic subjects nearly always completed the speech behavior test, even though their reports of distress in this situation were comparable to those of the phobic situations for snake phobics, who dropped out at a higher rate. Thus, these data may be indicative of a different organization and nature of fear in social vs. specific phobics (Öhman, 1986). Similarly, other data suggest that avoidance in behavior tests with agoraphobics does not strongly predict reports of panic, distress, or outcomes in therapy (Mavissakalian & Hamann, 1986). Thus, while behavior is sometimes seen as the premier, defining measure of a phobia, it is apparent that differences in fear behavior are critical to understanding differences between anxiety disorders.

Physiology

The psychophysiological data reviewed here represent only a tiny fraction of the extant such literature on the anxiety disorders (e. g., see Turpin, 1989). However, recently some investigators have questioned the utility of psychophysiological measurements. These objections seem to take two primary forms. One is the concern that physiological measures, such as heart rate, are not well suited as measures of treatment outcome, due to inconsistency and low agreement with other outcome measures (e. g., Himadi, Boice, & Barlow, 1986; Holden & Barlow, 1985). The other question regards the low reliability of physiological measures, in that test-retest correlations may be rather low

(Arena, Blanchard, Andrasik, Cotch, & Myers, 1983).

Both of these concerns seem to indicate an implicit viewpoint that physiological measures are reflecting an inner state of fear or other emotion. In spite of some discussion about three-systems measurement, the assumption seems to be that physiological measures ought to reflect faithfully some inner state. This view is possibly based in classical psychometric theory, with its emphasis on traits, measurement reliability, and so forth. From the current theoretical viewpoint, however, similar patterns and magnitude of physiological response would only be expected if the same memory structure for a fear is accessed in the same manner on successive occasions. As the above review has shown, this is much more likely to occur for simple phobics than for agoraphobics; thus, the very lack of consistency across occasions may be useful data for the researcher and clinician.

Another important point to bear in mind is that basic psychophysiological principles such as habituation are still operative in the clinical domain, and must be considered. Thus, the extent to which patients and normal controls show the same patterns, such as habituation, is once again a potentially interesting phenomenon; a lack of differences may be as informative as a significant differentiation. Relatedly, the results discussed above indicate that it is imperative to consider the context in which physiology is recorded. For example, lack of difference for snake phobics and socially anxious subjects in the speech behavior test (Lang et al., 1983) is best interpreted as reflecting the metabolic requirements of the task, rather than some indication that snake phobics were exhibiting an otherwise unobserved fear. Thus, in some sense, physiological responses might be considered to be always valid and reliable; it is up to the investigator to understand their meaning as a joint function of context, system, and subject.

Conclusion

The preceding section has attempted to address briefly some of the contemporary issues in anxiety disorders research in the context of the three-systems model. Development of the bioinformational theory, meanwhile, has proceeded concurrently with research in the Lang laboratory. In the latest extension of the model (Lang, Bradley, & Cuthbert, 1990), the emotional memory structures discussed previously are further conceived to be organized around a superordinate biphasic dimension of affective valence, marked by either approach and appetitive behavior (positive valence), or by aversion and withdrawal (negative valence). The primary basis for this work has been a series of studies with the startle reflex, specifically, the eyeblink which results from a sudden, intense noise or light flash. Such stimuli have been presented while subjects are engaged in a task with contents varying along several dimensions of affect, such as watching colored slides or imagining different situations. The blink response can be measured with electrodes placed over the orbicularis muscle, underneath the eye.

As the major findings are discussed in detail elsewhere in this volume (see chapter by Bradley & Vrana), the two major conclusions can be summarized succinctly here. First, the startle reflex becomes larger and faster with increasing aversiveness of the foreground task. Second, this effect does not appear to be due to the arousal or interest value of the material, as indexed by a variety of rating and other physiological measures. This work has important implications for the ongoing program of research in the anxiety disorders. First, it will be of interest to see how the startle reflex is related to phobic material – for instance, whether blink reflexes evoked in the context of phobic objects will be augmented even relative to highly negative, but non-phobic material. A related issue involves possible differences in such blink potentiation across the different anxiety disorders. Thus, while the current developments seem in some ways directed more toward emotion theory in general, an ongoing concern with the anxiety disorders remains in the forefront of the research program.

In conclusion, it has been the aim of this chapter to review the research related to anxiety disorders carried out in Peter Lang's laboratory over the past three decades. In this discussion we have attempted to show how the original three-systems model has been incorporated into subsequent developments in theory and research. Much of Lang's research seems to have involved threes: three systems of emotional response, three kinds of network information, three primary phobia groups. Thus, it is perhaps fitting to mark the span of his research program after three decades of contributions to basic research, clinical understanding, and psychophysiology.

References

Arena, J. G., Blanchard, E. B., Andrasik, F., Cotch, P. A., & Myers, P. E. (1983). Reliability of psychophysiological assessment. *Behavior Research & Therapy, 21,* 447–460.

Barlow, D. H. (1985). The dimensions of anxiety disorders. In A. H. Tuma & J. D. Maser (Eds.), *Anxiety and the anxiety disorders* (pp. 497–500). Hillsdale, NJ: Erlbaum.

Barlow, D. H. (1988). *Anxiety and its disorders: The nature and treatment of anxiety and panic* (pp. 499–532). New York: The Guilford Press.

Beck, A. T. (1985). Theoretical perspectives on clinical anxiety. In A. H. Tuma & J. D. Maser (Eds.), *Anxiety and the anxiety disorders* (pp. 183–198). Hillsdale, NJ: Erlbaum.

Beck, A. T., & Emery, G. (1985). *Anxiety disorders and phobias.* New York: Basic Books, Inc.

Cook, E. W. III, Melamed, B. G., Cuthbert, B. N., McNeil, D. W., & Lang, P.J. (1988). Emotional imagery and the differential diagnosis of anxiety. *Journal of Consulting and Clinical Psychology, 56,* 734–740.

Cuthbert, B. N., & Lang, P. J. (1984). Eye movements in visual imagery. *Psychophysiology, 21,* 574. (Abstract).

Cuthbert, B. N., Bradley, M. M., & Lang, P. J. (1990).

Valence and arousal in startle modulation. *Psychophysiology, 27,* S24. (Abstract)

Cuthbert, B. N., Vrana, S. R., & Bradley, M. M. (1991). Imagery: Function and physiology. In P.J. Ackles, J.R. Jennings, & M. G. Coles (Eds.), *Imagery: Function and physiology* (1–42). London: Jessica Kingsley Publishers.

Ellis, A. (1977). The basic clinical theory of rational-emotive therapy. In A. Ellis & R. Grieger (Eds.), *Handbook of rational-emotive therapy.* New York: Springer.

Hallam, R. S. (1985). *Anxiety: Psychological perspectives on panic and agoraphobia.* London: Academic Press.

Himadi, W. G., Boice, R., & Barlow, D. H. (1985). Assessment of agoraphobia: Triple response measurement. *Behaviour Research & Therapy, 23,* 311–323.

Himadi, W. G., Boice, R., & Barlow, D. H. (1986). Assessment of agoraphobia-II. *Behavior Research & Therapy, 24,* 321–332.

Hirota, A., & Hirai, H. (1986). Effects of stimulus- or response-oriented training on psychophysiological responses and the propositional structure of imagery. *Japanese Psychological Research, 28,* 186–195.

Hodes, R. L., Cook, E. W. III, & Lang, P. J. (1985). Individual differences in autonomic response: Conditioned association or conditioned fear? *Psychophysiology, 22,* 545–560.

Holden, A. E., Jr., & Barlow, D. H. (1986). Heart rate and heart rate variability recorded in vivo in agoraphobics and nonphobics. *Behavior Therapy, 17,* 26–42.

Hugdahl, K. (1981). A three-systems-model of fear and emotion—a critical examination. *Behaviour Research & Therapy, 12,* 319–326.

Izard, C. E., & Blumberg, S. H. (1985). Emotion theory and the role of emotions in anxiety in children and adults. In A. H. Tuma & J. D. Maser (Eds.), *Anxiety and the anxiety disorders* (pp. 109–130). Hillsdale, NJ: Erlbaum.

Johnson-Laird, P.N., Herrmann, D.J., & Chaffin, R. (1984). Only connections: A critique of semantic networks. *Psychological Bulletin, 96,* 292–315.

Jones, J. C., & Barlow, D. H. (1989). An investigation of Lang's bioinformational approach with sexually functional and dysfunctional men. *Journal of Psychopathology and Behavioral Assessment, 11,* 81–97.

Kemper, T. D. (1987). A Manichaean approach to the social construction of emotions. *Cognition and Emotion, 1,* 353–365.

Kozak, M. J., & Miller, G. A. (1982). Hypothetical versus intervening variables: A re-appraisal of the three-systems model of anxiety assessment. *Behavioral Assessment, 4,* 347–358.

Lader, M.H. (1967). Palmar skin conductance measures in anxiety and phobic states. *Journal of Psychosomatic Research, 11,* 271–281.

Lader, M. H., Gelder, M. G., & Marks, I. M. (1967). Palmar skin conductance measures as predictors of response to desensitization. *Journal of Psychosomatic Research, 11,* 283–290.

Lang, P. J. (1968). Fear reduction and fear behavior: Problems in treating a construct. In J. M. Shlien (Ed.), *Research in psychotherapy (Vol. 3).* Washington, DC: American Psychological Association.

Lang, P.J. (1970). Autonomic control or learning to play the internal organs. *Psychology Today,* October, 37–41.

Lang, P. J. (1977). Imagery in therapy: An information processing analysis of fear. *Behavior Therapy, 8,* 862–886.

Lang, P. J. (1978). Anxiety: Toward a psychophysiological definition. In H.S. Akiskal & W. L. Webb (Eds.), *Psychiatric diagnosis: Exploration of biological predictors* (365–389). New York: Spectrum.

Lang, P. J. (1979). A bio-informational theory of emotional imagery. *Psychophysiology, 16,* 495–512.

Lang, P. J. (1984). Cognition in emotion: Concept and action. In C. E. Izard, J. Kagan, & R. B. Zajonc (Eds.), *Emotions, cognitions, and behavior* (pp. 192–228). New York: Cambridge.

Lang, P. J. (1984). Dead souls: Or why the neurobehavioral science of emotion should pay attention to cognitive science. In T. Elbert, B. Rockstroh, W. Lutzenberger, & N. Birbaumer (Eds.), *Self-Regulation of the brain and behavior* (pp. 255–272). New York: Springer-Verlag.

Lang, P. J. (1985). The cognitive psychophysiology of emotion: Fear and anxiety. In A. H. Tuma & J. D. Maser (Eds.), *Anxiety and the anxiety disorders* (pp. 131–170). Hillsdale, NJ: Erlbaum.

Lang, P. J.,Kozak, M.J., Miller, G. A., Levin, D. N., & McLean, Jr., A. (1980). Emotional imagery: Conceptual structure and pattern of somatovisceral response. *Psychophysiology, 17,* 179–192.

Lang, P. J., & Lazovik, A. D. (1963). Experimental desensitization of a phobia. *The Journal of Abnormal and Social Psychology, 66,* 519–525.

Lang, P. J., Bradley, M. M., & Cuthbert, B. N. (1990). Emotion, attention, and the startle reflex. *Psychological Review, 97,* 377–395.

Lang, P. J., Lazovik, A. D., & Reynolds, D. J. (1965). Desensitization, suggestibility and pseudotherapy. *Journal of Abnormal Psychology, 70,* 395–402.

Lang, P. J., Levin, D. N., Miller, G. A., & Kozak, M. J. (1983). Fear imagery and the psychophysiology of emotion: The problem of affective response integration. *Journal of Abnormal Psychology, 92,* 276–306.

Lang, P. J., Melamed, B. G., & Hart, J. (1970). A psychophysiological analysis of fear modification using an automated desensitization procedure. *Journal of Abnormal Psychology, 76,* 220–234.

Lazarus, R. S. (1974). Cognitive and coping processes in emotion. In B. Weiner (Ed.), *Cognitive views of human motivation.* New York: Academic Press.

Mahl, G. F. (1956). Disturbances and silences in the patient's speech and psychotherapy. *Journal Abnormal Social Psychology, 53,* 1–15.

Mavissakalian, M., & Hamann, M. S. (1986). Assessment and significance of behavioral avoidance in agoraphobia. *Journal of Psychopathology and Behavioral Assessment, 8,* 317–327.

McNeil, D. W., Vrana, S. R., Melamed, B. G., Cuthbert, B. N., & Lang, P. J. (in press). Emotional imagery in simple and social phobia: Fear vs. anxiety. *Journal of Abnormal Psychology.*

Melamed, B. G. (1969). The habituation of psychophysiological responses to tones, and to filmed fear stimuli under varying conditions of instructional set. Unpublished doctoral dissertation, University of Wisconsin-Madison.

Michelson, L. (1986). Treatment consonance and response profiles in agoraphobia: The role of individual differences in cognitive, behavioral and physiological treatments. *Behaviour Research & Therapy, 24,* 263–275.

Öhman, A. (1986). Face the beast and fear the face: Animal and social fears as prototypes for evolutionary analyses of emotion. *Psychophysiology, 23,* 123–145.

Panksepp, J. (1982). Toward a general psychobiological theory of emotions. *The Behavioral and Brain Sciences, 5,* 407–422.

Patrick, C. J., Cuthbert, B. N., & Lang, P. J. (1989). Automaticity of emotional processing in anxious and nonanxious patients. *Psychophysiology, 26,* S47. (Abstract).

Pitman, R. K., Orr, S. P., Forgue, D. F., Altman, B., de Jong, J. B., & Herz, L. H. (1990). Psychophysiologic responses to combat imagery of Vietnam veterans with posttraumatic stress disorder versus other anxiety disorders. *Journal of Abnormal Psychology, 99,* 49–54.

Rachman, S., & Hodgson, R. J. (1974). Synchrony and desynchrony in fear and avoidance. *Behavior Research & Therapy, 9,* 231–247.

Reisenzein, R. (1983). The Schachter theory of emotion: Two decades later. *Psychological Bulletin, 94,* 239–264.

Robinson, A., & Reading, C. (1985). Imagery in phobic subjects: A psychophysiological study. *Behaviour Research & Therapy, 23,* 247–253.

Sheehan, P. W. (1967). A shortened form of Betts' questionnaire upon mental imagery. *Journal of Clinical Psychology, 223,* 380–389.

Skinner, B. F. (1953). *Science and human behavior.* New York: Macmillan.

Tuma, A. H., & Maser, J. D. (Eds.). (1985). *Anxiety and the anxiety disorders.* Hillsdale, NJ: Lawrence Erlbaum Associates Publishers.

Turpin, G. (Ed.). (1989). *Handbook of clinical psychophysiology.* Chichester: John Wiley and Sons Ltd.

Watson, D., & Friend, R. (1969). Measurement of social-evaluative anxiety. *Journal of Consulting and Clinical Psychology, 33,* 438–447.

Wolpe, J. (1958). *Psychotherapy by reciprocal inhibition.* Stanford: Stanford University Press.

Wolpe, J., & Lang, P. J. (1964). A fear survey schedule for use in behavior therapy. *Behaviour Research & Therapy, 2,* 27–30.

Zander, J. R., & McNally, R. J. (1988). Bio-informational processing in agoraphobia. *Behaviour Research & Therapy, 26,* 421–429.

Pathological Anxiety:
The Meaning and the Structure of Fear

Edna B. Foa and Michael J. Kozak*

Abstract

In this chapter we argue that anxiety disorders reflect pathological memories, and that meaning is an important aspect of such memories. We review several lines of evidence relevant to the representation and processing of threat-related information in fear structures. It is argued that anxiety disorders can be distinguished with respect to the specific threat material, and that individuals with an anxiety disorder show selective processing of threat material associated with their disorder. Finally, we consider possible mechanisms for modifying meaning in fear structures, including representations of the probability of harm and of negative valence.

Key words: anxiety, fear structure, meaning

Peter Lang's thinking has influenced many areas of psychology. His contributions in the field of anxiety and its therapeutic modification include studies of desensitization, autonomic self-regulation, and the psychophysiology of emotion. In the present chapter, we will focus on the impact of Lang's writings on current theory of pathological anxiety and its treatment. We will summarize Lang's theoretical work on imagery and emotion, review recent ideas of emotional processing, and consider clinical research that is either guided by these theories or is pertinent to it.

Inspired by the outcome research which demonstrated the efficacy of treatment by imaginal confrontation with feared situations (systematic desensitization, flooding), Lang and his colleagues (Lang, Melamed, & Hart, 1970) have pursued a line of research directed at understanding the role of imagery in therapy. Out of the early research which was designed to demonstrate the essential contribution of imagery

procedures themselves in fear reduction grew an interest in the theoretical underpinnings of imagery effects. An account of these effects was propounded in a paper on "Imagery in Therapy: An Information Processing Analysis of Fear" (Lang, 1977).

In this paper, Lang analyzed fear imagery from the perspectives of information processing theory and psychophysiology. He conceptualized fear as represented by information structures in memory. Adopting Pylyshyn's (1973) construal of a propositional network as an organization of concepts related to one another by other concepts, Lang (1977) suggested an analysis of the fear structure into propositions. Accordingly, fear is represented as a cognitive schema that includes propositions about the feared stimulus situation as well as about verbal, physiological, and overt behavioral responses. Such schemata are stored in long-term memory and can be viewed as programs for escape or avoidance.

---

*   Medical College of Pennsylvania

The Concept of Meaning in Fear Structures

In his paper, "A Bioinformational Theory of Emotional Imagery," Lang (1979) expanded the imagery construct to include semantically coded propositions about stimulus events, e. g., "snakes are dangerous." This addition enriched the theory to allow its broader application. Foa and Kozak (1985) extended the concept of meaning to include semantically and non-semantically coded information about stimuli, responses and their relationships. In that paper, we proposed that if the fear structure is indeed a program to escape danger, it must involve information that stimuli and/or responses are dangerous, as well as information about physiological activity preparatory for escape. Thus, a fear structure is distinguished from other information structures not only by response elements but also by certain meaning information it contains. For example, the programs for running ahead of a baton-carrying competitor in a race and for running ahead of a club-carrying assailant on a racetrack are likely to involve similar stimulus and response information. That which distinguishes the fear structure is the meaning of the stimuli and responses: Only the fear structure involves escape from threat.

Our position certainly does not imply that a fear structure is entirely available to consciousness. Although certain aspects may be identified through introspection, ample evidence (cf. Van Den Berg & Eelen, 1985) suggests that associations among stimuli, responses, and their meanings can exist in the absence of conscious knowledge about them. Just as a person may be unaware of some response information in a fear structure (e. g., information that underlies increased blood pressure), they also may be unaware of the meaning of those responses. This is not to say that people are always unaware of meanings associated with stimuli and responses, for they can indeed report beliefs and evaluations that reflect elements in their fear structures. Because of people's imperfect knowledge about their fear structures, non-introspective assessment of these structures is also desirable. In addition to recorded physiology, nonverbal behavior such as facial expressions, postural adjustments, overt actions, and so on would also be expected to reflect some elements. Any of these data can provide a basis for hypotheses about the elements of a fear structure and the relations among them.

Some but not all elements of an emotional memory are accessible by introspection. Therefore, theories of emotions must take into account what people tell us about their emotions, but these reports must be treated with caution. Two types of errors in conceptualizing introspective data can arise. One extreme is to ignore the inherent meaning of people's interpretation of their experiences, or to reject, *a priori*, their validity. Researchers who hold this position usually allow that self-reports could evidence some hypothetical construct but that the reports themselves have no content validity. At the other extreme, the content validity of subjective reports is taken for granted and becomes the basis for theories of emotion.

Meaning and Pathological Anxiety

Foa and Kozak's expanded notion of meaning in the fear structure allowed some understanding of the pathology of anxiety disorders and their reduction. Because distinctions between normal and pathological anxiety often depend on the interpretive meaning attached to feared events, a developed concept of meaning is important for understanding such distinctions. In addition, the differences among differ-ent anxiety disorders are often founded in differences in relationships among stimuli, responses and their meanings. Fear is considered to be pathological when it is disruptively intense and persists despite available information that it is unrealistic. A fear is considered to be unrealistic when its underlying memory structure contains stimulus-stimulus (S-S) associations which do not accurately represent relationships in the world. For example, for many obsessive-compulsive washers, floors are strongly associated with feces (and therefore are highly contaminated), whereas in reality, feces are rarely encountered on floors. Any associations between harmless stimuli and responses (S-R) preparatory to escape or avoidance are also disordered: escape from floors does not enhance an organism's survivability. Embedded in these disordered S-S and S-R associations is some of the erroneous meaning of the pathological fear structure.

Unrealistic meaning can also be coded semantically in the pathological structure. For example, anxiety-disordered individuals are reluctant to engage in fear-provoking experiences because of their evaluation that anxiety will persist until they escape. Also, the fear stimuli and/or responses can be estimated to have an unrealistically high potential for causing psychological (e. g., going crazy, losing control) or physical (e. g., dying, being ill) harm. In addition, the anticipated consequences often have a relatively high negative valence, i.e., are extremely aversive for the anxiety-disordered individual.

The anxiety disorders can be viewed as representing distinct fear structures. For example, the presence of a relationship between certain situations and fear responses in panicky agoraphobics and animal phobics indicates a pathological link among stimulus and response elements of their underlying fear structures. However, what distinguishes the agoraphobic structure from that of simple phobia and other anxiety disorders is erroneous meaning associated with the fear responses. Agoraphobics commonly perceive anxiety itself to be dangerous, rather than stimulus elements (e. g., supermarkets). In contrast, for animal phobics, the potential harm does stem from the stimulus situation (e. g., snakes, wasps, dogs).

Experimental Evidence for Pathological Fear Structures

Lang (1968) proposed that fear is best assessed multi-dimensionally. Influenced by this view, research on anxiety disorders has used multiple methods of assessment as converging measures of a hypothesized structure. Traditionally, psychophysiological measurement constituted one such assessment. More recently, the methods of cognitive experimental psychology have been used to understand the role of semantic meaning in anxiety disorders. Of course, behavior such as facial expressions, postural adjustments, overt actions, and so on would also be expected to reflect some elements. Any of these data can complement subjective reports as bases for hypotheses about emotional structures.

Threat Information in Fear Structures

Using a self-report method, Dattilio and Foa (1987) studied whether interoceptive responses are interpreted as dangerous by individuals with: specific phobias, generalized anxiety disorder, and panic disorder. Their interpretations were compared to one another and to those of non-anxious individuals. All received questionnaires assessing fear of fear (Chambless, Caputo, Bright, & Gallagher, 1984; Reiss, Peterson, Gursky, & McNally, 1986). A consistent picture emerged for all these measures: panic-disordered patients showed stronger response-danger associations than the other groups. Moreover, they overestimated the probabilities that feared interoceptive responses would occur, compared to the other groups but they did not overestimate the likelihood of general fear events. The same pattern emerged for ratings of valence: panic-disordered individuals rated feared interoceptive responses as more aversive than did the other groups, but general fear items were rated similarly by all groups.

Further support for the hypothesis that agoraphobics, but not simple phobics, show especially strong associations between interoceptive responses and danger comes from a psychophysiological study of imagery (Mansueto, Grayson, & Foa, 1987). Subjects were presented with four types of scenes: 1) external fear stimuli, 2) interoceptive fear responses,

3) stimulus plus response scenes, and 4) neutral (non-fear) stimuli. Self-report, skin conductance spontaneous fluctuations (SF), and heart rate (HR) were used to assess fear. Agoraphobics reported greater fear and had more SF's and higher HR's while imagining external, interoceptive, and combined scenes than when imagining neutral material. In contrast, simple phobics showed this response pattern only while imagining external and combined material, but not interoceptive material. These psychophysiological results converge with the questionnaire data of Dattilio and Foa (1987) to suggest that agoraphobic fear structures, unlike those for simple phobias, include the particular interpretive meaning that interoceptive responses are dangerous. This convergence of introspective and physiological data indicates that people's beliefs about the nature of their fears reflect elements of their fear structures.

Additional evidence for particular response-threat associations in the fear structures of agoraphobics emerges from a study comparing nine normal controls and nine untreated agoraphobics with nine agoraphobics who had been successfully treated via exposure and anxiety management techniques (McNally & Foa, 1987). All three groups received questionnaires with items pertaining to fear of interoceptive cues and the harm anticipated from them, as well as items about general fear situations that might also disturb non-anxiety-disordered individuals. The questionnaires were the same as those used by Dattilio and Foa (1987) above, and the results of the two studies were consistent. Untreated agoraphobics scored higher than normals when asked to estimate the probability and cost of interoceptive cues, but not of external fear situations. Also, as in the other study, when asked to consider scenarios describing either interoceptive responses or external stimuli, this group interpreted both types as more threatening than did normals. Interestingly, the treated agoraphobics did not differ from normals on any of the measures. These results not only evidenced a connection between symptoms and interpretive meaning in the hypothesized agoraphobic fear structure, but also suggested that change in the fear structure may underlie therapy outcome.

Selective Processing of Threat Information

Another method of assessing a fear structure is to examine selective processing of threat-information in anxiety-disordered individuals. Clinical observations of anxiety-disordered patients give rise to two hypotheses about the selective processing of threat information which is represented as a fear structure. The tendency of anxious patients to fearful avoidance suggests that the presentation of threat information may elicit defensive responses which are characterized by certain physiological response patterns and by information "rejection" (Graham, 1979). Cognitive resources recruited for such defensive responses may compete for capacity needed for other tasks, and this competition will interfere with performance.

Findings from perceptual threshold experiments seem to lend credence to the defensive response hypothesis (for review, see Dixon, 1981). In contrast, the finding that anxious patient orient *towards* threat information in a visual probe paradigm (MacLeod, Mathews, & Tata, 1986) seems to contradict this account. The MacLeod et al. (1986) finding points to an alternative explanation, namely that anxiety-disordered individuals have attentional bias toward threat stimuli (Williams, Watts, MacLeod, & Mathews, 1988). Accordingly, anxious individuals will evidence extra-sensitivity to threat information. i. e., they will show orienting, rather than defensive responses to such information.

If there is indeed selective processing of threat information, then paradigms that detect selective processing can reveal what is threatening for an individual and thus provide a way of examining the meaning elements of a fear structure.

Dichotic Listening Paradigm. Evidence for extra sensitivity of anxiety-disordered individuals to fear-relevant stimuli comes from experiments using dichotic listening paradigms. Typically, this experimental procedure involves presenting a subject simultaneously with two messages, one to each ear, and instructing the subject to repeat aloud the words presented to the dominant ear. Subjects can readily detect words in the attended but not in the unattended channel, unless the words are of particular significance. It is expected that "threat" words have special significance and would be detected in the unattended channel more readily than neutral words. Two studies using the dichotic listening paradigm illustrate how anxiety-disordered individuals show hypersensitivity to threat words related to their disorder.

Burgess, Jones, Robertson, Radcliffe, and Emerson (1981) compared agoraphobics, social phobics, and non-fearful controls using a dichotic listening task. It was hypothesized that in the unattended channel, phobics, but not controls, would detect critical words reflecting their fears (e. g., shopping alone, failure) more easily than neutral words (i.e., pick). As expected, no differences between phobics and controls were found in detecting target words in the attended passage. In contrast, phobics, but not controls, detected significantly more fear-relevant than neutral words in the unattended channel. These data suggest that individuals with anxiety disorders are more attentive to fear-relevant material.

The interpretation of these results is difficult because the fear-relevant stimuli were words that were likely to be used more frequently by patients than by controls. Foa and McNally (1986) noted that the increased attention to fear-relevant stimuli may reflect a greater familiarity with such material rather than its greater emotional salience.

To examine the fear versus familiarity issue, Foa and McNally (1986) repeated Burgess et al.'s study with obsessive-compulsive patients before and after three weeks of exposure and response prevention treatment. They hypothesized that if sensitivity to fear-relevant words is due to their emotional salience, it should *decrease* after treatment that was directed at reducing the specific fear associated with the words. Conversely, if the bias is due to familiarity, it should *increase* after treatment during which the specific fear material was continually discussed.

The results supported a fearfulness interpretation: patients detected more fear-relevant than neutral words in the unattended passage

before, but not after, treatment. Moreover, fear-relevant words produced larger skin conductance responses (SCRs) than did the neutral words prior to, but not following, behavior therapy. Such responses were repeatedly found to be associated with anxiety (Kozak, Foa, & Steketee, 1988; Rabavilas, Boulougouris, & Stefanis, 1977).

A subsequent study (Foa, Rowan, Krajnak, & Riggs, 1990) with obsessive-compulsives did not reveal hypersensitivity to fear-relevant words in the dichotic listening paradigm. A potentially important difference between the experiments is that fear-word length was shorter in this last study than in the earlier studies which demonstrated hypersensitivity. Notably, skin conductance magnitude was larger for fear than for neutral words in the attended channel only. This suggests that semantic discrimination between fear and neutral words occurred only in the attended channel. Perhaps there is a word-length threshold below which even fear-relevant words are not semantically processed if unattended, and that the short word-lengths of this study fell below the threshold.

This "threshold hypothesis" points to a more general methodological issue to be considered in evaluating the results of experiments which compare performance on different tasks such as the dichotic listening paradigm. If one task has greater discriminating power than another, performance differences may be attributable to differences in discriminative power rather than to some characteristics of the subjects (Chapman & Chapman, 1973). In the dichotic listening paradigm described above, subjects had two tasks: detecting neutral words and detecting fear words. The Burgess et al. (1981) finding that anxious subjects detected more fear words than neutral words whereas controls failed to do so may have been due to the greater discriminating power of the fear word task rather than to emotional content. For the results to be unambiguous, the neutral word should have been of equal length to that of the fear word. It is plausible that anxious subjects are *generally* more sensitive than non-anxious subjects and that with equally discriminating tasks, the anxious subjects would have been found to detect more fear words as well as more neutral words.

Stroop Interference Paradigm. Another paradigm that has been invoked to examine selective processing of threat information is the modified Stroop. The original Stroop task (Stroop, 1935) involved presenting subjects with either color words or meaningless stimuli; both were presented in different colors. Subjects were asked to name the color of the ink and to ignore the content of the words. Typically, color-naming time was faster for meaningless stimuli than for the words, suggesting interference of the meaning of the word with the task performance.

More recently, investigators have modified the Stroop (Ray, 1979) by substituting threat and neutral words for color words and requesting the subject to name the color of the ink. It is hypothesized that anxiety-disordered individuals who have pathological fear structures will be more attentive to threat words than to neutral words. This selective attention will interfere with color-naming and yield longer reaction times for color-naming of threat words than of neutral words.

Indeed, Watts, McKenna, Sharrock, and Trezise (1986) found longer reaction time for color-naming of spider words than for neutral words in spider phobics but not in normal controls. These results are subject to interpretations other than that fear accounts for performance differences. There is evidence to suggest that familiarity enhances interference (Warren, 1974). Perhaps phobics are more familiar with fear-relevant material than non-phobics. If familiarity accounts for performance interference then subjects who had similar experiences with the fear-relevant material will show equivalent performance. Rape victims provide an opportunity to study this issue because although all have been assaulted, not all develop chronic PTSD.

To examine this question, Foa, Feske, Murdock, Kozak, and McCarthy (1990) used the modified Stroop task to compare rape victims with and without PTSD and non-traumatized controls. Rape victims with PTSD showed longer color-naming latencies for rape-related words than for general threat words, neutral words, and non-words. Non-PTSD victims and non-victims had no performance differences

across words. These results indicate that fear, rather than familiarity, underlies the differential performance.

Mechanisms of Stroop Interference. How does fear interfere with color-naming of fear words? One hypothesis is that most anxiety-disordered individuals are *generally* anxious, and that anxiety may have interfered with performance on the Stroop task. It is well known that high anxiety interferes with information processing (Spielberger, 1966). Indeed, the PTSD victims in the Foa et al. study were more anxious and depressed than non-PTSD victims and controls. The general anxiety hypothesis predicts a general interference with color-naming, but such interference was found only for words matching the specific fear of the individual (e. g., spiders, rape) and not for general threat or neutral words. Therefore, general anxiety cannot account for the interference of specific threat words with the reactions of anxiety-disordered individuals.

Another explanation for Stroop interference is that 1) threat words specifically related to a given anxiety disorder are especially meaningful to the individuals who manifest that disorder, and that 2) more meaningful words cause more interference. Support for this explanation is found in results demonstrating that *any* common word produces more Stroop interference than does a row of X's (Klein, 1964). Furthermore, words associated with color (e. g., sky, grass) produced more interference with color-naming than did words unassociated with colors (Scheibe, Shaver, & Carrier, 1967), and interference is especially pronounced with antagonistic color names (Stroop, 1935). These results suggest the importance of the meaning of the stimulus for Stroop performance. If meaning is a mediator of Stroop interference and fear words interfere more than non-fear words, fear words may be more meaningful than non-fear words.

How does meaning mediate Stroop interference? Two approaches to understanding meaningfulness of a word can be considered: elaboration (complexity) of the cognitive schema associated with the word, and valence of the word.

The elaboration approach proposes that the meaning of a word is reflected in the number and pattern of associations representing that word, such that more meaning entails more associations. Accordingly, a more meaningful word in the Stroop task would evoke a more elaborate memory structure, and thus use more processing capacity. Interference would then occur because less capacity is available for the primary task of color-naming. Perhaps because of extensive experience with feared situations or extensive imaginal elaboration of fearful ideas, fear concepts are more elaborate than non-fear concepts, and this enhanced elaboration, in turn, accounts for the interference effects of fear words.

Support for the elaboration hypothesis comes from an experiment which manipulated the complexity of non-fear words before they were used for the Stroop (Hasher, 1990). Just prior to a Stroop task, some words were introduced in the context of sentences, and other words were introduced individually. More color-naming interference was later found for words previously presented in sentences, suggesting that context-related elaboration mediated the interference effects.

Evidence that the interference effect of fear words is *not* mediated by complexity alone comes from several sources. First, although only PTSD rape victims show Stroop interference to rape words, victims both with and without PTSD often describe elaborate memories of the rape. In fact, victims with PTSD seem to have greater difficulty recounting details of rape than non-PTSD victims. Second, as we have noted, Stroop interference has been found to be specific to the fear of the individual. However, Watts et al. (1990) have found that spider phobics recall fewer spider-related words than neutral words, compared to non-phobics. A similar finding was reported with speech phobics by Foa, McNally, and Murdock (1989). These results suggest that anxiety-disordered individuals may access fear memories with impoverished complexity of stimulus detail. It follows that the Stroop interference produced by fear words cannot be attributed simply to the enhanced elaboration of stimulus associations in a fear structure.

The foregoing discussion addressed complexity of *stimulus* details of a cognitive structure. Response propositions could also contribute to complexity, and thus may account for how meaning mediates Stroop interference. Whereas phobics may have difficulty accessing the stimulus details of fearful memories, they seem to access response propositions quite readily. Confrontation with feared objects or situations, either imaginally or *in vivo*, is well known to evoke palpable autonomic reactions in anxiety-disordered individuals (e. g., Lang et al., 1970; Boulougouris, Rabavilas, & Stefanis, 1977; Kozak et al., 1988). Moreover, fear imagery scripts which include certain response propositions are especially evocative of fear responses (Lang, Kozak, Miller, Levin, & McLean, 1980). These results suggest that despite an impoverished stimulus structure, a richly elaborated response structure for fear words could still occupy more available processing capacity than would neutral words, thus producing Stroop interference effects. Direct psychophysiological evidence that single fear words presented in the Stroop paradigm evoke an autonomic response is not available. However, indirect evidence comes from findings by McNally and Foa (1986) that skin conductance responding was larger for single fear words in a dichotic listening experiment.

If the elaborate response structure of fear material mediates color-naming interference, then one might expect that *any* emotional material, because of its elaborate response structure, would produce such interference. That is, both positive and negative affective content should produce this effect. Indeed, Martin, Williams, and Clark (1988) studying patients with generalized anxiety disorder, found greater Stroop interference for both positive *and* negative affective words than for neutral words. On the other hand, McNally, Kaspi, Riemann, and Zeitlin (1990) found that Vietnam veterans with PTSD showed greater interference from combat words than from words with positive affective content. Moreover, non-PTSD combat veterans showed no interference from threat words or positive words. In another study, Stroop interference was found for threat words, but not pleasant words, in a group of high trait anxious subjects (Richards & Millwood, 1989). These three studies lead to no clear conclusion about whether positive and negative content causes equivalent interference in the Stroop task. These equivocal results on the effects of positive affective content, taken together with the robust finding that specific threat words do cause interference, suggest that specific threat is an important mediator of interference.

In summary, evidence from different experimental paradigms converges to indicate that individuals who manifest specific fears show differential processing of fear-relevant material. We propose that threat meaning elements of a fear structure underlie both the fear symptoms and the selective processing in anxiety-disordered individuals.

Modifying the Fear Structure

It has been argued that anxiety disorders are founded in pathological fear structures. It follows that successful therapy requires modification of such structures. Elsewhere, we have proposed that regardless of the type of therapy selected, two conditions are required for the reduction of fear (cf. Foa & Kozak, 1986). First, fear-relevant information must be made available in a manner that will activate the fear memory. Accordingly, as suggested by Lang (1977), if the fear structure remains in storage but unaccessed, it will not be available for modification. Next, information made available must include elements that are incompatible with pathological elements of the fear structure, so that a new memory can be formed. This new information must be integrated into the evoked fear structure for an emotional change to occur. This change in the fear structure constitutes emotional processing.

We have identified three indicators of emotional processing which are associated with successful outcome of exposure treatment for anxiety. First, patients who improve with therapy show physiological responses and self-reports of fear that evidence activation of anxiety. Second, their reactions decrease gradually during confrontation with feared situations. Third, initial reactions to the fear decrease at successive confrontations. Support for the validity of these indicators comes from clinical outcome studies and experiments that have been reviewed by Foa and Kozak (1986). Recent data further buttress the argument for their validity.

Kozak, Foa, and Steketee (1988) explored the relationship between the three indicators and therapy outcome with obsessive-compulsives who were treated by exposure and response prevention. Treatment outcome was evaluated via ratings of target symptoms by the therapist, patient, and independent assessor. Processes during therapy were assessed through self-report of anxiety as well as by cardiac and electrodermal responses. The first indicator, activation of anxiety, was evident in both self-report and physiological measures during exposure sessions and predicted posttreatment improvement. As expected, treatment was successful overall, and the second indicator, habituation within sessions, was also evident in both self-report and physiology for the group as a whole. This indicator did not, however, predict individual differences in outcome, perhaps because most patients habituated within sessions. The third indicator, habituation across sessions, was found for the group only in self-report, but individual differences on this indicator (both heart rate and self-report) predicted outcome. In summary, the three hypothesized indicators of emotional processing were evidenced either by the group means or the correlations. The association among successful outcome and the three indicators supports our claim that these indicators reflect mechanisms of emotional processing.

The above results converge with those of another investigation of the process and outcome of therapy (Schwartz & Kaloupek, 1987) in which speech-anxious volunteers were treated with imaginal exposure. Outcome was evaluated by self-report, observations of speech performance, and cardiac and electrodermal activity. Process of therapy was assessed by self-report and physiological measures during imaginal exposure sessions. Greater responding and greater habituation within and/or between sessions predicted better outcome of therapy.

Mechanisms for Emotional Processing

As noted earlier, we have embraced Lang's view that fear is represented as a propositional network in memory which serves as a program for fear behavior. Pathological fear, we suggested, includes erroneous elements and/or associations among elements, such that change in the pathological network is the target of psychotherapy for anxiety disorders. Such change, which we have called emotional processing, requires the integration of information which is incompatible with the pathological elements of the structure. If we hypothesize that psychotherapy of fear promotes structural changes, we must specify what cognitive representations must be changed, that is, what needs to be learned.

Dissociation of Response Elements

We propose that pathological fear structures are characterized by stimulus-response associations in which the responses preparatory to escape or avoidance are unwarranted by the context. Exposure leads to physiological habituation within sessions which involves decreases in such preparatory responding. The absence of this responding in the fear context constitutes information that is incompatible with the existing structure, thereby weakening the pre-existing links between stimulus and response elements. Disordered response-response associations, as found in panic disorders, are also hypothesized to succumb to habituation.

Meaning

In addition to promoting changes in the S-S and S-R links of a fear memory via short-term physiological habituation, harmless confrontation with a feared situation also changes both semantic and non-semantic aspects of meaning. Such changes involve a reduction in the exaggerated probability associated with the feared harm and/or a change in the representation of its valence.

Reduction in probability of harm might occur in two ways. One obvious process is incorporation of new contingencies, e. g., a barking puppy dog on one's lap is not followed by painful bites, and thus, the association between bites and dogs is weakened. This type of change can be construed as weakening of S-S associations. Another way of modifying semantic representations of probability is via their replacement with incompatible content. For example, the instruction that AIDS cannot be communicated through handshakes changes the perceived probability of contracting AIDS, given handshaking. Perhaps weakening of S-S associations requires neither conscious awareness nor language, whereas modification of semantic representations of probability may require both.

Just as with probability, modification of negative valence might occur in two ways: weakening of S-S or S-R associations and changing semantic representations. In the case of harmless exposure to a dog, the weakened association between dog and biting from the dog also decreases negative valence: dogs are unlikely to bite, dogs are not bad. Likewise, habituation of fear responses results in weakening associations between fear stimuli and responses. The power of the stimulus to evoke the responses decreases. If the fear responses themselves are aversive, then their dissociation from the stimulus renders it less negatively valent. From these two examples, it is apparent that although probability of harm and valence are conceptually distinct, in practice they seem to covary with changes in strength of S-S and S-R associations. Such covariance may not occur when either valence or probability is modified semantically, by direct instruction or through observation. For example, the negative valence of contracting syphilis remains high even with the instruction that it is not contracted from toilet seats: the likelihood of syphilis changes but not the valence. Conversely, when one is instructed that syphilis is readily cured, the disease becomes less negative regardless of its probability of occurrence.

Indirect support for the notion that meaning also changes through unconscious S-S weakening comes from experiments on extinction of generalization gradients in aversive conditioning (Hoffman & Fleshler, 1961). Pigeons received shocks signalled by 1000 Hz tones and the generalization of extinction to different tones was then tested. Extinction was minimal to the original tone but increased gradually as the test tones grew less similar to the 1000 Hz CS. This sharpening gradient of extinction developed without either previous or concurrent differential reinforcement. This paradigm can be interpreted as analogous to exposure therapy procedures in which a feared stimulus is presented repeatedly. Accordingly, associated fear stimuli would be expected to lose potency more readily than the target stimulus itself.

Evidence supporting our suggestion that successful therapy changes the meaning of a feared situation comes from the earlier described experiment by Watts et al. (1986). Stroop interference for spider words was found in spider phobics before, but not after, desensitization. Similarly, Foa and McNally (1986) found that the hypersensitivity of obsessive-compulsives to their fear words in a dichotic listening procedure, disappeared after therapy. These results converge with those of McNally and Foa (1987) described earlier, in which untreated agoraphobics rated interoceptive sensations as more negatively valent and more likely than did treated agoraphobics, who did not differ from normals in their ratings.

Conclusion

We have argued here that anxiety disorders reflect pathological memory, and emphasized meaning as an important aspect of such memories. The evidence reviewed suggests that meaning must be considered in understanding fear. However, more experimental data on the relationship between change in meaning and fear reduction is needed, and a satisfactory information processing account of this relationship must be advanced. Lang's bioinformational theory might provide a foundation upon which such an account of meaning can be developed.

References

Boulougouris, J. C., Rabavilas, A. D., & Stefanis, C. (1977). Psycho-physiological responses in obsessive-compulsive patients. *Behaviour Research and Therapy, 15*, 221–230.

Burgess, I. S., Jones, L. M., Robertson, S. H., Radcliffe, W. N., & Emerson, E. (1981). The degree of control exerted by phobic and non-phobic verbal stimuli over the recognition behavior of phobic and non-phobic subjects. *Behaviour Research and Therapy, 19*, 233–243.

Chambless, D. L., Caputo, G. C., Bright, P., & Gallagher, R. (1984). Assessment of fear of fear in agoraphobics: The body sensations questionnaire and the agoraphobic cognitions questionnaire. *Journal of Consulting and Clinical Psychology, 52*, 1090–1097.

Chapman, L. J. & Chapman, J. P. (1973). Problems in the measurement of cognitive deficit. *Psychological Bulletin, 79*, 380–385.

Dattilio, F. M. & Foa, E. B. (1987). Fear of fear: A comparison of generalized anxiety disorder, panic disorder with and without agoraphobia, and simple phobia. Unpublished manuscript.

Dixon, N. F. (1981). *Preconscious processing.* London: Wiley. Foa, E. B., Feske, U., Murdock, T. B., Kozak, M. J., & McCarthy, P. R. (1990). Processing of threat-related information in rape victims. (Unpublished manuscript).

Foa, E. B. & Kozak, M. J. (1985). Treatment of anxiety disorders: Implications for psychopathology. In A. H. Tuma & J. D. Maser (Eds.), *Anxiety and the Anxiety Disorders*. Hillsdale, NJ: Lawrence Erlbaum Associates.

Foa, E. B. & Kozak, M. J. (1986). Emotional processing of fear: Exposure to corrective information. *Psychological Bulletin, 99*, 20–35.

Foa, E. B. & McNally, R.J. (1986). Sensitivity to feared stimuli in obsessive-compulsives: A dichotic listening analysis. *Cognitive Therapy and Research, 10*, 477–485.

Foa, E. B., McNally, R., & Murdock, T. B. (1989). Anxious mood and memory. *Behaviour Research and Therapy, 27*, 141–147.

Foa, E. B., Rowan, V. C., Krajnak, K., & Riggs, D. (1990). A dichotic listening analysis of sensitivity to fear relevant stimuli: A failure to replicate. (Unpublished manuscript).

Graham, F. K. (1979). Distinguishing among orienting, defense, and startle reflexes. In H. D. Kimmel, E. H. Van Olst, & J. F. Orlebeke (Eds.), *The orienting reflex in humans*. New Jersey: Lawrence Erlbaum, pp. 137–167.

Hasher, L. (1990). Personal communication.

Hoffman, H. S. & Fleshler, M. (1961). Stimulus factors in aversive control: The generalization of conditioned suppression. *Journal of the Experimental Analysis of Behavior, 4*, 374.

Klein, D. F. (1964). Delineation of two drug-responsive anxiety syndromes. *Psychopharmacology, 5*, 397–408.

Kozak, M. J., Foa, E. B., & Steketee, G. (1988). Process and outcome of exposure treatment with obsessive-compulsives: Psychophysiological indicators of emotional processing. *Behavior Therapy, 19*, 157–169.

Lang, P. J. (1968). Fear reduction and fear behaviors: Problems in treating a construct. In J. M. Schlien (Ed.), *Research in Psychotherapy: Vol. 3*. Washington, D.C.: American Psychological Association, pp. 90–103.

Lang, P.J. (1977). Imagery in therapy: An information processing analysis of fear. *Behavior Therapy, 8*, 862–886.

Lang, P. J. (1979). A bio-informational theory of emotional imagery. *Psychophysiology, 6*, 495–511.

Lang, P. J., Kozak, M. J., Miller, G. A., Levin, D. N., & McLean, A. (1980). Emotional imagery: Conceptual structure and pattern of somatic-visceral response. *Psychophysiology, 17*, 179–192.

Lang, P., Melamed, B., & Hart, J.D. (1970). A psychophysiological analysis of fear modification using automated desensitization. *Journal of Abnormal Psychology, 31*, 220–234.

MacLeod, C., Mathews, A., & Tata, P. (1986). Attentional bias in emotional disorders. *Journal of Abnormal Psychology, 95*, 15–20.

Mansueto, C. S., Grayson, J. B., & Foa, E. B. (1987). Assessment of the "fear of fear" component in agoraphobic versus specific phobic patients. (Unpublished manuscript).

Martin, M., Williams, R., & Clark, D. M. (1988). Does anxiety lead to selective processing of threat-related information? Paper presented at the World Congress of Behaviour Therapy, Edinburgh.

McNally, R. J. & Foa, E. B. (1986). Preparedness and resistance to extinction to fear-relevant stimuli: A failure to replicate. *Behaviour Research and Therapy, 24*, 529–535.

McNally, R. J. & Foa, E. B. (1987). Cognition and Agoraphobia: Bias in the interpretation of threat. *Cognitive Therapy and Research, 11*, 567–588.

McNally, R. J., Kaspi, S. P., Riemann, B. C., & Zeitlin, S. B. (1990). Selective processing of threat cues in post-traumatic stress disorder. *Journal of Abnormal Psychology, 99*, 398–402.

Pylyshyn, Z. W. (1973). What the mind's eye tells the mind's brain: A critique of mental imagery. *Psychological Bulletin, 80*, 1–22.

Rabavilas, A. D., Boulougouris, J. C., & Stefanis, C. (1977). Compulsive checking diminished when over-checking instructions were disobeyed. *Journal of Behavior Therapy and Experimental Psychiatry, 8*, 111–112.

Ray, C. (1979). Examination stress and performance on a colour word interference test. *Perception and Motor Skills, 49*, 400–402.

Reiss, S., Peterson, R., Gursky, D., & McNally, R. (1986). Anxiety sensitivity, anxiety frequency, and the prediction of fearfulness. *Behaviour Research and Therapy, 24*, 1–8.

Richards, A. & Millwood, B. (1989). Colour-identification of differentially valenced words in anxiety. *Cognitive Emotion, 3*, 171–176.

Scheibe, K. E., Shaver, P. R., & Carrier, S. C. (1967). Colour association values and response interference on variants of the Stroop test. *Acta. Psychol., 26*, 286–295.

Schwartz, S. C. & Kaloupek, D. G. (1987). Acute exercise combined with imaginal exposure as a technique for anxiety reduction. *Canadian Journal of Behavioral Science, 19*, 151–166.

Spielberger, C. D. (1966) (Ed.). The effects of anxiety on complex learning and academic achievement.

In *Anxiety and behavior*. New York: Academic Press.

Stroop, J. R. (1935). Studies of interference in serial verbal reactions. *Journal of Experimental Psychology, 18*, 643–662.

Van den Berg, O. & Eelen, P. (1985). *Unconscious processing and emotions*. Unpublished manuscript, University of Leuven, Department of Psychology, Belgium.

Warren, R. E. (1974). Association, directionality and stimulus encoding. *Journal of Experimental Psychology, 102*, 151–158.

Watts, F. N. et al. (1990). Memory for phobia-related words in spider phobics. Unpublished manuscript.

Watts, F. N., McKenna, F. P., Sharrock, R., & Trezise, L. (1986). Colour naming of phobia-related words. *British Journal of Psychology, 77*, 97–108.

Williams, J., Watts, F., MacLeod, C., & Mathews, A. (1988). *Cognitive Psychology and Emotional Disorders*. Chichester, England: Wiley.

Imagery and Brain Processes

N. Birbaumer, W. Lutzenberger, T. Elbert, H. Flor and B. Rockstroh*

Abstract

This chapter presents a Hebbian view of brain processes related to imagery. It continues with an investigation of the possible neurophysiological substrates of Lang's propositional network theory. An overview of electrophysiological and imaging studies of brain activity during imagery reveals that cortical processes in imagery do not differ from "actual" processing, storage and retrieval of information. The valence of emotional content is difficult to objectify on a cortical level.

A series of studies using non-linear (deterministic) chaos methodology of spontaneous EEG during imagery and other mental activities found the complexity of cortical network-interaction to be highest in emotional imagery.

The chapter concludes with a review of the clinical application of neuropsychological imagery research to various behavioral and neurological disorders: Psychopathy, schizophrenia and local destructions of the central nervous system.

Key words: imagery, evoked potentials, EEG, deterministic chaos

Neuronal Networks During Intentional or Nonintentional Imagery

In recent years, emotional imagery has been studied in the context of a bio-informational theory derived from contemporary models of information processing and associative memory (Lang, 1979). This theory posits that emotional imagery reflects the processing of neural activity within associative memory structures of the brain. In addition to information about *stimulus aspects* and their meaning, the bioinformational theory proposes that these networks also contain elements pertaining to *somatic responses* integral to the imaginal situation, which are activated when the image is produced. While these responses are presumed to be largely gated out from final overt implementation – one does not actually cry out,

run, etc. – small amounts of efferent activity nonetheless "leak" out to the periphery, and can be measured by appropriate psychophysiological techniques (Lang et al, 1990). However, since the "gating-out" mechanism is largely peripheral, brain processes of imagery reflect the actual processing of the image without distortion by peripheral gating.

Images are Pictures in the Head and Propositional Networks

One (of many) non-productive controversies in cognitive psychology is the question whether the representation of images in the brain is pic-

---

*   University of Tübingen.
     Supported by the Deutsche Forschungsgemeinschaft (SFB 307).

torial or if it involves processes fundamentally different from perception (Pylyshyn, 1984). Does an image of an object or a scene share the same representations as the percept and/or the memory of the percept?

If the memory of a "scene" consists of a representational neuronal network of Hebbian associative cell assemblies – as most neuroscientists agree these days (cf. Braitenberg, 1989) – then the image of that "scene" consists of the reactivation (recall) of either *all* elements of that network (which would be equivalent to an eidetic recall), or at least *parts* of that network. Thus, all rules and principles of learning and memory as formulated by psychology and biology of human cognition are valid for images and imagery production. No new or special theoretical concepts are necessary to explain the case of imagery.

Recall–image–dream–hallucination. There seems to be little evidence for structural differences between those neural and cognitive processes involved in recall, imagery, dream or hallucination. All four consist of the activation of one or several cell assemblies representing memories.

The term "recall" is used if an accessed cognitive representation precisely matches a specific memory; we name this cognitive representation an image if it does not precisely match a memory but contains a majority of common elements of a memory set, and is not identical with the actually present perception. A cognitive representation may be termed a dream if sensory afferent input and motor efferents approach zero or are substantially reduced, and memories which are not identical to the original perception are activated one after the other at high speed. Finally, we call a cognitive representation a hallucination if a new (non-expected) combination of memories is activated with such high attentional intensity that images are mistakenly judged as perceptions (cf. Hoffman 1986). Metaphorically spoken, hallucinations are "seizures of images" but they remain images.

The *aspect of active, conscious search* in imagery production is a special case of images stored as

propositional networks, but not a crucial requirement of a general definition of imagery. The generation of images is not related to imagery process per se, but represents a special case of human linguistic abilities. Language coded memory traces may activate memories in humans more frequently because of the enormous array of associative connections they form with memories in both hemispheres.

Propositional networks. P. Lang's (1979) notion of images as propositional networks is a rather useful specification of a general theory of images as loosely coupled associative memories. In humans with language capacity images are frequently activated and stored in a propositional mode. Specifically, the voluntary activation of images in most instances uses memories coded in propositional form. Imagery as it is explored in experimental psychology and psychophysiology involves propositionally coded memories for methodological reasons: language is an easy and fast tool to access associative memories.

Intentional and non-voluntary imagery. Like memory and voluntary movements we assume that all intentional images arise from a preconscious or subconscious level. The mechanisms of intentional memory and recall are the mechanisms of intentional imagery as explored in the fields of attention and learning; Table 1 lists some terms and processes which differentiate between memory and imagery arising from processes the subject is aware of or unaware of, as reviewed by Birbaumer & Schmidt (1990). The neuroanatomical and neurophysiological evidence for such a differentiation is reviewed by Daum (1989).

Table 1. Differences between conscious and non-conscious memory and imagery processes.

aware – intentional	unaware
Controlled attention and search	Automatic attention and search
Explicit memory	Implicit memory
Declarative learning	Procedural (habit) learning

There is a *continuum* from preconscious to intentional imagery, dependent upon attentional resources allocated for a given set of representational networks, as there is a continuum from automatic to controlled attentional processes (Birbaumer & Schmidt, 1990). Both are reflected in the amplitudes of local electrocortical negativities and positivities (Birbaumer et al. 1990, see also section II).

Emotional and non-emotional imagery. Lang's important theoretical discovery is the notion that the "emotionality" of an image is reflected in the degree of output-oriented involvement of peripheral physiology. As noted already by Lange (1885), emotional responses depend upon the reafferent input from the periphery as do emotional images. For this reason emotional imagery is probably inevitably linked to muscular-autonomic-limbic correlates of thinking and behavior. In part II of this chapter we provide experimental evidence that *cortical* networks involved in imagery may remain unaffected by the

emotional content of an image, but reflect motor involvement (active-passive dimension of an image) and cognitive aspects of the image (such as the spatial-verbal dimension, memory search, image maintenance etc.). The hedonic (positive-negative) valence enters into the cortical networks through subcortical-limbic structures.

The theoretical case of purely "cortical" imagery could be found in a person born completely paralyzed with no memory of reafferent feedback from the periphery, endocrine glands and even facial muscles. Such a person may have "purely" cognitive imagery without an emotional association attached to it. Since memories are cortically stored (in some romanic languages storage of memories is synonymous with imaging, i.e. in Italian "imagazzinare") such a person is perfectly capable of imaging, but the images remain "cold." There may be some psychopathological conditions close to this "ideal" of cognitive imagery such as amnesia and psychopathy.

Brain Activity and Imagery

Negative and Positive Deflections in the EEG and the Problem of Match-Mismatch in Propositional Networks

Mismatch negativity – match negativity. Translating Hebb's (1949) principle of the neuronal basis of recall from memory into the cognitive terms of propositional network theory, Lang (1979) formulated a match-mismatch mechanism for the activation of images.

With an increasing number of common propositional units between a stimulus configuration and the memory of that pattern the probability of activating a particular propositional network with all its associative connections is increased. The production of an image and its associated autonomic responses is particularly high if motor-response propositions are used as stimuli that match a motor-response element of the memory. Sensory, stimulus-oriented propositions or "meaning" propositions have a lower probability of guiding behavioral and autonomic outflow. Lang calls his model a *motor*

theory of emotions, emphasizing the primacy of efferent propositional structures.

From a neurophysiological perspective, there is no clear indication for a CNS-structure or mechanisms favoring the proposed *output-oriented* matching. The match-mismatch comparison is an automatic, preconscious attentional process. For simple stimuli the first comparison between actual and stored patterns is *completed* around the appearance of the P300 component of event-related potentials (ERPs). With respect to the timing of these hypothetical processes, stimulus comparison occurs first, response-oriented decision usually afterwards. Since a comparison of stored stimulus configurations has to be located on a cortical level (together with some subcortical and basal ganglia "assistance") ERPs should be a useful tool for observing match-mismatch processes. Following the sequence of components and their neocortical location, it should be possible to decide theoretical issues such as the one posed by Lang's notion of a "primacy" of efferent imagery for emotional behavior (apart from the trivial notion that behavior is efferent and therefore must result ultimately from an output-oriented comparison process).

Unfortunately, match *and* mismatch following simple stimuli or imagery tasks appear as a negative component around 200ms. Näätänen and Picton (1986) described the "mismatch negativity" N2a around 200 ms following physically discordant stimuli in the primary and secondary projection areas and a N2b unspecific orienting vertex response related to the "completion" – the "memory closure" – P300 wave (see Näätänen, 1990).

In visual imagery tasks, Farah & Peronnet (1989) described a negative occipital response around 170ms following the match of a presented letter with an expected imagined identical letter. From their work and our investigation (see below) we conclude that *negative components of slow electric brain waves seem to be responsible for the positive effects of imagery on performance of the imagined cognitive and motor activities (see part II).*

We are therefore confronted with a mismatch-negativity and a match-negativity appearing around the same latency after stimulus- or image presentation. Both are generated around the primary projection areas where stimulus configurations are supposedly stored; matching, however, results in an *earlier* negativity than mismatch (it is often called "processing negativity," see Näätänen 1990).

The neurophysiology of matching. Theory and empirical research in imagery and its ERP-correlates is usually free of references to possible neuronal substrates: A long tradition in cognitive psychology that ignored the biological basis of cognition led to paradoxes such as a seemingly identical neuronal substrate for clearly different processes as in the case of match and mismatch stimulus configurations. However, at a cortical level, the two processes may not be as different as one may think.

Any new incoming stimulus (mismatch) causes a large negative-positive deflection around 200 ms. If the stimulus-trace requires further processing or imaging the negative deflection is followed by a positivity, the duration

and amplitude of which depends on the processing demands (mental load) of that activity, such as predictability, difficulty etc. With repetitions of the same stimulus the negativity habituates as does the positivity. Perfect match (identity of presented stimulus and stored neural model) therefore leads to smaller amplitudes of all components, if the stimulus does not *call* for further processing (Öhman 1983). A "call" for further processing leads to threshold reduction for neuronal excitation caused by the stimulus trace or image trace. This is a continuous process (not all-or-none), which is dependent on the strength of past associative motivational connections of the activated network ("meaning").

In match-conditions which call for further processing, as in most imagery experiments, the negativity will remain more focused on the location of the memory store, while under mismatch conditions a more widespread "unspecific" negativity and positivity with longer latencies should be expected because of a wider cortical *distance* between the representation of the incoming stimulus trace and other memory representations, a prediction which could be tested empirically. Matching-negativity with following positivity appears *closer to primary projection areas* for the respective stimulus modality than mismatch negativity. Short-term memory for auditory delayed-matching-to-sample tasks, for example, is located in the superior temporal cortex, for visual discrimination tasks in the inferior temporal lobe, for rotating spatial material at inferior parietal locations (Colombo et al. 1990, Birbaumer & Schmidt 1990). If the matching stimulus is precued or primed as in most of Farah's experiments an anticipatory negativity will artificially cause larger matching negativities, because the trace of the matching stimulus "rides" on the anticipatory negativity.

Based on the assumption that all late (≥100 ms) negativities reflect the *same* cellular process of synchronous local depolarisation of apical dendrites ("cerebral potentiality"), and all late positivities reflect local actual processing and cellular interactions ("cerebral performance"), matching will give rise to negativity if the presented stimulus or generated image contains propositional elements (assemblies) which call for *preparation* of action or preparation of processing capacities. Matching will cause more positivity and less negativity if the activated network contains a call for active mental processing such as thinking. A mismatch usually does the same, the search process for matching elements may be prolonged and more widespread (see Birbaumer et al. 1990 for details of the neurophysiological model).

Imagery Measurement in the Human Brain

Regional cerebral blood flow (rCBF). Several studies recorded rCBF during mental imagery. A radioactive compound such as Xe122 is injected or inhaled and the distribution of the radioactive substance during the process of mental imagery is measured. Generally, a greater cerebral blood flow was detected in those cortical areas where neurophysiological knowledge could localize the appropriate perceptional function: increase in occipital posterior areas during visual imagery comparable to perception of the imaged stimulus (Roland, 1982). Goldenberg et al. (1987) measured greater flow in an imagery condition (imagining words) compared to non-imagery (memorizing the same words). Whereas blood flow shifted more to the posterior areas during imagery, it was more evenly distributed during memorizing or abstract thinking . The series of studies with SPECT in Deecke's laboratory (Goldenberg et al. 1987) indicates higher rCBF in the left hemisphere with verbally mediated imagery; however, slow wave recording during the same imagery stimulation did not confirm the hemispheric differences suggested by SPECT images. The authors concluded that rCBF reflects only the quantitative dimension of the image, while slow brain potentials are more sensitive to qualitative aspects such as imagery content. They found increased flow in right inferior temporal lobe during imagery of human faces, and decrease of flow during imagery of maps and colours. Maps and colours on the other hand caused increased flow at parietal and occipital sites.

Hallucinations in schizophrenic patients appear like intensive imagery in PET or rCBF measurements, causing higher absorption rates of glucose in left temporal and occipital areas with weaker action in the frontal lobe. Again, these data are in full accordance with older EEG recordings during hallucinations (Andreasen 1989).

Overall, both rCBF and PET studies reveal no difference between the cortical physiology of an actual perception and the physiology of a "picture in the mind."

Electrophysiological recording during imagery. Farah (1989) provides a review of the earlier EEG work: as in those studies using brain imaging techniques there is a clear correspondence between the stimulus modality of the image and the locus of EEG desynchronization: during images of tactile stimuli on the left or right hand, EEG-desynchronization appears at contralateral central locations, during visual imagery activation moves toward the occiput.

More specific information about cerebral processes during imagery can also be derived from the evaluation of *ERPs*. Several studies have been performed, one by Farah and associates who analyzed the components up to one second after image presentation, and studies from our laboratory and Deecke's laboratory concentrating on slow cortical potentials during intervals of 1 to 10 seconds (Birbaumer et al. 1988; Rockstroh et al., 1990; Cuthbert et al. in preparation, Uhl et al., 1990).

These studies provide evidence for dominant left-hemispheric image generation if verbal induction of visual imagery is used. In the study by Birbaumer et al. (1988) subjects were asked to imagine preparation of a movement with the right or the left hand; these images produced increased negative shifts over the hemisphere (dominating at the central electrode) contralateral to the hand involved in the imagery, relative to less negative shifts at ipsilateral recording sites. Under these conditions, no left-hemispheric dominance was demonstrated despite verbal instructions.

Farah's (1989) conclusion that image generation depends on left parietal lobe activity may constitute a premature generalization because it only holds for verbal-visual image generation and not for tactile images. Also visual neglect speaks against an imagery deficit dependent upon left hemispheric damage only. Since most unilateral visual neglect follows *right* parietal lesions with a consequent inability to imagine the left side of the visual field, at least imagery maintenance (in contrast to imagery generation) depends on the proper long-term memory storage locations in cortical networks.

Rösler (1990), in a series of long-term-memory search experiments, found left-frontal negativities under conditions of *search* for verbal material as well as for colors, and a left parietal negativity during search for spatial material (line drawings). His data indicate that memory search and the generation and maintenance of imagery ("recall") is accompanied by negativities while actual storage of the mate-

rial and "processing " of imagery results in long-lasting positivities at the cortical location primarily involved with the respective content (spatial, verbal, colorful etc.) (see Figure 6). "Processing" is defined here as the amount of attentional resources necessary for the actual/not anticipated storage and/or motor execution of a particular sensorimotor configuration. With increasing resources mobilized, the cortical d. c. level turns toward positivity.

Imagery ability and event related potentials. Whereas Farah measured imagery ability after the experiment by presenting the "Vividness of Visual Imagery Questionnaire," Birbaumer and collaborators measured imagery ability with the comparable "Questionnaire for Mental Imagery." Farah found much larger positive SPs (during the interval 300–700 ms) at occipital

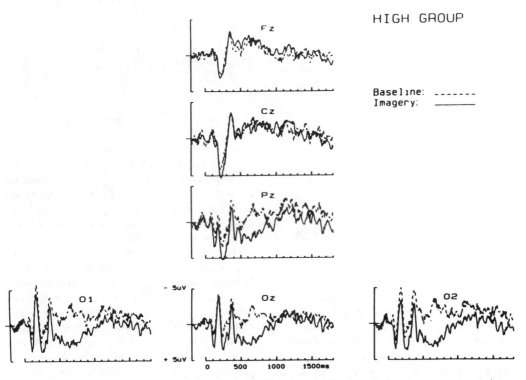

Figure 1. Average waveforms for abstract words baseline condition (broken line) and concrete words image generation condition (solid line), from 10 subjects with high vividness of mental imagery, recorded from 6 scalp locations. *Recording conditions:* The nose was the reference, the bandpass of the filters was 0.01–30 Hz, and the sampling interval was 8 ms. Eye movements were monitored with an infrared corneal reflectance eye tracker, and data from trials on which the eyes moved was excluded. (From Farah & Peronnet, 1989)

leads during imagery of concrete words compared to imagery of abstract words in subjects rating high on the vividness scale (see Figure 1).

Birbaumer et al. (1988) reported a significant correlation between imagery ability and the performance on a Slow Potential (SP) self-regulation task ($r = 0.37$): Ss had to generate differences between right and left central (C3-C4) SPs receiving visual feedback of and reinforcement for polarization between right- and left-central SPs. Ss with good imagery ability performed better, reaching larger local polarization between C3 and C4. Figure 2 illustrates the biofeedback paradigm.

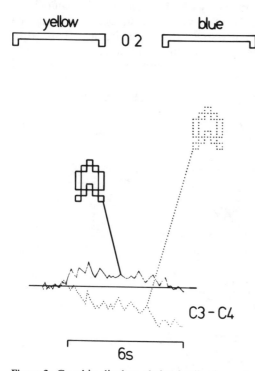

Figure 2. Graphic display of the feedback mode: Upon presentation of a yellow-light-S^D the rocketship should be directed at the yellow goal; upon presentation of a blue-light-S^D the blue goal should be reached. Reaching the required goal added a point to the counter between the goals. Left- or right-shifts of the rocket depended on the balance between left- and right-precentral SPs during the 6 s feedback interval. Increased left- and suppressed right-precentral negativity produced a movement as illustrated by the dotted lines.

In a second study, subjects were trained for five consecutive sessions using the same paradigm. Fig. 3 summarizes the achieved differentiation in the 5th session at the different recording sites.

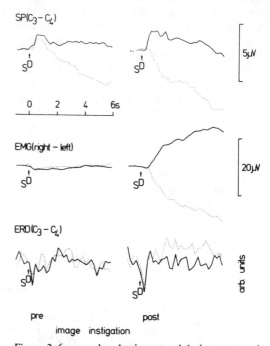

Figure 3. 6 sec – slow brain potentials (upper trace) for required left hemispheric negativity (——) and left-hemispheric positivity (- - - - -). Differentiation during transfer trials without feedback pre (left) and post (right) image instigation. Middle trace: EMG difference between right and left forearm before and after image instigation. The bottom trace represents the bipolar event-related desynchronization (ERD), i.e., the change in alpha power differentiation between the left- and right-precentral EEG recording across the 6-s feedback interval. ERD was analyzed by complex demodulation. While there is no obvious differentiation in ERD between the requirement for left-precentral increase in negativity and right-precentral SP suppression (solid lines) and the reverse polarization requirement (dotted lines) prior to image instigation, ERD is larger over the left hemisphere (less alpha power, solid lines) when left-precentral increases in negativity was required (and vice versa) (from Birbaumer et al., 1988, with kind permission).

During this session Ss imagined preparing for a rapid movement with the left hand, whenever an increase in right-hemispheric negativity (relative to left-central SPs) was required, while they imagined preparation for a right-hand movement, whenever left-hemispheric negativity increase was required. Instruction to imagine movement preparation with the contralateral hand facilitated the self-induced cortical differentiation: Ss with imagery instruction achieved significant left-right differences immediately on imagery instruction, while Ss without instruction needed two to three ses-

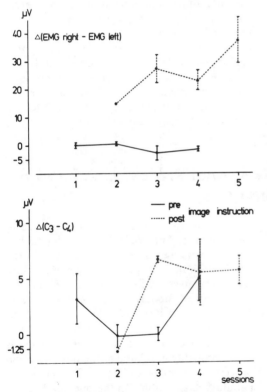

Figure 4. Mean bipolar (left-right recording) EMG responses (top) and SP (bottom) averaged for every experimental session for those subjects who had received the instruction for image instigation (post: - - - - -) and for those subjects who had not received this instruction (pre: ———) Sessions are arranged on the abscissa, the ordinate represents differentiation in µV (from Birbaumer et al., 1988, with kind permission).

sions to reach comparable performances (see Figure 4). Muscular or autonomic manipulations had no influence on cortical "performance" in the pre-imagery condition, while during imagery a clear "leakage" to peripheral channels (EMG) was observed as Lang's theory predicts.

Comparable predominance of contralateral surface-negative SP developed, when Ss anticipated tactile stimulation applied to the left or the right hand (Lutzenberger et al., 1986). When the tactile discrimination task was introduced after SP-modulation training, performance on the right-hand task was significantly improved on trials with self induced left-central negativity and performance with the left hand was improved on trials with self-induced negativity increase at C4 (Rockstroh et al., 1990).

Imagery and "thinking": It seems that electrocortical measures at present are more sensitive to subtle local cerebral variations in metabolic and/or attentional energy supply: studies measuring rCBF did not uncover clearcut differences between imagery of an event, the "real" perception of that event and the abstract, silent articulation of the event without imagery. In contrast, Cuthbert et al. (1990) found larger negative amplitudes over central (Cz) areas and less positive shifts over left temporal (T5) areas during imagery compared to silent articulation of the same scene. *During* actual imagery (concrete words with more active visual components compared to abstract words) Farah et al. observed larger positive shifts over occipital areas (see Fig.1), and similarly, Cuthbert et al. (1990) measured the more pronounced positive slow potentials at Pz under imagery (compared to silent articulation) conditions. Overall, imagery seems to require more attentional resources than actual perception; depending on the stimulus material, positivity seems to predominate over posterior areas. This of course does not imply that imagery is "more intense" than reality; the larger amplitudes may only reflect the fact that in a laboratory environment it may be easier to associate meaning and motivational elements with imagery of "private" events than with the reality of the laboratory. However, these data provide evidence against the widespread belief that imagery constitutes "a weak" reflection of reality.

Emotional content. Cuthbert et al. (1990) and Birbaumer et al. (1988) also varied the emotional content (fearful, pleasurable, neutral) and response disposition (active, passive) induced by the imagery scripts. Emotional content had an influence on peripheral variables (see chapter 5) but did not affect electrocortical measures, suggesting a rather nonemotional ("cognitive") character of neocortical projections. On the other hand, the response disposition as induced by the scripts influenced SPs irrespective of the task (imagery or silent articulation): Disposition towards active responding induced larger frontal but smaller centro-parietal negativity compared to "passive" scripts. Overall, the fronto-parietal gradient was significantly more pronounced for the active than for the passive disposition. However, response dispositions did not produce different SPs at the temporal sites.

This result is open to an alternative interpretation: increased frontal negativity during active images may reflect allocation of preparatory resources directed to the motor elements in the script , while the active response disposition may have induced more active processing in motor (central) areas as well as in parietal areas in which most of the memories for these images are located.

A dominance of left hemispheric activity during *generation* (not maintenance) of *visual imagery* was found in *split-brain* patients and patients with left hemisphere lesions. ERP studies also point in the same direction. However, the fact that communication in split brain patients with the right hemisphere of the patient is only possible at a nonverbal level makes it difficult to interpret the results. Farah (1989) provides a review of neuropsychological case studies, suggesting that the generation of a visual image is a process that is separable from the actual maintenance of the image which occurs at a different location.

The Non-Linear Dynamics of Neuronal Processes Related to Imagery

Chaos and EEG-Waves

The late components of event-related potentials (ERP) reflect depolarizations of relatively large areas of cortical tissue which – by way of their extraction from the EEG – are stimulus- or response-contingent. This, however, does not necessarily imply that all of the ongoing activity related to that particular event is represented in the ERP waveform. In contrast, it is well-known that event-related changes in the amplitude of alpha-waves may be totally unrelated to information available from decomposing ERP-waves (as reviewed by Elbert & Rockstroh, 1987).

However, over the last 60 years following Berger's discoveries most attempts to relate EEG-parameters, particularly the topographical pattern of the EEG with psychological phenomena have only met with limited success (see Lutzenberger et al. 1985 for an overview). This

disappointingly slow progress may be due to the limited methodologies available for analyzing the seemingly irregular variations in the EEG which never reproduce over time. Until recently analyses of EEG-data relied on linear mathematical models and linear thinking, an approach which obviously cannot account for the high variability in EEG-patterns. Therefore, most of the EEG-activity was dismissed as noise, probably unrelated to the ongoing brain processing under investigation. This created a paradoxical situation. On the one hand, it was assumed that the organism engages primarily in a certain task, on the other hand, it was agreed upon that most of the brain's activity remains unrelated to that activity.

EEG activity essentially results from the summation of postsynaptic potentials which originate primarily in the cerebral cortex and reflects the summed electrical activity of billions of neurons. Their interconnections form an extremely complex system. Given the high number of neurons with their infinite number of firing patterns, it is not obvious why systematic EEG activity can be observed at all when recorded from the scalp. The common explanation is that large numbers/populations of neurons are synchronized through thalamic afferent input so that their activity becomes superimposed. Simple examination of the waning and waxing of irregular waves might still lead one to infer that an infinite number of degrees of freedom contribute to the temporal development of the recorded voltage. However, this intuitive conclusion may be wrong. It has been demonstrated that a simple system with as few as three differential equations can generate totally irregular fluctuations of the system's variables – a phenomenon presently referred to as *deterministic chaos*. When a system produces irregularity in one of its variables, it is of interest, whether this behaviour results from randomness (meaning that the number of degrees of freedom is infinite), or whether a finite, and possibly small number of degrees of freedom has produced the chaos (meaning that the system is deterministic). The prominent features of chaos are unpredictability over extended time periods, and sensitive dependence on initial conditions. Once provided with specific initial values, the system's future might be totally different, from what it would have been had it started under slightly different initial conditions. The importance of this finding for the EEG is that this seemly disordered process may be governed by relatively few simple laws which could be determined.

How is it possible to characterize a (nonlinear) system? Every system of interest has a limited number of degrees of freedom. Otherwise, it is noise. At any point in time, the system may be characterized by a set of system variables which can be considered to define a multidimensional space, called phase space. If left undisturbed, the system is 'attracted' and follows distinct trajectories within this phase space. These are referred to as attractors. One of the classic quantitative measures of the attractor and thus of a complex dynamic system is that of its dimensionality. Assume an infinite

number of close trajectories in a plane of the phase space. The trajectories are one-dimensional. As there is an infinite number of infinitely close trajectories they may also form an area. A puzzling fact concerning 'strange attractors' is that their dimension lies in between, and therefore may be best described by a fractal dimension, lying between two integer numbers. Since it is possible to estimate the fractal dimension from a given time series, it is also possible to evaluate changes in the system's attractor.

Dimensional analysis of the EEG has not been applied to a large variety of cognitive and sensory tasks yet, thus it is difficult to make exact predictions of how sensory and cognitive activity would be reflected in an nonlinear analysis involving a variety of tasks. However, several EEG studies in the literature used deterministic chaos. For example, Babloyantz and her colleagues (Babloyantz et al., 1985, Babloyantz & Destexhe, 1986) have made dimensional calculations between states such as sleep stages, waking, and epilepsy, with higher dimension being found in the awake condition and lower dimenions in the sleep and epilepsy condition. Others (Mayer-Kress & Layne, 1987, Albano et al., 1986, Rapp, 1986) reported dimensions lower than 10 during the relaxed waking state with eyes either closed or open. Mayer-Kress & Holzfuß (1987) examined subjects who were either awake or under anesthesia and found higher dimensions in the anesthesized state. Lower dimensionalities have generally been reported during resting periods, particularly when eyes were closed, than during active engagement (Graf & Elbert, 1989, Mayer-Kress et al., 1988, Rapp, 1986). If such analyses are confirmed, one could conclude that the EEG results from a rather simple deterministic system with relatively few variables to be determined. Based on neuroscientific evidence, we (Birbaumer et al., 1990; Elbert & Rockstroh, 1987) have previously outlined means by which a chaotic time series of electrical activity might be generated by the brain's regulatory processes.

In our studies on imagery, we sought to extend the previous work in two ways. Firstly, we utilized imagery in order to investigate a system without external disturbances, which may make the system deviate from its attractor for some time. Secondly, whereas previous studies have been limited to only one or two electrode sites, we collected data from 15 electrode sites in one study. Thus, the study was designed to answer two major questions:

1) are there variations among images in terms of dimensionality, and
2) are there variations among sites in terms of dimensionality. In addition, the results may help us to delineate the question concerning whether the cortex functions as a single system in terms of connectivity, or represents more localized processes.

Experimental Evidence: The Fractal Dimension of the EEG During Imagery

In one experiment (Lutzenberger et al., in press) we utilized a variety of tasks that cut across sensory modalities including touch, vision, imagery, and verbal processing, which reflect neuropsychological processes that differentially utilize the frontal or more posterior areas of the cortex, or which are processed predominantly by the right or by the left sensorimotor areas.

Ten subjects participated in the experiment. EEG recordings were obtained from the following electrode placements: F7, F3, Fz, F4, F8, C3, Cz, C4, P3, Pz, P4, T5, T6, O1, O2. All leads were referenced to the vertex electrode for recording purposes and changed off-line to an average reference giving all electrodes equal weigth. Three eye movement measures served to control for ocular artifacts. The bandwidth ranged from 0.8 Hz to 40 Hz.

The sequence of two imagery tasks was counterbalanced across subjects. Four additional tasks were presented in a predetermined order which was incompletely counterbalanced due to the limited number of subjects. The six tasks were as follows: 1. observation of a swinging double pendulum ; 2. naming aloud nouns which started with the letter M (e.g. mouse, man, milk, morning); 3. determination which of six pieces of sandpaper was the smoothest with

the right index finger; 4. the same task with the left index finger; 5. imagery and experience of an extremely positive time in their past in which they had been in love (without actual sexual imagery) and 6. imagery of the same type of extremely positive experience which included a sexual experience.

Subjects were instructed that throughout the entire procedure, they were to keep their eyes open and during the tasks, and they were instructed to maintain a fixation point which was either the pendulum or a white cross in the center of the monitor screen.

For each task an interval of 16 s duration was selected for computation of the fractal dimension (for details see Lutzenberger et al., in press). Thus the length of each EEG-trace was 2048 points. The singular value decomposition was based on the autocovariation function with time-lags ranging from 0 to 32 points. A calcualtion of the dimension was performed separately for 32 equidistant points using the method of 'pointwise dimension' as proposed by Farmer et al. (1983).

The dimensional analysis for the six sensory tasks across the 15 electrode sites is shown in Figure 5. The highests dimensions were present on the imagery tasks and the lowest dimension in the verbal task. The observational task and the sensory touching task both produced similar dimensions. An ANOVA demonstrated a significant task difference across electrode sites ($F = 6.1$, df = 5,45, $p < .05$). Follow-up comparisons showed statistically significant differences between the tasks.

In terms of site, the electrodes were grouped in a rostal-caudal dimension with the frontal electrode grouping being composed of F7, F3, Fz, F4, and F8 and the more posterior electrode grouping being composed of T5, P3, Pz, P4, and T6. Figure 6 shows the dimensions for the frontal and posterior electrode groups for each of the six tasks. An ANOVA demonstrated a significant difference for electrode grouping ($F = 4.7$, df = 1,9, $p < .05$) and an electrode grouping by task interaction ($F = 7.8$; df = 5.45, $p < .05$). In general, the frontal and posterior groupings showed similar dimensions on the imagery tasks, whereas on the other four tasks smaller dimensions were found in the frontal as compared to the posterior electrode sites. The largest frontal-posterior difference appeared during the observation task (watching the pendulum). No significant right-left differences were found.

The results demonstrate clearly that imagery employs a significantly higher brain complexity than sensory stimulation at all brain sites, but particularly at frontal regions (see Fig. 5 & 6).

The chaos of passionate love. In another experiment we focussed on erotic images, comparing subjects who were actually in love with those who had only limited emotional involvement during the experimental investigation. Subjects in love carry their emotional "burden" like a snail's house into the laboratory of the physiologist. The vividness and readiness of their emotional imagery is particularly intense and easy to create under laboratory conditions. Using the questionnaire of passionate love

(Hatfield & Sprecher, 1986) a group of 10 students in love were selected out of a sample of 100 subjects and compared with a matched control group of 10 subjects not in love. Subjects had to imagine a positive scene with the beloved partner, a negative scene (jealousy) and a neutral scene (empty living room). EEG from the midline (Fz, Cz, Pz) was recorded and its fractal dimensions were estimated (using the method described by Graf & Elbert, 1988).

No meaningful between group or content differences resulted from these analyses. In line with the findings for the event-related potential scores, valence seems not to affect EEG measures in general. It is unlikely that more vivid imagination will create such differences as subjects passionately in love also failed to exhibit systematic differences.

Overall, the fractal dimensionality of the human EEG indicates that imagery employs anatomically more widespread (less localized) and more complex brain processes than sensory

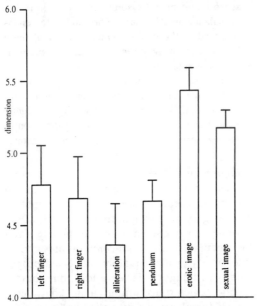

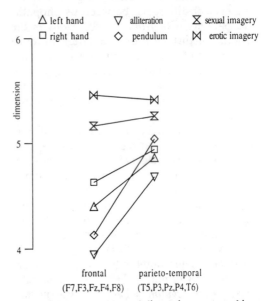

Figure 5. Number of fractal dimensions for the different tasks. ANOVA demonstrates significant difference for tasks across electrode sites (F = 6.1, df 5,45, P < .05), touching vs verbal (p < .01), touching vs imagery (p < .02), erotic vs sexual imagery (p < .001).

Figure 6. Number of fractal dimensions grouped in a rostral-caudal direction for the 6 tasks. ANOVA demonstrates significant electrode grouping by task interaction (F = 7.8, p < .05). In general, the frontal complexity remains high during imagery but is significantly reduced during the other cognitive activities.

tasks. The physiological nature of this increased complexity and variability remains to be determined. Frontal lobe mechanisms in particular seem to add imagery-related chaos compared to tactile or visual stimulation. However, before drawing final conclusions more comparative cognitive manipulation should be used. In general, non-linear analysis of physiological processes related to imagery constitutes a highly promising methodology for illuminating the basic physiological and psychological differences between imagery and other mental-neural activities; it may turn out that images are more than just pictures in the head.

IV. CNS-Pathophysiology of Imagery

Psychopathy. Recognizing the theoretical importance of psychopathy as a model-system for the understanding of imagery, Lang (see chapter 19) performed the first study on emotional imagery in psychopaths. The basic deficit in successful und unsuccessful (criminal) psychopaths is hypothesized to consist of an inability to experience anticipatory emotional imagery for aversive (but not appetitive) forthcoming stimuli. Emotional imagery (and conditioning) for rewarding stimuli is undisturbed and "cognitive" (non-emotional) imagery is intact. The crucial difference between psychopaths and patients with *frontal lobe lesions* is the general disturbance of the latter in most delayed reinforcement and anticipatory imagery tasks related to positive *and* negative reinforcement, while psychopaths present only a selective deficit related to anticipating fear-relevant cues.

To our knowledge, there are no studies in which cortical measures were used to investigate processes of imagery in psychopaths. CNV recordings in anticipation of aversive stimuli did not demonstrate consistent deviances in psychopaths. Using a two-stimulus-reaction-time paradigm, Forth and Hare (1989) observed enhanced frontal negativities for the initial CNV component (iCNV) in psychopaths but did not detect oddities for later preparatory slow waves (terminal tCNV). This illustrates nicely a *dissociation* between a hypernormal frontal ("cognitive")-cortical mechanism and obviously deficient subcortical and autonomic processes in psychopaths which may be derived from autonomic measures. Autonomic and hormonal recordings reflecting the processing of aversive and stressful events show consistent deficits such as a reduction in anticipatory skin conductance increase, reduced adrenal responding in the periphery and decreased platelet MAO.

Overall, psychophysiological results using imagery or classical conditioning are in accordance with Gray's (1982) and Fowles' (1984) notion of a loose or non-existing associative connection between cortical memories of aversive events and their subcortical "energizing" counterparts such as the septo-hippocampal-system and autonomic hypothalamic nuclei. Since the orbital frontal lobe is regarded as the final common pathway of these limbic energizing structures only magnetoencephalographic measures or sophisticated EEG source localization techniques may detect neural deficits in psychopaths. Positron emmission tomograohy (PET) imaging of limbic-hypothalamic structures may be a more promising direction to discover structural CNS changes in psychopaths.

Schizophrenia. Despite libraries of speculations on imagery in schizophrenics, virtually no systematic research has explored CNS function and imagery in schizophrenia. The lack of experimental work seems rather surprising given the fact that acoustic *hallucinations* may constitute loosely or inadequately connected propositions in imagery. Three additional characteristics which transform originally "harmless" propositional imagery into alien hallucinations may be important:

1) The energetic component: the "unconditioned" vividness of the images is extreme (probably caused by supersensitivity of D_2 receptors in reward structures)

2) The segmental set caused by a deficient selective attention system modifies imagined or real self-talk into a new and alien experience (such as listening the first time to one's own voice on a tape, Hoffman 1987).
Comparable to *computer viruses* propositional networks are infiltrated by new incontingent and incongruent associated cell assemblies, which tend to leak into other synchronized and consistent associative networks.

3) Because of the existing deficit in allocating attentional effort selectively to external or internal targets, persons with hallucinations judge vivid imagery incorrectly as external percepts (reality discrimination problem).

The *combination* of loose (delusional) associative connections between cortical memories and overactive energetic output from limbic-frontal brain structures forms the contrasting model-system to the study of imagery in psychopaths, where the associative connections on a cortical level are undisturbed but the energizing subcortical inflow "to feed the cortical connections with vividness" is lacking in anticipation of fearful events.

The above described situation in schizophrenia (at least Type I schizophrenia with positive symptoms) is reflected in event-related potential studies and regional cerebral blood flow during imagery in schizophrenia and subjects at risk for the disease (see chapter 20).

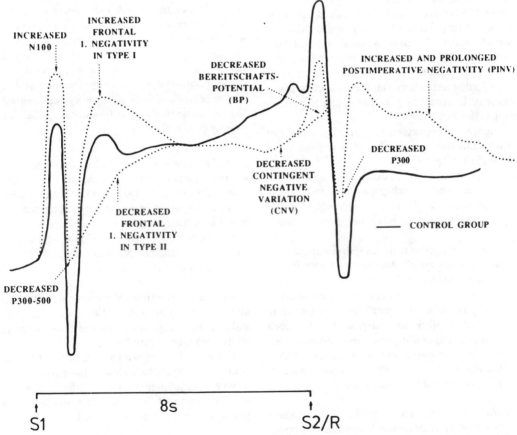

Figure 7. Idealized schema of event-related potential findings in type I and type II schizophrenia (- - - - -) in comparison with a normal control group (———). S 1 constitutes an acoustic stimulus followed by another acoustic S 2 8s later. Ss have to respond after S 2 as fast as possible.

The majority of rCBF studies demonstrate low prefrontal blood flow and increased flow at cortical localizations presumably active in processing visual or acoustic hallucinations at occipital or temporal sites. The decreased frontal activity (particularly of the left hemisphere) is interpreted as a defective attentional system, causing fragmented and unmodulated selective activation of posterior information processing areas, (probably caused by a degeneration of mesocortical dopaminergic fiber systems in contrast to an overactive mesolimbic dopamine system.). The partial breakdown of the attentional system may also be the cause of "chaotic" uncontrollable imagery in schizophrenia.

Another interpretation of hallucinations is in accordance with a low left frontal activity gradient: the judgment of an image as an image and not as reality may be dependent upon the *same* cortical structures responsible for the generation of images. Several studies (see above) indicate that the left frontal lobe may be in part responsible for both. At least auditory hallucinations could then be misattributions of internal imagery for external perceptions (Benfall 1990)

Figure 7 is representative of a large body of ERP- and slow potential studies in type I and type II schizophrenia.

There is no reason to doubt that these rather consistent results in schizophrenics and at-risk-groups are as valid for the processing of actual events as they are for imagining those events.

The overinclusive attentional system is reflected in large negative amplitudes around 100–200 ms, the defective and incomplete storage in small or non-existent P300, the segmental sets in reduced anticipatory negative slow waves; the over-energizing subcortical inflow may correspond to increased negativities after distractive input and remobilizing post-imperative-negative variations (PINV, see Rockstroh et al. 1989) in situations with already completed processing agendas.

Anxiety disorders. The crucial role of imagery in the development and maintenance of anxiety and phobias was extensively studied by Lang and co-workers (see chapters 13–16). On a CNS-level, Lang's notion of a supertightly con-

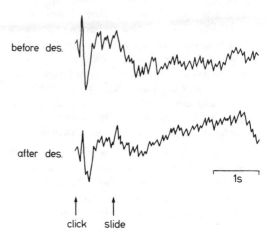

before des.

after des.

1s

click   slide

Figure 8. Slow brain potentials in test anxiety patients before (upper trace) and after (lower trace) behavioral treatment. A click (left) signals a slide (Dia) with the word "exam." Ss are instructed to imagine the exam-situation after slide presentation. Significantly smaller negativity between the cue (click) and smaller positivity during imagery after treatment indicates neutralization of anticipatory fear (negativity) and imagery vividness (positivity). (From Birbaumer & Tunner 1971).

nected propositional network of fear-response-memories was confirmed by increased negative slow waves vis-a-vis anxiety provoking stimulation (see chapter 14 by Sartory). The same is true for obsessive-compulsive disorders.

Birbaumer and Tunner (1971) were the first to use slow cortical potential negativity as a measure of treatment effects in desensitization of social phobies: with decreasing fear (= decreasing tightness of the specific network) slow negativity in anticipation of a slide provoking the imagination of the fearful scene decreased (see Figure 8).

These and other studies, mentioned in the previous paragraphs, indicate that cortical negativity in *anticipation* of a specific image is a good measure of the associative strength of a particular propositional network.

CNS-lesions. As described above, amnesia following bilateral temporo-hippocampal destruction results in a selective deficit of *declarative memory* leaving only habit memory and memory for procedures intact. Anectodal evidence of these cases, particularly H.M. described by B. Milner, suggests a deficit in *emotional imagery* as one element of that disorder. However, it is not clear whether the imagery deficiency is a consequence of the lost ability to form new memories of facts and episodes or is a consequence of a certain *visceral agnosia* for emotional arousal (Squire 1989).

In contralateral *neglect* the inability to imagine stimuli and/or movements of the (usually left) contralateral half-space of the patient's body seems to be more a consequence of the failure to distribute attentional resources in the respective cortical region than a genuine deficit in imagery. However, studies with contralateral neglect demonstrate again that the cerebral location of imagery is identical with the cerebral location of perception. Visual neglect is also imaginal neglect.

G. Sartori and R. Job (1988) described a curious deficit of remembering or imagining animals and fruits in a case of herpes-related destruction of the anterior temporal lobes. These and other reports suggest that

1) imagery is closely tied to the local cortical cell assemblies where a particular memory is stored,
2) that caution should be employed in ascribing imagery to left-hemispheric structures only,
3) that the cortical locations for imagery maintenance seem to be different from the cortical locations for image *generation*, the latter may be located in the *left* (posterior) *hemisphere* (Farah 1989).

References

Albano, A.M., Abraham, N.B., de Guzman, G.C., Tarroja, M.F.H., Bandy, D.K., Gioggia, R.S., Rapp, P.E., Zimmermann, I.D., Greenbaun, N.N., & Bashore, T.R. (1986). Lasers and brains: Complex systems with low-dimensional attractors. In: Mayer-Kress, G. (Ed.), *Dimension and entropies in chaotic systems* (231–252). Berlin/Heidelberg/New York/Tokyo: Springer-Verlag.

Andersen, P. & Andersson, S.A. (1968). *Physiological basis of the alpha-rhythm.* N.Y.: Appleton.

Andreasen, N.C. (Ed.) (1989). *Brain imaging: Applications in psychiatry.* Washington D.C.: American Psychiatric Press.

Babloyantz, A. (1985). Strange attractors in the dynamics of brain activity. In: Haken, H. (Ed.) *Complex systems – Operational approaches in neurobiology, physics, and computers* (116–122). Berlin: Springer-Verlag.

Balboyantz, A. & Destexhe, A. (1986). Low dimensional chaos in an instance of epilepsy. *Proc. Natl. Acad. Sci., 83,* 3513–3517.

Benfall, R.P. (1990). The illusion of reality: A review and integration of psychological research on hallucinations. *Psychol. Bull., 107,* 82–95.

Birbaumer, N. & Tunner, W. (1971). EEG, evozierte Potentiale und Desensibilisierung. *Archiv für Psychologie 123,* 225–234.

Birbaumer, N., Lang, P.J., Cook, E., Elbert, T., Lutzenberger, W., & Rockstroh, B. (1988). Slow brain potentials, imagery and hemispheric differences. *Int. J. Neuroscience, 39,* 101–116.

Birbaumer, N., Elbert, T., Canavan, A., & Rockstroh, B. (1990). Slow Potentials of the Cerebral Cortex and Behavior. *Physiological Reviews, 70,* 1–41.

Birbaumer, N. & Schmidt, R.F. (1990). *Biologische Psychologie.* Berlin/Heidelberg: Springer-Verlag.

Braitenberg, V. (1989). Some arguments for a theory of all assemblies in the cerebral cortex. In: Nadel, L. (Ed.), *Neural connections, mental computation.* London: MIT Press.

Colombo, M., D'Amato, M.R., Rodman, M.R., & Gross, Ch. (1990). Auditory association cortex lesion impair auditory short-term memory in monkeys. *Science, 247,* 336–338.

Daum, I. (1989). *Discrimination learning after temporal lobe lesions in man.* Unpublished Ph.D. thesis. University of London.

Elbert, T. & Rockstroh, B. (1987). Threshold regulation – a key to the understanding of the combined dynamics of EEG and event-related potentials. *J. Psychophysiology, 4,* 317–333.

Elbert, T., Ray, W., & Birbaumer, N. Nonlinear (chaotic) dynamics in physiological systems. Submitted.

Farah, M. & Peronnet, F. (1989). Event-related potentials in the study of mental imagery. *Journal of Psychophysiology, 3,* 99–109.

Farah, M. (1989). The neuropsychology of mental imagery. In: Goodplan, A. & Damanio, A.R. (Eds)

Handbook of neuropsychology. Vol. 2. Amsterdam: Elsevier.

Farmer, J.D., Ott, E., & York, J.A. (1983). Dimension of chaotic attractors. *Physica, 7D,* 153–180.

Forth, A. & Hare, R. (1989). Contingent negative variation in psychopaths. *Psychophysiology, 26,* 676–682.

Fowles, D.C. (1984). Biological variables in psychopathology. In: Adams, M. & Sutker, P. (Eds.), *Comprehensive handbook of psychopathology.* New York: Plenum.

Goldenberg, G., Podreka, I., Steiner, M., & Willmes, K. (1987). Patterns of regional blood flow related to memorizing of high and low imagery words. An emission computer tomography study. *Neuropsychologia, 25,* 473–486.

Graf, K.E. & Elbert, T. (1989). Dimensional analysis of the waking EEG. In: E.Basar & T.H. Bullock (Eds.), *Brain dynamics 2* (174–191). Berlin/Heidelberg: Springer-Verlag.

Gray, G. (1982). *Neuropsychology of Anxiety.* Oxford: Oxford University Press.

Hatfield, E. & Sprecher, S. (1986). Measuring passionate love in intimate relations. *Journal of Adolescence, 9,* 383–410.

Hebb, D.O. (1949). *The organization of behavior.* N.Y.: Wiley.

Hoffman, R. (1986). Verbal hallucinations and language production process in schizophrenia. *Behavior and Brain Sciences, 9,* 503–548.

Lang, P.J., Bradley, M. & Cuthbert, B. (1990). Emotion, attention, and the startle reflex. *Psychological Review, 91,* 377–395.

Lang, P.J. (1979). A bio-informational theory of emotional imagery. *Psychophysiology, 16,* 495–521.

Lange, C.G. (1922). *The emotions.* Williams & Wilkins, Balitmore (translation of 1885 edition).

Libet, B. (1985). Unconscious cerebral initiative and the role of conscious will in voluntary action. *Behavioral and Brain Sciences, 8,* 529–566.

Lutzenberger, W., Elbert, T., Rockstroh, B., & Birbaumer, N. (1985). *Das EEG.* Berlin/Heidelberg: Springer-Verlag.

Lutzenberger, W., Elbert, T., Ray, W.J., & Birbaumer, N. (in press). The scalp distribution of the fractal dimension of the EEG and its variation with mental tasks. *Brain Topography.*

Mayer-Kress, G. & Holzfuß, J. (1987). Analysis of the human electroencephalogram with methods from nonlinear dynamics. In: Rensing, L., an der

Heiden, U. & Mackey, M.C. (Eds.), *Temporal disorder in human oscillatory systems.* Berlin/Heidelberg/New York/Tokyo: Springer-Verlag.

Mayer-Kress, G., Yates, F.E., Benton, L., Keidel, M., Tirsch, W., Pöppl, S.J. & Geist, K. (1988). Dimensional analysis of nonlinear oscillations in brain, heart, and muscle. *Math. Biosciences, 90,* 155–182.

Näätänen, R. & Picton, T.W. (1986). The N2 wave of the human electric and magnetic response to sound: a review and analysis. In: McCallum, W.C., Zappoli, R. & Denoth, F. (Eds), *Cerebral psychophysiology: Studies in event related potentials* (169–173). Amsterdam: Elsevier.

Näätänen, R. (1990). The role of attention in auditory information processing as revealed by event-related potentials and other brain measures of cognitive function. *Behavior and Brain Sciences, 13,* 201–288.

Öhmann, A. (1983). The orienting response during Pavlovian conditioning. In: Siddle, D. (Ed.), *Orienting and habituation.* Chichester: Wiley.

Pylyshin, Z.W. (1984). *Computation and Cognition.* Cambridge, MA: MIT Press.

Rapp, P.E. (1986). Oscillations and chaos in cellular metabolism and physiological systems. In: Holden, A.V. (Ed.), *Chaos – Nonlinear science: Theory and application* (179–208). Manchester University Press.

Rockstroh, B., Elbert, T., Canavan, A., Lutzenberger, W., & Birbaumer, N. (1989). *Slow cortical potentials and behaviour* (2nd edition). München: Urban & Schwarzenberg

Rösler, F., Heil, M., & Glowalla, U. (1990). *Monitoring retrieval from long-term memory by slow event-related brain potentials.* Unpublished manuscript. University of Marburg.

Roland, P.E. (1982). Cortical regulation of selective attention in man. *Journal of Neurophysiology, 48,* 1059–1078

Sartori, G. & Job, R. (1988). The oyster with four legs: A neuropsychological study on the interaction of visual and semantic information. *Cognitive Neuropsychology, 5,* 105–132.

Squire, L.R. (1987). *Memory and Brain.* Oxford: Oxford University Press.

Strayer, D.L. & Kramer, A. (1990). Attentional requirements of automatic and controlled processing. *Journal of Exp. Psychology, Learning, Memory and Cognition, 16,* , 67–82.

Zuckerman, M. (1979). *Sensation seeking.* Hillsdale, NJ: LEA.

The Information Processing Approach to Human Sexuality

James H. Geer, Kevin J. Lapour and Sheryl R. Jackson*

Abstract

This chapter reviews some of the literature concerning the role of cognitive variables in and discusses models of cognitive functioning that may be usefully applied to the understanding of human sexuality. We approach this task by first considering Lang's Cognitive Model of Emotion and then reviewing other cognitive models that have addressed sexuality. The brief introduction to models is followed by a consideration of the application of the information processing approach to human sexuality. This entails a discussion of the approach and of the concepts and variables that it suggests are important. The main point of the chapter is that the information processing approach provides many useful heuristics that help organize and guide research. The literature on attentional processes is considered. Particular emphasis, in both the volume of research and its application to theory, can be found when considering the role of distraction in sexual arousal. We also discuss encoding and memory processes when examining the information processing approach. In that context, note is made of the implicit versus explicit distinction in memory. Finally, we suggest that particular attention be directed to the role of response processes in sexuality and to their contribution to gender differences.

Key words: sexuality, information processing, attention, memory, distraction, response processes

Preface by the Senior Author

I am very pleased to be a part of this collection of papers written in honor of Peter Lang. I was fortunate to have been one of Peter's first graduate students. That has afforded me the opportunity to have been student, colleague, and friend for more years than both of us wish to acknowledge. As Peter's student I was able to see first hand the rigor with which he approached research. I had the opportunity to learn from his insistence on dedication to scholarship and science. As colleague I have been able to witness the major contributions that he has made to behavioral science. The fields of psychophysiology, psychotherapy, and emotion theory have profited greatly from both his empirical and conceptual work. Finally, and most importantly, I have known Peter for a long time as a friend. I have felt and greatly appreciated his support and concern. If my work has made a contribution to our discipline, Peter must be recognized as having played a role. In the chapter that follows, I hope it is clear that while much of my research has focused on a different domain, it has been heavily influenced by my having had the privilege of knowing and having had continuing contact with Peter.

*   Louisiana State University, Baton Rouge, LA 70803, USA

This chapter takes as one of its objectives the task of demonstrating that our understanding of human sexuality will be aided by focusing attention upon cognitive variables. Additionally, we propose that using the heuristics provided by an information processing approach (IPA) provides a framework that furthers our understanding of cognitive variables in sexuality. We start with the assumption that cognitions are important in human sexuality. The extensive literature on the role of sexual fantasy, studies on the relationship between cognitive and physiological (genital) events, and a burgeoning literature from the experimental laboratory on cognitive phenomena in sexuality all make that point clear. We are not alone in our assumption. For example, Rosen and Beck (1988) in their book *Patterns of Sexual Arousal* note, "... theory and research in sexual psychophysiology have increasingly emphasized the role of *cognitive* factors in sexual arousal, leading to our cur-rent focus on the 'cognitive arousal' model of sexual response (p. 334)."

In the body of this paper we direct our attention to a brief consideration of cognitive models of emotion with a focus upon Lang's model. We then attend more specifically to concepts in cognitive theories that have dealt with the domain of sexuality. We follow the discussion of theories with an examination of the information processing approach as applied to the domain of sexuality. We will illustrate how the approach both helps us conceptualize studies and how it provides heuristics to guide further research. Next we will use the approach to help analyze a series of studies that we have undertaken to evaluate gender differences in response to elements in erotic stimuli. Finally, we will offer some brief observations on biological and evolutionary concepts in sexuality that far too often are ignored by investigators and theoriticians.

Models of Cognition in Emotion and Sexuality

Several models of emotion have been put forth that have as their goal a description of the role of cognitive variables. While these models deal with cognitive variables in emotion they only briefly, if at all, discuss sexuality. In what follows we will confine most of our discussion of models of emotion to the model presented by Lang. Given the nature of this collection of papers and its dedication to Lang, that seems appropriate. While others have made important contributions, (e. g. Bower, 1981, Lazarus et al , 1980, Leventhal, 1982, and Zajnoc, 1984) space limitations forces us to not detail their contributions. When it is necessary to discuss concepts from theoretical views other than Lang's, we shall introduce them. Following our presentation of Lang's views, we move to describe concepts from models that deal explicitly with cognitive variables in sexuality.

Lang's Cognitive Model of Emotion

Lang and colleagues (Lang, 1979; Lang, Kozak, Miller, Levin, & McLean, 1980) propose a bio-informational model of emotion that combines psychophysiology and cognitive psychology within the IPA. Lang proposes as the system's basic unit propositions which represent logical, non-linguistic relationships among concepts. Bower (1981) also offers a network theory of emotion. His theory is based on the concept of spreading activation. He proposes that memory units, which he identifies as clusters of semantic propositions, are linked in the brain within an associative network. Bower feels that each emotion node or memory is linked to propositions that describe events from the individual's life that had occurred when the emotion was activated. Activation of an emotion node spreads throughout the network. Lang adds specification to the notion of an associative network by proposing that there are at least three types of propositions in emotional structures. These are semantic propositions that hold semantic or content knowledge about the input stimulus. Response propositions hold information concerning the efferent outflow associated with the emotion network. The third type is meaning propositions which are the result of a synthesis of semantic propositions and response propositions. From this view, emotions are context based action dispositions. When stimuli are input into the system, they activate specific somatic and visceral response patterns that make up the emotional response.

Lang (Lang, Bradley, & Cuthbert, 1990) has recently augmented the bio-informational model of emotion with the suggestion that emotional networks can be usefully viewed as biphasic. Using an extensive series of investigations employing the startle reflex, they suggest that emotions may be meaningfully categorized as either appetitive or aversive.

Perhaps one of the most unique and important points of Lang's bio-informational model is the suggestion that response propositions are processed in parallel with semantic and are therefore a fundamental part of emotional meaning. Responses are not separated into an separate network nor are they seen as only the result of semantic activation; but, rather, they are vital as they are part of the meaning propositional network. Since it is suggested that meaning (semantic) propositions can be linked to other meaning propositions, the model could provide a link between emotions as well as individual concepts associated with a specific emotion. More will be discussed later concerning the implications of the bio-informational model for attentional processes and response generation.

Cognitive Models in Sexuality

Several cognitive models have been proposed that deal directly with sexuality. These have certain points of similarity as well as fundamental differences. In this section we wish to point to ideas that seem to be part of several theorists' view. Borrowing from Schachter's (1964) theory of emotion, Rook and Hammen (1977) suggest the importance of the individual's cognitive labeling of non-specific physiological arousal. Citing attribution research by Cantor, Zillman, and Bryant (1975), Rook and Hammen suggest that nonspecific physiological arousal, if labelled as sexual arousal, can lead to genital sensations and cause one to interpret a nonsexual situation as sexual. Other research (Dutton & Aron, 1974; Wolchik et al., 1980) has reported related findings. We may speculate that if the labeling process goes awry and erotic labeling never occurs, sexual behavior will not occur. Similarly, it is suggested that gross mislabeling may lead to arousal to socially unacceptable stimuli and paraphillia may result.

Walen and Roth (1987) suggest that sexual stimuli and subsequent sexual arousal and behavior must be perceived and evaluated positively by the individual. Positive evaluation of stimuli and behaviors provide for feedback that leads to increased arousal and greater willingness to engage in sexual behavior. They suggest that negative evaluation at any link in the sequence should result in decreased sexual responsiveness.

Barlow and associates have undertaken a program of research aimed at elucidating the role that anxiety and cognitive interference play in the sexual functioning of men. Barlow (1986) has described five key points in his analysis of anxiety and distraction in sexuality. First, contrary to popular notions that anxiety inhibits sexual arousal, Barlow has found that anxiety (operationally defined as shock threat), tends to facilitate physiological arousal in functional men, but is somewhat debilitating for dysfunctionals (e.g. Barlow, Sakheim, & Beck, 1983; Beck, Barlow, Sakheim, & Abrahamson, 1987). Second, neutral or non-erotic distractors have been shown to decrease arousal in normal males, but not in dysfunctional males (Abrahamson, Barlow, Sakheim et al., 1985). On the other hand, distractors that are relevant to the sexual situation (i.e. focusing on an aroused partner) enhance arousal in normals, but decrease arousal in sexually dysfunctional men (Beck, Barlow, & Sakheim, 1983; Abrahamson, Barlow, Beck, Sakheim, & Kelly, 1985). Fourth, Barlow notes preliminary evidence suggesting that dysfunctionals tend to under-report arousal levels, and outlines some clinical implications of this finding (Abrahamson, Barlow, Sakheim et al., 1985; Beck, Barlow, & Sakheim, 1982). Finally, Barlow borrows from the work of Byrne

(1983b) noting that dysfunctionals tend to be more erotophobic and react negatively to sex, while normal people tend toward more positive or erotophillic affect and evaluations of sex (Barlow, 1986). The model of sexual excitement that Barlow suggests takes the form of two feedback loops. A positive loop for functionals and negative loop for dysfunctionals. Barlow hypothesizes that expectancy effects and accurate/inaccurate perceptions gradually shape attentional focus toward erotic cues for functionals or on performance concerns for dysfunctionals. Attentional focus direct toward these respective stimuli becomes more efficient over time, leading to either functional/approach behavior or dysfunctional/avoidance behavior. Though in its early stages, this model is firmly grounded in empirical data and holds promise for further understanding of cognitive factors in sexuality.

Applying the Information Processing Approach to Sexuality

We believe, in agreement with the general models proposed by Bower and Lang, that the IPA holds real promise for advancing our understanding of emotion. We also would suggest that the efforts by Barlow and colleagues that deal with sexual dysfunctions are consistent with the IPA. We next would like to expand these ideas and examine the IPA to human sexuality is a systematic manner. We will supplement the general considerations by applying the approach to the specific problem of furthering our understanding of gender differences in processing erotica.

In the past 15 to 20 years human experimental psychology has had as its principal thrust the study of cognitive variables. Several general models have been proposed that provide heuristics to help formulate research. One of the more influential has been labeled the information processing approach (Anderson 1990). The model takes as its premise the proposition that humans can be usefully conceptualized of as information processors. That is, information is introduced into the system (the individual), either from without or within, and that information is acted upon (processed). The result of the various processes is behavior. We now present an outline of the approach noting some findings in sexuality that are relevant. We are not proposing a specific model. What we are suggesting is that the approach offers a general outline that instructs researchers to focus their efforts upon certain classes of variables and events.

In its most general sense, the IPA asserts that information is sequentially processed. Information enters into the system where it undergoes a series of processes. There is considerable disagreement on many details of the system. For example, is the processing strictly sequential in which information flows from one step to another or are there parallel processes that occur simultaneously and that influence each other? As a further complication, there can be feedback among processes so that the system can have self-regulatory functions. As we examine the approach, we must not lose sight of the fact that these events occur within a living organism. Care must be taken not to ignore the fact that there are constraints placed on the system because these processes reflect physiological activities. As we shall discuss at the end of this chapter, biological constraints seem particularly salient in the domain of sexuality.

It is usually assumed that the information processing system is in place and little attention has been directed to how it develops. Parenthetically, we note that the study of how cognitive systems and processes develop is becoming an increasingly important area of study. We feel that developmental studies are particularly important for understanding sexuality. The fact that sexual interests and preferences appear to be age related argues that point. In most analyses, however, it is assumed that the individual has the processing system and that it is operating.

Analysis of Attentional Processes

The first step in the system is the receipt of new information that enters into the processing stream. This typically occurs as stimulation from the environment but input can result from internal processes. Internal processes may include thoughts and images as well as non-conscious processes. Sexual thoughts are internal processes, and they provide important input in sexuality. We begin our description with the assumption that we are examining the situation in which stimuli originate in the environment. The first obvious step is the receipt of those stimuli by the sense receptors of the individual. The nature of the attentional processes that select among the broad range of stimuli that impinge upon sense receptors has been widely studied.

We are constantly bombarded by stimuli from the environment, yet we do not respond to all of it. Several concepts have been proposed to handle the fact that not all available information is taken into the system for processing. Concepts such as attentional bias and limited attentional capacity have been proposed to address these issues. What is clear is that only a subset of all accessible stimuli is available for further processing. Some theoretical proposals that deal with emotions lump these attentional processes into one system (e. g. Lazarus et al., 1970). Lazarus's view suggests that the first step in processing is "appraisal" of the stimulus as emotional. In the domain of sexuality this view suggests that the first step would be the recognition of the stimulus as sexual. In our view such recognition is the result of the stimulus activating memory structures. We would agree with Bower (1981) that consciousness is the sum of activated semantic propositions. Thus, appraisal appears to be the conscious aspect of activated sexual propositions. Since attentional processes do not necessarily involve awareness, we feel that appraisal is too broad a concept to handle the complex events that underlie receipt of and subsequent processing of sexual stimuli.

In considering attentional factors in sexuality we focus upon the case where the environment provides the information. Such information may be auditory, olfactory, visual, or tactile stimulation. Research on sexuality has focused almost exclusively upon auditory or visual stimuli. What are some of the findings concerning the influence of stimulus modality? For men, Abel, Barlow, Blanchard, and Mavissakalian (1975) have shown that visual stimuli produces greater genital responding than auditory. The problem with these types of studies is the difficulty in equating stimuli in different modalities on such variables as novelty, complexity, and context. Such experimental controls are extremely difficult to manage and leave us unsatisfied as to the final position concerning the influence of modality of stimulus input. We will return to this topic when we discuss evolutionary considerations.

Studies on distraction. Geer and Fuhr (1976) indirectly examined attention to erotic stimuli. They manipulated distraction from an erotic stimulus and studied the effect of that variable upon genital arousal. In that study males performed cognitive operations upon single digits presented to one ear via headphones. According to group assignment, tasks performed on the digits differed in the amount of attention that was required. While occupied with the tasks, subjects were presented an erotic story in their non-attended ear. The results showed that as the distracting property of the task increased, genital responses elicited by the erotic story decreased. In the most distracting task subjects showed essentially no genital arousal. Geer and Fuhr interpreted that study as indicating that attention to erotic stimuli is necessary for sexual arousal. In a study of sensory modality effects upon distraction, Przybyla & Byrne (1984) found that both males and females report decreased arousal when both the stimulus and distractor are auditory. Yet, when the erotic stimulus is visual only females report a decrease in arousal levels to auditory distraction. Unfortunately, this gender difference in cross-modality interference has not been shown with physiological data and therefore the results could be reflecting response biases. In an unpublished study Geer (1984) reported that women showed some evidence of learning to reduce the effects of auditory distraction on genital arousal.

The findings of the preceding studies are in line with the results of earlier correlational studies in which subjects are asked to control genital responding through cognitive means. For example, Laws and Rubin (1969) found that men could inhibit erections while watching an erotic film if asked to do so. Cognitive inhibition of arousal has also been demonstrated in homosexual men (Abel et al., 1975), paraphilliacs (Abel, Blanchard, & Barlow, 1981), and women (Cerny, 1978). We might speculate that the subjects distracted themselves from the erotic stimuli when they successfully reduced genital changes upon instruction. As will be further illustrated in the next section, distraction reliably reduces sexual arousal to erotic stimuli.

Studies on attentional focus. A series of studies by Barlow and associates on distraction effects in normal and dysfunctional men has implications for the role of attention in sexuality. These studies are of interest in that they attempt to isolate neutral distraction from erotic or performance related distraction. In examining the effect of non-erotic distraction on normal and dysfunctional individuals, Abrahamson, Barlow, Sakheim et al. (1985) had their subjects watch an erotic video tape while penile tumescence was measured. In the distraction condition, subjects listened to a neutral audiotape played simultaneously with the erotic film. They found that the neutral distractor resulted in decreased tumescence for sexually functional men, but produced little or no detumescence in dysfunctional subjects.

In an earlier study, Beck et al. (1983) reported that sexually relevant distractors also differentially affected arousal in normal and clinical subjects. These authors had sexually functional and dysfunctional men watch a sexually explicit film in which the female partner was portrayed as either highly aroused, not aroused, or a partner whose arousal level was unclear. Subjects were instructed to either focus upon the man or woman in the film but were asked only to identify with the man. The data indicated that in the high arousal condition, focus on the aroused partner in the film resulted in the highest level of penile tumescence for normally functioning subjects. Partner focus appeared to inhibit penile responding in dysfunctionals. Dysfunctional men produced greatest tumescence with self-focus (focus on the male) instructions in the high arousal condition.

A replication of that study, which utilized erotic audiotapes rather than videotapes, was conducted by Abrahamson, Barlow, Beck, et al., (1985) and produced similar results. In that study, analyses suggested that dysfunctional individuals are concerned with and attend to performance related cues. Heiman and Rowland (1983) reported similar findings in a study in which normal males were instructed to attend to the depiction of an aroused partner. Normal males showed more genital change to that condition than one in which they were instructed to attend to "internal sensations of arousal." The reverse was found for dysfunctional males. A direct test of differential attention by functionals and dysfunctionals was conducted by Abrahamson, Barlow, and Abrahamson (1989). In that study both neutral and performance related distrators were included. Findings confirmed that dysfunctional men were distracted by performance related cues (evidenced less arousal) but not by neutral distractors. Normal men showed the reverse pattern. Barlow and colleagues concluded that the direction of attentional focus is important for both normally functioning and sexually dysfunctional men. They venture that the same holds true for women (Barlow, 1986). We concur with that opinion, and urge further research in the area of attention and sexuality. We would add that the work of the above researchers was not undertaken using the IPA framework. We believe, however, the results are highly relevant.

Lang's bio-informational theory of emotion has implications for attentional processes. Lang's theory predicts different behavioral outcomes in experiments that vary the nature of the individual's focus of attention. The theory proposes that the variable of attending to stimulus versus response properties of imaginal stimuli will have important effects. A recent test of Lang's theory as applied to human sexuality was conducted by Dekker and Everaerd (1988). These researchers had male and female subjects either imagine a sexual interaction, view sexually explicit slides, or listen to an erotic story. In each of these conditions half the subjects were instructed to attend to only the situation and actions of their assigned sexual stimulus (hypothesized to activate stimulus propositions). The second set of subjects were to attend to both the situation and actions of the story and to their own responses and reactions (to trigger response propositions). In accord with Lang's theory, subjects given the latter instructions became physiologically more aroused. The effect was more widespread for men, who evidenced greater arousal with stimulus-response (S-R) instructions across all stimulus conditions (imagery, slides, and stories). Women showed greater arousal under stimulus-response instructions only in the imagery condition. That subjects generally responded with more arousal to S-R instructions over stimulus instructions indicates attentional focus is important in sexual arousal. Dekker and Everaerd suggested that idiosyncratic features of the story or slides may have distracted the women in this study.

Steinberg (1986) also conducted a test of the bio- informational model. She trained women to emphasize either stimulus propositions or response propositions when practicing visual imagery. In accordance with Lang's theory, those subjects who were trained to use response propositions showed greater genital responding when subsequently imagining sexual scenes. The most striking feature of that study was that training in imaging response propositions to non-sexual imagery resulted in increased genital responding to sexual imagery. This study combined with those cited above shows that attentional focus is a variable of importance in sexuality.

Saliency of erotic stimulation. Neilsen and Sarason (1981) used the IPA to examine the effects of emotional stimuli when presented in the unattended channel of a dichotic listening task. Using undergraduates, subjects were presented with word pairs in the shadowed channel. In the unattended channel, subjects were presented with one of four types of emotional target stimuli: Sexually explicit (taboo) words; hostility/aggression words; words concerning university life; or test anxiety words. A control condi-

tion was included in which subjects heard only neutral words in the unattended channel. The experimenters obtained data on shadowing error rates (distortions or omissions of shadowed words, or intrusions of unattended words) and confidence ratings. In confidence ratings subjects indicated how strongly they believed various target words were present in the unattended channel. The authors found that shadowing error rates for subjects in the taboo word condition were significantly higher than for those in the other experimental or control conditions. Taboo word intrusions appeared to account for a large proportion of errors, as 53% of the subjects in that condition reported hearing sexually explicit words. Only 20% or less of subjects in the other conditions reported hearing any target words in the unattended channel. Moreover, subjects in the taboo condition were significantly more confident of having heard taboo words in the ignored channel. Subjects in the other conditions were more confident of not having heard taboo words. Neilsen and Sarason conclude that sexual information can be highly salient within an individual's information processing abilities.

We have recently completed a study in our laboratory that bears on the issue of attention and sexuality. Using the IPA, Geer and Lapour (1990) examined individual differences in attentional biases for erotic, romantic, and neutral sentences. They used a modified form of the visual dot probe task (MacLeod, Mathews, & Tata, 1986) whereby male and female subjects were presented with pairs of sentences on a computer display. The sentences, one of which was always neutral, appeared one above the other. On some randomly determined trials, either the top or bottom sentence was probed by a small dot to which the subject responded by immediately pressing the keyboard spacebar. A measure of latency of responding to the dot was obtained. It was hypothesized that sentence types with shorter latencies to the associated dot probe had attention capturing qualities. The results were mixed. A general speeding effect was found for men across all sentences, though the effect was strongest for erotic sentences. Women responded slightly faster to romantic sentences and were slowest in detecting probes of erotic sentences, though this effect was nonsignificant. Thus weak evidence for a gender- linked attentional bias was found in this experiment. The modifications to the dot probe methodology do not allow us to say conclusively whether the pattern of results obtained is due primarily to attentional or to post attentional processes. We are conducting further research examining the hypothesis that there is a gender-linked attentional bias involved in sexual stimuli. Preliminary results do not support the hypothesis of gender based attentional biases with explicitly sexual or romantic words. If fact, preliminary analyses suggest that subjects may look away from erotic stimuli in the dot probe paradigm.

What can we say concerning our knowledge of the role of attention in the domain of sexuality? The evidence is clear that attention must be directed toward visual and auditory erotic stimuli for them to result in sexual arousal. We do not know if the same is true for tactile or olfactory stimuli. Most of the evidence for this view comes from distraction studies. We have some evidence that individuals can learn to reduce the effects of distraction. More research is needed to identify all the variables involved in distraction to map out parameters. We also know that differential focusing of attention influences sexual arousal. That finding has both theoretical (cf Lang's bio- informational model) and practical implications for sexual dysfunctions (see Barlow, 1986). Research has demonstrated the saliency of erotic stimuli and that the visual modality appears to yield the greatest response when contrasted with auditory stimuli and sexual thoughts.

Analysis of Encoding and Memory Processes

The next step in the IPA is encoding. By encoding most investigators refer to the processes by which material that is admitted to the system is prepared for and enters memory. The mechanisms surrounding the encoding of information in memory systems has been the focus of considerable research and theorizing. The fundamental notion is that upon entering the memory system the material influences and in turn is influenced by the current memory structures. The resultant memory structures form the basis of our updated knowledge representation.

Coding of sexual information. Some of the research on encoding has focused upon the nature of the code by which information is readied for storage. Is information coded differently from the different sensory systems or is the code similar regardless of the modality of input? For example, when we see an erotic word do we process that word in a fundamentally different manner than when the same word is spoken to us? These are extremely complex problems since the different sensory inputs are usually presented in considerably different contexts. These issues have not been studied in the domain of sexuality. The closest research on that topic of which we are aware was briefly described above. Przybyla and Byrne, (1984) showed that distraction could interfere with reports of sexual arousal across sensory modalities. Barlow and associates (Abrahamson, Barlow, Sakheim et al., 1985;) also showed cross-modality interference between and erotic film and neutral audiotape. They found that the interference effect varied as a function of the nature of the attentional focus and the clinical status of the subject. Regardless of the resolution of the issues surrounding the coding of the stimulus, the IPA suggests that next the stimulus code enters the memory system.

The suggestion of multiple memory systems. Before we discuss encoding in the domain of sexuality we must discuss a major complication. It is widely held that there are at least two major types of learning that are proposed to give rise to different memory structures (Schacter, 1987). These types of learning have been given various names by various investigators and theoreticians. Labels that have been used include explicit, strategic, declarative, and conscious on one hand and implicit, automatic, procedural, and non-conscious on the other. We propose to avoid questions concerning the details of these systems. For example, Tulving (1985) argued cogently for a ternary (three classification) system. Rather than enter a discussion of the details of the arguments concerning multiple memory systems, our point is to acknowledge the issue and point to its relevance to understanding sexuality. Some of the general models of emotion that we discussed earlier (e.g. Levinthal, 1982; Zajnoc, 1980) consider these issues under the heading of emotional versus cognitive learning. The approach that we are taking uses a different language, but we are often considering similar phenomena.

As support for the notion of multiple memory systems, we are impressed with the growing empirical literature that identifies different brain structures with the classes of learning (see Schacter, 1987). It is our belief that such evidence provides powerful support for the existence of at least two distinct but interacting learning systems. For our purposes it is important to note that both strategic, conscious, volitional memory (explicit) as well as non-conscious, automatic memory (implicit) play a role in sexuality.

The interaction between implicit and explicit memory. We are unable to specify in detail the nature of the interaction between the different types of memory in sexuality. However, if we accept the notion that subjective report indexes the explicit system and that genital changes involve the implicit system, considerable evidence of their interaction is available. For example, Hall, Binik, and Di Tomasso (1985) found stable individual differences across classes of stimuli in the individual's correlation between genital-subjective responding. Korff and Geer (1983) demonstrated that within the individual, the genital-subjective correlation can be influenced by instructional variables. These data as well as much that was cited in the section on the evidence of cognitive phenomena (e.g. Geer & Fuhr, 1976; Stock & Geer, 1982), force us to acknowledge that in sexuality implicit and explicit processes influence each other. We await further development of theory and additional research to complete our understanding of the importance of the interaction.

The issue of the interaction between the implicit and explicit memory structure has a long history in the study of emotion. Often it is couched in terms of the interaction between emotion and cognition. For example, many of the chapters in Clark and Fiske's (1982) *Affect and Cognition* are devoted to a consideration of the interface between emotion and cognition. Similarly, the book by Williams, Watts, MacLeod and Mathews (1989) notes the importance of strategic versus automatic processes. The notions automatic and strategic appear to have considerable overlap with the concepts of implicit and explicit. While Zajonc (1980) does not feel that cognition and emotion interact, we are not in accord with that view.

In sexuality, the issue of the interaction between the implicit and explicit processes takes on renewed importance. We have only the barest outline of the nature of the interaction. It appears to us that influence flows more readily from the cognitive or explicit to the implicit. We have empirical evidence that cognitive events can result in and influence genital responding. The influence of automatic and or physiological events upon the cognitive seem diffuse and weak relative to the reverse. There are anecdotal reports that non-sexual vibration, such as encountered in subways or on motorcycles, will result in erections. However, to our knowledge, this has not been studied empirically.

A series of investigations has shown that non-sexual arousal may be associated with increased sexual responding. Dutton and Aron (1974) had male passerbys approach an attractive female on either a fear-arousing or a non fear-arousing bridge. Those in the fear condition subsequently gave more sexual TAT responses. They also made more attempts to establish post-experimental contact with the female experimenter than subjects on a non-fear bridge or with a male experimenter. Cantor, Zillman and Bryant (1975) had males exercise, then obtained self-report ratings of arousal to and liking of an erotic film. The interval between exercise and film was varied. Self-rated sexual arousal was greatest with the most residual physiological activity (shortest interval). Wolchik et al. (1980) exposed males to emotionally arousing video tapes (depression and anger or anxiety and anger) or to a neutral tape. An erotic video followed. Genital change was measured during all videos. No difference was found to the initial film. However, arousal to the erotic tape was greater when it followed the anxiety and anger tape than when it followed the depression or neutral tapes. These studies, when taken together, demonstrate how non-erotic arousal can influence sexual arousal.

The usual interpretation of the above studies is that the non-sexual arousal becomes interpreted as sexual arousal. This then leads the individual to interpret the situation as sexual and subsequently elicits other sexual responses. The studies described above were stimulated by the Schachter and Singer (1962) model of emotion in which the physiological substrate of all emotions is similar. The definition by the individual of which emotion he or she is experiencing results from their interpretation of environmental cues. We view these findings as also important for their demonstration of the interaction between cognition and emotion, perhaps reflect interaction between explicit and implicit systems.

We cannot ignore the possibility that one type of memory process may transform itself into the other. It is recognized that well practiced strategic tasks can become automated. The example of driving a car is often noted as an example of that process. We don't know the degree to which similar processes may work in sexuality. It is possible that under certain conditions, the explicit can become implicit and visa versa. The study of this possibility is a challenge to sex researchers as well as researchers in emotion in general.

As a further complexity, many cognitive events often appear to be extremely fast while the more macro physiological events are by comparison slow. This difference in time course obviously is true for hormone effects. It is possible that hormone effects operate through selective excitation of brain structures that are involved with genital change. Different time courses complicate the issue but cannot be ignored. At this point we must admit that our understanding of the interactions between these systems is incomplete. Both theory development and additional data are needed to specify the nature of the interactions.

Studies on memory in sexuality. There now exists a substantial amount of literature that has examined memory in sexuality. Much of that literature was designed to test a schema- based model but many studies are relevant to network conceptualizations as well. Schema theories (Alba & Hasher, 1983) suggest that processed material is stored in cohesive units that reflect the current organization of memory. Scripting theories (Schank & Ableson, 1977) suggest a related conceptualization that typically describes quite specific situations. Other views of the structure of memory suggest that memory is best conceptualized as a network of associations or propositions. Bower's model and Lang's bio-informational model belong in that grouping. The assumption of both types of models is that encoded material when entering the memory system activates those components that are relevant to the encoded material. The implication of network conceptualization is that such activation also automatically influences associated parts of memory that were not directly activated through encoding. While there is considerable disagreement over the nature of the associative networks and/or schema, that clusters of information exist is an accepted formulation. The proposal is that the memory structures that exist following encoding reflect both the previous structure and changes brought about by the newly encoded material.

Several studies from our laboratory have investigated memory processes in sexuality. We shall discuss them in greater detail in the subsequent section on gender differences in response to erotica. At this point we wish to note how some of these studies are relevant to understanding memory structures. One of these studies (Geer & Broussard, 1990) examined the possibility that coitus is such a stereotyped behavior that it can be modeled using scripting concepts from computer modeling. That is, the Geer and Broussard investigation revealed the sequence of sexual acts that make up coitus is highly predictable. One of the prerequisites for scripting seems to be that the behavior under investigation is quite predictable. That study also revealed that scales of perceived level of arousal elicited by the steps in coitus differ markedly between the sexes.

Geer and McGlone (1990) designed a study to test suggestions grounded in schema theory that the genders differ in their responses to the elements contained in an erotic paragraph. In that study, students were given a paragraph to read that contained erotic, romantic, and neutral sentences. Later they were asked to recognize some of these sentences among distractor sentences. Males were faster and more accurate at recognizing erotic sentences and females were faster and more accurate at recognizing romantic sentences. Geer and Lapour (1990) partially replicated that experiment. They again found males to be faster when recognizing erotic sentences and females to be faster when recognizing romantic sentences although finding no differences in accuracy. A study (Geer & Judice, 1990) has been completed to examine the suggestion that the results of gender-based differences found in Geer and McGlone could be accounted for by examining reading times. There were significant differences between the reading times for the various categories of sentences. Erotic sentences were read longer than either the romantic or neutral, which did not differ from each other. Reading times could not explain memory effects since in this study the gender based differences failed to reach statistical significance. Since reading times did not predict recognition accuracy, the idea that reading times only index processing load must be modified when we consider the reading erotic of material.

The next study of interest is that of Kirsch-Rosenkrantz and Geer (1991). That investigation examined erotic story perspective (male or female) on memory. Although no differences were found in relation to the story perspective, an interesting gender difference was found. In comparison to females, males exhibited more erotic intrusions when recalling the story and fewer romantic intrusions. It is hypothesized that these intrusions are due to the activation of a more complex sexual schema in males. Preliminary data from our laboratory using Schvaneveldt's (Schvaneveldt, 1990) network producing algorithm "Pathfinder" indicates that males' cognitive network for sexual material is more complex than that found for females.

Providing further evidence for schema theory, Castille and Geer (1989) found that memory for an ambiguous story could be influenced by its context. By manipulating the title and a descriptor sentence, they were able to influence the theme remembered by subjects. The study revealed that subjects could be induced to interpret the same story as either sexual or non-sexual depending upon the title and descriptor sentence. According to schema theory, titles and descriptors function to structure the organization and interpretation of the story's theme. This study was described as demonstrating that sometimes sex is in the "eye of the beholder." Both Bower's (1981) and Lang's (1979) network theories can readily handle these findings.

These investigations show that memory structures are readily available for study in the domain of sexuality. Such experiments may well provide the opportunity to study the interaction between implicit and explicit process, both of which are important to sexuality. It can be demonstrated that gender differences exist in memory for erotic material and that subjects can be influenced to view ambiguous material as sexual if given a setting context.

Analysis of Response Production

The next step in the IPA is the translation of the memory representation into behavior. For the most part cognitive research has used traditional memory tasks (recall and recognition) to test details of the memory representation. These tests, such as described in the previous section, are seen as yielding information upon how knowledge is represented. Tasks can be designed to investigate how memory is organized, how structures interact, and how memory is modified by inputs. Generally it is suggested that knowledge, which can be read as memory structures, is used either to guide behavior or to facilitate problem solving. The concept of production systems has been proposed to embrace the obviously very complex processes that generate responses from knowledge.

When discussing the generation of responses, Lang's model of emotion has been more detailed than most in approaching the problem. As noted previously, the bio-informational model suggests that emotions may be usefully conceptualized as memory structures that involve meaning, stimulus, and response propositions. Response propositions function to yield behavior. In Lang's formulation autonomic activity is viewed as a crucial element in emotional states. In his model, when an emotional structure is activated, there is activation of autonomic nervous system response propositions. These response propositions are an integral part of the neural substrate that produces autonomic responses. This means that when an emotional memory structure is activated, autonomic activity occurs in addition to the overt behavior that is part of the response propositional structure. In the domain of sexuality genital responses are particularly important. Thus Lang's model, when applied to sexuality, must include genital response propositions. We will consider this point again in the section on evolutionary variables presented later.

An additional important point needs to be made concerning the use of knowledge available in memory structures. Literature on the IPA notes that post decisional processes may well influence subject's responses concerning the content of memory. In the domain of sexuality there likely are response biases that influence the production of output from the memory system. For example, it is probable that some subjects who retrieve several words from memory will be hesitant to report those words with sexual meaning. They may be reluctant to report what they view as socially undesirable words. Thus a response bias can influence the output from a knowledge representation. In any study, emotion investigators must be careful not to assume that the report of memory that he or she obtains reflects knowledge structures.

Research that is directly relevant to the notion of response bias in sexuality has been conducted. These studies have examined individuals' production of erotic associates when presented with double entendre words (e.g. Galbraith & Sturke, 1974). These studies were not conceptualized as investigating memory structures. Rather, they examined individual

difference variables such as sex guilt upon reactions to double entendre words. Galbraith and Sturke found that words rated as highly sexual yielded increased associative latencies. It is interesting that across all studies of this type, most individuals could produce sexual associates to ambiguous or double entendre words. This suggests that knowledge for sexual words is readily available for both sexes. Schwartz (1975) indicates that differential word association rates by those high and low in sex guilt is not a function of sexual knowledge. He argues the difference results from the "place sexual responses occupy in their (subject's) respective response hierarchies." In our parlance, the evidence suggests retrieval or response biases were operating in these studies.

The IPA suggests that knowledge representations, regardless of the argument over their form, act to direct behavior. The fact that production systems are carefully considered in the IPA is evidence of the attention directed toward mechanisms of responding. Lang's bio-informational model has been the most specific about this aspect of information processing. His concept of response proposition directs attention to this important aspect of the system. In sexuality, attention must be directed to genital responding. The concept of response propositions seems well suited to handle the matter. Additionally, the IPA literature on post-decisional processes alerts us to the notion of response biases. The work in our laboratory that has investigated gender differences in memory for erotic material provides a possible case in point for the operation of response biases. We will discuss this issue in some detail in the next section.

Information Processing Analysis of Gender Differences in Response to Erotica

We have noted that there are gender differences in memory for components of erotica. We now wish to present an analysis based on the IPA. This will serve to illustrate the heuristics available from the approach. We know that there are gender based differences in the report of memory for erotic material. These differences are consistent with the stereotyped gender difference in interest and response to erotic versus romantic stimuli. What is not clear are the mechanisms that underlie the differences. The IPA suggests that we consider attentional processes as one possible class of mechanisms. While it is possible that the genders differentially attend to erotic and romantic stimuli, as of this time direct evidence of the same is weak. Similarly, we have no definitive evidence that the genders differ in their coding of sexual stimuli. There have, however, been suggestions that such is the case. Symons (1987), arguing from an evolutionary perspective, suggests that the genders should differ in which sense modality is dominant in responding to sexual stimuli. Males should be aroused by distal (visual) stimuli more than females who should be more readily aroused by proximal (tactile) stimuli. That follows from the argument that males should be more readily aroused by females since it is in their reproductive interests to impregnate as many females as possible while females should be selective in mate selection. The study by Przybyla and Byrne (1984) provides partial support for that position. The jury is still out on the question of whether or not gender differences in response to erotica can be found in sense modality or attentional mechanisms. The findings and theoretical suggestions could, however, form the basis of a series of studies designed to investigate attentional processes and sense modality effects.

Our research has focused upon the question of whether knowledge structures relevant to sexual stimuli differ for the sexes. More specifically, when considering stimuli that contain erotic and romantic elements, do the genders differ in their processing of the material? The data that we have noted show that men and women process romantic and erotic stimuli differently (Geer & McGlone, 1990; Kirsch-Rosenkrantz & Geer, 1991; Geer & Lapour, 1990). That conclusion is drawn from studies designed to investigate the structure of memory. This leaves us tempted to say that for women knowledge representations concerning sexuality have more romantic elements and/or

those elements are more powerfully associated with each other. The same formulation would hold for males only now we are referring to erotic elements.

Of course, the world is not that simple. There is an alternative explanation for those findings that our studies do not eliminate. It is possible to obtain the results that we describe by appealing to processes that occur following accessing memory. It may be that women have the same knowledge representation as men, but when producing a response, biases or strategic processes intervene that modify it. For example, perhaps women are more hesitant than men to report explicitly erotic material due to social desirability concerns. Our findings (Geer & McGlone, 1990) that both sexes respond fastest to neutral stimuli is consistent with a response bias interpretation. It will take careful experimental study to tease out response biasing processes from memory differences. We believe that gender differences in both knowledge representations and response biases exist. The challenge will be to see under what conditions each operates and what are the interactions that occur.

We have shown how IPA has stimulated research on gender differences in response to erotica. The approach has been useful in providing insights into possible mechanisms to help explain the findings. Research has been conducted on attentional variables, knowledge structures, and post-decisional processes or response biases. We believe that the IPA has provided the most important function that a model has to offer, it has been a fruitful source of experimental hypotheses. Research is continuing on the question of sex differences, and we anticipate that the IPA will continue to provide interesting insights into the issues.

The Need to Consider Evolutionary Influences In Sexuality

One important missing factor in our proposed IPA is the need to acknowledge the importance of evolutionary features. Darwinian concepts force us to recognize that successful reproduction is the ultimate goal of evolutionary processes. The evolutionary approach to understanding sexuality emphasizes these considerations and demands that we seriously consider the issue (Symons, 1987).

Species survival requires that at least on some occasions genital responses occur in the presence of appropriate stimuli. That does not mean they must occur in their presence or that the stimuli must always be present for genital responses to occur. The argument is that over the course of evolution it is important that mechanisms have evolved that assure that sexual intercourse occurs. For our analysis this has several important implications. First, there must be a link between sexual stimuli and genital responding. That link, we would argue, must either be automatic or highly prepared. While one can readily demonstrate that the culture conditions the expression of sexuality, in no culture does sex exclude genital activity.

There is anecdotal evidence that in humans genital stimulation results in sexual arousal and pleasurable sensations in a reflexive or prepared manner. This evidence indicates that the link between genital stimulation and emotional responding does not require socialization or language. Serbin & Sprafkin (1987) note that genital stimulation in the non-verbal infant appears reflexively to yield pleasurable sensations. A similar observation can be made concerning the profoundly retarded. These individuals find genital stimulation very reinforcing and some individuals will spend much time in self stimulation. Our point is that on at least an anecdotal basis it can be observed that humans reflexively respond to genital stimulation as if it has positive or reinforcing value.

These observations mean that the IPA must recognize that emotional sexual memory structures will have strong links to genital responses. It appears that Lang's bio-informational model provides a conceptual framework that can recognize that relationship. The concept of response propositions can be invoked to denote the link between genital responding and sexual cognitive structures. What we would emphasize is that this link is either automatic or highly prepared and that any serious explanatory system that discusses sexuality must acknowledge that link. Lang does not address the question of genital activity in sexuality. However, the fact that his formulation can provide a framework from which to consider these issues speaks favorably to bio-informational model. Some theories ((Rook & Hammen, 1977; Steinberg, 1986/1987; Walen & Roth, 1987) have suggested a central role to the individual's recognition of his or her genital responding as being important. We would suggest that such an importance might flow from the recognition of the relatively automatic association between sexual stimuli, genital responding, and the reinforcing aspect of sexual arousal. The thrust of the preceding argument is that the IPA to sexuality has to recognize the powerful association of genital responding with the processing of sexual information.

Conclusions

We believe that the evidence is clear that concepts and ideas from the IPA have proven useful in furthering our understanding of sexuality. For example, any consideration of sexuality that fails to note the importance of attentional processes is doomed to be impoverished at best. Similarly, failure to account for the gender differences in memory without reference to contemporary cognitive concepts such as suggested by the IPA risks isolating sexuality from the mainstream of behavioral science. For us the IPA provides a rich source of experimental hypotheses. We feel that among the specific models that have put forward within the IPA framework that Lang's bio-informational model has the most to recommend its application to sexuality. Research already has established the model's relevance to sexuality. We look forward to its continued contribution to understanding sexuality.

We have described how cognitive activity (sexual thoughts) in the sexual domain can result in genital responding. We have used erotic paragraphs that are known to result in genital responses as stimuli in memory tasks. This means that researchers have the opportunity to study the interaction between genital and cognitive responding in established research paradigms. As of this date very little has been done to examine this potentially powerful paradigm. Exciting research opportunities await the investigator who combines these areas of research. This opportunity is surrounded by obstacles. There are practical problems that face that investigator. These include the different time course of cognitive and physiological (genital) systems and the myriad of problems faced by any investigator that conducts research on genital activity (Geer & Head, 1990). We recommend the IPA in combination with physiological recording for the serious consideration of scholars in sexuality.

References

Abel, G. G., Blanchard, E. B., & Barlow, D. H. (1981). Measurement of sexual arousal in several paraphiliacs: The effects of stimulus modality, instructional set and stimulus content. *Behaviour Research and Therapy, 19*, 25–33.

Abel, G. G., Barlow, D. H., Blanchard, E. B., & Mavissakalian, M. (1975). Measurement of sexual arousal in male homosexuals: Effects of instructions and stimulus modality. *Archives of Sexual Behavior, 4*, 623–629.

Abrahamson, D. J., Barlow, D. H., Sakheim, D. K., Beck, J. G., & Athansiou, R. (1985). Effects of distraction on sexual responding in functional and dysfunctional men. *Behavior Therapy, 16*, 503–515.

Alba, J. W., & Hasher, L. (1983). Is memory schematic? *Psychological Bulletin, 93*, 203–231.

Abrahamson, D. J., Barlow, D. H., & Abrahamson, L. S. (1989). differential effects of performance demand and distraction on sexually functional and dysfunctional males. *Journal of Abnormal Psychology, 98*, 241–247.

Abrahamson, D. J., Barlow, D. H., Beck, J. G., Sakheim, D. K., & Kelly, J. P. (1985). Effects of attentional focus and partner responsiveness on sexual responding: Replication and extension. *Archives of Sexual Behavior, 14*, 361–371.

Anderson, J. R. (1990). *Cognitive psychology and its implications* (3rd ed.). New York: Freeman.

Barlow, D. H. (1986). Causes of sexual dysfunction: The role of anxiety and cognitive interference. *Journal of Consulting and Clinical Psychology, 54*, 140–148.

Barlow, D. H., Sakheim, D. K., & Beck, J. G. (1983). Anxiety increases sexual arousal. *Journal of Abnormal Psychology, 92*, 49–54.

Beck, J. G., Barlow, D. H., & Sakheim, D. K. (1982, August). Sexual arousal and suppression patterns in functional and dysfunctional men. Paper presented at the American Psychological Association Annual Convention, Washington, D. C.

Beck, J. G., Barlow, D. H., & Sakheim, D. K. (1983). The effects of attentional focus and partner arousal on sexual responding in functional and dysfunctional men. *Behaviour Research and Therapy, 21*, 1–8.

Beck, J. G., Barlow, D. H., Sakheim, D. K., & Abrahamson, D. J. (1987). Shock threat and sexual arousal: The role of selective attention, thought content, and affective states. *Psychophysiology, 24*, 165–172.

Bower, G. H. (1981). Mood and memory. *American Psychologist, 36*, 129–148.

Byrne, D. (1983b). The antecedents, correlates, and consequents of erotophobia-erotophilia. In C. Davis (Ed.), *Challenges in sexual science: Current theoretical issues and research advances* (pp. 53–75). Philadelphia: Society for the Scientific Study of Sex.

Cantor, J., Zillman, D., & Bryant, J. (1975). Enhancement of experienced sexual arousal in response to erotic stimuli through misattribution of unrelated residual excitation. *Journal of Personlity and Social Psychology, 32*, 69–75.

Castille, C. O., & Geer, J. H. (1989, August). Sex is in the eye of the beholder. Paper presented at the American Psychological Association Annual Convention, New Orleans, LA.

Cerny, J. A., (1978). Biofeedback and the voluntary control of sexual arousal in women. *Behavior Therapy, 9*, 847–855.

Clark, M. S., & Fiske, S. T. (Eds.). (1980). *Affect and cognition: The seventeenth annual Carnegie symposium on cognition*. Hillsdale, NJ: Lawrence Erlbaum Associates.

Dekker, J., & Everaerd, W. (1988). Attentional effects on sexual arousal. *Psychophysiology, 25*, 45–54.

Dutton, D., & Aron, A. (1974). Some evidence for heightened sexual attraction under conditions of high anxiety. *Journal of Personality and Social Psychology, 30,* 510–517.

Geer, J. H., & Judice, S. L. (1990, August). Reading times of erotic material: Savoring the moment. Paper presented at International Academy of Sex Research Meeting, Sigtuna, Sweden.

Geer, J. H., & McGlone, M. S. (1990). Sex differences in memory for erotica. *Cognition and Emotion, 4,* 71–78.

Geer, J. H. & Head, S. (1990). Psychophysiology of sexual response. In Cacioppo, Tassiniari, & Petty (Eds.), *Principles of psycholphysiology: Physical, social, and inferential elements* (pp. 599–630). Cambridge: Cambridge University Press.

Geer, J. H., & Broussard, D. B. (1990). Scaling sexual behavior and arousal: Consistency and sex differences. *Journal of Personality and Social Psychology, 58,* 664–671.

Geer, J. H., & Lapour, K. J. (1990, June). The sexes differ in their processing of erotic, romantic, and neutral sentences. Paper presented at the American Psychological Society Annual Convention, Dallas, TX.

Geer, J. H., & Fuhr, R. (1976). Cognitive factors in sexual arousal: The role of distraction. *Journal of Consulting and Clinical Psychology, 44,* 238–243.

Geer, J. H. (1984). Distraction effects on female sexual arousal: Repeated exposure and possible recovery. Paper presented at the American Psychological Association Annual Convention, Toronto, Canada.

Hall, K., Binik, Y., & Di Tomasso, E. (1985). Concordance between physiological and subjective measures of sexual arousal. *Behaviour Research and Therapy, 23,* 297–303.

Heiman, J. R. & Rowland, D. L. (1983). Affective and physiological sexual response patterns: The effects of instructions on sexually functional and dysfunctional men. *Journal of Psychosomatic Research, 27,* 105–116.

Kirsch-Rosenkrantz, J., & Geer, J. H. (1991). Gender differences in memory for a sexual story. *Archives of Sexual Behavior, 28,* 295–305.

Korff, J., & Geer, J. H. (1983). Relationship between sexual arousal experience and genital response. *Psychophysiology, 20,* 121–127.

Lang, P. J. (1979). A bio-informational theory of emotional imagery. *Psychophysiology, 16,* 495–512.

Lang, P. J., Kozak, M. I., Miller, G. A., Levin, D. N., & McLean, A. (1980). Emotional imagry: Conceptual structure and pattern of somato-visceral response. *Psychophysiology, 17,* 179–192.

Laws, D. R., & Rubin, H. (1969). Instructional control of autonomic sexual response. *Journal of Nervous and Mental Diseases, 136,* 272–278.

Lazarus, R. S., Kanner, A. D., & Folkman, S. (1980). Emotions: A cognitive-phenomenological analysis. In R. Plutchik & H. Kellerman (Eds.), *Emotion: Theory, research, and experience* (pp. 189–218). New York: Academic Press.

Lazarus, R. S., Averill, J. R., & Opton, E. M., Jr. (1970). Toward a cognitive theory of emotion. In M. Arnold (Ed.), *Feelings and emotions* (pp. 207–231). New York: Academic Press.

Leventhal, H. (1982). The integration of emotion and cognition: A view from the perceptual-motor theory of emotion. In M. S. Clark & S. T. Fiske (Eds.), *Affect and Cognition: The Seventeenth Annual Carnegie Symposium on Cognition* (pp. 121–156). Hillsdale, NJ: Lawrence Erlbaum Associates.

MacLeod, C., Mathews, A., & Tata, P. (1986). Attentional bias in emotional disorders. *Journal of Abnormal Psychology, 95,* 15–20.

Nielsen, S., L., & Sarason, I. G. (1981). Emotion, personality, and selective attention. *Journal of Personality and Social Psychology, 41,* 945–960.

Przybyla, D., & Byrne, D. (1984). The mediating role of cognitive processes in self-reported sexual arousal. *Journal of Research in Personality, 18,* 54–63.

Rook, K. S., & Hammen, C. L. (1977). A cognitive perspective on the experience of sexual arousal. *Journal of Social Issues, 33* (2), 7–29.

Rosen, R. C., & Beck, J. G. (1988). *Patterns of sexual arousal.* New York: Guilford Press.

Schachter, S. (1964). The interaction of cognitive and physiological determinants of emotional state. In L. Berkowittz (Ed.), *Advances in experimental social psychology* (Vol. 1). New York: Academic Press.

Schachter, S., & Singer, J. (1962). Cognitive, social, and physiological determinants of emotional state. *Psychological Review, 69,* 379–397.

Schacter, D. L. (1987). Implicit memory: History and current status. *Journal of Experimental Psychology: Learning, Memory, and Cognition, 13,* 501–518.

Schank, R. C., & Abelson, R. (1977). *Scripts, plans, goals, and understanding.* Hillsdale, NJ: Lawrence Erlbaum Associates.

Schvaneveldt, R. (Ed.), (1990). *Pathfinder associative networks.* Norwood, N.J.: Ablex Publishing Co.

Schwartz, S. (1975). Effects of sex guilt on word association responses to double-entendre sexual words. *Journal of Consulting and Clinical Psychology, 43,* 100.

Steinberg, J. L. (1986). The psychophysiology of

sexual arousal: An information-processing approach (Doctoral dissertation, State University of New York at Stony Brook). *Dissertation Abstracts International, 48,* 574B.

Stock, W. S., & Geer, J. H. (1982). Study of fantasy-based sexual arousal in women. *Archives of Sexual Behavior, 11,* 33–47.

Symons, D. (1987). An evolutionary approach: Can Darwin's view of life shed light on human sexuality? In J. H. Geer & W. T. O'Donohue (Eds.), *Theories of human sexuality* (pp. 91–125). New York: Plenum Press.

Tulving, E. (1985). How many memory systems are there? *American Psychologist, 40,* 385–398.

Walen, S. R., & Roth, D. (1987). A cognitive approach. In J. H. Geer & W. T. O'Donohue (Eds.), *Theories of human sexuality* (pp. 335–362). New York: Plenum Press.

Williams, J. M. G., Watts, F. N., MacLeod, C., & Mathews, A. (1989). *Cognitive psychology and emotional disorders.* New York: Wiley.

Wolchik, S. A., Beggs, V., Wincze, J. P., Sakheim, D. K., Barlow, D. H., & Mavissakalian, M. (1980). The effects of emotional arousal on subsequent sexual arousal in men. *Journal of Abnormal Psychology, 89,* 595–598.

Zajonc, R. B. (1980). Feeling and thinking: Preferences need not inferences. *American Psychologist, 35,* 151–175.

Zajonc, R. B. (1984). On the primacy of affect. *American Psychologist, 39,* 117–123.

Physiology, Perceived Emotion and Memory: Responding to Film Sequences

Daniela Palomba and Luciano Stegagno*

Abstract

The present discussion focusses on factors influencing emotional information processing, production of relevant physiological outflow and integration of psychophysiological responses. According to Lang's bio-informational model of emotional imagery, the way in which emotional information is processes is critical in integrating psychological and physiological response levels to produce coherent emotional states.

Watching an emotional film is supposed to facilitate the production of emotional responses. Data are presented concerning the different psychophysiological patterns observed during the viewing of emotional film sequences. The hypothesis that subjects' involvement is a key factor for relevant emotional responses has been tested by presenting subjects with emotional scenes extracted from the movie. Subjects' judgements of emotion, and their memory for dialogues, objects and environments showed in the film, have also been studied. The relationship between expected and actual physiological arousal during emotion-eliciting film sequences is discussed in the last section. Data suggest that the integration of psychophysiological responses is based upon cognitive strategies which reduce possible discordance among levels.

Key words: emotions, movie, physiology, memory

The acquisition of an emotional set disposition and the occurence of specific emotional responses in selected contexts, is the result of integration processes between subjects' physiological changes and their evaluation and memory of the emotional event. Laboratory studies, however, often show poor correlations between physiological and cognitive emotional responses (Lang, 1964; Lacey, 1967). The fractionation and specificity of psychophysiological reactions (Lacey & Lacey, 1970; Obrist, 1982), as well as the unreliability of subjects' visceral perception mechanisms (Hirschman & Clark, 1983; Stegagno & Palomba, 1986), contribute to the lack of covariation.

In the light of Lang's bio-informational theory of emotional imagery (Lang, 1979; 1984), it can be hypothesized that a better integration between the two levels occurs under circumstances which enhance the matching between the input information and emotional information stored in memory.

Emotions are defined as action disposition sets which include overt behaviour, verbal reports and physiological changes. They are organized in memory as informational networks which are accessed to produce an emotional response. As obvious in Lang's model, the way in which emotional information is processed is critical in integrating psychological and physiological levels to produce coherent emotional states. Thus, the perception of the emotional stimulus, subjects' judgement and memory, as well as their physiological responses are integrated through informational shaping processes based upon consistent stimuli.

*   Department of General Psychology, University of Padova, Italy

Two main consequences follow from this discussion:

a) to some extent, the probability of eliciting coherent responses should improve with the number of relevant cues at the input stage. In addition, the psychophysiological patterns associated with emotional imagery may be enhanced by promoting the processing of information relative to the *stimulus*, to *responding* in that stimulus context, and to the *meaning* of input and output. This can be accomplished through training, instructional scripts, dramatic playlettes, or role-plays (Lang et. al, 1983; Palomba, 1988). These effects interact with pre-existing response dispositions, such as subjects' vividness of imagery, and the coherence and compatibility of contextual cues (Miller et al. 1987; Watts & Blackstock, 1987). The effects of this interaction, however, are difficult to assess in the standard laboratory settings

b) The organization and eventual integration of psycho-physiological response systems should be based upon cognitive strategies which operate to reduce possible discordance among levels.

As mentioned above, it is reasonable to assume that greater concordance between reported arousal and actual activation occurs when subjects are encouraged (by means of adequate instruction) to attend to physiological changes. It can also be hypothesized that subjects' expectancy of arousal affects the emotional response by inflencing the matching of actual physiological changes to the emotional image stored in memory. Some data will be discussed below with respect to these assumptions.

Responding to Emotional Film Stimuli

Watching an emotional film, or models and actors playing a drama, often facilitates the production of emotional responses. This emotional response is usually accounted for by the subject's involvement in the film, that is cognitive and emotional empathy (Davis et al., 1987). The subject's judgement and memory (and possibly his/her physiological responses) to the affective events showed in the movie are shaped by the complex interaction between their responses to emotional cues and the context in which they occur.

Data suggest that subjects watching a movie produce patterned psychophysiological responses which may help to identify the autonomic nervous system changes and their interaction with central nervous system activity in emotions (Sternbach, 1962; Carruthers & Taggart, 1973; Levi, 1972; Dimond & Farrington, 1977). The subjects' cognitive strategies in emotional involvement or detachment (see Lazarus, 1972) have also been shown to play a major role in determining the psychophysiological response to film stimuli. In the Sternbach (1962) study sympathetic inhibition (rather than the expected sympathetic activation) was shown in conditions judged as sad. A similar result was reported by Carruthers & Taggart (1973) in subjects watching the violent sequences of the movie "Clockwork Orange." A heart rate decrease occurred during the viewing of violent scenes even though cathecolamine excretion increased. As suggested by Levenson (1988), complex response patterns may be associated with emotions such as surprise or sadness. Even so, the subjects' involvement in the film could equally well account for the different physiological patterns.

We have recently performed some experiments to investigate the organization of emotional responses during the viewing of a highly involving movie. The selected film was the spy story "The eye of the needle" directed by R. Marquand from the novel by Ken Follett "Storm Island."

We analyzed first the different heart rate, respiration and electromyographyc responses to emotional film scenes. Then, the same experimental scenes were extracted from the film in order to check whether the emotional psychophysiological response was influenced by the subjects' involvment in the film plot.

Data were also collected concerning subjects' judgements of emotion, as well as memory for dialogues, objects and enviroments. The research is part of a co-operative study perfomed in our laboratory (Baroni, Cornoldi et al., 1989).

Subjects' Psychophysiological Changes while Viewing a Film

The method of the first experiment will be described in some details since the following studies will refer to it.

Fifteen undergraduate students, both males and females, participated in the experiment. None of them had seen the film or read the book from which the movie was taken.

The subjects saw the spy-story film recorded on a Warner Homevideo VHS videocassette. Nine scenes (referred to as experimental scenes), which had been judged in a pilot study as representative of neutral (n = 3), sad (n = 3) and fearful (n = 3) conditions, were selected from the film. Their duration ranged from 1 to 1.40 min. (these differences were due to the duration of the actions performed in the scenes), and were equally distributed along the film. All the scenes included dialogues among the characters, except one scene of fear, which was mainly based on action.

Scenes depicting landscapes were inserted in the film so that each experimental scene was preceded by the vision of a standard scene (lasting 1 min.) which served as baseline for the computation of physiological changes.

The film was projected by a videorecorder on a personal monitor located 2 meters in front of the subject

The subjects saw the whole film. During the viewing of the experimental scenes heart rate (HR), respiration rate (RR) and forearm electromyographic (EMG) measures were taken.

The film was shown in an acoustically shielded, darkened room. The physiological recording equipment and the viodeorecorder were located in an adjacent room.

When the subject arrived in the laboratory he/she was seated in a semireclined armchair and the electrodes were positioned. Then there

was a fifteen minutes adaptation phase to allow the subject to familiarize him/herself with the experimental environment before the film was started.

Physiological measures were recorded during each fixed landscape slide (1 min. baseline to allow change scores to be computed for the experimental conditions) and the following experimental scene. Three other scenes were presented in the same way as the experimental scenes (preceded by the landscape slide) as filler scenes; no physiological measures were taken during these scenes. Immediately after viewing each experimental scene, subjects rated the intensity of emotion they felt by marking a visual analog scale 10 cm. long, anchored at the ends "none at all — extremely strong."

Results

A one factor repeated measures design was used for each physiological measure and the visual analog scale (in millimeters).

Figure 1 shows the physiological pattern (HR, RR, EMG) as related to the emotional content of the scene.

Fearful scenes produced a clear arousal response, while sad and neutral scenes showed a similar pattern with a cardiac-respiratory dissociation mainly related to the sad condition.

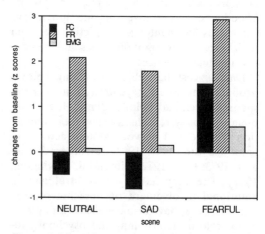

Figure 1. Mean heart rate, respiration and EMG changes during neutral, sad and fearful film sequences.

Heart rate differences among the three emotional conditions were significant ($F_{2/28}$ = 8.61; p < .01). Post-hoc comparisons (Tukey tests) showed that neutral and sad scenes were not significantly different from each other, but both of them were significantly below the fear condition.

Respiration ($F_{2/28}$ = 10.06; p < .01) and EMG ($F_{2/28}$ = 11.38; p < .01) also produced a significant emotional differentiation. Post-hoc comparisons showed that the neutral and sad scenes did not differ significantly from each other, while both of them significantly differed from the fear scene. Among these responses, the cardiac pattern is of special interest, as it indicated a directional fractionation of the cardiac response depending on the affective valence of the stimulus.

The neutral scenes did not show clearcut physiological differences from the sad ones. Indeed, in the field of psychophysiology of emotion, it is often difficult to obtain "neutral" physiological responses; it is even more difficult if the stimuli to be compared belong to the same emotional spy-story film.

The subjects' evaluation of the emotional intensity (see also Figure 3) varied according to the emotions represented in the film, increasing from the neutral to the fearful condition. The ANOVA showed a significant difference between the three emotional conditions ($F_{2/28}$ = 52.6; p < .001). Post-hoc comparisons showed significant differences between neutral and fearful scenes, between neutral and sad scenes and between sad and fearful ones.

Correlations between physiological and subjective measures showed a significant relation between the visual analog measure and respiratory changes in the fear condition (r = .45; p < .05), while the HR and EMG responses did not covary with rated emotional intensity. This result is in line with the hypothesis that HR and EMG tend to vary with the affective valence and not with the arousing dimension of emotion (Greenwald et al., 1989). Also, it is of special interest that the most arousing scene, the fear scene, resulted in significant correlations between two response levels (physiology and subjects' reports).

To sum up, the psychophysiological response to film sequences is related to the the emotional content of the particular clip. The data support the hypothesis that sadness implies a simpathetic inhibition rather than a sympathetic activation (Sternbach, 1962). The HR response to sad scenes is interesting considering the cardiac-respiratory dissociation. As shown in previous research in our laboratory (Chiappelli, Palomba & Stegagno, 1988) a similar pattern occurred when subjects listened to musical phrases played in major or minor mode. Considered as patterns, the emotional responses indicated a clear arousing effect during the fearful condition, while the sad condition showed a mixed autonomic effect which cannot be differentiated from the neutral condition. The subjects' judgement of the emotion induced by the scenes varied according to the intensity dimension, and was poorly related to the different physiological patterns.

Viewing the Whole Film versus Sequences Extracted from the Film

In the *second study* the same scenes already considered in the previous experiment were extracted from the film in order to check whether the emotional psychophysiological response was influenced by the subjects' involvment in the overall film plot.

Three balanced series of the 9 isolated scenes were made up, each of them in a different sequential order from that they had in the film. 15 new subjects, both males and females were examined. The same methods as in the first study were used for recording physiological functions and for subjects' evaluation of emotional intensity.

Results

The main physiological results are shown in Figure 2. Similar physiological patterns as in the previous study were produced when subjects were shown scenes isolated from the film context. To some degree, the general activation response was less strong, but the differentiation between conditions was even more clearcut. An arousing response occurred in the fear con-

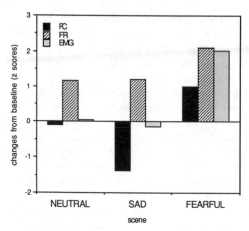

Figure 2. Mean heart rate, respiration and EMG changes during emotional scenes extracted from the film.

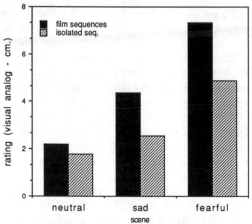

Figure 3. Subjects' rating of the emotional intensity of the film's scenes. Data of the two studies (whole film and isolated scenes) are compared.

dition and a physiological dissociation (stronger than in the "whole film" condition) in the sad scenes. HR ($F_{2/28}$ = 5.25; $p < .05$) and EMG ($F_{2/28}$ = 28.8; $p < .01$) showed the main differences due to emotions. The three sequences of presentation yielded no significant effect.

The data suggest that physiological differentiation in emotions was mainly related to the affective content of the stimulus. This is a stable effect independent of subjects' involvement in the film. On the other hand, viewing the whole film increased the intensity of the response without affecting the shape of the pattern.

Subjects' rating of emotional intensity in the "isolated scenes" condition was compared with the rating of the "whole film" condition in Figure 3.

The evaluation of emotion intensity was similar when subjects saw the whole film and scenes isolated from the film. In the "isolated scenes" condition there was a significant differ-

ence between emotions ($F_{2/28}$ = 14.5; $p < .01$). Even so, however, the film context seemed to amplify the subjects' evaluation.

Considered as a whole the results indicate that the patterned physiological responses observed in subjects viewing emotional film sequences seemed to be emotion-specific. Among the physiological responses, however, respiration showed a more clearcut arousal effect as compared to HR and EMG. The observed cardiac-respiratory dissociation also suggested interactive facilitatory/inhibitory effects of the two branches of the autonomic nervous system. These results were supported by data observed in an experiment which investigated electrogastrographic (EGG), HR and respiration changes to emotional film sequences (Baldaro et al., 1990). The hypothesized stimulus-specific response occurred for HR whilst inhibitory EGG and activational respiration changes indicated an arousal effect.

Memory for Emotional Film Sequences

The state dependent model of recall and memory, implies that the affective valence of the stimuli, and the context in which they occur, play a major role in memory (Bradley et al., 1987; Foa et al., 1989). In the dimensional ap-

proach different emotional states vary in terms of affective evaluation and level of arousal. This bidimensional structure has been found to influence retrieval from memory as well (Clark et al.,1984; Bradley et al., 1987).

These findings fail to support the classical psychophysiological theories of emotion which have emphasized the role of arousal in affective memory (see Craik & Blankstein, 1975 for a review). More specifically, they challenge the general assumption that short-term retention shows an inverted-U relationship – and even a negative relation – to arousal, whilst long-term retention is a positive function of arousal.

Arousal level is no more than a component of the affective network stored in memory; in retrieval processes its effect continuosly interacts, through associative pathways, with emotional information both stimulus and context-bounded (Bower & Cohen, 1982).

The above perspective in studying affective memory yields two major consequences. First, data have recently been provided that attempt to assess which dimension of emotion affects memory and how dimensions interact with each other (Clark et al., 1984; Greenwald et al., 1988). Second, it raises more general questions about the cognitive-emotional relationship (Vrana et al., 1989; Le Doux, 1989). Affective memory implies further cognitive work-load related to the retrieval process itself, or to the stimulus processing activity (Jennings, 1986), which it is difficult to assess independently . This limitation is even more relevant since the great majority of memory studies rely on verbal material.

Some data will be reported below with regard to subjects' memory for dialogues and environments during the viewing of emotional film sequences. Both dialogues and environments are relevant components of the associative schema stored in memory; moreover, their interactive effects have a closer relationship to how people respond in everyday-life emotional conditions.

It can be hypothesized that processing the meaning of a sentence requires less awareness or, at least, less attentional focussing than the grammatical or semantic comprehension which is necessary for dialogue processing (Hjelmquist, 1984). On the other hand, several studies on emotion underline that processing affective stimuli implies low levels of awareness or, more generally, it requires a reflexive automatic activity independent of cognition (Zajonc, 1980; Shiffrin & Schneider, 1977; Battacchi et al., in press).

Investigations in the field of environmental psychology* have provided a large body of data suggesting that in a low, incidental attention condition subjects generally remember the structural elements of interiors (that is the more schema-expected** items) better than the furniture objects (that is the more schema-compatible items), while the opposite is true in a high, intentional attention condition (Salmaso, Baroni, Job & Mainardi Peron, 1983).

As far as attention allocation is concerned, the condition of viewing a film differs from both a "classical" incidental memory condition, as the subject *intends* to pay some attention to the story, and from a "classical" intentional memory condition, as generally people are not supposed to memorize as much as possible of the scenes they saw.

When viewing a film, subjects are supposed to be interested in the story (namely the actions and/or the dialogue of the characters) whilst environments should attract little attention except when they are relevant to the story itself. With regard to the emotional content of the scenes, it can be hypothesized that the "neutral" scenes are experienced as neutral because they yield poor involvement in the story and low levels of arousal. The "sad" scenes are essentially based upon the dialogue and the attitude of the characters, and it can therefore be assumed that subject's attention will focus mainly on these aspects. The "fear" scenes are understood as fear provoking mainly because of the characters' actions, but this emotion can be generally considered more involving and context-bounded. Results at the multiple

---

*   Part of the research presented here is published under the title "Ti ricordi dove?" ("Do you remember where?") by E. Mainardi Peron. In Baroni, Cornoldi et al., 1989.

**   According to the matching modality model in the acquisition of knowledge for place schemata schema-expected items are those whose presence is necessary to define a place; schema-compatible items are those whose presence is compatible even if not necessary to define a place.

choice Memory for Environments task* (see Fig. 4) showed a significant difference between the kinds of scene: the sad scenes showed less recall than the fear scenes, which in turn were remembered equally as well as the neutral scenes.

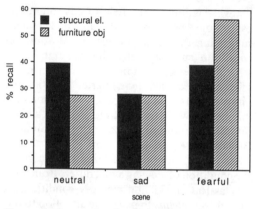

Figure 4. Memory for the environment elements of the neutral, sad and fearful film sequences. Percent recall of structural elements and furniture objects.

The fear scenes appeared to induce a generally higher level of attention leading to a better memory for environment in both structural and furniture elements.

On the other hand, in the neutral scenes the relative lack of importance of what the characters did or said allowed the subjects to pay some attention to the environment, therefore remembering it better than in the sad scenes, in which their attention appeared to be captured by the characters. Relative to fearful scenes, in the neutral scenes structural elements were better remembered than furniture objects.

As far as memory for dialogues is concerned (see Baroni & D'Urso, 1989), a similar hypothesis can be put forward: the recall of the *core*** of the dialogue was expected to be bet-

ter in highly emotional scenes than in neutral scenes. The *secondary elements* of the dialogue as well as the *verbatim memory* were expected to show the reverse trend. Again, attentional allocation on the meaningful elements of the sequence was supposed to interefere with other ongoing cognitive activity (namely processing secondary elements, grammatical and structural features of the sentences) (Hjelmquist, 1984; Isen, 1984; D'Urso, 1988).

As expected, fearful sequences yielded the highest recall both in the free recall task and in the multiple choice verbatim task (see Fig. 5).

Secondary elements of the dialogues, in any case, lead to worse performance in comparison to the other memory tasks.

It is noteworthy that the recall of the secondary elements as well as the verbatim memory varied as a function of the intensity of emotion (see also Fig. 3). In the recall of the core of the dialogue, the sad sequences showed a detrimental effect as compared to the fearful sequences

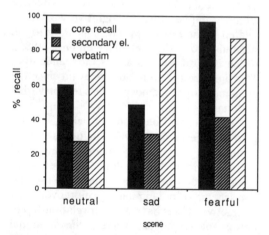

Figure 5. Memory for the dialogues of neutral, sad and fearful film sequences. Percent recall of the core and secondary elements of the dialogue and verbatim memory.

---

*   This consisted in giving to each subject a booklet of ten pages, the first one of instructions and then one for each experimental scene. The kind of environmental elements consisted of structural elements vs. furniture objects.

**   Memory for dialogues has been assessed by means of a free recall test aimed at identifying the meaning core of the dialogue as well as a certain number of associated propositional units. Subjects were also presented with a multiple choice recognition task for the verbatim memory.

and also to the neutral ones. Taken as a whole these data suggest that the sad condition was much more based on detailed elements of the scene; environments were therefore worse remembered, as were central elements of the narrative structure of the sequence. The complex memory pattern observed in the sad sequences resembled the observed physiological pattern (see Fig. 1, 2) suggesting that some emotional states, such as sadness, produced fractional effects to a greater extent than others, such as fear.

The fear scenes, on the other hand, were generally more attention-capturing and were therefore better remembered in all memory tasks. In addition, a heightened level of arousal accounted for the observed results, at least for the fearful scenes. These scenes were those which showed a clearcut general arousing pattern; this in turn facilitated cognitive retrival strategies. Data concerning the vividness (Cornoldi & De Beni, 1989) of the sequences during retrieval supported this hypothesis since vividness of the fear sequences was always higher than vividness of the sad and neutral scenes.

Expected Physiological Changes and Emotional Responses

This section is concerned with the problem of psycho-physiological interaction (and eventually integration) in emotions. It is suggested that physiological responses to emotional conditions are affected both by the stimulus (and the context in which it occurs) and by the subjects' expectancy of their own arousal changes. As noted at the beginning of the present discussion, a large body of data suggest that what the subject expects will change, or believes is changing in his/her physiology, does not always correspond to what is actually changing (Lang, 1964; Lacey, 1967; Stegagno & Palomba, 1986). In addition, as the widely known Valins experiments demonstrated (see Valins, 1966), subjects' reports of emotion were based primarily on their *belief of* being or not being aroused, regardless of actual changes (Valins & Ray, 1967).

In the field of psychophysiology of emotion, this argument was central to the widely known "cognition arousal" theory of emotion, which was primarily based on the findings of Schachter & Singer (1962). In their model, emotional experience was determined by cognitive appraisal of the relevant emotional cues. A state of generalized physiological arousal, combined with the cognitive appraisal of the stimulus, determined the emotional experience. More precisely, rather than actual arousal, perceived arousal was critical to the subjects' emotional experience.

There are, however, two intriguing points in this model. First, both perception and attribution of arousal are based on cognitive mechanisms sensitive to misleading manipulation (Valins, 1970; Harris & Katkin, 1975; Jacono et al., 1983). Second, it is difficult to predict in what way cognitive perception and appraisal can reduce discordance between the two response levels (subjects' judgment and their physiology) once it occurs. According to Lang's bio-informational model of emotional imagery, integration between the two response systems occurs under conditions of increased matching information, mainly cued by instructions (Lang, 1984)

We have recently studied subjects' judgment of emotion as well as their cardiac and respiration responses to visual stimuli after having induced an expectancy of physiological changes (Battacchi et al., 1990). Basically, the experimental paradigm resembles that of the placebo effect paradigm, in which subjects' expectation about a drug shapes physiological or cognitive changes following ingestion of the drug.

In the *present study* 54 subjects were given an injection of an inactive substance (saline solution) at the beginning of the experimental session. Subjects were randomly assigned to one of three groups: the first group was falsely informed about the arousing effect of the injection, the second was informed about its relaxation effect, while a neutral explanation (with no mention of either arousing or relaxation effects) was given to the third group.

About fifteen minutes after the injection, subjects watched two short film sequences (lasting about 2 minutes), the first being upsetting (an assault ending with mutilation) and the second neutral (a walk along a river).

Three baselines (three min. each) were recorded for the physiological measures: the first baseline before the injection, the second after it, the third in the interval between the two film sequences. Physiological measures were taken during the viewing intervals as well.

Subjects were also given two self-rating scales to rate both bodily perception (eight item perception questionnaire adapted from Mandler, Mandler & Uviller, 1958) and the emotion they felt during the film sequences (eigth items emotional scale adapted from Nowlis Mood Adjective Checklist (Nowlis & Nowlis, 1956)

Results

After the injection, HR decreased significantly, while respiration rate increased independently of the information about the drug effect. However, no significant difference was found in the perception questionnaire data suggesting that the subjects' perception of their own physiological changes was independent of expected and actual physiological changes.

As shown in Figure 6, heart rate showed a significantly larger increase during the emotional sequence as compared to the neutral one. The information about the injection did not lead to significant differences between groups. Even so, the arousing information led to a general amplification of the HR response to both the neutral and the emotional sequences. On the other hand, in the control group (no relevant information about the injection effect) the physiological differentiation between the two sequences was most clearcut.

To some extent, subjects' expectancy seemed to influence their physiology in the "arousing effects" group; in this group, indeed, an enhanced HR change occurred during both the neutral and emotional sequences. Neverthe-

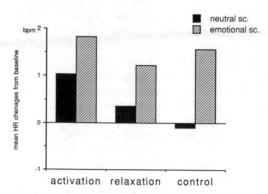

Figure 6. Mean heart rate changes during emotional and neutral film sequences in the expected activation, expected relaxation and control groups

less, emotion induced responses overcame expectation induced responses. Respiration also showed a larger increase during the emotional sequence as compared to the neutral sequence while no significant difference was produced by the information about the substance.

Subjects' rating of emotion did not change significantly among groups. Interestingly, however emotional ratings turned out to differ significantly within the relaxation and control groups.

Again, the expectation of *arousing* effects appeared to be an obstacle to possible differences between the emotional ratings. Thus, significant differences between emotion and neutral ratings occurred only in the relaxation and control groups.

The results indicate that emotion-induced changes were significant independently of the information about the drug effect. Even so, an expectancy of increased levels of arousal influenced, to some extent, both subjects' self-reports of emotion and their cardiac responses. The expectancy effect is less evident in the "relaxation" and "control" groups. According to Lang's theory it is likely that an expectancy of arousing changes focuses the attention on the physiological responses of the emotional image to a greater extent than an expectancy of relaxing changes. Certain contexts may, therefore, emphasize the processing of physiological events. Otherwise, cognitive and physiological measures are supposed to change indepently from each other even if they both are emotion-specific. The result that physiological changes were reliable indicators of ongoing emotional states, while cognitive measures were more sensitive to cognitive misleading influences, supports Zajonc's hypothesis (Zajonc & Markus, 1984) which states that physiological responses represent the essential (hard) component of emotion which precedes emotional appraisal.

The latter is responsible for "milder" emotional experience.

If a conflict is induced between the two levels in an emotional context, this would prompt a need for cognitive consonance in order to avoid the conflict. Therefore all the variables belonging to the same response level (namely cognitive) are forced to match, becoming thus more coherent.

Conclusions

The experiments reviewed here represent an effort to investigate those instances which facilitate integration among the different components of an emotional state. Subjects' verbal reports, their behaviour, as well as their physiological responses to an emotional event are supposed to be included in context-bounded response set dispositions. The inclusion in the same set, however, does not mean that the three systems will covary in a linear fashion both in laboratory and real-life situations. In Lang's theory of emotional imagery (1979; 1984), it is suggested that in each context the emotional response depends on specific information processing mechanisms. It is also suggested that both the number of relevant cues at the input stage and the focusing attention on the physiological changes, facilitate greater and more coherent responses.

Data obtained in subjects viewing emotional film sequences indicate that physiological changes parallel memory responses. The fearful sequences yielded an activation response, which seemed to heighten subjects' attention to both the meaning of the dialogues and the environments in which they take place. In the sad condition subjects' physiological responses showed a mixed autonomic influence which affected heart rate, respiration and EMG activity differently. Memory data seemed to reflect this patterned response. During the viewing of the sad sequences subjects paid less attention to environments and to the core of the dialogues. On the other hand, memory for the sad sequences was much more based on detailed elements of the scene. The complex pattern

observed in both physiological and memory responses during the sad sequences suggested that interactive dimensional effects must to be taken into account in the production of emotional states. These interactions are more easily accessed when increased arousal responses are induced.

The data concerning cognitive manipulation of subjects' expectancy of physiological changes added further information about the integration between physiological and cognitive events in emotions. Both the cardiac response and subjects' judgment were pertinent to the emotional content of the stimulus. Their changes were independent of the induced expectancy. Even so, an enhanced heart rate change occurred during both the neutral and emotional sequences, in subjects who expected arousing drug effects. This suggested that subjects' responses tended to accomplish a greater coherence under conditions of expected activation.

Nevertheless the fact that subjects' emotional responses were more differentiated when they expected relaxing or no drug effects indicated a cognitive influence which partially supports the Schachter model of emotions.

An alternative explanation may be suggested as well. The data presented here clearly indicate that stable, emotional response dispositions produced a reliable physiological output which also yielded coherent memory responses. The emotion-specific effect was independent of subjects' involvement or detachment in the situation, as well as of the influence of cognitive misleading information. When a misleading information was introduced, an attempt to reduce possible discordance was made. This does not automatically imply that this will influence actual physiological activity. If not specifically included in the cognitive schema (by means of

adequate instructions or contextual links) physiological measures will respond to environmetal stimuli regardless of their cognitive representation.

References

Baldaro, B., Battacchi, M. W., Trombini, G., Palomba, D., & Stegagno, L. (1990). Effects of an emotional negative stimulus on the cardiac, electrogastrographic and respiratory responses. *Perceptual and Motor Skill, 71,* 647–655.

Baroni, M. R., Cornoldi, C., De Beni, R., D'Urso, V., Palomba, D., Mainardi Peron, E., & Stegagno, L. (1989). *Emozioni in celluloide: Come si ricorda un film.* Raffaello Cortina. Milano.

Baroni, M. R. & D'Urso, V. (1989). Le parole ricordate. In Baroni, M. R., Cornoldi, C., De Beni, R., D'Urso, V., Palomba, D., Mainardi Peron, E. & Stegagno, L., *Emozioni in celluloide: Come si ricorda un film.* Milano: Raffaello Cortina.

Battacchi, M. W., Palomba, D., Stegagno, L., & Baldaro, B. (1990). Attivazione, percezione dell'attivazione ed esperienza emotiva. *Giornale Italiano di Psicologia, XVII,* 3, 487–504.

Bower, G. H. & Cohen, P. R. (1982). Emotional influences on learning and cognition. In Clark, M. S. & Fiske, S. J. (Eds.), *Affect and Cognition.* Hillsdale, N.J.: Erlbaum, 263–289.

Bradley, M. M., York, D. J., & Lang, P. J. (1987). Emotion as context in memory. *Psychophysiology, 24,* 581 (abstract)

Carruters, M. & Taggart P. (1973). Vagotonicity of violence: Biochemical and cardiac responses to violent films and television programmes. *British Medical Journal, 3,* 384–389.

Chiappelli, M., Palomba, D. & Stegagno, L. (1988). Psychophysiological reactions to minor and major musical phrases: the influence of musical competence. Annual Meeting DGPA, München. *Journal of Psychophysiology, 2,* 131–132 (abstract).

Clark, M. S., Milberg, S., & Erber, R. (1984). Effects of arousal on judgments of others' emotions. *Journal of Personality and Social Psychology, 3,* 551–560.

Cornoldi, C. & De Beni, R. (1989). Il ricordo di immagini filmiche. In M. R. Baroni, C. Cornoldi, R. De Beni, V. D'Urso, D. Palomba, E. Mainardi Peron & L. Stegagno, *Emozioni in celluloide: Come si ricorda un film.* Milano: Raffaello Cortina.

Craik, F. I. M. & Blankstein, K. R. (1975). Psycho-

physiology and human memory. In P. H. Venables & M. J. Christie (Eds.), *Research of psychophysiology.* London: Wiley.

Davis, M. H., Hull, J. G., Young, R. D., & Warren, G. G. (1987). Emotional reactions to dramatic film stimuli: the influence of cognitive and emotional empathy. *Journal of Personality and Social Psychology, 52,* 126–133.

Dimond, S. J. & Farrington, L. (1977). Emotional response to film shown to the right or left hemisphere of the brain measured by heart rate. *Acta Psychologica, 41,* 255–260.

D'Urso, V. (1988). Stati emotivi e memoria. In V. D'Urso & R. Trentin (Eds.), *Psicologia delle emozioni.* Bologna, Il Mulino.

Foa, E. B., McNally, R., & Murdock, T. B. (1989). Anxious mood and memory. *Behavior Research and Therapy, 27,* 141–147.

Greenwald, M. K., Bradley, M. M., Hamm, A. O., & Lang, P. J. (1988). Emotion and pictorial stimuli: Affective judgments, memory and psychophysiology. *Psychophysiology, 25,* 451 (abstract)

Greenwald, M. K., Cook, E. W., & Lang, P. J. (1989). Affective judgement and psychophysiological response: Dimensional covariation in evaluation of pictorial stimuli. *Journal of Psychophysiology, 3,* 51–64.

Harris, V. A. & Katkin, E. S. (1975). Primary and secondary emotional behavior: an analysis of the role of autonomic feedback on affect, arousal and attribution. *Psychological Bulletin, 82,* 6, 904–916.

Hirschman, R. & Clark, M. (1983). Bogus physiological feedback. In J. T. Cacioppo & R. E. Petty (Eds.), *Social psychophysiology: A sourcebook.* New York, Guildford Press.

Hjelmquist E. (1984). Memory for conversation. *Discourse Processes, 7,* 321–336.

Isen, A. M. (1984). Toward understanding the role of affect in cognition. In R. S. Wyer & K. T. Srull (Eds.), *Handbook of social cognition.* Hillsdale, N.J.: Erlbaum.

Jacono, G., Belelli, G., Lanza, L., Morelli, M., & Valerio, P. (1983). Emozione e valutazione dell'input autonomico: un contributo di ricerca.

Rivista di Neurologia, Psichiatria e Scienze Umane, 3, 100–127.

Jennings, J. R. (1986). Memory, thought and bodily response. In M. G. H. Coles, E. Donchin, S. W. & Porges (Eds.), *Psychophysiology: Systems, processes and applications* (290–308). New York: Guilford Press.

Lacey, J. I. (1967). Somatic response patterning and stress: some revisions of activation theory. In M. H. Appley & R. Turnbull (Eds.), *Psychological stress: Issues and research.* New York: Appleton Century Crofts.

Lacey, J. I. & Lacey, B. C. (1970). Some autonomic-central nervous system interrelationships. In P. Black (Ed.), *Physiological correlates of human emotion.* New York: Academic Press.

Lang, P. J. (1964). Experimental studies of desensitization psychotherapy. In J. Wolpe (Ed.), *The conditioning therapies.* New York: Holt, Reinehart & Winston.

Lang, P. J. (1979). A bio-informational theory of emotional imagery. *Psychophysiology, 16,* 495–512.

Lang, P. J. (1984). Cognition and emotion: concept and action. In C. E. Izard, J. Kagan & R. B. Zajonc (Eds.), *Emotion, cognition and behavior.* New York: Cambridge University Press.

Lang, P. J., Levin, D. N., Miller, G. A., & Kozak, M. J. (1983). Fear behavior, fear imagery and the psychophysiology of emotion: the problem of affective response integration. *Journal of Abnormal Psychology, 92,* 276–306.

Lazarus, R. S. (1972). The self-control of emotional reactions to stressful film. *Journal of Personality, 21,* 25–29.

Le Doux, J. E. (1989). Cognitive-emotional interactions in the brain. *Cognition and Emotion, 4,* 267–289.

Levenson, R. W. (1988). Emotion and the autonomic nervous system: A prospectus for research on autonomic specificity. In H. L. Wagner (Ed.), *Social psychophysiology and emotion: Theory and clinical applications.* Chichester: Wiley.

Levi, L. (1972). Stress and distress in response to psychosocial stimuli: Laboratory and real life studies on sympatho-adreno-medullary and related reaction. *Acta Medica Scandinava, CXCI,* Suppl. 528

Mainardi Peron, E. (1989). Ti ricordi dove?. In M. R. Baroni, C. Cornoldi, R. De Beni, V. D'Urso, D. Palomba, E. Mainardi Peron & L. Stegagno, *Emozioni in celluloide: come si ricorda un film.* Milano: Cortina.

Mandler, G, Mandler, J. M., & Uviller, E. T. (1958). Autonomic feedback: the perception of autonomic

activity. *Journal of Abnormal and Social Psychology, 56,* 367–373.

Miller, G. A., Levin, D. N., Kozak, M. J., Cook E. W. III, McLean, A., & Lang, P. J. (1987). Individual differences in perceptual imagery and psychophysiological response in emotion. *Cognition and Emotion, 1,* 367–390.

Nowlis, V, & Nowlis, H. H. (1956). The description and analysis of mood. *Annals of the New York Academy of Sciences, 65,* 345–355.

Obrist, P. A. (1982). Cardiac-Behavioral Interactions: A critical appraisal. In J. T. Cacioppo & R. E. Petty (Eds.), *Perspectives in cardiovascular psychophysiology.* New York: Guilford Press.

Palomba, D. (1988). Risposte efferenti ed immaginazione emozionale: un'indagine con la tecnica dell'improvvisazione teatrale. 7th Annual Meeting Basic Research in Psychology, Palermo, 139–141 (abstract)

Salmaso, D., Baroni, M. R., Job, R., & Mainardi Peron, E. (1983). Schematic information, attention and memory for places. *Journal of Experimental Psychology: Learning, Memory and Cognition, 9,* 263–268.

Schachter, S. & Singer, J. E. (1962). Cognitive, social and psychological determinants of emotional states. *Psychological Review, 69,* 379–399.

Shiffrin, R. M. & Schneider, W. (1977). Controlled and automatic human information processing: II. Perceptual learning, automatic attending, and a general theory. *Psychological Review, 84,* 129–190.

Stegagno, L. & Palomba, D. (1986). Cognitivo vs. fisiologico? Autocontrollo della frequenza cardiaca tramite feedback concordante o discordante con le istruzioni. *Archivio di Psicologia, Neurologia e Psichiatria, 1,* 53–68.

Sternbach, R. A. (1962). Assessing differential autonomic patterns in emotions. *Journal of Psychosomatic Research, 6,* 87–91.

Valins, S. (1970). The perception and labeling of bodily changes as determinants of emotional behavior. In P. Black (Ed.), *Physiological correlates of emotion.* New York: Academic Press.

Vrana, S. R., Cuthbert, B. N., & Lang, P. J. (1989). Processing fearful and neutral sentences: Memory and heart rate change. *Cognition and Emotion, 3,* 179–185.

Watts, F. N. & Blackstock, A. J. (1987). Lang's theory of emotional imagery. *Cognition and Emotion, 1,* 391–405.

Zajonc, R. B. (1980). Feeling and thinking: preferences need no inferences. *American Psychologist, 35,* 151–175.

Zajonc, R. B. & Markus, M. (1984). Affect and cognition: the hard interface. In C. E. Izard, Y. Kagan & R. B. Zajonc (Eds.), *Emotion, cognition, and* *behavior*. Cambridge, MA: Cambridge University Press.

Prompts – Leitmotif – Emotion
Play it Again, Richard Wagner!

D. Vaitl*, W. Vehrs** and S. Sternagel*

Abstract

In this chapter, the heuristic validity of Lang's emotional imagery approach is examined for the field of music. Music differs from verbally induced emotions by the fact that something occurs in time, something that is not arbitrary, but regulated, following precise rules. For this purpose, the leitmotifs of Richard Wagner's opera "The Mastersingers of Nuremberg" were selected. These are short-term pieces of music, which are repeated several times in order to deepen and refine the psychophysiological aspect of the characters by reinforcing a specific associative emotional network. In a field study, three listeners were psychophysiologically examined during the three acts of the opera. Electrodermal responses, respiratory activity, and ratings of emotional arousal were continuously recorded and analyzed during the leitmotifs. It was shown that physiological responses differ quite markedly with respect to the leitmotifs and their musical features (melody, rhythm, continuation). Interestingly, the correspondence between emotional arousal ratings and physiological responses was very weak. It is hypothesized that the somato-visceral responses reflect the operation of the acoustic associative network prompted by the very beginning of an individual leitmotif and correspond with the listeners experience. Instead of studying heterogeneous musical stimuli, it seems, therefore, sensible to study individual musical motifs which can be analyzed with regard to the context of the plot (semantic representation), their musical features, and their performance practice.

Key words: arousal ratings, emotion and music, electrodermal responses, expectancy theory, leitmotif, R. Wagner

Introduction

Music is an event in time. Despite its fleeting character, it evokes emotions that often have an unescapable quality. If we are interested in the emotional impact of music it appears a logical choice to examine the music of a composer with a reputation to stir up emotions. Nobody knew better than Richard Wagner how to use music to create moods, affects, and emotions. Hector Berlioz called his music "bone-marrow music," and Friedrich Nietzsche, once an enthusiastic supporter of Wagner and later one of his fierc- est critics, accused him of aiming solely at the "effect on the listener's nerves." To this day, the views on Wagner's music remain characterized by fierce controversy. Fortunately enough, however, such controversy has not prevented his operas from appearing on the programme of every aspiring theatre. They represent a constant challenge for musicians, singers, producers, conductors and, last but not least for the audience.

* University of Giessen, Giessen, Germany
** University of Bayreuth, Bayreuth, Germany.
Acknowledgements: We are indebted to Wolfgang Wagner for his excellent support of this study and his permanent help during our visit at the festival theatre of Bayreuth.

Lang's Theory of Emotion: Application to the Effect of Music

The starting point for our psychological analysis of music is Lang's (1979; 1984) model of emotion, where emotions are interpreted in terms of propositional networks in memory composed of stimulus, reponse and meaning information. In contrast to the method, preferably used by Lang and his group, which mainly relies on the use of verbal scripts to induce emotional imagery, our intention is to discuss the heuristic validity of this approach for the field of music. Music differs from verbally induced emotions by the fact that something occurs in time, something that is not arbitrary, but regulated, following precise rules, a "fixed composition." By means of this indispensable regularity, constituting the very essence of a musical piece of art, the aesthetic effect with all its associated emotions is achieved. Herein lies, in our opinion, the main difference between musical stimuli and verbally induced images and their accompanying emotions. Visual images, for instance, permit us to imagine processes in reverse, but with music, there is only a forward movement. Emotional responses which are linked to such images should therefore have a similar development in time.

One element of Lang's (1979; 1984) conception, which is significant in the analysis of the effects of music, is his explanation of how certain emotions are created in connection with certain images. Emotional responses occur whenever a prompting external or internal stimulus activates an associative network, which contains semantic codes, stimulus representations, and response programmes. These networks provide information about the adequate corresponding stimuli and the significance of the context, in which the stimuli are found about the "action set" with all its accompanying visceral-motoric adjustments. The emotion information network is a sort of prototype or schema which, when a critical number of propositions are accessed (through a match to environmental stimuli or internal associations, or both), is processed as a unit (Lang, 1985).

If we apply this concept to the field of music psychology, such an associative network, stored in memory, would correspond to an imagined piece of music (e. g. a simple melody, passages of an orchestral piece, or mono- or polyphonic singing). Thus, we are no longer dealing with "propositions," as in the case of visual images, but with a progressing sequence of sound"-images" and tone"-pictures." They are stored in our memory and linked by a network of associations. In comparison to visual associative networks they are far more structured and clearly defined. Ideally, the "production specifications" explicitly written into a score could serve as a frame of reference. This suggests an analogy with the associative networks of phobics, which are prototypical for a tightly knit associative network, as Lang's experimental studies have revealed (Lang & Cuthbert, 1984). Such networks are activated by a minimally matching stimulus which may serve as network specific "prompts." In a similar vein, the first few bars of a familiar piece of music can evoke the full sequence of tones "in the mind," and once such a network is initiated, the associated somato-visceral response schemes are activated as well, leading to affective responses.

Emotional Stimuli in Music: The Role of Leitmotifs

By which stylistic means does music try to produce emotions? This is done in two different ways. If, for instance, instrumental music wants to create the impression of emotionally evocative images (thunder, chirping of birds, sunrise, fearful lamentation), it tries to imitate these factual events by tones and melodies. It has an indicative function, suggesting what the listener is supposed to experience (e. g. patriotic feelings when listening to the national anthem).

The so-called leitmotifs have a similar, though far more subtle function in music, especially in the opera. They are concise, recurring musical passages (melodic, rhythmic, harmonic) which fulfill a specific purpose in the course of an opera. They symbolize a person, a place, a state of mood, and so forth, and they convey emotional understanding within the context of the dramatic event. They recall the past and point to the future. Richard Wagner referred to them as "emotional sign-posts" and "anticipatory motifs." They are techniques which, coupled with the dramatic-poetic lyrics, help to deepen and refine the psychological aspect of the characters. On the experiential level, they suggest structures that the text by itself cannot reveal in such a subtle form. The skillful technique of the recollection motif appeared even before Wagner's times in literature on music (e.g. the "idée fixe" of H. Berlioz in symphonic works). F. W. Jähn (1871) first coined the term "leitmotif" in his analysis of the works of C.M. von Weber, and then H. von Wolnzogen (1876) applied it to the works of Richard Wagner. It is beyond doubt, however, that Richard Wagner alone deserves the credit for applying this technique in his music dramas in such an elaborate and almost inexhaustable multitude, that he became a model for numerous opera composers to follow (e.g. Verdi, Puccini, Massenet). Of course, the uniqueness of his musical creations does not end here, for an opera does not solely consist of a mere line-up of such "leitmotifs." They constitute only a fraction of the whole duration of an opera. Wagner integrated them into the symphonic structure of his music at points that were important for the characterization of the feelings and moods of his characters. They are vehicles for expressing the expectations, fears, and intentions of the characters. Such structures of associations are built up in the listener in the course of the opera, particularly by means of repetition, which help to strengthen and establish them in the memory. Recognition is thus the first step which allows the listener to understand what the composer has tried to "say." The associative structures are reinforced by the fact that the leitmotifs do not appear isolated, but are embedded in contexts, that is, within networks of connotations, woven through the duration of the opera in connection with the overall musical interpretation of the events. This intended redundancy serves as an element of style in Wagner's music dramas, and it can lead to a special "welter of emotional thrills." For this reason, the operas of this composer seem to be exceptionally suitable for the examination of the emotional impact of music. In addition, as we shall see, his constructions of the leitmotifs are very similar to the verbal methods by means of which visual images and somatovisceral effects are induced in research on emotion. Thus Wagner provides us with the suitable tonal material for the examination method under discussion.

Empirical Evidence on Emotional Effects of Music

First of all, however, there is the general question to what extent music can create emotions. Is there any empirical evidence that music can influence physical responses and our inner experience? If so, what features of music lead to such responses?

Physiological Responses While Listening to Music

The scientific literature on this subject appears to confirm that music can exert an influence on physical responses in man. Each of us has experienced that listening to a piece of music sent a shiver down our spine, moved us to tears or made our hearts miss a beat. But what elements of music cause such strong effects? Is it the melody which moves and stirs us? Is it the rhythm, the dynamics, the tone, or just the tempo? Here are some examples from literature to illustrate the difficulty which this question brings up.

Already Dogiel (1880) found out that listening to music can lead to changes in breathing, heart rate, blood pressure, and muscle tonus. Binet and Courtier (1895) reported similar responses of their subjects when they listened to R. Wagner's "Walkürenritt." Breathing frequency and pulse rate accelerated as the tempo of a piece of music increased (Allesch, 1981). Pronounced rhythmics (as e.g. in L. Strawinsky's Sacre du Printemps) cause an increase in blood pressure as well (Destunis & Seebrandt, 1958). According to the same authors, blood pressure decreased when the subjects listened to soothing music. Likewise – and exactly as expected – lullabys from different cultures had a calming effect on heart rate and breathing (Kneutgen, 1970). In Elam's (1971) opinion small variations in the dynamics hardly lead to physiological responses (SCR), whereas large dynamic variations resulted in correspondingly strong physical responses. Jansen and Klensch (1964) found that large variations in cardiac output, heart rate, and blood pressure occurred when their subjects listened to the first movement of Bruckner's 9th Symphony as well as to the allegros and adagios of the 3rd Brandenburg Concert of Johann Sebastian Bach. Harrer, together with Pöldinger, Revers and Simon, did extensive experimental studies on physiological responses to music (cf. Harrer, 1982). They recorded electroencephalography (EEG), electromyography (EMG), skin conductance, heart rate, plethysmography, and breathing frequency. They reported the following conclusions: a) the impact of music can be as strong as physical strain; b) the intensity of responses is modulated by individual willingness to respond; c) the strongest psycho-vegetative responses occurred when listeners allowed themselves to be totally absorbed by the music; d) in pieces of music with increasing rhythm, breathing frequency and pulse rate adjusted to the tempo ("pulse and breathing driving"); e) active playing caused much stronger vegetative changes than mere listening. From these individual response patterns, Harrer evolved the thesis that each person had an organ system which was particularly responsive to music (in psychophysiology this is known as individual response specificity).

Unfortunately, these psychophysiological studies do not allow any general conclusions about the physical impact of music. This is due to the complexity of the stimuli as well as to the reported high level of variation in physiological responses from individual to individual. If we restrict the complexity of the musical presentations to allow better control of the experiment, and merely use simple tone structures, we will loose the very essence of music, that is, the skillful structure of various interrelated musical features. On the other hand, with too much complexity, or even with heterogenous pieces of music of different styles and genres, the stimuli become experimentally uncontrollable. Some authors suggest an intra-individual approach, that is, controlled case studies as a way out of this dilemma. If this method succeeds in revealing systematic differences in the physiological responses, dependent on the respective musical elements and features, the first step is accomplished to a better understanding of the emotional impact on the audience.

Subjective Impact of Music

Music influences the inner experience of the listener. Musical structures, as for instance tempo, pitch level, modulations, or motifs, provoke distinctive impressions and emotional experiences. Several authors have attempted to characterize the emotional content and the impression quality of extremely heterogenous pieces of music by means of lists of adjectives and polarity profiles (Hevner, 1936; Wedin, 1972; Scherer & Oshinsky, 1977; Brown 1981). Wedin (1972) requested his subjects to rate 40 parts of pieces of music by means of a list of 125 adjectives and submitted the ratings to a cluster analysis. He found 3 dimensions of impression qualities : "energy vs. relaxation," "gaity vs. gloom," and "light vs. solemn and serious" and compared these 3 clusters with the musical characteristics of the presented pieces. The characteristics "staccato," "articulation," and "sound volume" were associated with the dimension "energy-relaxation"; "gaity-gloom" was associated with consonant harmony, light flow of rhythm, D major and a relatively high pitch of the melodies. The pieces that were regarded as serious and solemn were loud, slow, deep in pitch and usually composed in a minor key. These results show that certain characteristics of a composition are judged in a relatively consistent way, that is, according to their general impression qualities.

Brown (1981) provided a more detailed analysis. He asked musicians and non-musicians to listen to six pairs of classic and romantic composition and then to compare these according to the emotions and moods they conveyed. They were asked to disregard any previous knowledge of the composers, the music style, tempo, and so forth. The evaluation was performed in two different ways. First, similar to Wedin's (1972) study, a list of adjectives was used as a frame of reference, and second, the pieces had to be classified without this verbal aid. The consistency in rating served as criterion for the validity of classification. The results showed that both non-musicians and musicians were able to grasp the emotional contents of the pieces precisely, with or without the reference guide of verbal characterizations of emotions. It is particularly interesting that the rating of the musicians showed better consistency when no reference guide was given. Brown (1981) explained this result by suggesting that any given set of descriptions of emotions distract musicians from applying their own standards of judgement, which they have developed earlier and usually apply when they analyze music. Brown (1981) further pointed out that a context is necessary for the listener in order to understand and interpret the emotions provoked by music. This is especially true for opera or ballet, where the plot and the acting characters are jointly responsible for conveying the underlying message.

A serious limitation that all these studies have in common is that musical experience is only assessed retrospectively, when the music performance has been completed. A continuous evaluation of moment-to-moment emotional changes in experiences probably is necessary to obtain reliable results reflecting the whole range of impression qualities experienced during longer pieces of music with their rapidly changing climaxes, condensations, and blendings. Vehrs (1986) was the first investigator to successfully evaluate the dimension "arousal-relaxation" on a continuous basis in longer passages of music, as for instance in the prelude to Wagner's opera "Die Meistersinger von Nürnberg", by means of a response lever, especially designed for this task. His results revealed close connections between the musical elements of this symphonically composed prelude and the assessment of emotions experienced by individuals. This method appears promising for use in field studies, e.g. during concerts or opera performance, or if we want to establish relations between subjective emotions and simultaneously recorded physiological responses.

Explaining the Emotional Impact of Music: Attempts and Alternatives

Expectancy Theories

The basic psychological approaches to music aesthetics have been founded on the phenomena of tension and relaxation. According to Meyer's "Theory on the Significance of Music," music is structured to induce expectations (Meyer, 1956). Fulfilling or violating such expectations brings about tension, maintains or relaxes it. Aesthetic pleasure is achieved if temporary tensions can be eased by stylistic features in the music. Meyer supported his view by numerous examples of such musical features (for instance, the laws of good continuation, completion and closure, the weakening of shape, and the tonal organization). Berlyne (1971) shared a similar view in his "experimential aesthetics" and saw the real "arousal potential" of music in its complexity, its novelty, its suprise effects, or its ambiguity. According to Berlyne, once these factors, which modulate level of arousal, balance out at a medium level, aesthetic pleasure and delight is achieved. The optimum psycho-physiological activation level constitutes the decisive condition for this phenomenon. If a piece of music is too complex or contains too many suprise effects, the listener will get aroused in the beginning but will soon loose arousal and "switch off." Exactly the same will happen if a piece of music is too simple and scarcely contains surprises. At which point an optimum balance is reached between a high and low level of arousal is, of course, assumed to depend on the musical sophistication of the listener. Werbik (1971) believed that an optimum alternation between fulfilled and violated expectations was a basic prerequisite for aesthetic experience, reflecting a medium activation level to which the organism tends innately . More recent studies on music aesthetics, as for instance by Raab (1981), or by Konecni and Flath-Becker (1984), do not differ fundamentally from Berlyne's psychology of aesthetics, although they consider far more influencing factors.

Conditioning Theories

In addition to these attempts of explanation based on information theory, there is another theory based on the psychology of learning and conditioning. We often observe that a tune evokes memories and moods of persons, events, and places. Consequently, pieces of music can function as conditioned stimuli to evoke emotional effects according to Pavlov's principles of classical conditioning. This means two different things: on the one hand, a piece of music can act as an unconditioned stimulus, due to the nature of its composition (sound volume, rhythm, dynamics, melody), and provokes certain affects and moods. On the other hand, however, a melody, once it has been associated with a certain situation, can bring about moods and affects similar to the ones provoked at the first time (cf. Eifert, Craill, Carey & O'Connor, 1988).

The basic thought of these theories sounds plausible, yet it disregards some important phenomena of music reception. In the following you will find some reflections which shall lead us to a more efficient explanatory approach.

Problems with Expectancy Theories

The expectancy theories all presume that when listening to a melody, the listener has a certain expectation of the development of the melody. Thus, even in simple cases (e.g. a melody of 8 bars) an "idea innata" should exist defining a good musical "shape," and providing bases for

expectation, but is also determined by listening habit. Meyer (1956) supplied plenty of examples to support such notions. But what about the complex, polyphonic and orchestrated pieces? When listening to a piece of music for the first time, it is almost impossible, particularly in case of a symphonic network of thematic interconnections and theme development, to detect all these violations of the "expectations," their pleasure-producing resolutions and to enjoy them at the same time (for example, Dowling & Harwood, 1986, p. 218 offered to demonstrate such a surprise effect in support of our view: Chopin's Waltz in C sharp minor Op. 62, No. 2, Bar 25!). If the expectancy theories should remain valid, additional suppositions must be made. Dowling and Harwood refer to one of these directly by saying: "... the musically untrained listener subconsciously marks deviations from the tonality he or she is used to, is aroused by them, and subconsciously finds meaning in their resolution" (p. 219). Meyer (1956) even goes further by suggesting that the conscious processing of musical information spoils the musical pleasure. However, by shifting the actual process of "violated expectation" to the subconscious level of information processing, the problem is not solved but becomes even more complicated. If there is pre- or subconscious information processing of this type, then, the activation level should increase in an untrained listener as soon as a piece of music constantly employs the stylistic element of quick changes, surprise modulations and violations of expectations on different tone levels. But just the opposite is often true: such music leaves the listener unmoved, or he or she just "switches off."

Each of us can listen endlessly to our favourite tune or piece of music. Over and over again, it is a source of aesthetic pleasure. No nuances are left to discover, we know every little detail and still it triggers the same psychophysiological states of arousal. According to the "expectancy theories," and in particular Berlyne's aesthetic theory, habituation, particularly of the associated physiological effects, should occur. But plain experience proves the contrary.

Changes in the musical structure often require time, allowing the reconstruction of the musical event in the mind. This is true especially for an unprepared listener. However, when tension is resolved within short passages of time, it is debatable whether our mental apparatus has sufficient resolution power to grasp such quick changes. This aspect deals with the great demands made on the listener. According to another quotation from Dowling and Harwood (1986, p. 219): "Music involves several overlapping schemata operating simultaneously so that subconscious interruptions are occurring by turn on different levels. The subconscious information-processing machinery of the brain is kept very busy by an attentive listener" (p. 219).

Associative Network Theory is an Alternative

In this context the theory of tonal associative networks presents itself as an alternative, because of the heuristic function which Lang's (1979; 1984) concept of emotion provides for the analysis of the impact of music. According to this model it is not necessary to produce cognitive incongruency to expectations, and so forth, in order to provoke psycho-physiological activation; it rather depends directly on listening and re-listening. It is the sequential structure of tonal associative networks that contains a high degree of predictability, which probably is responsible for the fact that things once heard (e. g. one's favourite tune) seldom lead to decreases in affective responses. This explains why such responses fail to habituate as they ought to if violated expectations, novelty, or surprise effects were the actual stimuli for them.

So far, we have implicitly assumed that such associative networks for particular pieces of music already exist. However, this is true, only for a listener who is familiar with the piece of music in question. It is a different situation, however, if the listener is exposed to a piece of music for the first time. In this case the context, out of which the network evolves, constitutes an important prerequisite. This includes, for instance, knowledge of style, listening habits and listening preferences (analytic compared to holistic approaches), memories of familiar pieces of music, and so forth. Or a piece of music is composed in such a skillfull "didactic" way that the listener is guided to the most important elements in the piece. Recurring themes (as for instance in a fugue) and leitmotifs can have this function. They provide the structural frame, within which an associative network can be built up in the course of a polyphonic composition or within the context of the plot of an opera. A good way to achieve this purpose is to appeal to the affects and thus ensure that pleasure and a positive mood is evoked in the listener. By recruiting an already existing "response program" the familiarity of the listener with a piece of music can be promoted. Once a shiver runs down the spine, tears are shed, or the listener is deeply moved there is the possibility of implementing further musical elements into the so far rudimentary network, consisting mainly of somato-visceral response components. In analogy to the vividness of a visual image (that has numerous perceptual components) the " tonal re-living" of a piece of music and its tonal sequence have to be seen over time. Once again, ideally, it would correspond to re-listening to a piece of music in the mind in the exact way as it is laid down in the score, a skill which one tends to ascribe to good composers. Many levels of musical expertise exist between this ability and a naive delight in music.

Let us return to Richard Wagner.

A Psychophysiological Field Study
of the Emotional Impact of Opera

Introduction: The Music Dramas of Richard Wagner

From the field studies conducted in the festival theatre in Bayreuth in 1987 and 1988 we have chosen to present data from one of Richard Wagner's operas to illustrate what has been said so far: "Die Meistersinger von Nürnberg." We start by some remarks on Wagner's work to ensure a better understanding of this music drama. The term "music drama" calls for an explanation. The semantic context in Wagner's operas is primarily found in the lyrics of the libretto, for which the music serves as an interpretation. However, the music is not only an embellishment of the words, it has a value of its own. The unity of the symphonic movements serves as a model for the music, composed to befit the poetry (cf. Wagner "On the Application of Music on the Drama"). For its time, this was a unique attempt, and for Wagner's contemporaries it seemed like "pure dreams of the future" (Wagner, 1860). It led to a unity of drama and music (universal art work), which was achieved by a gradual development from a network of basic themes woven through the whole work. Like in a symphonic movement they may oppose or complement one another, take on different shapes, be divided or combined: with the only restriction that the plot of the opera lays down the rules of division and combination (cf. Wagner, 1860). This principle was presented in its most fully developed and clearest form in "Die Meistersinger von Nürnberg." For Wagner one of the crucial points in the "Meistersinger" score was to make the dramatic dialogue the main subject of the musical performance. This called for an especially elaborated technique of motifs. The musical development of the orchestral melody requires the listener to reconstruct the previous musical development to find the cardinal point from which the motifs or their prototypes stem or first opposed one another (cf. Dahlhaus, 1986). Remembering the previous development of the leitmotifs, and the meaning attached to them in earlier situations, constitute the basic prerequisite for the aesthetic impression of a closely knit coherence, of a steady continuity, for the impression of a "never-ending melody." The "magic of relations," so typical for Wagner's compositions, results from remembering the past of the leitmotifs – their context –, and it is this "magic of relations" which leads to the development of a tonal associative network.

As it is often the case with field studies, the criticism may be raised that it is not the melody and the orchestration to which the listeners react, but solely the voice of the protagonist. However, Hanslick (1981) observed that in "Die Meistersinger" the singing voice by itself is not only incomplete but of no importance at all. "The accompaniment means everything, it is an independent symphonic creation" (Hanslick, 1981, p. 226). The orchestral accompaniment, developing the melody, produces the coherent and independent tone structure, the singing voice adjusts itself to it. Harmony is one of Wagner's most important stylistic elements to provide his texts with an interpretation. Timbre and dynamics become essential factors of the musical performance, as they are directly linked to the structural processes in this opera. In combination with the theatrical gestures, dynamics has the function to elucidate certain affects expressed on stage. Where words fail and do not suffice, music comes in and reveals as "tonal" silence the things which speech and scenic presentation cannot convey.

Method

In 1987 and 1988, psycho-physiological field studies on the impact of Wagner's music were conducted in the festival theatre in Bayreuth. A total of 27 subjects took part in the studies. The operas "Lohengrin," "Tannhäuser," "Parsifal" as well as "Die Meistersinger von Nürnberg" were the subjects of examination. However, in this chapter, we will report only the findings from "Die Meistersinger von Nürnberg."

Subjects

Three subjects (1 male, 2 female) took part in the study. They were selected according to prior knowledge of music, because theoretical considerations suggested that identifying and recognizing musical motifs is a crucial condition for experiencing solid musical coherence. Each subject participated in only one of the three acts of the opera.

The Festival Theatre

The festival theatre in Bayreuth is a unique place for performances compared to other opera houses. Experts unaminously agree that the festival theatre in Bayreuth, due to its special construction, is the best suited for the performances of Wagner's operas. As a result of the special arrangement of the orchestra in the pit and the vaulted sounding-board above it, a unique blend of sounds is achieved, which makes the orchestra sound as an entirety without emphasizing any instruments. Because the ceiling of the festival theatre is made of cloth, a pleasant dampening and scattering of the acoustic waves is guaranteed, which further reinforces the famous Bayreuth blend of sounds. The auditorium, shaped like an antique amphitheatre, is supported by a wooden construction which serves as a huge sounding-board. The resulting sound patterns is impossible to reproduce by any sound technique, no matter how sophisticated it may be. Changes in dynamics are a distinctive feature of Wagner's style of composition. Even if modern technology does allow the reproduction of much wider dynamic ranges, than previous ones, there is still a considerable difference in quality between the dynamic changes heard in a festival theatre and those heard from CD-playback. In addition, for all sound-carriers, irrespectible of their quality, the recording depends on the "philosophy" of the sound mixer who decides what is to remain and what is to be filtered out. Many parts of the singers in Wagner's operas are of such wide dynamic range that they cannot be reproduced in their entire richness by modern equipment. For our examinations, a box, usually offering room for about 10 audi-

tors during a performance, was converted to provide room for 2 subjects and the recording equipment for the physiological responses.

Apparatus

Electrodermal responses (skin conductance responses; SCR), respiration and changes in finger pulse volume (not reported here) were recorded by a Watanabe physiopolygraph. In order to synchronize physiological responses and music during the course of an entire act of the opera, a trained musician marked each bar during the performance by pressing a button corresponding to the tempo of the music. These digital signals were also recorded by the physiopolygraph. In addition, a video camera recorded the physiological data displayed on the polygraph simultaneously with the music on the sound-track of the video-camera. The music was picked up by an additional microphone placed on the stage. This allows an unambiguous synchronization of music, bars of the score book, physiological recordings and scaling of emotions. The continuous scaling of emotion was achieved by means of a gear shift-like stick (for details cf. Vehrs, 1986) which could be easily moved backward and forward. The subjects were instructed to move this stick according to their emotional arousal (forward=high arousal, backward=low arousal). During previous practice sessions, they were trained to use the stick for scaling of their arousal level. The analog output signal from this apparatus was fed into the polygraph and registered on the paper sheet.

All the data recorded by the polygraph were sampled and stored on an IBM compatible PC. These digitized data were used for subsequent analyses.

Test Material

The opera "Die Meistersinger von Nürnberg" comprises three acts and lasts approximately five hours (first act: 87 min, 45 sec; second act: 66 min; third act: 127 min, 15 sec). The director was Wolfgang Wagner, and the conductor Michael Schoenwandt. With respect to the motifs, some of them appear only once, while others are repeated in their original version or con-

Motif	Name	Tempo ♩=	1st Act Frequency	1st Act Duration (sec)	2nd Act Frequency	2nd Act Duration (sec)	3rd Act Frequency	3rd Act Duration (sec)
1	Meistersinger [Meistersingers]	108/112	8	192	-	-	7	340.5
2	Zunftmarsch [March of the Guild Masters]	108/112	4	34	-	-	9	244
3	Liebe [Price Song]	76	6	159.5	2	27	12	359.5
4	Anmut [Grace]	76	1	17.5	5	73	11	154.5
5	David	72	8	114	-	-	7	85.5
6	Schuster [Shoemaker]	116	3	25	15	164.5	5	35
7	Beckmesser	84	4	56	-	-	8	95
8	Lenz [Springtime]	88	5	36	5	106.5	3	21
9	Stolzing	92	5	68.5	1	10	-	-
10	Johannistag [Midsummer's Day]	84	7	144	-	-	3	46
11	Melodie der Johannisnacht [Melody of Midsummer's Eve]	76	-	-	6	101.95	1	28
12	Sorge [Worry]	84	1	5	6	46	-	-
13	Freundschaft [Friendship]	112/116	-	-	-	-	9	128
14	Wahn [Delusion]	56	-	-	-	-	9	180.5

Table 1. Motifs (name, frequency, duration) and tempi during the three acts of the opera.

Table 1 continued

Motif	Name	Tempo ♩ =	1st Act Frequency	1st Act Duration (sec)	2nd Act Frequency	2nd Act Duration (sec)	3rd Act Frequency	3rd Act Duration (sec)
15	Traum [Dream]	76	-	-	-	-	10	371
16	Prügel [Fight]	184	-	-	-	-	5	67.5
17	Sehnsucht [Yearning]	69	-	-	-	-	1	12.5
18	Wach-Auf-Choral [Wake up Hymn]	48	-	-	-	-	1	107
	Total duration of the act:		87.45 min		66 min		127.15 min	
	Total duration of the motifs:		851.5 sec (= 14 min, 12 sec)		528.5 sec (~ 8 min, 49 sec)		2275.5 sec (~ 37 min, 56 sec)	
	Mean duration of motifs:		X = 16.4 sec		X = 11.5 sec		X ~ 22.5 sec	

tinued by different melodies (i.e., motifs with continuation). As explained in the introduction section the leitmotifs served as the basic stimulus material for the study. For this purpose, 18 motifs were chosen which are described in detail in table 1. The mean duration of the leitmotifs during the first act was 16.4 seconds, during the second act 11.5 seconds, and during the third act 22.5, seconds. Hence, they are not too short to be recognized. Their durations are comparable to the scripts used in Lang's studies on emotional imagery. In this context, it is important to emphasize that the leitmotifs are not always found among the singing voices, usually they are just intonated by the orchestra. Consequently, the stimulus material we are dealing with in this study consists of repeated presentations and of tone passages clearly defined musically and in duration.

Data Analysis

The first inspection of the data showed that the most marked physiological and emotional re-

spones (arousal ratings) occurred during characteristic musical events, in particular during passages involving leitmotifs. Therefore, in a first step, appropriate "windows" for data analysis had to be determined. According to the assumption that trained listeners in contrast to inexperienced ones respond anticipatorily, that is prior to the real appearance of a specific melody, the windows had to be relatively wide in this step. However, the data showed that the most pronounced responses occurred during the melodic passage of the leitmotifs. This allowed us to narrow the windows, and to look at responses temporally close to the individual leitmotif. In addition to the melodies of leitmotifs, formal characteristics of musical pieces such as tempi were analyzed with respect to their emotional impact on emotional arousal and physiological responses.

The leitmotif-related electrodermal responses (magnitude of SCR amplitudes and the number of spontaneous electrodermal fluctuations per minute) were determined. Whenever responses occurred at least 3.5 seconds apart, they were considered as two separate responses. Since electrodermal responding to stimuli requires some latency, the leitmotif-related window was extended 4 seconds after the leitmotif has been terminated. The analog signals of continuous arousal-scaling were treated in the same fashion as the electrodermal responses.

In addition to the leitmotif, the tempi of the music were of special interest. By means of a metronom the tempi of the entire opera were post hoc determined. We found very long passages of 30–80 bars which were played in the same tempo. In contrast, passages with rapidly changing ritardandi and accelerandi did not allow reliable determination at the actual tempo. They were excluded from further analyses. If the tempo of a music piece has any impact on emotional responses this effect should come into appearance when comparing passages with slow ($\downarrow$ = 56 – $\downarrow$ = 76) and fast ($\downarrow$ = 112 – $\downarrow$ = 208) tempi. Besides electrodermal responses respiration provides a promising variable to reflect changes induced by different tempi. Therefore, the number of respiratory cycles were determined across 40–80 second passages with different tempi. A leitmotif-related analysis of respiratory activity was nearly impossible because of their relatively short duration. Consequently during leitmotifs we looked only at deep inhalations (sights) or exhalations or breath stopping.

Results

For each act of the opera, data of one listener are reported here. They may only be taken as anecdotal reports which were chosen to demonstrate possible outcomes of this psychophysiological approach to music-emotion interaction.

First act

In this listener, electrodermal responses varied with the different leitmotifs of the first act (Figure 1). The strongest responses were observed during rhythmically intonated motifs, especially during the Mastersingers-, the Stolzing-, the Midsummer's Day-, and the David-motif. Interestingly, the March of the

Guild Masters- and the Beckmesser-motif did not elicit any electrodermal responses. Among the lyrically intonated motifs, the largest SCR amplitudes could be observed during the Price Song. The spontaneous electrodermal fluctuations increased whenever the Worry-motif was intonated. This listener responded in a similar way to motifs with and without continuation, which may reflect that emotional responses were elicitated at the very beginning of a leitmotif. The electrodermal activity was influenced by the tempi of the music (Figure 2). During slow tempi larger electrodermal responses (SCR-amplitudes) occurred than during fast tempi. The respiratory activity, however, was unaffected by the tempi.

The arousal-scaling showed a quite different picture. According to the arousal-rating, this listener was emotionally very much affected by the Price Song. Similarly high ratings were observed for the Springtime- and the Mastersingers-motif. This listener, however, was not moved by the Beckmesser-motif. Among the other motifs, neither the rhythmically and lyrically intonated motifs, nor the different tempi had any impact on the subjective feelings of arousal (Figure 2).

No correlations between physiological responses and subjective scaling could be found. This discrepancy was particularly evident during the Spring Time-, the Stolzing-, and the March of the Guild Masters-motifs. During these motifs, the listener appeared to respond emphatically according to arousal-ratings, but the electrodermal responses at the same time suggested "physiological silence."

Second Act

This listener, too, exhibited different electrodermal responses according to the various leitmotifs of this act (Figure 3). Among them the melody of the Midsummer's Eve elicited the largest SCRs. In general she responded more strongly during the five lyrically intonated motifs compared to the two rhythmically intonated motifs of this act. The spontaneuous electrodermal fluctuations were clearly enhanced during the Spring Time-motif and the

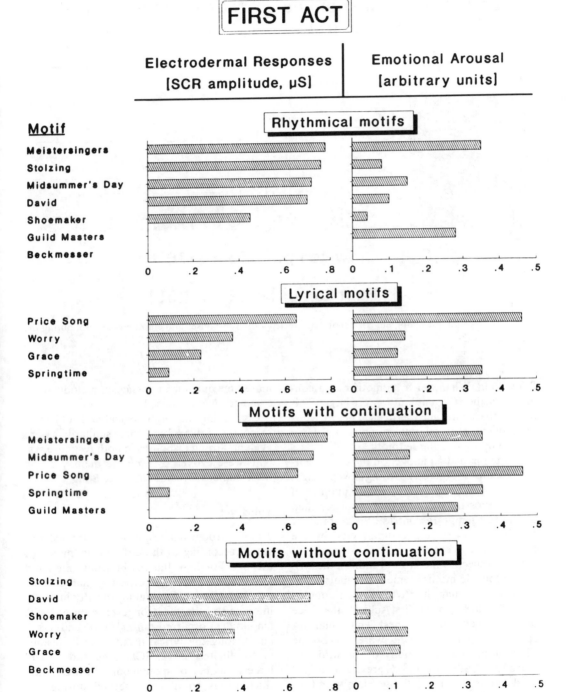

Figure 1. Electrodermal responses (SCR amplitudes) and emotional arousal (continuous scaling of arousal) of one listener (M. H., female) during different motifs (see Table 1).

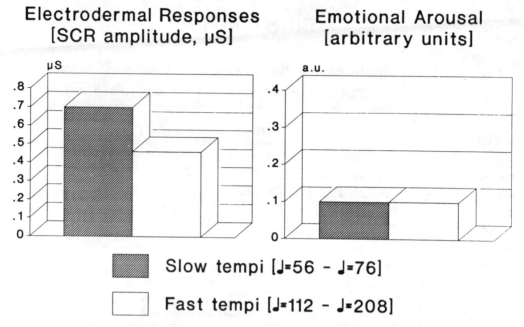

Figure 2. Slow and fast tempi and corresponding electrodermal responses and emotional arousal during the first act.

Price Song. Whenever a leitmotif had a continuation, the SCR amplitudes were larger. This implies that some time was needed before a distinguishable electrodermal response has been elicited by a particular leitmotif.

The tempi had an impact on the electrodermal responses (Figure 4). During slow passages both the SCR amplitudes and the number of spontaneuos fluctuations were stronger than during fast tempi. In contrast, the respiratory activity remained largely unaffected by the tempi to a large extent.

With respect to the arousal-ratings, the lyrically intonated motifs seemed to stimulate this listener more than the rhythmically intonated ones. Similarily to the first subject, the Price Song evoked the strongest emotional responses. Equally arousing were the Spring Time-motif and the melody of the Midsummer's Eve. Both these motifs are characterized by slow tempo. Among the seven leitmotifs of the second act, four are played with continuation. This listener felt less aroused by motifs without continuation. Presumably, she needed

more time or a longer passage of melody to become positively aroused.

Comparing the physiological and subjective responses of this subject some similarities were evident. Strong responses in both response systems were evoked by both the melody of the Midsummer's Eve and the Price Song.

Third Act

The electrodermal responses of this listener varied according to the different leitmotifs of this act. For him, the rhythmically intonated motifs elicited stronger responses than the lyrical ones (Figure 5). Among the rhythmically intonated motifs, the strongest responses (SCR amplitudes) occurred during the David-motif, and among the lyrical motifs, the Delusion-motif elicited large SCR amplitudes. The largest number of spontaneous electrodermal fluctuations could be observed during the Yearning-motif and the Price Song. Motifs with and without continuation did not have any impact on the electrodermal responding of this

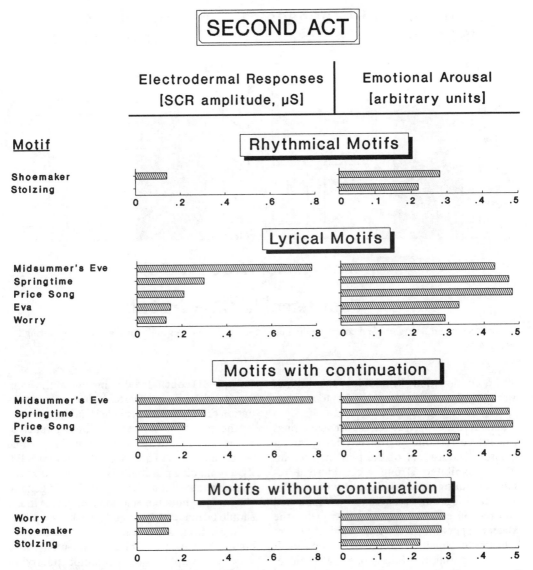

Figure 3. Electrodermal responses (SCR amplitudes) and emotional arousal (continuous scaling of arousal) of one listener (A.M., female) during different motifs (see Table 1).

listener. The tempi of the musical passages, however, evoked different SCR amplitudes. Again, as in the other two listeners, these electrodermal responses were larger during passages of slow tempi (Figure 6).

The arousal ratings were also affected by the various motifs. Among the rhythmically intonated motifs, the highest ratings were prompted by the Mastersingers-motif, followed by the Yearning-, the March of the Guild Masters-, and the Midsummer's Day motif. Within the group of lyrical motifs, this listener felt strongly aroused by the Price Song and the melody of the Midsummer's Eve. Whenever the motifs had continuations, he was more positively stimulated than during motifs without

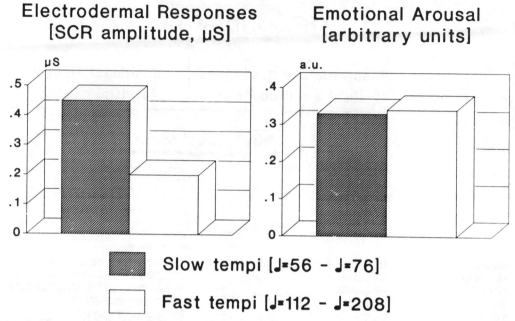

Electrodermal Responses [SCR amplitude, µS]

Emotional Arousal [arbitrary units]

Slow tempi [♩=56 – ♩=76]

Fast tempi [♩=112 – ♩=208]

Figure 4. Slow and fast tempi and corresponding electrodermal responses and emotional arousal during the second act.

such a continuation. In addition, this listener was more pleasantly aroused by fast tempi than by slow ones (Figure 6).

Similar to the first listener, the arousal ratings did not correspond to the physiological responses. The listener of the third act, for instance, exhibited strong electrodermal responses during the David-motif whereas the arousal-ratings during the same motif indicated "no response." The opposite is true for the Mastersingers-motif: strong subjective responses, but small electrodermal responses. It was only during the Price Song that both response modes seemed to correspond.

Discussion

These preliminary data show that the listeners respond physiologically and emotionally to music, and that their responses depend on the musical structure at specific points in time. Furthermore, they are related to motif passages. It comes as no surprise that individual responses may vary widely. Even studies using controlled experimental conditions (e. g., Al-

lesch, 1981) concluded that in view of the complexity of the muscial performance, only examination of single cases provide a viable approach to the question of the emotional impact of music. In view of the restrictions in possible conclusions, due to questionable external validity, a remaining possibility is to homogenize the stimulus material as far as possible. If general statements about the emotional effects of music should be made, they should be based on pieces of music from one and the same style only. To compare fugues by Johann Sebastian Bach, rock and pop music, symphonic poetry or operas of the most diverse centuries, offended the principle of commensurability. For reasons derived from the history of music and the technique of composition, we used one of the central and most mature operas of Richard Wagner for our investigation. This opera provides the repetition and the systematic integration of different motif groups in the context of a plot. Admittedly, there is no way to differentiate clearly between the effects of the music and the plot. It was obvious, however, that all subjects reacted very strongly to the "Love-motif." Sub-

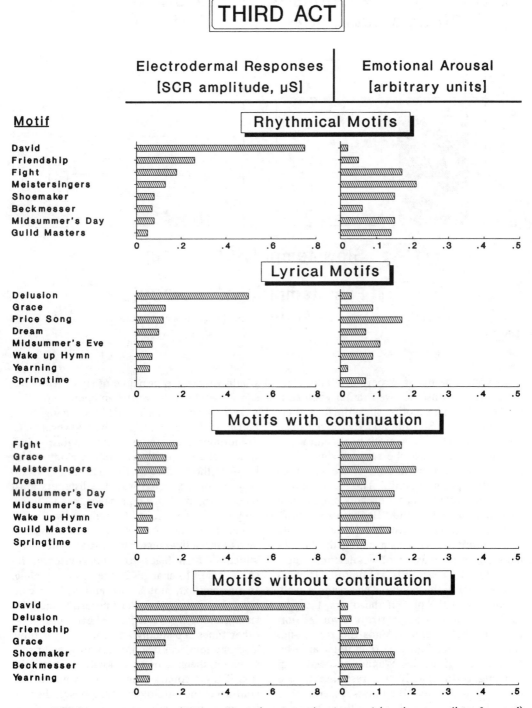

Figure 5. Electrodermal responses (SCR amplitudes) and emotional arousal (continuous scaling of arousal) of one listener (G. H., male) during different motifs (see Table 1).

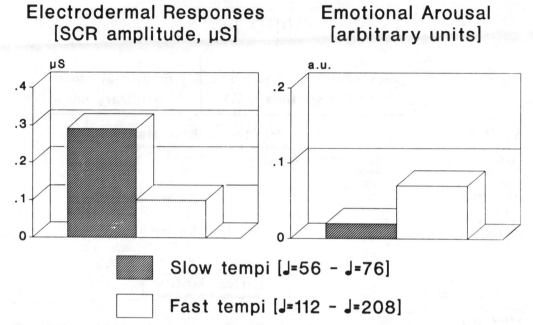

Figure 6. Slow and fast tempi and corresponding electrodermal responses and emotional arousal during the third act.

jective statements of experience and electrodermal responses showed rather good concordance for these motifs. Since the love affair between Walter Stolzing and Eva is the focal point of the opera, this motif is of central importance. In contrast, the subjects showed almost no physiological and subjective responses to the "Beckmesser-motif." The "Love-motif" can be characterized as a broadly emphasized triad melody, while the "Beckmesser-motif" represents a rather narrow, bumpy descent. The "Love-motif" is written in major, the "Beckmesser-motif" consists of whole-tone steps, which results in very different timbres. The two motifs differ in the rhythmic character as well. According to the plot of the opera, the personality of Beckmesser portrays a worried, unloved bachelor who defends the traditional rules of a singers' guild, a rival not feared by Walther Stolzing. Has Wagner succeeded in bringing forth exactly this response in the listeners with the "Beckmesser-motif"? A seperation of music and plot for the purpose of a controlled quasi-experimental manipulation would violate the principle of style. An opera simply would no longer be an opera.

The various motifs in "Die Meistersinger von Nürnberg" are scattered over several acts. Sometimes they underlie the singing voices which follow a totally different melody, as for instance the "David-motif." Thus, in order to react in the expected way, the listeners must have recognized these passages, even though they may be very short. Consequently, the imminence of a motif, or the first few bars of it, lead to the activation of an associative network, which in turn leads to somato-visceral responses and to changes in the arousal-scaling. In this context, motifs with and without continuation are of particular interest. Sometimes such a motif rings out for a short moment, at other times repeatedly and for a longer time. The physiological responses show greater sensitivity in the case of a motif without continuation. They become stronger if it is continued. In contrast to the physiological responses, the subjective arousal-scalings seem more inert: either there is no response at all – mostly with motifs without continuation – or it begins to build up only as soon as a motif has a continuation. The distinctive subjective responses to the "Love-motif" can be explained by the facts that this motif is repeated very often and that it is usually continued. We could conclude from this discussion that subjective experience, or the transmission of it, does occur with considerable delay in time. In this and in other operas of Richard Wagner, which have been subjected to the same method of examination in the festival theatre in Bayreuth ("Tannhäuser," "Lohengrin," "Parsifal"), we have gained the impression that particularly the inexperienced listeners need strong musical stimulation in order to react both physiologically and subjectively. Typically this requires that melodies have a long performance duration (for instance choral singing), that musical passages are performed in a loud and rhythmic fashion or that they otherwise are already familiar (for instance the wedding melody in the 3rd act of "Lohengrin": "Treulich geführt ..."). Weak or missing responses, which are often observed in these listeners, can be theoretically attributed to their lack of correspondingly elaborated and complex associative network. Although all of them stated that they loved and appreciated the music of Richard Wagner, their response patterns suggested that they remain "unmoved," particularly with regard to their physiological responses.

Psychophysiological data suggest that electrodermal responses, and particularly SCR-amplitudes, provide signs of short-term, stimulus-bound activation. As a rule, the more intense a simple acoustic stimulus, the larger the amplitudes. This is altogether different with music reception. The largest responses occured with very low and restrained passages. In the 2nd act of "Die Meistersinger von Nürnberg," strikingly high SCR amplitudes were prompted by the melody of "Midsummer's Eve." The essential characteristic of this melody is its extremely tender and mysterious character. Strong electrodermal responses were observed in the 3rd act, too, again following a motif with low sound volume, that is, the "Delusion-motif." Both motifs sound like "a presentiment from another world," "go under your skin" and

"send a shiver down your spine." Apparently these dynamic features influence the physiological responses. So far, the influence of dynamics has only been noted in a few studies. According to Elam (1971), small variations in dynamics lead to hardly any skin resistance responses, large variations, however, cause considerable changes in these variables. Variations in the dynamics are part of Wagner's unique style of composition. This can only be detected and heard in a concert hall. Due to the unique construction of the festival theatre Bayreuth, it is particularly conducive to conveying such experiencing.

The importance of rhythm for the experience of music has always been stressed in previous studies. Traxel and Wrede (1959), as well as Rötter (1987), found a clear relation between rhythmic elements of music and electrodermal responses. Frank (1975) even succeeded in synchronizing physiological responses such as breathing and heart rate with rhythm. In our field study, the rhythmically accentuated motifs had a stronger impact on at least one test person's electrodermal responses, compared to the rhythmically less accentuated motifs. With regard to the musical characteristics of the tempo, however, the findings of our studies were less equivocal. All three subjects showed significant effects in their skin conductance responses, but to our surprise, the effects were in opposite directions: the largest electrodermal responses occured not with fast tempi, but with slow ones. Yet this feature had only a weak influence or none at all on the subjective arousal-scaling. Unlike our findings, Kohler and his colleagues (Kohler et al., 1971), as well as Schmidt (1984), reported significant skin resistance responses depending on the musical tempi. This discrepancy in findings is probably due to the fact that in the "Die Meistersinger von Nürnberg" more motifs are presented in slow tempi than in fast ones. This could be an indirect clue that our subjects were more stimulated by the motifs themselves than by the tempi. That is all the more astonishing since both groups of tempi did not only comprise a few bars, like the motifs, but lasted for relatively long periods, that is to say, 30 to 80 bars. Obviously, this feature of a piece of music cannot provoke the responses in music experts which it may provoke in other cases, as for instance in the laboratory studies with non-musicians conducted by Miles and Tilly (1935) or by Destunis and Seebrandt (1958).

Concluding Comments

This chapter should be understood as an encouragement to study the emotional effects of music in the light of theory and with appropriate stimulation material. Lang's (1979; 1984) model of associative network not only serves an important heuristic function in the clinical sphere, but also in the psychology of music. Its primary advantage is the assistance it provides in illustrating important aspects of music reception, such as the fact of quick physiological responses and the slow habituation when listening repeatedly to one's "favourite melody." Concerning the musical "material" of such studies, it does not seem promising to compare the effects of very heterogenous pieces of music, for every work contains so many musical features, coming forth at the same time and closely interwoven with each other, that the desired controllability of a study is inevitably undermined. Rather, it seems sensible to study individual musical motifs, which can be better analyzed with regard to the context of the plot (semantic representation), their musical features, and their performance practice. This limitation should not impair the validity of the scientific examination. If the heuristic function of the associative network is to be taken seriously, persons should be chosen who are experienced with regard to the music in question, that is, optimum conditions should be established.

Research on expert behavior (expert – novice issue; cf. Chi, Glaser & Farr, 1988) has revealed that experts, unlike novices, possess a larger storage capacity of short term and long term memory and do have faster access to the stored material.

Comparable studies about musical expertise have not been published so far, particularly with regard to somato-visceral "response-sets." A fertile cooperation between musicians and psychophysiologists would suggest itself in this respect.

References

Allesch, C.G. (1981). Untersuchungen zum Einfluß von Musik auf Puls- und Atemfrequenz. *Zeitschrift für Klinische Psychologie und Psychotherapie*.

Berlyne, D.E. (1971). *Aesthetics and psychobiology*. New York: Appleton.

Binet, A., & Courtier, J. (1895). Influence de la musique sur la respiration. Le coeur et la circulation capillaire. Rev. *Scient.*, 7, 257–263.

Bradshaw, J.L. (1985). Funktionsteilung im Gehirn. In H. Bruhn, R. Oerter, & H. Rösing (Hrsg.). *Handbuch der Musikpsychologie* (70–78). München, Wien, Baltimore.

Brown, R.W. (1981). Music and language. In *Documentary Report of the Ann Arbor Symposium* (233–265). Reston, VA.

Chi, M.T.H., Glaser, R., & Farr, M.J. (Hrsg.) (1988). *The nature of expertise*. Hillsdale, N.J.: Erlbaum.

Dahlhaus, C. (1986). Die Musik. In U. Müller & P.

Wapnewski (Hrsg.). *Richard-Wagner-Handbuch* (197–221). Kröner.

Destunis, G. & Seebandt, R. (1958). Beitrag zur Frage der Musikeinwirkung auf die zwischenhirngesteuerten Funktionen des Kindes. In H.R. Teirich (Hrsg.). *Musik in der Medizin* (34–42). Stuttgart: Fischer.

Dogiel, J. (1880). Über den Einfluß der Musik auf den Blutkreislauf. *Arch. Anat. Physiol. Abt. Psychol.*, 416–428.

Dowling, W.J. & Harwood, D.L. (1986). *Music cognition*. New York: Academic Press.

Dreher, R.E. (1947). *The relationship between verbal reports and galvanic skin responses to music*. Diss. Indiana. Quoted after Farnsworth, 1976, 205.

Eifert, G.H., Craill, L., Carey, E., & O'Connor, C. (1988). Affect modification through evaluative conditioning with music. *Behav. Res. Ther.*, 26(4), 321–330.

Elam, R.W. (1971). *Mechanisms of music as an emotional intensification stimulus.* Doctoral thesis, Univ. of Missouri.

Farnsworth, P.R. (1976). *Sozialpsychologie der Musik.* Stuttgart: Kohlhammer.

Frank, C. (1975). Die Auswirkungen rhythmischer Elemente auf vegetative Funktionen. In G. Harrer (Hrsg.). *Grundlagen der Musiktherapie und Musikpsychologie* (79–90). Stuttgart: Fischer.

Hanslick, E. (1981). Die Meistersinger von Richard Wagner. In A. Csampai & D. Holland (Hrsg.). *R. Wagner "Die Meistersinger von Nürnberg"* (217–227).

Harrer, G. (Hrsg.). (1982). *Grundlagen der Musiktherapie und Musikpsychologie.* Stuttgart: Fischer.

Hevner, K. (1936). Experimental studies of the elements of expression in music. *American Journal of Psychology, 48,* 248–268.

Jansen, G. & Klensch, H. (1964). Beeinflussung des Ballistogramms durch Schallreize und Musik. *Internationale Zeitschrift für angewandte Physiologie einschließlich Arbeitsphysiologie, 20,* 258–270.

Kneutgen, J. (1970). Eine Musikform und ihre biologische Funktion. Über die Wirkungsweise der Wiegenlieder. *Zeitschrift für angewandte Psychologie und Charakterkunde, 17,* 245–265.

Kohler, M., Böttcher, C., Köhler, C., Roth, N., & Schwabe, C. (1971). Physiologische und psychologische Untersuchungen zur rezeptiven Einzelmusiktherapie. In C. Kohler (Hrsg.), *Musiktherapie. Theorie und Methodik* (57–71). Jena: Fischer.

Konecni, V. & Flath-Becker, S. (1984). Der Einfluß von Streß auf die Vorlieben für Musik. Theorie und Ergebnisse der neuen experimentellen Ästhetik. In *Jahrbuch der deutschen Gesellschaft für Musikpsychologie. Band 1* (23–51).

Lang, P.J. (1979). A bio-informational theory of emotional imagery. *Psychophysiology, 16,* 495–512.

Lang, P.J. (1984). Cognition in emotion: Concept and action. In C. Izard, J. Kagan & R. Zagoni (Eds.), *Emotion, cognition, and behavior* (192–225). New York: Cambridge University Press.

Lang, P.J. (1985). The cognitive psychophysiology of emotion: Fear and anxiety. In A.H. Tuma & J. Maser (Eds.), *Anxiety and the anxiety disorders* (131–170). Hillsdale, NJ: Erlbaum.

Lang, P.J. & Cuthbert, B.N. (1984). Affective information processing and the assessment of anxiety. *Journal of Behavioral Assessment, 6,* 369–396.

Meyer, L.B. (1956). *Emotion and meaning in music.* Chicago: University of Chicago Press.

Miles, J.R. & Tilly, C.R. (1935). Some physiological reactions to music. *Guy's Hospital Gazette, 49,* 319–322.

Peretti, P. & Swenson, K. (1974). Effects of music on anxiety as determined by physiological skin responses. *Journal of Research in Music Education, 22(4),* 278–283.

Petsche, H., Pockenberger, H., & Rappelsberger, P. (1985). Musikrezeption, EEG und musikalische Vorbildung. *EEG-EMG, 16,* 183–190.

Raab, E. (1981). Ästhetik und Neugier. In H.G. Voss & H. Keller (Hrsg.), *Neugierforschung* (263–308). Weinheim: Beltz.

Rötter, G. (1987). Elektrische Hautwiderstandsänderungen als Abbild musikalischer Strukturen. *Jahrbuch der deutschen Gesellschaft für Musikpsychologie, 4,* 139–147.

Scherer, K.E. & Oshinsky, J.S. (1977). Cue utilization in emotion attribution from auditory stimuli. *Motivation & Emotion, 1,* 331–346.

Schmidt, B. (1984). Empirische Untersuchung emotionaler Wirkungen verschiedener Tempi bei rhythmisch betonter Musik. *Jahrbuch der deutschen Gesellschaft für Musikpsychologie, 1,* 149–159.

Traxel, W. & Wrede, G. (1959). Hautwiderstandsänderungen bei Musikdarbietungen. *Zeitschrift für Experimentelle & Angewandte Psychologie, 6,* 293–309.

Vehrs, W. (1986). *Nicht-verbale Erlebnisbeschreibung.* Göttingen: Hogrefe.

Wagner, R. (1860). *Zukunftsmusik. An einen französischen Freund.* Leipzig: Insel-Verlag.

Walker, J.L. (1977). Subjective reactions to music and brainwave rhythms. *Physiological Psychology, 5(4),* 483–489.

Wedin, L. (1972). A multidimensional study of perceptual-emotional qualities in music. *Scandinavian Journal of Psychology, 13,* 1–17.

Werbik, H. (1971). *Informationsgehalt und emotionale Wirkung von Musik.* Mainz: Schott & Söhne.

Zakharova, N.N. & Avdeyev, V.M. (1982). Functional changes in the CNS during perception of music: On the problem studying positive emotions. *Zhurnal Vysshei Nernoi Deyatel'nosh, 32(5),* 915–924.

Section C.
Acquisition of Fear

The Associative Network of Fear: How Does It Come About?

Gudrun Sartory*

Abstract

Does the associative network of fear come about by a gradual strengthening of the association of its elements, or do some elements take precedence, with others being gradually added? An attempt is made to collate the available evidence on the genesis of phobic reactions with regard to this question. Although scarce, data suggest that phobic responses can come about by a number of routes, the most frequent being by an initial conditioning event, the next being via vicarious learning and occasionally simply via adverse information. Different routes and forms of phobic anxiety seem to predominate at different stages in life, with conditioning events in adulthood being the more frequent mode of onset in agoraphobia. Conditioning gives rise to a compound of visceral responses and negative stimulus appraisal. Among the facilitating factors are individual differences and preparedness, but also the affective intensity of the conditioning event. There is good evidence that avoidance behaviour is consequent upon the visceral response-stimulus appraisal compound. It is concluded that the associative network of fear is the result of a process whereby visceral and appraisal elements bring about avoidance behaviour and are strengthened by it in turn.

Key words: phobic anxiety, fear network, etiology of phobic anxiety, preparedness, fear conditioning, vicarious learning

Fear and Propositional Network Theory

Until quite recently fear was considered to be adequately assessed by a single measure, be it a questionnaire measure, an eye-blink or electrodermal activity (EDA). Reviewing the utility of clinical assessments of fear, Lang (1971) argued that multiple measures of fear had to be taken to obtain a comprehensive account of fear responses. He proposed a tri-modal approach to the assessment of emotional responses, namely the assessement of verbal-cognitive, motor-behavioral and physiological responses. Not only would such an approach allow for an exhaustive clinical assessment of a client's fear and for the full evaluation of treatment outcome, but the three modes were also considered to be the relevant observable manifestations of the hypothetical construct that was fear.

This conceptualisation of fear raises the question of how the response modes are related. Lang (1979,1985) answered this question by suggesting that fear constituted an associative network in memory which included information about the stimulus, its appraisal and the range of possible responses. A sufficiently matching stimulus would activate the whole structure of the associative network, and thereby also the efferent verbal, visceral and

* Department of Psychology, University of Wuppertal, Germany

motor responses, manifesting themselves in the often observed compound of subjective or reported fear, behavioural avoidance and cardiac acceleration, among others.

In order to prove experimentally and clinically valid, theoretical models of fear need also explain how fear reduction or emotional processing (Rachman, 1980) comes about. Foa and Kozak (1986) developed a model of emotional processing based on Lang's (1979) bio-informational theory. They proposed that, first of all, the associative network had to be accessed or activated for emotional processing to occur. The other essential ingredient was thought to be the availability of information which invalidated, or was in some way incompatible with, any elements of the fear structure. Therapeutic emotional processing was thus thought to represent exposure to corrective information leading to the uncoupling or disintegration of stimulus, appraisal and response elements. A more detailed account of the model of emotional processing is provided in another chapter of this book. In the present chapter, the remaining question will be addressed, namely, that of the genesis of the associative network of fear.

This is little disagreement that just as its processing, the development of phobic anxiety requires time. Is it then the case that the associative network is at first tentatively formed, to become better established by frequent activation of its pathways (in the Hebbian sense)? Neurophysiological research has yielded a body of data which, when collated, provides a model of the growth of associative networks. There is evidence of post-synaptic memory mechanisms as well as of axonal and dendritic growth, and diversification and linkage within and between neuronal cell assemblies. These models tend to require temporal contiguity between stimuli, or stimuli and reactions, for such linkages to occur. Once established, all elements of the thus associated network will be activated. Within the context of fear it is, however, unlikely that all elements of the fear structure are present from the beginning, to be further strengthened by repeated temporal contiguity. Instead, it is more likely that the genesis of some elements of the fear structure takes precedence over, or indeed brings about, others.

A similar suggestion was made with regard to emotional processing. Rather than hypothesizing a slow fading of the associative network, Foa and Kozak (1986) proposed that fear processing was conditional upon certain steps without which the fear structure could not be changed. In their conception of the fear network, stimulus and meaning or appraisal elements, are linked by intense visceral responses such as tachycardia and hyperventilation. Consequently, the authors argue, an uncoupling of stimulus elements and their appraisal of being dangerous and fear-inducing can come about only by attenuation of the physiological responses. Drawing on empirical evidence, the authors also proposed that within-session habituation, i.e., attenuation of physiological responses during activation of the fear structure, needs to take place before between-session habituation, or the permanent encoding of that attenuation. Following the line of argument that attenuation of physiological responses can lead to the collapse of the fear structure it is likely that their development will also constitute an important building block. It should also follow that phobic anxiety is initiated by traumatic or distressing events. This is, however, not always the case as studies of the modes of fear acquisition showed.

Retrospective Studies on the Acquisition of Phobic Anxiety

The validity of retrospective studies is subject to a number of constraints. One shared with all assessments of phenomena after the fact is the difficulty in interpreting cause and effect; for instance, individual differences between subjects are just as likely to be the result rather then the cause of an anxiety disorder. Another constraint is bias in memory or simply memory performance. The precipitant event may have been forgotten or never verbally encoded if it occurred before development of language functions. Different modes of fear acquisition have nonetheless been identified. Some patients recall a highly distressing event at the onset of their phobia, e.g. dog phobics may report having been bitten by a dog or agoraphobics may report having been shut in a tightly packed train compartment during an outing when heat and distress prompted an anxiety attack. Such accounts are identified as conditioning experiences. Other phobics may recall that a parent of theirs was frightened of a particular situation or animal which the patient is now frightened of, too. In such a case fear is considered to have come about through vicarious learning. In some cases patients report that they were given instructions to avoid certain dangerous places or animals by their parents. Such an account would be rated among 'information or instruction' as having caused the phobic anxiety. Patients may, however, be unable to recall any particular event and state that they have always had their fear.

As shown in table 1, a varying and sometimes substantial number of animal phobics has indeed reported not to be able to recall a precipitant event, from 10% (Öst & Hugdahl, 1981) to 68% (McNally & Steketee, 1985). The number of phobics reporting a traumatic or conditioning onset also varies considerably, from none (Kleinknecht, 1982) to 81% (Öst & Hugdahl, 1983). Similar disagreement has been found regarding the proportion of patients recalling vicarious learning namely, from 3% (Rimm et al. 1977) to 34% (Kleinknecht, 1982). The proportion of phobics becoming anxious as a result of information about the dangerousness of the phobic object

Table 1: Percentages of subjects who have no recall of precipitants of their phobic anxiety (have always had it), who report a distressing conditioning event, a vicarious learning event or who report having been given information about the danger of the phobic object/situation at the onset of phobic anxiety.

Sample	N	% no recall	% conditioning event recalled	% vicarious event recalled	% information about danger
Mixed analogue phobics (Rimm et al., 1977)	45	29	36	3	4
Tarantula analogue (Kleinknecht, 1982)	43	17		34	61
Dog analogue (Di Nardo et al., 1988)	16	–	56	–	–
Animal phobics (Öst & Hugdahl, 1981)	40	10	47.5	27.5	15.0
Animal phobics (Mc Nally & Steketee, 1985)	22	68	23	4	4
Claustrophobics (Öst & Hugdahl, 1981)	35	11.4	68.6	8.6	11.4
Social phobics (Öst & Hugdahl, 1981)	31	26.0	58.1	12.9	3.0
Agoraphobics (Öst & Hugdahl, 1983)	80	10.0	81.3	8.7	

ranges from none (Öst & Hugdahl, 1983) to 61% (Kleinknecht,1982).

It has been suggested that a conditioning experience at the onset of phobic anxiety would lead to greater severity than anxiety resulting from information about the object (Rachman, 1978). There is, however, no appreciable difference between analogue and clinical populations regarding the proportion reporting a conditioning event (among animal phobics). Taken together, there seems to be a high proportion of subjects giving informational and vicarious learning accounts among snake and spider phobics. Murray & Foote's (1979) subjects reported that they were given instructions to avoid snakes by their parents and had been made anxious by films depicting snakes as dangerous. Actually being bitten by a snake is indeed a rare event in urban society. Social phobics, claustrophobics and agoraphobics reported more frequent conditioning events at the onset than animal phobics. This appears counterintuitive since being adult at the onset, agoraphobics, for example, should be more amenable to informa-

tion about danger. It has to be noted, however, that a greater proportion of animal than other phobics fail to remember events occurring at the onset of their phobias.

If conditioning initially engenders physiological responses, then it might be expected that individuals with a traumatic onset would exhibit larger cardiac reactions than those with indirect precipitants. Öst & Hugdahl (1981) found that groups with a conditioning experience showed HR increases that were higher by some 5 bpm than those of 'indirect' groups, but the difference was significant only for claustrophobics. In contrast, claustrophobics with 'indirect' onset showed more avoidance and reported a higher level of subjective anxiety than those with a 'conditioning' onset. It is unclear why this should be the case for claustrophobics rather than, for instance, for social or agoraphobics (Öst & Hugdahl, 1983). It can, however, be concluded at present that the fear network can develop through a variety of precipitants, conditioning being only one of them.

The Rise of the Visceral Response

Given that visceral responses are thought to constitute an essential building-block in phobic anxiety (Foa & Kozak, 1986), due consideration must be given here to the development of these responses. Visceral responses in phobic anxiety are characterised by cardiac acceleration, peripheral vasoconstriction, an increase in systolic and diastolic blood pressure, as well as far-reaching endocrine changes, such as an increase in adrenaline and noradrenaline level, in the levels of cortisol, of insulin and of the plasma growth hormone (Nesse et al., 1985). These responses are partly consistent with a sympathetic discharge.

In keeping with the tenet that visceral reactivity is subject to conditioning, it has been argued throughout this century that reactivity pertaining to phobic reactions is also the product of a conditioning process. It has, however, been curiously difficult to obtain empirical support for this notion. Classical aversive conditioning procedures of heart-rate, for instance, have usually resulted in decelerative responses (see also the chapter by Hamm and Vaitl, this volume). Are we to think that they are the seed of the latter heart-pounding observed in phobics?

Eysenck (1968) came to the rescue of the declining classical conditioning paradigm by proposing an incubation model of fear. Pondering clinical reports of the slow development of phobic reactions and the lack of repeated CS/UCS pairings, Eysenck proposed that phobic anxiety was the result of a single trial of aversive classical conditioning after which the individual encountered only the CS. Since the CS had acquired aversive qualities during the conditioning trial, it was in itself capable of strengthening the aversive reaction in further trials. An essential condition for incubation of fear to take place was the duration of CS exposure: Long exposure would induce habituation and only short exposure was likely to lead to incubation because the anxiety response had not enough time to diminish.

The model was in agreement with the empirical evidence available at the time. Measuring blood pressure responses in dogs, Napalkov (1963) had observed that repeated pairings of a light flash and UCSs such as toy-pistol shots or pulling the dogs on straps to the ceiling, resulted in a response decrement over trials, that is, the dogs habituated to the UCS. If, however, a single paired trial was followed by administration of the CS only, the blood pressure response increased over trials. Although these experiments were less than stringent, the data are nevertheless remarkable. The blood pressure response generalised to the room in which the experiments were carried out as well as to others if the CS was presented there. Some dogs also exhibited a chronically hypertensive state. Corroborative evidence for an incubation process of fear was also supplied by data on the effect of short exposure to intensely fear-arousing material. While long exposures (1–3 hrs) had the expected therapeutic effect, short ones (2 min) tended to produce an increase in fear (Rachman, 1966).

Empirical tests of the incubation model in rats, however, have produced inconsistent results, some showing a systematic increase in avoidance behaviour after short compared to no or long exposures to the CS (Rohrbaugh and Riccio, 1970), others failing to find this effect (Sartory and Eysenck, 1976). It is likely that the failures to reproduce Napalkov's data convincingly have been due to the choice of the response measure, namely, passive avoidance rather than a visceral variable. More convincing data have been supplied by behavioural endocrinology (Eysenck & Kelley, 1987). Injections of ACTH or adrenalin given after acquisition training and prior to an extinction trial produced an increase in the fear response rendering it chronic without further injections (Haroutunian & Riccio, 1979). The question arises whether or not stresses of the kind that bring about endocrine changes can also turn the concurrent aversive reaction into a persistent phobic response. There is anecdotal clinical evidence suggesting that life stresses can sensitise phobic anxiety reactions. It is thus possible that the current endocrine status determines conditionability and thereby the genesis of the visceral response.

Factors Influencing the Conditioned Acquisition of Fear Responses

Individual Differences

It is frequently argued that the experience of stress is less dependent upon the nature of the stressor than upon the way the individual perceives and processes it. Such a formulation implies that individual differences may explain some of the variance found in acquisition and extinction of fear responses. Animal data support this notion. Rats bred selectively for emotionality, i.e., a high defecation response in the the open field test, acquired and maintained conditioned fear responses more rapidly than those bred for non-emotionality (Sartory & Eysenck, 1976). Laboratory experiments in humans differing in anxiety-proneness, i.e.,

Neuroticism, however, produced inconsistent results (Sartory, 1983).

Support for the importance of individual differences is nonetheless also provided by real-life 'experiments' in humans. Although post-traumatic-stress disorder (PTSD) in war veterans represents a variety of different disorders, a conditioned fear response to relevant stimuli, such as battle noise, has been isolated (Pallmeyer et al., 1986). Longitudinal studies of soldiers with battle experience revealed personality factors which rendered combatants prone to subsequent PTSD. Locus of control (Rotter, 1966) was one of the predictors of the outcome of such intensely life-threatening experiences. Subjects with external locus of control were more likely to develop PTSD than those with internal locus of control (Solomon et al., 1989). Individual differences thus appear to contribute to the maintenance of acquired fear reactions.

Preparedness

Surveying the nature of phobias which occur clinically, Seligman (1971) noted that not all stimuli were equally likely to attract a lasting fear response, but rather that stimuli such as spiders or snakes were among the most frequently observed targets. In contrast, other stimuli commonly paired with pain or danger, such as dentists or knives, only rarely present as objects of phobic anxiety. He thus contested the notion of equipotentiality of stimuli for becoming a target of phobic avoidance and proposed that some stimuli were genetically 'prepared'. Along the path of evolution, natural selection was to have favoured those who were frightened of stimuli that threatened species survival. Fear of those stimuli was more easily acquired and more resistent to extinction than fear of unprepared stimuli – hence the preponderance of snake and spider phobics among simple phobics (see the chapter by Öhman, this volume). A full discussion of the clinical and laboratory data of this influential theory theory has recently been provided by McNally (1987) and will not be reiterated here. The basic notion, however, that avoidance of some stimuli represents a selective advantage is ultimately untestable. We have no access to causes of morbidity down the phylogenetic scale but it is conceivable that communities perished through volcanic movement of the earth, through floods (Genesis 7:12) or that individuals disappeared down the aesophagi of assorted large predatory animals (as is still sometimes the case). Yet the number of thunder-, water- or bear/tiger-phobics represents a minority among simple phobics.

Attempts at substantiating the notion that fear responses are more easily conditioned to phylogenetically relevant stimuli than to neutral stimuli show a chequered history (McNally, 1987) but large-scale studies such as one involving 292 Ss (Cook et al., 1986) showed that preparedness makes a significant contribution to the conditioned cardiac accelerative response usually observed in phobics when confronted with the phobic object. When comparing accelerators with decelerators (Hodes et al, 1985), it could also be shown that the former underwent a change of stimulus appraisal during the conditioning procedure. Afterwards, the stimulus was considered less pleasurable and more dominant then before. These data support the notion that some stimuli are more easily conditioned than others. It is an enduring problem for experimental studies, however, that the conditioning histories of subjects prior to the experiment, 'cultural-preparedness' for want of a better term, is difficult to ascertain.

Belongingness

Phobics rarely report that they are anxious of a painful outcome of an encounter with the phobic object, i.e. of being throttled or injected with venom by a snake, in the case of snake phobia, or of being bitten or cocooned in a web by a spider, in the case of spider phobia. Nonetheless, dog phobia for instance seems to have been initiated frequently by an early experience of having been bitten by man's best friend (Di Nardo et al, 1988). The nature of the UCS or rather the type of combination of stimuli and reinforcer may then be important as to whether or not conditioning occurs. Thus a UCS such as lithium chloride (which, when ingested, results in gastric upset) produces more pronounced conditioning when paired with a taste CS (saccharin) than with a visual CS (light) (Garcia & Koelling, 1966). The functional relationship between stimulus and reinforcer has been variously called 'belongingness' by these authors, or 'relevance' by Mackintosh (1983). Mackintosh (1983) argues that 'there may be no physical characteristic that serves to identify those combinations that are readily associated from those that are not'. In animal research, it has indeed been difficult to predict why, for instance, pigeons should show aversive conditioning to a tone rather than a light and the converse with appetitive conditioning (Force & Lolordo, 1973, cit. Mackintosh, 1983), i.e., belongingness could often be discovered only after the fact.

In humans, it is likely that belongingness of stimuli is a function of previous experience. When asked to rate the extent of belongingness between stimuli, subjects considered an angry face and a 100 dB scream as being more closely related than the angry face and an electric shock (Hamm et al., 1989). In the course of normal human experience an angry face presumably signals a loud voice somewhat more often than it signals the administration of an electric shock. Within the context of fear conditioning it could be argued that the possible painful consequences peculiar to the phobic object will also constitute the most potent reinforcer. In accordance with that notion, a tactile stimulus paired with slides of snakes and spiders produced a more pronounced conditioned cardiac response than did an auditory stimulus (Cook et al., 1986). Unfortunately, this effect does not seem to be robust (McNally, 1987).

Intensity of UCS

A high proportion of agoraphobic patients who recall a conditioning event as precipitant, report a traumatic event, such as being shut into a situation and feeling sick as triggering off subsequent gradual avoidance. In any case, patients frequently report the initial experience as having been intensely aversive or even life-threatening.

Surveying the literature on fear conditioning, it becomes obvious that the employed UCS is typically a mild one, despite the fact that it is probably one of the oldest tenets of classical conditioning that more intense negative UCSs result in stronger CRs. There exist, of course, justified ethical constraints concerning the extent of suffering that can be inflicted on animal or human subjects in an experimental situation which curtail this line of enquiry. Nonetheless, it is surprising that failures to create affective responses in the laboratory are rarely explained in terms of the mild stimulation administered. The only study, in which subjects experienced the UCS in a single trial as 'terrifying' led quite unequivocally to instantaneous conditioning and avoidance (Campbell et al., 1968). Without prior information, subjects were administered succinylcholine chloride dihydrate which interrupted, among other things, their ability to breathe. A tone was associated with the onset of paralysis. Subjects later described the experience as having been more horrifying than acutely life-threatening combat situations during World War II. Further administrations of the tone by itself resulted in enhanced EDRs and finally flight and avoidance of the building in which the experiment had taken place.

Similarly, instances of highly traumatic experiences have been reported by veterans with PTSD and also by victims of violence and rape, resulting in intense fear states when confronted with related stimuli and situations. It is likely that a variety of simple phobias with a childhood onset are also the result of traumatic experiences, even if they are not remembered at all at a later stage. Alternatively, they may not be remembered as having been life-threatening at the time because of a change of appraisal of the stimulus with the passage of time. It must not be forgotten that children are likely to experience particular situations or stimuli as more or less fear-inducing than do adults.

Fear Acquisition via Information and Vicarious Learning

Comparatively few studies have been carried out on social learning and the acquisition of phobias. It could be argued that social learning constitutes a form of conditioning. If a child observes the upset of the mother confronting a spider, s/he may suffer from her withdrawal and come to associate that aversive state with the phobic object thereby becoming phobic him/herself. But social learning is not restricted to conditioning. Experiments on vicarious learning in which children observed a peer apparently receiving a shock were successful in creating fear if not a persistent one (Bandura and Rosenthal, 1966).

Highly persistent fears were shown to develop through vicarious learning in monkeys (Mineka & Tomarken, 1989). Exposing a previously unafraid lab-reared monkey to another wild-reared one exhibiting fear of snakes resulted in intense and persistent fear of snakes in about 3/4 of the observers. These results strongly support the view that phobias can develop through social learning. It is likely that the same factors influencing the long-term outcome of conditioning, such as individual differences, present mood, phylogenetic or cultural preparedness, will also modulate the outcome of social learning.

As to factors influencing social learning in monkeys, Mineka and Tomarken (1989) report that the intensity of the model's expression of fear greatly determined that of the observer. Conversely, the observing monkeys could be immunised against fear acquisition by prior exposure to a model who was unafraid of snakes (Mineka & Cook, 1986). Controllability of the aversive event and previous experience of control or 'mastery' also influenced fear acquisition (Mineka et al., 1986). Monkeys who had experienced control over their environment were less anxious or habituated more rapidly to fear-provoking situations and were therefore less prone to develop persistent fear reactions. Similarly, an emotionally robust child living in an educational context rich on possibilities to experience control may react less strongly to models experiencing fear or information delivered with an anxiety-ridden voice than an anxious child.

Developmental Aspects

No student of phobic anxiety can ignore the data about onset times of different kinds of fears. Any etiological model of phobic anxiety will also have to explain why particular situations or stimuli are prone to engender phobic reactions at different stages of life. In attempting to explain why animal phobias start in childhood, Öhman (1986) has argued that young primates are highly vulnerable to predators. Fear of other species could therefore promote their survival. As noted above, it is not quite obvious why it should be fear of snakes and spiders rather than of large furry animals, some of whom are deadly carnivorous, that provides a selective advantage.

The onset of social phobias coincides frequently with adolescence. Öhman has argued that this is also the time of 'intraspecies' strife and struggle for a dominant position in the social hierarchy within the peer group. Sensitivity towards manifestations of dominance and social threat may also ensure a superior conditionability to such stimuli during adolescence. Hormonal and concurrent behavioural changes related to sexual maturation may also provide a focus for the development of social phobia in adolescence.

The phylo- and ontogenetic functionality of agoraphobia remains unclear. Assuming that there is none, it is surprising that a high proportion of agoraphobics report an initial conditioning event out of which, completely unaided by a collective phylogenetic memory, grows the disorder. Animal phobias, although thought to be prepared, have a higher proportion of informational and vicarious learning onsets. Could it be that preparedness facilitates fear acquisition via these two pathways whereas conditioning is less dependent on phylogenetic factors? Given that agoraphobics have had extensive experience with the situations they later avoid, it could be argued that a traumatic event is necessary to turn them into a phobic stimulus. Less intense experiences such as those provided by social learning may suffice to turn a comparatively novel stimulus into a phobic one. Small children are also more dependent on models to learn about their environment than are adults and may therefore also be uniquely sensitive to social learning.

Beyond the Precipitant Event

It is unlikely that a single event will serve to establish the associative network of fear with its ready and immediate efferents observed in a phobic. Di Nardo et al. (1988) found that students who had been previously bitten showed elevated heart-rate when being confronted by a dog. Only a proportion of them, however, reported to be fearful or avoided the animal. It is generally agreed upon that avoidance and lack of exposure strengthen the fear response, and thereby have their share in bringing it about. Given that a visceral response has occurred, are cognitive, that is, conscious processes that can be verbalised by the individual, necessary to mediate behaviour? Öhman (1988) has recently summarised the evidence on nonconscious control of autonomic responses concluding that emotional processes and their physiological correlates do not require conscious control. By the same token, various lines of evidence point at nonconscious control of behaviour mediated by emotional processes. Nisbett & Wilson (1977) and others showed that priming of contents influenced choice behaviour without subjective awareness as to why a particular choice had been made. Extensive evidence is also provided by Lewecki (1987) that behavioral performance, in this case, reaction time, can be a function of non-conscious processing of information. Le Doux' (1989) work also demonstrates that reactions to stimuli previously made aversive remain intact following ablation of the primary cortical region which processes the fear stimulus. It can be assumed then that a stimulus made aversive by either conditioning, vicarious learning or information/instruction will subsequently be avoided even if the individual is not aware of feeling anxious.

Avoidance Threshold

Little is known about factors that promote the first avoidance response of a stimulus that has turned aversive. There are likely to exist individual differences regarding the threshold above which situations or stimuli are avoided, i. e. some individuals may avoid a stimulus or situation after minimal information of its negative consequences whereas for others only a major traumatic event will do to prevent approach. Extensive individual differences can be observed when phobics are given the option to approach as much or as little as they choose (Sartory, et al., 1982). Although highly anxious, some are determined to get as near as possible to the feared situation while others are equally determined to remain at a distance from which they do not experience fear at all. Accordingly, the correlation between behavioural and subjective anxiety is commonly reported to be low or even negative. It has therefore been proposed that avoidance behaviour is not linearly related to emotion of anxiety (Sartory et al., 1982) but is accounted for by at least two factors although it is uncertain what the other one might be. Rachman (1978) boldly called it 'courage' and indeed, it may constitute tolerance of aversive states although this has not as yet been shown. Individual differences may contribute to setting the threshold for the avoidance response similar to those provoking a visceral response and a change to a negative appraisal of that stimulus in the first place.

Extensive avoidance is thought to strengthen the fear response be it because avoidance prevents habituation or because it does not allow for corrective information to enter the associative fear network, or both, as Foa and Kozak (1986) argue. Other processes that serve to strengthen the fear response have recently been laid open. Rachman and Lopatka (1986a, b) showed that individuals who expected not to be fearful in a situation but had a panic attack and had to leave it instead, felt more fearful of it afterwards. It is likely that such processes contribute to the development of the associative network of fear.

Genesis of the Fear Network: Summary (Fig. 1)

The network model of phobic anxiety stresses the unity of the various components of phobic anxiety and accounts better for their concurrent activation than could previous models of phobic anxiety. It is at present, however, a stationary model or at best one in which links between elements are evenly strengthened owing to their temporally contiguous activation. It is proposed here that the elements of the fear network are assembled sequentially, i. e., that activation of some elements brings about others. Special importance is attached to the visceral response element. It is either the product of a traumatizing event which gave rise to avoidance behaviour, thereby compounding the fear structure or else the product of information/instruction about the phobic object or

situation which is followed by avoidance. Long-term avoidance is then capable of giving rise to visceral responses upon exposure. Some data (Öst & Hugdahl, 1981) point at predominance of subjective fear following the information/avoidance route compared with a relative predominance of visceral responses following the conditioning/avoidance route.

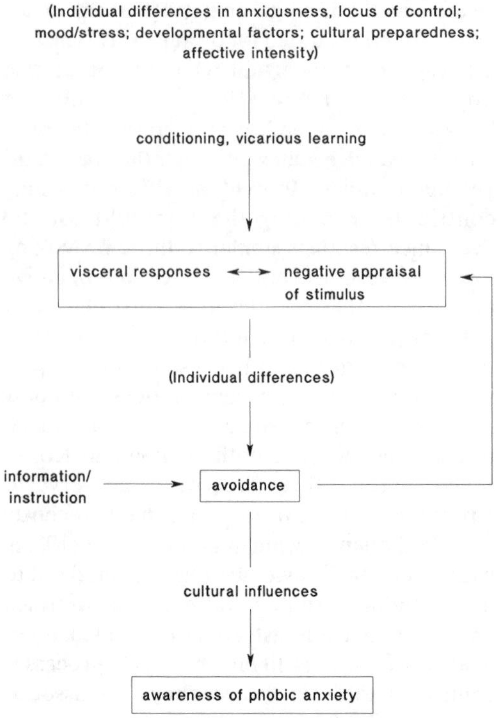

The processes leading to the fear network as well as contributing factors are summarised in Fig. 1. Accordingly, it is proposed that a conditioning, i. e., distressing event or similarly distressing vicarious learning will give rise to visceral responses and negative stimulus appraisal. Whether or not this effect will be achieved depends on traits of the individual; anxiousness and an external locus of control have been pinpointed in empirical reasearch so far. State factors such as mood and stress appear to be important as well. Different situations are likely to attract negative appraisal upon a distressing event at different ages; developmental factors therefore play an important role. Previous experience with the phobic object or situation e. g., fears portrayed in films or books, will also contribute to conditionability since it represents a form of vicarious learning. Finally, the affective impact of the distressing event interactively determines whether or not the chain of events leading to the emergence of a fear network will be set in motion. Given a vulnerable individual and a developmentally and culturally prepared object/situation, minor upset may trigger off the visceral response – negative stimulus-appraisal compound. Alternatively, an intensely distressing event may not need support from other quarters to become stored with negative connotations and autonomic responses. Little is known about factors leading to avoidance following the initial event. But it is likely and in any case, parsimonious to assume that the same factors, i. e., vulnerability and developmental and cultural preparedness and now also the intensity of the visceral response – negative stimulus appraisal compound will lead to behavioural avoidance. While there is agreement that long-

Figure 1. Summary of modes of onset and factors leading to the genesis of the fear network. Contributing factors are in brackets and observable elements of the fear network in boxes.

term avoidance will strengthen the fear network, little is known about the underlying processes. Avoidance may increase anticipatory anxiety before renewed exposure but it may also merely serve to increase the novelty of the stimulus/situation contributing to the intensity of the reaction. Avoidance may also be punctuated by short exposures to the phobic situations with outcomes more distressing than anticipated. As noted above, a small proportion of phobics (Tab. 1) report negative information and instruction to avoid the phobic object/situation at the onset of phobic anxiety. It is likely that vulnerability and developmental factors/cultural preparedness make a contribution to the development of the fear network via this route, too. Finally, cultural influences seem to determine the degree of awareness of the phobic state and its related processes.

References

Bandura, A. & Rosenthal, T.L. (1966). Vicarious classical conditioning as a function of arousal level. *Journal of Personality and Social Psychology, 3,* 54–62.

Campbell, D., Sanderson, R.E. & Laverty, S.G. (1964). Characteristics of a conditioned response in human subjects during extinction trials following a single traumatic conditioning trial. *Journal of Abnormal and Social Psychology, 68,* 627–339.

Cook, E.W. III, Hodes, R.L. & Lang, P.J. (1986). Preparedness and phobia: Effects of stimulus content on human visceral conditioning. *Journal of Abnormal Psychology, 95,* 195–207.

Di Nardo, P.A., Guzy, L.T. & Bak, R.M. (1988). Anxiety response patterns and etiological factors in dog-fearful and non-fearful subjects. *Behaviour Research and Therapy, 26,* 245–251.

Di Nardo, P. A., Guzy, L.T., Jenkens, J.A. Bak, R.M., Tomasi, S.F. & Copland, M. (1988). Etiology and maintenance of dog fears. *Behaviour Research and Therapy, 26,* 241–244.

Eysenck, H.J. (1968). A theory of the incubation of Anxiety/ Fear responses. *Behaviour Research and Therapy, 6,* 309–321.

Eysenck, H.J. & Kelley, M.J. (1987). The interaction of neuro- hormones with Pavlovian A and Pavlovian B conditioning in the causation of neurosis, extinction, and incubation of anxiety. In G. Davey (Ed.), *Cognitive processes and Pavlovian conditioning in humans.* Chichester: Wiley.

Foa, E.B. (1979). Failure in treating obsessive-compulsives. *Behaviour Research and Therapy, 17,* 169–176.

Foa, E.B. & Kozak, M.J. (1986). Emotional processing of fear: Exposure to corrective information. *Psychological Bulletin, 99, 1,* 20–35.

Garcia, I. & Koelling, R.A. (1966). The relation of cue to consequences in avoidance learning. *Psychonomic Science, 5,* 123–124.

Hamm, A.O., Vaitl, D. & Lang, P.J. (1989). Fear conditioning, meaning and belongingness: A selective association analysis. *Journal of Abnormal Psychology, 4,* 395–406.

Haroutunian, V. & Riccio, D.C. (1979). Drug-induced 'arousal' and the effectiveness of CS exposure in the reinstatement of memory. *Behavioral and Normal Biology, 26,* 115–120.

Hodes, R.L., Cook, E.W. III & Lang, P.J. (1985). Individual differences in autonomic response: Conditioned association or conditioned fear? *Psychophysiology, 22,* 545–560.

Kleinknecht, R.A. (1982). The origins and remission of fear in a group of tarantula enthusiasts. *Behaviour Research and Therapy, 20,* 437–443.

Lang, P.J. (1971). The application of psychophysiological methods to the study of psychotherapy and behavior modification. In A.E. Bergin & S.L. Garfield (Eds.), *Handbook of psychotherapy and behavior change.* New York: Wiley.

Lang, P.J. (1979). A bio-informational theory of emotional imagery. *Psychophysiology, 1979, 16,* 495–512.

Lang, P.J. (1985). The cognitive psychophysiology of emotion: Fear and anxiety. In A.H. Tuma & I.D. Maser (Eds.), *Anxiety and the anxiety disorders.* Hillsdale, N.J.: Erlbaum.

LeDoux, J.E. (1989). Cognitive-emotional interactions in the brain. *Cognition and Emotion, 3,* 267–289.

Lewecki, P. Czyzewska, M. & Hoffmann, H. (1987). Unconscious acquisition of complex procedual knowledge. *Journal of Experimental Psychology: Learning, Memory and cognition, 13,* 523–530.

Mackintosh, N.J. (1983). *Conditioning and associative learning.* London: Oxford University Press.

McNally, R.J. (1987). Preparedness and phobias: a review. *Psychological Bulletin, 101,* 283–303.

McNally, R.J. & Steketee, G.S. (1985). The etiology

and maintenance of servere animal phobias. *Behaviour Research and Therapy, 23,* 431–435.

Mineka, S. & Cook, M. (1986). Immunization against the observational conditioning of snake fear in rhesus monkeys. *Journal of Abnormal Psychology, 95,* 307–318.

Mineka, S. & Tomarken, A.J. (1989). The role of cognitive biases in the origins and maintenance of fear and anxiety disorders. In T. Archer & L.-G. Nilsson (Eds.), *Aversion, avoidance and anxiety.* Hillsdale, N.J.: Erlbaum.

Murray, E.J. & Foote, F. (1979). The origins of fear of snakes. *Behaviour Research and Therapy, 17,* 489–493.

Napalkov, A.V. (1963). Information Processes of the brain. In N. Wiener & J.P. Schade (Eds.), *Progress in brain research, Vol. 2: Nerve, brain and memory models.* Amsterdam: Elsevier.

Nesse, R.M., Curtis, G.C., Thyer, B.A., McCann, D.S., Huber-Smith, M.J. & Knopf. R.F. (1985). Endocrine and Cardiovascular Responses during phobic anxiety. *Psychosomatic Medicine, 47,* 320–332.

Nisbett, R.E. & Wilson, T.D. (1977). Telling more than we can know: Verbal reports on neutral processes. *Psychological Review, 54,* 231–259.

Öhman, A. (1986). Face the beast and fear the face: Animal and social fears as prototypes for evolutionary analyses of emotion. *Psychophysiology, 23,* 123–145.

Öhman, A. (1988). Nonconscious control of autonomic responses: A role for Pavlovian conditioning? *Biological Psychology, 27,* 113–135.

Öst, L-G. & Hugdahl, K. (1981). Acquisition of phobias and anxiety response patterns in clinical patients. *Behaviour Research and Therapy, 19,* 439–447.

Öst, L.-G. & Hugdahl, K. (1983). Acquisition of agoraphobia, mode of onset and anxiety response patterns. *Behaviour Research and Therapy, 21,* 623–631.

Pallmeyer, T.P., Blanchard, E.B. & Kolb, L.C. (1986). The psychophysiology of combat-induced posttraumatic stress disorder in Vietnam veterans. *Behaviour Research and Therapy, 24,* 645–652.

Rotter, J.B. (1966). Generalized expectancies for internal versus external control of reinforcement. *Psychological Monographs: General and Applied, 80*(1), Whole No. 609.

Rachman, S. (1966). Studies in desensitisation: II. Flooding. *Behaviour Research and Therapy, 4,* 1–6.

Rachman, S. (1978). *Fear and courage.* San Francisco: Freeman.

Rachman, S. (1980). Emotional processing. *Behaviour Research and Therapy, 18,* 51–60.

Rimm, D.C., Janda, L.H., Lancaster, D.W., Nahl, M. & Dittmar, K. (1977). An exploratory investigation of the origin and maintenance of phobias. *Behaviour Research and Therapy, 15* 231–238.

Rohrbaugh, M. & Riccio, D. (1970). Paradoxical enhancement of learned fear. *Journal of Abnormal Psychology, 75,* 210–216.

Sartory, G. (1983). The orienting response and psychopathology: Anxiety and phobias. In D. Siddle (Ed.), *Orienting and habituation: Perspectives in human research.* Chichester: Wiley.

Sartory, G. & Eysenck, H.J. (1976). Strain differences in acquisition and extinction of fear responses in rats. *Psychological Reports, 38,* 163–187.

Sartory, G., Rachman, S. & Gray, S.J. (1982). Return of fear: The role of 'rehearsal'. *Behaviour Research and Therapy, 20,* 123–133.

Seligman, M. E. P. (1971). Phobias and preparedness. *Behavior Therapy, 2,* 307–320.

Solomon, Z., Mikulincen, M. and Benbenishty, R. (1989). Locus of control and combat-related posttraumatic stress disorder: The intervening role of battle intensity, threat appraisal and coping. *British Journal of Clinical Psychology, 28,* 131–144.

Affective Associations: The Conditioning Model and the Organization of Emotions

Alfons O. Hamm and Dieter Vaitl*

Abstract

The present chapter emphasizes the importance of multi-system approach to analyse conditioned emotional reactions, notably fear conditioning. After reviewing three important paradigms, employed to study affective associations, data of a series of conditioning experiments are presented. These data indicate that conditioned startle reflex potentiation and electrodermal response differentiation reflect two different processes involved in Pavlovian conditioning. Evidence is presented that conditioned startle reflex modulation is a function of the change in affective valence of the conditioned stimulus as a result of its association with the aversive event. Resistance to electrodermal extinction, on the other hand, shows a straightforward covariation with reports in arousal change of the reinforced CS. Comparing aversive and non-aversive US-conditions, it will be demonstrated that only fear conditioning involves a *hedonic* association and that this learning process is preceded by a non-associative sensitization of the startle response. Potentiation of protective reflexes thus indexes the acquisition of an avoidance disposition – whereas skin conductance learning follows changes in arousal level induced by the association of a stimulus with a significant event.

Key words: startle reflex potentiation, preparedness, fear conditioning, sensitization, eyeblink response, skin conductance

Introduction

Conditioned Emotional Reactions (CER): Early Paradigms

In their famous article "Conditioned emotional reactions" from 1920, John Watson and Rosalie Rayner demonstrated for the first time that emotional responses can be acquired by Pavlovian conditioning. Eight month old Little Albert showed a so called fear response (crying; trying to crawl away) to white rats or other furry objects as a result of having the presence of furry animals (rat, dog, rabbit) (conditioned stimuli) paired with the sounding of a loud noise (unconditioned stimulus). This affective association enables a formerly neutral stimulus to elicit avoidance – a much more complex behavior than the muscle and gland reponses (e. g. the salivation reflex) studied before by the Russian school (Pavlov, 1927; Bechterev, 1932). However, it is not at all clear that this avoidance was really acquired by Pavlovian or "classical" conditioning (Overmier & Archer, 1989).

*   Department of Clinical Psychology, University of Giessen, Giessen, Germany
    This research was supported by National Institute of Mental Health (NIMH) Grants MH 37757, MH 41950 and MH 43975, to Peter J. Lang, by the Deutsche Forschungsgemeinschaft (German Research Society) Grant VA 37/13–3 and by a Research Fellowship of the Deutsche Akademische Austauschdienst (German Academic Exchange Service) to the first author.

Estes and Skinner (1941) developed the so called suppression paradigm or better known as CER-procedure, to demonstrate the quantitative properties of conditioned emotional responses. The amount of suppression of an ongoing appetetive instrumental response (i. e. hunger motivated bar-pressing or licking) during a CS predicting the occurence of a noxious event is taken as a measure of conditioned fear.

Taking complex avoidance or alteration of operant performance as an index of a CER (e. g. fear) raises some serious problems. There is a lot of evidence of clear dissociation between the conditioned emotional response and extended avoidance performance (Kamin, Brimer & Black, 1963; Mineka & Gino, 1980). Furthermore, instrumental response measures presumably not only reflect the effects of conditioned fear but are also influenced by other factors (e. g. by the strength of the instrumental response itself).

Thus, if we want to study affective associations it might be wise to borrow some ideas from the field of emotion theory.

The Three-System Theory of Emotion

Major theories and conceptualizations of emotions agree that there are three measurement systems of emotions, including verbal reports, physiological responses and overt motor acts (Miller & Kozak, this volume; Izard, Kagan, & Zajonc, 1984; Lang, 1968, 1985). Therefore studying the conditioning process of emotions also requires a multi-system approach, including efferent events which appear in all three behavioral systems.

Using pictures of happy and angry faces as conditioned stimuli, and a 100 dB noise US in a differential conditioning paradigm, Dimberg (1987) examined for the first time the three component model in an emotional conditioning context. He demonstrated that persistent conditioning effects could be obtained for corrugator muscle activity, skin conductance response frequency and recovery time, as well as for self reported fear, respectively, if angry faces were reinforced by an aversive noise. If happy faces signalled the occurence of the noise, there was only poor differential conditioning in the three efferent systems.

Although this was an elegant approach to study the three behavioral systems, the data obtained were not totally conclusive. In the rating data reported by Dimberg (1987) it remains unclear, whether differences between the conditioned and the control stimuli could be attributed to conditioning. The higher fear ratings obtained for the angry compared to the happy facial expressions could rather be due to pre-conditioning differences (Greenwald, Hamm, Öhman, Vaitl, & Lang, 1990), than being a result of the learned associations. Furthermore, conditioning effects in the EMG of the corrugator muscle were obvious only during extinction and only if angry faces were used as CSs. No reliable conditioning effects in facial muscle activity could be detected during acquisition. Thus, the facial expressive behavior seems not to be very sensitive to Pavlovian Conditioning. This is also supported by data of Vaughan and Lanzetta (1980) who showed in a vicarious conditioning paradigm that the reinforced CS did tend to elicit higher activity in the orbicularis oculi, the masseter and the frontalis muscle, but those effects were neither statistically significant nor stable across experiments. The difficulty to obtain anticipatory somatic responses in a Pavlovian conditioning design (using longer ISIs) is not restricted to facial muscles as could be demonstrated in an experiment done by Kimmel and Davidov (1967). Those experimenters could demonstrate clear electrodermal response differentiation but no learned anticipatory response of an aversive shock US (ISI: 5 seconds) could be detected in EMG activity measured from the extensor digitorum muscle, irrespective whether the shock was adminstered ipsi- or contralaterally.

These difficulties to demonstrate emotional conditioning in the somatic system lead back to the dissociation problem between fear and avoidance discussed above.

Nevertheless, the idea of studying the conditioning process in all three behavior systems is certainly worth pursuing. However, the central issue in this context is, whether there are sensitive indicators of emotional conditioning in all three measurement systems, and, if so, how they can be specified.

In the following section, we will review some paradigms used in conditioning research which might provide hints of how to study the principles of affective associations using the three-system approach.

Motor System: Modulation of Protective Reflexes

The Potentiated Startle-Paradigm

Brown, Kalish, and Farber (1951) used the probe-stimulus technique to study affective associations. Starting from the clinical observation that anxiety patients often exhibit exaggerated startle reactions to sudden loud sounds, these investigators undertook a probe study of classical fear conditioning. Startle probes (toy pistol shots) presented to rats in the context of cues (light-buzzer compound) previously paired with shock were shown to evoke larger whole body startle reflexes than did probes administered during control stimuli. This phenomenon has been termed the "fear-potentiated startle effect" and has been replicated with both animal and human subjects either using loud sounds or air puffs as probe stimuli (Spence & Runquist, 1958; Ross, 1961). More recently, Michael Davis and his associates produced data further supporting the hypothesis that probe reflexes are enhanced in conditioned fear (see Davis, 1986).

Davis and coworkers have reported extensive anatomical and pharmacological research of the potentiated startle reflex in rats. Anxiolytic drugs (diazepam, clonidine etc.), for example, decreased the startle reflex potentiation as a result of fear conditioning (Berg & Davis, 1984). In addition, antagonistic drugs, which induce anxiety in normal people, increased potentiated startle in rats (Charney, Heninger & Breier, 1984). Electrical stimulation and lesion experiments done by this group demonstrate that the central nucleus of the amygdala is a central core of the fear conditioning/startle circuit.

The Startle Reflex and Emotional Valence

In a persuasive series of experiments Lang and his associates found that startle reflex magnitude was linearly related to affective valence engaged by a visual foreground (Bradley & Vrana, this volume; Lang, Bradley, & Cuthbert, 1990). The startle response was augmented while subjects processed unpleasant material, whereas blink magnitude was inhibited when the subjects viewed pleasant stimuli. This startle valence effect occurred regardless of the modality of the probe (Bradley, Cuthbert, & Lang, 1990). Without going into detail (see Bradley & Vrana, this volume) these data have some interesting implications for the mechanisms of affective associations.

Thus, the potentiation of the startle reflex observed in the conditioning studies might be a function of the change in affective valence of the conditioned stimulus as a result of its association with the aversive event. It might be possible that a formerly neutral stimulus might acquire negative affective valence and thus become able to elicit an avoidance disposition as a result of aversive conditioning (see Lang et al., 1990). This disposition then potentiates protective reflexes.

Autonomic Responses: Indices of Emotional Conditioning

The Preparedness-Paradigm

Starting from Seligman's concept of prepared learning (Seligman, 1971), Öhman and his co-workers in Norway and Sweden have convincingly shown that Pavlovian conditioning to emotional, – or strictly speaking – potentially phobic stimuli differs from conditioning to presumably neutral cues (see Öhman, this volume; Öhman, Fredrikson, Hughdahl, & Rimmö, 1976; Öhman, Dimberg, & Öst, 1985; Öhman, 1986). Typically, this work used a differential conditioning paradigm, with a mild electric shock as the US and common phobic stimuli (pictures of snakes, spiders and angry faces) and neutral cues (pictures of flowers, mushrooms or neutral faces etc.) as CSs. Contents of conditioned stimuli were varied between groups. Basically, it could be shown that conditioned skin conductance – or finger pulse volume responses, became more *resistant to extinction* than responses to pictures of flowers or mushrooms as a result of contiguous association with an electric shock US (Fredrikson & Öhman, 1979; Öhman, 1986).

Although the mechanisms of these selective associations are still under discussion (Hamm, Vaitl & Lang, 1989) resistance to extinction of the skin conductance response might be a suitable index for determining course and characteristics of emotional conditioning.

Skin Conductance Responses and Autonomic Arousal

In a recent experiment, Greenwald, Cook & Lang (1989) could demonstrate that skin conductance change to pictorial stimuli was closely related to the arousal judgements of the slides. The electrodermal response system is a very good candidate to reflect arousal because the neural control of the sweat gland activity – the basic mechanism of electrodermal phenomena (Fowles, 1986) – is entirely by way of the sympathetic branch of the autonomic nervous system. Thus, it might be reasonable to hypothesize that the resistance to electrodermal extinction covaries with changes in the autonomic arousal of the conditioned stimulus, as a result of the association with the US.

Verbal Reports: Changes in Affective Ratings

The Evaluative Conditioning-Paradigm

In an elegant experiment, Levey and Martin (1975) demonstrated that pairing affectively neutral pictures with pleasant or unpleasant stimuli resulted in a hedonic shift of the neutral cues. Average ratings and number of preferences assigned to the neutral stimuli differed significantly depending upon whether a disliked or a liked cue followed the CS. The neutral CS was evaluated more negatively if it was followed by a disliked cue and rated as more positive when it was paired with a liked picture. This hedonic transfer was acquired very rapidly and occurred in absence of any detailed processing of the stimulus features i.e. without any "awareness" (see Levey & Martin, 1987). Although accounting for the major proportion of variance, the affective valence studied by Levey and Martin (1987) is only one of the three basic dimensions in which emotional language can be organized (Russell, 1980). Besides pleasure-displeasure, the arousal (calm-aroused) and dominance dimension have to be included to get a comprehensive picture of the affective reports. Using a computer generated graphic display, called SAM (for Self-Assessment Manikin) (Lang, 1980), derived from work on the semantic differential by Mehrabian and Russell (1974), Hodes, Cook & Lang (1985) demonstrated that affective ratings changed significantly as a result of emotional conditioning for all three dimensions. The conditioned stimulus which was followed by an aversive 110 dB noise during acquisition became associated with less pleasure, more arousal, and less perception of dominance after conditioning.

This procedure seems to be a versatile method to assess verbal report in a conditioning experiment.

Experimental Investigations of the Principles of Affective Associations

Integrating all three paradigms Hamm, Greenwald, Bradley and Lang (in press), Hamm, Stark and Vaitl (1990), conducted a series of conditioning experiments to study the principles of affective associations.

It was hypothesized that changes in affective valence of the CSs as a result of conditioning are reflected in changes of the startle reflex magnitudes. Furthermore, arousal shifts after the conditioning procedure should be reflected in the electrodermal response system. It was further hypothesized that the physiological changes after conditioning covary systematically with changes in the verbal report as a result of the affective associations.

Affective Associations and the Emotional Features of the CS

In a recent conditioning study, Hamm, Greenwald, Bradley and Lang (in press) used slide stimuli as CS materials.

Those visual stimuli varied systematically in emotional valence and arousal, including pictures of mutilated bodies (highly negative/highly arousing), snakes and spiders (moderately negative/moderately arousing), common household objects (neutral/low arousing), opposite sex nudes (moderately positive/highly arousing) and nature scenes (highly positive/moderately arousing). There were two exemplars in each content category, yielding 10 slides which were rated for valence, arousal and dominance by all subjects prior to conditioning (using the SAM-methodology, described by Hodes, Cook & Lang, 1985). After the rating phase, the electric shock US was introduced and set to a level which the subjects described as highly annoying but not painful. After shock workup, subjects were presented with two different slides (from the same content cate-

gory) resulting in five independent groups. Each slide was presented for four 8 sec habituation trials. The same slides were then repeated, each for eight acquisition trials, in which one of the slides was always followed by the shock. Subsequently, extinction trials were administered (12 for each slide). After the extinction phase, subjects rated the whole series of ten slides again for pleasantness, arousal and dominance. Acoustic startle probes were administered during three of the four habituation presentations of each slide. Two startle simuli were presented during the interstimulus intervals and each slide was presented once without the probe stimulus. This testing pattern was repeated during extinction. No probes were administered during acquisition phase. The startle response was measured by recording EMG from the orbicularis oculi muscle underneath the left eye.

There were clear conditioning effects, both in the skin conductance and in the blink responses. Startle reflexes and skin conductance responses were larger to the reinforced CS than to its control stimulus. However, the amplitude of this conditioning effect varied systematically, depending upon the content of the CS-materials and the response system analysed. Figure 1 shows the amount of differential conditioning during extinction for all five content groups. The upper part of figure 1 shows the differences in the startle response magnitudes between CS+ and CS–, the lower part displays the same measure of differential conditioning for the skin conductance responses.

For the startle reflex, differential conditioning linearly increased with the pleasantness of the CS-materials. Thus, for mutilation slides the difference between the control and the conditioned slide was smallest compared to all other contents. Largest differential startle reflex potentiation on the other hand was obtained for the initially most pleasant nature scenes.

Differential conditioning of the skin conductance responses showed a markedly different pattern (see lower part of Figure 1). Resistance to electrodermal extinction was strongest for the snake/spider group, followed by the book/basket and the flower/landscape group, thus demonstrating the typical preparedness effect, described by Öhman and his collegues (Öhman, Fredrikson, Hugdahl & Rimmö, 1976). What is intriguing, however, is the poor electrodermal conditioning for the two groups viewing highly arousing CS-materials. Thus, whereas conditioned startle reflex magnitude seemed to be related to the affective valence of the conditioned slides, resistance to electrodermal extinction covaried with the arousal level of those stimuli. To test this relationship in more detail the subjects were distributed according to their own pre-conditioning valence and arousal ratings of the to be conditioned stimuli. The top panel of Figure 2 shows the conditioned changes in the physiology (differences between CS+ and CS– during extinction) and in the bottom panel changes in reported valence and arousal levels of the reinforced CS as result of conditioning are displayed.

The valence-startle pattern was again confirmed; the conditioning effect linearly increased with the pleasantness of the slides. Furthermore, subjects showed a greater post-conditioning increase of judged aversiveness to slides that they had previously reported to be more pleasant, exactly paralleling the startle reflex results. Resistance to electrodermal extinction on the other hand, showed straightforward covariation with reports of arousal change. Thus, largest differences between CSs and control stimuli were found for slides that were initially rated as low in arousal. These slides also showed the highest increase in rated arousal after conditioning.

In this study, startle reflex magnitude and skin conductance seemed to be independent measures of valence and arousal changes of the CSs as a result of conditioning.

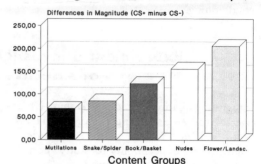

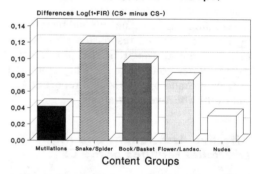

Figure 1. Top panel: Mean differences in startle magnitude between CS+ and CS– during extinction for each of the five content groups. Bottom panel: Mean differences in the skin conductance response magnitudes (log-values) between CS+ and CS– during extinction for each of the five content groups.

In the bottom panel the position of the flower/landscape- and the nude group are interchanged to give a better picture of the corresponding arousal differences in the contents.

Affective Associations and the Aversiveness of the US

In a very recent series of conditioning studies, Hamm, Stark, and Vaitl (1990) replicated and extended the findings described above.

In principle the same conditioning design was applied as in the previous study but for some minor

Changes in Physiology

Startle Responses

Differential Startle Reflex Potentiation during Extinction (Valence Groups)

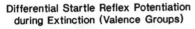
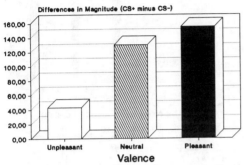

Electrodermal Responses

Average Resistance to Electrodermal Extinction (Arousal Groups)

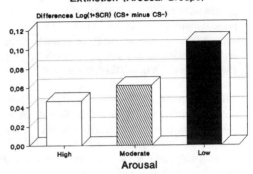

Changes in Verbal Report

Valence Ratings

Changes in the Valence Ratings of the CS+ from Pre- to Post- Conditioning

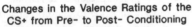
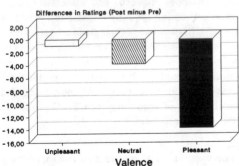

Arousal Ratings

Changes in the Arousal Ratings of CS+ fro Pre- to Post- Conditioning

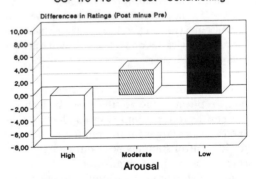

Figure 2. Top Panel: Mean differences in the blink reflex magnitude (left) and the skin conductance response magnitude (log-values) between CS+ and CS– during extinction for each of three groups, arranged either by subject's pre-conditioning valence or arousal ratings of the to be conditioned stimuli. Bottom Panel: Mean differences in valence or arousal ratings, respectively, of the reinforced stimulus between pre- and post-conditioning for each of the three valence or arousal groups.

procedural changes. Rather than presenting two different slides for four habituation trials after the shock workup, the pre-conditioning phase was altered. Subjects viewed – prior to conditioning – a series of 27 different slides, depicting pleasant/arousing, neutral/calm and unpleasant/arousing scenes and objects. The to be conditioned stimuli were included in this series. Acoustic startle probes were presented during and between slide presentations. Startle reflex and skin conductance data replicated previous results reported by Lang and his associates (see Lang, Bradley & Cuthbert, 1990; Bradley & Vrana, this volume).

After this pre-conditioning phase, the unconditioned stimulus was introduced. Two different types of US-conditions were employed. In the *aversive conditioning* procedure, shock electrodes were attached and shock intensity was increased to a level which the subjects described as highly annoying, but not painful. In the *non-aversive conditioning* procedure a neutral but arousing reaction time task was employed as US. A vibratory stimulus signalled to the subject to press a button as quickly as possible immediately after slide offset. Speed of reaction determined the amount of money won by the subject. Instead of the shock workup, five practice trials of the task US (without CS) were given. After this procedure, subjects were presented with two slides for eight acquisition trials, one of which was followed by the shock, or in the other group, by the reaction time task US (RT-US). Subsequently extinction trials were administered (12 for each slide). In these studies the probe stimulus was presented both during acquisition and extinction.

The data of the *aversive conditioning* experiment replicated the results described above; i.e. startle reflexes and skin conductance responses were larger for the reinforced CS than for its control stimulus both during extinction (as seen before) and acquisition.
    Administering probe stimuli during acquisition phase revealed some interesting results. Startle response magnitudes to the noise bursts administered during and between CS presentation dramatically increased from the prephase (where subjects had no shock electrodes attached) to the first trial block of acquisition.

Startle Reflex Potentiation during Acquisition

Aversive Conditioning Procedure

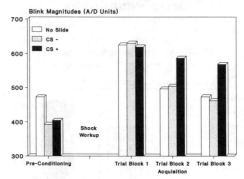

Aversive vs Non-Aversive Conditioning

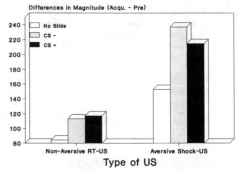

Figure 3. Top panel: Mean blink reflex magnitude to acoustic startle probes presented during and between slide viewing both prior to conditioning (without shock electrodes attached) and again after shock workup and during acquisition (there are blocks of two trials). Bottom panel: Changes in acoustic startle response as a function of the experience of an aversive (shock) or non-aversive (reaction time task) unconditioned stimulus. (Difference scores of startle response magnitudes between pre-conditioning and first trial block of acquisition for CS+, CS– and the probe alone presentation).

The upper part of Figure 3 shows this strong sensitization of the startle reflex occuring immediately after the shock workup.
    Learned response differentiation then developed throughout the course of acquisition. Probes presented during the reinforced stimulus continued to elicit strong reflexes, whereas response magnitudes during the con-

Changes in Physiology

Startle Responses

Differential Startle Reflex
Potentiation during Extinction

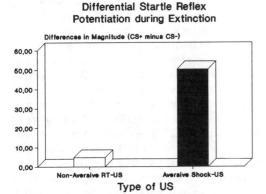

Electrodermal Responses

Average Resistance to
Electrodermal Extinction

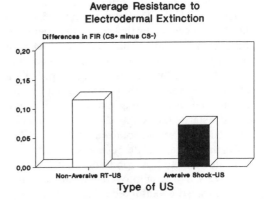

Changes in Verbal Report

Valence Ratings

Changes in Valence Ratings of
CS+ from Pre- to Post-Conditioning

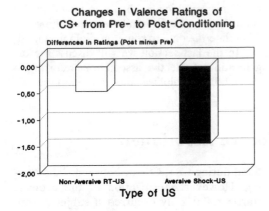

Arousal Ratings

Changes in Arousal Ratings of
CS+ from Pre- to Post-Conditioning

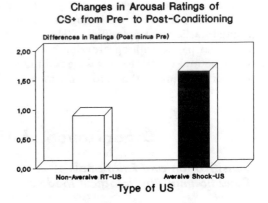

Figure 4. Top panel: Mean differences in the startle reflex magnitude (left) and the skin conductance response magnitude between CS+ and CS– during extinction for each of the two conditioning groups. One group was presented with an aversive shock US, the other with a non-aversive reaction time task during acquisition. Bottom panel: Mean differences in either valence or arousal ratings of the conditioned stimulus between pre- and post-conditioning for the two groups having either experienced the shock or reaction time task US.

trol stimuli decreased. The same decrease in magnitude could be observed for reflexes elicited between slide presentation.

However, if instead of an electric shock the *non-aversive* RT-US was introduced after the pre-conditioning phase, there was no such sensitization of the startle reflex after the training procedure. The bottom part of Figure 3 shows the differences in startle magnitudes between the pre-conditioning phase and the first trial block of acquisition (for CS+, CS−, and no slide control) for the two conditioning groups having either experienced the shock workup or the reaction time task training. Sensitization of the acoustic startle reflex only occurred, if the aversive shock US was introduced.

Furthermore, startle response magnitudes were not affected by conditioning if the non-aversive US was employed. Probes administered during the reinforced CS did not elicit significantly stronger startle responses than those presented during CS−.

Skin conductance responses, on the other hand, showed clear differential conditioning both during acquisition and extinction, irrespective of the type of US used. There were larger skin conductance responses to the conditioned stimulus (followed either by the electric shock or the arousing RT-US) than to the unreinforced CS. Thus, associating a stimulus with an aversive and arousing US, produced clear electrodermal conditioning and a substantial startle reflex potentiation. However, if a CS was paired with an arousing but affectively neutral event, there was clear differential conditioning in the autonomic measure,

but no conditioning effect in the startle reflex. The upper part of Figure 4 illustrates this response pattern.

Differential startle reflex potentiation (differences in magnitudes between CS+ and CS− during extinction) was only obvious if an aversive US was employed in the conditioning procedure, whereas the type of US had no significant influence on the differential electrodermal conditioning during extinction.

As in the previous study, changes in physiology covaried systematically with the changes in the verbal report. The lower part of Figure 4 displays changes in reported valence and arousal levels of the reinforced CS as a result of conditioning. Those subjects who experienced an aversive US rated their conditioned stimulus significantly more negative after conditioning than the group with the non-aversive US, again exactly paralleling the startle reflex results. Both groups, however, showed the same increase in rated arousal after conditioning, again showing straightforward covariation with resistance to electrodermal extinction.

The data of these conditioning studies suggest that startle reflex modulation and electrodermal response differentiation reflect two different processes involved in Pavlovian conditioning. In the following paragraph we will discuss some implications of these data to the mechanisms which might be involved in the conditioning of emotional responses. First, we will relate the data to some physiological models. In the last section we will discuss the organisation of affective associations referring to Peter J. Lang's biphasic theory of emotion.

Organization of Affective Associations

Sensitization and Emotional Conditioning: Physiological Models

If the subjects were exposed to a number of electric shocks there was a marked increase of the startle reflex amplitudes after these presentations (see Figure 3). This sensitization effect was obvious across all stimulus conditions, i. e. irrespective whether the probe was adminis-

tered during CS+, CS− or between slide viewing. However, sensitization of the acoustic startle reflex only occurred if subjects were preexposed for a *noxious* or *aversive* stimulus (see bottom panel of Figure 3). These results are totally concordant with animal data recently reported by Davis and his group. Administration of a single footshock or a series of 5–10 footshocks markedly increased the amplitude of the acoustic startle reflex in rats during 5–20 min after presentation of shock (Davis, 1989). Furthermore, bilateral lesions of the central nucleus of the amygdala blocked shock sensitization of startle (Hitchcock, Sananes & Davis, 1989). Thus, the same brain structure which is involved in the modulation of the fear-potentiated startle in aversive conditioning also regulates shock sensitization. According to Davis and our data sensitization might be the pre-condition to aversive classical conditioning. First, there is a non-associative learning in which the organism learns to strengthen its defensive reflexes to a range of stimuli after it has been exposed to a potentially threatening and noxious stimulus (e.g. the electric shock). After temporally contiguous pairing of the aversive US with a specific stimulus, the general response enhancement is then associated with the reinforced CS (see upper panel of Figure 3). These data relate nicely to invertebrate models of classical aversive conditioning, in *Aplysia* (Hawkins & Kandel, 1984). The mechanism of classical conditioning of the siphon- and gill withdrawal reflexes is an elaboration of the mechanism of sensitization of the reflexes: presynaptic facilitation in the sensory neurons – also involved in sensitization – becomes pairing-specific (Hawkins, Abrams, Carew & Kandel, 1983).

Non-aversive conditioning, on the other hand, seems to be rather independent of the process of sensitization (Berger, Berrry & Thompson, 1986). Furthermore, whereas the amygdala are the central core of aversive conditioning different brain structures (e.g. the interpositus nucleus in the cerebellum) seem to mediate non-aversive learning (Thompson, 1986).

Avoidance Disposition and Arousal: The Biphasic Emotion Theory

According to the biphaisc emotion theory described by Lang and his associates, emotions "appear to be organized around two broad strategic dimensions, valence and arousal" (Lang, Bradley, & Cuthbert, 1990). The valence dimension defines the general *direction of be-havior* and refers to the organism's disposition either to approach (i.e. activating an appetitive behavioral set) or to avoid (i.e. favoring a defensive or protective action set). The arousal dimension on the other hand, is an *intensity factor* and refers to the organism's disposition to react with varying degrees of energy. This dimensional organization also holds for the verbal behavior, i.e. affective language can be ordered along the two basic dimensions valence and arousal (Mehrabian & Russell, 1974; Russell, 1980).

On the basis of the theoretical conceptualization of emotions developed by Lang and his group, a model of affective associations can be derived. After experiencing a series of noxious events, the organism is in a general disposition to avoid, resulting in an enhancement of defensive reflexes to a variety of previously weak or neutral stimuli: After pairing the aversive event contiguously with one stimulus this "response disposition" or "action set" (e.g. Lang, 1984) is associated with the reinforced stimulus, thus, enabling the conditioned cue to evoke the affective response disposition by itself (after a number of learning trials). The efferent motor system is tuned according to this action disposition, i.e. protective reflexes – such as the startle reflex – are potentiated. This change in the efferent output covaries with verbally reported changes of the affective valence of the conditioned stimulus as a result of conditioning. If a positive event is associated with the conditioned cue, the organism might acquire a disposition to approach and thus, alimentary or preservative reflexes (Konorski, 1967) might be potentiated accompanied by an inhibition of the protective reflexes. Independent of this hedonic conditioning there are changes in the arousal induced by the conditioned stimulus as a result of its association with an arousal generating unconditioned stimulus. This arousal change is depicted in the process of electrodermal conditioning. Changes in the autonomic responses covary with verbally described changes of the arousal level of the CS. Thus, emotional conditioning always implies associative changes along the basic strategic dimensions of emotions accompanied by efferent changes in the corresponding behavioral systems.

References

Bechterev, V.M. (1932). *General principles of human reflexology.* New York: Oxford University Press.

Berg, W.K., & Davis, M. (1984). Diazepam blocks fear-enhanced startle elicited electrically from the brainstem. *Physiology & Behavior, 32,* 333–336.

Berger, Th.W., Berry, St.D., & Thompson, R.F. (1986). Role of the hippocampus in classical conditioning of aversive and appetetive behaviors. In R.L. Isaacson & K.H. Pribram (Eds.), *The Hippocampus, Vol. 4* (pp. 203–239). New York: Plenum Press.

Bradley, M.M., Cuthbert, B.N., & Lang, P.J. (1990). Startle reflex modification: Emotion or attention. *Psychophysiology, 27,* 513–522.

Brown, J.S., Kalish, H.I., & Farber, I.e. (1951). Conditioned fear as revealed by magnitude of startle response to an auditory stimulus. *Journal of Experimental Psychology, 41,* 317–328.

Charney, D.S., Heninger, G.R., & Breier, A. (1984). Noradrenergic function in panic anxiety. *Archives of General Psychiatry, 41,* 751–763.

Davis, M. (1986). Pharmacological and anatomical analysis of fear conditioning using the fear-potentiated startle paradigm. *Behavioral Neuroscience, 100,* 814–824.

Davis, M. (1989). Sensitization of acoustic startle reflex by footshock. *Behavioural Neuroscience, 103,* 495–503.

Dimberg, U. (1987). Facial reactions, autonomic activity and experienced emotion: A three component model of emotional conditioning. *Biological Psychology, 24,* 105–122,

Estes, W.K., & Skinner, B.F. (1941). Some quantitative properties of anxiety. *Journal of Experimental Psychology, 29,* 390–400.

Fowles, D.C. (1986). The eccrine system and electrodermal activity. In M.G.H. Coles, E. Donchin, & St.W. Porges (Eds.), *Psychophysiology* (pp. 51–96). Amsterdam: Elsevier.

Fredrikson, M. & Öhman, A. (1979). Cardiovascular and electrodermal responses conditioned to fear relevant stimuli. *Psychophysiology, 16,* 1–7.

Greenwald, M.K., Cook, E.W., & Lang, P.J. (1989). Affective judgement and psychophysiological response: Dimensional covariation in the evaluation of pictorial stimuli. *Journal of Psychophysiology, 3,* 51–64.

Greenwald, M.K., Hamm, A.O., Öhman, A., Vaitl, D., & Lang, P.J. (1990). Dimensional analysis of affective significance and preparedness: A cross cultural study. Unpublished manuscript.

Hamm, A.O., Greenwald, M.K., Bradley, M.M., &

Lang, P.J. (in press). Emotional learning, hedonic change, and the startle probe. *Journal of Abnormal Psychology.*

Hamm, A.O., Stark, R., & Vaitl, D. (1990). Startle reflex potentiation and electrodermal response differentiation: Two indicators of two different processes in Pavlovian conditioning. (Abstract). *Supplement to Psychophysiology, 27,* 37.

Hamm, A.O., Vaitl, D., & Lang, P.J. (1989). Fear conditioning, meaning, and belongingness: A. selective association analysis. *Journal of Abnormal Psychology, 98,* 395–406.

Hawkins, R.D. & Kandel, E.R. (1984). Is there a cell-biological alphabet for simple forms of learning. *Psychological Review, 91,* 375–391.

Hawkins, R.D., Abrams, T.W., Carew, T.J., & Kandel, E.R. (1983). A cellular mechanism of classical conditioning in Aplysia. Activity-dependent amplification of presynaptic facilitation. *Science, 219,* 400–405.

Hitchcock, J.M., Sananes, C.B., & Davis, M. (1989). Sensitization of the startle reflex by footshock: Blockade by lesions of the central nucleus of the amygdala or its efferent pathway to the brain stem. *Behavioral Neuroscience, 103,* 509–518.

Hodes, R.L., Cook, E.W., & Lang, P.J. (1985). Individual differences in autonomic response: Conditioned association or conditioned fear? *Psychophysiology, 22,* 545–560.

Izard, C.E., Kagan, J., & Zajonc, R.B. (1984). *Emotions, cognition and behavior.* Cambridge: University Press.

Kamin, L.J., Brimer, C.J., & Black, A.H. (1963). Conditioned suppression as a monitor of fear of the CS in the course of avoidance training. *Journal of Comparative and Physiological Psychology, 56,* 497–501.

Kimmel, H.D. & Davidov, W. (1967). Classical GSR conditioning with concomitant EMG measurement. *Journal of Experimental Psychology, 74,* 67–74.

Konorski, J. (1967). *Integrative activity of the brain: An interdisciplinary approach.* Chicago: University of Chicago Press.

Lang, P.J. (1968). Fear reduction and fear behavior: Problems in treating a construct. In J.M. Sclien (Ed.). *Research in Psychotherapy, Vol. 3* (pp. 90–103). Washington DC: American Psychological Association.

Lang, P.J. (1980). Behavioral treatment and bio-behavioral assessment: Computer applications. In J.B. Sidowski, J.H. Johnson, & T.A. Williams

(Eds.), *Technology in mental health care delivery systems* (pp. 119–137). Norwood, N.J.: Ablex.

Lang, P.J. (1984). Cognition in emotion: Concept and action. In C.E. Izard, J. Kagan, & R.B. Zajonc (Eds.), *Emotions, cognitions, and behavior.* (pp. 192–228). New York: Cambridge University Press.

Lang, P.J. (1985). The cognitive psychophysiology of emotion: Fear and anxiety. In A.H. Tuma & J.D. Maser (Eds.), *Anxiety and the anxiety disorders* (pp. 131–170). Hillsdale, N.J.: Erlbaum.

Lang, P.J., Bradley, M.M., & Cuthbert, B.N. (1990). Emotion, attention, and the startle reflex. *Psychological Review, 97*, 377–395.

Levey, A.B., & Martin, I. (1975). Classical conditioning of human "evaluative" responses. *Behavior Research and Therapy, 13*, 221–226.

Levey, A.B., & Martin, I. (1987). Evaluative conditioning: A case of hedonic transfer. In H.J. Eysenck and I. Martin (Eds.), *Theoretical foundations of behavior therapy* (pp. 113–132). London: Plenum.

Mehrabian, A., & Russell, J.A. (1974). *An approach to enviromental psychology.* Cambridge MA: MIT Press.

Mineka, S. & Gino, A. (1980). Dissociation between conditioned emotional response and extended avoidance performance. *Learning and Motivation, 11*, 416–502.

Öhman, A. (1986). Face the beast and fear the face: Animal and social fears as prototypes for evolutionary analyses of emotion. *Psychophysiology, 23*, 123–145.

Öhman, A., Dimberg, U., & Öst, L.G. (1985). Animal and social phobias: A laboratory model. In S. Reiss & R.R. Bootzin (Eds.), *Theoretical issues in behavior therapy* (pp. 123–175). Orlando, FL: Academic Press.

Öhman, A., Fredrikson, M., Hugdahl, K., & Rimmö, P.H. (1976). The premise of equipotentiality in human classical conditioning: Conditioned electrodermal responses to potentially phobic stimuli. *Journal of Experimental Psychology: General, 105*, 313–337.

Overmier, J.B. & Archer, T. (1989). Historical perspectives on the study of aversively motivated behavior: History and new look. In T. Archer and L.G. Nilsson (Eds.), *Aversion avoidance, and anxiety* (pp. 3–39). London: Lawrence Erlbaum Associates, Publishers.

Pavlov, I.P. (1927). *Conditioned reflexes: An investigation of physiological activity of the cerebral cortex.* New York: Oxford University Press.

Ross, L.E. (1961). Conditioned fear as a function of CS-UCS and probe stimulus intervals. *Journal of Experimental Psychology, 61*, 265–273.

Russell, J.A. (1980). A circumplex model of affect. *Journal of Personality and Social Psychology, 39*, 1161–1178.

Seligman, M.E.P. (1971). Phobias and preparedness. *Behavior Therapy, 2*, 307–321.

Thompson, R.F. (1986). The neurobiology of learning and memory. *Science, 233*, 941–947.

Vaughan, K.B. & Lanzetta, J.T. (1980). Vicarious instigation and conditioning of facial expressive and autonomic responses to a model's expressive display of pain. *Journal of Personality and Social Psychology, 38*, 909–923.

Watson, J.B., & Rayner, R. (1920). Conditioned emotional reactions. *Journal of Experimental Psychology, 3*, 1–14.

Stimulus Prepotency and Fear Learning: Data and Theory

Arne Öhman*

Abstract

The notion of prepotent stimuli implies that there are genetic programs that contribute to the emotional potency of some stimuli, that these effects are not automatic or fixed, and that they are modified by learning. This chapter examines some of the implications of this notion with particular emphasis on results from the so called "preparedness paradigm," that is, differential autonomic conditioning to fear-relevant (e. g., snakes and spiders) or fear-irrelevant (e. g., flowers and mushrooms) stimuli. Typically, such paradigms result in conditioned autonomic responses with enhanced resistance to extinction for fear-relevant stimuli. Failures to replicate this result are reviewed and analysed critically. A section on critical issues in conditioning to fear-relevant stimuli examines the specificity of the effect, belongingness between the conditioned and the unconditioned stimulus, the nature of the conditioned response, and the role of cognitive factors. In discussing possible theoretical mechanisms behind the observed results, it is argued that a satisfactory theoretical account needs to consider the organization and modification of associative structures between conditioned and unconditioned stimulus, the organization of emotional responding, and the role of preattentive mechanisms in the evocation of fear. The importance of the latter mechanism is illustrated by some new data on conditioning to masked conditioned stimuli.

Introduction

Reviewing the "Psychophysiology of Emotion," Lang, Rice and Sternbach (1972) noted that "the stimuli of many of the gross fears of man are similar to those of other primates (snakes, being stared at, mutilated bodies, etc.)" (p. 627). Mainly on the basis of ethological data they went on to argue that genetically prepotent stimuli "apparently do instigate unusual nervous activity, perhaps in the diffuse projection system of the central nervous system and the autonomic nervous system, and furthermore, they seem to demand some adjustive response. These responses may be avoidant, aggressive, sexual: the specific characteristics are determined by context and learning" (p. 627). The important points here are that (a) genetic programs may contribute to the emotional potency of some stimuli; (b) the effect is not fixed or automatic; and (c) it is modified by learning.

Similar ideas have been voiced by other authors. About 20 years earlier, in a classical paper, Neal Miller (1951) suggested that "certain cues that do not spontaneously arose fear may have a latent tendency to elicit it, with the result that ... the subject will learn to fear these

* Department of Clinical Psychology, University of Uppsala, Uppsala, Sweden
Acknowledgement: Preparation of this chapter was facilitated by a series of grants from the Swedish Council for Research in Social Sciences and the Humanities. The assistance of Ulf Dimberg, Francisco Esteves, Cristina Parra and Joaquim Soares is greatfully acknowledged.

cues much more quickly than others .... In other words, fear may be high in the innate hierarchy of responses to a stimulus without being the dominant response" (p. 445). Much in the spirit of Lang et al. (1972), Marks (1969) reviewed extensive ethological data attesting to the genetic prepotency of fear stimuli in his monograph on "Fears and phobias." At about the same time, Seligman (1971) applied his notion of "prepared learning" (Seligman, 1970) to the acquisition of phobias. He argued that phobias occur to stimuli that are biologically prepared (i.e., genetically prepotent) to easily become associated with fear, given an aversive context.

The idea that fear stimuli may enlist some of their potency from genetic programs has important ramifications (see Öhman & Dimberg, 1984; Öhman, Dimberg, & Öst, 1985). However, the concepts of "stimulus prepotency" and "preparedness" are not synonymous (see e.g., McNally, 1987). For example, as suggested in the quote from Lang et al. (1972) above, their concept of prepotency merely suggest that prepotent stimuli have "unusual effects," which may be channelled in widely different direc-

tions ("avoidant, aggressive, sexual"). Seligman's (1970; 1971) preparedness concept, on the other hand, specifically denotes associability between particular stimuli and particular responses, such that, for example, potentially hazardous stimuli, say, those denoting an active predator, easily become associated with escape and avoidance, but not with approach. However, the two concepts also have shared meaning in suggesting that genetic design is important in determining the effect of some stimuli, and in suggesting that learning plays a crucial role in mediating these effects. The first component of this shared meaning, the presumed genetic basis, remains quite inaccessible for direct experimental verification in studies of human subjects. Therefore, in this paper, I shall focus on a somewhat diluted version of the basic question and review experimental work purporting to demonstrate special properties of common fear stimuli in the context of Pavlovian conditioning. In the concluding part of the paper, I shall deal specifically with attempts to account for the mechanisms behind these special properties.

Autonomic Conditioning to Fear-Relevant Stimuli

Original Findings

In a series of papers published during the seventies, my coworkers and I reported research examining human autonomic conditioning to potentially phobic stimuli such as pictures of snakes and spiders, or threatening human faces (see reviews by Öhman, 1979a and McNally, 1987). Our data indicated that the most pervasive effect of pairing a potentially phobic stimulus with an aversive event such as a mild electric shock to the fingers, was enhanced resistance to extinction. Typically, we used a differential conditioning paradigm where one cue (e.g., a picture of a snake) was followed by an electric shock unconditioned stimulus (US) whereas another, equally "prepotent," cue (e.g., a picture of a spider) was not. The difference in, e.g., skin conductance re-

sponse (SCR), to the reinforced cue (the positive conditioned stimulus, CS+), and the nonreinforced cue (the negative conditioned stimulus, CS-), for such a fear-relevant group was then compared to the differential response to the CS+ and the CS- in a control group given fear-irrelevant stimuli (e.g., pictures of flowers and mushrooms). Invariably in our findings, the resistance to extinction when the US was omitted was larger with fear-relevant than with fear-irrelevant stimuli (e.g. Fredrikson & Öhman, 1979; Öhman, Fredrikson & Hugdahl, 1978; Öhman, Fredrikson, Hugdahl, & Rimmö, 1976). Similar results were obtained with a single cue conditioning paradigm (Öhman, Eriksson, & Olofsson, 1975) and with angry faces as CSs (Öhman & Dimberg, 1978). The effect was not dependent on actual presentation of the US, but occurred with instructed shock threat (Hugdahl, 1978; Hugdahl & Öhman, 1977) or vicariously through the observation of a model exhibiting fear (Hygge & Öhman, 1978). Finally, responses to fear-relevant CSs were not abolished by instructed extinction, that is, instructions that the US would be omitted inhibited responses to fear-irrelevant stimuli but left responses to fear-relevant stimuli unaltered (Hugdahl & Öhman, 1977).

Failures to Replicate

These findings have occasioned a large interest in the fear literature, and several authors have reported attempts to replicate and extend them. Many of these attempts have been interpreted as failures to replicate the original findings. Several of these studies have introduced procedural variations, which make the findings difficult to evaluate. For example, McNally (1981) reported immediate reversal of SCRs to fear-relevant CSs+ and CSs– after instructions that the shock US would now follow the CS–. He took this finding as inconsistent with the presumed lack of cognitive control over responses to prepared stimuli (Seligman, 1971). However, the results are less than convincing. Most importantly, McNally (1981) failed to observe conditioning effects prior to the instructed reversal of the cue significance. Thus, the conditioning arrangement appeared ineffective, and it is difficult to tell whether the immediate differential response after instructions represents anything more than the already demonstrated sensitivity of fear-relevant stimuli to threat of shock (Hugdahl & Öhman, 1977), particularly as a fear-irrelevant control group was lacking from the design. Similarly, McNally and Riess (1982, 1984) did not observe inferior safety-signal conditioning to fear-relevant stimuli (unless the subjects had prior fear of the CS, McNally & Riess, 1984), which they interpreted as inconsistent with the preparedness theory. However, the theory explicitly deals only with excitatory conditioning, so the weight of these findings is hard to assess.

Similar failures have been reported by other authors on the basis of findings from experi-

ments which deviates in significant parameters from those used by us (e. g. Deitz, 1982; Emerson & Lucas, 1981; Maltzman & Boyd, 1984; Vaitl, Gruppe & Kimmel, 1985). However, occasional positive findings have also been reported from other types of paradigms. For example, Eifert and Schermelleh (1985) reported more rapid acquisition and slower extinction to a picture of a snake than to a picture of a rabbit in a single cue paradigm with noise as US, and a "language conditioning" procedure intervening between acquisition and extinction. Similarly, Siddle, Power, Bond, and Lovibond (1988) found more rapid acquisition to fear-relevant than to fear-irrelevant stimuli in a differential conditioning paradigm, although postacquisition manipulations of the US precluded straight-forward interpretation of extinction effects. Furthermore, Siddle and coworkers have reported that fear-relevant CSs were more effective in supporting second-order conditioning to neutral stimuli than were fear-irrelevant CSs (Bond, Siddle & Schaafsma, in press; Siddle, Bond, & Friswell, 1987). However, of more immediate interest are the studies which explicitly have sought to use the procedures used in the Uppsala laboratory.

McNally and Foa (1986) used the type of differential conditioning paradigm that we have been using, yet failed to observe any differences in SCRs between groups exposed to fear-relevant (snake and spider) and fear-irrelevant (strawberry and flower) stimuli. However, rather than using unselected subjects as we have done, they selected their subjects to be either low (lowest quartile of distribution) or high (highest quartile of distribution) in snake and/or spider fears. Furthermore, they systematically selected the most feared stimulus as the CS+ in the high-fear, fear-relevant group. This procedural differences immediately preclude a meaningful comparison with our data. In spite of this artificially created bias to observe enhanced responding to the fear-relevant CS+, which in fact would have undermined the interpretability of positive findings, no differences emerged between fear-relevant and fear-irrelevant groups. This is peculiar, given the preponderance of reports of enhanced responding to feared stimuli among high fear subjects (e. g.,

Fredrikson, 1981; Hare & Blevings, 1975), and cast serious doubts on the sensitivity of their experimental procedure.

Merckelbach, van der Molen and van den Hout (1987) used a similar procedure (albeit with fewer trials both in acquisition and extinction), and again, failed to obtain differences between fear-relevant and fear-irrelevant stimuli during extinction. However, their most basic failure to replicate does not concern the "preparedness effect," as their title implies, but rather a failure to obtain any convincing evidence of conditioning to either fear-relevant or fear-irrelevant stimuli. Thus, for the SCR measure corresponding to the one typically reported by us (the first interval anticipatory response, see Öhman, 1983), there was no main effect of conditioning, and only weak and statistically unsubstantiated evidence of differential response on the last training trials. Lacking convincing evidence of conditioning in either the fear-relevant or the fear-irrelevant group, it is not surprising to find that none of the groups showed differential response during extinction. This hardly qualifies as a "failure to replicate the preparedness effect" given that the prerequisite for such a demonstration, clear differential response during acquisition, was not fulfilled.

The most distressing failures to replicate the preparedness effect has been reported by Björkstrand (1990), in research carried out at the University College of Örebro in Sweden, partly under my supervision. This work follows closely the procedures used by us, yet in two independent experiments Björkstrand (1990) failed to obtain any evidence of superior resistance to extinction of fear-relevant stimuli. The basis for these failures remains elusive, and they suggest that the effect is not a strong and pervasive one. Subsequent unpublished work by Björkstrand continues to fail in observing standard preparedness effects, but he has been able to demonstrate, and replicate, enhanced reinstatement of responses to potentially phobic stimuli after unpaired presentation of the US, following extinction (see Rescorla & Heth, 1977), even though these stimuli did not differ from neutral stimuli during acquisition and extinction. In a study, which, similar to the one by

Björkstrand (1990), was primarily interested in the effect of CS preexposure, Booth, Siddle and Bond (1989) also failed to obtain differences in conditioning and extinction between fear-relevant and fear-irrelevant stimuli, using convincing differential conditioning procedures. Thus, it is clear that the effect must be regarded as somewhat elusive. However, there are also many successful replications in the literature.

Successful Replications

Work on conditioning to fear-relevant stimuli began in Lang's laboratory in the midseventies. A series of six experiments was reported by Cook, Hodes and Lang (1986). These experiments used procedures closely mapped on those used in Uppsala. However, in the first four experiments aversive noise was substituted for electric shock as the unconditioned stimulus. Although one of the studies showed clearly superior resistance to extinction to potentially phobic (snakes and spiders) as compared to technologically dangerous stimuli (weapons), the consensus of the experiments using noise CS was that no difference in SCRs between potentially phobic and neutral stimuli emerged, primarily because resistance to extinction was quite substantial to the neutral stimuli. However, in the last two experiments, either adding a tactile component to the noise or using an electric shock US, statistically significant differences were obtained in resistance to extinction between potentially phobic and neutral stimuli. Furthermore, a combined analysis including 292 subjects demonstrated that significant resistance to extinction was observed to potentially phobic but not to neutral stimuli with a tactile US, whereas fear-relevance had no effect with the noise US.

Dawson, Schell and Banis (1986) used a considerably more complicated differential conditioning design in which fear-relevant (snakes and spiders) or fear-irrelevant (flower and mushrooms) CSs were embedded among other pictures in an alleged visual memory task. The purpose of this task was to hamper and retard the subjects' discovery of the CS-US contingency in order to assess potentially non-aware learning effects. In spite of the different procedure, their results closely replicated our basic "preparedness effect" in that superior resistance to extinction was observed to fear-relevant as compared to fear-irrelevant stimuli, particularly for subjects given an extended extinction series and being uninformed about shock omission.

These data were extended in a study by Schell, Dawson and Marinkovic (1991). During a first session, they exposed subjects to four different types of pictures: snakes, spiders, flowers and mushrooms. Half of the subjects had a fear-relevant CS+ (snake or spider) with the other fear-relevant stimulus serving as CS–, whereas the other half of the subjects had a similar arrangement involving fear-irrelevant CSs+ and CSs-. Only an adaptation and an acquisition series were given during this session. At a second session, occurring either one or six months after the first, the subjects' retention of the CS-US contingency was first tested, by asking the subjects to recall the events of the first session and to indicate which of the stimuli had been followed by shock. Then followed a reinforced CS+ presentation and nonreinforced presentations of the other stimuli, before an extended extinction series was given. The data demonstrated superior resistance to extinction to the potentially phobic stimuli independently of retention interval, and no differences during acquisition or immediately after the conditioning trial preceding the extinction series.

Using facial expression as stimuli in a differential conditioning paradigm (cf. Öhman & Dimberg, 1978), Orr and Lanzetta (1980) reported better conditioning to fear-relevant (fearful) than to fear-irrelevant (happy) facial expressions. Follow-up research using compound stimuli found that a fearful face in compound with a tone overshadowed the tone, whereas the tone overshadowed a happy face; a neutral face, finally, did not differ from the tone (Lanzetta & Orr, 1980, 1981). These data suggest that the fearful face was an effective excitatory CS, and that the happy face was an effective inhibitory stimulus. Similar conclusions were reached by Dimberg (1986). In a close replication of the study reported by Öhman and Dimberg (1978), Pitman and Orr (1986) exposed anxiety patients and controls to series of angry and neutral faces. Half of the subjects had a shock US follow the angry faces, and for the other half the contingency was reversed. All subjects were informed that no shocks would be presented during extinction and had the shock electrodes removed. The results indicated better acquisition with an angry than with a neutral face as the CS+, irrespective of diagnosis. During extinction, however, significant differential response was obtained only in the anxiety patients conditioned to an angry CS+, which was taken as suggesting irrational responding in this clinical group, given the instructed extinction.

Taken together, the studies reviewed here show that a fear-relevance or preparedness effect of enhanced resistance to extinction is a common but not invariable finding in the human conditioning literature. Many of the alleged "failures to replicate" do not stand up to critical scrutiny, and positive findings have been reported from many different laboratories. Furthermore, there are other bodies of data available which provide more convincing demonstrations that fear-relevant stimuli are very effective CSs in an aversive conditioning context. Thus, Mineka and coworkers (see e.g. Mineka and Tomarken, 1989, for a review) have demonstrated that rhesus monkeys rapidly acquire fear of snakes by observing a conspecific behave fearfully in the presence of live or toy snakes. By use of videotape techniques, it was possible to demonstrate that the same fear display in the model did not result in learned fear to fear-irrelevant stimuli, such as flowers (Cook and Mineka, 1989). Because the prior experience of snakes and fear of snakes can be controlled in these studies, they provide the strongest data available in support of a genetic basis for the effects.

Thus, although the effect from the human conditioning studies may appear somewhat fragile and my have clear boundary conditions, it is nevertheless of interest to consider theoretical mechanisms which may account for the superior resistance to extinction to fear-relevant stimuli. To do so, it is necessary to examine more closely how conditioning to potentially phobic stimuli differ from conditioning to neutral stimuli. First, the specificity of the effect will be examined with particular attention paid to the phenomenon of "belongingness" between the CS and the US. Second, we will examine studies suggesting that the nature of the response conditioned to fear-relevant stimuli is different from that conditioned to fear-irrelevant stimuli. Finally, it is imperative to discuss the role of "cognitive control" in conditioning to potentially phobic stimuli. It is only when these issues have been dealt with that it is meaningful to analyse the mechanism that may account for the observed findings.

Critical Issues in Conditioning to Fear-Relevant Stimuli

Specificity of the Effect

The obvious first question to ask regarding the enhanced resistance to extinction of fear-relevant stimuli concerns the boundary condition for the effect in terms of stimulus content. Do similar effects occur to any fear-relevant stimulus or are they restricted to particular subsets of such stimuli? In particular, do the effects occur more readily to stimuli for which an evolutionary association with fear is likely?

This question was addressed by Cook et al. (1986). They compared differential conditioning to fear stimuli of likely evolutionary origin, snakes and spider, with conditioning to fear-relevant stimuli for which such an origin is highly unlikely, hand-guns and rifles. Their data demonstrated significantly larger resistance to extinction of conditioned SCRs to snakes and spiders than to weapons. However, some of the impact of this finding is reduced by the results for the control group exposed to presumably neutral stimuli, common household objects, which occupied a position in between the other two, not significantly different from either of them.

This result was extended by Hugdahl and Kärker (1981). They reasoned that snakes and spiders may be easily associated with shock-induced aversion because of their common negative connotations. Therefore, it would be of interest to compare conditioning to snakes and spiders with conditioning to other classes of stimuli which are readily integrated into associative structures encompassing shock-induced aversion, but where the common associative core is more likely to have on ontogenetic than a phylogenetic origin. Hugdahl and Kärker (1981) decided that pictures of electrical cords and equipments would fulfil the criteria for such a class of stimuli. Their result demonstrated larger resistance to extinction of conditioned SCRs to snakes and spiders than of responses conditioned to electrical wallsockets or control stimuli consisting of simple geometrical forms. In combination these two results suggest, but by no means prove, that the fear relevance effect may be specific to fear stimuli that derive the potency from evolutionarily determined sources.

Dimberg and Öhman (1983) showed that the general stimulus dimension of direction of the threat implied in a fear-relevant stimulus is a powerful determinant of conditioning. They compared the effect of directing an angry face towards or away from the observer, and found significant resistance to extinction only in the former condition. In a second experiment, they demonstrated that it was the direction of the angry display during extinction which was the critical manipulation. Thus, subjects conditioned to an angry face looking away, showed significant resistance to extinction, if the direction of the face was switched so that the stimulus person directed his anger towards the observer, during extinction. Subjects switched in the other direction, from towards to away, on the other hand, showed no resistance to extinction. These effects were further elucidated by Dimberg (1986), who, among other things, showed that the inhibitory effect of a happy face on conditioning, could be reduced by having the happy display directed away from the observer during extinction. Finally, Hugdahl and Johnsen (1989) showed direction of the threat to be a powerful modulator of the effects of guns on SCR conditioning and extinction (see below).

CS-US Belongingness

More important than specificity with regard to CS properties is demonstrations of specificity with regard to particular CS and US couplings. This is because Seligman's (1970) preparedness concept concerns the associability of particular CSs with particular USs and not simply CS or US properties. Thus, as pointed out by Lo-Lordo (1979), demonstrations of such *selective associations* require that more than one US is used in double dissociation paradigms. That is to say, not only must it be demonstrated that evolutionary fear-relevant CSs result in superior conditioning with an aversive US, but it must also be shown that such CSs *do not* result in superior conditioning with a non-aversive US. Ideally, a double dissociation requires that one CS is superior with one US, whereas the alternative CS is superior with an alternative US, such as in the famous demonstration of belongingness in taste aversion learning by Garcia and Koellig (1966). They showed that taste CSs were superior to visual and auditory CSs with malaise as unconditioned response (UR), but that tone and light stimuli were superior with shock induced aversion as the UR. If the latter condition does not hold, the effect in the former condition would simply have been due to CS salience rather than to CS-US associability.

Öhman et al. (1978) tried to address this problem by comparing conditioning to fear-relevant and fear-irrelevant stimuli with aversive and non-aversive USs. As in previous work, the aversive US was a mild electric shock to the fingers. The non-aversive US was the imperative stimulus for a reaction-time task, which was signaled either by fear-relevant (snake, spiders) or fear-irrelevant (flowers, mushrooms) stimuli. Such a stimulus arrangement typically results in differential autonomic responses to the CS+ and the CS– (e. g., Öhman, Nordby and d'Elia, 1986). The data showed superior resistance to extinction to fear-relevant stimuli with the shock US, and actually superior resistance to extinction for fear-irrelevant stimuli with the non-aversive US (Öhman et al., 1978), which provides evidence for a double dissociation effect. However, to some extent, the im-

pact of this finding is reduced by the lack of conditioning effects observed during acquisition with the imperative stimulus as the US (LoLordo & Droungas, 1989). No doubt such independent evidence of the effectiveness of the conditioning procedure would have been desirable, but the situation is not as damaging as suggested by LoLordo and Droungas (1989). First, there is convincing evidence that this procedure does result in reliable differential response. In particular, Öhman et al. (1986) reported reliable differential SCR, heart rate and finger pulse volume responses to the CS+ and the CS– in this type of task for normal subjects (but not for schizophrenics). Second, given the constraints of the procedure, it is very hard to come up with an alternative explanation (except for chance) for the findings with the reaction time task. Most likely, the results by Öhman et al. (1978) merely suggest that differential response during acquisition was less sensitive than the extinction data to pick up the underlying associative effect which provided the basis for the observed differential response during extinction. If this conclusion is accepted, the findings by Öhman et al (1978) represents a valid demonstration of belongingness between fear-relevant CSs and aversive USs.

This problem was brought a significant step further by the finding of Cook et al. (1986) which were reviewed above. They reported that a fear relevance effect for SCRs was observed only with USs including a tactile component (either noise plus a vibratory stimulus to the hand, or electric shock to the fingers). With noise alone, conditioning was as good with neutral as with potentially phobic stimuli. This finding suggests that the belongingness for evolutionary fear-relevant small animal stimuli is not restricted to aversive stimuli in general, but concerns specific aversive stimuli implying damage to the skin.

Hamm, Vaitl and Lang (1989) noted that belongingness had not been explicitly operationalized in previous research. They measured CS–US belongingness directly by asking subjects to rate the belongingness of three CSs and five USs, as well as indicating which of two CS-US pairs showed most belongingness in a pairwise comparison procedure.

On the basis of the psychophysical data, they selected a high belongingness CS-US combination, an angry human face combined with a loud human scream, and a low belongingness combination, a landscape and the scream, for use in conditioning experiments. The conditioning experiments examined differential conditioning to compound stimuli consisting of CSs from high or low belongingness CS-US combinations and background illumination in the room (blue or yellow). In the first experiment, the high belongingness subjects saw two angry faces, one of which was paired with the scream US during acquisition. Low belongingness subjects differentiated between two landscape pictures by having one followed by the scream. For half of the subjects the background light was yellow and for half it was blue. The background stimulus was on for 1 to 1.5 minutes during which time a CS (8-sec duration) was presented. Thus, for a given subject, only the pictorial stimuli provided discriminative information about US occurrence, because the background was always the same. With this stimulus arrangement, significantly better conditioning and resistance to extinction of finger pulse volume responses (but not for SCRs) was observed in the high belongingness group. In the second experiment, the stimulus contingencies were reversed, by having the two light conditions of the background stimulus providing discriminative information of the US, using the same pictorial CS both on reinforced (e.g., angry face, blue light) and nonreinforced (e.g., angry face, yellow light) trials. With this stimulus arrangement, less differential response both in SCRs and finger pulse volume was observed for the high than for the low belongingness pair, which suggests that the subjects were unable to disregard the content of the CS in the high belongingness CS-US combination. Thus, they did not utilize the alternative cue in the compound, the background light, to prepare for the US. In combination, these two experiment demonstrate that high belongingness between a CS and a US results in superior excitatory conditioning and in overshadowing of discriminative cues if the contingencies are reversed. This is illustrated in Figure 1, which shows the data from the Hamm

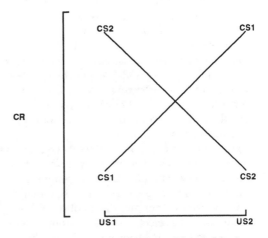

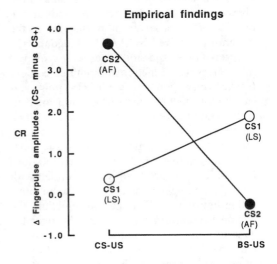

Figure 1. Double dissociation of different belongingness according to the theoretical model proposed by LoLordo (1979) (upper panel) and the empirical data obtained by Hamm, Vaitl, and Lang (1989) (lower panel). AF = angry face; LS = landscape; BS = background stimulus. Reprinted by permission.

et al. (1989) study in relation to the expected effects from the Lolordo (1979) model. Thus, these findings provide a nice double dissociation demonstration in the context of human aversive conditioning. Although they used CSs which we have regarded as prototypical evolutionary fear CSs, that is, angry human faces (Öhman & Dimberg, 1984), Hamm et al. (1989) were careful in restricting their discussion to semantic associations between CSs and USs, and they make no claims for a genetic preparedness basis of their effect.

Hugdahl and Johnsen (1989) combined manipulation of a CS property, direction of threat, and potential CS-US belongingness, by examining snakes versus guns as CSs, direction of threat (towards or away from observer) and US (noise versus electric shock), within a single SCR conditioning experiment. The subjects were required to differentiate between either snakes directed towards and to the side of the observer, or held guns directed towards and to the side of the observer, by having one of the directions followed by the US. Hugdahl and Johnsen (1989) did not observe any overall differences as a function of stimulus content (snakes versus guns) or type of US (noise versus shock) which, on the surface, appears contrary to findings reported by Cook et al. (1986). However, these overall failures were modified by important interactions between the independent variables which make interpretations less straight-forward (and less in conflict with previous findings). First, according to an interaction between CS content and direction, the effect of threat direction was much larger for guns than for snakes both during acquisition and extinction. Furthermore, according to three-way interactions between CS content, direction, and type of US, the best conditioning and resistance to extinction with snake CSs occurred when the snakes were directed towards the observer and followed by shock rather than noise. With guns as CSs, on the other hand, the best conditioning and resistance to extinction, similar to the snake condition, occurred when they were directed towards the observer, but when noise was the US. In fact, the a priori association between a directed gun and noise appeared so strong that it resulted in reversed dis-

crimination when the CS+ was a gun directed to the side of the observer. That is to say, the presence of the noise appeared to sensitize the response to the CS−, the directed gun, to such a degree that it elicited larger responses than the CS+, the gun directed aside, even though the noise was coupled with the latter stimulus. Follow-up Tukey test suggested that the best conditioning was observed to the directed gun with a noise US. This condition resulted in significantly better resistance to extinction than all other conditions *except* the directed snake conditioned with a shock US. Thus, the data imply a belongingness between snakes and shock, on the one hand, and guns and noise on the other, which is similar to the conclusion reached by Cook et al. (1986) for belongingness between small animals and USs involving a tactile component. Furthermore, the much larger effect of direction of threat with the gun stimuli suggest that their effect was mediated at a more controlled-conscious level, which is consistent with a "cultural" hypothesis. The relative small direction effect with snake stimuli, on the other hand, is consistent with an evolutionarily based, non-conscious automatic mediating mechanism (see Öhman, 1986: Öhman, Dimberg & Esteves, 1989).

Finally, quite convincing double dissociation effects have been reported by Cook and Mineka (1990) for observationally acquired fear in the rhesus monkey. Thus, they reported better conditioning to real and toy snakes than to flowers from observing a fearful model express fear in conjunction with these stimuli. However, these CSs did not differ as signals for food in a food-reinforced visual discrimination task.

In summary, the research reviewed in this section appears to indicate that the effect of fear-relevant stimuli on resistance to extinction is particularly evident for fear stimuli for which a case can be made that their potency is of an evolutionary origin. The effect, however, is modulated by the direction of the threat implied in the stimulus. Furthermore, this effect is not related to stimulus properties *per se*, but resides in a special belongingness between fear-relevant stimuli and aversive events. For small animal CSs, this belongingness appears to be specific for US implying an insult to the skin, that is to say, USs involving a tactile stimulus component, such as electric shock. For other classes of fear-relevant stimuli, such as angry faces, auditory stimuli such as loud screams may be particularly effective (Hamm et al., 1989), although this has not been formally tested with different USs. Finally, rapid conditioning and high resistance to extinction is not restricted to evolutionary fear stimuli. Given some specific conditions, such as directed threat with guns and intense auditory USs, very good conditioning may be observed to other classes of stimuli (Hugdahl & Johnsen, 1989).

Nature of the Conditioned Response

Öhman et al. (1978) launched the appealing hypothesis that much of the different effects observed in conditioning with fear-relevant stimuli would be accounted for if one assumed that a different type of response was conditioned to such stimuli. In particular, they argued that SCR conditioning to neutral stimuli primarily involves modification of orienting responses (see Öhman, 1983, for an extensive discussion and documentation of this point). As such, it is highly dependent on cognition and conscious expectations. Conditioning to evolutionary fear-relevant stimuli, on the other hand, would entail the acquisition of another, more primitive, type of response, a defense response (Sokolov, 1963; Graham, 1979), which would be expected to be less dependent on cognition and to behave more in accordance with the traditional conditioned response (CRs) notion. Based on Edelberg's (1973) theorizing on the SCR effector mechanism, Öhman et al. (1978) measured SCRs both from the palmar and the dorsal sides of the hand. The hypothesis was that palmar responses would include both orienting and defense components, whereas dorsal recording would reflect the orienting response only. Their results supported their hypothesis. A fear relevance effect on resistance to extinction was observed only in palmar recordings; the dorsal data did not differentiate between fear-relevant and fear-irrelevant conditions, showed short lasting stimulus pairing

effects, and more pronounced habituation across trials than palmar data. However, given the criticism which has been directed towards Edelberg's (1973) theory (e. g., Bundy & Fitzgerald, 1975), these results must be regarded as less than conclusive.

More conclusive data were reported by Cook et al. (1986). They used a more accepted index of the defense response, heart rate acceleration, which is sharply distinguished from the heart rate deceleration which is associated with orienting (Graham, 1979). With electric shock as US, they reported reliable conditioning of heart rate acceleration to potentially phobic stimuli. This contrasted markedly with the lack of accelerative conditioning observed to neutral stimuli. In fact, male subjects showed reliable conditioning of a long latency decelerative response to neutral but not phobic stimuli. These results are similar to data obtained by Öhman, Dimberg and Nordby (reported by Öhman et al., 1985). Pooling data from six individual experiments (N = 292), Cook et al. (1986) reported highly reliable conditioning of heart rate acceleration which was unique to potentially phobic stimuli, particularly when the US included a tactile component. A similar tendency was observed also with the noise US, but it fell slightly short of significance. These data are illustrated in Figure 2. It is noteworthy, however, that the heart rate effects have been observed during acquisition rather than extinction. Partly, these may be due to the competitive interaction between orienting and defense response in the heart rate response. Thus, extinction, involving as it does stimulus change, may result in orienting with its associated deceleration, which thus masks the accelerative response indexing defense.

The interpretation of these results is assisted by data reported by Hodes, Cook and Lang (1985). They found that subjects who showed a tendency to accelerate their heart to the to-be-come CSs during preconditioning habituation trials were likely to show conditioned heart rate acceleration, enhanced resistance to extinction of SCRs, and a change in rated evaluation of the CSs in the direction of negative valence and increased arousal. In combination, these effects suggests that conditioned heart rate accelera-

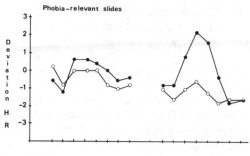

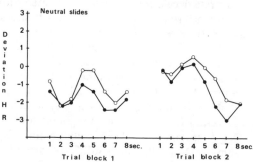

Figure 2. Changes in heart rate (HR) from pres-timulus level during post-stimulus seconds elicited by phobia relevant or neutral slide conditioned stimuli (snake or spider, and flower or mushroom, respectively) followed (CS+, filled circles) or not followed (CS– open circles) by the shock unconditioned stimulus. Data are displayed separately for the first and second half of acquisition (Trial block 1 and 2). (Data replotted from Cook et al., 1986: Reprinted by permission).

tion may be related to more genuine acquisition of fear. Cook et al. (1986) concluded that conditioning to fear-relevant stimuli may involve "two related psychological processes: (a) conditioned mobilization for avoidance (the cardiac defense response) when an aversive stimulus is both recent and presumed to be imminent and (b) conditioned stimulus significance (the electrodermal orienting response), which persists much longer, reflecting the new meaning (negative valence) of the stimulus. Thus, cardiac responses are more likely to occur during acquisition trials, when the aversive US is presented on immediately preceding and/or subsequent trials. The electrodermal effects are more salient at extinction when the US is not presented, reflecting continued vigilance

rather than immediate mobilization against the threat" (p. 205). Thus, in this way, they were able to account for the fact that the heart rate effects occurred during acquisition, whereas the SCR effects most typically have been observed during extinction.

The Role of Cognitive Factors

Seligman (1970) surmised that prepared learning was "noncognitive" in the sense that it was unrelated to expectancies, but rather involved changes in the perceived qualities of the CS. The noncognitive nature of prepared conditioning was then used to explain the irrationality (cf. Marks, 1969) of phobias (Seligman, 1971).

Merely assuring the phobic that her fear is irrational in the sense that it severely overestimates the real danger involved, typically represents lost therapeutic efforts. To capture this aspect of phobic fear, Hugdahl and Öhman (1977) first conditioned subjects to either fear-relevant or fear-irrelevant stimuli and then instructed half of them about shock omission during extinction. Furthermore, the shock electrodes were removed for instructed subjects. This manipulation effectively took away differential response to fear-irrelevant stimuli but left responses to fear-relevant stimuli virtually intact. This result was taken as support for the presumed "noncognitive" nature of conditioning to fear-relevant stimuli. However, this should not be interpreted as suggesting that responding to fear-relevant stimuli is completely independent of instruction-manipulated cognitions. In a second experiment, Hugdahl and Öhman (1977) showed that a verbal threat that a shock would follow a particular cue was much more effective if the cue was fear relevant rather than fear-irrelevant. This was interpreted as an example of the presumed "minimality of input" required for prepared learning (Seligman, 1970).

Cook et al. (1986) failed to confirm the lack of effect of instructed extinction on SCRs to fear-relevant stimuli. Rather they reported powerful instruction effects both with fear-relevant and fear-irrelevant stimuli with both shock and noise plus tactile stimulus as USs.

Dawson et al. (1986) subjected the hypothesized noncognitivity of conditioning to fear-relevant stimuli to an intense analysis. As already noted, they replicated the basic effect of enhanced resistance to extinction of SCRs to fear-relevant stimuli (snakes and spiders) in a complex differential conditioning paradigm, which was embedded in an alleged visual memory task. The purpose of this arrangement was to retard discovery of CS-US contingencies. Verbal awareness (or rather US expectancy) was assessed on a trial-by-trial basis. Half of the subjects were informed that the US would be omitted during the last part of the experiment. Dawson et al. (1986) hypothesized that conditioning to fear-relevant stimuli should be less dependent on reported awareness of CS-US contingencies than conditioning to fear-irrelevant stimuli (see Öhman, 1983, for a review of the role of awareness in human autonomic conditioning). No support for this hypothesis was found either when comparing subjects classified as aware and nonaware of the CS-US contingency, or in responses to the CSs+ and the CSs- presented before the point in time when the subjects became aware. Secondly, on the basis of the data reported by Hugdahl and Öhman (1977), Dawson et al. (1986) hypothesized that responses conditioned to fear-relevant stimuli would persist even after extinction of the expectancy of the US. In general, they reported an association between enhanced resistance to extinction of SCRs and resistance to extinction of verbal expectancies of the USs to fear-relevant stimuli. However, when comparing differential response before and after expectancy extinction, they did not obtain any effect of fear relevance. Rather, differential response decreased from before to after expectancy extinction, but remained statistically reliable to both classes of stimuli even after the subjects had stopped to expect the US.

The results from the Dawson et al. (1986) study was followed-up and extended in a study by Schell et al. (1991). In addition to further examining post expectancy extinction differentiation in SCRs to fear-relevant and fear-irrelevant stimuli, they investigated retention of expectancy and SCR differentiation over one or six months intervals in subjects conditioned

to fear-relevant stimuli with a .5 or 8 sec CS-US interval. Following the early work by Öhman and colleagues (e. g., Öhman et al., 1976), practically all investigators have used a long (about 8 sec) CS-US interval (but see Hugdahl & Öhman, 1980).

As noted above, Schell et al. (1991) reported larger resistance to extinction of SCRs to phobic stimuli regardless of retention interval. This effect held across all extinction trials, whereas a similar effect of enhanced resistance to extinction of expectancy to fear-relevant stimuli only was valid for the first few extinction trials. This implies that subjects in the fear-relevant groups continued to differentiate between CS+ and CS- in SCRs even after the extinction of the expectancy. Direct analysis of post expectancy extinction differentiation in SCRs confirmed this possibility. This analysis showed that subjects conditioned to fear-relevant and fear-irrelevant CSs reached expectancy extinction at about the same point in time. When post expectancy extinction trials were examined, differential responding was still significantly better to fear-relevant than to fear-irrelevant stimuli. This effect, however, interacted strongly with the CS-US interval during training. Thus, reliable post expectancy extinction differentiation in SCRs was observed only for the fear-relevant group conditioned with the .5 sec CS-US interval. Thus, "irrational" SCRs in the sense that they persisted in spite of the extinguished verbal expectancy was observed in this study, similar to the original findings reported by Hugdahl and Öhman (1977). However, Schell et al. (1991) found this effect only with a short CS-US interval in the range traditionally associated with optimal conditioning. Confirming this observation, Soares and Öhman (1992), in an experiment to be detailed below, and using a .5 sec CS-US interval, found that instructed extinction abolished responding to fear-irrelevant stimuli but only reduced differential responding to fear-relevant stimuli (snakes and spiders) (see right panels of Fig. 3).

Schell et al. (1991) also examined the relation between SCRs and retention of verbal expectancies, measured as recall and recognition of which stimuli were followed by shock. They found better retention of expectancies to potentially phobic stimuli than to neutral stimuli, particularly with a six as opposed to a one month retention interval. However, when looking for the hypothesized retention of SCRs to fear-relevant stimuli even in subjects who had forgotten the CS-US contingency according to verbal expectancies, they did not find any evidence of differential response either to fear-relevant or fear-irrelevant CSs. Among remembering subjects, on the other hand, significant SCR differentiation was obvious both to fear-relevant and fear-irrelevant stimuli. Thus, differential SCRs appeared restricted to subjects who were able to remember and verbally report the specific CS-US contingency.

Except for the dissociation between SCRs and verbal expectancies during extinction reported by Schell et al. (1991), there is a general relation between verbal expectancies and SCRs to fear-relevant stimuli during acquisition (Siddle et al., 1988), retention (Schell et al., 1991) and extinction (Dawson et al., 1986). In general, paralleling SCR findings, the aversive US is more readily expected after a fear-relevant than after a fear-irrelevant CS. To some extent, therefore, SCR findings may reflect a covariation bias in humans to perceive "illusory" correlations between fear-relevant stimuli such as pictures of snakes and spiders, on the one hand, and aversive USs, on the other, even though the events are objectively uncorrelated (Tomarken, Mineka & Cook, 1989). Tomarken et al. (1989) exposed high- and low-fear subjects to series of slides (snakes/spiders, flowers and mushrooms) followed by three different outcomes: shock, a control condition (tone or chime sound/flashing lights) or nothing. Slides and outcomes were uncorrelated, that is, shock (as well as the other outcomes) was as likely to follow each of the three types of slides. The base rate for the critical outcome, shock, was .33 in two experiments and .33 or .50 in the third experiment. After exposure to such a series, subjects were asked to indicated how likely the shock was to follow each of the slide events. High-fear subjects invariably rated shock as much more likely after a phobic slide (snake or spider) than after the other slides (.5-.6 when the actual probability was .33; .6 when it was .5). Low-fear sub-

ject showed only a weak illusory correlation effect when the base rate of shock was low (.33) but equalled high-fear subjects in illusory correlation when shock base rate was high (.5). In addition, shock was rated as more painful when it followed phobic slides than neutral ones, particularly among high-fear subjects. Tomarken et al. (1989) interpreted their data as demonstrating a cognitive bias, particularly among high-fear subjects, to perceive danger as associated with fear-relevant stimuli, and to perceive the danger to be more intense (increased pain) when it occurred in association with such stimuli. The effect of this bias is to help maintain the fear. Because a similar bias is operating in low-fear subjects, albeit under more restricted conditions, it may provide a basis for the preparedness effect observed in human conditioning studies. So far however, the association is merely correlational, and it is impossible to tell whether the cognitive bias results from conditioning or whether the conditioning data merely reflect the cognitive bias. Nevertheless, the data reported by Tomarken et al. (1989) suggest that there are cognitive structures biased to connect potentially phobic stimuli with aversive outcomes. One possibility, therefore, is that the conditioning procedures we have used activate such structures and that the increased resistance to extinction of SCRs which typically has been reported from conditioning studies is merely a manifestation of this covariation bias. This possibility points to a possible mechanism behind the findings reviewed in this chapter. This mechanism, however, is as likely a result of phylogenetic as of ontogenetic contingencies. For example, Tomarken et al. (1989) cite unpublished work failing to demonstrate similar illusory correlations between pictures of electrical equipment and electric shock (cf. Hugdahl & Kärker, 1981).

Summary

To sum up, this section has documented that fear-relevant or potentially phobic stimuli are particularly likely to enter into associations with aversive events to produce quite lasting conditioned autonomic responses. When the fear-relevant stimuli consists of small animals such as snakes and spiders, there is some basis for suggesting that aversive USs involving a tactile component are particularly effective. Such "prepared" CS-US contingencies (or contingencies showing "belongingness" between CS and US) are likely to result in the conditioning of a defense type of response marked by heart rate acceleration, whereas other types of contingencies typically results merely in modification of orienting behavior. Finally, at least under some conditions, the resulting responses are not easily modified by or reduced to cognitive expectancies. Any theory with the ambition to account for the data on human conditioning to potentially phobic stimuli would have to account at least for this set of findings.

Theoretical Interpretations

Associative structures

The work of Hamm et al. (1989) and Tomarken et al. (1989) suggest that fear-relevant stimuli are coded in memory in easily accessible associative connections with aversive events. According to Hamm et al. (1989) the availability of such semantic connections may form the basis for demonstrations of CS-US belongingness effects. According to common assumptions, these semantic relations may be thought of as associative nodes linking concepts in memory (see Lang, 1984; Öhman, 1979b). However, both the nature of the changes in these nodal connections brought about by conditioning training and the necessary conditions for them remain obscure. Partly the changes must include access to memory nodes representing emotional responding (Lang, 1979). Recently, Lang, Bradley and Cuthbert (1990) have proposed that conditioning results in changes in valence of the CS in the direction of the valence of the US. Thus, aversive conditioning results in more negative evaluation of the CS. Furthermore, Lang et al. (1990) proposed that these changes in valence are most directly reflected in changes in startle blink reflexes to auditory probe stimuli as a result of conditioning. Their data suggested that such conditioned changes in startle amplitude followed the Rescorla and Wagner (1972) model for conditioning. That is to say, changes in valence as a result of conditioning was postulated to be inversely related to the initial valence of the CS. For example, relatively small changes were observed in startle blinks elicited during negatively valued visual stimuli such as mutilated bodies, whereas large changes occurred in startle elicited during positively evaluated stimuli, such as pictures of attractive landscapes. However, whereas changes in startle blink may index an important underlying process in aversive conditioning, this process does not account for SCR findings, because Lang and coworkers (Greenwald, Cook & Lang, 1989; Vrana, Spence & Lang, 1988) have demonstrated that SCR was related to experienced arousal rather than experienced valence of stimuli. Lang et al. (1990) hinted that the Rescorla-Wagner rule also may help explain SCR findings as changes in arousal. Thus, they found better SCR differentiation as a result of differential conditioning for stimuli initially rated low (e.g., snakes) rather than high (e.g., mutilated bodies) in arousal. However, this cannot provide a general account of the fear relevance resistance to extinction effect, because to the extent that preconditioning differences have been obtained between fear-relevant and fear-irrelevant stimuli, the former invariably elicited larger SCRs than the latter (see, e.g., the discussion of Schell et al., 1991). Thus, although Lang et al. (1990) have provided an interesting start in the direction of a dimensional analysis of human conditioning to various classes of stimuli, considerable more work is needed in spelling out and testing the postulated relationships. However, because encoding and organization of various types of CSs and USs, their potential relations in memory, and their access to memory information about emotional responses, are central issues for the understanding of conditioning to fear-relevant stimuli (or any other stimuli, see Öhman, 1979b), this remains a high priority task. In particular, notions have to be developed that can envision how phylogenetic effects on fear relevance are represented in memory, and how such covariation biases differ from those of ontogenetic origin.

Organization of Emotional Responding

If it is difficult to detail the mechanisms responsible for the changes in memory representations which underlie conditioning to phobic stimuli, it is even more difficult to develop a theory which can account for the organization of emotional responses to such stimuli. However, again, a start has been provided by Lang and coworkers. Lang et al. (1990) defined emotions as action dispositions and introduced a distinction between strategical and tactical responses to emotional situations. The former can be described in terms of valence and arousal. At the behavioral level, the valence dimension corresponds to an approach-avoidance dimension. Thus, in general, the state of an organism is determined by situations prompting various degrees of approach or avoidance and various degrees of intensity in these behaviors. The emotional state determines the strategical dispositions of the organism in terms of the likelihood of approach or avoidance of various stimuli. It is most conveniently defined by help blink reflexes to startle probes (valence) or autonomic indices such as SCR (arousal). However, within this state, a multitude of tactical responses are possible, some of which may even appear contrary to the overall strategy (as in tactical retreat, or defensive attack).

In terms of strategical dispositions, conditioning to fear-relevant stimuli no doubt results in enhanced avoidance tendencies. However, within this general strategy, different types of fear-relevant stimuli may prompt different tactical responses. Öhman et al. (1985) argued at length for the proposition that animal and social fears represent behavioral systems of different evolutionary origin, promoting different types of responses. In particular, they argued that animal fears, as derived from a predatory defense system, were associated with mobilization of physiological responses for metabolically taxing defenses such as flight or attack. Thus, the conditioned heart rate accelerations to fear-relevant stimuli observed by Cook et al. (1986) were consistent with this view. Social fears, on the other hand, were conceived as part of a social submissiveness system (Öhman et al., 1985). Within such a system avoidance of threatening dominants is more often achieved through a repertoire of submissive gestures than through direct flight. This response tactic represents an important evolutionary development, because it allows the animal to handle the threat, yet remain in the relatively protected position of a group member (see Gilbert, 1989). Thus, the immediate response to social threat is not automatic sympathetic mobilization to support flight. Part of the evolutionary basis for this difference from animal fears may be that the visible concomitants of sympathetic mobilization, e. g., pupillary dilation and piloerection, may have communicative functions. That is to say, for the dominant threater, it may be hard to distinguish whether a sympathetically aroused victim is about to flee or attack. This ambiguity may actually escalate the threat and eventually provoke an attack, which may hurt the submissive animal or propel it out of group protection. Indeed, data reported by Lang, Levin, Miller and Kozak (1983) showed that socially fearful subjects were less physiologically reactive, particularly in heart rate, than animal phobics during both actual and imagined social and animal fear scenes.

A remaining issue concerns how information about tactical responses is coded in memory and how they may be accessed as part of a memory structure of emotion. Lang (1979; 1984) has argued that emotions are organized in memory to include response information. When such memories are accessed, not only do we recall the situation where the emotion was evoked, but we also relive some of the associated responses that were part of the emotion. Thus, part of the memory codes that are activated during emotions is held to represent emotional responding, such as behavioral avoidance, sweaty palms and racing heart. Indeed, including such response information as part of a fear image results in much more obvious mobilization of physiological responses (e. g., Lang et al., 1983). From this perspective, it appears plausible to assume that, e. g., the defense response described by Sokolov (1963), can be thought of in terms of a memory representation which can be associatively activated from, say, a fear-relevant CS. Thus, part of the story of conditioning to fear-relevant stimuli may be that they make easy access to particular types of already coded responses, such as the defense response, or behavioral avoidance.

The Role of Preattentive Mechanisms

An important component in any theory accounting for the present phenomena may be hidden in the preattentive processes which provide preliminary recognition of stimuli and preliminary mobilization of responses (Öhman, 1979b; 1986; 1987, 1992). Indeed, it may be at this level that the strategical dispositions in terms of approach or avoidance postulated by Lang et al. (1990) is determined. In developing a theory to account for habituation of the orienting response and conditioning to neutral stimuli (Öhman, 1979b), I had to admit that the resulting model simply was too "rational" to account for conditioning to fear-relevant stimuli, or, for that matter, phobic fears in general. A suggested way out of this dilemma (Öhman, 1979b, p. 465) was that responses to fear-relevant stimuli were prone to become controlled from preattentive mechanisms. As such, they would be much less accessible to controlled, conscious processing mechanisms than responses to fear-irrelevant stimuli (see Öhman, 1992).

The preattentive mechanisms were presumed to be rapid, effortless, parallel processing, not accessible to introspection, and automatic in the sense that they were independent of intentions. The conscious, controlled processing mechanisms, on the other hand, were presumed to be slow, effortful, serial, sensitive to intentions, and conscious, at least in the sense that results of processing would be available to introspection (Öhman, Dimberg, & Esteves, 1989). The preattentive processing mechanisms were postulated to achieve automatic recognition of stimuli in relation to the information held in short term memory (Öhman, 1979b). An important component was assumed to be automatic evaluations of stimulus significance. When stimuli were encountered which did not match memory elements available in short term memory, or which were evaluated as significant, the orienting response was elicited as part of a "call for processing resources" in the controlled processing mechanism. Subsequently, it was suggested that this call was just a subset of the priming of response systems for efficient action, once the situation had been analysed at the controlled processing level (Öhman, 1986; 1987).

In subsequent work, some implications of this general model has been subjected to empirical scrutiny (see Öhman, 1992; Öhman et al., 1989). These studies have all used backward masking as a techniques to separate preattentive from controlled processing. Thus, it is assumed that by presenting a stimulus for a very short duration (about 30 ms) and then having it masked by an immediately following stimulus, the first stimulus, the target, can only be processed preattentively, and does not enter controlled processing stages.

Using target-mask intervals that preclude conscious recognition of the target (about 30 ms), we have demonstrated that responses conditioned to fear-relevant stimuli (angry faces) elicits reliably enhanced responses even when masked by neutral facial stimuli (e. g., Öhman et al., 1989). These studies used a standard differential conditioning paradigm during acquisition, and then presented the CS+ and the CS– (e. g., and angry and a happy face, respectively) masked by a neutral face during extinction. This basic effect has been replicated several times, and it seems to be mediated from the right cerebral hemisphere, because it occurred only when the stimulus was presented in the left visual field (see Öhman, 1992, for review). The subjects were unable to recognize the target stimuli, but they might be able to dis-

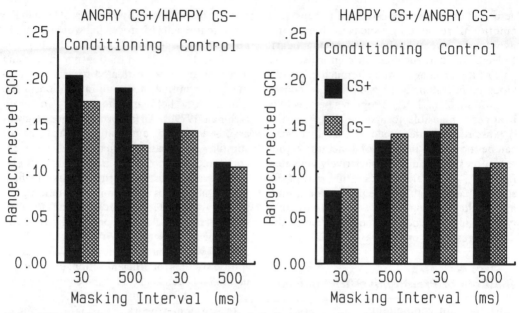

Figure 3. Mean skin conductance responses (SCR) during extinction to unmasked and unreinforced presentations of angry and happy faces. Subjects were conditioned to masked angry (CS+, left panel) or happy (CS+, right panel) faces with the other facial expression presented without shock (CS–). Subjects in the control conditions were exposed to nonpaired presentations of the CSs and the shock unconditioned stimulus. The masking interval during acuqisition either prevented (30 ms) or allowed (500 ms) conscious recognition of the CSs. (Note that the data for the controls are the same in the two panels).

criminate the stimuli in terms of affective ratings, although the data so far are equivocal. If this turns out to be a reliable effect, it is important, because it may be interpreted as suggesting that the effect of stimuli in terms of emotional dispositions (Lang et al., 1990) occurs very early in the processing chain.

Not only seem fear-relevant stimuli able to elicit conditioned responses from a preattentive level, but data also suggest that responses can be conditioned to masked stimuli, provided that the stimuli are fear-relevant. Esteves, Dimberg, Parra and Öhman (1992) exposed subjects to targets followed by masks at masking intervals that precluded or allowed conscious recognition (30 and 500 ms, respectively). Half the subjects had a fear-relevant stimulus as the CS+ (angry face) and a fear-irrelevant stimulus as the CS– (happy face). For the other half, the CS–US contingency was reversed. Control groups received the same stimuli but unpaired with the US. During extinction, targets were

presented for 2 sec without any masks. As shown in Figure 3, the results showed reliable conditioning effects, that is, CS+ - CS– differentiation, only in subjects conditioned with an angry face as CS+, and regardless of the target-mask interval. No differential response was observed with happy faces as the CS+ or in the unpaired control groups. Thus, conditioning effects were observed even with the short, effective masking interval. These data replicate and extend previous results (see Öhman et al., 1989), and they suggest that conditioning to fear-relevant stimuli may occur at a preattentive level not requiring conscious processing of the stimuli. Given the strong data showing that conditioning to neutral stimuli requires controlled processing (see Öhman, 1983), this conclusion is quite remarkable, and suggests that the effects of fear-relevant stimuli are sharply different from those of fear-irrelevant stimuli.

In a recent series of studies, Öhman and Soares (1992; Soares & Öhman, 1992) have extended these finding to another class of fear-relevant stimuli, pictures of snakes and spiders, with flowers and mushrooms as fear-irrelevant control stimuli. The masks have been pictures of the same objects, which have been randomly cut to pieces and then randomly reassembled. In this way, the central object has been taken away, but the general background has been the same as in the target stimuli. So far, three experiments have been performed, all of them showing enhanced responding to the fear-relevant stimuli during masked extinction. In one of these experiments, 128 subjects were randomly allocated to one main group conditioned to fear-relevant stimuli and another main group conditioned to fear-irrelevant stimuli (Soares & Öhman, 1992). A standard differential paradigm was used with shock as the US, but with

a short (.5 sec) CS-US interval. After 12 acquisition trials (10 reinforced), half the subjects were extinguished with masks preventing recognition of the CSs, whereas the other half were extinguished without masks. Half of the subjects were informed about US omission during extinction and had the shock electrodes removed. Thus, the design of the experiment was a 2 (fear-relevant vs fear-irrelevant CSs) × 2 (mask vs no mask during extinction) × 2 (informed or noninformed about US omission) involving 8 groups of 16 subjects each. The dependent variable was SCR. The results from extinction are shown in Figure 3. The upper right panel shows reliable differential response during extinction both to fear-relevant and fear-irrelevant stimuli without mask and without instruction. Instruction, however, com-

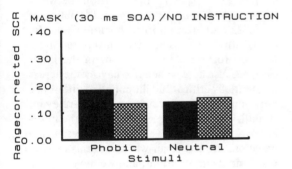

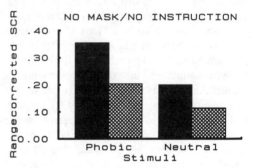

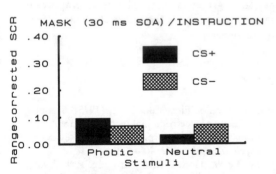

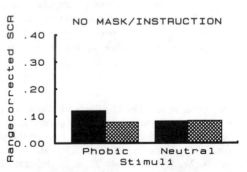

Figure 4. Mean skin conductance responses (SCR) to masked (left panels) or non-masked presentations (right panels) of potentially phobic (snakes, spiders) or neutral (flowers, mushrooms) conditioned stimulus followed (CS+) or not followed (CS–) by an electric shock unconditioned stimulus during a training series preceding the extinction sessions from which the displayed data derive. Half the subjects were instructed that no shock unconditioned stimulus would be presented during extinction (lower panels) and half were not (upper panels). The masking interval for groups having masked CS presentations was 30 ms (SOA = stimulus onset asynchrony).

pletely took away differential response to fear-irrelevant stimuli, but left reliable differential response to fear-relevant stimuli (lower right panel). The mask was effective in abolishing differential responding to fear-irrelevant stimuli, but left reliable differential response to fear-relevant stimuli (upper left panel). Instructions in the masked groups, finally, reduced overall responsiveness but did not abolish differential response to the fear-relevant stimuli (lower left panel).

These data demonstrate that SCRs to fear-relevant stimuli, in contrast to SCRs to fear-irrelevant stimuli, were controlled from a pre-attentive level, inaccessible to instructed controlled and conscious processing, after conditioning. Thus, they suggest "preferred preattentive processing of potentially phobic stimuli" and underscore a fundamental difference between the ways in which different types of stimuli are processed. This characteristic helps to understand why responses to fear-irrelevant stimuli, and possibly phobic fear, is difficult to modulate by instructions reassuring the subject that there is no objective ground for the fear. In a recent article (Öhman, 1992), my original theory (Öhman, 1979b) has been revised to account for this type of findings. The revised theory posits that fear-relevant stimuli associated with aversion preattentively "pop out" from the visual background to capture attention and controlled processing (see Hansen & Hansen, 1988). It is only when the stimulus has received controlled processing that an orienting response is elicited. Because of the

pop-out effect, fear-relevant stimuli receive processing priority so that attention may be briefly switched to the target stimulus, before processing is interupted by the mask. This brief attention investment may be sufficient for eliciting the orienting response, and to allow some learning about the stimulus.

This new theory (Öhman, 1992) presents a mechanism-oriented account of the fear-relevance effects discussed in this chapter, but the theoretical account remains insufficient to account for the whole spectrum of data. Thus, rather than presenting a neat package of theoretical propositions accounting for stimulus prepotency in human autonomic conditioning, this section has only been able to suggest various avenues that appear fruitful to explore for this purpose. Thus, much more work is needed to specify the relation between stimulus prepotency and memory, the nature of response mobilization to such stimuli, and the information processing mechanisms required. Maybe progress is most obvious in the latter case, because here we seem to have come across a potentially critical and illuminating difference between fear-irrelevant and fear-relevant stimuli, which suggests a difference at the information processing level. Nevertheless, many questions are left to answer about this mechanism and its implications, and we haven't even started to relate it to memory and response generating mechanisms. This is an important task which is left for the future students of fear to pursue.

References

Björkstrand, P.-Å. (1990). Effects of conditioned stimulus preexposure on human electrodermal conditioning to fear-relevant and fear-irrelevant stimuli. *Biological Psychology, 30,* 35–50.

Bond, N. W., Siddle, D. A. T., & Schaafsma, M. (submitted). Effects of stimuilus fear-relevance and first-order extinction on retention of second-order electrodermal conditioning in humans.

Booth, M. L., Siddle, D. A. T., & Bond, N. W. (1989). Effects of conditioned stimulus fear-relevance and preexposure on expectancy and electrodermal measures of human Pavlovian conditioning. *Psychophysiology, 26,* 281–291.

Bundy, R. S., & Fitzgerald, H. E. (1975). Stimulus specificity of electrodermal recovery time: An examination and reinterpretation of the evidence. *Psychophysiology, 12,* 406–422.

Cook, E. W., Hodes, R. L., & Lang, P. J. (1986). Preparedness and phobia: Effects of stimulus content on human visceral conditioning. *Journal of Abnormal Psychology, 95,* 195–207.

Cook, M., & Mineka, S. (1989). Observational conditioning of fear to fear-relevant versus fear-irrelevant stimuli in rhesus monkey. *Journal of Abnormal Psychology, 98,* 448–459.

Cook, M., & Mineka, S. (1990). Selective associations

in the observational conditioning of fear in rhesus monkeys. *Journal of Experimental Psychology: Animal Behavior Processes, 16,* 372–389.

Dawson, M. E., Schell, A. M., & Banis, H. T. (1986). Greater resistance to extinction of electrodermal responses conditioned to potentially phobic CSs: A noncognitive process? *Psychophysiology, 23,* 552–561.

Deitz, S. R. (1982). Individual differences in electrodermal response conditioning and self-report of discomfort: A phobia analogue. *Physiological Psychology, 21,* 239–245.

Dimberg, U. (1986). Facial expression as excitatory and inhibitory stimuli for conditioned autonomic responses. *Biological Psychology, 22,* 37–57.

Dimberg, U. & Öhman, A. (1983). The effect of directional facial cues on electrodermal conditioning to facial stimuli. *Psychophysiology, 20,* 160–167.

Edelberg, R. (1973). Mechanisms of electrodermal adaptations for locomotion, manipulation, or defense. In E. Stellar, & J. M. Sprague (Eds.), *Progress in physiological psychology. Vol. 5* (155–209). New York: Academic Press.

Eifert, G. H., & Schermelleh, K. (1985). Language conditioning, emotional instructions, and cognitions in conditioned responses to fear-relevant and fear-irrelevant stimuli. *Journal of Behavior Therapy and Experimental Psychiatry, 16,* 101–109.

Emerson, E., & Lucas, H. (1981). "Preparedness" and the development of aversive associations. *British Journal of Clinical Psychology, 20,* 293–294.

Fredrikson, M. (1981). Orienting and defensive reactions to phobic and conditioned fear stimuli in phobics and normals. *Psychophysiology, 18,* 456–465.

Fredrikson, M., & Öhman, A. (1979). Cardiovascular and electrodermal responses conditioned to fear-relevant stimuli. *Psychophysiology, 16,* 1–7.

Garcia, J., & Koellig, R. A. (1966). Relation of cue to consequence in avoidance learning. *Psychonomic Science, 4,* 123–124.

Greenwald, M. K., Cook, E. W., III, & Lang, P. J. (1989). Affective judgment and psychophysiological response: Dimensional covariation in the evaluation of pictorial stimuli. *Journal of Psychophysiology, 3,* 51–64.

Hamm, A. O., Vaitl, D., & Lang, P. J. (1989). Fear conditioning and belongingness: A double-dissociation analysis. *Journal of Abnormal Psychology, 98,* 395–406.

Hansen, C. H., & Hansen, R. D. (1988). Finding the face in the crowd: An anger superiority effect.

Journal of Personality and Social Psychology, 54, 917–924.

Hare, R. D., & Blevings, G. (1975). Defensive responses to phobic stimuli. *Biological Psychology, 3,* 1–13.

Hodes, R. L., Cook, E. W., III, & Lang, P. J. (1985). Individual differences in autonomic arousal: Conditioned association or conditioned fear? *Psychophysiology, 22,* 545–560.

Hugdahl, K. (1978). Electrodermal conditioning to potentially phobic stimuli: Effects of instructional extinction. *Behavioural Research and Therapy, 16,* 315–321.

Hugdahl, K., & Johnsen, B. H. (1989). Preparedness and electrodermal fear-conditioning: Ontogenetic vs phylogenetic explanations. *Behavioural Research and Therapy, 27,* 269–278.

Hugdahl, K., & Kärker, A. C. (1981). Biological vs experiential factors in phobic conditioning. *Behavioural Research and Therapy, 19,* 109–115.

Hugdahl, K., & Öhman, A. (1977). Effects of instruction on acquisition and extinction of electrodermal responses to fear-relevant stimuli. *Journal of Experimental Psycholog: Human Learning and Memory, 3,* 608–618.

Hugdahl, K., & Öhman, A. (1980). Skin conductance conditioning to potentially phobic stimuli as a function of interstimulus interval and delay versus trace paradigm. *Psychophysiology, 17,* 348–355.

Hygge, S., & Öhman, A. (1978). Modeling processes in the acquisition of fears: Vicarious electrodermal conditioning to fear-relevant stimuli. *Journal of Personality and Social Psychology, 36,* 271–279.

Lang, P. J. (1979). A bio-informational theory of emotional imagery. *Psychophysiology, 16,* 495–512.

Lang, P. J. (1984). Cognition in emotion: Concept and action. In C. E. Izard, J. Kagan, & R. B. Zajonc (Eds.), *Emotion, cognitions, and behavior* (192–228). New York: Cambridge University Press.

Lang, P. J., Bradley, M. M., & Cuthbert, B. N. (1990). Emotion, attention, and the startle reflex. *Psychological Review, 97,* 377–395.

Lang, P. J., Levin, D. N., Miller, G. A., & Kozak, M. J. (1983). Fear behavior, fear imagery, and the psychophysiology of emotion: The problem of affective response integration. *Journal of Abnormal Psychology, 92,* 276–306.

Lang, P. J., Rice, D. G., & Sternbach, R. A. (1972). The psychophysiology of emotion. In N. S. Greenfield, & R. A. Sternbach (Eds.), *Handbook of psychophysiology* (623–643). New York: Holt, Rinehart & Winston.

Lanzetta, J. T., & Orr, S. P. (1980). The influence of facial expressions on the classical conditioning of fear. *Journal of Personality and Social Psychology,* *39,* 1081–1087.

Lanzetta, J. T., & Orr, S. P. (1981). Stimulus properties of facial expressions and their influence on the classical conditioning of fear. *Motivation and Emotion, 5,* 225–234.

LoLordo, V. M. (1979). Selective associations. In A. Dickinson & R. A. Boakes (Eds.), *Mechanisms of learning and memory: A memorial volume to Jerzy Konorski* (367–398). Hillsdale, NJ: Erlbaum.

LoLordo, V. M., & Droungas, A. (1989). Selective associations and adaptive specializations: Taste aversion and phobias. In S. B. Klein & R. R. Mowrer (Eds.), *Contemporary learning theory.* Vol. 2 (145–179). Hillsdale, NJ: Erlbaum.

McNally, R. J. (1981). Phobias and preparedness: Instructional reversal of electrodermal conditioning to fear-relevant stimuli. *Psychological Reports, 48,* 175–180.

McNally, R. J. (1987). Preparedness and phobias: A review. *Psychological Bulletin, 101,* 283–303.

McNally, R. J., & Foa, E. B. (1986). Preparedness and resistance to extinction to fear-relevant stimuli: A failure to replicate. *Behavioural Research and Therapy, 24,* 529–535.

McNally, R. J., & Riess, S. (1982). The preparedness theory of phobias and human safety-signal conditioning. *Behavioural Research and Therapy, 20,* 153–159.

McNally, R. J., & Riess, S. (1984). The preparedness theory of phobias: The effects of initial fear level on safety-signal conditioning. *Psychophysiology, 21,* 647–652.

Maltzman, I., & Boyd, G. (1984). Stimulus significance and bilateral SCRs to potentially phobic stimuli. *Journal of Abnormal Psychology, 93,* 41–46.

Marks, I. M. (1969). *Fears and phobias.* London: Heineman Medical Books.

Merckelbach, H., van der Molen, G. M., & van den Hout, M. A. (1987). Electrodermal conditioning to stimuli of evolutionary significance: Failure to replicate the preparedness effect. *Journal of Psychopathology and Behavioral Assessment, 9,* 313–326.

Miller, N. E. (1951). Learnable drives and rewards. In S. S. Steven (Ed.), *Handbook of experimental psychology* (435–472). New York: Wiley.

Mineka, S., & Tomarken, A. J. (1989). The role of cognitive biases in the origin and maintenance of fear and anxiety disorders. In T. Archer & L.-G. Nilsson (Eds.), *Aversion, avoidance and anxiety* (195–229). Hillsdale, NJ: Erlbaum.

Öhman, A. (1979a). Fear relevance, autonomic conditioning, and phobias: A laboratory model. In P.-O. Sjödén, S. Bates, & W. S. Dockens III (Eds.), *Trends in behavior therapy* (107–134). New York: Academic Press.

Öhman, A. (1979b). The orienting response, attention, and learning: An information processing perspective. In H. D. Kimmel, E. H. van Olst, & J. F. Orlebeke (Eds.), *The orienting reflex in humans* (443–472). Hillsdale, NJ: Erlbaum.

Öhman, A. (1983). The orienting response during Pavlovian conditioning. In D. A. T. Siddle (Ed.), *Orienting and habituation: Perspectives in human research* (315–369). Chichester: Wiley.

Öhman, A. (1986). Face the beast and fear the face: Animal and social fears as prototypes for evolutionary analyses of emotion. *Psychophysiology, 23,* 123–145.

Öhman, A. (1987). The psychophysiology of emotion: An evolutionary-cognitive perspective: In P. K. Ackles, J. R. Jennings, & M. G. H. Coles (Eds.), *Advances in psychophysiology.* Vol. 2 (79–127). Greenwich, CT: JAI Press.

Öhman, A. (1992). Orienting and attention: Preferred preattentive processing of potentially phobic stimuli. In B. A. Campbell, R. Richardson, & H. Haynes (Eds.) *Attention and information processing in infants and adults: Perspectives from human and animal research* (263–295). Hillsdale, NJ: Erlbaum.

Öhman, A., & Dimberg, U. (1978). Facial expressions as conditioned stimuli for electrodermal responses: A case of "preparedness"? *Journal of Personality and Social Psychology, 36,* 1251–1258.

Öhman, A., & Dimberg, U. (1984). An evolutionary perspective on human social behavior. In W. M. Waid (Ed.), *Sociophysiology* (47–86). New York: Springer-Verlag.

Öhman, A., Dimberg, U., & Öst, L.-G. (1985). Animal and social phobias: Biological constraints on learned fear responses. In S. Reiss & R. R. Bootzin (Eds.), *Theoretical issues in behavior therapy* (123–178). New York: Academic Press.

Öhman, A., Dimberg, U., & Esteves, F. (1989). Preattentive activation of aversive emotions. In T. Archer & L.-G. Nilsson (Eds.), *Aversion, avoidance and anxiety* (169–193). Hillsdale, NJ: Erlbaum.

Öhman, A., Eriksson, A., & Olofsson, C. (1975). One trial learning and superior resistance to extinction of autonomic responses conditioned to potentially phobic stimuli. *Journal of Comparative and Physiological Psychology, 88,* 619–627.

Öhman, A., Fredrikson, M., & Hugdahl, K. (1978). Orienting and defensive responding in the electrodermal system: Palmar-dorsal differences and recovery rate during conditioning to potentially phobic stimuli. *Psychophysiology, 15,* 93–101.

Öhman, A., Fredrikson, M., Hugdahl, K., & Rimmö, P.-A. (1976). The premise of equipotentiality in human classical conditioning: Conditioned electrodermal responses to potentially phobic stimuli. *Journal of Experimental Psychology: General, 105*, 313–337.

Öhman, A., Nordby, H., & d'Elia, G. (1986). Orienting and schizophrenia: Stimulus significance, attention, and distraction in a signaled reaction time task. *Journal of Abnormal Psychology, 95*, 326–334.

Orr, S. P., & Lanzetta, J. T. (1980). Facial expressions of emotion as conditioned stimuli for human autonomic responses. *Journal of Personality and Social Psychology, 38*, 278–282.

Pitman, R. K., & Orr, S. P. (1986). Test of the conditioning model of neurosis: Differential aversive conditioning of angry and neutral facial expressions in anxiety disorder patients. *Journal of Abnormal Psychology, 95*, 208–213.

Rescorla, R. A., & Heth, C. D. (1975). Reinstatement of fear to an extinguished conditioned stimulus. *Journal of Experimental Psychology: Animal Behavior Processes, 1*, 88–96.

Rescorla, R. A., & Wagner, A. R. (1972). A theory of Pavlovian conditioning: Variations in the effectiveness of reinforcement and nonreinforcement. In A. H. Black, & W. F. Prokasy (Eds.), *Classical conditioning II: Current research and theory* (64–99). New York: Appleton-Century-Crofts.

Schell, A. M., Dawson, M. E., & Marinkovic, K. (1991). Effects of the use of potentially phobic CSs on retention, reinstatement, and extinction of the conditioned skin conductance response. *Psychophysiology, 28*, 140–153.

Siddle, D. A. T., Bond, N. W., & Friswell, R. (1987). Effects of stimulus content on second-order electrodermal conditioning. *Psychophysiology, 24*, 439–448.

Siddle, D. A. T., Power, K., Bond, N. W., & Lovibond, P. F. (1988). Effects of stimulus content and devaluation of the unconditioned stimulus on retention of human electrodermal conditioning. *Australian Journal of Psychology, 40*, 179–193.

Seligman, M. E. P. (1970). On the generality of the laws of learning. *Psychological Review, 77*, 406–418.

Seligman, M. E. P. (1971). Phobias and preparedness. *Behavior Therapy, 2*, 307–320.

Sokolov, E. N. (1963). *Perception and the conditioned reflex.* Oxford: Pergamon Press.

Tomarken, A. J., Mineka, S., & Cook, M. (1989). Fear-relevant selective associations and covariation bias. *Journal of Abnormal Psychology, 98*, 381–394.

Vaitl, D., Gruppe, H., & Kimmel, H. D. (1985). Contextual stimulus control of conditioned vasomotor and electrodermal reactions to angry and friendly faces: Transswitching - Yes! Preparedness - No! *Pavlovian Journal of Biological Sciences, 20*, 124–131.

Vrana, S. R., Spence, E. L., & Lang, P. J. (1988). The startle probe response: A new measure of emotion? *Journal of Abnormal Psychology, 97*, 487–491.

Section D.
Emotion and Reflex Modification:
Clinical Implications

Emotion, Arousal, Valence, and the Startle Reflex

Peter J. Lang, Margaret M. Bradley and Bruce N. Cuthbert*

Abstract

Recent evidence suggests that the vigor of the startle reflex varies systematically with an organism's emotional state. A theory is presented to elucidate this relationship, suggesting how the amplitude of the eyeblink response to an abrupt, task-irrelevant probe may be modulated by the affective content of ongoing perception and thought. The present approach defines emotions as *action dispositions*, founded on brain states that organize behavior along a basis appetitive-aversive dimension. It is postulated that all affects are primitively associated with either a behavioral set favoring approach, attachment, and consummatory behavior or a set disposing the organism to avoidance, escape, and defense. The efferent system as a whole (including exteroceptive reflexes) is presumably tuned according to the current status of this central affect-motivational organization. Thus, reflexes associated with an appetitive set (e.g., the salivary response to a sucrose probe) would be enhanced if activated when a subject was already engaged in a positive emotional response; conversely, the startle reflex to a sudden loud noise is viewed as an aversive or defensive response and would be augmented if it occurred in the context of an ongoing aversive emotion. In short, reflexes that match a concurrent, tonic affective process will be amplified. A reciprocal rule is also postulated: A mismatched reflex (e.g., a defensive reflex initiated during a pleasant state of affairs) will show relative inhibition or attenuation.

The Startle Reflex and the Eyeblink

Early interest in the human startle response was stimulated by the work of Landis and Hunt (1939). A pistol shot activated the startle reflex in their experiments, and subsequent movement was recorded with high-speed motion pictures. Drawings of the rapidly unfolding, whole-body startle were frequently reproduced in textbooks (e.g., Woodworth & Schlosberg, 1956).

Its gross features include a forward thrusting of the head and a descending flexor wave reaction, extending through the trunk to the knees. The first, fastest, and most stable element in the sequence is the sudden closure of the eyelids. The primacy of the eyeblink has been confirmed by subsequent research, which further showed that lid flexion alone may occur to stimuli not sufficiently strong to engage the whole reflex. Because of these response properties, the eyeblink has become an important tool in experiments probing such diverse phenomena as classical conditioning and cognitive resource allocation in attention. Although studies vary widely in subject population and theoretical orientation, they consistently show that variations in the intensity of the blink indexes the brain's receptivity to information input.

Eyeblink is occasioned by rapid contraction of the orbicularis oculi muscle (see Figure 1). It occurs reflexively 30–50 ms after the onset of

* University of Florida.
This research was supported by NIMH grants MH 37757, MH 41950, and MH 43975.
Reprinted from: Lang, P. J., Bradley, M. M., & Cuthbert, B. N. (1990). Emotion, attention, and the startle reflex. *Psychological REview, 97*, 377–395; Excerpt: pp. 377–382.

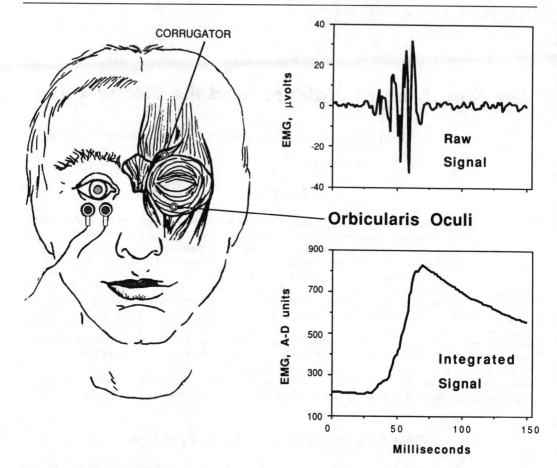

Figure 1. Left panel: Illustration of the orbicularis oculi and corrugator muscles on the left side of the face and the placement of the eyeblink recording electrodes when positioned beneath the right eye. *Top right panel:* A muscle action potential from orbicularis, recorded during a blink reflex. *Bottom right panel:* An integration of this same signal, which is the response waveform scored for peak amplitude and latency in most human subject studies of the probe reflex. (EMG = electromyogram; A–D = analog-to-digital conversion.)

an abrupt acoustic stimulus. The primary characteristic of the eliciting stimulus is its rapid rise time (ideally, instantaneous), with intensity secondary. The blink reflex shows a regular course of habituation with repeated presentation at short interstimulus intervals. However, it dishabituates quickly and thus can be evoked repeatedly within a relatively brief period (as many as 40–50 probe trials are practical in a half-hour experimental session). The response is variously recorded – by photography; using a potentiometer attached with a thread to the eyelid; by the electro-oculogram, where abrupt pen movements indicate the lid passing rapidly over the corneal surface; or indeed, inadvertently by electroencephalogram, in which the recording of the reflex may appear as a troubling artifact. The electromyographic measurement of orbicularis muscle during eyeblink is shown in Figure 1. This method captures events most proximal to the neural path of innervation and is thus preferred by most investigators.

Context and Reflex Evocation

The reliability of the knee jerk as a neurological sign depends on the bedside manner (as well as the motor skill) of the diagnostician who delivers a percussive tap to the patellar tendon. This fact, that reflexes vary with the psychological context in which they are evoked, has long been practical knowledge for health-care workers and was a focus of study for scientists before the turn of the century (Bowditch & Warren, 1890; Ison & Hoffman, 1983; Sechenov, 1863/1965). More recent research on the startle reflex has contributed importantly to two major topics in psychology – the study of attention and the study of conditioned fear.

Attention

Frances Graham and her associates have reported a series of experiments based on an innovative startle-probe methodology (e. g., Anthony & Graham, 1985; Graham, 1975, 1979). In this research, various stimuli, tasks, and instructional manipulations are used to guide the subject's attentional focus. While the subject is thus engaged, brief nonsignal startling stimuli are presented, with the expectation that the eyeblink reflex will be enhanced or attenuated according to the amount of attentional resources allocated to the primary task.

Several important phenomena have been shown in this work. For example, instructions to attend to the probe stimulus itself prompt an augmentation of the reflex (e. g., Bohlin & Graham, 1977; Hackley & Graham, 1984). Conversely, reflex attenuation results if unsignaled probes are presented in the foreperiod of a reaction time task. In this latter case, attention is not directed to the startle stimulus but is presumably focused on the anticipated go signal. This probe reflex reduction is greatest, furthermore, when the go signal is imminent (and attention to it most needed), as corroborated by greater late-foreperiod heart rate deceleration – a common measure of stimulus "orienting" (Graham & Clifton, 1966). These

studies and related work, as well as an attentional theory of the startle probe, have been admirably reviewed by Anthony (1985).

Of particular interest for this presentation are a group of cross-modality experiments. In this procedure, the subject's attention is directed to either a visual or auditory foreground task while startle probes are administered in either the same of the alternate sensory channel. The hypothesis examined is that attentional resources are limited and are allocated a priori according to modality. Thus, when subjects engage in a visual task (e. g., viewing pictures), resources available to the auditory system are reduced, and the reflex response to an acoustic startle probe is expected to be attenuated. Results from Anthony and Graham's (1985) test of this view are presented in Figure 2. Both infants and adults show blink reflexes that are smaller and slower when the modality of the probe does not match the modality of foreground stimulation.

A further aspect of this research concerns the interest value of the foreground stimulus. Anthony and Graham (1985) proposed that more interesting stimuli (e. g., slides of human faces or music) engage attention to a greater extent than do less interesting stimuli (e. g., blank slides or single pure tones), and thus cross-modality probe response attenuation should be greater with interesting than with dull foregrounds. Again, both infants and adults show this effect. Recently, Simons and Zelson (1985) undertook a test of this hypothesis, using stimuli that were more evocative of emotion. Subjects viewed two content classes of photographic slides as a foreground task: *interesting content*, a varying series of attractive nude men and women, and *dull content*, a picture of a small wicker basket, repeatedly presented. Unpredictable auditory startle probes were presented during both slide presentations. As expected, the blink reflex was significantly smaller for interesting than for dull slide content.

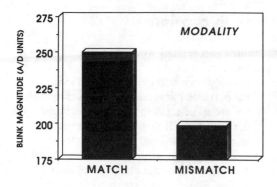

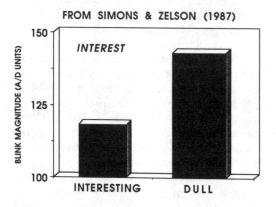

FROM SIMONS & ZELSON (1987)

Figure 2. Top panel: Blink magnitude data, which show the difference in mean reflex response when the probe modality matched the foreground modality (e. g., an acoustic probe with a foreground of recorded music) and when there was a probe-foreground modality mismatch (e. g., an acoustic probe with a pictorial slide foreground). *Bottom panel:* Data obtained using a probe-foreground mismatch design; mean reflex magnitude to an acoustic probe was smaller when a pictorial slide foreground was interesting (attractive nudes) than when it was dull (a household object, repeatedly presented). (A/D = analog-to-digital conversion. *Note:* Top panel redrawn from "Blink Reflex Modification by Selective Attention: Evidence for the Modulation of 'Automatic' Processing" by B.J. Anthony and F.K. Graham, 1985; *Biological Psychology, 21,* p. 51. Copyright 1985 by Elsevier/North-Holland. Adapted by permission. Data in bottom panel are from "Engaging Visual Stimuli and Reflex Blink Modification" by R.F. Simons and M.F. Zelson, 1985, *Psychophysiology, 22,* p. 46. Copyright 1985 by the Society for Psychophysiological Research. Adapted by permission.)

Fear Conditioning

Brown, Kalish, and Farber (1951) undertook a probe study of classical fear conditioning, based on a very different theory of startle modulation. The investigators noted that anxiety patients often show exaggerated startle responses. Presuming this was a function of a high drive state (Hull, 1943), they reasoned that animals conditioned to be fearful would show a similar enhanced startle when startle probes were presented during the conditioned stimulus (CS) at extinction. Their experiment used male rats as subjects, a light-buzzer compound CS, and a shock unconditioned stimulus (US). The startle probe was a toy pistol shot, and the whole-body startle was measured by a stabilimeter table. As shown in Figure 3, their results conformed to expectation. Startle probes

presented in the context of CSs early in extinction evoked larger reflexes than those presented during control stimuli. These general findings were subsequently replicated with both animal and human subjects (Ross, 1961; Spence & Runquist, 1958). More recently, Michael Davis and his associates produced data further supporting the hypothesis that probe reflexes are enhanced in conditioned fear. For example, consistent with the hypothesis that the probe response is related to level of fear, laboratory rats showed a systematic increase in reflex response to startle probes (presented concurrently with the CS in extinction) with increased intensity of the previously presented shock US (Davis & Astrachan, 1978). Furthermore, significant attenuation of the reflex was found after administration of anxiolytic drugs (Berg & Davis, 1984).

The CS used in Ross's (1961) study of human subjects, as well as that chosen by the Davis group (e. g., Berg & Davis, 1984) for their animal learning study, was a change in illumina-

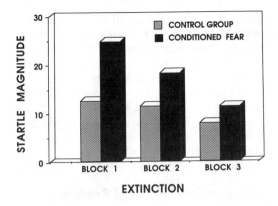

Figure 3. Brown, Kalish, and Farber (1951) reported augmented probe-startle reflexes for fear-conditioned stimuli. (The mean whole-body startle reflex, recorded by stabilimeter of rats is shown. An acoustic startle probe was presented during extinction of conditioned stimuli, previously paired with electric shock, and nonconditioned stimuli [unpaired].)

tion. It is interesting to consider these experiments in the context of Graham's attention theory. From this perspective, the light CS presented during extinction was clearly a foreground stimulus, and it was visual. The probe stimulus was acoustic. This amounts to a conditioning version of the cross-modality-attention paradigm (e.g., Anthony & Graham, 1985; Simons & Zelson, 1985). However, the attention theory makes a prediction opposite to drive theory. The CS at extinction is more engaging, or of greater interest, than the control stimulus. A primary visual cue should direct attentional resources to the visual modality, making less attention available for the auditory channel. Thus, a logical conclusion is that a context-irrelevant acoustic probe, presented during this visual signal stimulus, should produce an inhibited startle reflex. As we have seen, the actual results are otherwise. The amplitude of the acoustic startle reflex is significantly increased during presentation of a visual CS.

Emotional Valence and Reflex Excitation: Background

A goal of this article is to present some theoretical considerations that may help to resolve apparently inconsistent results from these two lines of research. It seems clear that attention and modality modulate startle amplitude, and it seems equally clear that the probe startle is augmented by conditioned fear. The theoretical conflict arises in the neglect of affective motivation. Thus, it is suggested that attentional effects cannot be clearly assessed if the emotional valence of foreground and probe are ignored; with reference to both attention and conditioning research, positive and aversive affective cues may modulate the startle response differently, and a context's emotional valence may have an influence on the reflex that is independent of arousal.

Hebb (1949) suggested that the significant dimensions of behavior are direction and vigor. Similarly, we propose that the emotional significance of behavior can be understood in terms of two primitive strategic dispositions, valence

and arousal. *Valence* refers to the organism's disposition to assume either an appetitive or defensive behavioral set. *Arousal* refers to the organism's disposition to react with varying degrees of energy or force. This article focuses on the significance of emotional valence for cognition and behavior. Arousal is considered to be an intensity factor, which must be brought under experimental control if the effects of valence are to be clearly observed.

Strategic and Tactical Aspects of Motivated Behavior

As described by Karl von Clausewitz in his classic treatise *On War* (1832/1976), *tactics* are diverse, specific, context-bound patterns of action; *strategy* is a unitary, underlying organization that marshals individual actions in the cause of broad end goals. Tactics serve strategies but do not mirror them. Thus, a tactical situation may call for defensive behavior, even though the overall strategic plan is to attack.

Applying this metaphor to motivated behavior, the emotions appear to be organized around two broad strategic dimensions, valence and arousal. These dimensions are called *strategic* because they define the general direction of behavior (either appetive or defensive) and the amount of energy resources to be allocated without specifying exact patterns of action. The organism's strategic state – its valence and arousal predisposition – differentially primes or inhibits subsequent behavior. These parameters are set by conjunctions of internal and external stimuli, integrated through subcortical structures, and represent for a given period the background framework of transactions between the organism and its environment.

Emotions that are subordinate to a specific valence level are various. Several theorists (e. g., Ekman, 1973; Izard, 1977) have suggested that affect is further organized into a set of broad, survival-related categories such as fear, aggression, and pleasure (as in consummatory or sexual approach), each of which has its own associative structure and logic. However, there is no agreement on a fundamental list, and importantly, emotions are clearly tactical in any specific instance of expression. For example, widely different behavioral programs have been classified as fear related. These include anxious vigilance, freezing, spontaneous defecation, disruption of motor control, or headlong flight. Indeed, appetitive-appearing behaviors, such as mock aggressive or sexual displays, also may occur in primates under threat (e. g., van Lawick-Goodall, 1971, p.172). It is this tactical variability in emotional behavior that has frustrated efforts to discriminate positive from negative affects (much less individual emotions) in terms of specific and reliable psychophysiological response measures (e. g., see Mandler, 1984, pp. 27–34).

We suggest that the probe reflex methodology may provide a partial solution to the problem of emotion measurement. It is proposed that the exteroceptive reflexes are differentially primed according to the existing, strategic set of the organism. It is further hypothesized that this priming extends across

different specific affects and is independent of differences in tactical response pattern. Finally, whereas tonic activation has been shown to sometimes increase reflex strength (e. g., Davis & File, 1984; Putnam, 1976), new research suggests that this effect strongly depends on the valence parameter. That is, individual reflexes are either enhanced or inhibited, depending on whether the organism's strategic, valence disposition is appetitive or defensive.

Emotional Valence and Behavior

Motivated, emotionally relevant behavior is seen as having an underlying biphasic organization, primitively based on functionally opposed approach and withdrawal reactions. A scheme of this sort was proposed formerly by Schneirla (1959). His orientation was biological and evolutionary:

> In general, what we shall term the A-type of mechanism, underlying approach, favors adjustments such as food-getting, shelter-getting, and mating; the W-type, underlying withdrawal, favors adjustments such as defense, huddling, flight, and other protective reactions. Also, through evolution, higher psychological levels have arisen in which through ontogeny such mechanisms can produce new and qualitatively advanced types of adjustment to environmental conditions. (p. 4)

Konorski (1967, p. 9) also advocated a biphasic model. Unconditioned reflexes were organized into two classes, preservative (e. g., ingestive, copulation, and nurture of progeny) and protective (e. g., withdrawal from or rejection of noxious agents), based primarily on their biological, motivational role. He was at pains to point out that both types of responses involved arousal, and he thus differentiated his classification from the ergotrophic-tropotrophic distinction of Hess (1957). Dickinson and Dearing (1979) developed Konorski's dichotomy into two opponent motivational systems, aversive and attractive, each activated by a different but equally wide range of unconditioned stimuli. These systems were held to have reciprocal inhibitory connections that modulated learned responses and reactions to new, unconditioned input.

More recently, making a similar distinction between approach and avoidant behavior in animals, Masterson and Crawford (1982) conceived negatively valent behaviors to be organized into a "defense motivation system"; this system "selectively potentiates or primes a set of innate defense reactions that include fleeing, freezing, fighting and defensive burying" (p. 664). They suggested that affective reactions in humans (e. g., fear, anger, anxiety, and apprehension) can be construed as a phylogenetic development of the mammalian line and represent output of the same defense system. Presumably, positive affects would be similarly related to an appetitive motivational system.

Emotional Valence and Semantic Judgments

The conclusion that emotion-motivational systems are biphasic has also been reached by most investigators studying verbal behavior. For example, recent work on natural language categories (Ortony, Clore, & Collins, 1988; Shaver, Schwartz, Kirson, & O'Connor, 1987) suggests that people's knowledge about emotions is hierarchically organized and that the subordinate division is between positivity (love and joy) and negativity (anger, sadness, and fear). A similar deduction was made by Osgood and his associates (e. g., Osgood, Suci, & Tannenbaum, 1957) on the basis of their classic studies of the semantic differential. Using factor analysis, they determined that emotional descriptors were mainly distributed (in terms of the most variance accounted for) along a bipolar dimension of valence. Despite wide differences in the dictionary definition of the words used, the primary affective meaning of stimuli was captured by a single dimension from attraction to aversion, pleasure-displeasure. A smaller but significant portion of the total variance was controlled by a second dimension, arousal or engagement. Although minor details vary, this general conception has received wide support from a host of independent investigators (e. g., Mehrabian & Russell, 1974; Russell, 1980; Tellegen, 1985).

Biobehavioral and language dimensions of arousal and valence are presumed to be roughly coupled. That is, language and behavior (and even to some extent its physiology) can be shaped independently (Lang, 1968, 1985), but central associative connections are assumed to exist between semantic and behavioral representations of emotion. Thus, barring an active dissociative process, subjective affective judgments about stimuli are expected to be positively correlated with related emotional behaviors.

Biphasic Emotion Theory

The Startle Probe in an Affective Foreground

The overview developed earlier asserts that affective behavior is organized biphasically at all levels of response complexity, from cognitive events to the exteroceptive reflexes. Many reflexes can be classified as either appetitive (e. g., the salivary reflex) or defensive (e. g., pain withdrawal and startle). Both classes are seen to be augmented or diminished, depending on whether the behavioral context in which the specific reflex is instigated is a valence match or mismatch. For example, when a foreground stimulus engages an appetitive response, a negative probe of that foreground should prompt a reflex of lower amplitude and slower latency; if the foreground stimulus is aversive, an augmented reflex is anticipated.

Theoretical Hypotheses

Several hypotheses are derived from this position. They concern how startle amplitude varies with the perception of aversive or appetitive stimuli and with the retrieval of pleasant or unpleasant memories. The first two are basic and can be derived neither from the attentional explanation of the startle probe nor from the view of activation (drive) as a nonspecific motivating factor in behavior. The remaining hypotheses are parsimonious collaterals, also generated from the biphasic emotion view:

1. The startle-probe reflex indexes the strategic valence disposition of the organism. Thus, reflex amplitude will be enhanced linearly as foreground stimuli vary from highly positive, appetitive content to highly negative, aversive content. This effect is determined by valence and is not a simple function of the interest value or arousal level of the foreground.

2. The covariation between probe reflex amplitude and foreground valence is based on an affective (not modality) stimulus match or mismatch. Therefore, it is independent of probe modality and should occur with a visual as well as an acoustic startle probe.

3. Probe reflex amplitude will change if the affective valence of a foreground changes. Thus, following conditioned association of a foreground stimulus with an aversive event, the probe response to that foreground will be increased in magnitude, relative to a control stimulus.

4. Research suggests that the right cerebral hemisphere is dominant in the processing of emotional stimuli. Thus, it is presumed that the emotional valence of foreground stimuli will have a greater influence on reflex amplitude when acoustic probes are presented to the left ear.

5. If reflexes are modulated by a central, affective response disposition, then the reflex-valence relationship should hold even when there is no sensory foreground, that is, when subjects retrieve and process emotional memories.

References

Anthony, B. J. (1985). In the blink of an eye: Implications of reflex modification for information processing. In P. K. Ackles, J. R. Jennings, & M. G. H. Coles (Eds.), *Advances in psychophysiology* (Vol. 1, pp. 167–218). Greenwich, CT: JAI Press.

Anthony, B. J., & Graham, F. K. (1985). Blink reflex modification by selective attention: Evidence for the modulation of "automatic" processing. *Biological Psychology, 21,* 43–59.

Berg, W. K., & Davis, M. (1984). Diazepam blocks fear-enhanced startle elicited electrically from the brainstem. *Physiology & Behavior, 32,* 333–336.

Bohlin, G., & Graham, F. K. (1977). Cardiac deceleration and reflex blink facilitation. *Psychophysiology,14,* 423–430.

Bowditch, H. P., & Warren, J. W. (1890). The knee jerk and it physiological modifications. *The Journal of Physiology, 11,* 25–64.

Brown, J. S., Kalish, H. I., & Farber, I. E. (1951). Conditioned fear as revealed by magnitude of startle response to an auditory stimulus. *Journal of Experimental Psychology, 41,* 317–328.

Davis, M., & Astrachan, D. I. (1978). Conditioned fear and startle magnitude: Effects of different footshock or backshock intensities used in train-

ing. *Journal of Experimental Psychology: Animal Behavior Processes, 4,* 95–103.

Davis, M., & File, S. E. (1984). Intrinsic and extrinsic mechanims of habituation and sensitization: Implication for the design and analysis of experiments. In H.V. S. Peeke & L. Petrinovich (Eds.), *Habituation, sensitization, and behavior* (pp. 287–324). New York: Academic Press.

Dickinson, A., & Dearing, M. F. (1979). Appetitive-aversive interactions and inhibitory processes. In A. Dickinson & R. A. Boakes (Eds.), *Mechanisms of learning and motivation* (pp. 203–231). Hillsdale, NJ: Erlbaum.

Ekman, P. (1973). Introduction. In P. Ekman (Ed.), *Darwin and facial expression: A century of research in review* (pp. 1–10). New York: Academic Press.

Graham, F. K. (1975). The more or less startling effects of weak prestimulation. *Psychophysiology, 12,* 238–248.

Graham, F. K. (1979). Distinguishing among orienting, defense, and startle reflexes. In H. D. Kimmel, E. H. van Olst, & J. F. Orlebeke (Eds.), *The orienting reflex in humans. An international conference sponsored by the Scientific Affairs Di-*

vision of the North Atlantic Treaty Organization (pp. 137–167). Hillsdale, NJ: Erlbaum.

Graham, F. K., & Clifton, R. K. (1966). Heart rate change as a component of the orienting response. *Psychological Bulletin, 65*, 305–320.

Hackley, S. A., & Graham, F. K.(1984). Early selective attention effects on cutaneous and acoustic blink reflexes. *Physiological Psychology, 11*, 235–242.

Hebb, D. O. (1949). *The organization of behavior: A neuropsychological theory.* New York: Wiley.

Hess, W. R. (1957). *The functional organization of the diencephalon.* New York: Grune & Stratton.

Hull, C. L. (1943). *Principles of behavior.* New York: Appleton-Century-Crofts.

Ison, J. R.,& Hoffmann, H. S. (1983). Reflex modification in the domain of startle: II. The anomalous history of a robust and ubiquitous phenomenon. *Psychological Bulletin, 94*, 3–17.

Izard, C.E. (1977). *Human emotions.* New York: Plenum Press.

Konorski,J. (1967). *Integrative activity of the brain: An interdisciplinary approach.* Chicago: University of Chicago Press.

Landis,C.,&Hunt, W.A. (1939). *The startle pattern.* New York: Farrar.

Lang, P. J. (1968). Fear reduction and fear behavior: Problems in treating a construct. In J. M. Schlien (Ed.), *Research in psychotherapy* (Vol. 3, pp. 90–103). Washington, DC: American Psychological Association.

Lang, P. J. (1985).The cognitive psychophysiology of emotions: Fear and anxiety. In A. H. Tuma & J. D. Maser (Eds.), *Anxiety and the anxiety disorders* (pp. 131–170). Hillsdale, NJ: Erlbaum.

Mandler, G.(1984). *Mind and body: Psychology of emotions and stress* (pp. 27–34). New York: Norton.

Masterson, F. A., & Crawford, M. (1982). The defense motivation system: A theory of avoidance behavior. *The Behavioral and Brain Sciences, 5*, 661–696.

Mehrabian, A., & Russell, J. A. (1974). *An approach to enviromental psychology.* Cambrigde, MA: MIT Press.

Ortony, A., Clore, G. L., & Collins, A. (1988). *The cognitive structure ot emotions..* Cambridge, England: Cambridge University Press.

Osgood, C., Suci, G., & Tannenbaum, P. (1957). *The measurement of meaning.* Urbana: Univesity of Illinois.

Putman, L. E. (1976). The human startle reaction: Mechanisms of modification by background acoustic stimulation (Doctoral dissertation, University of Wisconsin-Madison, 1975). *Dissertations Abstracts International, 36*, 6419B.

Ross, L. E. (1961). Conditioned fear as a function of CS-UCS and probe stimulus intervals. *Journal of Experimental Psychology, 61*, 265–273.

Schneirla, T. C. (1959). An evolutionary and developmental theory of biphasic processes underlying approach and withdrawal. *Nebraska Symposium on Motivation: 1959* (pp. 1–42). Lincoln: University of Nebraska Press.

Sechenov, I. M. (1965). *Reflexes of the brain* (S. Belsky, Trans.). Cambridge, MA: M.I.T. Press. (Original work published 1863).

Shaver, P., Schwartz, J., Kirson, D., & O'Connor, C. (1987). Emotion knowledge: Further exploration of a prototype approach. *Journal of Personality and Social Psychology, 52*, 1061–1086.

Simons, R. F., & Zelson, M. F. (1985). Engaging visual stimuli and reflex blink modification. *Psychophysiology, 22*, 44–49.

Spence, K. W., & Runquist, W. N. (1958). Temporal effects of conditioned fear on the eyelid reflex. *Journal of Experimental Psychology, 55*, 613–616.

Tellegen, A. (1985). Structures of mood and personality and their relevance to assessing anxiety, with an emphasis on self-report. In A. H. Tuma & J. D. Maser (Eds.), *Anxiety and the anxiety disorders* (pp. 681–706). Hillsdale, NJ: Erlbaum.

Woodworth, R. S., & Schlosberg, H. (1956). *Experimental psychology.* New York: Holt.

Reflexes as Probes for Studying Cognitive Processes

Jean Requin and Michel Bonnet*

Summary

Differences in the organizing principles of the neural pathways responsible for the blink and limb reflexes make the former more suitable for studying attentional modulation of sensory processes and the latter more suitable for studying preparatory modulation of motor processes. Such a distinction is confirmed by an overview of the experimental data currently available, in which both kinds of reflex responses were used as probes for investigating cognitive processes. Moreover, as emphasized by the "synergistic" theory of emotion developed by Peter Lang, reflex responses cannot be considered as "neutral" probes with respect to the cognitive processes investigated:predictions from this theory closely depend upon the functional relationships between the mechanisms underlying the blink reflex and those associated with the behavioral expression of emotional processes. Considering the differences in the behavioral function of the blink and limb reflexes, one might thus expect opposite effects of emotional valence upon either reflex response. Although the results of a preliminary experiment using limb reflexes did not clearly confirm this prediction, it must be stressed, however, that, by diversifying the functional types of reflexes used as probes for studying cognitive processes, one may undoubtedly get a deeper insight in the understanding of these processes.

Key words: emotion, attention, motor preparation, blink reflex, stretch reflex

Introduction

Reflex movements may be defined as "stereotyped and previsible responses to triggering stimuli, as if the latter reflect on the body periphery in the form of motor outputs with the stringency of a physical law" (Morin, 1971). The innate and unavoidable features as well as the obvious finality of reflexes do not imply, however, that reflex responses have no degree of freedom with respect to their triggering cause. Parameters, such as latency and/or amplitude of these obligatory responses show some variability which expresses changes in the state of activity, or reactivity, of the neural structures included in the reflex pathways. Pro-vided that these changes may be related to well-controlled experimental factors, reflexes may then be considered as tools opening "a window in the central nervous system" (Brunia and Boelhouver, 1988). In such a perspective, the structural organization of reflex pathways, as shown by anatomical and neurophysiological studies, has been exploited to use reflexes as probes to localize changes in activity of neural structures associated with cognitive processes (see, for example, Hackley and Graham, 1991; Requin et al., 1991). The first aim of this paper is to draw some methodological implications for the study of sensory attentional and motor

* Cognitive Neuroscience Laboratory, CNRS, 31, Chemin Joseph-Aiguier, 13402 Marseille Cedex 9, France

preparatory processes from a comparison of the structural organizations of the blink reflex and of the limb reflexes. However, both kinds of reflexes result from activating neural pathways whose structural organization determine the functional features and, therefore, the behavioral significance of the reflex responses. Consequently, it is likely that the basic methodological principle that a probe must not "interfere with what it is designed to measure (Bohlin et al., 1981) is often more or less violated. Furthermore, such an interference between the probe and the psychological process under investigation may have important implications for modelling this process. The "motor" theory

of emotion developed by Lang must be considered as a privileged example is this way. The theory predicts that the effect of any affective state on the features of a reflex response depends upon the functional "proximity," i. e. the common behavioral meaning, of the "action disposition" which is associated with this affective state and of the reflex response. Data collected by using the blink reflex has already provided strong support for the theory. The second aim of this paper is to present arguments and preliminary data suggesting that the use of reflexes functionally different from the blink reflex, e. g. limb reflexes, could add supplementary evidence for the Lang theory of emotion.

Structural Organization of the Pathways of the Blink and Limb Reflexes

Among the large number of reflex pathways which can be activated in humans, only those whose stimulus and response parameters are unequivocally standardized and measured are currently used. The blink reflex and the limb reflexes elicited by stimulating the muscular and cutaneous afferents have been particularly well-investigated (cf. Figure 1).

The Blink Reflex

A new input in any sensory modality is able, when it reaches a sufficiently high physical intensity, to trigger a transient increase or decrease of the background tonic muscular activity associated with the general level of alertness, the so-called "startle pattern" (Landis & Hunt, 1939).

Because of its low sensitivity to habituation, the blink reflex, or startle blink, is the most reliable element of the startle pattern. It can be elicited, in a wide range of species, by a transient increase in intensity of an auditory, visual, or mechanical stimulation, as well as of a cutaneous electrical stimulation. A number of arguments drawn from the effects of either experimental or pathological lesions indicate that the startle pattern is mediated by subcortical structures, the efferent pathway including the

reticulospinal tract. The final common pathway for the blink component is the facial nucleus which innervates the muscle orbicularis oculi. However, Asher (1965) and Buser et al. (1966) reported that in anaesthetized cats, the ablation of a cortical primary sensory area (visual, auditory or somaesthetic) reduced the amplitude of the startle response elicited by a stimulation in the corresponding sensory modality.

Acoustically Elicited Blink Reflex

A tone or white noise of high intensity triggers a blink which results from the activation of the orbicularis oculi, whose mean latency and duration are both of about 30 msec. This muscular response mainly results from the activation of a subcortical pathway including successively the auditory nerve, the cochlear nucleus, the inferior colliculus, the nucleus reticularis pontis caudalis and the facial nucleus. The specific involvement of the auditory cortex in gating the acoustically elicited blink reflex remains controversial. Patients with extensive cortical lesions exhibit an exaggerated blink reflex with less habituation (Wilkins et al., 1986). In contrast, bilateral lesions of the temporal lobe, including the auditory cortex, suppress the blink reflex (Woods et al., 1984). After having ex-

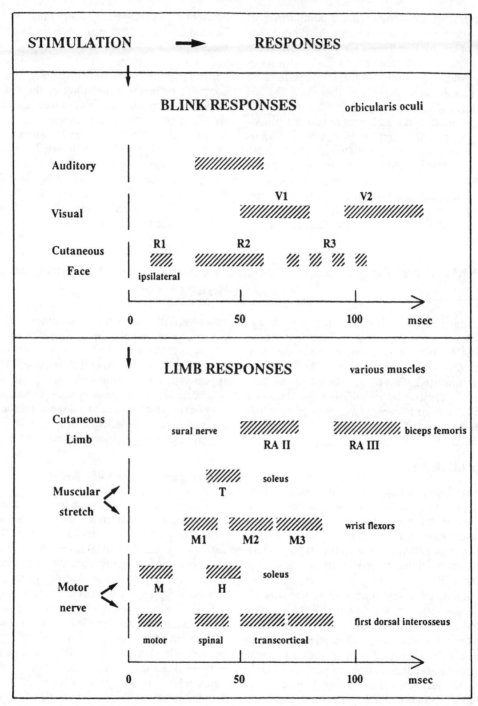

Figure 1. Onset latency of the EMG reflex responses elicited 1) in the orbicularis oculi by various stimulations of face receptors (blink reflex) and 2) in various limb muscles by various stimulations of limb receptors (limb reflexes).

amined the acoustically triggered general activation of spinal structures in a group of patients with well-circumscribed lesions in one hemisphere, Liegeois-Chauvel et al. (1989) concluded that the startle pattern could involve a cortico-cortical pathway connecting primary and associative auditory areas with frontal premotor and motor areas. Moreover, a modulatory control of the blink reflex exerted directly by the auditory cortex on the inferior colliculus cannot be excluded (Andersen et al., 1980).

The acoustically elicited blink reflex progressively decreases in amplitude when the stimulation is repeated (habituation) and is inhibited by a brief stimulus occurring shortly before the eliciting stimulus (prepulse inhibition). The reactivity of the blink reflex pathway depends upon the level of alertness. A correlation was found between the blink reflex amplitude and the frequency of the EEG recorded immediately before the occurrence of the eliciting stimulus (Gogan, 1970). However, the depressive effect of a prepulse does not depend upon the level of alertness, which suggests that the prepulse inhibition does not result from high level central processes (Silverstein, Graham & Calloway, 1980).

Visually Elicited Blink Reflex

The need to fixate gaze on a visual display, a condition which results in an active inhibition of spontaneous blinks, makes the elicitation of a blink reflex with a visual stimulus more difficult than with an auditory stimulus. However, a flash of light of high intensity triggers a blink response, the latency of which shows large variations, from 50 to 150 msec. Anthony and Graham (1983) have identified two components of the visually elicited blink response, the first of short latency (40 to 70 msec), the second of longer latency (90 to 130 msec). The threshold intensity depends on the retinal area stimulated, exposure time and color, the threshold intensity for a yellow stimulus being, for example, lower than for a white stimulus (Hopf et al., 1973). Moreover, there is no general agreement in the literature about the neural circuitry involved in the visually elicited blink, al

though most authors underlined the likelihood of a retinotectal afferent pathway.

Cutaneously Elicited Blink Reflex

A mechanical tap or an electrical stimulation applied to the periorbital area triggers on blink reflex. More precisely, a percutaneous, unilateral electrical stimulation of the supraorbital branch of the trigeminal nerve results in a sequence of EMG activity in the palpebral musculature (cf. Kugelberg, 1952). In the orbicularis oculi, the first response (R1), ipsilateral to the stimulation site, with a latency and duration of 10 msec, is followed by a second, bilateral response (R2), with a latency and duration of 30 msec (Rushworth, 1962).

When painless stimuli of 1 msec duration are used, the intensity threshold is roughly identical for R1 and R2 (Penders & Delwaide, 1973), which suggests that both responses result from the activation of fibers of same diameter in the trigeminal nerve. The first R1 response involves an oligosynaptic trigemino-facial pathway. The second R2 response involves the ipsilateral trigemino-spinal tract, the lateral reticular formation and the facial nucleus on both sides. While R2 can be elicited by a stimulation delivered anywhere on the face, R1 is triggered only by an ipsilateral stimulation of the periorbital area.

An important feature of the R2 component, as well as of the other cutaneously elicited polysynaptic reflexes, is its progressive disappearance when the stimulation is repeated. It has been shown that such an habituation may be transferred from one to another sensory modality used to evoke the blink reflex. For example, after the habituation which results from repeating an auditory or visual stimulus, the habituation of the stimulation of the trigeminal nerve is accelerated. This phenomenon suggests that a network of interneurons is likely involved, as a common relay for the trigeminal, auditory and visual afferents (Rimpel, Geyer & Hopf, 1982). In contrast, the R1 component was shown insensitive to habituation. Moreover, both blink response components are affected differently by a prepulse (Sanes & Ison, 1979), the level of alertness (Kimura & Horada, 1979) the task performance (Boelhouver & Brunia, 1977) and a variety of mental processes in humans (Anthony, 1985).

Note that a blink reflex can be elicited by cutaneous electrical stimulation of any body part, provided that this stimulation is sufficiently transient and intense. The latency of the blink response closely depends upon the site of the stimulation, i. e. upon the distance between the stimulated area and the orbicularis oculi.

The Limb Reflexes

In both animal and human neurophysiology, special emphasis has been placed on investigations of monosynaptic stretch reflexes, partly because of their relative simplicity.

Muscular Stretch Reflexes

The tendon jerk is a reflex of proprioceptive origin triggered by the activation of neuromuscular spindle receptors. The latter are sensitive to any change in muscle length. A sudden muscle stretch elicits action potentials in the sensory fibers of large diameter (group Ia) which innervate the primary sensory terminals of spindle receptors. Because spinal collaterals of these Ia fibers are directly connected to the alpha motoneurons of the stretched muscle, a volley of synchronized afferent impulses results in predominant depolarization with a single synaptic delay. This two-neuron pathway forms the structural basis of the monosynaptic stretch reflex. The latency is perfectly constant in any one subject, as it depends only on the distance between the muscle and the spinal cord and on the conduction time of the nerve fibers. Since the monosynaptic reflex response triggered by a tendon tap, the so-called T-reflex, appears as a triphasic EMG potential representing the synchronous activity of motor units, its amplitude is directly proportional to the number of motoneurons activated.

Variations in T-reflex depend upon stimulus parameters and upon changes in the excitability of the active elements of the reflex pathway. The latter include: 1) the sensitivity of the neuromuscular spindle to stretch, which is controlled by gamma motoneuronal activity; 2) the

efficiency of the primary endings of the neuromuscular spindle in transmitting afferent inputs to alpha motoneurons, which is controlled by the action of the spinal interneurons responsible for presynaptic inhibition; and 3) the excitability level of the alpha motoneurons determining reflex response amplitude, which depends upon various factors of peripheral and central origin.

The variations inherent in the application of a mechanical stimulus to the tendon can be avoided for certain muscles by using, instead, an electrical stimulus applied to the motor nerve. For instance, in humans, electrical stimulation can be used so as to transcutaneously stimulate the sciatic nerve at the level of the popliteal fossa. A weak stimulation, 1 msec duration, selectively activates the largest Ia afferent fibers; this activation in turn provokes reflex contraction of the soleus muscle. This is known as the Hoffmann or H reflex (Hoffman, 1918). An electrical stimulus of sufficient intensity can activate not only the Ia fibers but also the alpha-motor fibers. This direct motor response (the M response) can serve as a reference for evaluating both the level of recruitment for H or Achille-tendon reflex and, technically, the constancy of electrical stimulation (Desmedt, 1973).

The simultaneous comparison of soleus H and T reflexes provides insight into spindle receptor sensitivity and activity state of the gamma loop (Paillard, 1959). The controversial concept of fusorial tonus has now been confirmed by direct recordings of gamma fibers activated in awake man (Ribot et al., 1986). An oligosynaptic contribution to the human ankle jerk and the H reflex was suggested by Burke et al. (1983) who described the complex spinal mechanisms responsible for H and T responses (Van Boxtel, 1986). Proprioceptive spinal reflex studies in humans have been focused mainly on the soleus muscle, which presents, in response to electrical motor nerve stimulation, an exceptional reflex sensitivity related to some of its anatomical and functional features (Bonnet et al., 1981). The depressant effect of repetitive stimulation of the H-reflex has been widely reported, although this phenomenon has never been termed "habituation" (Hoehler et al.,

1981); no depression is observed when stimulus frequency is inferior to 0.2 Hz.

The conditioning of the H-reflex by a previous stimulation allows the study of those supraspinal structures which are known to be responsible for the effects of this conditioning. Thus, the facilitory effect exerted by a brief and sudden tone on the monosynaptic spinal reflex excitability (i.e. the audiospinal facilitation) has been investigated during the foreperiod of a reaction time task (Bonnet, Requin & Semjen, 1980). A facilitation of the reticular reactivity modulated by the force to be applied during response execution, was identified as a component of the pattern of preparation to react.

When muscles, such as the forearm flexors, are tonically activated, the sudden application of a load resulting in a muscle stretch triggers a sequence of three successive components of the EMG reflex response. On the basis of their latency, these components have been labelled by Lee and Tatton (1975) as M1 (about 20 to 40 msec), M2 (about 40 to 60 msec) and M3 (about 60 to 80 msec). The M1 component involves the well-known spinal monosynaptic reflex pathway. The neural structures which are responsible for the late components have been extensively discussed. The most common view since Milner-Brown, Stein and Lee (1975), Desmedt (1978), Wiesendanger and Miles (1982) and Cheney and Fetz (1984) is that M2 may result from an oligosynaptic transcortical pathway and that an additional transcerebellar loop possibly exists for M3. The hypothesis of a transcortical reflex loop comes from a study by Phillips (1969) on the monosynaptic corticomotoneuronal connexions that concern the distal muscles of anterior limbs in the monkey.

In primates, the input-output organization of the cortical efferent zone that controls, for instance, the flexor muscle of a digit, is such that the stretching of this muscle activates neurons in its efferent zone (Asanuma, 1975). Ascending branches of Ia fibers in the spinal cord follow two fast conduction pathways: the spinocortical pathway responsible for the M2 response or the assumed transcortical pyramidal reflex (Evarts, 1973), and the spino-cerebellar pathway, which could be the ascending limb of the long loop responsible for the M3 response.

These long ascending pathways show a high level of somatotopical organization.

The phasic functioning features of the transcortical loop originating in spindle receptors are comparable to those of the peripheral spinal loop. Being triggered by a muscle stretch that results from the overloading of an activated muscle, both reflex loops tend towards a compensatory action with respect to the muscular overload (Marsden et al., 1981).

Primary spindle afferents are modulated by a permanent presynaptic control that attenuates their transmission capacity to the motoneuron pool and possibly explains the lack of H-reflex responses in upper limb muscles at rest (Person & Kudina, 1978). However, during a voluntary sustained contraction, the H-reflex has been reliably obtained, for example, from tibialis anterior muscle and forearm muscles. Moreover, a moderate electrical stimulation of the motor nerve of a tonically active muscle triggers several synchronous EMG activities with stable latencies (Upton, McComas & Sica, 1971; Milner-Brown, Stein & Lee, 1975; Iles, 1977). After stimulation of the median nerve at the wrist, four successive responses emerge from EMG activity of the first dorsal interosseus muscle: 1) the direct motor response with a mean latency of 5 msec, corresponding to the activation of alpha fibers; 2) the spinal reflex response (H-reflex or M1) with a mean latency of 29 msec; 3) a M2-type response with a mean latency of 56 msec; 4) a M3-type response with a mean latency of 83 msec. These M3 responses are not observed in all subjects. When they occur, they must not be confounded with the voluntary response, which is triggered by stretching and has a comparable latency (Jaeger, Gottlieb & Agarwal, 1982).

Cutaneous Elicited Limb Reflexes

The flexion reflexes are defense responses to noxious stimulation of the skin. The pattern of the muscles activated in the response is in accordance with its biological function, that is the withdrawal of the limb away from the offending stimulus (Hagbarth, 1960; Kugelberg, 1962). For instance, if a train of electrical pulses of 20 msec duration and of suitable amplitude is applied to the skin of the concave part of the foot, it evokes a reflex response in m. tibialis anterior after a latency of 50 to 80 msec. The EMG discharge, that consists, most of the time, of two bursts of activity, is due to the activation of groups of afferent fibers with different conduction velocity. The first component has a low threshold and is mediated by group II afferents, which elicit a tactile sensation. It is called Reflex Afferents II (RA II, Hugon, 1973). The second component, due to the activation of high-threshold slow conducting group III afferents, which evoke pain, is called Reflex Afferents III (RA III). Several arguments suggest that both components can be organized at the spinal level. The presynaptic gating mechanisms that control the inflow of sensation and reflex activity through the posterior gray horn of the cord (Melzack & Wall, 1965) play a prominent role in modulating reflex reactivity.

The cutaneous reflexes of the biceps femoris elicited by electrical stimulation of the sural nerve have been shown and extensively studied by Hugon (1973). The cutaneous sural nerve was percutaneously stimulated with a 1 msec-duration pulse, single or in train, by skin electrodes placed below the external malleolus.

With correct positioning, subjects experienced a tactile sensation along the outer side of the foot and the small toe. Flexion reflex responses involve first the biceps femoris capitis brevis and then spread to other flexor muscles such as biceps femoris capitis longus and tibialis anterior. They finally concern the adductors when the stimulus is increased. Hugon found that the short biceps consistently yielded the best responses for threshold stimulation. The tactile reflex (RAII) is elicited by a train of stimuli with a threshold equal to 1.5 time that of tactile perception and a latency of between 40 and 60 msec. The nociceptive component (RA III) is induced by a single pulse (threshold: 3 times that of tactile perception) with a latency of 85 to 120 msec. Both components are depressed by a tactile prepulse. A progressive reduction in reflex response to repeated stimulation is a characteristic of RAII. On the other hand, RAIII progressively increases in amplitude and duration as stimulation frequency reaches .5 Hz. However, the tendinous reflex of the short biceps is not changed when it is elicited simultaneously. Finally, the subject's apprehension or anxiety can be seeen to exert a strong effect on reflex performance (Young, 1973).

Methodological Implications of the Structural Organization of Reflex Pathways for Using Reflexes as Probes

The neural pathways responsible for the reflex responses evoked by stimulating 1) the visual, auditory and cutaneous receptors of the face – i. e. those used for triggering the blink reflex – and, 2) the muscular and cutaneous receptors of the limbs – i. e. those used for triggering limb reflexes – show similarities and differences in their structural organization, which must be underlined.

A same organizing principle characterizes the anatomical circuits of the blink reflex and of the limb reflexes. First, both involved *parallel input pathways*. When the blink reflex is considered, input pathways are formed by the auditory nerve and cochlear nucleus for auditory stimuli, the trigeminal nerve and nucleus for cu-

taneous (tactile and nociceptive) stimuli, the optic nerve and tectum for visual stimuli. When limb reflexes are considered, input pathways are formed by the muscular and cutaneous (tactile and nociceptive) afferents conveyed by the spinal nerve. Second, before reaching their output pathway, both circuits can involve various central nervous structures via a series of *hierarchically-organized loops*: thalamic and, may be, cortical structures for the blink reflex, bulbomesencephalic, cortical and, may be, cerebellar structures for limb reflexes. This explains that the same sensory stimulus can evoke successive EMG responses according to the length of the nervous pathways and the number of synapses involved. Third, both circuits end with a *common output pathway*, i.e. the nucleus reticularis pontis caudalis and, then, the motor nucleus of the facial nerve for the blink reflex and the motoneuron pool of the ventral horn of the spinal cord for limb reflexes.

The main difference between the anatomical organization of the blink reflex and that of limb reflexes is that the former is unique, i.e. specific of the cephalic part of the body, whereas the latter is multiple, i.e. is replicated at different levels of the segmental organization of the spinal cord. Consequently, there is only one output pathway for the blink reflex, which controls the orbicularis oculi, while, for the limb reflexes, several output pathways controlling different limb muscles, are sequentially distributed along the spinal cord. Each of them is either selectively or preferentially involved when the stimulus is located in the same segment as the activated muscle. Note, however, that this opposition between the unique-output pathway of the blink reflex and the multiple-output pathways of limb reflexes is not entirely true. The circuits of both kinds of reflexes are not, in fact, completely independent, but interact because of cutaneous afferents, a sensory modality which is common to face and limbs. Cutaneous stimulations of both these body areas converge on the midbrain reticular formation, explaining that a stimulation of the face can evoke not only a blink reflex but also, via the reticulo spinal tract, an activation of the limb muscles (a component of the startle pattern), while stimulation of one limb can evoke not only a flexion reflex, but also a blink reflex via the motor nucleus of the facial nerve.

Similarities and differences in this structural organization of the pathways responsible for the blink and limb reflexes have methodological implications when reflexes are used as probes for the neural mechanisms associated with cognitive processes. The parallel-input, but common-output pathways of both kinds of reflexes offer, in principle, the opportunity to identify the central processes which intervene in sensory processing, as already underlined by Graham (1979; see also Hackley and Graham, 1990) for the blink reflex. The rationale of the method is that if such a central process (as, for instance, attention) is supposed to act selectively upon the sensory processing which takes place in one input pathway, the reflex response will differ whether the reflex stimulus involves the same or a different input pathway. However, the fundamental difference between exteroceptive and proprioceptive stimuli makes the blink reflex a tool much more suitable than limb reflexes for studying the neural mechanisms of cognitive processes. Visual, auditory and cutaneous stimuli, used for triggering the blink reflex, give rise to a conscious perception, while only stimulations of the cutaneous but not of the muscular receptors used for triggering limb reflexes, have access to consciousness. Such a difference makes it much more easier to use the blink reflex than limb reflexes in experiments aimed at studying the effects of manipulating cognitive factors upon sensory processing. This manipulation is expected to result not only in changes in the reactivity of reflex pathways but also in parallel changes in the performance of sensory tasks, such as detection, discrimination or judgment tasks, which require a conscious perception of stimuli. Note, however, that the conscious perception of tactile and nociceptive, cutaneous stimulations used to evoke limb flexion reflexes makes it possible to conduct such kind of experiments with limb reflexes.

In contrast to the advantage that the blink reflex presents, as compared to limb reflexes, for studying cognitive factors which act upon sensory processing, the multiple, segmentary distributed output pathways of limb reflexes, as compared to the unique output pathway of the blink reflex, offers a privileged tool for identifying cognitive processes which act selectively upon motor processing. The rationale of the method is that if such a cognitive factor (as, for instance, preparation) is supposed to act selectively upon the motor processing which takes place in one output pathway, the reflex response will differ whether the reflex stimulus activates the same or a different output pathway. This rationale is that followed when examining the effects of preparatory processes on the reactivity of spinal motor structures (cf. Brunia and Boelhouver, 1988; Requin et al., 1991; Bonnet et al., 1981). It must be underlined that the unconscious feature of the proprioceptive stimulations generally used for evoking limb reflexes does no matter and, even, is a convenient condition for studying the effects of manipulating cognitive factors supposed to act selectively upon motor processes, that can be inferred from the associated changes in the performance of a motor task, as reaction time. However, the fact that a conscious cutaneous stimulation is unavoidably associated with a tendon tap or an electrical stimulation of a motor nerve makes such a convenient condition difficult to be currently realized; it is, therefore, always necessary to control that cognitive factors acting upon sensory processing, such as attending to reflex stimuli, do not interfere with the cognitive factors supposed to selectively affect motor processing. Note, finally, that the privileged conditions which limb reflexes offer for studying cognitive processes acting upon motor processes do not mean that such a study is totally excluded by using the blink reflex. It is still possible to compare (cf. for example, Brunia and Boelhouwer, 1988) the blink reflex when cognitive processes are supposed to act either upon the blink reflex output pathway, as when a voluntary blink response must be performed, or upon a limb reflex output pathway, as when a limb movement must be performed.

Finally, the hierarchical organization of reflex loop superimposed upon the basic reflex arc, which is a common feature of both blink and limb reflex pathways, makes it possible to locate precisely the modulatory effect of cognitive processes in neural structures. From a differential effect of a cognitive factor on the successive reflex responses evoked by a same stimulus, inferences can be drawn on the target structure upon which this factor acts. If, for example, an early R1 response does not change but a later R2 response does, one could infer that the site of the effect responsible for this change is a structure which is included in the reflex pathway involved by R2. Note that, because of this superimposition of reflex loops, the reverse pattern of results, i.e. R2 does not change but R1 does, is much more unlikely. This is because the target structures, supposed to be located in the reflex pathways responsible for R1, are, in principle, necessarily included also in the reflex pathways responsible for R2. Some data, however, have been found which violate this one-way "inclusion law," due to exceptions in this basic looping organization of reflex pathways. Moreover, a common modulation of both R1 and R2 under the effect of a cognitive factor may not be a necessary consequence of the inclusion law, but may indicate that both the structures included in R1 and R2 reflex pathways are targets for the modulating effect. The responsability for this effect of the neural structures included in R1 and R2 circuits respectively, can be evaluated, as already underlined (cf. Requin et al., 1991), by applying some kind of substractive method to the changes observed in R1 and R2: while changes in R1 are an index of the contribution of the neural structures included in the R1 reflex pathways, changes in the difference R2-R1 may be viewed as an index of the specific contribution of the neural structures included in the R2 reflex pathways to the changes observed in R2.

Basic Findings of Reflex Studies of Attentional and Preparatory Processes

The methodological implications of the similarities and differences in the organization of the neural pathways activated by the blink and limb reflexes may be summarized as follows: the blink reflex appears as a privileged tool for investigating the cognitive processes which modulate differentially sensory processes, while the limb reflexes appear more suitable for studying cognitive processes which modulate differentially motor processes. Moreover, for both blink and limb reflexes, the superimposition of reflex loops involving hierarchically-organized neural structures makes it possible to determine the locus of these modulatory effects by comparing the changes in the features of the successive reflex responses evoked by the same stimulus. These implications may be illustrated by reviewing briefly two sets of experimental data devoted to the study of selective attention on one hand, and of selective preparation on the other. The common paradigm of both these kinds of experiments is to ask subjects to pay attention to a particular stimulus (or to prepare for a particular response) and to compare the features (latency or amplitude) of the same reflex response when triggered by a stimulus either "similar" to, or "different" from that which the subject is waiting for (or to compare the features of a reflex response, elicited by the same stimulus, either "similar" to, or "different" from the response which the subject prepares for). The notions of "similarity" and "difference" between stimuli refer to the subdivision of the sensory sphere into sensory modalities, or "channels": two stimuli may be different either because they involve different sensory modalities – in such case one talks about "between-sensory channels" difference – or because they involve the same sensory modality but differ in one or several feature(s) (as intensity or frequency) – in such case one talks about "within-sensory channel" differences. In the same way, the notions of "similarity" and "difference" between responses may be used in reference to the subdivision of the motor system into muscles, or "response channels": two responses may be different either because they result from the activation of different muscles – in such case one talks about "between-response channels" differences – or because they result from activating a same muscle but with different feature(s) (as force or muscle structuring) – in such case one talks about "within-response channel" differences.

Between-Sensory Channels, Selective Attentional Set

The experiment conducted by Anthony and Graham (1985; see also Hackley and Graham, 1985) may be considered as prototypical for the use of the blink reflex as a probe for identifying attentional processes acting differently between sensory channels. Either visual or auditory stimuli were presented to the subjects for 5 sec. They were either interesting and attention-engaging stimuli, when slides of human faces or melody segments were presented, or dull and not attention-engaging, when blank slides or tones of fixed frequency were presented. At the end of stimulus presentation a blink reflex was either visually or acoustically elicited. Data showed that the amplitude of the EMG reflex response was increased when the sensory modalities of the stimulus eliciting the blink and of the attention-engaging foreground stimulus match, in reference to conditions in which these sensory modalities mismatch. These results therefore support the hypothesis that attentional set selectively facilitates stimulus processing in a particular sensory modality. Moreover, from the anatomical organization of the blink reflex pathways, one can infer that such an attentional facilitation acts before the convergence of visual and auditory afferents on the midbrain reticular formation, i.e. may be at the level of the first relay of sensory pathways.

As expected, no experiment dealing with the problem of a between-sensory channels bias in attentional set has been performed using limb reflexes as probes. While the unconscious feature of stimulations of muscular receptors most likely precludes the design of a task in which subjects would be required to pay attention to these stimulations, the triggering of limb reflexes by conscious, cutaneous stimuli make such investigations in principle possible. For example, a differential change in the magnitude of the tactile (RA II) and nociceptive (RA III) components of the cutaneously elicited limb reflexes could be hypothetized when subjects are asked to pay attention – by using, for instance, a judgment task – either to the tactile feature or to the painful feature of the reflex stimulus. As far as we know, such an experiment has never been performed, although data collected in a study where cutaneously elicited limb reflexes during the foreperiod of a RT task suggested such a differential effect of selective attentional set on the two reflex response components (cf. Bonnet and Requin, 1972). However, some data obtained in animal experiments are indirectly relevant for an attentional control of cutaneous reflex pathways (cf. Maitte et al., 1985; Ciancia et al., 1988). In an RT task, cats were required to pay attention to either a vibration of the foot or a tone, as a response signal for releasing foot pressure. Changes in the sensory potential evoked in the medial lemniscus, thalamus and association cortex by a cutaneous, electrical stimulation of the same foot were used as probes. Results showed that the evoked potentials recorded in the thalamus and cortex were significantly depressed when animals paid attention to the tactile stimulation but not when they paid attention to the tone. However, the absence of this differential effect at the level of the medial lemniscus suggested that the reactivity of the afferent pathways of the cutaneously elicited limb reflexes was probably not changed when attention was directed toward the tactile stimulus.

Within-Sensory Channel, Selective Attentional Set

The use of the blink reflex as a probe for evidencing an attentional bias in differently processing the features of a sensory event in the same modality is especially well-illustrated by a series of experiments conducted by Hackley and Graham (1987; see also Hackley et al., 1987). After a visual warning signal, a loud tone was randomly presented to the left ear, the right ear or both ears (thus perceived at the midline) of subjects. In order to easily discriminate the location, the three tones also differed in pitch. Subjects had to judge the tone duration at one location-pitch and to ignore the others, this to-be-attended location-pitch being varied across blocks of trials. The latency of the blink EMG response to the tone was significantly reduced when attention was directed toward the location-pitch of the reflex-eliciting tone, as compared to when attention was directed away. In a second experiment, the property of the blink reflex to be inhibited by a "prepulse" stimulus delivered immediately before the reflex-eliciting stimulus was used, with the same design as in the first experiment. The blink reflex was elicited by a tactile, airpuff stimulus on the orbital region 100 msec after the differently located-pitched tone was presented to the subjects. The inhibitory effect of the tone on the cutaneously elicited blink reflex was found to be greater when tone duration had to be judged than when the tone was to be ignored. These data therefore support the hypothesis of a "within-sensory channel" selective attentional set, i.e. that attention can facilitate the processing of a particular stimulus feature, such as the location and/or pitch of an auditory stimulus, within the same sensory modality. Once again, the structural organization of the afferent pathways of the blink reflex makes the hypothesis of an "early" anatomical location of this attentional bias likely.

For similar reasons to these invoked when the "between-sensory channels" attentional bias was considered, it is not surprising that, as far as we know, no data based upon the limb reflex methodology has demonstrated a "within-sensory channel" selective attentional set. Note, again, that such a study would, in principle, be possible using cutaneously elicited limb reflexes. Moreover, the conditioning of the blink reflex by a "prepulse" may be a possible way to modulate by a prior stimulus the reflex responses triggered by a stimulation of the muscular afferents. It is well-known that the amplitude of the H and T reflexes is enhanced by presenting, about 100 msec before the reflex pathway is activated, a loud tone or a flash of high intensity (cf. Bonnet et al., 1981). Supposing, for example, that subjects have to pay attention to either a visual or an auditory task (or a task which involves to process either a high or a low pitch tone), one may hypothesize that any attentional facilitation of performing the task in a particular sensory modality (or in a particular band frequency...) must result in a larger increase of the H or T reflex amplitude when following a conditioning stimulus in the same sensory modality (or in the same band frequency...), than in a different sensory modality (or in a different band frequency). However, no experiment based on these principles, which could provide data interpretable in the same way as Hackley and Graham's data, has been performed.

Between-Response Channels, Selective Preparatory Set

The use of limb reflexes as probes of selective preparatory set acting on the output pathways of the motor system is well-documented (see Bonnet et al., 1981; Brunia and Boelhouver, 1988; Requin et al., 1991, for reviews). Prototypical experiments aimed at demonstrating a "between-response channels" preparatory bias may be found in Requin (1969; see also Requin et al., 1977). Spinal H and T reflexes were bilaterally elicited in the soleus muscles during the foreperiod of a RT task in which subjects had to perform either a right or a left foot pressure, a movement which mainly involved an activation of the soleus muscle. It was found repeatedly that the magnitude of the H and T reflex evoked at the end of the foreperiod was relatively depressed when elicited in the muscle to be involved in movement performance, as compared with reflexes elicited in the contralateral, non involved muscle. Whatever the functional interpretation and physiological mechanism of this phenomenon, data thus showed that intending to perform a movement in a particular "response channel" resulted in a selective modulation of the reactivity of the reflex output pathways in this particular "response channel."

Experiments based on the same principles and conducted with a similar design have been done with the blink reflex as a probe of a selective "between-response channels" preparatory bias (Boelhouver, 1982; see also Brunia and Boelhouver, 1988). In a simple RT-task, subjects had to perform either a voluntary blink or a button push with both hands in response to a tone which ended a 3-sec foreperiod. Blink reflexes were elicited by an electrical stimulation of the supra-orbital branch of the trigeminal nerve at various, randomly distributed times during the foreperiod. Neither the amplitude of the short-latency (R1) nor that of the long-latency (R2) components of the blink reflex significantly differed between response conditions. There is therefore no experimental evidence for concluding that preparing for a voluntary blink selectively changes the reactivity of the output pathways of the blink reflex.

Within-Response Channel, Selective Preparatory Set

The rationale of the experiments which aim to demonstrate the selectivity of preparatory set between different response channels has been also applied when the features of the response performed within the same response channel, i.e. by a particular muscle, were considered. Relevant data in this way may be found, for example, in Bonnet (1983); see also Bonnet et al. (1991). Subjects were required to perform, in a simple-RT procedure, either a flexion or an extension of the wrist, thus moving a handle to point at either a left-located or a right-located target. Limb reflexes were elicited, at various, unpredictable times during the foreperiod, by stretching either the forearm extensor or forearm flexor muscles, so that the amplitude of the three components of the EMG reflex response might be compared when the stretched muscle was involved either as an agonist or as an antagonist in movement performance. Data showed that the amplitude of the latest (M3) component of the muscular reflex was enhanced when the stretched muscle was announced as to be activated during movement performance, and was depressed when the muscle was announced as to be relaxed during movement performance. These data thus supported the hypothesis of a motor preparatory bias modulating differently the output pathways of the reflexes elicited by stimulating muscular afferents, according to the role of the muscle in a forthcoming motor action. However, both the earlier (M1 and M2) components of the stretch reflex did not show such a differential change in amplitude. This finding confirmed previous data collected with the H and T reflexes (Requin et al., 1977), suggesting, therefore, that the selective preparatory set for response features, i.e. within a particular response channel did not act at a spinal, but at a more central level of reflex pathways (cf. Requin et al., 1991).

It is not surprising that data is not available for such a within-response channel selective preparatory set with blink reflex. The fact that blinks are not usually done under voluntary control makes it difficult to manipulate the biomechanical features, as for example force or direction (up and down), of such a mainly automatic movement. Moreover, the negative results obtained when looking for a selective motor preparation of the blink output pathways, as compared with an alternative limb response, makes the demonstration of a motor preparatory set selective for one of the parameters of the voluntary blink response quite unlikely.

Theoretical Implications of the Functional Organization of Reflex Pathways in the Understanding of Cognitive Processes

The differences in the organizing principles of the pathways responsible for the blink and limb reflexes, which seem to be more quantitative than clear-cut, not only have consequences on the probe methodology when the site of action of modulatory processes in neural structures is considered. Such structural differences are obviously related closely to functional, behaviorally significant differences between both types of reflexes, which may be summarized as follows. Although the functional meaning of the blink reflex remains a controversial question (cf. Graham, 1979), the blink reflex participates in the startle reflex 1) which is triggered by aggressive sensory inputs in both the sensory modalities (auditory and visual) that mainly provide information about the extrapersonal space, 2) which interrupts the ongoing actions and suspends any new action until sensory inputs will be analyzed for re-orienting behavior, and, 3) which transiently protects processing systems against a new unexpected aggression. Briefly, the blink reflex may be thus defined as part of a "negative-closing" mechanism regarding extraneously driven events. In contrast – and this conception may be also challenged – limb reflexes may be viewed as resulting from a mechanism 1) which is triggered by non aggressive inputs mainly in the sensory modality (muscular receptors) that provide information about the body space, 2) which assist ongoing actions, and 3) which prepare for subsequent actions by making motor systems available for processing new outputs. Briefly, limb reflexes may thus be defined as "positive-opening" mechanisms regarding intraneously driven events. Note, once again, that cutaneously elicited reflexes participate in both these functionally different reflex modes, on one hand in the "negative-closing" mode, through the widely distributed muscular activation of the startle reflex as well as withdrawal, avoiding reflexes, on the other hand in the "positive-opening" mode, through the collaboration of cutaneous reflexes in the planning and assistance of motor actions.

These functional, behaviorally significant differences between the blink and limb reflexes have a fundamental consequence when reflexes are used as probes for studying cognitive processes. Briefly, it is questionable to consider the reflex probe as "neutral" relative to these processes. More likely and most often, the probe and processes investigated interfere, so that the interpretation of experimental data will depend closely upon the functional relationships between the mechanisms underlying the reflex responses used as probes and these mechanisms supposed to be associated with the behavioral expression of cognitive processes. However, such an interference or interaction must not be viewed as an artifact, requiring supplementary technical refinements, but rather as the consequence of the fundamental unitary organization of behavior and its neural substrate. It is in this perspective that must be viewed the theory of emotion developed by Lang (cf. Lang et al., 1990), which explicitly bears upon, and exploited the theoretical and methodological implications of such an integrative psychophysiological concept. Emotions are defined as "action dispositions," or covert, even implicit, response sets, that drive behavioral activities according to a binary, "appetitive-aversive" dimension. At the core of the theory is the concept that emotional states "are primitively associated with either a behavioral set favoring *approach, attachment and consummatory behavior,* or alternatively, a set disposing the organism to *avoidance, escape and defense.* It is presumed that the efferent system as a whole is tuned according to the current status of this central affect-motivational organization" (Lang et al., 1990).

The predictions drawn from this "motor" theory bear upon the way – agonistic vs antagonistic – in which the action disposition associated with the emotional state and the functional significance of the blink reflex interplay. The basically "aversive response" meaning of the blink would mismatch the "positive, approach response disposition" triggered by positively valent stimuli, resulting in an inhibitory effect and would match" the negative, avoidance response disposition" triggered by negatively valent stimuli," thus resulting in one enhancement effect. A large number of experiments conducted by Lang and his group (cf. Lang et al., 1990) supported these predictions. In the paradigm used, a set of slides of negative, neutral or positive emotional content, which were rated on emotional valence and arousal, are presented randomly, each during a 6 sec exposure time. Negatively valent slides show mutilations, spiders, snakes ... etc, neutral slides show usual objects and positively valent slides show opposite-sex nudes, cuddly animals, flowers ... etc. A typical set of results is shown in Figure 2, where the magnitude of the EMG response of the orbicularis oculi is expressed as a function of slide emotional valence. In reference to neutral slides, the blink reflex magnitude increases for negatively valent slides and decreases for positively valent slides, in agreement with the predictions of the theory.

From the comparison of the functional features and behavioral meaning of the blink and limb reflexes, one may propose that the blink reflex probe methodology could be usefully complemented by using limb reflexes for investigating response disposition, i. e. covert motor set, associated with emotional processes. According to the synergistic theory of Lang, it is reasonable to expect that cutaneously-elicited limb reflexes, insofar as they share the "negative, closing" functional meaning that charac-

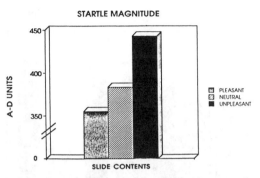

Figure 2. Magnitude (arbitrary units) of the acoustically elicited blink EMG response as a function of slide content emotional valence (from Lang, Bradley and Cuthbert, 1990).

terizes the blink reflex, would show a similar differential effect according to affective valence of foreground stimuli. In contrast, limb reflexes elicited by activating muscular afferents, insofar as they express a "positive, opening" functional significance, must show the reverse differential effect: positively valent foreground stimuli must be associated with an activation and negatively valent stimuli with an inhibition of reflex pathways.

In a pilot experiment, Bradley et al. (unpublished results) have begun to examine such a prediction using the muscular reflex elicited by a tendon tap (T reflex). With an experimental design and a set of visual stimuli similar to that used in previous experiments with the blink reflex, T reflexes were evoked bilaterally in soleus muscles, 500 msec, 2 sec or 4 sec after the onset of each 5-sec slide presentation. Preliminary data collected on 10 subjects are shown in Figure 3. The mean amplitude of the reflex EMG response, data recorded in both legs being pooled, is expressed separately for the three slide affective valences, as a function of the time of the reflex eliciting stimulus during slide presentation. Results were quite clear. When probe reflexes were triggered 500 msec after the onset of slide presentation, there was a general increase in reflex amplitude which did not significantly differ according to the slide content valence. When the probe was triggered either 2 sec or 4 sec after the onset of slide pre-

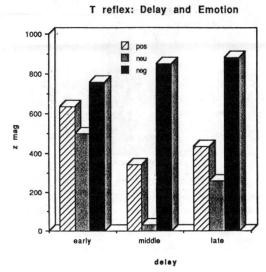

Figure 3. Amplitude of the T reflexes elicited 500 msec (early), 2 sec (middle) or 4 sec (late) after the onset of slide presentation, as a function of slide content emotional valence. Reflex amplitude is expressed in Z score with reference to the distribution of reflexes elicited between slide presentation (Bradley, Bonnet, Lang and Requin, unpublished results).

sentation, the increase in reflex amplitude was larger for both pleasant and unpleasant slides than for neutral slides, but significantly larger for unpleasant than for pleasant slides.

These results may be interpreted by postulating a combination of the effects of two, unspecific and specific factors, arousal and emotional valence. The former would explain that the reactivity of reflex pathways was increased by any kind of emotional stimulus, the latter would explain that such an increase in reactivity was larger for negatively than for positively valent slide content. This specific emotional valence effect thus does not support the predictions derived from Lang's "synergistic" theory, i.e. a "match" between the approach, appetitive action disposition, or motor set associated with pleasant stimuli and the

"positive, opening" functional significance of muscular reflexes. In contrast, the results are, in this respect, very similar to those obtained using the blink reflex and, therefore, lead to a similar interpretation. Taking into account – as already underlined – the unavoidable mixture of cutaneous and muscular afferent activations when a tendon tap and, a fortiori, a slightly painful electrical stimulation were used for eliciting T and H reflexes, respectively, one may suggest that these preliminary data reflect a mixture of two emotionally specific effects. The first would result from the "mismatch" between the "positive" functional significance of muscular reflexes and the action disposition set up by the unpleasant slides. The second effect would result from the "mismatch" between the "negative" functional significance of cutaneously elicited reflexes and the action disposition set up by the pleasant slides. Provided 1) that this second effect is larger than the first one, and 2) that mismatches result in larger effects than matches (as is suggested by the blink reflex data shown in Figure 2), results would thus remain entirely understandable in the framework of Lang's theory, without calling upon some arousal effect which was discarded in blink reflex studies.

Although data collected in this preliminary experiment do not deserve further speculation, yet need further investigations, it must be stressed that, by diversifying the functional types of reflexes used as probes for studying cognitive processes, one may undoubtedly expect a substantial benefit in the understanding of these processes. Conversely, the modelling of cognitive processes in a psychophysiological perspective may likely provide a deeper insight into the functional, behavioral significance of the physiological mechanisms underlying the activation of reflex pathways. The emotion theory of Lang offers, in this two-way perspective, a privileged example of such a cross-fertilization between the cognitive and neuroscience approaches of behavior.

References

Andersen, R.A., Knight, P.L. & Merzenich, M.M. (1980). The thalamocortical and corticothalamic connections of AI, AII and the anterior auditory field (AAF) in the cat: evidence for two largely segregated systems of connections. *Journal of Comparative Neurology, 194*, 663–701.

Anthony, B.J. (1985). In the blink of an eye: Implications of reflex modification for information processing. In P.J. Ackles, J.R. Jennings & M.G.H. Coles (Eds.), *Advances in Psychophysiology, Vol. 1*. Greenwich, CT: JAI Press Inc.

Anthony, B.J. & Graham, F.K. (1983). Evidence for sensory-selective set in young infants. *Science, 220*, 742–744.

Anthony, B.J. & Graham, F.K. (1985). Blink reflex modification by selective attention: Evidence for the modulation of "automatic" processing. *Biological Psychology, 20*, 43–59.

Asanuma, H. (1975). Recent developments in the study of the columnar arrangement of nervous within the motor cortex. *Physiological Review, 55*, 143–156.

Ascher, P. (1965). La réaction de sursaut du chat anesthésié au chloralose. *Thèse de Doctorat ès Sciences*. Paris.

Boelhouver, A.J.W. (1982). Blink reflexes and preparation. *Biological Psychology, 14*, 277–285.

Bohlin, G., Graham, F.K., Silverstein, L.D. & Hackley, S.A. (1981). Cardiac orienting and startle blink modification in novel and signal situations. *Psychophysiology, 18*, 603–611.

Bonnet, M. (1983). Anticipatory changes of long latency stretch responses during preparation for directional hand movements. *Brain Research, 280*, 51–62.

Bonnet, M. & Requin, J. (1972). Variations des réflexes polysynaptiques cutanés au cours de la période préparatoire au TR simple chez l'homme. *Psychologie Française, 17*, 101–112.

Bonnet, M., Requin, J., & Semjen, A. (1980). Intervention d'influences réticulaires dans une réorganisation des structures motrices spinales pendant la préparation au mouvement. In J. Requin (Ed.), *Anticipation et Comportement*. Paris: Editions du CNRS, 367–381.

Bonnet, M., Requin, J., & Semjen, A. (1981). Human reflexology and motor preparation. In D. Miller (Ed.), *Exercise and Sport Sciences Reviews, 9*. Philadelphia: Franklin Institute Press, 119–157.

Bonnet, M., Requin, J., & Stelmach, G.E. (1991). Changes in electromyographic responses to muscle stretch, related to the programming of movement spatial parameters. *EEG and Clinical Neurophysiology, 81*, 135–151.

Brunia, C.H.M. & Boelhouwer, A.J.W. (1988). Reflexes as a tool: a window in the central nervous system. *Advances in Psychophysiology, 3*, 1–67.

Burke, D., Gandevia, S.C. & McKeon, B. (1984). Monosynaptic and oligosynaptic contributions to human ankle jerk and H-reflex. *Journal of Neurophysiology, 52*, 435–448.

Buser, P., Saint Laurent, J. & Menini, C. (1966). Intervention du colliculus inférieur dans l'élaboration et le contrôle cortical spécifique des décharges cloniques au son chez le chat sous chloralose. *Experimental Brain Research, 1*, 102–126.

Cheney, P.D., & Fetz, E.E. (1984). Corticomotoneuronal cells contribute to long-latency stretch reflexes in the rhesus monkey. *Journal of Physiology (London), 349*, 249–272.

Ciancia, F., Maitte, M., Honoré, J., Lecoutre, B. & Coquery, J.M. (1988). Orientation of attention and sensory gating: an evoked potential and RT study in the cat. *Experimental Neurology, 100*, 274–287.

Desmedt, J.E. (1973). A discussion of the methodology of the triceps surae T and H reflexes. In J.E. Desmedt (Ed.), *New developments in electromyography and clinical neurophysiology*. Basel: Karger, 773–780.

Desmedt, J.E. (Ed.) (1978). Cerebral motor control in man: long loop mechanisms. *Progress in Clinical Neurophysiology, 4*, 338 p.

Evarts, E.V. (1973). Motor cortex reflexes associated with learned movements. *Science, 179*, 501–503.

Gogan, P. (1970). The startle and orienting reactions in man. Study of their characteristics and habituation. *Brain Research, 18*, 117–135.

Graham, F.K. (1979). Distinguishing among orienting, defense, and startle reflexes. In H.D. Kimmel, E.H. Van Olst & J.F. Orlebeke (Eds.), *The orienting reflex in humans*. Hillsdale, NJ: Erlbaum, 137–167.

Hackley, S.A. & Graham, F.K. (1983). Early selective attention effects on cutaneous and acoustic blink reflexes. *Physiological Psychology, 11*, 235–242.

Hackley, S.A. & Graham, F.K. (1987). Effects of attending selectively to the spatial position of reflex-eliciting and reflex-modulating stimuli. *Journal of Experimental Psychology: HPP, 13*, 411–424.

Hackley, S.A. & Graham, F.K. (1991). Passive and active attention to input: active attention and localized, selective analysis. In J.R. Jennings & M.G.H. Coles (Eds.), *Handbook of cognitive psy-*

chophysiology: Central and autonomic nervous system approaches (299–356). Chichester: Wiley.

Hackley, S.A., Woldorff, M. & Hillyard, S.A. (1987). Combined use of microreflexes and event-related brain potentials as measures of auditory selective attention. *Psychophysiology, 24*, 632–647.

Hagbarth, K.E. (1960). Spinal withdrawal reflex in the human lower limbs. *Journal of Neurology, Neurosurgery and Psychiatry, 23*, 222–227.

Hoehler, F.K., McCann, M.A. & Bernick, K.D. (1981). Habituation of the Hoffmann reflex. *Brain Research, 220*, 299–307.

Hoffmannn, P. (1918). Uber die Beziehungen der Sehnenreflexe zur Willkürlichen Bewegungen und zur Tonus. *Zeitschrift für Biologie, 68*, 351–370.

Hopf, H.C., Bier, J., Brener, B. & Scheerer, W. (1973). The blink reflex induced by photic stimulation. In J.E. Desmedt (Ed.), *New developments in electromyography and clinical neurophysiology, 3*, 666–672.

Hugon, M. (1973). Exteroceptive reflexes to stimulation of the sural nerve in normal man. In J.E. Desmedt (Ed.), *New developments in electromyography and clinical neurophysiology, 3*, 713–729.

Iles, J.F. (1977). Responses in human pretibial muscles to sudden stretch and to nerve stimulation. *Experimental Brain Research, 30*, 451–470.

Jaeger, R.J., Gottlieb, G.L. & Agarwal, G.C. (1982). Myoelectric responses at flexors and extensors of human wrist to step torque perturbations. *Journal of Neurophysiology, 48*, 388–402.

Kimura, J. & Harada, O. (1976). Recovery curves of the blink reflex during wakefulness and sleep. *Journal of Neurology, 213*, 189–198.

Kugelberg, E. (1952). Facial reflexes. *Brain, 75*, 385–396.

Kugelberg, E. (1962). Polysynaptic reflexes of clinical importance. *EEG and Clinical Neurophysiology, suppl. 22*, 103–111.

Landis, C. & Hunt, W.A. (1939). *The startle pattern.* New York: Farrar and Rinehart.

Lang, P.J., Bradley, M.M. & Cuthbert, B.N. (1990). Emotion, attention, and the startle reflex. *Psychological Review, 97*, 377–395.

Lee, R.G. & Tatton, W.G. (1975). Motor responses to sudden limb displacements in primates with specific CNS lesions and in human patients with motor system disorders. *Canadian Journal of Neurological Sciences, 2*, 285–293.

Liégeois-Chauvel, C., Morin, C., Musolino, A., Bancaud, J. & Chauvel, P. (1989). Evidence for a contribution of the auditory cortex to audiospinal facilitation in man. *Brain, 112*, 375–391.

Maitte, M., Ciancia, F. & Coquery, J.M. (1985). Modulation chez le chat des potentiels évoqués cutanés

au cours de la période préparatoire à un temps de réaction. *Physiology and Behavior, 34*, 665–669.

Marsden, C.D., Merton, P.A., Morton, H.B., Rothwell, J.C. & Traub, M.M. (1981). Reliability and efficacy of the long-latency stretch reflex in the human thumb. *Journal of Physiology, 316*, 47–60.

Melzack, R. & Wall, P.D. (1965). Pain mechanisms, a new theory. *Science, 150*, 971–979.

Milner-Brown, H.S., Stein, R.B. & Lee, R.G. (1975). Synchronization of human motor units: possible roles of exercise and supraspinal reflexes. *EEG and Clinical Neurophysiology, 38*, 245–254.

Morin, G. (1971). *Physiologie du système nerveux central.* Paris: Masson, 350 p.

Paillard, J. (1959). Functional organization of afferent innervation of muscle studied in man by monosynaptic testing. *American Journal of Physical Medicine, 38*, 239–247.

Penders, C.A. & Delwaide, P.J. (1973). Physiologic approach to the human blink reflex. In J.E. Desmedt (Ed.), *New developments in electromyography and clinical neurophysiology 3*, 649–657.

Person, R.S. & Kudina, L.P. (1978). On "tuning" mechanism of segmentary apparatus before voluntary movement. *Neurophysiologi (Kiev), 10*, 322–325.

Phillips, C.G. (1969). Motor apparatus of the baboon's hand. *Proceedings of the Royal Society, London, ser. B 173*, 141–174.

Requin, J., Bonnet, M. & Semjen, A. (1977). Is there a specificity in the supraspinal control of motor structures during preparation ? In S. Dornic (Ed.), *Attention and Performance VI.* Hillsdale, NJ: Erlbaum, 139–174.

Requin, J., Brener, J. & Ring, C. (1991). Preparation for action. In J.R. Jennings & M.G.H. Coles (Eds.), *Handbook of cognitive psychophysiology: Central and autonomic nervous system approaches* (357–448). Chichester: Wiley.

Ribot, E., Roll, J.P. & Vedel, J.P. (1986). Efferent discharges recorded from single skeletomotor and fusimotor fibres in man. *Journal of Physiology, 375*, 251–268.

Rimpel, J., Geyer, D. & Hopf, H.C. (1982). Changes in the blink responses to combined trigeminal, acoustic, and visual repetitive stimulation, studied in the human subject. *EEG and Clinical Neurophysiology, 54*, 552–560.

Rushworth, G. (1962). Observations on blink reflexes. *Journal of Neurology, Neurosurgery and Psychiatry, 25*, 93–108.

Sanes, J.N. & Ison, J.R. (1979). Conditioning auditory stimuli and the cutaneous eyeblink reflex in humans: differential effects according to oligosynaptic or polysynaptic central pathways. *EEG and Clinical Neurophysiology, 47*, 546–555.

Silverstein, L.D., Graham, F.K. & Callaway, J.M. (1980). Preconditioning and excitability of the human orbicularis oculi reflex as a function of state. *EEG and Clinical Neurophysiology, 48*, 406–417.

Upton, A.R., McComas, A.J. & Sica, R.E. (1971). Potentiation of "late" responses evoked in muscle during effort. *Journal of Neurology, Neurosurgery and Psychiatry, 34*, 699–711.

Van Boxtel, A. (1986). Differential effects of low-frequency depression, vibration-induced inhibition, and post-tetanic potention on H-reflexes and tendon jerk in the human soleus muscle. *Journal of Neurophysiology, 55*, 551–568.

Wiesendanger, M. & Miles, T.S. (1982). Ascending pathway of low-threshold muscle afferents to the cerebral cortex and its possible role in motor control. *Physiological Review, 62*, 1234–1270.

Wilkins, D.E., Hallett, M. & Wess, M.M. (1986). Audiogenic startle reflex of man and its relationship to startle syndromes. *Brain, 109*, 561–573.

Woods, D.L., Knight, R.T. & Neville, H.J. (1984). Bitemporal lesions dissociate auditory evoked potentials and perception. *EEG and Clinical Neurophysiology, 57*, 208–220.

Young, R.R. (1973). The clinical significance of exteroceptive reflexes. In J.E. Desmedt (Ed.), *New developments in electromyography and clinical neurophysiology 3*, 697–712.

The Startle Probe in the Study of Emotion and Emotional Disorders

Margaret M. Bradley* and Scott R. Vrana**

Abstract

The reflexive response to a startle probe (e. g., a sudden loud noise) includes an easily measurable eyeblink component. Recent studies implicating the blink reflex as a new measure of emotion are reviewed, highlighting applications to the study of psychopathology. The magnitude of the startle reflex has proved sensitive to differences in the emotional valence of foreground processing in contexts including viewing emotional pictures, imagining emotional events, and anticipating or receiving electric shocks. Links are draws between these data and the potential usefulness of the startle methodology in terms of clinical assessment, diagnosis, and treatment outcome. In addition, startle research addressing issues related to fear, anxiety, and psychopathy is discussed. All indicators suggest the startle probe methodology is a useful tool in the study of emotional disorders.

Key words: emotion, startle reflex, conditioning, imagery, pictures, anxiety, fear, phobia, psychopathy, psychophysiology, psychopathology, laterality, aversive, appetitive

Theory and research regarding emotional disorders is perhaps on strongest footing when it is linked to basic research on emotion. The startle reflex response, which has recently been suggested as a new measure of emotion (Lang, Bradley, & Cuthbert, 1990; Vrana, Spence, & Lang, 1988), may be a promising new tool in the assessment of emotional disorders as well. In this chapter, a framework for thinking about emotion is presented, and research and theory relating the startle probe response to emotion briefly reviewed. Then, we turn our attention to applying the startle probe methodology in the study of emotional disorders, particularly in the anxiety disorders and in the study of psychopaths. While relatively little research exists to date which relates startle reflexes to psychopathology, what little there is suggests that the startle probe may be a productive tool for understanding and investigating both abnormal, as well as normal, emotional reactions.

Introduction: A Dimensional Approach to Emotion

One way to view emotion is to define the dimensions underlying emotional expression, and to subsequently organize behavior along these dimensions. This is the approach taken by Lang and his colleagues (Greenwald, Cook, & Lang, 1989; Lang et al., 1990; Lang, Greenwald,

*   University of Florida
**   Purdue University
        This research was supported by National Institute of Mental Health (NIMH) Grants MH37757, MH41950 and MH43975 to Peter J. Lang.

Bradley, & Hamm, in press). According to this conception, emotional behavior can be defined by 1) a dimension of affective valence, which controls the direction of emotional engagement, favoring either a stance based on approach (appetitive responses) or withdrawal (aversion responses), and 2) a dimension of arousal, which dictates the intensity or amount of activity involved in the behavior. Proposing these two dimensions as important for emotional behavior has historical continuity: Hebb (1949) suggested that the significant dimensions of behavior were direction and vigor, and the work of Osgood, Suci, & Tannenbaum (1957) using the semantic differential identified these dimensions as accounting for most of the variance in verbal reports of emotional experience.

If the goal is to measure emotion, this dimensional view suggests that indices of both affective valence and arousal should be sought to characterize emotional response. Verbal report regarding these dimensions is not a sufficient index, since subjective reports are vulnerable to demand characteristics, can be discordant with other emotional indices (Lang, 1968), and can not be obtained from infants, animals, and other non-verbal populations. As Lang (1968, 1978) has made clear, verbal report is merely one avenue of emotional response – both behavioral actions and physiological responses comprise relevant (and sometimes independent) response systems in the expression of emotion. For instance, it is possible to adequately index the arousal dimension using a physiological measure – skin conductance responses appear to show a clear, one-to-one relationship with reports of emotional arousal. The data from several studies have indicated that the size of the peak skin conductance response for visually-depicted emotional materials shows a significant linear relationship with subjective ratings of arousal (Lang et al., in press). The same relationship can be inferred when large skin conductance responses occur to materials that are rated as either highly pleasant or unpleasant, since these materials tend to have higher arousal ratings (see Bradley, Greenwald, & Hamm, this volume; also Lang et al., 1991). Both Manning & Melchiori

(1974) and Winton, Putnam, & Krauss (1984) obtained larger skin conductance responses for items rated at either extreme of the valence dimension. The former study obtained the relationship using verbal materials, whereas Winton et al. used emotionally evocative slides. The relationship between arousal and electrodermal responding is sensible, since skin conductance activity is mediated solely by the sympathetic branch of the autonomic nervous system, which is important for mobilizing and sustaining emotional responses.

Several potential physiological candidates exist for measuring affective valence. The cardiovascular system has been profitably measured in the past to index the valence of affective processing and, in general, confrontation with unpleasant material is associated with increased heart rate and blood pressure. However, these measures are also influenced by other factors, including physiological mobilization for somatic or cognitive effort (Obrist, Webb, Sutterer & Howard, 1970; Vrana, Cuthbert & Lang, 1986) and intake/rejection of external stimuli (Lacey & Lacey, 1970). Thus, cardiovascular responding in emotional contexts is also dependent on specific task requirements (Lang, 1985; Lang et al., 1990). For example, many studies have shown accelerated heart rate responses while subjects imagined fearful events (see Cuthbert, Vrana & Bradley, 1991, for a review). Studies also consistently show that, for normal subjects, the heart rate response to pictures of unpleasant material is heart rate deceleration (Lang et al., 1991; Winton et al., 1984). These data suggest that while heart rate may be able to discriminate the valence of emotional processing, its direction (e. g., acceleratory or deceleratory) is quite context-dependent.

Facial electromyographic (EMG) response is currently under investigation for its ability to index the direction of emotional responding (see Fridlund & Izard, 1983; Tassinary & Cacioppo, 1989). Studies conducted recently have been encouraging, and indicate that the amount of activity in the corrugator (frown) EMG recording is related to the unpleasantness of visually-depicted materials; similarly, zygomatic (smile) EMG activity appears at its greatest during the processing of pleasant material (Lang et al., in press). The same relationship between facial EMG and valence has been obtained in studies of emotional imagery (Schwartz, Brown, & Ahern, 1980).

These data are promising in suggesting that facial EMG activity may index the affective valence of emotional processing. As usual, however, this system of measurement has both its advantages and disadvantages. Chief among the difficulties is the voluntary nature of facial reactions, which can be influenced by the subject's knowledge concerning appropriate re-

sponses in the experimental or assessment context. Thus, facial EMG recordings may sometimes reflect a non-spontaneous display of affective response. Recently, Tassinary & Cacioppo (1989) have sought to determine whether EEG activity might discriminate between spontaneous and voluntary facial activity. The addition of EEG measurement to the facial EMG recording procedure may help clarify the effects, but also increases somewhat the complexity of the measurement, especially for clinical applications.

The Startle Probe as an Index of Emotional Valence

Lang and his colleagues recently proposed the startle probe reflex as a new measure of emotion (Lang et al., 1990; Vrana et al., 1988). A reflexive startle response occurs at the abrupt onset of an intense stimulus, such as a loud noise, a bright light, or an electric shock. While including several behavioral characteristics (including head, trunk, and limb movements), a reliable, easy-to-measure component of the human startle reflex is the reflexive eyeblink. The blink reflex to a startle probe is rapid, typically occurring within 50 ms of stimulus onset; and is difficult, if not impossible, to voluntarily inhibit. The peak magnitude and the onset latency of the blink can be measured by recording EMG activity from the orbicularis oculi muscle, which surrounds the eye socket. (Anthony [1985] provides an excellent description of this, and alternative methods, of blink measurement.)

The magnitude and latency of the blink response appear to be reliably related to the affective valence of ongoing processing: Blink magnitude is larger, and its onset latency shorter, during the processing of unpleasant, relative to pleasant, events (see Lang et al., 1990). For instance, Vrana et al. (1988) used color slides that varied in affective valence from pleasant to unpleasant, and presented a brief acoustic startle stimulus during the the slide viewing interval. The magnitude of the eyeblink response to these acoustic startle probes

increased systematically in magnitude with the unpleasantness of the affective foreground, as Figure 1 illustrates. Subsequently, this affect-startle effect, indicating larger and faster-onset blink reflexes for unpleasant, relative to pleasant materials, has proved to be a relatively reliable and stable phenomenon: The effect has been repeatedly replicated in Lang's laboratory (Bradley, Cuthbert, & Lang, 1990a, 1990b, 1991; Bradley, Lang, & Cuthbert, 1990; Cuthbert, Bradley, & Lang, 1990a, 1990b; Lang et al., 1990; Vrana & Lang, 1990), as well as at other sites (Cook, Hawk, Davis, & Stevenson, 1991; Hamm, Stark, & Vaitl, 1990).

Lang et al. (1990) attribute the affect-startle effect to a synergistic match between the affective valence of ongoing emotional processing and the affective valence of the startle probe. In their view, emotional behavior is presumed to be organized along a basic appetitive-aversive (i. e., valence) dimension, which defines the current direction of emotional responding. According to this scheme, emotional valence can be considered a behavioral set favoring appetitive responding, which includes approach, attachment or consummatory behaviors, or alternatively, a set indicating aversive responding, including avoidance, defense or escape. The affective direction of the current motivational set is reflected in the priming of matching responses. Thus, when a foreground stimulus is aversive (e. g., an unpleasant slide), an aversive probe (e. g., a startle stimulus) delivered concurrently will match the behavioral disposition and augment the blink reflex; conversely, when the foreground stimulus is pleasant, a mismatch occurs, and the startle response is diminished.

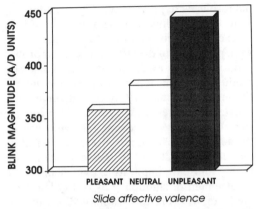

Figure 1. Blink magnitude to an acoustic startle probe presented during the viewing of pleasant, neutral, or unpleasant slide foregrounds.

Emotion and Attention

The matching account proposes that the magnitude of the blink reflex is directly related to the affective valence of ongoing emotional processing. To reliably index emotional valence, however, the measuring instrument – in this case, the probe reflex – should be minimally affected by processes other than those indicating emotional response. In fact, an alternative, attentional account of the affect-startle relationship should be explored before the role of emotional valence in startle modulation is clearly indicated.

The attentional account of startle modulation has been proposed and tested by Graham and her colleagues (Anthony & Graham,1985; Hackley & Graham,1984), Simons and Zelson (1985) and others. It maintains that attentional resources are limited, and are allocated according to the sensory modality of foreground processing. Thus, when a subject engages in a visual task (e. g., viewing pictures), resources available to the auditory system are reduced, and the reflex response to an acoustic startle

probe will be attenuated. To the extent that the stimulus in the visual modality is extremely interesting, it will draw even more attentional resources, resulting in minimal resource allocation to the acoustic modality. This account easily explains (indeed predicts) the attenuated acoustic startle reflexes found during the viewing of pleasant slides (Anthony and Graham, 1985; Simons and Zelson, 1985). The augmented startle to aversive slides, on the other hand, is a challenge for the attention account. However, if it is assumed that nocent events are implicitly rejected, the attention hypothesis satisfactorily accounts for the blink modulation. In this case, resources withdrawn from the aversive visual stimulus (an unpleasant slide) would be available for processing the auditory channel, resulting in an augmented startle to an acoustic probe.

Bradley et al. (1990) conducted an experiment comparing the attention and emotion hypotheses. Slides were used as emotional prompts, and a visual startle stimulus, in addition to an acoustic stimulus, was used as a probe during slide processing. For the visual startle probe, the two theoretical accounts predict opposite results for reflex modulation by affective foreground. According to the stimulus rejection (attention) hypothesis, an aversive visual foreground should act to close down that input modality. Unpleasant slides should block the allocation of attentional resources to the visual modality, such that reflexes elicited by a visual startle probe should be reduced; pleasant slides should attract resources, and the visual probe response should be augmented. On the other hand, if it is emotional valence that modulates the reflex, the same relationship between reflex magnitude and affective valence should be observed as when an acoustic startle stimulus serves as the probe.

As Figure 2 illustrates, the results were clear: Both types of startle probes produced increasing startle reflex magnitude as a function of decreasing slide valence, as previously found in the Vrana et al. (1988) study. Thus, even when the startle reflex is elicited using a visual probe, blink magnitude during the viewing of unpleasant slides was larger than during pleasant slides. The weight of evidence disconfirms a

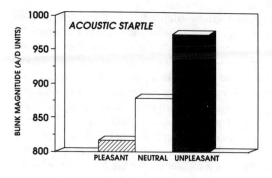

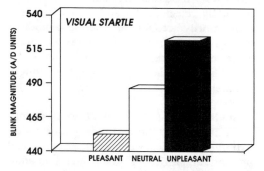

Figure 2. Blink reflexes elicited by a visual startle stimulus (bottom panel) or an acoustic startle stimulus (top panel) produced the same linear relationship as a function of the affective valence of a slide foreground.

simple attentional explanation for the modulation of startle by the valence of the foreground material, although effects of attention on startle reflex magnitude do occur in different probe paradigms (Anthony, 1985). The affect-startle effect also appears to be sensitive to hemispheric laterality of emotional processing. Bradley, Cuthbert, and Lang (1991) presented monaural acoustic startle probes to either the left- or right-ear while the subject viewed an array of emotionally evocative slides. The initial results were provocative: Significant modification of the blink reflex as a function of slide valence only occurred when the acoustic probes were presented to the left ear. Right-ear probes produced little evidence of affective startle modulation. Since two-thirds of the neural fibers in the auditory system diverge contralaterally, these data suggest a strong role for right hemisphere processing (as evidenced by the left-ear probe condition) in the affective modulation of startle. This is consistent with theory and data implicating right hemisphere involvement in emotion (Ley & Bryden, 1982; Heilman, Watson, & Bowers, 1983). Interestingly, the effects of startle modulation by ear of presentation were identical regardless of whether the blink reflex was measured from the left or right eye. The data from this initial exploration of laterality are impressive, in that the slide stimuli were not confined to a single hemisphere (e. g., by presenting the slide to a specific visual field). Obtaining hemispheric effects with this relatively weak manipulation of laterality suggests a clear role for the startle probe in clinical and neuropsychological investigations involving laterality and emotion.

Startle Magnitude and Fear

The relationship of the startle probe response to emotion clearly indicates its use in clinical manifestations of emotional disorders, particularly the anxiety disorders. Since both fear and anxiety constitute aversive response sets, it is expected that fear processing will prime the startle reflex and augment the reflexive eyeblink response. In fact, an abundance of evidence demonstrates that a fear state facilitates the startle reflex. Two major sources of data on this issue come from classical conditioning procedures in which a new fear response is elicited to a previously neutral stimulus, and from imagery or slide paradigms that present fear materials to the subject.

Fear Conditioning

Classical conditioning procedures have long provided a laboratory paradigm for studying fear (Estes & Skinner, 1941), and are a standard meeting ground for animal and human models of fear (Mineka, 1985). Davis, Hitchcock and Rosen (1989) list many advantages of startle potentiation as a measure of fear in animals. Among these are: 1) the measure is sensitive, because it involves a within-subject difference in startle magnitude in the presence versus the absence of the fear-conditioned stimulus, 2) it allows an evaluation of specific effects (startle reduction in the presence of the conditioned stimulus) versus nonspecific startle-diminishing qualities of fear-reduction treatments, and 3) the startle response itself does not involve any operant behavior. The latter point is particularly important, and is clearly related to Lang et al.'s (1990) conception of what startle reflex facilitation indexes: central aversive dispositions (like fear), rather than specific, tactical behavioral responses. Scientists interested in generalizing from animal models to human fear might add to this list the fact that the startle reflex in man and animals involves similar morphological characteristics, and the functional relationship between the startle response and its many modulatory processes is very similar in humans and animals (Hoffman & Ison, 1980).

Many studies, extending back four decades (Brown, Kalish, & Farber, 1951; Kurtz & Seigel, 1966) confirm that the presence of a fear-conditioned stimulus facilitates the startle reflex in rats. In this procedure, a rat learns to fear a previously neutral stimulus (e.g., a light) through contingent pairing of the stimulus with an electric shock. Presentation of the conditioned light stimulus (in the absence of shock) results in an augmented startle response, relative to a control stimulus. This fear-potentiated startle response is specific to the explicit pairing of a conditioned stimulus with electric shock, and does not occur when the light and shock are not explicitly paired (Davis & Astrachan, 1978). The effect is so robust that startle potentiation is an accepted method of testing for drug treatments that reduce fear (Davis et al., 1989).

Studies that involve human subjects have used experimental procedures similar to those used in animal experiments and have also found that an augmented startle reflex is a reliable component of conditioned fear (Cook,

Spence, Gray, & Davis, 1988; Ross, 1961; Spence & Runquist, 1958). Hamm, Greenwald, Bradley, & Lang (in press) used the startle stimulus as a probe in an aversive conditioning study in which affective slides served as conditioned stimuli. In this experiment, the subject viewed two different slides, each presented in an habituation, acquisition, and extinction phase. During acquisition, one of the two slides was always followed by an aversive electric shock; during habituation and extinction, the two slides were presented without shock reinforcement. An acoustic startle probe was presented while the subject viewed the slides (and during some interslide intervals) at habituation and extinction.

Results indicated that the size of the blink response decreased dramatically from habituation to extinction for slides that had not been paired with shock. However, blink magnitude for slides conditioned to the shock stimulus continued to elicit a strong reflex, which was significantly larger than blink responses occurring to the non-shocked slide. Thus, the startle response in this study clearly indexed the (newly learned) aversiveness of the conditioned slide stimulus. This probe response was concordant with ratings of the conditioned stimulus: Subjects reported an increase in unpleasantness from habituation to extinction only for slides associated with shock.

Fear Imagery

Producing an aversive state using classical conditioning procedures is one method for eliciting fear behavior experimentally, and has the virtue of allowing a direct comparison between startle effects obtained in human and animal research. Human emotions, however, can also be elicited through symbolic processes. Lang and his associates (Cuthbert and Lang, 1989; Cuthbert, Bradley, & Lang, 1990b; Miller, Levin, Kozak, Cook, McLean, & Lang, 1987; Vrana, Cuthbert, & Lang, 1986, 1989; Vrana & Lang, 1990) have successfully elicited emotional responses using mental imagery. In one study, Vrana and Lang (1990) found that startle probes presented during imagery of unpleasant events produced larger startle reflexes than those occurring during neutral imagery; similar effects of startle magnitude during unpleasant imagery have been obtained by Cook et al. (1991) and Cuthbert et al. (1990b). The materials used to prompt unpleasant images in the Vrana and Lang study consisted of almost exclusively fear material, including a description of a dental examination, an intruder in the night, speaking before a group, and an observed automobile accident. Greater blink magnitude obtained during imagery of these materials suggests that the startle probe easily measures fear states.

The utility of the startle probe for clinical research would greatly increase if there was evidence that the startle probe showed the additional property of sensitivity to specific manifestations of fear within and across individuals. Some evidence suggests this may be the case. In the Vrana and Lang (1990) study, each subject post-experimentally rated the fearfulness of each of the imagined events. Within individual subjects, startle magnitude during fear imagery increased in an orderly, linear fashion as the rated fearfulness of the situation increased. Thus, startle magnitude appeared to measure the degree of fearfulness associated with each imagined scene for a given subject. Also, as is discussed later in this chapter, patients seeking treatment for severe simple phobias show greatly amplified magnitude (as well as faster onset latency) for startle reflexes occurring during imagery of content related to their phobia (Vrana & Constantine, 1990).

In summary, blink magnitude and latency is facilitated when fear is evoked. This effect is obtained 1) in both animals and human beings and 2) regardless of the method by which fear is elicited. The startle reflex response may prove to be a useful measure in the experimental study of fear and phobias, as well as a potentially useful clinical assessment tool with phobic disorders. A full-scale experiment investigating the startle reflex during processing of phobic material in patients diagnosed with a variety of anxiety disorders (e. g., simple phobia, agoraphobia, generalized anxiety disorder) is currently underway at the University of Florida Anxiety Disorders Clinic, which is directed by

Lang and his colleagues. When these clinical populations are assessed, it will be interesting to note whether, at extremely high levels of fear, startle facilitation begins to decrease, as it does for rats fear-conditioned to electric shocks of very high intensity (Davis & Astrachan, 1978).

Applying the startle methodology to phobic disorders will surely prove interesting. Whereas simple phobia provides a relatively straightforward case of fear and avoidance (or escape) behavior elicited by a distinct external instigator, both agoraphobia and social phobia may include startle-modulating attentional components. Agoraphobics tend to be vigilant toward interoceptive physiological, in addition to environmental, stimuli (Barlow & Cerny, 1988). Social phobics closely monitor their own social performance and are hypervigilant to cues of social evaluation, but do not regularly withdraw from feared social situations (Heimberg, Dodge & Becker, 1987). It remains to be seen whether, in addition to emotional modulation, the components of sensory-channel-specific attention inherent in these disorders modulate the startle response as suggested by the attentional hypothesis described earlier.

Post-Traumatic Stress Disorder

The use of the startle probe methodology in the clinical domain is clearly relevant in the study of another disorder related to fearfulness – posttraumatic stress disorder (PTSD). The diagnostic label of PTSD is assigned when, after undergoing "an event that is outside the range of usual human experience and that would be markedly distressing to almost anyone," a person persistently reexperiences the trauma (through nightmares, intrusive thoughts, or flashbacks), plus exhibits symptoms of avoiding stimuli associated with the trauma, numbing of general responsiveness, and increased arousal (American Psychiatric Association, 1987, p. 250). The diagnosis of PTSD requires a fear conditioning etiology, and so the studies of fear conditioning and startle described earlier appear fully relevant to this disorder as well. Since PTSD entered the diagnostic lexicon (American Psychiatric Association, 1980), one of the diagnostic criteria of increased arousal has been an "exaggerated startle response." This criterion emerged from clinical impressions, however and no assessment of the actual startle response has been undertaken. When the startle phenomenon is addressed, it is generally assessed through patient's self-report (e.g., Fairbank, DeGood & Jenkins, 1981).

Physiological reactivity, albeit without assessment of startle responses, has been assessed in populations with combat-related PTSD. For example, Blanchard and his associates (Blanchard, Kolb, Pallmeyer, & Gerardi, 1982; Pallmeyer, Blanchard, Kolb, 1986; Blanchard, Kolb, Gerardi, Ryan, & Pallmeyer, 1986) and Malloy, Fairbank, & Keane (1983) have examined subject's psychophysiological responses to combat-related stimuli, presented on audiotape and videotape, respectively. These studies found that autonomic reactivity in PTSD patients (particularly heart rate acceleration) was specific to relevant combat stimuli, and was not obtained with non-PTSD controls with similar combat experience. Pitman and his colleagues (Pitman Orr, Forgue, de Jong, & Claiborn, 1987) have evaluated responses during imagery of combat, and found similar high autonomic reactivity for the PTSD patients, relative to various control groups. At least in terms of autonomic responses, it appears that this clinical population is reactive to perceptual stimuli relevant to their trauma. However, it is clearly desirable to assess the reflexive eyeblink in a PTSD population.

An initial study assessing the startle response in patients suffering from PTSD was recently reported by Ornitz and Pynoos (1989). They measured the blink reflex in six children, ages 8 to 13 years, who had been under sniper fire on their school playground. The children all met diagnostic criteria for PTSD, including report of exaggerated startle response. Surprisingly, the PTSD children showed smaller amplitude blink responses to a 104 dB white noise burst when compared with children matched for age and sex but not suffering from PTSD.

However, the children with PTSD did show abnormal reflexes in two established startle modulation paradigms. A brief "prepulse" stimulus occurring between 15–400 ms before a

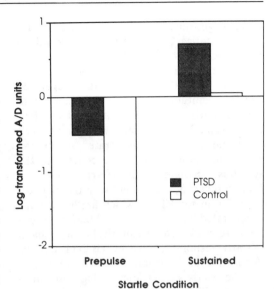

Figure 3. Modulation of the acoustic startle response by an acoustic prepulse (occurring 120 ms prior to the startle probe and a sustained tone (beginning 2000 ms prior to the startle probe), in children with and without posttraumatic stress disorder (PTSD). Adapted from E.M. Ornitz and R.S. Pynoos, Startle Modulation in Children with Posttraumatic Stress Disorder, American Journal of Psychiatry, Vol. 146, No. 7, pp. 866–870, 1989. Copyright 1989, the American Psychiatric Association. Adapted with permission.

startle stimulus reliably inhibits reflexes to the startle probe, and a sustained stimulus beginning 800 ms or longer before the probe facilitates reflexes to a startle stimulus (Graham, 1975). Figure 3 illustrates the response of children with and without PTSD in these two conditions. When compared with the normal controls, PTSD children exhibited relatively less inhibition to a prepulse tone and more facilitation to a sustained tone. Thus, although children with PTSD showed small startle responses to isolated noise bursts, modulation of responses to these bursts was in the direction of larger responses – less inhibition and greater facilitation – when compared to children not suffering from PTSD.

This provocative study raises more questions than it answers. First, the attenuated startle response in the PTSD subject is clearly contrary to the diagnostic criteria that formalized the report of countless PTSD patients. Ornitz and Pynoos suggest that the small reflexes may be due to numbing of general responsiveness (another symptom of PTSD), and that exaggerated startle magnitude may occur only upon confrontation with stimuli associated with the traumatic event. While consistent with conditioning phenomena that demonstrate augmented startle responses only in the context of the stimulus associated with electric shock, this formulation is not consistent with the diagnostic criterion for PTSD, which implies a tonic exaggerated startle. Since the DSM-III-R criteria are not based on empirical measurement of startle responses, however, it is likely that the description of "exaggerated startle response" may be overly simplistic as a diagnostic criterion for PTSD.

In fact, the abnormal modulation of the startle by preceding prepulse and sustained stimulation may be the key to understanding the reported clinical phenomena. Lack of inhibition by transient stimulation and exaggerated response during a sustained stimulus may best mimic the startle response in a naturalistic set-

ting, in which startling stimuli occur in the midst of other perceptual input. If so, the interaction of prepulse modulation with emotional modulation of startle promises to be an exciting avenue of future research. On the other hand, the differences found – less inhibition and greater facilitation with PTSD patients – may be simply an artifact of the smaller baseline startle responses in these children. Finally, it is unclear whether this pattern of results will be obtained in adults with PTSD. Startle modulation by prior stimulation is a rather late-developing nervous system phenomenon. Both of the abnormal effects found in the 8- to 13 year-olds with PTSD are characteristic of normal five-year-olds (Ornitz, Guthrie, Kaplan, Lane & Norman, 1986). This raises the possibility that the trauma resulted in delayed or regressed nervous system development. In any case, use of the startle methodology with an adult population of PTSD patients will allow a better assessment of the validity of the DSM-III-R criteria, the nature of posttraumatic stress disorder, and the generality of Ornitz and Pynoos' results.

Anxiety and Startle Modulation

Conceptualizing and organizing the many manifestations of fear and anxiety has always been a controversial business. One distinction that is fairly well accepted is between fear and anxiety, in which fear is conceived of as a response to a specific, identifiable object or situation, whereas anxiety is considered to be more "free-floating," usually of less intensity but longer duration, and less tied to any tangible aspect of the environment. Davis' work (Davis et al., 1989), tying both fear and anxiety neurobiologically to the amygdala, suggests that high levels of fear or anxiety should increase startle reflex response.

Davis et al. (1989) provide evidence that, in fact, "anxiety" does produce startle potentiation. In their study, two different groups of rats heard a habituation series of 40 acoustic startle stimuli; one group then experienced 10 unsig-

naled electric footshocks. Both groups were subsequently probed with one startle noise burst every 30 seconds for 20 minutes. The shocked rats responded more robustly to the startle stimuli than previously, while the rats receiving no shocks evidenced continued habituation. Interestingly, the difference between the two groups was not evident until 90 seconds after the last shock, did not peak until 10 minutes after shock cessation, and lasted for at least 20 minutes following the electric shocks. Thus, this result seems more indicative of an anxious state, rather than a response to a specific fear-provoking stimulus.

A human analogue to the footshock studies conducted on rats by Davis et al. (1989) was recently obtained by Greenwald, Bradley, Cuthbert, and Lang (1990) as well as by Hamm et al. (1990). In these experiments, blink magnitude to a startle probe occurring after a series of shocks had been presented was larger than reflexive blinks prior to shock experience. The startle response during viewing of affective slides was measured both before and after a shock workup session was conducted for a classical conditioning experiment. In the workup procedure, the subject was exposed to a series of shocks at increasing levels of intensity until the level was rated by the subject as 'uncomfortable, but not painful'. Finding larger blinks to startle stimuli occurring after shock workup suggests that the procedure may have produced an aversive, or 'anxious' state which led to startle potentiation. Again, these experiments tie together nicely data from animal and human populations.

Putnam (1975) found that the human eyeblink response to a startle stimulus was augmented with increasing levels of background noise. In her study, increasing intensity of an acoustic background stimulus potentiated the startle response to both an acoustic and a tactile startle stimulus, indicating the phenomenon is probably due to general aversiveness of the background noise, rather than some specific relationship between acoustic probe and background stimulus. Subsequently, Putnam and Roth (1990) determined that, in addition to increases in blink magnitude, judgments of the degree to which a startle stimulus was disturbing increased linearly with increases in the duration of the startle probe. Similarly, Davis (1974; Davis & File, 1984) has found that the startle response in rats increased as background noise changed to either a higher intensity or a longer duration stimulus.

On the basis of these data, one might expect larger reflexes in subjects who find the startle probe itself differentially aversive. Bradley et al. (1990) required their subjects to post-experimentally rate the aversiveness of both a light and noise stimulus, each presented multiple times as a startle probe earlier in the experiment. In general, most subjects rated the acoustic probe as aversive. For the light probe, however, subjects were divided into two groups, depending upon whether the probe was rated as aversive or not. Subjects finding the visual probe aversive produced significantly larger

blinks to all materials, relative to those who rated the visual probe as non-aversive. Since there are typically quite large between-subject differences in blink reflex magnitude, these data encourage the view that the aversiveness of the experimental situation may account for some of this variance. Subjects finding the visual startle stimulus aversive also showed a significantly larger affect-startle effect, which is expected if the effect is due to a synergistic match between an aversive probe and an aversive foreground stimulus.

How might trait anxiety affect startle reflex magnitude? Cook et al. (1991) selected subjects on the basis of high or low scores on the Fear Survey Schedule (indicating high or low levels of general anxiety), and subsequently involved these subjects in an imagery experiment. Twelve trials of each of seven different affective events (i.e., fear, sadness, anger, joy, pleasant, relax, neutral) were imagined; acoustic startle probes were presented during the imagery period. Results indicated that persons with high fear showed larger startle potentiation (i.e., larger difference in reflex magnitude between unpleasant and pleasant images) than the low fear subjects. Cook, Hawk & Stevenson (1990) found a similar difference in the size of the affect-startle effect for high and low fear subjects viewing affective slides.

A clear clinical extension and prediction from these data is that people with generalized anxiety disorder will evince larger baseline (unmodulated) responses to a startle probe than will less anxious people, as well as a stronger affect-startle effect. The between-subject element of this prediction, however, mitigates one of the major advantages of startle probe methodology: powerful and elegant within-subject effects. It is possible that irrelevant between-sessions and between-individual differences in electrode placement or hearing acuity, to name just two, add error variance to these comparisons. Other "state" differences, like caffeine intake (Blumenthal & Verma, 1988) or menstrual cycle (Gescheider, Verrillo, McCann & Aldrich, 1984) can also affect startle magnitude. These may mediate anxiety level as well. Understanding the factors that contribute to an individual's baseline startle response will be an interesting avenue of future research. That the affect-startle effect itself should be modulated by anxiety disorders, however, seems clear.

Startle Responses and Psychopathology

If the startle reflex indexes affective state, it is possible that it can be used to investigate emotional aberrance as well. Psychopaths have sometimes been described as affectively deficient, less empathic, or less emotionally reactive, especially with respect to aversive events. In conditioning and anticipatory paradigms, for example, psychopaths have typically demonstrated weak skin conductance responses in anticipation of aversive stimuli, relative to nonpsychopaths (for a review, see Hare, 1978). One explanation for these data is that stressful events fail to mobilize the psychopath (Hare, 1978). As discussed above, however, skin conductance activity might be a better index of arousal (i.e., intensity of behavioral mobilization) rather than specifically indexing the direction of the behavioral disposition activated by emotional stimuli. A specific deficit in aversive responding might be better indexed by a lack of startle potentiation during processing of unpleasant materials.

Patrick, Bradley, and Lang (in press) recently tested this hypothesis. In their study, startle reflex modulation by affective valence was assessed in a group of psychopathic subjects. The subjects were 54 members of a prison treatment program for sexual offenders and were diagnosed as psychopathic or non-psychopathic using Hare's (1980) Psychopathy Checklist. Each prisoner viewed a set of slides that varied in affective valence, ranging from pleasant to unpleasant contents. An acoustic startle probe was presented during the slide viewing period on two thirds of the trials.

Results indicated that for the 18 subjects diagnosed as psychopaths, the typical affect-startle effect was not obtained. As Figure 4 illustrates, reflexes obtained during the viewing of pleasant slides for these subjects were similar to college students and non-psychopathic prisoners in that blink magnitude was inhibited rela-

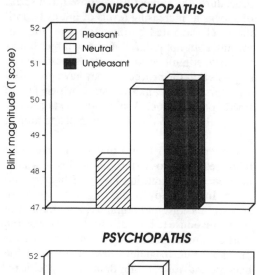

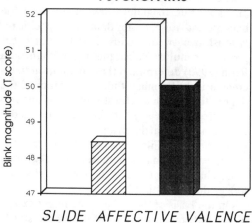

SLIDE AFFECTIVE VALENCE

Figure 4. Blink magnitude to an acoustic startle probe for psychopathic prisoners and non-psychopathic prisoners; psychopaths did not show the typical affect-startle effect.

tive to neutral slides. However, instead of showing an augmented response during the processing of aversive stimuli, the startle reflex of psychopaths during viewing of aversive slides was inhibited, relative to neutral slides. Thus, for psychopaths, a significant quadratic trend was obtained, indicating diminished blink reflexes to both pleasant and unpleasant materials, relative to neutral. Non-psychopathic prisoners produced reflexes that showed the typical linear trend across slide valence categories. These data are consistent with the hypothesis that psychopaths show a distortion in emotional processing, and are perhaps specifically less reactive to psychologically aversive events.

Assuming startle reflex magnitude is primarily an index of affective valence, a tentative hypothesis based on these data is that, for psychopaths, aversive materials are 'positive', in the sense that they prime an approach, rather than avoidance, disposition. This explanation relies on interpreting the pattern of reflex magnitude obtained for pleasant and neutral slides as indicating normal affective responding to positive events. In this case, the focus is on the abnormal response to unpleasant slides, and the most straightforward explanation is in terms of affective valence: these materials appear to be similar to pleasant stimuli for the psychopathic subject. Alternatively, it is possible that the affective valence dimension in psychopaths is generally disordered, and the startle reflex data obtained here are primarily effects of attention. In this case, for instance, the diminished magnitude to pleasant and unpleasant slides merely indexes that the psychopath failed to process the acoustic probe as fully when resources were directed visually. Use of a visual startle probe would assist in addressing these alternative hypotheses (Bradley et al., 1990).

It is significant that psychopaths and non-psychopaths did not differ in their affective judgments of how pleasant and arousing the slide materials were. Verbal reports on these dimensions for slides presented during the experiment showed no difference in either affective valence or arousal ratings as function of whether the prisoner was diagnosed as psychopathic or not. Rather, all subjects demonstrated congruence with the ratings of college students and reported, for example, that slides categorized a priori as negative were, indeed, unpleasant and arousing.

As demonstrated above, however, the startle modulation effects were drastically different, producing a disassociation between verbal report and reflex responses for the psychopaths. It is likely that verbal report data relies heavily on cultural/societal learning, whereas the reflexive defense response (i. e., the startle reflex) may be a better index of the central motivational state activated by an emotional stimulus. Thus, while the psychopath, in a sense, 'knows' what to say about the affective valence of environmental events, the behavioral disposition appropriate to this judgment is not activated. This discordance in response systems has serious ramifications for treatment outcome indices in populations of this type. More generally, Patrick et al.'s (in press) initial exploration generates interesting questions concerning the use of the startle methodology in investigating the psychopath specifically, and other disorders of emotional responding in general.

Treatment Outcome and Startle Modulation

Behavior therapists have long sought an adequate measure of pathology and treatment outcome in the anxiety disorders. The two measures most often used – self-report and behavioral avoidance tests – are each under voluntary control and therefore manipulable through experimenter/therapist or situational demand (Nietzel, Bernstein & Russell, 1988). The startle probe methodology may be an ideal

laboratory assessment of phobic severity and treatment outcome, since the startle response is reflexive and therefore not subject to the strong demand characteristics of other measures.

Several lines of theory and research suggest that the startle response might prove to be a sensitive index of treatment outcome, specifically with respect to anxiety disorders. If the startle response is facilitated in the context of aversive information, as Lang et al. (1990) hypothesize, treatments that reduce or eliminate the aversiveness of a fear-producing stimulus should reduce or eliminate startle facilitation during confrontations with the stimulus. Further, the linear relationship between blink magnitude and the valence of an affective foreground that is typically found implies that the startle amplitude ought to decrease in an orderly way as treatment successfully progresses. Two preferred treatment modalities exist for anxiety-based disorders: pharmacological and exposure therapy. Interestingly, there is evidence that, when fear is reduced by either type of therapy, response to a startle probe during phobia confrontation is also reduced.

Pharmacological Treatment

Michael Davis' work with fear-potentiated startle in rats is of central import here. In a recent review, Davis et al. (1989) list several substances that block startle potentiation in the presence of a fear-conditioned stimulus. These drugs, including diazepam, morphine, alcohol, flurazepam, buspirone and clonidine, have all been found to reduce anxiety in human beings. Several drugs (piperoxane and yohimbine) that increase anxiety in people also increase startle facilitation to a fear-conditioned stimulus.

Drugs that block the fear-potentiated startle response generally do so without reducing baseline response to a startle probe; thus the effect is not a non-specific damping of responsiveness. Interestingly, Davis et al. (1989) report that drugs that decrease serotonin levels do not reduce fear-potentiated startle. Serotonin has been implicated in the neurobiology of anxiety, primarily because serotonin antagonists reduce several measures of animal anxiety. However, Soubrie (1986) argues persuasively that serotonin antagonists actually reduce response inhibition. Since anxiety typically dampens operant activity, renewed activity (which could result from either reduced anxiety or reduced response inhibition) is a common test for identifying anxiolytics in animal studies. Davis et al. (1989) argue that, while other measures of anxiety tap the effect of serotonin on

operant behavior, the startle response indexes the conditioned fear state of the animal. Thus, the startle probe is advantageous in that it measures an aversive state, rather than tactical, situation-dependent operant responses. These startle modulation data are also consistent with human anxiety treatment research on this point: There is no good evidence that serotonin antagonists serve to reduce human anxiety (Marks, 1987).

Exposure Therapy

The experimental analog of exposure-based therapy is the procedure of extinguishing a conditioned fear response. In extinction studies using animals, the fear-potentiated startle effect obtained to a light paired with shock gradually diminishes with repeated unreinforced presentations of the light (Brown et al., 1951; Davis & Astrachan, 1978). This phenomenon mimics the desired outcome in exposure-based therapy. Spontaneous recovery of the fear response, a common finding in the conditioning literature, is also evident in startle potentiation (Brown et al., 1951). Frustrative non-reward, when used as an aversive unconditioned stimulus, also produces a conditioned response that includes potentiated startle, which diminishes during extinction (Wagner, 1963). These data suggest that the startle probe methodology will successfully mirror changes in behavior associated with exposure-based therapy.

A recent pair of case studies (Vrana & Constantine, 1990) demonstrated that exposure-based treatment does appear to reduce fear-potentiated startle in human clinical patients. Two females seeking treatment for small animal phobias were probed with 95 dB white noise during imagery of pleasant or phobia-relevant fear scenes. This assessment occurred before and after treatment for their phobia, with treatment consisting of 6–7 sessions of imaginal desensitization.

As expected, before treatment both of the patients exhibited facilitated reflexes to the startle probes during imagery of fear material, relative to imagery of pleasant material (see

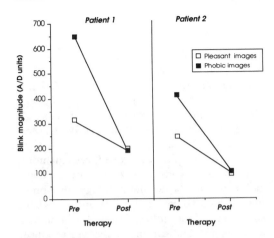

Figure 5. Latency to startle response during phobic and non-phobic fear imagery for two patients (patients 1 & 2) before and after exposure treatment. Response during fear imagery is subtracted from response during pleasant imagery; positive numbers indicate startle facilitation to fear relative to pleasant imagery.

Figure 5). Following treatment, the startle reflex evidenced general habituation with both patients showing approximately the same amount of decrease in blink magnitude during pleasant imagery. More importantly, both patients reported less fear during imagery of the phobic situations, and for phobic scenes reported as not fearful after treatment, startle magnitude was greatly reduced. As Figure 5 illustrates, for scenes reported as no longer fearful blink magnitude during imagery was practically identical to startle responses elicited during images of pleasant events. Interestingly, Patient 1 reported a decrease of fear in all phobic scenes, and blink magnitude decreased for each scene from pre- to post-treatment for this patient. Patient 2, however, reported behavioral improvement and no remaining fear to two of the phobic scenes after treatment, but continued to report maximum fear to a third phobic situation. Whereas startle magnitude decreased during the scenes reported as not

fearful (Figure 5), she continued to show a heightened response to the phobic scene identified as continuing to produce fear (mean startle response = 184 A/D units).

While animal research and the case studies discussed above are suggestive, full-scale experimentation is clearly needed to confirm that startle modulation adequately tracks treatment outcome in human anxiety disorders. Among the questions that should be addressed are whether the startle probe will assess successful treatment in exposure-based, pharmacological, and other forms of clinical treatment, and whether the startle probe is a useful measure for anxiety disorders other than simple phobias. Specific questions arise on the basis of anomalies in the data. For example, Davis et al. (1989) report that anxiolytics reduce fear-potentiated startle in rats, without reducing baseline startle response. If generalized anxiety (which anxiolytics alleviate) produces high baseline startle response (as some evidence suggests), will this pharmacological treatment attenuate baseline startle reflexes in this group of patients?

Finally, another clear application of the startle methodology is in predicting treatment outcome. Patients who exhibit physiological activation (increased heart rate, skin sweat activity, etc.) when exposed to phobic material have a higher probability of positive treatment outcome than people who do not respond physiologically (Lang, Melamed & Hart, 1970; Beckham, Vrana, May, Gustafson & Smith, 1990). This is presumably because physiological activation is a marker that emotional processing of the phobic material, necessary for fear reduction, is occurring (Foa & Kozak, 1986). Autonomic physiological variables seem to reflect specific tactical (i.e. context-dependent) responses in the situation, whereas the startle response presumably reflects an emotional disposition activated by the stimulus. Comparing the startle probe response and autonomic measures as predictors of treatment outcome might more clearly specify the type of processing necessary for successful fear reduction.

Conclusion

The recent success of the startle methodology in indexing affective valence holds promise in the study of emotion and emotional disorders. Clearly, many facets of the relationship between the startle reflex response and emotional valence remain to be explored. These include parametric questions, such as the role of stimulus modality, arousal, and intensity in affective modulation of the startle reflex, as well as properties of the startle probe itself, including its intensity, duration and predictability. Questions concerning the development and sustenance of emotional responses over time can also be addressed with the probe methodology. The startle probe appears to be an excellent measure of emotion: It is reflexive, reliably indexes the affective valence of ongoing emotional processing, and appears to be relatively uncontaminated by processes other than those indicating emotional engagement. As such, the startle reflex might be preferred over other potential measures of affective valence, such as facial EMG responses, cardiovascular measures or EEG measurement.

The startle probe methodology has accumulated a large data base in the assessment of conditioned emotional responsivity in animals (Davis et al., 1989), and in the assessment of human cognitive and perceptual processes (Graham, 1975). These data bases (and accompanying theoretical viewpoints) will be important in future investigations of startle modulation and human emotion; the former because of the obvious advantage in integrating animal and human theories of emotion (Mineka, 1985), the latter as the inseparability of cognitive and emotional processes is increasingly recognized (Lang, 1985; Williams, Watts, MacLeod & Mathews, 1988).

In terms of clinical procedures, including assessment, diagnosis, and treatment, the application of the startle methodology may prove quite useful. To date, the startle probe has been shown to reliably reflect fear states in animals and humans, and can index changes produced by drugs or extinction procedures. Its use in the study of anxiety disorders and PTSD therefore seems clear. The inital data obtained by Patrick et al. (1991) in a psychopathic sample suggests that the startle probe may be potent in measuring emotional behavior in groups for which specific deficits in affective processing are hypothesized. Obvious candidates are anhedonics, schizophrenics, and people suffering from depression. Disorders in which stimulus-specific approach/ avoidance tendencies are hypothesized, such as eating disorders or substance abuse disorders, are also good candidates for investigation with the startle methodology. Finally, the startle response may be an important tool for assessing the emotional responses in populations with deficient language ability, such as infants, and adults with language-impairing strokes or other neuropysychological disorders.

References

American Psychiatric Association (1980). *Diagnostic and statistical manual of mental disorders* (3rd. Edition). Washington D.C.: Author.

American Psychiatric Association (1987). *Diagnostic and statistical manual of mental disorders* (3rd. Edition – revised). Washington D.C.: Author.

Anthony, B.J. (1985). In the blink of an eye: Implications of reflex modification for information processing. In P.K. Ackles, J.R. Jennings, & M.G.H. Coles (Eds.), *Advances in psychophysiology, Vol. 1.* Greenwich, CT: JAI Press.

Anthony, B.J., & Graham, F. (1985). Blink reflex modification by selective attention: Evidence for the modulation of "automatic" processing. *Biological Psychology, 21,* 43–59.

Barlow, D.H. & Cerny, J.A. (1988). *Psychological treatment of panic.* New York: Guilford Press.

Beckham, J.C., Vrana, S.R., May, J.G., Gustafson, D.J., & Smith, G.R. (1990). Emotional processing and fear measurement synchrony as indicators of treatment outcome in fear of flying. *Journal of Behavior Therapy and Experimental Psychiatry, 21,* 153–162.

Blanchard, E.B., Kolb, L.C., Gerardi, R.J., Ryan, P.,

& Pallmeyer, T.P. (1986). Cardiac response to relevant stimuli as an adjunctive tool for diagnosing post-traumatic stress disorder in Vietnam veterans. *Behavior Therapy, 17*, 592–606.

Blanchard, E.B., Kolb, L.C., Pallmeyer, T.P., & Gerardi, R.J. (1982). A psychophysiological study of post-traumatic stress disorder. *Psychiatric Quarterly, 54*(4), 220–229.

Blumenthal, T.D., & Verma, A. (1988, April). The effects of low levels of caffeine on the human startle reflex. Paper presented at the Southeastern Psychological Association Convention, New Orleans.

Bradley, M.M., Cuthbert, B.N., & Lang, P.J. (1990a). Startle reflex modification: Emotion or attention? *Psychophysiology, 27*, 513–523.

Bradley, M.M., Cuthbert, B.N., & Lang, P.J. (1990b). Probe intensity and startle modulation. *Psychophysiology, 27*, S18. [Abstract].

Bradley, M.M., Cuthbert, B.N., & Lang, P.J. (1991). Startle and emotion: Lateral acoustic probes and the bilateral blink. *Psychophysiology, 28*, 285–295.

Bradley, M.M., Lang, P.J., & Cuthbert, B.N. (1990). Habituation and the affect-startle effect. *Psychophysiology, 27*, S18. [Abstract]

Brown, J.S., Kalish, H.I., & Farber, I. e. (1951). Conditioned fear as revealed by magnitude of startle response to an auditory stimulus. *Journal of Experimental Psychology, 43*, 317–328.

Cook, E.W. III, Hawk, L.W., Jr., Davis, T.L., & Stevenson, V.E. (1991). Emotional dysfunction and affective modulation of startle. *Journal of Abnormal Psychology, 100*, 5–13.

Cook, E.W. III, Hawk, L. W., Jr., & Stevenson, V.E. (1990). Fearfulness and affective modulation of startle. *Psychophysiology, 27*, S7. [Abstract]

Cook, E.W. III, Spence, E.L., Gray, J.D., & Davis, T.L. (1988). Acoustic startle is modulated by affective associative learning. *Psychophysiology, 25*, 440–441. [Abstract]

Cuthbert, B.N., Bradley, M.M., & Lang, P.J. (1990a). Valence and arousal in startle modulation. *Psychophysiology, 27*, S24. [Abstract].

Cuthbert, B.N., Bradley, M.M., & Lang, P.J. (1990b). Affective imagery and startle modulation. *Psychophysiology, 27*, S24. [Abstract].

Cuthbert, B.N., & Lang, P.J. (1989). Imagery, memory, and emotion: A psychophysiological analysis of clinical anxiety. In G. Turpin (Ed.), *Handbook of clinical psychophysiology*. Chichester: Wiley.

Cuthbert, B.N., Vrana, S.R., & Bradley, M.M. (1991). Imagery: Function and physiology. In P.K. Ackles, J.R. Jennings, & M.G.H. Coles (Eds.), *Advances in psychophysiology IV*.

Davis, M., & Astrachan, D.I. (1978). Conditioned fear and startle magnitude: Effects of different footshock or backshock intensities used in training. *Journal of Experimental Psychology: Animal Behavior Processes, 4*, 95–103.

Davis, M., & File, S.E. (1984). Intrinsic and extrinsic habituation and sensitization: Implications for the design and interpretation of experiments. In H.V.S. Peeke and L. Petrinovich (Eds.), *Habituation in the Behaving Organism* (287–323). New York: Academic Press.

Davis, M. (1974). Sensitization of the rat startle response by noise. *Journal of Comparative and Physiological Psychology, 87*, 571–581.

Davis, M., Hitchcock, J.M., & Rosen, J.B. (1989). Anxiety and the amygdala: Pharmacological and anatomical analysis of the fear-potentiated startle paradigm. In G.H. Bower (Ed.), *The psychology of learning and motivation, Vol. 21*. New York: Academic Press.

Estes, W.K., & Skinner, B.F. (1941). Some quantitative properties of anxiety. *Journal of Experimental Psychology, 29*, 390–400.

Fairbank, J.A., DeGood, D.E., & Jenkins, C.W. (1981). Behavioral treatment of a persistent post-traumatic startle response. *Journal of Behavior Therapy and Experimental Psychiatry, 12*, 321–324.

Foa, E.B., & Kozak, M.J. (1986). Emotional processing of fear: Exposure to corrective information. Psychological Bulletin, 99, 20–35.

Fridlund, A.J., & Izard, C.E. (1983). Electromyographic studies of facial expressions of emotion and patterns of emotion. In Cacioppo, J.T. & Petty, R.E. (Eds.). *Social Psychophysiology* (243–280). New York: Guilford Press.

Gescheider, G.A., Verrillo, R.T., McCann, J.T., & Aldrich, E.M. (1984). Effects of the menstrual cycle on vibrotactile sensitivity. *Perception & Psychophysics, 36*, 586–592.

Graham, F.K. (1975). The more or less startling effects of weak prestimulation. *Psychophysiology, 12*, 238–248.

Greenwald, M.K., Bradley, M.M., Cuthbert, B.N., & Lang, P.J. (1990). The acoustic startle reflex indexes aversive learning. *Psychophysiology*. [Abstract].

Greenwald, M.K., Cook, E.W., & Lang, P.J. (1989). Affective judgment and psychophysiological response: Dimensional covariation in the evaluation of pictorial stimuli. *Journal of Psychophysiology, 3*, 51–64.

Hackley, S.A., & Graham, F.K. (1984). Early selective attention effects on cutaneous and acoustic blink reflexes. *Physiological Psychology, 11*, 235–242.

Hamm, A.O., Greenwald, M.K., Bradley, M.M., & Lang, P.J. (in press). Emotional learning, hedonic change, and the startle probe. *Journal of Abnormal Psychology*.

Hamm, A.O., Stark, and Vaitl, D. (1990). Classical fear conditioning and the startle probe reflex. *Psychophysiology*. [Abstract].

Hare, R.D. (1978). Electrodermal and cardiovascular correlates of psychopathy. In R.D. Hare & D. Schalling (Eds.), *Psychopathic behavior: Approaches to research* (107–143). Chichester: Wiley.

Hare, R.D. (1980). A research scale for the assessment of psychopathy in criminal populations. *Personality and Individual Differences, 1*, 111–119.

Hebb, D.O. (1949). *The organization of behavior: A neuropsychological theory*. New York: Wiley.

Heilman, K.M., Watson, R.T., & Bowers, D. (1983). Affective disorders associated with hemispheric disease. In K.M. Heilman & P. Satz (Eds.), *Neuropsychology of human emotion* (45–64). New York: Guilford.

Heimberg, R.G., Dodge, C.S., & Becker, R.E. (1987). Social phobia. In L. Michelson and M. Ascher (Eds.), *Cognitive behavioral assessment and treatment of anxiety disorders*. New York: Plenum Press.

Hoffman, H.S., & Ison, J.R. (1980). Reflex modification in the domain of startle. I. Some empirical findings and their implication for how the nervous system processes sensory input. *Psychological Review, 87*, 175–189.

Kurtz, K.H. & Seigel, A. (1966). Conditioned fear and magnitude of startle response: A replication and extension. *Journal of Comparative and Physiological Psychology, 62*, 8–14.

Lacey, J.I. & Lacey, B.C. (1970). Some autonomic-central nervous system interrelationships. In P. Black (Ed.), *Physiological correlates of emotion* (205–227). New York: Academic Press.

Lang, P.J. (1968). Fear reduction and fear behavior: Problems in treating a construct. In J. Schlien (Ed.), *Research in psychotherapy, III*. Washington, DC: APA.

Lang, P.J. (1978) . Anxiety: Toward a psychophysiological definition. In H.S. Akiskal & W.L. Webb (Eds.), *Psychiatric diagnosis: Exploration of biological predictors* (365–389). New York: Spectrum.

Lang, P.J. (1979). A bio-informational theory of emotional imagery. *Psychophysiology, 16*, 495–512.

Lang, P.J. (1980). Behavioral treatment and bio-behavioral assessment: Computer applications. In J.B. Sidowski, J.H. Johnson, & T.A. Williams (Eds.), *Technology in mental health care delivery systems* (119–137). Norwood, NJ: Ablex.

Lang, P.J. (1985). The cognitive psychophysiology of emotion: Fear and anxiety. In A.H. Tuma & J.D. Maser (Eds.), *Anxiety and the anxiety disorders* (131–170). Hillsdale, N.J.: Laurence Erlbaum.

Lang, P.J., Bradley, M.M., & Cuthbert, B.N. (1990). Emotion, attention, and the startle reflex. *Psychological Review, 97*, 377–398.

Lang, P.J., Greenwald, M.K., Bradley, M.M., & Hamm, A.O. (in press). Looking at pictures: Affective, facial, visceral, and behavioral reactions. *Psychophysiology*.

Lang, P.J., Melamed, B.G., & Hart, J. (1970). A psychophysiological analysis of fear modification using an automated desensitization procedure. *Journal of Abnormal Psychology, 76*, 220–234.

Ley, R., & Bryden, M. (1982). A dissociation of right and left hemispheric effects for recognizing emotional tone and verbal content. *Brain & Cognition, 1*, 3–9.

Lykken, D.T. (1957). A study of anxiety in the sociopathic personality. *Journal of Abnormal & Social Psychology, 55*, 6–10.

Malloy, P.F., Fairbank, J.A., & Keane, T. M. (1983). Validation of a multimethod assessment of post-traumatic stress disorders in Vietnam veterans. *Journal of Consulting and Clinical Psychology, 51*, 488–494.

Malloy, P.F., Fairbank, J.A., & Keane, T.M. (1983). Validation of a multimethod assessment of post-traumatic stress disorders in Vietnam veterans. *Journal of Consulting and Clinical Psychology, 51*, 488–494.

Manning, S.K., & Melchiori, M. P. (1974). Words that upset urban college students: Measured with GSRs and rating scales. *Journal of Social Psychology, 94*, 305–306.

Marks, I.M. (1987). *Fears, phobias, and rituals*. New York: Oxford: Oxford University Press.

Miller, G.A., Levin, D.N., Kozak, M.J., Cook, E.W. III, McLean, A., & Lang, P.J. (1987). Individual differences in emotional imagery. *Cognition and Emotion, 1*, 367–390.

Mineka, S. (1985). Animal models of anxiety-based disorders: Their usefulness and limitations. In A.H. Tuma and J.D. Maser (Eds.), *Anxiety and the anxiety disorders* (199–244). Hillsdale, N.J.: Laurence Erlbaum.

Nietzel, M.T., Bernstein, D.A., & Russell, R.L. (1988). Assessment of anxiety and fear. In A.S. Bellack and M. Hersen (Eds.), *Behavioral assessment: A practical handbook* (3rd. Edition) (280–312). New York: Pergamon Press.

Obrist, P.A., Webb, R.A., Sutterer, J.R., & Howard, J.L. (1970). Cardiac deceleration and reaction time: an evaluation of two hypotheses. *Psychophysiology, 6,* 695–706.

Ornitz, E.M., & Pynoos, R.S. (1989). Startle modulation in children with posttraumatic stress disorder. *American Journal of Psychiatry, 146,* 866–870.

Ornitz, E.M., Guthrie, D., Kaplan, A.R., Lane, S.J., & Norman, R.J. (1986). Maturation of startle modulation. *Psychophysiology, 23,* 624–634.

Osgood, C., Suci, G., & Tannenbaum, P. (1957). *The measurement of meaning.* Urbana, IL: University of Illinois Press.

Patrick, C.J., Bradley, M.M., & Lang, P.J. (in press). Emotion in the criminal psychopath: Startle modulation. *Journal of Abnormal Psychology.*

Pitman, R.K., Orr, S.P., Forgue, D.F., de Jong, J.B., & Claiborn, J.M. (1987). Psychophysiologic assessment of post-traumatic stress disorder imagery in Vietnam combat veterans. *Archives of General Psychiatry, 44,* 970–975.

Putnam, L.E., & Roth, W.T. (1990). Effects of stimulus repetition, duration, and rise time on startle blink and automatically elicited P300. *Psychophysiology, 27,* 275–297.

Putnam, L.E. (1975). The human startle reaction: Mechanisms of modification by background acoustic stimulation (Doctoral Dissertation, University of Wisconsin, 1975). *Dissertation Abstracts International, 36,* 6419-B.

Ross, L.E. (1961). Conditioned fear as a function of CS-UCS and probe stimulus intervals. *Journal of Experimental Psychology, 61,* 265–273.

Schwartz, G.E., Brown, S.L., & Ahern, G.L. (1980). Facial muscle patterning and subjective experience during affective imagery: Sex differences. *Psychophysiology, 17,* 75–82.

Simons, R.F., & Zelson, M.F. (1985). Engaging visual stimuli and reflex blink modification. *Psychophysiology, 22,* 44–49.

Soubrie, P. (1986). Reconciling the role of central serotonin neurons in human and animal behavior. *The Behavioral and Brain Sciences, 92,* 319–364.

Spence, K.W., & Runquist, W.N. (1958). Temporal effects of conditioned fear on the eyelid reflex. *Journal of Experimental Psychology, 55,* 613–616.

Tassinary, L.G., Cacioppo, J.T., & Geen, T.R. (1989). Characterizing organismic-environmental transactions: The use of the readiness potential as a mark of voluntary facial behavior. *Psychophysiology, 26,* S60. [Abstract]

Vrana, S.R., Cuthbert, B.N., & Lang, P.J. (1986). Fear imagery and text processing. Psychophysiology, 23, 247–253.

Vrana, S.R., Cuthbert, B.N., & Lang, P.J. (1989). Processing fearful and neutral sentences: Memory and heart rate change. *Cognition and Emotion, 3,* 179–195.

Vrana, S.R., & Constantine, J.A. (1990). The startle reflex response as an outcome measure in the treatment of simple phobia. *Psychophysiology, 27,* S74. [Abstract].

Vrana, S.R., & Lang, P.J. (1990). Fear imagery and the startle probe reflex. *Journal of Abnormal Psychology, 99,* 189–197.

Vrana, S.R., Spence, E.L., & Lang, P.J. (1988). The startle probe response: a new measure of emotion? *Journal of Abnormal Psychology, 97,* 487–491.

Wagner, A.R. (1963). Conditioned frustration as a learned drive. *Journal of Experimental Psychology, 2,* Vol. 66, 142–148.

Williams, J.M.G., Watts, F.N., MacLeod, C. & Mathews, A. (1988). *Cognitive psychology and emotional disorders.* New York: Wiley.

Winton, W.M., Putnam, L.E., & Krauss, R.M. (1984). Facial and autonomic manifestations of the dimensional structure of emotion. *Journal of Experimental Social Psychology, 20,* 195–216.

Wolpe, J., & Lang, P.J. (1964). A fear survey schedule for use in behavior therapy. *Behavior Research & Therapy, 2,* 27–30. Reprinted in *Behavior modification procedure: A sourcebook.* New York: Aldine-Atherton, 1974.

Emotion-Processing in Anhedonia

Robert F. Simons, Lee Fitzgibbons and Evelyn Fiorito*

Abstract

Using Lang's bio-informational theory of emotion as a conceptual base, three studies were conducted to investigate the nature of emotion processing in subjects reporting a trait-like inability to experience pleasure (physical anhedonia). In the first two studies, emotion processing was induced with a standardized set of color-slide stimuli, while self-report (valence and arousal ratings), behavior (viewing time), and a variety of physiological reponses were measured. Relative to control subjects, anhedonics consistently rated the positive slides as less positive, though the two groups did not differ behaviorally nor in the modulation of startle by the affective content of the slide stimuli. Between-group differences were noted in two valence-sensitive physiological reponses (facial EMG and heart rate) supporting a valence-based hypothesis for the emotion-processing deficit in anhedonia. The third study used imagery instructions to induce emotion processing and again found evidence for a valence-based deficit. As in the previous studies, the two groups differed in verbal report of emotion and in the physiological responses which normally covary with stimulus (imagery) valence. Together with a general report of less vivid imagery from anhedonics, these results suggest that the emotion-processing deficit in anhedonia may be associated with the nature of their emotion representations in long-term memory.

Key words: anhedonia, emotion, valence, arousal, imagery, startle

For somewhat more than a decade, a major focus of our research program has been the idiosyncratic behavior of two subject groups – those who on paper and pencil inventories report an inability to experience pleasure and those who report an unusually high number of perceptual distortions, mostly surrounding the body image. Subjects selected for this research are identified based on high scores (+2 SD) on either the Physical Anhedonia Scale (Chapman, Chapman & Raulin, 1976) or the Perceptual Aberration Scale (Chapman, Chapman & Raulin, 1978). These two test instruments were constructed for the purpose of identifying young-adults in the college undergraduate population who evinced trait-like personality characteristics frequently associated with schizophrenia. The hypothesis which underlay the development of the questionnaires was that 'normal' young adults who possessed such schizotypal features may stand at higher risk for schizophrenia than individuals in whom these features are absent.

It was hypothesized at the outset that the two questionnaires would identify distinct subject groups and this has been well borne out in the laboratory. Many studies have succeeded in identifying features in anhedonic or perceptual aberration subjects that are often noted in schizophrenics, but the constellation of these fea-

* University of Delaware. Preparation of this manuscript was supported, in part, by an NIMH grant (#42465) to F. K. Graham and the first author. Portions of this reseach have been submitted by the second author to the University of Delaware in partial fulfillment of the requirements for the Master of Arts degree and portions of this work have been presented at the 30th annual meeting of the Society for Psychophysiological Research (Boston, October, 1990). All of the research described in this manuscript was stimulated directly or indirectly by interactions with Peter Lang.

tures differs substantially between the two groups. While both groups produce deviant Rorschach protocols (Edell & Chapman, 1979) and to some extent have also shown deviant eye tracking (Simons & Katkin, 1985) and reaction-time crossover (Simons, MacMillan & Ireland, 1982a), many studies revealed schizophrenia-like deficits in only one group, and the particular group evincing the deficit has varied from study to study.

Haberman, Chapman, Numbers and McFall (1979), for example, assessed social skills in a laboratory simulation and reported that subjects with physical anhedonia had poorly developed social skills while the social skills of perceptual aberrators were normal. When subjects were confronted with a standard clinical interview (Chapman, Edell & Chapman, 1980), subjects with perceptual aberrations admitted to a variety of psychotic experiences (e.g. thought withdrawal, thought insertion) while anhedonic subjects did not. Perceptual aberrators frequently showed evidence of major affective disorder; anhedonic subjects did not. In the psychophysiology laboratory, anhedonic subjects have consistently produced small P300 components in their event-related brain potentials (Josiassen, Shagass, Roemer & Straumanis, 1985; Miles, Perlstein, Simons & Graham, 1987; Simons, 1982; Simons & Russo, 1987). Similarly, both Simons (1981) and Bernstein (1987) have observed that anhedonic subjects tend to be skin conductance hyporesponders – i.e. they frequently fail to respond or produce very small responses which tend to habituate rapidly. In both the P300 and the SCR contexts, the data from perceptual aberration subjects was indistinguishable from that produced by normal controls.

On the other hand, we have recently begun investigating the hypothesis that subjects in our two schizotypy groups would show deficits in stimulus gating which have long been hypothesized to be a central feature of schizophrenia, perhaps underlying the disordered attention described clinically by McGhie and Chapman (1961). While stimulus gating has been studied in a variety of ways in the laboratory, our studies have employed the prepulse inhibition paradigm described by Graham (1975; 1979). In

this procedure, a startle-eliciting stimulus is presented shortly after a weak prestimulus. With short stimulus onset asynchronies (SOAs), the weak prepulse markedly inhibits the startle reflex, and this prepulse inhibition effect has been reported to be weaker in schizophrenic patients (Braff, Stone, Calloway, Geyer, Glick & Bali, 1978). We have conducted a number of studies of this phenomenon with our subjects, and though the results are not always consistent, when differences between our schizotypes and control subjects are present, it is always between controls and perceptual aberrators. Anhedonic subjects have not differed from control subjects on any measure in any study in this series (e.g. Perlstein, Fiorito, Simons & Graham, 1989; Simons & Giardina, in press).

Taken together, both the clinical and laboratory/psychophysiological studies seem to suggest two things. First, that subjects with perceptual aberrations and physical anhedonia share several characteristics with subjects known to fall within the schizophrenia spectrum. Second, that the two groups of subjects identified with the schizotypy questionnaires are distinct. The phenomenology is different as is the performance of the two groups across a wide variety of experimental situations. While these general conclusions can be easily deduced from the data just described, it is less clear how to interpret the nature of the differences between the two groups – that is, the specific deficits unique to each subject group and particularly those that might augur the development of future psychopathology.

Our working hypothesis, based partly on the questionnaire items themselves and partly on early conceptions of schizophrenia as a splitting or disintegration of the various functions of the intact 'personality' (e.g. Bleuler, 1950), is that subjects with perceptual aberrations evince dysfunctional *information* processing (i.e. a cognitive deficit) while subjects with anhedonia have intact cognition but evince dysfunctional *emotion* processing (i.e. an affective deficit). This is not meant to imply that anhedonic subjects are more predisposed to clinically significant affective disorder than to schizophrenia. In fact, the evidence suggests that there are more affective *diagnoses* among perceptual aberrators (Chapman & Chapman, 1985; Chapman et al., 1980). Rather, it is primarily through dysfunctional cognitive or affective systems that subjects in each group may enter the schizophrenia pipeline.

To this end, our current research has begun to focus more intensively on the specific cognitive or affective deficits that might characterize the two subject groups. Our investigations with perceptual aberrators center around the possibility of a specific input dysfunction (see above) and we are using a variety of permutations of the basic startle modification paradigm to address a number of interesting questions. For example, if perceptual aberrators are characterized by reduced prepulse inhibition, is this accompanied by changes in evoked potential components such as the P50 discussed by Freedman, Adler, Gerhardt, Waldo, Baker, Rose, Drebing, Nagamoto, Bickford-Wimer & Franks, (1987) in their studies of stimulus gating? If the startle stimulus is less effectively 'gated' by the prestimulus among perceptual aberrators, is this also accompanied by subjective reports of greater intensity (i. e. loudness)? And are there similarities between these phenomena and the perceptual anomalies by which these subjects were initially identified for investigation? While these are intriguing questions and constitute a substantial portion of our research efforts, the remainder of the present paper will focus on our recent attempts to understand the processing of affect and affective stimuli in subjects who report physical anhedonia.

Emotion and Anhedonia

The Physical Anhedonia Scale (Chapman et al., 1976) is a 61-item true/false inventory that attempts to assess a wide variety of positive physical experiences. Examples of test items include:
- The beauty of sunsets is greatly overrated. (T)
- One food tastes as good as another to me. (T)
- The bright lights of a city are exciting to look at. (F)

Since anhedonia is defined as an inability to experience pleasure, the questionnaire does not include items which target experiences of negative affect. Thus, it is empirically unclear whether subjects identified with this instrument have an affect-processing deficit that is specific to positive emotion, as the definition would suggest, or whether the deficit is more general – that is, whether the entire range of emotional behavior is restricted as the clinical descriptor, 'flat' affect, might imply. A first goal of our present research then, is to examine the specific versus general question by utilizing a wide variety of stimuli which have been developed to invoke the full range of human emotion.

A second major goal of our research is to examine the emotion deficit in anhedonics across multiple emotion output systems. We were stimulated to do this in part theoretically, as Lang has repeatedly argued that there is often little correlation among response systems in emotion contexts (e. g. Lang, 1984; 1985), but also by some unpublished data from an experiment of Berenbaum, Snowhite, and Oltmanns (1987) which suggested that anhedonics may sometimes report less pleasure than control subjects but at the same time produce facial expressions (coded from videotape) that can not be differentiated from those produced by controls (Berenbaum, personal communication). Our present research consistently attempts to assess emotion-processing in anhedonics not only through verbal-report measures, but by examining a variety of visceral responses such as heart rate and skin conductance, by assessing facial expressiveness using electromyographic measurements, and by measuring overt behavior whenever possible. Our goal is to determine whether anhedonia is limited to a stylistic difference in self report, or whether a more basic and pervasive deficit in emotion-processing can be identified.

In order to initiate these investigations, some

preliminary decisions were necessary regarding how emotion would be conceptualized and how it would be elicited and quantified in the laboratory. While the purpose of the present paper is not to consider in detail the many theories of emotion, it is necessary to mention in brief the two competing conceptualizations that have to some extent guided the beginning phase of our research program with anhedonics. The first approach to the study of emotion holds that there are a small and finite number of specific emotions that are common to the human species. They have evolved across the millennia similar to many other human characteristics and can be recognized in all cultures. This approach to human emotion has been taken by a variety of investigators, most notably Izard (1971) and Ekman (1982). Izard's Differential Emotion Theory posits the existence of twelve discrete emotions – interest, joy, sadness, anger, fear, disgust, shyness, contempt, shame, guilt, pain/distress and surprise. The laboratory sine qua non for the identification of each emotion is the appearance of a distinct facial expression, though the subjective experience of each emotion is also distinct and it is generally believed that each emotion also carries a distinct visceral signature. Assessment of emotion experience is usually done with paper and pencil instruments such as Izard's Differential Emotions Scale (DES; Izard, Dougherty, Bloxom, & Kotsch, 1974) or Zuckerman's Inventory of Personal Reactions (ZIPERS; Zuckerman, 1977) and a number of systems have been developed to systematically code facial expression (Ekman & Friesen, 1978; Izard, 1979). The identification of distinct visceral physiologies associated with emotions has had a mixed history in psychophysiology, though some recent success has been reported in that regard by Ekman, Levinson and Friesen (1983).

An alternative to the discrete-emotion approach to emotion research has been championed recently by Lang (1984; 1985). Based generally on the work of Russell and Mehrabian (1977; Mehrabian & Russell, 1974), Lang has begun to conceptualize emotion as behavior existing within a three-dimensional emotional space. The three orthogonal dimensions are valence, arousal and dominance.

Valence appears to be the primary factor and is most easily thought of as a dimension with positive (approach) and negative (avoidance) poles. 'Discrete' emotions such as interest or joy would be located toward the positive pole, while emotions such as anger and fear would cluster toward the negative pole. Arousal is a dimension which runs from high to low and generally involves energetic aspects of emotional behavior. Sadness, for example, would be a negative-valence, low-arousal emotion while anger would be characterized as an emotion that is negative, but with high arousal. The third dimension, dominance, seems to correspond to control aspects of behavior. Lang (1985) sites fear and anger to illustrate the potential importance of the dominance dimension since both fear and anger are negative, high arousal emotions but are distinctly different on dominance; fear is a low-dominance and anger a high-dominance emotion.

Though each dimension in this three-dimension emotional space may be important for a precise description of behaviors usually thought to involve emotion, most of the work by Lang and colleagues has focussed on the two primary dimensions, valence and arousal. This work has been successful on a number of fronts, but perhaps most importantly, they have shown repeatedly and in a variety of different contexts that the two dimensions are associated with different physiological response systems. Ratings of valence are consistently related to activity in the muscles of facial expression (corrugator and zygomatic) and to changes in heart rate, while electrodermal activity (skin conductance) covaries consistently with ratings of arousal (e. g. Greenwald, Cook & Lang, 1989).

While we have not completely eschewed the discrete emotions perspective in our research with anhedonics, we do feel that the dimensional approach has several advantages. From a self-report perspective, the use of Lang's self-assessment manikin (SAM; Lang, 1980) as an instrument for rating subjective valence and arousal is easy to use and makes far fewer demands on subjects' for subtle internal state discrimination than devices used to assess the variety of discrete emotions. Similarly, from a psychophysiological perspective, the relationships between valence and arousal and physiology is at present less ambiguous than the relationship between discrete emotions and their physiological substrates. Finally, the simplicity of the dimensional strategy provides a natural starting point for our research program. That is, while the definition of anhedonia (i. e. a 'pleasure' deficit) would suggest the involvement of positive emotions (see above), we might now ask whether the deficit can be located more specifically along either the valence or arousal dimension.

Our hypotheses at the outset were unclear as there was evidence to suggest that either or both dimensions might be involved. Some initial laboratory work (Simons, 1982) pointed to an arousal deficit (see also Bernstein, 1987) since a number of anhedonic subjects were electrodermally hyporesponsive. On the other hand, the items which constitute Physical Anhedonia Scale, when rated, are arousal neutral and valence positive. Thus, the scale itself would suggest that anhedonic subjects would show difference in valence self report and perhaps also in the physiological responses associated with the valence dimension. In our only previous study with anhedonics using stimuli chosen to provoke positive affect (Simons, MacMillan & Ireland, 1982b), the stimuli employed (opposite sex nudes) are were high on both valence and arousal. Though anhedonic subjects were less physiologically responsive in anticipation of these slides than were normal controls, the results of this study are ambiguous with respect to the valence versus arousal hypothesis.

Emotion and the Probe-Startle Paradigm

In a series of studies by Lang and his colleagues (Lang, Bradley & Cuthbert, 1990), startle stimuli (e. g. loud sounds or bright light flashes) have been delivered to subjects concurrently engaged in the processing of emotional stimuli. These emotion-stimuli were either color slides, well standardized with known emotion-eliciting properties (Lang, Ohman & Vaitl, 1988) or imaginal, with the imaging based on brief sentences describing common emotional scenes. With both slide (Vrana, Spence & Lang, 1988) and imaginal stimuli (Vrana, Cuthbert & Lang, 1989), the magnitude of the startle response (eye blink) evoked during the emotion-processing task varied directly with the valence of the foreground stimulus. That is, slides or images with negative valence ratings were associated with larger eyeblink reflexes than slides or images with positive valence ratings. Most commonly, stimuli with neutral valence were associated with responses of intermediate magnitude. Interestingly, this relationship between foreground content and startle response magnitude was specific to valence, with no relationship present between startle magnitude and the *arousal* value of the foreground. Lang et al. (1990) interpret these data as consistent with their more general notion of emotions as action tendencies or response dispositions. In short, a stimulus with negative valence activates to some extent motor elements consistent with a general avoidance tendency such that stimuli simultaneously encountered which evokes a similar action tendency are essentially synergistic and the response will be augmented (i. e. the startle response will be larger). The opposite outcome would be expected when the foreground stimulus primes motor programs associated with approach. Startle stimuli then elicit a reflex that is antagonistic to the approach posture and the net result is a reflex with a diminished amplitude.

The specificity of the relationship between foreground valence and startle response amplitude as well as its general reliability provided a convenient starting point for our investigations of emotion-processing in anhedonia. To this end, thirty-six slides from the larger international slide set developed by Lang and his colleagues (Lang et al., 1988) were chosen for use as foreground stimuli in a probe-startle experiment with anhedonic and normal control subjects. The slides were grouped into three equal size valence groups (12 positive, 12 neutral and

12 negative) with the three valence groups equated as closely as possible on arousal ratings. That is, within each valence group there were three slides with high arousal ratings, three with medium and three with low arousal ratings. The mean arousal ratings of the positive and negative valence slide groups were comparable, though arousal ratings associated with the neutral valence slides were somewhat lower.

The general procedures employed in this study were very similar to those employed by Vrana et al., 1988). Thirty-six 35 mm color slides were presented to all subjects during two phases of the experiment. In the first phase, a 40 ms, 104 dB white noise stimulus with uncontrolled rise and fall time was presented to subjects over headphones at some point during the six-second slide viewing time. A total of 36 startle stimuli were presented during this phase of the experiment, 9 associated with positive slides, 9 with neutral and 9 with negative slides. An additional 9 startle stimuli occurred during interslide intervals which varied randomly around 30 seconds and during 9 slide presentations, no startle stimulus was delivered. An integrated electromyographic (EMG) signal obtained from the eyelid portion of m. obicularis oculi was used to quantify the startle reflex.

Following the startle-probe phase of the experiment, the slides were presented to all subjects for a second viewing. The purpose of this phase of the experiment was two-fold. First, it was used to collect the self-report ratings of slide valence and slide arousal. This was accomplished using a five-point paper and pencil version of Lang's self-assessment manikin (Lang, 1980). Subjects were also asked to provide ratings of interest. The second goal of the self-report procedure was to obtain measures of viewing time. This was done surreptitiously by allowing subjects to initiate the onset and offset of each slide during the rating task while at the same time the laboratory computer which controlled the experiment was recording the duration of the full slide exposure.

Results

The ratings (interest, valence and arousal) of the slides as a function of a priori valence categories are presented in Figure 1. There was a significant between-group difference in interest ratings, and this difference was most pronounced when the slides were positive. Lang et al. (1990) have shown that quadratic functions with valence, such as the interest/valence relationship seen in the left-hand panel of Figure 1, often suggest strong mediation by arousal, and this valence/arousal relationship can be seen in the remainder of the figure. When the valence and arousal ratings were evaluated statistically, anhedonic subjects were found to rate the posi-

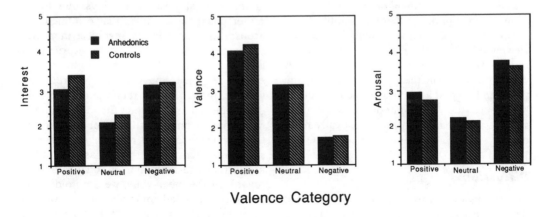

Valence Category

Figure 1. Self-report of interest, valence and arousal from anhedonic and control subjects viewing slides previously defined as positive, neutral or negative.

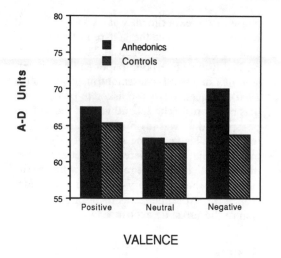
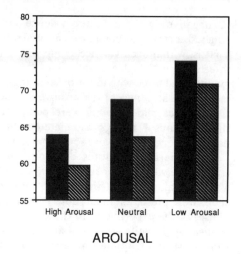

Figure 2. Reflex blink magnitude as a function of slide valence and arousal ratings.

tive slides as less positive than controls, but there were no between-group differences in ratings of arousal.

Startle-response magnitude is presented in Figure 2 as a function of valence and slide arousal. Contrary to the results of Lang et al. (1990), our subjects showed a distinct, strong and inverse relationship between startle magnitude and slide arousal while the relationship between startle magnitude and slide valence was not significant. As Figure 2 also suggests, there were no differences between anhedonic and control subjects in their overall response to the startle probe nor the modulation of the response by the content of the foreground stimulus.

The relationship between slide valence and viewing time for both subject groups was quadratic, with both positive and negative slides viewed longer than the neutral slides. Again, this would suggest a mediating role for arousal. Differences between anhedonic and control subjects were small and not statistically reliable.

Discussion

The results of this experiment are somewhat difficult to evaluate. On the one hand, there were clear differences in the groups' verbal re-

sponse to the stimuli with anhedonics rating the positive slides as less interesting and less positive. Since no similar differences were found between groups when either viewing time or startle-response magnitude was examined, one might conclude that the 'deficit' observed in anhedonic subjects is limited to verbal report and that this stylistic difference between subjects is unaccompanied by behavioral or physiological differences in emotion processing. On the other hand, if the deficit in anhedonia is specific to affective valence, as the questionnaire would suggest, then the present study mitigated against positive findings due to the rather unexpected and intrusive influence of arousal on our primary response measures. Lang (personal communication, April, 1990) has recently noted that the modulation of startle response magnitude by foreground valence, though highly reliable, may be more dependent on arousal than first believed. New data from his ongoing studies seem to indicate that the valence effect may only occur when slides have high arousal values as well and we are currently re-examining our own data in this regard. In the meanwhile, we are holding the probe startle paradigm in abeyance as we continue to pursue our interests in the nature of emotion-processing in anhedonia.

The Face of Anhedonia

One of the more popular psychophysiological techniques of the past decade or so has been facial electromyography. A number of very interesting studies have been reported (e. g. Schwartz, Fair, Mandel, Salt, Mieske & Klerman, 1978) from which valuable information about subjects' affective state has been provided by recording the activity in muscles normally involved in the facial expression of emotion. As indicated above, Lang has further specified the nature of these relationships by demonstrating that facial EMG (at least when recorded from the zygomatic and corrugator muscles) relates to the valence but not the arousal dimension of emotion. Though facial expression can be measured, perhaps more directly, by coding videotaped records of the whole face, this is a very time- and labor-intensive procedure. EMG, though itself nontrivial technologically, can be more readily computer scored and may be more sensitive to low levels of activity than the videotape procedures. It is possible, for example, that lack of sensitivity underlay the Berenbaum et al. (1987) finding that anhedonic and control subjects did not differ in facial expression when the two groups were exposed to emotion-provoking film clips. That is, when videotaped records are coded, actual movement of the muscles is required before an expression can be scored. Facial EMG, on the other hand, can be used to indicate the presence of covert expressions – expressions which involve identical muscles, but at levels of activity insufficient to produce actual changes in facial features.

The present experiment evaluated facial EMG from the corrugator and zygomatic muscles as well as heart rate and skin conductance. Heart rate was of interest for two reasons. First, as a measure also sensitive to affective valence, it might serve as a within-experiment replicate for valence specific deficits in anhedonia. Second, it is a visceral response and thereby less amenable to volition and perhaps less susceptible to the demand characteristics of the experimental context. Skin conductance, on the other hand, was measured for its discrimi-

nant validity. Since SCRs have been shown to covary with arousal and not valence, the combination of skin conductance and the valence-sensitive EMG and HR measures should go a long way toward the clarification of the ambiguities of our probe-startle results.

The experiment consisted of six-second presentations of the same 35 mm color slides studied by Greenwald et al. (1989). Of the 21 slides, 7 had positive valence, 7 were neutral and 7 were negative. Greenwald et al. report that within this slide set, there was no correlation between valence and arousal, although unlike our probe-startle experiment, the slides were not specifically chosen for this characteristic. The experiment was conducted in three phases. In the first phase, slides were presented to subjects every 25 to 35 seconds. The subjects task was simply to attend to each slide as it was presented. During this phase, the physiological data was collected. Integrated EMG from the corrugator and zygomatic were recorded for two seconds prior to slide onset and during the six-second viewing period. An EMG pattern score was computed by subtracting corrugator change from zygomatic change and this derived score served as the dependent variable. A positive pattern score reflected a relative increase in zygomatic activity and a negative pattern score was indicative of a relative increase in corrugator activity.

The heart rate response to each slide was obtained from an EKG by timing (in milliseconds) inter-R intervals for two prestimulus seconds and eight poststimulus seconds and converting them into heart rate in beats per minute (BPM) for each half second real-time interval using the procedures described by Graham (1980). A measure of the heart-rate acceleration associated with each slide was obtained from the HR response curve by computing change scores (subtracting the two-second base period) and then identifying the fastest half-second HR value during seconds 2 to 8 following slide onset.

Skin conductance, recorded from electrodes placed on the palmar surface of the nondominant hand, was digitized at 24 cps and scored by identifying response onset and maximum on a graphics display terminal. For all physiological measures, across-stimulus averages were obtained as a function of both slide valence and slide arousal.

During the second phase of the experiment, each slide was again presented for six seconds. The subject was instructed to provide valence and arousal ratings using SAM's five-point paper and pencil version following the offset of each slide. At the completion of this phase of the experiment, the experimenter, using a ruse, provided the subjects with free access to the slide carrousel while at the same time obtaining viewing-time measurements. This constituted phase three of the experiment.

Results

The valence and arousal ratings are presented in Figure 3. Similar to the results of the startle-probe experiment, anhedonic subjects rated the positive (and neutral) valence slides as less positive than did the control subjects, but the two groups did not differ in their ratings of the negative slides. Once again, this self-report difference was specific to valence. As Figure 3

suggests, there were no group differences in their self-report of arousal.

While the physiology collected in the startle-probe experiment was somewhat at odds with our expectations, the physiological data in the present experiment were entirely consistent and the control-subject data replicated in all respects the results described by Lang (Greenwald et al., 1989). Figure 4 contains the data from both the control and anhedonic subjects for EMG pattern score (top) and HR acceleration (bottom) as a function of slide valence. As in Greenwald et al. there were significant linear relationships between slide valence and both facial EMG and HR acceleration. More importantly, significant differences emerged between the two groups. First, and quite surprisingly, anhedonic subjects produced more facial EMG than control subjects and this was true in response to both positive and negative slides. Furthermore, when activity from the corrugator and zygomatic activity was examined separately, differences between groups were evident in both muscles. That is, anhedonic subjects produced more corrugator activity in response to slides with negative valence as well as more zygomatic activity in response to slides with positive valence. The opposite was true for the measure of heart-rate acceleration, how-

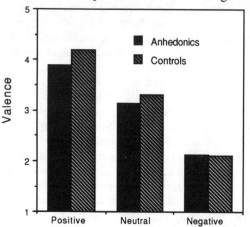

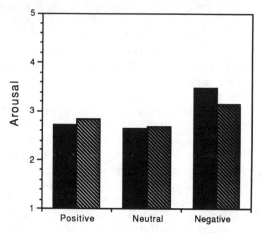

Valence Category

Figure 3. Self-report of valence and arousal for slides grouped into positive, neutral and negative (valence) categories.

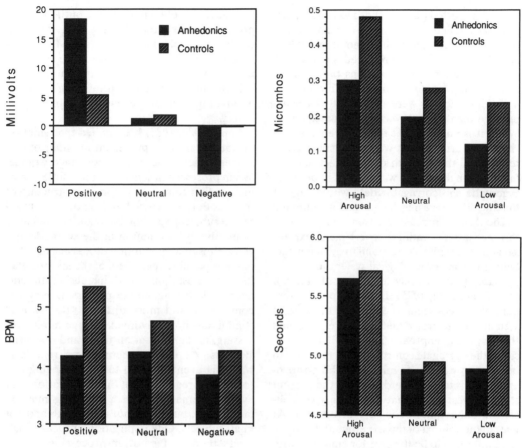

Valence Category

Figure 4. EMG pattern score (zygomatic-corrugator; top panel) and heart rate (bottom panel) as a function of slide valence ratings.

Figure 5. Skin conductance response magnitude (SCR; top panel) and viewing time (bottom panel) as a function of arousal ratings.

ever. Not only did anhedonics produce less acceleration in general, but there was no significant relationship between their HR acceleration scores and slide valence. As indicated above, for control subjects this relationship was significantly linear.

The SCR data from the present experiment, along with viewing times, are presented in Figure 5. On both measures, the between-group differences did not approach significance, though consistent with Lang (Greenwald et al., 1989), the two measures were each significantly related to arousal.

Discussion

The results of this experiment are intriguing, although they do not suggest that the difference in emotion processing between anhedonic and control subjects is a simple one. The primary purpose of the study was to explore with physiological measures, sensitive specifically to valence and arousal, whether the deficit in emotion processing presumed to be associated with anhedonia could be localized to one of these two dimensions. The results seem positive in this regard. Of the three measures demonstrating significant between-group differences, all were associated with valence. Anhedonic subjects reported positive slides to be less positive, they failed to show any association between heart-rate change and emotional valence and at the same time produced significantly greater covert facial expressions than normal control subjects. Of course, the finding that anhedonic subjects were significantly *more* expressive than controls was wholly unexpected. While it is possible that that this represents a chance occurrence that would not stand up to replication, the strength of the effect and the fact that the difference was present in both the zygomatic and corrugator data would suggest that the difference may be real and meaningful.

The three dependent measures employed in this study, SAM ratings, covert facial expression and heart rate, correspond to the language, behavioral and physiological systems discussed by Lang in his three-systems view of emotion (e.g. Lang, 1984; 1985). In fact, the data from our anhedonics seem to exemplify the kind of systems-desynchrony that gave rise to Lang's three-systems approach initially. If one considers the aggregate control-subject response to be close to what Lang might call the positive-emotion prototype, the data from the present study suggest either that this prototype is absent in anhedonics or is very incoherent. At least in the context of this experiment, the same does not seem to be the case for emotions with negative valence.

Lang has argued that as evidence that subjects have activated an emotion prototype, one can turn to the visceral physiology. While language, and most likely facial expression, may be modulated by accessing only parallel semantic information associated with the emotion prototype, the deep structure of the emotion contains the motor program and its physiological support. Activation of the deep structure

necessarily involves measurable outflow. In the present context, the visceral data (HR) recorded from anhedonic subjects was flat. Interestingly, a similar inability to produce an appropriate visceral physiology to an affective stimulus has been reported by Lang (1984) in his investigations of subjects with poor imagery ability.

Lang (1984; 1985) has implied that emotion prototypes may be processed in either of two modes – a semantic mode or an imagery mode. When processed in semantic mode, little, if any, information contained in the deep structure of the emotion is accessed and reports produced by the subject regarding the emotion are based primarily on information in the semantic network. Presumably, emotion processing in either mode is possible regardless of the specific eliciting stimulus, though with increasing stimulus degradation image-mode processing may become more and more difficult. 'Real-world' stimuli may normally invoke image-mode processing, though not at all times and not in all subjects. As events become less real (e.g. watching events happen to others, seeing pictorial or reading text representations of events), semantic-mode processing may be more likely, but again, not at all times and not in all subjects. One implication of such a dual-mode theory of emotion-processing is that meaningful individual differences in how and when subjects engage in semantic- v. image-mode processing may exist. While anhedonic subjects seem to have a less coherent prototype, at least for positive-valence emotions, it may also be true that they are less likely or less able to access emotion in the imagery mode. This hypothesis was tested in the following experiment.

Anhedonia and Emotional Imagery

Sixty-four subjects participated in the imagery experiment – 33 anhedonic and 31 normal controls. During the experiment, 8 standardized scenes were presented to each subject verbally through headphones. The description of each

scene lasted 20 seconds and was followed by a 20 second period in which subjects were to imagine the scene that had just been presented as vividly as possible, i.e. as if they were participating in the activity described. The scenes were chosen to elicit a wide range of positive and negative affect and were developed based on intensive interviewing of undergraduates to determine situations that would generate fairly uniform verbal report across subjects. After the completion of the eight standardized scenes, two additional imagery trials were presented. On the ninth trial, subjects were instructed to imagine an event from their own life experience that they recalled as particularly negative, and on the final trial they were to recall a life event that was particularly positive. For each subject, the content of the two final scenes was chosen prior to the experiment based on a short interview that took place during the informed consent procedure and while the physiological recording devices were put in place. At the outset of the experiment, all subjects were required to complete the Questionnaire on Mental Imagery (QMI; Sheehan, 1967), the instrument used in Lang's research to divide subjects into good and poor imagery groups, and at the conclusion of each imagery period, subjects were asked to fill out a modified version of the ZIPERS (Zuckerman, 1977). Our particular version of the ZIPERS contained thirteen items designed to assess specific emotions such as fear, anger, happiness etc., but in addition, two items were included in order to obtain self reports of visceral arousal (heart rate and respiration).

As in the previous experiment, heart rate, skin conductance and integrated facial EMG were recorded on each trial prior to the delivery of the imagery script, during delivery, and during the visualization period. EMG was scored as in the previous experiment by computing zygomatic-corrugator differences. Skin conductance was quantified by counting the number of nonspecific fluctuations which occurred during the three measurement periods, while heart rate was quantified by calculating the mean for each period. The scores for the presentation as well as the visualization period were computed for each measure as change from the final 10 seconds of the predelivery baseline.

Results

As a first test of the hypothesis that anhedonics were similar to poor imagers, the QMI data from the two groups were compared. The QMI is a 35 item scale which requires subjects to rate the vividness of their imagery. High scores on the QMI are associated with poor imagery. In support of the poor imagery hypothesis, anhedonic subjects scored significantly higher than controls (91.7 v 79.2).

Though we eventually intend to look closely at the issue of specific emotions, our initial analysis of the emotion self-report was based on a factor analysis of the entire set of ZIPERS data. While the optimum number of factors to consider is always debatable and the interpretation of factors can be even more so, the results of the factor analysis suggested to us that the majority of the variance could be explained most easily by a two-factor solution. The first, and by far the most substantial factor, grouped all the positive-emotion questions at one pole and all the negative-emotion questions at the opposite pole. We tentatively identified this as the valence factor. The second factor was composed essentially of the two physiology items. We identified this factor with arousal.

To determine the validity of these identifications, we asked whether the two factors behaved as SAM ratings do with respect to both the subject-group variable and each of the physiological measures. Toward this end, factor scores representing the two factors on each trial were constructed by selecting the items from the ZIPERS which had the highest weights on each factor and then summing across these items for each imagery trial. Since the first factor had both a strong positive and negative pole, two scores were obtained in this manner. These derived scores were subjected to analysis of variance in order to evaluate both between-trial and between-group differences. The top panel of Figure 6 illustrates the positive valence aspect of Factor 1 for each trial and the center panel illustrates the negative valence aspect. Not surprisingly, there was a clear dichotomy among the different imagery trials which is evident in both panels of the figure. The pleasant scenes were associated with high positive

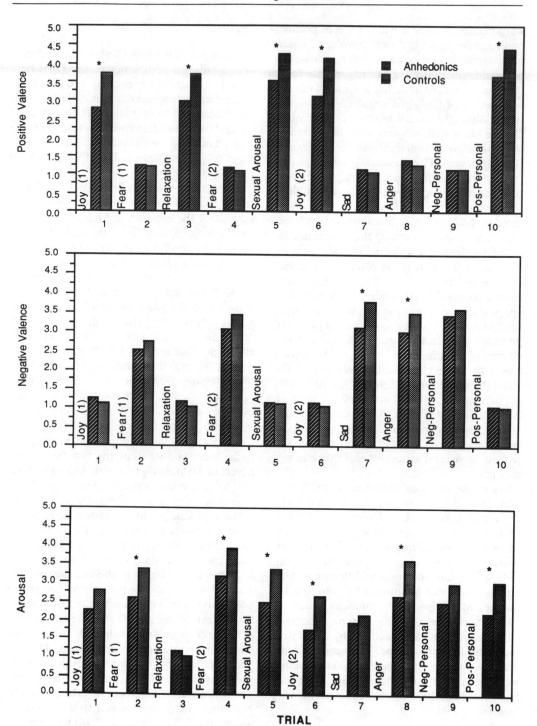

Figure 6. Positive, negative and arousal self-report following each of the ten imagery scripts. Significant group differences are denoted by asterisk.

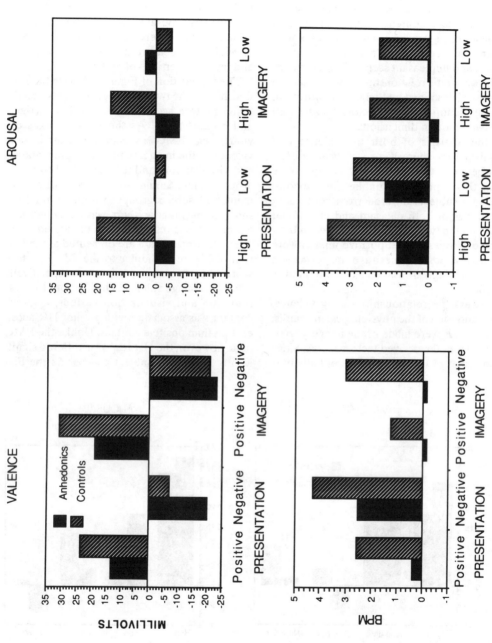

Figure 7. EMG pattern (top) and heart rate (bottom) as a function of valence and arousal ratings. Data are presented for both presentation and imagery periods.

valence scores (and low negative valence) and the unpleasant scenes were associated with high negative valence scores (and low positive valence). The relationship between arousal scores and scene content depicted in the bottom panel of Figure 6 was more complex with high arousal associated with a number of both pleasant and unpleasant scenes. This is not unlike the quadratic relationship between valence and arousal described by Lang and confirms, in part, the identification of Factors 1 and 2 with these two emotion dimensions.

In the analysis of both the valence and arousal factors, there were significant differences between the two subject groups. Note that in this experiment, unlike the previous, anhedonic subjects differed from controls in their ratings of both pleasant and unpleasant scenes and the two groups also differed in their ratings of arousal. Thus, positive images were rated as less positive, negative images as less negative and high arousal images were rated as less arousing.

To assess the relationship among valence, arousal and each of the physiological measures, two groupings were made of the imagery trials on the basis of the derived factors scores. Since the two poles of Factor 1 were essentially mir-

ror images, the grouping of trials on the basis of this factor was based only on the positive factor score. With a simple median split, five high and five low valence trials and five high and five low arousal trials were identified. Separate ANOVAs were then conducted on each physiological measure during the presentation and imagery portions of all trials.

The top portion of Figure 7 depicts the relationship for the two subject groups between the EMG pattern score and both valence (right) and arousal (left). As the Figure makes obvious, facial EMG is specifically related to the valence of the image, both during presentation and visualization, and it is unrelated to image arousal value. Similar to our previous experiment, both subject groups showed this relationship, but in this case, there was no evidence of a more intense response from the anhedonics.

The heart rate data are presented at the bottom of Figure 7. Similar to the EMG pattern scores, heart rate responsivity was specifically related to image valence. During both the presentation and visualization periods, negative content was associated with greater HR acceleration than positive content. Unlike the EMG data, however, the HR response differed significantly in the two subject groups. As the Fig-

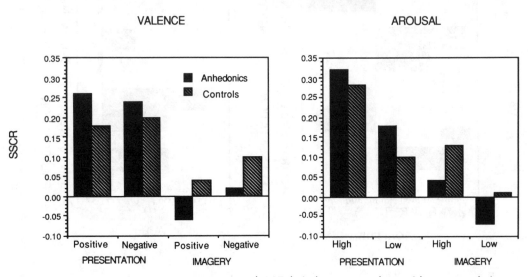

Figure 8. Spontaneous skin conductance responses (SSCRs) during presentation and imagery periods as a function of valence and arousal ratings.

ure illustrates, anhedonic subjects produced smaller responses than control subjects during both the presentation and visualization periods. Though a significant relationship with valence was present in this group during the presentation period, there was no HR response from anhedonic subjects when they were engaged in the imagery task.

Unlike the facial pattern and heart-rate scores, there was no significant relationship between the number of spontaneous skin conductance responses (SSCRs) and image valence. On the other hand, the relationship between SSCRs and image arousal was highly significant. These data are presented in Figure 8. As was true in our previous experiment, there were no differences between anhedonic and control subjects either in overall amount of skin conductance activity or in the within-group relationship between SSCR and arousal.

Discussion

This experiment was conducted in part to determine whether anhedonic subjects were poor imagers. In general, we believe the data provide good support for this hypothesis. First, on the QMI, anhedonics scored higher (indicative of poor imagery) than controls. Second, regardless of the particular aspect of emotion made prominent in an image description, anhedonics rated that dimension lower than controls. It is important to note that this does not seem to reflect a response 'style' in which all verbal report is less extreme since their scores on the QMI were actually higher than controls. Nor do anhedonics stylistically answer questions in the 'deviant' direction since their scores on scales such as the Perceptual Aberration Scale (Chapman et al., 1978) or the Beck Depression Inventory (Beck, Ward, Mendelson, Mock & Erbaugh, 1961) do not differ from those provided by normal controls. Finally, the heart-rate response, which in Lang's work has been sensitive to the good/poor imager distinction, was clearly

aberrant in anhedonics, particularly when they were asked to image.

The results of this experiment seemed impressive in another regard. While we originally intended to focus on discrete emotions, the data provide compelling support for the dimensionality approach to emotion research. This is particularly evident in the striking relationships that emerged between the physiological measures and the self-report factors obtained from the ZIPERS ratings. As discussed above, experiments which assess valence and arousal directly, using SAM for example, consistently find that facial EMG and HR relate to the valence dimension while SCR relates to self-report of arousal. This is precisely the pattern obtained here. EMG and HR were strongly related to Factor 1 (Valence) and unrelated to Factor 2 (Arousal), while the opposite was true for the skin conductance measure. These relationships must be particularly robust since neither the verbal report nor the visceral physiology (HR and SSCR) were assessed as they were by Greenwald et al.(1989) nor as they were in our own study using the slide stimuli. Rather than assessing the acceleratory peak in a phasic heart rate response, the present study used heart rate means – a much more tonic measure. While during imagery high heart rate is associated with negative valence and not positive valence as it is when phasic responses to discrete stimuli are assessed, it is still valence and not arousal that modulates the response. Similarly, in the present experiment, skin conductance was assessed by counting spontaneous fluctuations, not by measuring the amplitude of a discrete response, yet its relationship to arousal, not valence, was unequivocal. Though a more detailed analysis of the present data, vis-à-vis the discrete emotions, remains to be done, the power and parsimony provided by the dimensionality approach is impressive and would suggest that it is an approach to emotion-research whose time has come.

Emotion-Processing in Anhedonia

The purpose of the present research was to determine whether anhedonic and normal control subjects could be differentiated experimentally when confronted with emotion-provoking stimuli or instructions. If evidence for an emotion-processing deficit could be found, we wished to ascertain its generality across emotions (or within the emotional space) and across output systems constituting the emotional response. To some extent, the research described here answers these questions, but as is often the case, our research just as surely raises others.

There is little doubt that anhedonic subjects do not process affective stimuli in the same manner as do normal controls. In all three experiments, differences between groups were observed in the verbal report measures and in two of the three experiments between-group differences were observed in the physiological measures as well. Although the facial EMG was somewhat inconsistent across these two experiments, the heart-rate data in both cases indicate that the emotion-processing deficit in anhedonia goes beyond verbal report. Thus, at least two of the three response systems (verbal report, visceral physiology) involved in emotion production have been sensitive to subject group membership. Implications for the third system (overt behavior) are less clear. No differences between the two groups were evident when viewing times were assessed and facial EMG differences were evident only in one of the two studies in which it was measured. The interpretation of these data is complicated, however, first by the fact that viewing time was primarily a function of arousal, and second by the ambiguity surrounding the proper positioning of facial expression in the general structure of emotion. While Lang (1985) includes facial expression among the overt behaviors associated with emotion, he also speculates that the face, like language, may become detached from affect in the service of social communication. A high priority as we continue to investigate emotion in anhedonia is to develop a variety of behavioral measures by which this aspect of emotion could be assessed more comprehensively.

While the data seem to suggest that all response systems are implicated in the way anhedonics respond to affective stimuli, there remains ambiguity regarding the range of emotions affected. Most consistently, the evidence implicates positive emotion and more specifically the valence aspect of these emotions. On the other hand, anhedonics showed more covert facial expression to both positive *and* negative slides in the second experiment and under imagery instructions produced no HR acceleration during imagery regardless of the scene's valence. Furthermore, during imagery, between-group verbal report differences were present not only in response to positive imagery, but to scenes with negative valence and to scenes rated high on arousal irrespective of valence. This pattern of results suggests a deficit more general than one involving only positive emotion.

It is possible that the fundamental difference between anhedonic and normal control subjects involves the structure of *all* emotion prototypes. In particular, we suggest that the two groups differ in terms of the coherence of these prototypes and that there is systematic variance among the prototypes in anhedonics such that positive-emotion prototypes are less coherent than negative-emotion prototypes. A coherent prototype is one in which associations among and within levels of the prototype are strong and one which can therefore be accessed even with highly degraded stimuli. Incoherent prototypes are only loosely structured and require a stronger match between the prototype and the invoking stimulus before complete processing will occur. With very incoherent prototypes, such as the positive-emotion prototype of anhedonics, even realistic (nondegraded) stimuli such as color slides fail to provoke 'image-mode' processing with its associated visceral outflow. These stimuli are adequate to insure such processing of negative-emotion prototypes, however. With more degradation, such as moving from slides to text to imagery, differences between the two subject groups are no longer limited to positive valence items. During imagery, negative emotions were rated as less intense by anhedonics and their processing was associated with no commensurate heart rate increases.

In sum, the data presented here strongly support a fundamental difference in emotion-processing between anhedonic and normal subjects and suggest that the difference likely resides in the representation of emotion in memory. We have speculated somewhat over the nature of this representation and with this as background we would suggest (albeit briefly) that our results have implications for issues relevant to remediation and to the study of affect in other subject groups. For instance, Lang (1985) describes the focal phobic-patient as one with a particularly coherent memorial representation, and though often isolated can be triggered easily and is often processed in toto. A variety of treatments may be effective, but

their end result may be to reduce the coherence of the fear prototype and render it much less accessible. If the positive-emotion prototype in the anhedonic lacks an appropriate coherence and is too inaccessible, can the converse be done with these subjects? What elements would such a treatment contain? Similarly, though we know that anhedonics are not necessarily depressed, we wonder why not? What is the difference between the representation of emotion in anhedonics and its representation in subjects who are depressed? And what of the disorganized emotion in schizophrenia? These are among the questions currently commanding our attention and we have every confidence that the work of Lang, his colleagues and students will continue to be a major source of inspiration as we continue what we feel is an interesting and exciting line of research.

References

Beck, A.T. Ward, C.H., Mendelson, M., Mock, J. & Erbaugh, J. (1961). An inventory for measuring depression. *Archives of General Psychiatry, 4,* 561–571.

Berenbaum, H., Snowhite, R. & Oltmanns T.F. (1987). Anhedonia and emotional responses to affect evoking stimuli. *Psychological Medicine, 17,* 677–684.

Bernstein, A. S. (1987). Orienting response research in schizophrenia; where we have come and where we might go. *Schizophrenia Bulletin, 13,* 623–640.

Bleuler, E. (1950). *Dementia praecox.* New York: International Universities Press (originally published 1911).

Braff, D.L., Stone, C., Callaway, E. Geyer, M., Glick, I., & Bali, L. (1978). Prestimulus effects on human startle reflex in normals and schizophrenics. *Psychophysiology, 15,* 339–343.

Chapman, L.J., & Chapman, J.P. (1985). Psychosis proneness. In M. Alpert (Ed.), *Controversies in schizophrenia* (157–194). New York: Guilford.

Chapman, L.J., Chapman, J.P., & Raulin, M.L. (1976). Scales for physical and social anhedonia. *Journal of Abnormal Psychology, 85,* 374–382.

Chapman, L.J., Chapman, J.D. & Raulin, M.L. (1978). Body-image aberration in schizophrenia. *Journal of Abnormal Psychology, 87,* 399–407.

Chapman, L.J., Edell, W.S., & Chapman, J.P. (1980).

Physical anhedonia, perceptual aberration, and psychosis proneness. *Schizophrenia Bulletin, 6,* 639–653.

Edell, W. S., & Chapman, L. J. (1979). Anhedonia, perceptual aberration, and the Rorschach. *Journal of Consulting and Clinical Psychology, 47,* 377–384.

Ekman, P. (1982). *Emotion in the Human Face* (2nd ed.). NY: Cambridge University Press.

Ekman, P. & Friesen, W.V. (1978). *Facial Action Coding System (FACS): A Technique for the Measurement of Facial Action.* Palo Alto, CA: Consulting Psychologist Press.

Ekman, P., Levenson, R.W. & Friesen, W.V., (1983). Autonomic nervous system activity distinguishes among emotions. *Science, 221,* 1208–1210.

Freedman, R., Adler, L.E., Gerhardt, G.A., Waldo, M., Baker, N., Rose, G.M., Drebing, C., Nagamoto, H., Bickford-Wimer, P. & Franks, R. (1987). Neurobiological studies of sensory gating in schizophrenia. *Schizophrenia Bulletin, 13,* 669–678.

Graham, F. K. (1975). The more or less startling effects of weak prestimulation. *Psychophysiology, 12,* 238–248.

Graham, F. K. (1979). Distinguishing among orienting, defense, and startle reflexes. In H. D. Kimmel, E. G. van Olst, & J. F. Orlebecke (Eds.), *The orienting reflex in humans* (137–167). Hillsdale, NJ: Lawrence Erlbaum Associates.

Graham, F.K. (1980). Representing cardiac activity in relation to time. In P.H. Venables & I. Martin (Eds.), *Techniques in psychophysiology* (192–197). NY: John Wiley and Sons.

Greenwald, M., Cook, E., & Lang, P. (1989). Affective judgment and psychophysiological response; dimensional covariation in the evaluation of pictorial stimuli. *Journal of Psychophysiology, 3,* 51–64.

Haberman, M.C., Chapman, L.J., Numbers, J.S. & McFall, R. M. (1979). Relation of social competence to scores on two scales of psychosis proneness. *Journal of Abnormal Psychology, 88,* 675–677.

Izard, C.E. (1971). *The face of emotion.* New York: Appleton-Century-Crofts.

Izard, C.E. (1979). *The maximally discriminative facial movement coding system (Max).* Newark, DE: Office of Academic Computing and Instructional Technology, University of Delaware.

Izard, C.E., Dougherty, F.E., Bloxom, B.M. & Kotsch, W.E. (1974). The DES: A method of measuring the subjective experience of discrete emotion. (Unpublished manuscript). Vanderbilt University, Nashua, Tennessee.

Josiassen, R.C., Shagass, C., Roemer, R.A. & Straumanis, J.J. (1985). Attention-related effects on somatosensory evoked potentials in college students at risk for psychopathology. *Journal of Abnormal Psychology, 95,* 507–518.

Lang, P.J. (1980). Behavioral treatment and biobehavioral assessment: Computer applications. In J.B. Sidowski, J.H. Johnson & T.A. Williams (Eds.), *Technology in mental health care delivery* (119–137). Norwood, NJ: Albex Publishing Corp.

Lang, P.J., (1984). Cognition in emotion: Concept and action. In C.Izard, J. Kagan & R. Zajonc (Eds.), *Emotion, Cognition and Behavior* (196–226). NY: Cambridge University Press.

Lang, P.J. (1985). The cognitive psychophysiology of emotion: Fear and anxiety. In A.H. Tuma and J.D. Maser (Eds.), *Anxiety and the anxiety disorders* (pp.131–170). Hillsdale, NJ: Erlbaum.

Lang, P.J., Bradley, M.M. & Cuthbert, B.N. (1990). Emotion, attention & the startle reflex. *Psychological Review, 97,* 377–395.

Lang, P.J., Ohman, A., & Vaitl, D. (1988). *The International Affective Picture System* (photographic slides). Gainesville, FL: Center for Research in Psychophysiology, University of Florida.

McGhie, A. & Chapman, J. (1961). Disorders of attention and perception in early schizophrenia. *British Journal of Medical Psychology, 34,* 103–115.

Mehrabian, A. & Russell, J.A. (1974). *An approach to Environmental Psychology.* Cambridge, Massachusettes and London, England: MIT Press.

Miles, M.A., Perlstein, W.M., Simons, R.F., &

Graham, F.K. (1987). ERP and HR components of active and passive orienting in a long-ISI paradigm: Anhedonic and normal controls. *Psychophysiology, 24,* 601. (Abstract).

Perlstein, W.M., Fiorito, E., Simons, R.F., & Graham, F.K. (1989). Prestimulation effects on reflex blink and EPs in normal and schizotypal subjects. *Psychophysiology, 26,* S48. (Abstract).

Russell, J. & Mehrabian, A. (1977). Evidence for a three-factor theory of emotion. *Journal of Research in Personality, 11,* 179–183.

Schwartz, G.E., Fair, P.L., Mandel, M.R., Salt, R., Mieske, M. & Klerman, G.L. (1978). Facial electromyography in the assessment of improvement of depression. *Psychosomatic Medicine, 40,* 355–360.

Sheehan, P.Q. (1967). A shortened form of Betts' questionnaire upon mental imagery. *Journal of Clinical Psychology, 23,* 386–389.

Simons, R.F. (1981). Electrodermal and cardiac orienting in psychometrically defined high-risk subjects. *Psychiatry Research, 4,* 347–356.

Simons, R.F. (1982). Physical anhedonia and future psychopathology: An electrocortical continuity? *Psychophysiology, 19,* 433–441.

Simons, R.F. & Giardina, B.D. (in press). Reflex modification in psychosis-prone young adults. *Psychophysiology.*

Simons, R.F. & Katkin, W. (1985). Smooth pursuit eye movements in subjects reporting physical anhedonia and perceptual aberrations. *Psychiatry Research, 14,* 275–289.

Simons, R.F., MacMillan, F.W. & Ireland, F.B. (1982a). Reaction-time crossover in preselected schizotypic subjects. *Journal of Abnormal Psychology, 91,* 414–419.

Simons, R.F., MacMillan, F.W. III & Ireland, F.B. (1982b). Anticipatory pleasure deficit in subjects reporting physical anhedonia: Slow cortical evidence. *Biological Psychology, 14,* 297–310.

Simons, R. F. & Russo, K. R. (1987). Event-related potentials and continuous performance in subjects with physical anhedonia or perceptual aberrations. *Journal of Psychophysiology, 4,* 401–410.

Vrana, S.R., Cuthbert, B.N. & Lang, P.J. (1989). Processing fearful and neutral sentences: Memory and heart-rate change. *Cognition and Emotion, 3,* 179–195.

Vrana, S.R., Spence, E.L. & Lang, P.J. (1988). The startle probe response: A new measure of emotion? *Journal of Abnormal Psychology, 97,* 487–491.

Zuckerman, M. (1977) The development of a situation-specific trait-state test for the prediction and measurement of affective responses. *Journal of Consulting and Clinical Psychology, 45,* 513–523.

Subject Index

List of Contributors

Niels Birbaumer
Universität Tübingen
Department of Physiological Psychology
Gartenstrasse 29
D-7400 Tübingen
Germany

and

Università Degli Studi
Dipartimento Psicologia Generale
Piazza Cavour
I-35139 Padova
Italy

Margaret M. Bradley
University of Florida
Center for Research in Psychophysiology
Box J-196 JHMHC
Gainesville, FL 32610
USA

Michel Bonnet
Cognitive Neuroscience Unit
CNRS-LNF1
31 Chemin Joseph Aiguier
Marseilles Cedex 9 13402
France

Bruce N. Cuthbert
University of Florida
Center for Research in Psychophysiology
Box J-196 JHMHC
Gainesville, FL 32610
USA

Thomas Elbert
Universität Münster
Institute of Experimental Audiology
Kardinal-von-Galen-Ring 10
D-4400 Münster
Germany

Evelyn Fiorito
University of Delaware
Department of Psychology
230 Wolf Hall
Newark, Delaware 19716
USA

Lee Fitzgibbons
University of Delaware
Department of Psychology
230 Wolf Hall
Newark, Delaware 19716
USA

Herta Flor
Universität Tübingen
Department of Physiological Psychology
Gartenstrasse 29
D-7400 Tübingen
Germany

Edna B. Foa
The Medical College of Pennsylvania
Department of Psychiatry
Center for the Treatment and Study of Anxiety
3200 Henry Avenue
Philadelphia, Pennsylvania 19129
USA

James H. Geer
Louisiana State University
Department of Psychology
Baton Rouge
Louisiana 70803-5501
USA

Mark K. Greenwald
Center for Research in Psychophysiology
University of Florida
Box J-196 JHMHC
Gainesville, FL 32610
USA

Alfons O. Hamm
Department of Psychology
Section of Clinical Psychology
Justus-Liebig-Universität Giessen
Otto Behaghel Strasse 10
D-6300 Giessen
Germany

Sheryl R. Humphrey
Louisiana State University
Department of Psychology
Baton Rouge
Louisiana 70803-5501
USA

Michael J. Kozak
The Medical College of Pennsylvania
Department of Psychiatry
Center for the Treatment and Study of Anxiety
3200 Henry Avenue
Philadelphia, Pennsylvania 19129
USA

Peter J. Lang
University of Florida
Center for Research in Psychophysiology
Box J-196 JHMHC
Gainesville, FL 32610
USA

Kevin J. Lapour
Louisiana State University
Department of Psychology
Baton Rouge
Louisiana 70803-5501
USA

Werner Lutzenberger
Universität Tübingen
Department of Physiological Psychology
Gartenstrasse 29
D-7400 Tübingen
Germany

Barbara G. Melamed
Ferkauf Graduate School of Psychology
Mazer Hall
Albert Einstein College of Medicine Campus
1300 Morris Park Avenue
Bronx, NY 10461
USA

Gregory A. Miller
Department of Psychology
University of Illinois
603 E. Daniel Street
Champaign, IL 61820
USA

Arne Öhman
University of Uppsala
Department of Clinical Psychology
P.O. Box 1225
S-751 42 Uppsala
Sweden

Daniela Palomba
Università Degli Studi
Dipartimento Psicologia Generale
Piazza Capitaniato, 3
I-35139 Padova
Italy

Jean Requin
Cognitive Neuroscience Unit
CNRS-LNF1
31 Chemin Joseph Aiguier
F-13402 Marseilles Cedex 9
France

Brigitte Rockstroh
Fachbereich Psychologie
Universität Konstanz
P. O. Box 556
D-7750 Konstanz 1
Germany

Gudrun Sartory
Clinical Psychology
University of Wuppertal
Max-Horkheimer-Str. 20
D-5600 Wuppertal 1
Germany

Robert F. Simons
University of Delaware
Department of Psychology
230 Wolf Hall
Newark, Delaware 19716
USA

Luciano Stegagno
Universitá Degli Studi
Dipartimento Psicologia Generale
Piazza Capitaniato, 3
I-35139 Padova
Italy

Sigrid Sternagel
Department of Psychology
Justus-Liebig-Universität Giessen
Otto Behaghel Strasse 10
D-6300 Giessen
Germany

Dieter Vaitl
Department of Psychology
Section of Clinical Psychology
Justus-Liebig-Universität Giessen
Otto Behaghel Strasse 10
D-6300 Giessen
Germany

Wofgang Vehrs
Kulturwissenschaftliche Fakultät
University of Bayreuth
Geschwister-Scholl-Platz 3
D-8580 Bayreuth
Germany

Scott R. Vrana
Purdue University
Department of Psychological Sciences
West Lafayette, IN 47907
USA